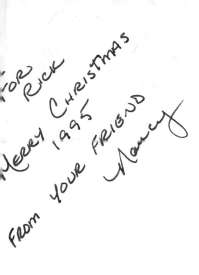

For Rick

Merry Christmas
1995

From your FRIEND

Nancy

D0405443

THE STEINWAY SAGA

An American Dynasty

D. W. Fostle

SCRIBNER
NEW YORK   LONDON   TORONTO   SYDNEY   TOKYO   SINGAPORE

To Betty Sue, who read each word aloud and thought
before she spoke.

Scribner
Rockefeller Center
1230 Avenue of the Americas
New York, New York 10020

Copyright © 1995 by D. W. Fostle

All rights reserved, including the right to reproduce this book or portions therein,
in any form whatsoever.

All family images are from the collection of Henry Z. Steinway.

SCRIBNER and colophon are registered trademarks of Simon & Schuster Inc.

Designed by Anne Scatto/PIXEL PRESS

Manufactured in the United States of America

1   3   5   7   9   10   8   6   4   2

Library of Congress Cataloging-in-Publication Data

Fostle, D. W. (Donald W.)
The Steinway saga : an American dynasty / D.W. Fostle.
p.   cm.
Includes index.
1. Steinway family.   2. Steinway & Sons—History.   3. Piano
makers—New York (N.Y.)—History.   I. Title.
ML424.S76F7   1994
786.2′197471—dc20   94-7842   CIP
MN
ISBN 0-684-19318-3

CONTENTS

Contents

ACKNOWLEDGMENTS

For more than ninety years there lived near the shores of the St. Lawrence River a man named Lucius Britton. He had made his way through life as a draftsman, mechanic, boatbuilder, and hardware store owner. Seated one summer evening on the porch of the home he built for his family, Lou Britton, sometime mechanic, sentient remnant of the nineteenth century, and full-time philosopher, told a story.

Late one night an officer of the law chanced upon a drunk who, on his hands and knees, was urgently examining the sidewalk beneath a streetlight. "What are you looking for?" queried the officer. "Housekeys," slurred the inebriate. "Is this where you lost them?" asked the policeman. "No, officer, but the light is better here . . ."

Following is the register of a few of the writer's streetlights; readers will naturally form their own views as to whether the correct keys were found. No claims are made, other than diligent search and the collection of certain flat metallic objects that, upon trial, irregularly opened small doors in the edifice of time.

One who early shed much light was Roland Loest, then the curator of a small piano museum and now an independent piano technician and re-storer in Manhattan. It was Roland who first made sensible, with the greatest of patience, the remarkable technological and aesthetic accomplishments of men long forgotten: Bacon and Raven, Dunham, Mathushek, the Nunns, and the Lindemanns, among others, who were contemporaries and later the vanquished competitors of the Steinways. For his descriptions of the subtleties of mechanism and insight into Steinway manufacturing practice, the counsel of piano technician and educator Bill Garlick likewise proved useful, as did the researches of Roy Kehl, whose work showed that piano design was never a static discipline.

Rummages in the attic of Victorian technology would have been nearly impossible without an immense and original directory of nineteenth-century Manhattan musical instrumentmakers by Nancy Groce. Nancy also provided an introduction to Vera Lawrence, whose contributions transcend the occasional citation as found in the notes; these were simultaneously ineffable and essential.

It is customary to cite the persons at repository institutions who have assisted in research; there are many of these, but for assistance beyond the routine, several deserve specific mention. At the New York County Clerk's Division of Old Records Joe Van Nostrand and Bruce Abrahms refuted the general proposition that the words civil and service are meaningless in modern governmental organizations; they not only found on request beribboned packets of court papers by the dozens but functioned as deft guides to still more documents, many untouched for a century or more. Of the Steinways, their allies and adversaries, much less would be known were it not for the assistance of these two men. Evelyn Gonzalez of the New York City Municipal Archives unflinchingly caused to be excavated cartloads of documents; among those tens of thousands of pages were found the few dozen that limned a poignant epoch in the lives of the children of Henry Steinway, Jr., after his death in 1865. Bill Asadorian of the Queens Public Library graciously gave access to large quantities of uncataloged material and key documents on the manifold enterprises of William Steinway.

If proof is somehow required that the local library is the foundation of the nation's cumulative knowledge, this writer submits in evidence the name of Judy Gessel, at the Sussex County (New Jersey) Public Library, who processed innumerable requests for periodical arcana while showing spectacular deftness in searching and decoding the cryptic databases indigenous to her profession. Much time was saved; much information was gained.

There is in this volume a chapter which, if it cannot be called original, at least deserves the description peculiar. It has as its prime topic what has been called the "Steinway sound." That there is such a sound is taken as a fact of which proof is thought superfluous by many artists and critics, but not all. It was therefore decided to compare with acoustical measurements the sound of selected grand pianos, and thanks are due, alphabetically, to Baldwin, Bosendorfer, Steinway, and Yamaha for providing subject instruments. Pianos are mute without a player, and Mordecai Shehori functioned as executant, coaxing the pianos ever closer to, and sometimes

Acknowledgments

beyond, their musical limits as engineer Marc Aubort digitally recorded the event. Wade Bray provided the systems, software, and skill that hacked a small clearing in the jungles of perception in which he and the writer deliberated, comfortably seated on stacks of empirical data. The interpretations of the data are, however, the sole responsibility of the writer.

There are others whose lights illumined the search for keys in highly specific ways; they are acknowledged in the notes, as the contributions were generally of a scholarly nature. Undoubtedly, there have been omissions, and to those persons apologies are tendered with full assurances of inadvertency.

In 1989 this writer met for the first time Mr. Henry Z. Steinway, an affable man with a marked distaste for the pretentious. He is retired and plays no role in the management of the firm that bears his name. The topic was technological: the involvement of his grandfather William Steinway with Gottlieb Daimler, a gas engine pioneer. Mr. Steinway riffled through the grey metal files that line the walls of his office producing, almost magically, multiple packets of Daimler data. The writer knows now that those files contain documents by the thousands, spanning all the generations of family and business history.

This volume was later proposed, and during the years of its development Henry Steinway never tried to influence the direction of research; never did he shrink from a question or dissemble in response. With what can only be termed courageous generosity, he made available without restriction his archive and gave, gladly it seemed, countless hours to the instruction of the writer in the ways of pianomakers. That tutelage would fill several books, but sadly there was only one to write. If anything of merit or interest is found in the pages that follow, credit is likely due Henry Z. Steinway. Mr. Steinway, like the policeman in Lou Britton's tale, is also admired for his forbearance.

—D.W.F.

RITORNELLO

Forty-first and Berrian Boulevard, Steinway, Long Island City, Queens, New York. *He lies there, spread-eagled on his back, permanent and vacant joy stitched on the grey fake-fur face. The Taiwan-counterfeit Bugs Bunny, a four-foot sunbather in an industrial desert, reclines on a bright blue door, artfully angled on the remains of a seventeen-inch Sylvania. Bugs, the door, and the television repose in an oasis of iridescent green liquid thickened by rotting bags of masonry cement and pool filter sand. Overhead a Delta Heavy clears its four throats and staggers over Bowery Bay into the sky. The roar strangles a bandsaw screaming at metal in the Gottlieb Iron Works. An Imperial Sanitation Corporation garbage packer grinds up Forty-first, clanking through the potholes. The breeze shifts; smells segue from hot metal to number two Diesel to sewage.*

Bugs's lone Lucite eye stares. Follow his sight line, past the tires, the toilet seats, the dog excrement bleaching white in the sun, over the corrugated metal fence autographed by Jack the Wack, and it is there. William Steinway's mansion towers like a granite butte in the wilderness, the 140-year-old French slate roof still glowing in the gritty urban light.

Children once played croquet in the carefully sculpted gardens. Where the sewage plant now gurgles and hisses, a steam yacht was moored. The Steinway mansion was an incubator of power, prestige, and progress, a place where a man of ability repaired to be with those who mattered most: his family.

The five-story axed Italian granite tower still scratches at the sky, topped by

1

an octagonal cupola. From that cupola William Steinway looked down on the village he built and called Steinway. Homes dotted the rectangular grid with streets named for Henry and Theodore, William's brothers; William Steinway held the mortgages on those homes, the occupants' savings secure in Steinway banks. At night the windows glowed with the yellow gaslight from the Steinway Illuminating Company.

To the north flowed the East River, and on it William saw Steinway ferries, black smoke coursing from their stacks, plying the waters to Manhattan two miles distant. To the south lay the school he built for the village children, his Protestant church, its copper steeple shimmering in the summer heat, and his prim white village library. All were interconnected by the Steinway trolleys that clanged along the village streets and throughout Long Island City. To the east, where La Guardia Airport now stands, thousands crowded his North Beach Amusement Park to splash away the heat in Bowery Bay, row rental skiffs on crystal waters, and listen to brass bands play Sousa on Sunday afternoons.

To the west, in a parklike setting upholstered with green grass and fringed with old-growth oaks, discretely distanced from the homes, the piano manufactory covered a city block with red-brick buildings four stories high; one thousand one hundred men labored sixty hours each week to build the instruments that were the foundation of Steinway wealth and power. In the shadow of Steinway & Sons other enterprises flourished: a lumberyard, a dye company, and William's vision of the future, the Daimler Motor Company. The fledgling maker of motorboats and horseless carriages would one day be Mercedes-Benz.

One hundred and five model years later, the words "Golden Garage" are sprayed in yellow on William Steinway's carriage house. In the mud lie the oxidizing exoskeletons of Mercedes, FIATs, MGs, Jaguars, and Sunbeams. The iron fence bulges, unable to restrain the mass of bumpers, fenders, and doors piled against it. West on Steinway Place the piano works are dwarfed now by the forest green storage tanks of the Castle Astoria Oil Depot. Though all is transmogrified without, within is a Victorian preserve, a museum of manufacturing that still manufactures.

The plant is half-empty now; leather notebooks of German foremen are gone, replaced by cathode ray tubes, glowing cold and green. There are no longer Steinways at Steinway. Caribbean accents supplant those of Europe. The grey-bearded men who grew poinsettias are dead. Soft drinks succeed lagerbier at lunch. For a few, pianomaking jobs still remain the doorway to the American Dream. One hundred years ago Steinway pianos were the best; they are still the best, some claim. William Steinway would understand why. Jack the Wack would not. . . .

Chapter 1

HIS EXCELLENT CONSTITUTION

"Henry E. Steinway was born February Fifteenth, Seventeen Hundred Ninety-seven, at the little village of Wolfshagen, in the Harz Mountains. He was the baby in a big brood of twelve. . . . It was a happy, busy, economical group, where the garden gave vegetables, the mountain-stream fish, the forest fuel. The simple life of a forester and his family was bounded by six square miles. Their days were full of work and quiet homely joys," wrote Elbert Hubbard in *The Fra* magazine in 1909.

Into the pastoral goodness of Wolfshagen rode "the army of the Corsican," which "devoured the substance of the villagers." Nine-year-old Henry E. Steinway fled to the mountains with his mother to escape the "red tooth and claw" of war. "Up there with the foxglove, alone with God and her children, worn by worry, hunger and cold, the Mother of Henry Steinway passed away. Her children covered her worn-out form with a pile of rocks, and left her tired body there on the mountainside. Several of the motherless children gave up the struggle and cried themselves to sleep, to awake no more," recounted Hubbard in his *Story of the Steinways*.

Father Steinway and the older brothers were in the Prussian army far away when Henry returned to the village, "only to find it a mass of blackened ruins." In this chronicle the surviving children built a house of stone and logs for themselves and once again planted a garden. Notwithstanding the carnage of war, "Henry Steinway had his dreams of books and study and the world of art, seen by him in fancy as soldiers and travelers told their tales around campfires when the sun went down."

With the suspension of the Napoleonic Wars, the life of young Heinrich Englehard Steinweg presumably resumed its pastoral quality until a fateful day in the summer of 1812. An 1882 volume called the *Contemporary Biography of New York* provides an account, "as often repeated by Mr. Steinway." Fifteen-year-old Heinrich, his father, three older brothers, and two hired men were out in the forest when "they were surprised by a violent thunder shower accompanied by a most terrific hurricane." The party sought shelter in a hut made of tree bark when "a blinding flash of lightning filled the hut with living fire, and . . . the young lad was stretched in a semi-unconscious state on the earthen floor of the hut."

Regaining consciousness, Heinrich found the forms of his father, brothers, and friends "stiff and almost cold." "The body of his eldest brother still retaining some warmth, he placed his ear to his breast just in time to perceive the last faint pulsations of his heart." Now orphaned and penniless, Heinrich was "forced to earn his living by hard, ill-paid labor" until he "answered the call to arms against Napoleon issued by the Duke of Brunswick."

In what appears as an exemplary military career, the young man earned a silver medal for bugling during the Battle of Waterloo. The occasion, according to legend, was an advance by Marshal Blücher in valiant support of the troops of the Duke of Wellington. In another martial adventure young Heinrich leapt from a bridge into the ice-filled waters of the river Oker in pursuit of a prisoner making his escape. "A fearful struggle ensued . . . until the arrival of aid," when both the prisoner and Steinway were pulled from the "deep and rapid" waters "and the young soldier personally delivered his prisoner to headquarters." Due to "his excellent constitution" Heinrich rapidly "recovered from all the effects of his exploit" and was commended before the garrison.

Heinrich's musical talents were reportedly not limited to the bugle; "he enjoyed the reputation among his acquaintances of being a musical genius." He constructed of spruce a cithara that was "greatly admired for its superior tone" and he "beguiled the tedium of garrison life by mastering the art of playing." Soldier Steinweg accompanied the "whole company of his stalwart companions" as they sang "the liberty-breathing and heroic songs of Korner and Schenkendorf."

About 1818, the mythos records that Heinrich Englehard Steinweg was honorably discharged from the army after declining a promotion to sergeant and made his way to the nearby village of Goslar. There he tried to work as a cabinetmaker but was impeded by the guild system, which required a five-year apprenticeship and a further five years as a journeyman before an artisan could set up his own business. "Self-made business men were almost unknown in Germany at that day, for whoever attempted to rise above the

narrow limits set by the guilds was considered a revolutionist and a dangerous subject," informed *Contemporary Biography*. The truly rigid guild system
forced Heinrich to work with an organmaker in the nearby village of Seesen;
apparently the power of the church was sufficient to deflect the force of the
guilds, and the result was a less structured craft.

In the somewhat garbled chronology, it was ostensibly during this time
that Heinrich Englehard Steinweg built his "masterpiece—a costly writing
desk with inlaid drawers." Political power and a local catastrophe intervened
to provide twenty-eight-year-old Heinrich with an opportunity for a stable
life. The power was in the form of the chief justice of Seesen who "admired
and sought to purchase" Heinrich's desk, and the catastrophe was an 1825
fire that burned much of Seesen. Skilled men were needed to rebuild the
village and, through the efforts of the justice, Heinrich again evaded the
strictures of the guilds and opened a shop in Seesen.

The verifiable is a rarity in the German life of Heinrich Steinweg, but
records clearly show that on Wednesday, October 7, 1829, he bought from
a debt-ridden laborer named Johann Heinrich Roder some stalls and sheds
in Seesen for five hundred thalers, one hundred thalers down and the
assumption of a mortgage. The property, as purchased, may have been
nothing more than a pigsty and possibly a garden; the record is unclear as
to whether a home was included or if the property suffered greatly during
the village conflagration. It may be inferred, however, that both Heinrich
and his lender were sufficiently confident of his ability to repay the loan.

By the time of the property purchase Heinrich had married Julianne
Thiemer and fathered three children. Christian Freidrich Theodor was
nearing age four, Johanna Dorothee Juliane was two and one-half, and
Christian Karl Gottlieb was a nine-month-old infant. With a family and
property, Heinrich must have had a viable trade, but what it was, other
than "cabinetmaker," is unclear. According to the family legend, shortly
after the birth of his first son, Heinrich began to build a piano, purportedly
in the evenings at the kitchen table, so that the "boy should have the
advantages early in life which he himself had been unable to encompass."
Yet another account has him completing his first piano in a year; even
allowing for another year's error in these tales, a piano does not seem a
suitable instrument for a two-year-old.

In Hubbard's redaction of these distant events, Heinrich built his first
piano not for his son but for his bride as a wedding gift. On its case, carved
in relief, were cupids that frolicked among flowers. The piano for son
Theodore took fourteen years to complete and was exhibited at the state fair
in Brunswick in August 1839. "Musicians came from distant cities to see
and hear this wonderful musical instrument. The tinkle, tinkle, tin-pan
tones of the harpsichord were gone. Here was full, clear, vibrant expression." It earned its maker a "special gold medal . . . , the highest honor
that could be paid." In another, more probable account, three Steinweg

pianos were displayed at the fair and one obtained a medal as well as praise "for tone and workmanship."

That some small number of pianos did emerge from the shop in the Steinweg homestead is certain; beginning when or how many in total will never be known. Who might have bought these instruments in the surrounding hamlets that were connected to Seesen only by the most primitive dirt trails cannot be divined. If a living were made from them alone, it was modest. A more likely scenario is that Heinrich Steinweg built the occasional piano, tuned and repaired any he could find, sold and fixed second-hand instruments of all kinds, and kept a large vegetable garden and livestock out of necessity.

He did value education, perhaps because he had none; his two oldest sons, later known in America as Theodore and Henry, attended a private academy in Seesen known as the Jacobson School. Given was Heinrich's perseverance; war, famine, and revolution were woven into the fabric of his family's life. That Heinrich Steinweg was industrious is conspicuous; in a subsistence economy where government permission was needed before cutting even one of the abundant trees, he somehow accreted enough wealth to own a four-thousand-square-foot building and a veneer-cutting machine.

Though the writers of the hagiographies of Heinrich Englehard Steinweg reported incorrectly, this is of little consequence. In fact, his birthday was February 25, 1797, not February 15. He was the fourth of eight children, not the last of twelve, not the son of a "forester" but of a *kohlermeister*, or charcoalmaker. He was no orphan; a stepmother, a half-brother, and a brother still survived well into Heinrich's adulthood. These were tales of the distant boyhood of a man already long dead.

It was claimed that Heinrich's ancestors served as officers in the Thirty Years' War and were "well-known and well-to-do patricians" in the "fortified city" of Stralsund on the Baltic Sea. Connected to aristocracy only by a surname meaning "stone road," in truth his forebears lived serflike lives in the hamlets of the Harz Mountains for at least three generations before he was born. Eager to impart meaning to the impenetrable and drama to the mundane, Heinrich's sons fabricated these foreshadowings of a future as successful as it was improbable. Perhaps they believed in them. Although the *instrumentenmacher* Steinweg was born in Germany, his fame, after nearly a lifetime of incubation, was hatched in the New World. The Steinweg story is a story of America.

Chapter 2

DID A WHITE MAN
DO THAT?

"We have entered upon a new year in the reckoning of time and a new epoch has commenced in the history of our revolution, or rather, we are again in the same stage of our political history in which the commencement of the revolution found us. Not a trace is left to remind us of the glorious March days, save the ruins, and heaps of dust and ashes in the streets. Not one of our glorious liberties, so much boasted of, remains to console us for the loss of blood and property, for the death of our most able and brave champions of freedom, for the devastation of trade and commerce."

The words were those of an anonymous German correspondent to the *New York Herald*, written in the opening week of 1849. In the twenty-nine United States, the Whig Zachary Taylor was president, Millard Fillmore was vice president, and gold was discovered in California. The *Herald* correspondent continued, "The news of the immense gold districts in California has created no little sensation here. America has long been considered, by the destitute and indigent working classes of Europe, as a desirable place of refuge, and all who could, by any means, scrape together a sufficient sum of money to pay their passage across flocked thither. But since the fabled Eldorado of old has turned out to be a mere desert to the glittering plains of California, the mania for emigration has arrived at alarming heights." So it was throughout much of Europe in the bleak winter of 1849.

When the Commissioners of the Ports of Entry to the United States of

America closed the books on the year 1849 and toted their sums, they found that 297,024 persons had emigrated to America, an increase of 31 percent over 1848. Of these, 54 percent were Irish, 20 percent German, 19 percent English, and 3 percent Canadian. Save for the uncounted that walked to America from Mexico or Canada, they came by boat: ships, barks, brigs, and schooners, from six hundred to a dozen souls per vessel, entered at ports from New Orleans to Camden, Maine.

The locus of emigration was the Port of New York; the city was a funnel for humanity. In 1848 eight of every ten immigrants landed there. In 1849 it was three out of four, averaging 605 men, women, and children per day, every day, for a total of 220,603 persons, a number nearly half the city's permanent population.

Not all who made the journey did so by choice. At Liverpool the practice was to ship paupers to America. Each October the almshouse was purged of its residents; and the poor, no matter how diseased or aged, were deported to the United States. The decision was economic: it cost five pounds sterling to feed a pauper through the winter, but passage to America could be obtained for two pounds, or about ten dollars. These men and women knew their fate. In the words of one pauper, "We came out of a poorhouse and must go into it again at New York." To combat exportation of the defeated and dying, it was proposed that the "Commutation Tax," a landing fee to cover hospitalization and other immigrant services, be raised from $1.50 to ten dollars. The tax was not increased, for the New York commissioners reckoned it was better to seasonally feed a few thousand "out-of-doors poor" than staunch the flow of the able by punitive landing taxes.

The vessels in which most immigrants came were designed for cargo, not passengers. Bunks were built of secondhand lumber, to be torn out at the destination when goods such as cotton or grain were taken aboard. Each emigrant was allocated a berth six feet long, three wide, and three high. In this space, roughly the size of a coffin, men, women, and children lived and slept for the duration of the voyage, up to three months in "light airs." They provided their own bedding and food; many did not have a change of clothes. Though reformers pushed for regulations that would require "each man to have three shirts," the practical policy makers knew that to be impossibly restrictive. Even in America, three shirts meant a gentleman.

Baggage, boxes, and pots, along with the treasures and ephemera of lives in the Old World, were piled in the aisles between tiers of bunks. Steerage was a lightless place; there were no portholes, and flame from candle or lamp was banned for fear of fire. A democratic darkness was the only privacy. No bathing facilities were provided, for nothing was as precious at sea as fresh water. Dried sausage was a favorite food of the Germans; potatoes were preferred by the Irish, while the English elected oatmeal and bacon. Cooking was done on deck, where a communal stove was shared by all. To prepare food, emigrants formed groups, usually of eight persons, and negotiated time at the stove. The gallant dictum of the sea, "Women and children first," did not apply to table etiquette on immigrant vessels.

Fair weather was spent on deck playing cards or socializing, swapping facts, rumors, and suppositions, extrapolating to the future in a New World. In heavy weather the passengers were sent below and the afterhatch secured. There they would remain for the duration of the storm, be it hours or days. If so inclined, they might drink water from communal buckets and eat dry biscuits as they huddled in their damp bunks in a hold devoid of ventilation and light as the vessel rolled, pitched, and yawed through the seas. Above could be heard the howl of the wind in the rigging. Nearby in the darkness the decks and carlings creaked, the sick groaned, and children screamed while beneath them, stinking but unseen, sloshed the bilge.

Bilge water was a mephitic mix of seawater, tar, pitch, turpentine, vomit, dead rats, and the residues of cargo breakage: wine, flour, wheat, corn, cotton, salt, sugar, fats, and oils. Until reaching a depth of more than half a foot, the bilge was not pumped because the "free-water" posed no threat to the safety of the vessel. The "unctuous, oily, black, green, purple and yellow, thick, muddy fluid, the stench of which is intolerable, is so filthy and pungent that none but 'nightmen' can withstand its disgusting and overwhelming fetor," reported A. C. Castle, M.D., a surgeon and dentist who had seen conditions aboard "during my peregrinations of a large surface of the earth."

With the rising barometer emigrants would once again be allowed on deck, usually to find that the fire in the stove had been extinguished by rain or wind. But by then sunlight and sea air must have meant more than hot food to those who survived. In less than three months in the fall of 1853, 17,400 persons embarked for America; 16,100 arrived. Over 1,300 died at sea from disease, roughly one of every thirteen passengers. Though likely unaware, voyagers to America were living Patrick Henry's oratorical choice: "Give me Liberty or give me Death."

Though the emigrants could not have known it, the probability of survival varied widely depending on the flag of the vessel boarded. They were about half again more likely to die on a British or German registry vessel than on an American one. Fortunately for the emigrants, almost two-thirds of them shipped in American bottoms. Some years were less deadly, but even in the relative safety of 1849, more than one thousand died during crossings. Were travel equivalently fatal today, roughly 160,000 persons would die each year on international airline flights. But the statistics do not resonate as do the manifests of the vessels themselves: "Ship *Montezuma*, from Liverpool to New York, April 13, 1849, containing 332 adults and 10 infants, of which 6 have died. Sworn, A. B. Lowher, Master."

Monday, June 11, 1849, was an entirely ordinary summer day in the City of the Kickerbockers when the English bark *England's Queen*, 311 tons burthen, in ballast, made the Port of New York with 104 souls surviving

9

on board, forty-five days out of the free city of Bremen. Lloyd's rated her as a vessel of the Second Class. She was sent down the ways in 1842 with extensive repairs to her hull in 1847, probably required by a collision or grounding.

On June 13, 1849, after two days presumably spent in quarantine, her master, Robert Robinson, came ashore at the customs house and presented his manifest and log. The manifest, number 720 for the year 1849, listed the names, ages, and occupations of the immigrants as hastily scratched by the captain before the four-masted vessel cleared Bremen. On this crossing the column labelled "Died on the Voyage" bore no marks.

"I, Robert Robinson do solemnly, sincerely and truly swear that the following List or Manifest of Passengers, subscribed with my name and now delivered by me to the Collector of the Customs for the District of New-York contains, to the best of my knowledge and belief, a just and true account of all Passengers received on board The English Bark *England's Queen* whereof I am Master, from Bremen. So help me God." Among the farmers, stonecutters, and carpenters was an *instrumentenmacher* who declared his intention to reside in the United States, his country of origin as Germany, his age as twenty years, and his name as Carl Steinweg.

Had he been able to understand English and been inclined to give two cents to the grimy, ragged street urchins who sold the eight-page *New York Herald*, Carl would have read, "The tide of immigration which is setting so strongly towards our shore must largely increase the amount of taxable property in our Western States. . . . The arrival of immigrants, at this point averages about 1,000 per day, most of which immediately take in their line of travel for the West where they at once locate themselves and bring thousands upon thousands of acres under cultivation." Immigrants are desirable, James Gordon Bennett seemed to be saying in yet another variation of Horace Greeley's "Go West, Young Man, Go West" theme— as long as they do not stay in New York.

Bennett's was not a universal opinion. There was a strong nativist sentiment among the city's population, about half of whom were American-born. Bakers, tailors, painters, carpenters, stonemasons, bricklayers, cigarmakers, draymen, and general laborers were among those who felt that the "foreigners" depressed wages, eliminated jobs, and drove up rents. For these men and their families every immigrant was a threat, a person who might one day soon seize his job, no matter how menial, and his home, however rude and filthy. This was not a groundless fear; the capitalists, owners, master stonemasons, boss-carpenters, and others sensed that labor supply exceeded demand. They hired and paid in rational, if parsimonious, response to the market.

The result was a virulent xenophobia that percolated through the city. "Did a white man do that? No, it was a Dutchman," went a common joke. In 1857 a New York State Housing Commission reported that landlords preferred to rent to blacks rather than Germans since the "colored people are greater respecters of property." Crude jokes, street brawls, bar fights, and occasional beatings of hapless immigrants were routine manifestations of these social sentiments.

After Carl Steinweg debarked at the Port of New York, he obtained employment as a cabinetmaker according to the family legend. Where, when, or with whom is unknown; public records show what Carl Steinweg did *not* do: he was not arrested, not hospitalized at public cost, and not remanded to the almshouse or the lunatic asylum. About sixty thousand of his fellow New Yorkers—12 percent of the population—were not as fortunate in the year 1849.

The city's social pathologies were a minor menace in the summer of 1849, for an Asiatic cholera epidemic had once again begun. The 1834 epidemic in New York struck down over 3,500 persons. Roughly 2 percent of the population was killed by "the most fatal and severe of all diseases." By mid-June 1849, when Carl Steinweg arrived, about one-fourth of all deaths in the city were due to cholera. Fatalities increased in rough proportion to the mean temperature, and the epidemic peaked that summer in the week ending July 21 when 714 persons succumbed to the "Indian disease."

Treatment, such as it was, consisted of opium pills, then starch enemas and "counter-irritants" of mustard plasters and turpentine applied to the abdomen. "Effervescing drinks" were given. Stimulants such as ammonia and brandy were tried, but only when the patient "threatens to sink." In the summer of 1849, 5,083 New Yorkers "sank" from cholera, their black-lipped corpses even more grisly than their deaths: "The bodies of persons dying of Cholera are found to remain long warm, and their temperature may even rise after death. Peculiar muscular contractions have been observed to take place after death, so that the position of the limbs may become altered.

"Every article of clothing which has been in contact with a Cholera patient should be burnt," declared medical authority. But among New York's poor, a shirt, coat, or sheet was an asset not easily condemned to flame. Instead, a *chiffonnier* was called. The ragman might pay a nickel for each item and carry it off to be sold again. Even cloth too ragged or soiled to be sold was "recycled." By grinding the fabric and mixing the shreds with lampblack and chicory, a passable imitation of coffee was created, then sold back to the poor at outdoor markets or dispensed in restaurants.

Carl Steinweg survived the Cholera of '49, and according to legend, he was "sent as an *avant courier* to examine the localities, the institutions and manufactures, and report upon the chances. His report will be understood, when the immigration of the whole family is mentioned as the result." The reconnaissance, to the extent it occurred, was a brief one. Given the speed of international mails, not more than four letters could have been exchanged between Carl in New York and his family in Germany.

On Thursday, January 10, 1850, Heinrich Englehard Steinweg sold his home/workshop, grounds, garden, and outhouse to the Jacobson Institute to be used as a school. The price was 2460 thaler, which, after satisfaction of the mortgage and other debt, netted the family about 1000 thaler, approximately $780. The amount was the equivalent of fifteen to eighteen months' wages for a journeyman mechanic in New York. Given Heinrich Steinweg's prudence, he probably had few other assets, for he would have most likely used them to reduce his debt. Failure to pay a debt in Germany at this time could have meant prison. Continuing to follow the approved procedure, Heinrich Steinweg appeared before the duchy of Brunswick police and declared his intention "to emigrate in the spring to North America." A public notice of the family's desire to leave Germany for this remarkably vague destination was published on March 20, 1850.

On Sunday, May 19, 1850, the *instrumentenmacher* Heinrich Steinweg, 53 *Jarhe alt*, *Ehefrau* Juliane, 46, *Tochter* Dorothee, 22, *Sohn* Heinrich, 19, *Tochter* Minna, 17, *Sohn* Wilhelm, 15, *Sohn* Hermann, 13, *Sohn* Albert, 9, and *Tochter* Anna, 7, boarded the *Propellor Helena Sloman* under the command of Captain P. N. Paulson at Hamburg, destination New York. The Steinwegs made their way into steerage along with 224 other passengers while 66 others were berthed in the relative light and comfort of the first and second cabins. Ship's records show that the Steinwegs brought with them nine cases, one for each family member. For purposes of the trip, Heinrich declared his occupation as "farmer." Perhaps he knew that farmers were welcome in America; perhaps this false occupation was merely the caution of a man familiar with the ways of authoritarian governments.

This was the maiden voyage of a new vessel using innovative technology. Instead of sidewheels, the steamer *Sloman* had a single propellor, novel for its time. Like most new ideas, this one gave trouble, and the *Helena Sloman* broke a propellor gear, forcing her to put in at England for repairs. What should have been a two-week voyage stretched to six weeks. But under the protection of a huge Bermuda High, the Steinwegs crossed the Atlantic on glassy-calm seas, a slow summer boatride in clean if not luxurious surroundings. Theirs was not the typical immigrant voyage, crewed by vermin, stewarded by disease, and captained by death.

This was more a matter of chance than planning. Later that year, in the cavelike blackness of an Atlantic night, somewhere near latitude 42 degrees 13 minutes and longitude 61 degrees 30 minutes, the *Propellor Helena Sloman*, abandoned with fires out, foundered on the green, white-flecked, heaving seas in the only weather she ever encountered. A newspaper report listed the names, ranks, and residences of drowned crewmen and saluted their heroism. The account concluded with the words, "Also five steerage passengers of Germany." In Manhattan everyone knew that there were many more in the places from which those five had come; there was no point in printing their names.

By count, 212,796 immigrants disembarked at the Port of New York during 1850, a number equal to 41 percent of the city's population. An equivalent influx today would require the arrival of more than four million persons. But in this wash of humanity Heinrich Englehard Steinweg was a statistical rarity. Only 8 percent of immigrants were over the age of 40. In a time when the life expectancy of a European male was roughly 45 years, Heinrich Steinweg, at 53, was actuarily ancient, a man who had overdrawn the account of his natural time.

When the Steinweg family landed on Saturday, June 29, 1850, the city was in preparation for one of its great holidays: "Every kind of preparation is being made for the celebration of the Fourth of July. The military parade will be on a grand scale and the fireworks will be magnificent. All the little boys are appropriating their pocket money to the purchase of rockets and crackers, serpents and snakes, blue lights and Roman candles. . . . The 'children of larger growth' are also making their preparations, purchasing firearms and ammunition to blaze away in honor of the great day of American Liberty." The evening of Independence Day was an assault on the ears as firecrackers popped and banged, candles whooshed, rockets whistled, and the narrow streets of the city reverberated with the blasts of shotguns, the whine of rifle bullets, and the rapid-sequence cracks of black-powder revolvers. Overhead, pyrotechnics traced graceful, glowing incendiary arcs in the sky, their reports rumbling through Manhattan streets like distant summer thunder. What nine new immigrant Steinwegs from a pastoral village in northern Germany thought that night is unknown.

Later during that first Steinway summer in America, the mock-mayhem became real. The cycle of socioeconomic anger peaked and ebbed during much of the nineteenth century. At the peaks, labor unrest, radical rhetoric, strikes, and violence became the norm. In the late 1830s a thousand children in the Paterson, New Jersey, textile mills struck to have their workday reduced from thirteen to eleven hours. Among the strikers were seven-year-olds. The children were victorious. The pianomakers also struck, declaring, "That as labor is the only merchandise which the journeymen have in the market, they have a right to set a price on it, and those who will not enjoy the privilege are slaves, and we recommend them and their masters to the attention of the Abolitionists." The workers tarred and feathered a piano superintendent for "working under wages" in a show of their conviction. The "unhealthy excitement" was often most acute among the tailors, who, depending upon social philosophy, would have been considered either great leaders or dangerous radicals. In 1835 Judge Savage of the New York Supreme Court sent down a decision that the cordwainers (shoemakers) and tailors were guilty of conspiracy for "their organizing societies for the avowed purpose of self-protection." Several tailors were jailed for forming what would later be called a union.

The bells of the social alarm clock rang again in the summer of 1850, eleven days after the Steinways arrived. On Wednesday, July 10, in a rare display of ethnic unity, the English- and German-speaking branches of the tailors' still-illegal protective association met to draft a new scale of piecework prices. These were naturally rejected by the employers, who maintained that since tailors worked at home, they often took goods and did not return them. Five days later the strike began, continuing throughout July with marches, rallies, and meetings.

In early August a fight broke out at the home of a tailor still working for less than scale. The tailor, Frederick Wartz, was beaten and his home destroyed. Unclear is whether the house was ransacked by the tailors or the police. Later that day, a group of German tailors marching in protest were beaten by the police. Two tailors were killed and dozens injured, the first known deaths associated with the American labor movement. The events of August 4, 1850, would become known as the "Tailor's Riot," with the marches and rallies labelled as "striking illustrations of socialism" by even the most liberal large-circulation newspapers.

In years to come, the Steinways would be enmeshed in similar conflicts. It was probably sometime in the summer of 1850 that they moved into their newly rented home at 199 Hester Street, owned by John Short. Located eight blocks north and four blocks east of City Hall Park, the site of choice for labor demonstrations, Hester Street was and is in the city's Fourteenth Ward, Sixth Election District, just above Canal Street and slightly west of Bowery in what is now Chinatown.

Hester between Orange (now Baxter) and Mulberry streets was a thin strip of cobblestone, a scant 195 feet long. The lots on the street, as in most of the city, were only twenty-five feet wide, encouraging the building of structures that were narrow, long, and high. There were no alleys. Walkways of a tunnellike two and a half feet led to the rear of such buildings, where other structures were often built. The walkways also allowed access to the nightmen who pumped the privies. This caused landlords expense, and was done only occasionally. In poorer neighborhoods the scent of overflowing privies permeated the air; effluvia seeped into basements and ran into the gutters. The water supply for such structures usually consisted of a spigot in the courtyard. Number 199 was a brick dwelling of four stories with a slate or metal roof. It was the only brick building on the street—a distinct advantage in the frequent case of fire— and had a storefront on the first floor. Since 199 Hester was a "first class" structure, its outdoor privy may have been connected to the sewer. Garbage was placed in wooden boxes at the curb, where it was irregularly removed by the city's sanitation contractor. In many areas residents threw garbage and slops out their windows, knowing that the trip to the street up and down four to six flights of unlighted stairs would be unrewarded by disposal.

Writing a few years later—the city did not change quickly—a doctor gave his impression of the Fourteenth: "One half of the inhabitants are of the lower order and have little regard for cleanliness. They live by their daily labor or keep small shops. These are mostly Irish and German, the former nationality prevailing." The Steinway family's neighbors on Hester Street were a diverse lot: At 193 lived Andrew Miller, a grocer. At 195 were James Rigan and Daniel Kelly, a bootmaker and organmaker respectively. Next door at 197 lived a peddler, a laborer, and another bootmaker. At 199, where the Steinways now lived, the premises had been previously rented by two Irish tailors and a sailmaker. In 201 Hester resided Samuel Dunshee and his wife, who owned several of the buildings on the block. At 203 lived J. W. Bard and Joseph Pine, who apparently declined to provide an occupation to the canvasser. Living at 205 were J. H. Ming, a printer, Gefert Wetjen, a grocer, and a carpenter named John Myer.

Across the street was a bakery, a fish merchant, and the omnipresent dramshop. The socially conscious were fond of pointing out that "a man had ten opportunities to buy a drink in this city for every one he has to buy bread." Hyperbolic when cast this way, the statement was based on statistical truth. The city had a saloon for every fifty-five residents over the age of fifteen. Other vices were openly available within convenient walking distance. At 168 and 169 Hester were a brothel and a house of assignation, the latter being the Victorian appellation for an establishment renting rooms for liaison by the hour. This house of assignation obtained a fleeting infamy a few years later when a Brooklyn schoolteacher placed a gun to the head of a female fellow instructor and pulled the trigger before turning the weapon on himself.

It was not ethnic affinity which brought Heinrich Steinweg to Hester Street. Of the Fourteenth Ward's total population of 1855, only 13.3 percent were German. Had he desired to live with his countrymen, he would have chosen the Tenth or Eleventh Ward, known, condescendingly, as *Klein Deutschland*, where fully a third of the residents were German.

The ward of the Steinways was distinctly Irish. The "Sons of Erin" made up 36.2 percent of the ward's population. The proportion of "native Americans," a Census Bureau term, was below average at 42.6 percent. The Steinweg family was not drawn by the spaciousness of the place, for the Fourteenth's 0.15 square miles held people with bean-can density at a rate of 165,027 per square mile, four times the average for the city. Including all streets, sidewalks, residences, stores, and businesses, each resident was allotted an average space of about 170 square feet, roughly the area in the living room of a modest modern home.

The accommodations themselves at Hester Street bore no resemblance to the stolid but spacious stone home Heinrich Steinweg sold in Seesen. If typical—no pictures or plans of the building can be found—199 was a warren of windowless rooms, cubicles really, of roughly ten by twelve feet or twelve by fifteen feet. A spacious room was twelve by eighteen feet. On the upper floors room sizes shrank to as small as six by ten feet, the minimum needed to accommodate a bed, chair, and dresser. Hallways and inner rooms were unventilated and unventilatable, never seeing sunlight. With the stable next door at 197 and its inevitable manure pile, a lack of ventilation may have been a blessing. Many rooms were unheated in these buildings, a single fireplace or stove sufficing for the entire flat. Residents carted coal or firewood up the flights of stairs and stored it in their apartments.

Heinrich Steinweg did not move to the Fourteenth for pastoral peace or freedom from crime. If there was an ethnic group more reviled by the natives in the city than the Germans, it was the Irish. Whether it was cause, effect, an iterative combination of cause and effect, or simply prejudice, the Irish were the most arrested ethnic group in the city. A person of Irish origin—of any age and either sex—had an average chance of about one in five of being arrested in any year. In 1860, a typical midcentury year, the city's Irish accounted for 58.6 percent of all arrests but about 25 percent of the population.

The crimes of the general population were not of great gravity by contemporary standards. Intoxication was the most common, and it accounted for almost one in three of total arrests. Assault and battery was the second-ranking crime at one in seven arrests. This violence was not constrained to men. Women were arrested in one-fifth of the assault and battery cases. The combination of disorderly conduct plus "disorderly and intoxicated" accounted for one in four arrests with nearly four out of ten of these being of the "gentler sex." If the records can be believed, the City of the Knickerbockers was truly the City of Drinkers.

The precise aggregations of the crime reports do not show the tragedies of individual cases: "At 10 o'clock on Thursday night, TIMOTHY and CATHERINE HARRISHAM, both Irish, were found in a state of gross intoxication in Cherry Street, by the Fourth Ward Police, having with them the body of their dead child in a pine coffin which they had brought from Hampton, N. J. They were taken to the station-house, and having no physician's certificate, the Coroner was notified and the parties detained."

In total, about one in every 12 Gothamites was arrested that year, but perpetrators of major mayhem were rare, or at least rarely apprehended. There were only 57 arrests for murder, 135 for attempted murder, 30 for rape, and 24 for attempted rape. Burglaries, robberies, suspicion of, and attempts at same comprised scarcely 1 percent of all arrests. Of those arrested for theft, many were servants who stole from their employers. There were also the crimes indicative of the time: almost 200 were arrested for bastardy and 16 runaway apprentices were apprehended. There were also 16 prostitution arrests, although the prostitute population was variously estimated at up to twenty-five thousand women.

Nor did Heinrich Steinweg come to New York to educate his children. On Mulberry Street was Colored School #1, one of two in the city. Around the corner on Orange Street, 125 child-sized paces from their new home, was Ward School 17, but the Steinweg children did not attend there. The Steinwegs were not defective in this by the standards of the time. In 1849, ninety-five thousand students were enrolled in city schools, but the average daily attendance was about thirty-five thousand or roughly one-third of the enrollment. Thousands of children were never enrolled. To eat, many children had to work.

There were ample employment opportunities in the Fourteenth Ward. Shoemaking, cabinetmaking, and carriage building were among them. For those whose prime skill was a strong stomach, a four-block area only four short blocks north of Hester provided many opportunities in some of the city's grisliest trades, for it was there that the *abbatoir*, tanners, fat-boilers, and candlemakers, concentrated. To reach the *abbatoir*, herds of cattle were driven through the streets, past residences, past the retail stores on the Bowery, and into the pens to be slaughtered and butchered. Nearby a school lay between a butchery and a fat-boiler. At these establishments huge piles of animal remains littered the ground, oozing liquids across the sidewalks and into the streets.

Fat-boiling was the vilest of these activities but a necessary one. The fat-boilers took the waste of butchered animals, combined it with the carcasses of dead horses, and boiled the remains, dozens of animals at a time, in large vats. The fats that rose to the top were skimmed and delivered, still warm, to the neighborhood candlemakers or used to make coarse soap. In due time, the flesh separated from the bones. The meat was piled in the yards and allowed to decompose for about a year, after which it was sold as fertilizer to uptown farms. Uptown in the 1850s was north of Forty-second Street. The bones were allowed to dry in the sun, whereupon they were ground into meal. In the four square blocks lived roughly five thousand persons whose health risks from the activity, aesthetics aside, were immense by modern standards.

But fat-boiling and the related trades were tolerated for a very simple reason: they were essential to the disposal of the city's twenty-five thousand licensed horses. The animals died at a rate of four thousand to five thousand per year, implying a life span of perhaps five to six years. For decades, the dead animals were thrown into the rivers around the island. Most carcasses did not float away with the currents but simply moved to and fro with the tides, often beaching on the muddy shores at low water. Now there were too many horses to continue this practice.

By the time the Steinwegs arrived, fat-boiling became the preferred method of disposal, although an animal might lie in the street where it had dropped for days or weeks before being dragged away by the sanitation contractor. Dogs and cattle were also left where they died to be removed by the sanitation men. One month the duly-filed report listed the removal of 454 dead horses, 103 cattle, and miscellaneous other animals, including one alligator, the latter perhaps unable to live any longer in the sewers.

Of an entirely different nature, there was another industry concentrated in the Fourteenth, one devoted to principles as ethereal as its economic neighbors were base. That trade was piano manufacturing. While piano*making* on a small scale was centered in the Eighth Ward but scattered throughout the city, piano *manufacturing*, producing instruments by the hundreds annually, was heavily concentrated in the Fourteenth. On Broome Street were the works of Lighte, Newton & Bradbury. Lighte, whose name was Anglicized from Leuchte, gave Heinrich Steinweg employment making soundboards at six dollars per week. Also in the ward, a few hundred yards from 199 Hester, were the works of Bacon & Raven. The greying senior partner of that firm, George Bacon, witnessed Carl Steinweg's American citizenship application in 1854. The piano actionmakers, Stebbins and Smith and Francis Bonnean, conducted business on Centre Street as well. Abraham Bassford, whose sprawling business occupied a full block's depth at 63 and 64 Centre Street and three other locations, was a force in the industry. Bassford made not only pianos but pool tables and, almost predictably, a combination piano and pool table. He also operated an iron foundry that provided castings to the trade and was active in ivory turning. Completely neglected by music historians, Bassford pianos were apparently fine instruments, and he was able to obtain endorsements for them from noted artists, including New Orleans–born Louis Moreau Gottschalk, the first American piano virtuoso to be acknowledged as such in Europe.

That Heinrich Steinweg placed himself and his family at the epicenter of this activity is almost certainly not accidental. On the twenty-two square miles of Manhattan Island there were perhaps fifteen thousand dwellings from which the family might have chosen, but they elected 199 Hester Street, a ground-zero for the economic and artistic explosion that was to come. This cannot have been chance or luck; whether through astute analysis or the guidance of friends whose names are lost, the Steinwegs settled in the right place at the right time. That the Fourteenth Ward was a social petri dish, oozing with ethnic animosity, squalor, crime, vice, and the grossest affronts to the senses, is true, but it is also true that from this place Heinrich Steinweg and his sons founded a dynasty of excellence that became synonymous with the highest achievement in art and science.

Chapter 3

IN THEIR OWN
NAME AND STYLE

"The pianoforte is the most universal of instruments. Scarcely a family in this country, beyond the ordinary means of subsistence, is without one," wrote the editor of the *New York Musical Times* in 1852. "Lady," he continued, "you are, perhaps seated at a pianoforte. Possibly you are engaged in the laudable task of mastering the 'elements.' Perhaps you have got beyond all that . . . and you can make adventurous voyages on the open sea of the seven-octave pianoforte from pole to pole of the instrument, untroubled by flats, shoals, sharps, sudden modulations, or any of the harmonious quicksands, which reckless composers delight to scatter in the path of the musical voyager."

Several more prefatory and patronizing paragraphs later, editor Oliver Dyer connected with the core of his essay, a visit to the largest and most advanced piano manufactory in America: the Chickering works in Boston. Not one factory but four produced approximately thirteen hundred pianos per year with a staff of three hundred. Jonas Chickering's manufacturing operations were run on the latest principles; his was not a shop of individual craftsmen where leather-aproned, grey-bearded men custom-crafted singular instruments of distinction for the virtuoso. He relied on the tripartite concepts of automation, division of labor, and technological advance as they were then understood.

Joseph Whitworth, a renowned English engineer, reported to the British government that the sophisticated machinery found in plants such as Chickering's was commonplace in America: "A large proportion of the mechanical power of the United States has . . . been directed to wood, this being the material on which it has been requisite to operate for so many purposes, and which is presented in great abundance." Whitworth also suggested that the reason for the emphasis on automation was found in the higher pay rates of American workers. Skilled labor was scarce, commanding large wages; and "to this very want of human skill, and the absolute necessity for supplying it, may be attributed the extraordinary ingenuity displayed in many of the labour-saving machines, where automatic action so completely supplies the place of the more abundant hand-labour of older manufacturing countries."

Those whose understanding of the process and economics of manufacturing were less profound than the august British engineer's could still be impressed: "Some of these Yankee workshops are exciting places for a novice to visit. There are so many saws, and augers, and plains [*sic*], and turning-lathes buzzing, and boring, and skirring, and whirring around, that, unless one looks sharp he will find an auger hole through him, or have a shaving taken off him, before he knows what he is about," commented Oliver Dyer as he watched oak, rock maple, pine, spruce, and other woods, some seasoned for up to four years, transformed into pianoforte componentry.

Moving from the water-powered Lawrence, Massachusetts, milling operation to the final assembly plant at 334 Washington Street in Boston, Dyer commented on finishing operations: "The term 'finishing' is very comprehensive, the business being divided into upwards of twenty departments, or classes. To each department a certain number of men is assigned. . . . The same men always do the same things from year's end to year's end. For example, the man who makes *hammers* never does anything else. . . . Mr. Chickering has a man in his factory who has done nothing but make hammers to pianofortes for thirty years!! . . . This minute subdivision of labor secures, of course, the greatest possible uniformity and perfection."

In the action-making department Dyer watched the men assemble the sixty pieces of wood, leather, cloth, felt, brass, iron, and steel that made up the mechanism for each *key* into a complete module of eighty-five keys, which, when finished, contained fifty-one hundred parts. Similar levels of complexity would not be achieved in other products for the home for decades to come; a half century later, a quality automobile such as a Cadillac had less than one thousand parts, less than one-fifth the number in one Chickering & Sons piano action.

Writing to a friend in the New York trade, Chickering outlined his views on sales promotion: "It should be the duty of every piano man in this country . . . to instill in his neighbors a true and lasting love of music." He went on to describe his prescriptions for artist relations, composition, publishing, and instruction, closing with the words, "And most important, he should keep music as close to his heart as is his God, his family and his enterprise, for in doing so his enthusiasm will infect his neighbors, to mutually good effect." One of those effects, as Chickering undoubtedly knew, was increased piano sales.

Nearly a century and one-half after Jonas Chickering's apogee, it is difficult to comprehend the power of the name to the cultured American of his era. Wrote Dyer, "We looked upon Chickering as one of our most important 'institutions,' and used to mix his name up with the Tariff, National Bank, Free Trade, River and Harbor Improvements, the Eastern Boundary, and other great national questions." Heinrich Steinweg and Jonas Chickering were men of about the same age, yet as Chickering was reaching the heights of his career in America, Steinweg was just beginning his ascent. With predictable unpredictability, fate interceded. In December 1852 the Boston Chickering works was burned to the earth on which it once stood. Chickering began to build a new plant, but one year later, during a meeting "upon the interests of the Female Medical College," Chickering's head dropped to his chest; he vomited and lost consciousness. Bleeding was tried as a last resort, and Jonas Chickering died. His sons inherited the firm.

Below Chickering & Sons on the midcentury pyramid of success were dozens of other makers, all smaller but not necessarily inferior. Every port city of the eastern seaboard and some inland towns could claim at least a few pianomakers. Many of these enterprises served their local markets, insulated in part from national competition by regional pride and the primitive state of transportation and communications.

In Manhattan alone there were over thirty such firms at midcentury, their proprietors and partners (corporations were not yet in legal vogue) unlikely to voluntarily relinquish their limited success to an immigrant family named Steinweg. The tradesmen were not seekers after the universal truth in the ultimate piano tone, although some did their best to convince potential customers that this was their sole objective.

James Pirsson, a New York builder of quality instruments including a remarkable "American Double Grand Piano Forte" on which up to seven persons could play at once, gave up the business when he received an offer to buy the real estate that housed his shop. Amazed by the amount proffered, Pirsson accepted and took up real estate development. Before his career change, Henry Steinweg, Jr., worked for Pirsson making keyboards; two per week earned wages of seven dollars. Henry, Jr., quickly saw that Pirsson's double grand, though absurd as an instrument, generated much publicity and business; he also took note of the technical innovations Pirsson used, particularly an iron frame that saved making a number of wooden parts. Henry, Jr., further learned that J. Pirsson was an indefatigable experimenter with piano mechanism, and undoubtedly met many of the city's musicians, for Pirsson was also a double-bass player in the young

New York Philharmonic Orchestra. Both Pirsson's home and nearby sales-room were the scenes of many chamber music performances. Within a few years Henry Steinweg, Jr., would show that he had profited from his employment far beyond the wages earned.

James Pirsson was not unusual in changing occupations. Movement into, around, or out of the trade was common. The always-observant Whitworth noted the fluidity of occupation among Americans: "The citizen of the United States . . . seems really to pride himself in not remaining over long at any particular occupation, and being able to turn his hand to some dozen different pursuits in the course of his life." Compared to the ossified productive systems of Europe where, for example, a journeyman might be required by law or guild fiat not simply to make chairs, and only chairs, but to make a single type of chair in a fixed and small quantity, the freedom of America must have been heady to some and terrifying to others. The Steinwegs would show that they could adapt.

As well as the many who moved between the related crafts of wood-turning, carpentry, ivory-turning, varnishing, cabinetmaking, and carpentry in the New York piano trade, there were also a few men who specialized in deadly economic predation. One such was appropriately named Wake, an attorney who also sold pianos and supplied hardware, tuning pins, strings, agraffes, and other exotic bits of metal needed in pianomaking. Wake's technique for economic gain was simple: he sold hardware on credit to a struggling pianomaker. When a sufficient debt was accrued, payment was demanded. If prompt payment was not made, forced bankruptcy followed, assets were seized and the business liquidated, with Wake retaining both the debt owed with interest and the profit of the liquidator. A fat stack of yellowing cards in the New York county clerk's judgment files tell the story. Each contains a terse record of a man or firm who fell prey to Wake, the liquidator. He never lost.

In 1853 one of Wake's liquidations involved the assets of the pianomaker William Nunns, a three-decade veteran of the New York trade. One of those scarred by the financial claws of the predator Wake was William Steinweg. The three hundred dollars in back wages due young William for his labor in Nunns's shop were never collected from Nunns or Wake, the liquidator. For a "new man," the sum represented eight months' work, six days per week, up to twelve hours per day. William's brother Charles also worked for Nunns as a casemaker, but apparently had gone to another shop before Nunns failed.

Four decades later the experience of the boy resonated with the immediacy of yesterday in the mind of the man, now famous, powerful, and wealthy. Contributing by invitation, along with du Pont, Colgate, Pillsbury, Armour, Lorillard, and others in a book describing American industrial progress, William Steinway (Steinweg) wrote, "The despicable 'truck' system prevailed throughout the country. The skilled workman was not paid his hard-earned wages, which were from $6 to $10 a week; he would receive, say, from $2 to $3 of his weekly earnings in cash and some of the rest in orders on grocers, tailors and shoemakers. The remainder would be retained by his employer, who acted as a self-constituted savings bank for his employ- ees, without paying interest, and sometimes not even paying the princi- pal. . . . There were piano factories and other manufacturers who were each thus constantly owing over $100,000 in wages to their workmen." A man so wealthy that he could donate fifty thousand dollars to bring the World's Fair to New York and could give gifts of thousands to virtual strangers in need, still remembered the loss of three hundred dollars in his youth to men long dead.

Besides the transient, the quixotic, and the deadly, the Gotham piano milieu also supported firms of substance and reputation. Largest among them was Lighte & Newton, which employed 164 men and six boys to produce about $250,000 in pianos at mid-decade. Pennsylvania-born piano-maker Henry J. Newton teamed with a German, Ferdinand C. Leuchte, in 1848. Adding the capital, reputation, and influence of William B. Brad-bury, a prominent Maine-born conductor, organist, and hymnologist in 1854, the firm scrambled to the top of the trade during the early Steinway years in the city. After a ballistic rise the enterprise splintered, and the partners separated to become competitors. The ever-permuting nature of the partnerships, economic marriages of convenience often with the longevity of warm milk, would prove to be an advantage to the Steinwegs, who, as a family, had the benefits of sanguineous if not always sanguine relationships.

The total employment at Lighte, et alia, of 170 men and boys was an impressive number for its time when the average American manufacturing establishment employed about eight persons. Likewise, Lighte's revenues of $250,000 represented large-scale sales considering that, by official defini-tion in Massachusetts, a manufacturer was anyone making products worth more than five hundred dollars per year. Lighte's workers were not employ-ees in a contemporary sense, nor were those of other manufacturers. There were no paid holidays, no sick leave, no benefits, no overtime, no formal path to promotion; and the men provided their own tools and workbenches. The benches of the dismissed might be placed in the street to be carted away by the freshly unemployed if a separation were acrimonious. The men were not paid by the month, week, or hour; they were paid by the piece on a scale negotiated between the worker and the employer. Two to three dollars might represent the price for a piano sounding board. How long it took to produce such a component was up to the individual worker, but the employer or his foreman was the sole judge of acceptable quality. If rework were needed, it was done on the worker's time. In some specialties workers employed helpers, who were paid a portion of the piece price.

When there was work, the men came to the shop. When there was not, they stayed home or set about the task of finding a shop where they were needed. Onerous by modern standards, the piecework system was highly valued by the workers, at least by the more efficient. In one case, strike threats resulted from the mere rumor that hourly wages might be substituted for piece prices. The piano trade was not a particularly brutal one; its labor practices were conventional for the time.

The piano workers were relatively well paid. A man varnishing pianos might make 15 to 25 percent more than a man varnishing cabinets, basically the same task. Piano casemakers had the same skills as cabinetmakers, but again the pay differential favored piano work. According to the *New York Times*, but by computations unknown, a "mechanic" with a family of four could live well in New York on six hundred dollars per year in 1853. Of this 45.5 percent went for food, 22 percent for clothing, 20 percent for household items, 15 percent for rent, 5 percent for light and heat, and 2 percent for medical expenses. The reporter calculated that this left a few dollars to be spent on a *Times* subscription, a library fee, and a church donation. It was assumed that the mechanic walked to work, for if he had ridden on a nickel horsecar, the church, the library, and the *Times* would all have lost their support.

The second-largest firm in the city may have been one of the more pleasant and profitable places for the workman. Adam H. Gale & Company had its roots in the strikes and riots of the late 1830s when a group of roughly twenty pianomakers banded together in the best socialist fashion. They formed the New York Pianoforte Manufacturing Company as a cooperative operating a works at Third Avenue and Thirteenth Street. Within a few years the cooperative went the way of most enterprises based on faith in human nature and was purchased by Gale, who was one of the participants in the experiment. Apparently hewing to the socialist prescription, Gale & Company produced relatively inexpensive instruments, receiving about $230 per piano and making roughly 650 of them per year, about 14 percent of the city's 1855 output of roughly 4,500 pianos per year.

At the opposite pole of the social sphere were the pianofortes produced by Nunns & Clark, the third of New York's pianistic big three. Nunns & Clark produced very expensive instruments, averaging five hundred dollars each. The case work was magnificent, exhibiting rare woods and the heavy application of ornamentation and carvings. There is little doubt that making pianos the Nunns & Clark way was very profitable. If the Steinwegs had a local strategic target when they entered the trade as manufacturers, it was most likely Nunns & Clark; for the company's formula of high prices, high quality, and proven technology needed change in only one word: *proven* would be transmuted by the Steinwegs to *advanced*.

In the medium-priced niche was another large manufacturer, Bacon & Raven, operating from 160–62 Centre Street, just a few hundred feet from the Steinwegs at 199 Hester. Producing five hundred medium-priced instruments per year with revenues of $120,000, George Bacon and Richard

Raven formed one of the trade's more stable partnerships in 1841, a business arrangement that continued until Bacon's death about 1855. It was probably through an association with Bacon & Raven that the Steinwegs entered the New York piano trade. Not only was Charles Steinweg well enough known to George Bacon that the elderly and distinguished American businessman witnessed Carl's citizenship application in 1854, an act not unlike being the best man at a wedding; but a former partner of Bacon's, one Thomas H. Chambers, also played a prominent role in the early success of Steinway & Sons.

That the family faced truly formidable competition when they entered the piano business is clear. Confronting them was an array of talented men with hundreds of years of aggregate experience. Whether "native" or English, the Steinweg competitors had the financial resources, the market knowledge, the network of contacts, the dealer relationships, and all the other advantages of the entrenched. The Steinwegs had the further burden of their ethnic origin. The only highly successful German in the trade was Lighte, whose partners were American-born. Though many Germans worked as pianomakers, there was but one other who had established and maintained his own business, which, after more than a decade, was only a modest success. That pioneer was William Lindeman, who employed fifteen men. Short and slightly bowlegged Heinrich Steinweg had survived wars, revolution, epidemics, famine, and a lightning bolt during his first fifty years. To such a man, the odds of success may have appeared less daunting than they really were.

To understand and reconstruct the reality of the early Steinweg years in America, a beginning can be made with the standard legend. A tale oft-repeated, with suitable modifications and elaborations over a period of four decades by the family, the story is still told today by Steinway & Sons. Stripped to its essence, the legend holds that the Steinwegs came to America and lived at 199 Hester but worked in various other shops until they opened their own business on March 5, 1853, as Steinway & Sons at 85 Varick Street. From that fateful Saturday the Steinways ascend to greatness with uninterrupted majesty. The Stein*wegs* became the Stein*ways* about this time for business purposes. Legal name changes, approved by the courts, were slower in coming. Henry, Jr., had his name changed in the Court of Common Pleas in June 1864. He had already been a citizen for more than eight years.

Of the legend, even the date is in doubt, for in sworn 1876 testimony William Steinway stated the company "commenced operations on the First of May 1853." Historically, the May date is more plausible than March due to a New York custom called May Day. As the *Times* explained in 1858: "New comers in New York from foreign countries and the rural districts, who happen to be here on the first of May, seeing how recklessly and good-naturedly half the population change their residences and place of business on that day, conceive the wild idea that New Yorkers rather enjoy the miseries of moving. . . . But though moving to many is a misery which cannot be avoided, its discomforts are greatly mitigated by having one day out of the year devoted expressly to it, like New Year's Day for visiting and the Fourth of July for fireworks." March 5 had an entirely different significance for the enterprise: it was William Steinway's birthday.

A factor undoubtedly contributing to the Steinway's decision to begin the manufacture of their own instruments was the labor unrest percolating through the city in the spring of 1853. More or less quiescent for several years, the city's workers were once again organizing, raising the specter of mayhem, murder, strikes, and riots that haunted the memories of adult New Yorkers.

The pianomakers met to consider the advisability of a strike against those firms which had not acceded to their wage demands. Two hundred men, half Germans, attended the meeting, again in the Fourteenth Ward. James Young, chairman of the group, had previously issued a communiqué in suitably diplomatic and noble language, proposing that "journeymen piano-forte makers of this city of New York organize themselves into a society for the purpose of regulating and establishing uniform prices for their labor, and receiving communications and suggestions from their employers that may tend to the legitimate interest and welfare of the trade." Astutely worded to avoid the charges of a felonious conspiracy that throttled earlier union activity, the message was no less clear to the makers: a price increase or a strike was inevitable. The bosses, as was customary, threatened to fire men joining protective societies. During that spring other rumblings were heard from the trades, among them the shipjoiners, coachmen, and coal hoisters, all threatening to strike.

Thus the spring of 1853 was an ideal time to begin manufacture of pianos. If a pianomakers strike occurred, dealers would be unable to obtain pianos, creating opportunities for a new maker; strikers would be seeking supplementary work; trade suppliers would be generous with terms on goods they could not sell elsewhere; and, of course, the Steinways themselves would be deprived of their regular incomes. The legend simply states that the Steinways worked for other firms, then went out on their own, a seemingly straightforward decision. The reality is much more complex.

The essence of the truth is that the Steinways built pianos at 199 Hester Street, probably for others in the trade, and were apparently not eager to admit this fact. A further probable truth emerges: during the early years the family built pianos not only under "their own name and style" but also for a dealer who likely sold them under his own name. This was, and is, called "stencilling." The dealer bought a cheap, generic piano, and a "stencil" was used to apply the name of his choice to the instrument. The potential for misleading buyers though stencilling is obvious and not infrequent in the nether reaches of the trade. One favorite device was to apply the name of a famous composer to the instrument; others used stencil names with great similarity to a reputable maker. This might result in a piano marked *Chickoring & Son*, to be sold at a very large profit. For a firm and family of fame, professing the highest standards of art, science, and craft in a climate of moral absolutism, expedient participation in the stencil business could not be admitted; a suitably sanitized legend was necessary.

The mosaic of Steinweg activity in this period has been shattered by time, but shards remain. A city directory published in 1851—the Steinwegs were not yet in America for a year—carries the listing on its mildewed pages: "Henry Steinweg, Piano Manufacturer, 199 Hester St." So it can be seen that after a few months' stay in America Heinrich Steinweg had at least the aspiration to be a *manufacturer*, not simply a pianomaker who worked for others. He, or the printer, had also partially anglicized his name.

Detailed maps of New York City produced by civil engineers and sold to insurance companies to assess fire risks provide another clue: 199 Hester appears on these maps colored in pale green with three carefully inked small circles. The map's legend shows the code to mean "Third Class Hazardous Manufacturing," including, among others, bleaching works, candlemakers, rectifiers of liquors by fire and heat, omnibus stables, and flour mills. On the long list of activities likely to precipitate palpitations among the underwriters was yet another: *pianoforte makers*. The presence of wood shavings, lacquers, varnishes, paints, mineral spirits, and fires kept for the steam-bending of wood plus, of course, the standard luminaries—open gaslights and oil lamps—meant that pianomaking was not an activity loved by insurance companies. With its combination of combustible materials, volatile chemicals, and open flames, a piano works was a holocaust waiting to happen, and they commonly burned to the ground, taking surrounding structures with them.

Thus insurance maps reveal a truth the Steinways preferred to conceal in later years: pianos were made at 199 Hester Street. That the Steinways themselves were involved is of little doubt, for a company account book for 1856 contains the entry, "Hoistway at 199 Hester . . . $60." A hoistway was a wooden or iron frame with block and tackle used to lift large and heavy objects, usually into the upper floors of a building. There is further evidence of commercial activity on Hester: a classified newspaper ad for a reconditioned piano (or pianos) appeared in the *Times*—"Enquire No. 199 Hester st., upper floor."

The ultimate evidence of a Steinway piano works at 199 Hester comes from a New York State Census for the Fourteenth Ward. There, captured in the fatigued scrawl of the enumerator who trudged from building to building and floor to floor in the stifling heat of the city summer, are family numbers 338, 339, 340, and 341. Enumerated as family 338 are the "Stimways": Henry; Julia, wife of Henry; Charles, son; his wife. Sophia; Henry, son; William, son; Albert, son; and Anna, daughter. The "Stimways" had done well during their five years in America, and living with them was a 23-year-old servant from Germany, Eva, one-year resident in America.

Also at 199 were Frederick Rahaus, 36, a pianomaker, his wife, Christina, and two young daughters, Henrietta and Mary, listed as family 339. Family 340 was Henry Vogel, 26, a pianomaker, with his wife, Mina, and 2-year-old daughter, Lizzie. Family 341 consisted of Henry Rapp, 25, a varnisher, with his wife and daughter, both named Lena.

The residents of 199 Hester formed the classical economic unit of nineteenth-century New York, a group of families that lived and worked at the same address; the census shows hundreds of such units in virtually every trade, from shoemaking to goldbeating. Almost invariably they lived in buildings, like 199 Hester, with a storefront underneath from which they sold the products of their labors. The Hester Street arrangements proved transient, and before 1858 neither Rahaus nor Rapp nor Vogel was a part of Steinway operations. These men and their families had dispersed throughout the city to live separate lives of anonymity.

By the time of the 1855 census, operations at 199 Hester had grown well beyond the minor family enterprise, for other records show that thirty men labored for the Steinways in their Fourteenth Ward manufactory. Paid an average of forty dollars per month to produce a declared two hundred pianos per year, this was a hard-working group, producing almost seven pianos per man, in contrast to the more typical four to five.

However, the remarkable productivity at 199 is ignored in the official Steinway version of events. The company legend avers that the business began at 85 Varick Street. The same still-crisp, bright white maps that revealed Hester as a commercial location show that 85 Varick was a "Fourth Class Stone Dwelling" with a shingle roof. Unlike Hester, it had no storefront underneath. Occupied in 1851 to 1852 by a bookkeeper, the building was used in 1853 by Heinrich Steinweg, but he stayed only one year. In 1854, 85 was occupied by pianomaker Charles Krall, in 1855 by two other pianomen, Otto Scheutze and Augustus Luedolph, and in 1856 was again in use by the Steinwegs for keymaking. More than simply consecutive occupants at 85 Varick, Krall, Scheutze, and Luedolph were intertwined with the Steinwegs. They, along with Charles and Heinrich, all had commercial relationships with the well-established makers Bacon & Raven. Krall was later employed by Steinway & Sons as a piano finisher. The most plausible explanation of the revolving door tenancy at 85 Varick involving all these men is that the shop was used to build components, or perhaps complete pianos, for Bacon & Raven and others in the trade.

Number 85 Varick Street was located between Watts and Canal streets and is now paved over as part of the egress from the Holland Tunnel. The building was situated at the western edge of the city's Eighth Ward, not far from the shore of the North (Hudson) River. Reaching Varick from

Hester meant traversing some of the city's most notorious "fever nests," the area between Varick and Wooster where dysentery, typhus, typhoid, and cholera were common.

The Eighth was notorious for vice among its roughly 120,000 inhabitants. Reporting on conditions in the ward, the Council on Hygiene and Public Health cited "the vicious habits of thousands who inhabit this section and who follow a nightly vocation of assignation, thereby contaminating and spreading widely the syphilitic disease and other maladies."

Many families in the ward lived in basements, eight to ten individuals per small room, "where the floor was perfectly saturated with water" or overflow from the sewers. "The negroes who inhabit some of these cellars are fond of excluding light by placing dark curtains in the windows"; in other cellars ventilation was available only by opening doors. Cellar dwellers, it was reported, were easily identifiable on the streets by their "cadaverous appearance." Nor was this all. There were "the filthy habits of the occupants, in not keeping their persons and apartments clean; allowing vermin to infest everything . . ." According to a doctor, "The moral condition of many portions of this section is lamentable; abounding with thieves, pickpockets, gamblers, and all sorts of bad men and women, who are ready to do anything for money."

While the men of the Steinway family must have endured assaults to the senses, health, and person in the crosstown commute from Hester to Varick streets, they were at least partially compensated by the low rents of the district. It is unlikely, though, that the "Lady" to whom Oliver Dyer addressed his remarks on Chickering's manufactory would have willingly endured the conditions of the Eighth, simply to purchase that symbol of civility and genteel culture, a piano. It is most likely that the Steinways used 85 Varick solely as a manufacturing site for their expanding operations.

The more than forty-five hundred pianos made each year in New York City, and representing perhaps half the nation's total output, were naturally sold from a variety of locations, but the retail trade was centered along Broadway; of the 116 firms listed in directories as makers, dealers, and tuners, almost a third were located on Broadway. In the 300 to 500 blocks of Broadway there was a heavy concentration of piano dealers on both sides of the avenue, forming a sort of musical checkerboard on city maps. Ladies and gentlemen of refinement did not venture into the ruder sections of the city to purchase pianofortes. They bought them on Broadway in ornate emporia, commercial temples of culture.

Customers might, of course, have ventured slightly off the thoroughfare onto one of the side streets if there were a reason to do so. At 88 Walker, 265 feet east of Broadway, just two blocks below Canal, there was a reason. Number 88 had for many years been a place where pianos were sold. The "Second Class Store" there, right next to a lumberyard and sawmill, had been occupied by James Pirsson in the 1840s and after that by William

Nunns. On the other side of 88 at 86 Walker was the cabinet shop of Robert Ward. In 1854 the premises at 88, all of 25 feet wide, were also rented by the Steinways. On one corner of Broadway and Walker was the popular Panorama Hall with its depictions of battles and historic scenes; on the other was the Florence Hotel. Though Walker Street was easy to find, it was not a place from which one could sell the declared 200 pianos a year of 1855, more than one every other day. From this location the Steinways sold a total of only 29 pianos directly to metropolitan New Yorkers, about 26 percent of their total production in 1855.

In fact, the Steinways did not make 200 pianos by mid-1855 as they told the census. According to the company's own records, they made 112 in the entire year. The total number of men working for the Steinways was 55, making them the city's sixth-largest piano employer, an impressive accomplishment if true, for a German family living in America for only five years.

The balance of 83 pianos was sold through a sophisticated but small system of dealers, travelling salesmen, and at least one piano teacher. Among the dealers was Thomas H. Chambers, a part of the city's commercial/musical community since 1835. A former partner in Dubois, Bacon & Chambers, he was himself a pianomaker. In the early Steinway years Chambers was operating a retail showroom at 385 Broadway, less than two hundred paces from the Steinway store at 88 Walker. In 1855 Chambers took delivery of 24 instruments from Steinway & Sons.

An aggressive promoter, Chambers advertised heavily: "Thomas H. Chambers invites purchasers to call at his old established warerooms, 385 Broadway, and examine his pianofortes, which never fail to give perfect satisfaction, as his numerous patrons will testify. These instruments contain all the latest improvements and are warranted to stand the action of any climate, having been thoroughly tested, and are preeminent for their durability, tone, touch and elegance of finish. Call, see and be convinced," read a mid-1854 insertion in the *Times*.

Though he bought many, Chambers never advertised Steinway pianos, and the advertisements convey the message that he was selling his own instruments. That two stores would be selling the same brand of instruments, one run by the builder and another run by a dealer, within 545 feet of each other does not seem commercially sensible. The alternative explanation is that Steinway & Sons was stencilling pianos for Chambers and continued to do so into 1857 when Chambers left the Broadway location.

Selling nearly as many instruments as Chambers in the early years was a travelling salesman named J. T. Hammick. Moving indefatigably around New York State, Hammick sold Steinway-built instruments in what would now be called "upstate" New York. At towns along the newly opened Erie railroad such as Calicoon, Hancock, Deposit, and Binghamton, J. T. Hammick sold the products of Steinway & Sons. A large number of units went to Catskill, New York; Hammick also made occasional forays into New Jersey, selling at Jersey City, as far north into Chickering territory as Hillsdale, Massachusetts, where he sold two pianos, and west perhaps as far as Buffalo.

Also selling for the Steinways in a more limited way, but still critical in the early years, was Francis A. Blanchard, a music teacher who lived upstate in the Columbia County town of Hudson, New York, with his wife Jane and daughter Mary. Residing in a commercial area, Blanchard undoubtedly found that recommending the pianos of Steinway & Sons was a profitable way to augment his already comfortable net worth of $8,000.

Blanchard, Chambers, and Hammick were involved with the Steinways from the beginning of Steinway & Sons, each taking at least one of the first dozen pianos built. But within two years of the first sale the Steinways were engaged in building a national dealer organization patterned after major producers such as Chickering. A dealer named Petri soon joined in Baltimore, where Knabe was the powerful local builder. In Washington, D.C., Steinway pianos were sold by F. C. Reichenbach; in Louisville, Kentucky, they were available from D. P. Faulds; and in Savannah, Georgia, from Zogbaum & Company. The Zogbaums were also active as New York musical dealers at the same time, but, interestingly, did not offer Steinway-built instruments at their Maiden Lane store in Manhattan.

The early Steinway years in America are both more complex and impressive than the legend. Likely beginning with the manufacture of components for the trade at 199 Hester and later at 85 Varick, the family began to manufacture complete pianos under their own name in the first half of 1853. They made a scant dozen units that year and nurtured the early relationships on which they built their success throughout the mid-1850s.

Again the activity of the Steinways slips into darkness. The firm's early records are confusing, fragmentary, and written over by several hands. As the story is told, instrument number 483 was the first Steinway & Sons piano, and it exists today, covered with a blanket, in the climate-controlled basement of New York's Metropolitan Museum of Art. Number 483 was sold on the sixteenth of September 1853 to a Mr. Griswold of Brooklyn. However, according to the "number book," which tracks Steinway production through the generations to this very day, eleven days earlier 484 was sold to a Mr. Fox on East Broadway. Surfacing eighty-eight years later, number 484 was destroyed by Steinway & Sons in 1941.

The question of the "first Steinway" is not necessarily trivial or arcane; it was germane to a court decision rendered as late as 1980. In reference to the oft-told tale, Heinrich Steinweg built pianos in Germany, and upon immigration to America continued to number them consecutively. The courts did not consider that Heinrich could neither read nor write in *any* language, thereby bringing his recordkeeping abilities into general doubt. There are also the words of Charles (aka Carl) Steinweg. Speaking publicly in 1860, he commented on "their immense business in Brunswick of ten pianos per year, the supply always exceeding the demand." Taken at a generous face value, the Steinwegs could not have produced more than 150 pianos in Germany and probably made many fewer. With the numbering beginning in America at 483, there are at least 333 missing pianos in the series.

While the Steinwegs probably produced pianos for the stencil trade, it seems unlikely that they could have built over three hundred instruments in the three years before they began pianomaking under their own name. Perhaps there was nothing more to this than a desire on the part of the family to appear as a larger maker than they were, beginning their serial numbers in the hundreds, rather than with the number one. They would not have been the first, nor the last, manufacturer to adopt that ploy. But there is a second set of books, a ledger kept by William Steinway. Its entries begin in the *middle* of the page with number 483. Why William began in the middle of the page or what he might have recorded, had he the time or inclination, cannot be known fourteen decades later.

But the records do show that from the very beginning the Steinways had other employees. On the first eighteen serial numbers the books carefully note the work of five different casemakers. The Steinways themselves did not work long at the bench. Eighteen-year-old William Steinway was the "bellyman" who installed the sounding board and frame in the case, while his older brother, Henry, Jr., 21, was a finisher, and Charles, now age 23, was responsible for "regulating," that critical set of operations in which the instrument receives its final adjustments. Their father Heinrich did not work in the shop as a craftsman according to the records. Henry was the first son to leave his bench, after only nine units were completed. He was replaced by one of the Decker brothers, who had also worked for Bacon & Raven. A decade later the Deckers founded their own firm, beginning, ironically, at 85 Varick Street, and grew to be potent competitors of Steinway & Sons.

After roughly forty units were built, William ceased his work as a bellyman. He was replaced by Henry Kroeger, an impressively competent pianoman who could make any part of a piano and also design with the best. Kroeger's career with the family lasted for over a quarter-century, and for many years he was paid a royalty on each piano built, the only non–family member ever to be paid anything but a salary.

Only Charles remained in the shop—well into 1856—in the critical role of regulator, but he forsook his bench to be replaced by Theodore Vogel, the husband of one of Heinrich's daughters, Wilhelmina. The brothers were now "managers." In modern terms a structure evolved. Charles focused on manufacturing operations while Henry, Jr., specialized in research and development and William concentrated on marketing. That Heinrich was ultimately in charge, there can be little doubt.

The Steinways' rapid evacuation of the shop floor was in marked contrast to the behavior of Jonas Chickering, who, even in his final years, greeted artists and members of the press wearing a shop apron and often carrying a plane or brace and bit. Whether this was an affectation on Chickering's part, designed to amuse or perhaps shock his visitors, or whether it reflected his daily behavior is unknown. It was not expected that a millionaire would greet important guests in the rough garb of a mechanic. Mechanics were not held in high esteem, and manual work of any kind was considered coarse by many prosperous enough to avoid it.

Oliver Dyer illuminates the attitude toward pianos and the men who made them: "To most minds, it is simply a mechanical arrangement of wood, iron, ivory, steel, wire, leather and various other vulgar materials, which, when taken separately, are beneath the notice of any well-bred lady or gentleman;—it is merely a mechanical affair, and the maker is, of course, only a mechanic." Chickering, the institution, the wealthy Yankee, could flaunt stereotype and prejudice with impunity. Immigrant German mechanics, scratching to gain a handhold in a perilous trade, could not. And so the family left the domain of "buzzing and boring and skirring and whirring" machinery and the "vulgar" men who tended lathes and augers to begin a long journey though time. At the end of that journey pianos would no longer be seen as machines but as works of art and the men who built them as artists, partners with the composers and the virtuosi who created musical history.

Chapter 4

NOT STRICTLY LEGITIMATE, BUT GOOD

"After the concert Liszt stands there like a victor on the battlefield, like a hero at a tournament. Daunted pianos lie around him; torn strings wave like flags of truce; frightened instruments flee into distant corners; the listeners look at each other as after a cataclysm of nature . . . and he stands there leaning melancholically on his chair, smiling strangely, like an exclamation point after the outbreak of general admiration. Thus is Franz Liszt." The words were those of critic Moritz Gottlieb Saphir, after witnessing one of Franz Liszt's more than three thousand public performances.

For roughly five decades of his life Liszt was a living icon, the apotheosis of the nineteenth-century piano virtuoso. He would perform to the accompaniment of medals clanking on his chest in a variety of bizarre costumes, Turk, cossack, and military among them, sometimes puffing on a cigar. The story is told that one woman, after retrieving a Lisztian cigar end from a group of other admirers equally determined to possess it, carried it in her bosom for the rest of her life. Two countesses, in a contest for Liszt's snuffbox, fought to exhaustion on the floor. Other devotees framed broken strings from his pianos. Mobs of women clamored to touch the master on stage during performances.

Liszt's genius as a showman was equal to his musicianship. He might faint on stage or kick the piano stool away; he might jump up and down. His handsome countenance would assume forms seen "in the paintings of

Our Savior by some of the early masters." He was occasionally carried off the stage by friends while in "fits of hysterics." In one case Liszt reported, with great amusement, that he had cuffed his piano tuner for trying to repair his instrument during a performance after the maestro had called the technician on stage.

Franz Liszt never came to America, but he apparently contemplated the idea. A letter to Liszt from Hector Berlioz admonished Liszt: "Your project for a tour of the United States seems violent to me—to cross the Atlantic to make music for Yankees who just now are only thinking of California gold!" Horrifying though it may have been for the cognoscenti to contemplate, the record suggests that Franz Liszt and Phineas T. Barnum based their respective popular successes on similar principles of showmanship.

European musical artists were of at least two minds on cultural sophistication in the United States. Max Maretzek, an opera impresario, summed them up in 1855: "Some believe it to be a literal Eldorado. . . . The inhabitants are wealthy, confiding and generous in the extreme." The other view, as sketched by Maretzek, was that America "contains a race of people who eat raw meat and devour uncooked vegetables, who chew tobacco, and void their rheum upon ladies' dresses and Turkish carpets, who drink unheard of quantities of brandy, schnapps, ale and Monogahela whiskey." Maretzek did not analyze why these two views could not both be simultaneously true. It was generally conceded that while Americans might build the best clipper ships, telegraphs, and railroads, they were not a people of high aesthetic refinement by European standards.

"Justly or unjustly," wrote the *New York Times* in 1852, "an idea is abroad that the musical ideals of the American press are not, to use the gentlest phrase, what they should be. In Paris they call our commentaries on ALBONI, SONTAG, and the rest, 'dilettantism run mad,' when as they have been penned in the soberest humor, and with the best available lights to aid us. Is it not possible that we are in want of teachers? Are not some canons of criticism needed?" The editorialist went on to suggest support for a series of musical lectures being offered by William Henry Fry, a composer and musical critic who had worked for six years in Europe as a newspaper correspondent. The lectures "will save a vast deal of transcendentalism and extravagance among gentlemen who feel impelled to say much when they know little. . . . We propose in fact that MR. FRY organize a special class of musical editors, with reference to the correction of vulgar taste." American taste, whether vulgar or refined, spawned an active business in cultural arbitrage in which European musical, dramatic, and literary figures placed their performance standards at risk in return for potentially large rewards bestowed by American cultural consumers.

The pioneer pianist to venture across the sea to the land of coonskin caps and cotton gins was Leopold De Meyer. Forgotten now, when not dismissed as a charlatan, the Lion Pianist (Liszt was the King of Pianists) blazed trails that can be traced to the present, including the playing of "Yankee Doodle Variations" and other patriotic melodies.

Landing and leaving well before the Steinways arrived, De Meyer's mode of operations would prove prototypical for later artist tours promulgated by pianomakers, including the legendary Steinway-sponsored national tours of Anton Rubinstein and Ignace Paderewski. The Lion's first New York appearance was playing during intermissions between one-act comedies with titles such as *The Dumb Belle*. From this fragile platform, De Meyer launched into instantaneous fame. "It is difficult to afford an adequate idea of the unparalleled enthusiasm—it might be called frenzy—with which [he] was received . . . everybody looked so excited, that a stranger . . . could have fancied himself in a lunatic asylum, with De Meyer—the only one who looked reasonable—as the keeper," wrote the *New York Herald*.

A scant three weeks from landing in America and after only six nights of intermission performances, Leopold De Meyer was playing to sold-out houses of three thousand persons at a converted church on Broadway known as the Tabernacle. A performance with the New York Philharmonic materialized. Two more Manhattan performances followed, again to sold-out houses, and New Yorkers were able to bask in self-congratulatory claims of superior municipal tastes in matters musical. Within six months of his arrival in America, Leopold De Meyer grossed a sum larger than a carpenter would earn working for thirty years. This was only the beginning, and De Meyer soon toured the major cities.

During his American sojourn The Lion played principally on his "custom-made" Erards, but not exclusively. He also endorsed—and played locally— the instruments of Emilius Scheer of Philadelphia. In Boston he played, much to the pleasure of the residents, a Chickering grand. A rumor was floated in the press that Jonas Chickering was building a special instrument for De Meyer. In New York De Meyer wrote that he felt the pianos of Stodart & Dunham to be of "superior quality . . . but also, through durability in workmanship, superior to any other manufactory." De Meyer was undoubtedly aware that performing on an indigenous piano played to emotions more than musical; it generated local pride and with it increased ticket sales.

Promiscuous endorsements of pianos by artists was a long-standing European tradition, practiced by the best. Chopin owned instruments by three competing makers but opined he had no time to play any of them. Liszt's homes were veritable warehouses of pianos in an ever-changing inventory that would have been the envy of any Broadway piano dealer. A half-century later Paderewski chose to play Steinways in the United States and Erards in Europe, commenting that while anyone could make a Steinway "sing," it took real genius and mastery to accomplish this on an Erard. Three-quarters of a century after that, Leonard Bernstein endorsed Bosendorfer in Europe and Baldwin in America, apparently out of loyalty for an early and crucial favor. Baldwin had loaned Bernstein an instrument when no one else would.

De Meyer's performances on American instruments were an early signal that domestic pianomakers were fast closing on their European counterparts. Sometimes playing his hallowed Erards and American pianos on the same stage the same night, De Meyer was demonstrating, inadvertently, that the Americans were achieving parity in instrument making. If they had not felt that they could withstand comparison to the famed Erard, local makers would not have allowed their instruments on the same stage under the same talented hands.

Press opinion on De Meyer bifurcated after a time; few challenged his pianistic competence and skills, but the "puffing" and "humbug" of his promotional techniques offended many. In his second year in America De Meyer was enmeshed in one of New York's many newspaper wars in which the editors of the city's daily papers flagellated each other with accusations of corruption, incompetence, greed, and bad taste, all in the interest of circulation building. There were charges of paying for reviews, sabotaging the concerts of competing artists, and plagiarism. De Meyer lost a twenty-five-dollar lawsuit brought by a journalist for translation services. None of this hurt the Lion Pianist's ability to draw audiences, and he continued to play to full houses at the Tabernacle.

What did damage De Meyer was the arrival from France of another European virtuoso, Henri Herz. In less than a year, news of De Meyer's American success had brought forth competition from the Old World. A formidable amalgamation of talents, European virtuoso Henri Herz not only played and composed in the conventional manner; he was also a successful teacher and piano manufacturer. Playing a stylistic counterpoint to De Meyer, Herz appeared reserved and diffident, almost immediately winning the favor of the cognoscenti. Herz's performances were suave and gentle, again a contrast to the bombast of De Meyer.

Before long Herz acquired a manager, the young Bernard Ullmann, who became one of New York's most powerful impresarios. They worked together for almost five years developing listener-pleasing routines such as on-the-spot improvisations to melodies called out by the audience ("Home, Sweet Home" was a favorite), a popular eight-piano arrangement of the *William Tell* Overture, and, of course, the requisite "Yankee Doodle" variations.

In response to the Herz incursion, Leopold De Meyer made a "southern tour," as he had the year before, but it was less successful. Astute in many ways, De Meyer failed to consider the potent effects of novelty in his earlier triumphs. Returning to New York in the summer of 1847, The Lion sold his Erards and left American shores for Europe, making a strange promise to return in twenty years.

Leopold De Meyer did, in fact, appear in America two decades later. "We . . . take pleasure in informing our dealers that the celebrated pianist

LEOPOLD DE MEYER (who created such a furore during his first visit to this country twenty years ago) has arrived here a few days since," wrote William Steinway on September 1, 1867. "He intends to give Concerts only in New York, Boston and intermediate places, Philadelphia, Baltimore and Washington during the coming season, but will probably make a more extensive concert tour next spring." In a strange flip of fate, De Meyer, the first European piano virtuoso to tour America in 1845, had become the first European artist to tour for Steinway & Sons in 1867.

"DE MEYER'S playing continues still to be remarkable for its fire and impetuosity, while with those peculiarities is mingled a rarer excellence— only acquired by years of practice—supreme delicacy of touch, which gives true poetic expression to everything he puts his finger to. . . . As of yore, he seats himself at his instrument, then ungloves . . . before he enters the arena to grapple for the crown of victory." The *Times* review of the Steinway Hall performance was positive, but this was not enough, and the audiences waned.

The Lion had been declawed by time and changing tastes. There were just three more New York performances, all shared with other artists, the last two of them with second billing. Before long the Steinway & Sons sponsorship evaporated, and De Meyer stepped from the pages of American musical history. Whatever can be said for or against Leopold De Meyer, one thing is certain: in coming to America he went where few artists had gone before; after him, there were many. On the night of De Meyer's second American debut at Steinway Hall, Tuesday, October 1, 1867, William Steinway was not in the audience, nor is there any evidence that he ever actually met The Lion. Had William comprehended De Meyer's significance, he would certainly have made a personal contact. Twenty years before, while the Steinway family was suffering from famine in Germany, Leopold De Meyer first lit the lamp of musical interest that still burned in New York City. Along with many others, that lamp illuminated the path of the Steinways.

If De Meyer lit the lamp, it was Phineas Taylor Barnum who turned up the wick. Beginning his career as a showman by selling his grocery store and purchasing a female slave for one thousand dollars in 1835, Barnum engaged Philadelphia's Masonic Hall. There the public was invited to see "one of the greatest natural curiosities ever witnessed, viz., Joice Heth, a negress, aged 161 years, who formerly belonged to the father of General Washington. She has been a member of the Baptist Church for 116 years, and can rehearse many hymns and sing them according to former custom," as the advertisement said. The people came and paid.

By 1842 Barnum was, through "a shrewd stroke of business," the owner of the American Museum in New York City. Located at Broadway and Ann Street, the museum became the commercial home of the Fee-Jee Mermaid, the Woolly Horse, the Original Bearded Woman, a parade of dwarfs and giants without limit, sea lions, and other attractions. Offering what today might be called "A Total Entertainment Experience," Barnum's museum regularly produced plays and musical concerts, usually light operas, "of a most interesting, instructive and moral character."

In 1848 Barnum contracted with Jenny Lind, the Swedish Nightingale, for an American tour. With a portfolio of endorsements from Haydn, Rossini, Moscheles, and Mendelssohn and a dozen years of success as an operatic soprano in Europe behind her, Lind first performed in America at New York's Castle Garden on September 17, 1850, less than three months after Heinrich Steinweg's arrival. Legend has that the Lind performance was the Steinway's first musical experience in America. Through an advertising campaign of unprecedented intensity Barnum fanned the embers of the American taste for European music and musicians to a fire storm of popularity. Leaving Barnum in 1851 with a statement that she did not like his sensational advertising, Lind's proceeds after ninety-five concerts were reported as $176,675.09 or roughly two and one-half million current dollars. There were no taxes; gross was net.

"The city was music-mad in 1851 and 1852," said one journalist, nor did the madness abate. It reached a higher peak in the summer of 1854 with another P. T. Barnum–promoted event, the Grand Musical Congress, with fifteen hundred performers. The *Chef de Orchestre* for the "first musical reunion" was Louis George Maurice Adolphe Roche Albert Abel Antonio Alexandre Noe Jean Lucien Daniel Eugene Joseph-le-brun Jeseph Bareme Thomas Thomas Thomas-Thomas Piere Arbon Pierre-Maurel Emanuel Barthelmi Artus Alphonse Bertrand Dieudonne Emanuel Jose Vincent Luc Michel Juiles de-la-plane Jules-Bazin Julio Cesar Jullien. M. Jullien was immersed in music from birth and was unconventionally named for thirty-six godfathers, all members of a philharmonic society. A child prodigy billed as the "Paganini of the Alps" by his bandmaster father, he was no stranger to the arts of promotion and publicity when he combined with Barnum at age forty-two.

A survivor of three duels and at least as many bankruptcies before he arrived in America, M. Jullien had conducted concerts in London for fifteen years. The fare was a musical tossed salad of symphonic excerpts, solos, waltzes, and his own quadrilles. While occasional concerts were devoted to the compositions of Mozart or Beethoven, Jullien was known to modify the works. In one instance he added drums and a saxophone to Beethoven's Fifth Symphony; canonical reverence for master composers was not yet widespread. Wearing sequinned gloves, he grasped a jewelled baton when conducting. It was brought to him on a silver platter by an assistant. On stage, solely for the use of the maestro, was a red velvet chair. While Jullien's pioneer use of the baton, sans diamonds, has persisted to the present, the comfortable but monarchically grandiose velvet chair has not.

In his American series of concerts—more than 200 in one year—Jullien conducted the "best orchestra ever heard in this country," according to his *New York Times* obituary. So it was that on the night of Thursday, June 15, 1854, 24,000 persons jammed into Manhattan's recently built Crystal Palace at Forty-second Street and Sixth Avenue. Of these, 20,000 paid fifty cents to stand and 4,000 paid two dollars to be seated. The price of the tickets included public transportation from anywhere in the metropolitan area. The audience heard roughly two-dozen choral and musical societies, sometimes simultaneously.

The evening's pièce de résistance was composed for the occasion by M. Jullien and named *The Fireman's Quadrille*. Before the quadrille, P. T. Barnum cautioned the audience "that they should not be alarmed at the frightful effects which would be introduced." During the performance a fire bell sounded while companies of city firemen marched and played. The fire erupted, and the men rushed off to fight the blaze amidst the sounds of crackling wood and hissing steam. "The fire is reached, and all the excitement of a struggle with the mighty element is produced in its wildest mood." Offstage drums of oil were ignited to produce the requisite smoke and flickering light, while onstage a house collapsed at the finale. A reviewer was moved to comment that there were "other devices, not strictly legitimate, but good," that were a part of *The Fireman's Quadrille*. "In short the Musical Congress last night was a triumph in every respect," commented the *Times* from its customary posture as arbiter of tastes and morals. "The triumph extended even to the architects of the Palace, for, notwithstanding the enormous pressure on the building, there was no perceptible deflection in any important rod or support about it." Jullien's "triumph" did not provide him with a foundation for prosperity and philanthropy in the manner of Jenny Lind. In 1860, after attempting suicide, M. Jullien died a pauper's death in a Paris lunatic asylum.

Strange as it may seem that Beethoven and firefighters would appear on the same program, this was entirely acceptable to at least 24,000 nineteenth-century New Yorkers (4 percent of the population) and to many reviewers of the time. Charles, Henry, and William Steinway, the latter an indefatigable concertgoer throughout his life, may very well have seen the Crystal Palace performance. Within a few years several of the featured artists in the Jullien/Barnum extravaganza were endorsing Steinway pianos. Carl Bergmann, the director of the Germania Society, a twenty-four-piece professional orchestra and the first in America, tendered his approval of Steinway instruments, as did Aptommas, the harpist, and George F. Bristow, an American composer whose works were performed by Jullien's orchestra.

To the contemporary mind another peculiarity occurs in the accounts of Jullien's extravaganza: there is a marked preponderance of Teutonic surnames on the program. The Eurocentric preferences of musical audiences created a strange inversion in which the Germans, held in stereotypically low esteem by the city's "natives" in most matters, were revered as musicians.

In response a group called the American Music Association was formed to promote the performance of American works by American musicians. The members wished it "to be clearly understood, that we consider the prevalent opinion that the birth of an individual on American soil renders null and void his claim to original genius a disgrace to the age we live in."

This claim brought forth a rejoinder from an anonymous *Times* writer: "The evil that we see . . . is that Americans do not work together. . . . The consequence is that the Germans who *do* cooperate with each other have command of all the avenues that lead to the public." Roughly a year later the *Times* interred the American Musical Association with a report that the American musician was "nothing but a superfluous appendage to the skirts of Germany: he sings German songs, plays German music, drinks German Lager Bier." In advancing their music the Americans, it appears, chose to emulate the Germans. A century later a similar strategem would be used by white musicians who expropriated black music in the early days of rock and roll. But by the values of the mid–nineteenth century, this was strange behavior for anyone, musician or not. Nativism was still a very potent force.

On a quantitative basis the Germans did have dominance over many aspects of New York's musical life. In 1855 a tally of the city's instrumentmakers revealed the existence of 826 of them; the largest proportion—39 percent—were German. About 34 percent were native-born, while the remaining 27 percent came from a dozen other nations. Interest in music was growing rapidly, undoubtedly stimulated by the promotions of Barnum, Bernard Ullmann, and other impresarios. Between 1855 and 1865 the number of music teachers in New York State grew 44 percent, four times faster than the rate of population growth. The population of music dealers grew 216 percent, more than tripling during the same time period. The professional musicians did not fare as well; their number increased 10.8 percent, roughly the same rate as the general population, which grew 10.4 percent.

The evidence suggests that the growth was in amateur music, music at home. Music of any kind was still a rare event, a fact difficult to appreciate in the late twentieth century when the click of a button will instantaneously access dozens of musical choices via radio. (The average American home had 6.8 radios in 1990.) Another button commands both images and music to appear on a television screen at any hour of the day or night; television sets are turned on for an average of 7.1 hours per day in each home, fed by 1,182 broadcast stations and 6,600 cable television systems. Rarity has been transformed to ubiquity.

Yet music was once not only rare; it was a fugitive, transient phenomenon, each note lasting no longer than the time it took to play it and, once played, was gone forever, save for its memory. Today, a button will cue a digital recording, one of fifty thousand released each year, and repeat, identically, a performance as many times as may be desired or tolerated. Over half of United States households can record a television program. Technology has transmogrified the transient to the permanent and the uncommon to the omnipresent, with access on demand.

One hundred and thirty years ago, there were no such choices. The musical auditor either listened to live performance or performed himself. Outside of a few metropolitan areas such as New York, Boston, Philadelphia, and New Orleans, professional musical performances could rarely be heard and the appearance of a virtuoso was the rarest of events. "But once in a lifetime we who are far distant from the great cities of the world, are privileged to hear such melody," wrote a journalist from the *Atlanta Examiner* after the 1858 concert of another European pianist, Sigismond Thalberg. After Henri Herz and his "assistants" played Mobile, Alabama, in 1847, the local editor opined that the experience "will be cherished in the recollection of all who are moved by the concord of sweet sounds."

When the immigrant Germans established their perceived popular ascendance in music, they controlled social and economic powers of great magnitude. It was a form of cultural oligopoly from which, ultimately, the Steinways would profit immensely.

Given the relative stability of human nature and the verities of economic competition, contemporary sociological studies of the Japanese in California, the Cubans in Florida, and immigrants to Australia provide insight into the experience of the Steinways. One key to the economic success of an immigrant group is economic hegemony. In such a hegemony, an ethnic group controls an economic activity to such an extent that it is difficult or impossible for buyers to avoid transactions with the group. That the Germans in Victorian Gotham had a command of pianomaking is clear from their ubiquity in these trades at least at the level of individual tradesmen in these occupations. Roughly half of all pianomakers were German, as were about one-third of the musicians.

Modern studies show that entrepreneurship is much greater among immigrant groups who speak a language different from the majority of their host nation. Under this theory, it was more likely that Germans would open small businesses than would the Irish who spoke English. A language difference ultimately proves, surprisingly enough, to be advantageous to the immigrants.

First, the immigrants are paid less than natives because of the communications difficulties created for native employers by the language difference. This was true in the case of Heinrich Steinweg, who was paid six dollars a week when making keyboards at Lighte & Newton. Had he spoken English, which he refused to learn, he would have been offered seven dollars. The wage differential causes the more entrepreneurial immigrants to open their own businesses. In this they have a cost advantage because they are able to pay their countrymen somewhat less, just as the native employers do. Research indicates that while immigrant employers do pay lower wages than natives receive for the same work, they pay labor rates somewhat *higher* to their countrymen than do native employers. In sum, an immigrant employer is able to take economic advantage of the "language barrier" while at the same time benefitting his "coethnics" by providing them jobs at marginally better wages. In the case of the Steinways, they were able to draw on a large labor pool—numbering in the high hundreds—of German pianomakers with whom they shared a common culture. The Steinwegs would have the advantage of greater efficiency in employing these men—no language impediments—and somewhat reduced costs. This tradition was so powerful that German was the operating tongue at the Steinway factory on Long Island until well into the middle of the twentieth century.

In the highly Germanic New York musical scene the Steinways had another advantage. The German-born and German-trained musicians of New York could serve as endorsers of Steinway pianos, and this they did. Not only did Carl Bergmann, who went on to conduct the New York Philharmonic, endorse Steinway early on, but so did Theodore Thomas. Thomas for many years conducted his own symphony orchestra as an entirely credible rival of the Philharmonic. Hermann Wohlenhaupt, now entirely forgotten, was a New York–resident piano virtuoso who also promoted Steinway. Massachusetts-born William Mason, who studied in Germany with Liszt, was another pioneer Steinway proponent. German ethnicity, a liability in American society at large, could be used advantageously in the manufacture and sale of pianos.

Steinway & Sons used another strategem characteristic of successful ethnic businesses. They integrated vertically by almost instantaneously opening their own retail store. In doing so, they came to control their own distribution in what was then, as it is now, the largest retail market for pianos in the nation. When, in 1857, the Steinways and Thomas H. Chambers discontinued their retail relationship in the city, it may be surmised that this was done by the Steinways. They no longer needed a native American to provide a credible outlet for their pianos in New York. Though Chambers remained in business for many years, he did not sell Steinways. In less than a decade after taking exclusive control of retail sales in New York, the Steinways accomplished yet another step in their vertical integration. They opened their famed concert hall on Fourteenth Street with a capacity of about 2,500 persons. It was in this hall that the eclipsed De Meyer performed in 1867. With control of their manufacturing and retail facilities well in hand, a hall providing an outlet for performances—still a novel service in high demand—made perfect economic and promotional sense.

There is little question that the social forces at work in the city and the nation—sociological, musical, and economic—were significant in the success of Heinrich Steinway and his sons. But such forces have about them a brutally blind impartiality. The Steinways were no more or no less favored by the socioeconomic vectors of the time than the 96,000 other German residents in the City of the Knickerbockers. All were struggling to at least survive, if not succeed, in the New World during those hot summer days of 1855 when they were tallied, undoubtedly with indifference if not contempt, by the politically appointed state census enumerators. Almost all of those 96,000 lives—men, women, and children alike—would be lived in anonymity. Such was not the fate of the Steinways, for they were about to demonstrate a spectacular facility with a potent weapon. It was the weapon of Fulton, Whitney, McCormick, Pullman, Colt, Edison, Westinghouse, Bell, the Wrights, and Ford: *technology*.

Chapter 5

AN UNFRIENDED PIANO OF THE SQUARE KIND

"It is not a long time ago—so short a time, in fact, that anyone who remembers the pleasant but unfortunate Crystal Palace in Reservoir Square may recall it—that an unfriended piano of the square kind was discovered by certain gentlemen of the musical jury in an exhibition of the American Institute." The writer of these words in 1864 was Charles C. Bailey Seymour, the *New York Times* music critic from its founding in 1851 until his death in 1869. C.C.B.S., as he sometimes signed his reports, was well qualified to reminisce on the American Institute Fair at the Crystal Palace in 1855; he had been chairman of the jury for musical instruments and played a key role in deciding the awards, along with fellow jurors W. H. Sage, Theodore Hagen, and the twenty-five-year-old pianist William Mason, who had recently returned to America after studies with Liszt and Moscheles.

"The judges were pursuing their rounds, and performing their duties with an ease and facility that promised a speedy termination to their labors, when suddenly they came upon an instrument that, from its external appearance—solidly rich, yet free from the frippery that was then rather in fashion—attracted their attention. One of the company opened the case, and carelessly struck a few chords. The others were doing the same with its neighbors, but somehow they ceased to chatter when the other instrument began to speak. One by one the jurors gathered round the strange polyphonist and without a word being spoken, everyone knew that it was the best piano in the exhibition." The judges had discovered Steinway & Sons serial number 550.

On exhibition 550 was stared at and stroked by the interested among the more than one hundred thousand persons who had paid twenty-five cents to see the wonders of the fair, probed by the eyes and hands of competitors, and finally, on October 22, vetted by experts.

"The jurors were true to their duties. It is possible that some of them had predilections in favour of other makers; it is certain that one of them had—the writer of the present notice. But when the time for the award came, there was no argument, no discussion, no bare presentment of minor claims, nothing, in fact, but a hearty endorsement of the singular merits of the strange instrument," recalled the critic Seymour.

The opinion of the judges was unanimous; of the nineteen pianos entered into competition, that of Steinway & Sons was the best. A note, as brief as it was grammatically inept, recorded the opinion of the judges: "(Entry) #1541 is the best. The exhibitor of this instrument has two other instruments of interest in the Fair. The present one (#1541) & the two others in a less degree is characterized by purity of tone, elasticity of action and equality of scale. Gold Medal." One silver medal was also awarded, as were two diplomas, to Steinway competitors.

The gold medal of the American Institute cost the management sixteen dollars, but to a winner the value could be immense, as the award was widely recognized as a verification of quality. In the two dozen years from 1828 through 1852 perhaps forty thousand objects ranging from sculpture to steam engines and needlepoint to navigation instruments had been displayed at American Institute Fairs. Among the exhibits were Morse's telegraph and Colt's revolvers. During this same time only ninety gold medals were awarded. At something in excess of one in four thousand, the chances of winning one of these small aureate emblems were remote. The medals and diplomas, along with gifts of books to meritorious minors, were traditionally dispensed at the close of the fair with great gravity and ceremony.

"Old gentlemen, young ladies, demure madammes, whose big cases of millinery stood perched up-gallery, machinery men and artists huddled together, everybody believing in his heart that he was sure to win a gold medal, or, at the very least, two silver medals and a diploma," were present according to a *New York Times* reporter sent to cover the ceremonies on Wednesday, November 14, 1855. It is likely that the Steinways were among the "several hundreds of persons" awaiting the results of the judging. If so, they were disappointed since for the first time, "the Managers deemed it best to forgo the verbal announcement of the list. . . . When these excellent gentlemen retired with big bundles of unread awards under their arms, the audience retired in great disgust, turning, as they always do, for consolation and comfort to the representatives of the DAILY TIMES, several of whom are always on hand whenever anything is about to happen." The assembled hopefuls were told that they could learn of the awards in the next morning's papers as presenting them all would take too long.

Deprived, perhaps, of a moment of personal glory the Steinways were quick to advertise "GOLD MEDAL PIANOS!" The conquering number 550 was not, however, immediately sold. It remained with the Steinways for almost two more months, long after its twin instrument, number 549, was sold to Thomas H. Chambers for his Broadway emporium. Pianos were then built in pairs so that the casemaker could work on one instrument while waiting for the glue to set in another.

Steinway & Sons left one exhibition, held at a recently built rockpile called the Smithsonian Institution, with a first prize for best two- and three-stringed pianos. This was a modest victory in a minor place, for Washington was inhabited by only forty thousand persons, a reflection of the relative importance of the federal government in the mid–nineteenth century. Brooklyn was twice as large as Washington City; Providence, Rhode Island, was the same size, and at least three New York wards had populations larger than the nation's capital. For the Steinways the Washington, D.C., Metropolitan Mechanics' Institute Exhibition was a rehearsal.

The choice of places to exhibit depended, at least in part, on which makers were competing. There were subtleties here. A late entry would permit an assessment of the competitors and chances of an award, but an early entry might preempt minor makers, particularly those with established reputations based on a medal or two in the distant past. New firms, such as Steinway, had little to lose since they were essentially reputationless. A defeat in competition had little impact on status, while a victory, particularly a gold medal, could greatly enhance reputation. So Steinway & Sons aggressively entered the arena and accreted a claimed thirty-five awards by 1862, an accomplishment they promoted untiringly for decades.

In the medals race the Steinways were not alone. In 1866 Chickering & Sons advertised that they had been awarded "Sixty-five First Premiums, Gold and Silver Medals over all competitors at the principal fairs in this country." The Steinways and their dealers would have undoubtedly rejoined that it took Chickering four times as long to get them. At least one of the Steinways did not have great personal respect for their competitor: "an ignorant, arrogant ass" was Henry Steinway, Jr.'s assessment of Colonel Frank Chickering. But exhibition entries in Chickering's Boston were notably absent in the Steinway portfolio. In at least one early case where documentation survives of a Steinway versus Chickering competition, it was the Steinways who placed second.

At the Crystal Palace Fair of 1856, Chickering took home a gold medal and the Steinways a silver, both for grand pianos. Two pianists were on the jury: the renowned Louis Moreau Gottschalk and the lesser-known but entirely competent Hermann Wohlenhaupt. Gottschalk was regularly provided with Chickering pianos, free transportation, and a piano tuner at no cost for his concerts, while Wohlenhaupt was an endorser of the Steinways. Equivocal and confounded interests of this type were common behind the curtain, but on stage the public saw only the results. Throughout the nineteenth century, fairs and exhibitions were the terrain for brutal battles between rival commercial interests: no strategem was too devious, no tactic too corrupt, no public statement too outrageous, no manipulation too excessive if it resulted in a plausible claim of victory, real or imagined. There was a reason.

The fairs and exhibitions themselves were tremendously popular, and millions paid admissions to gaze at the implements of American industrial power and productivity: stationary steam engines, lathes, mills, multispindle drill presses, and hundreds of other machines, now long forgotten. This was the capital equipment that made consumer goods possible. Fantastically finished in glowing greens, supersaturated reds, and the blackest of blacks, edges defined in silver striping, ornamented with gold leaf and decorated with flowers, machinery was pridefully displayed on glowing mahogany floors and set in forests of ferns.

To mid-Victorian sensibilities, at least those uninvolved in the arts, the machines were no less wonderful than the goods they produced, for they promised not only delightful devices such as sewing machines, pianos, and plows, but a release from drudgery itself in some vaguely envisioned automated future. The machines were not feared as replacers of men; in 1860 the Steinways proudly announced that their machinery performed the work of nine hundred. This was a sign of a progressive industrial attitude with an implicit guarantee of superior quality. The natural and undesirable variability of the human hand was to be eliminated and replaced by the invariant perfection of the machine-made. In this emergent mechanical Utopia many in the crowds came to wonder at not only the machines which they could buy, but the machines which made the machines. The mechanics, coarse though they might be, were capable of amazing things, almost all of which were for sale.

There was a certain panmaterialistic quality to the exhibitions. Sculptures, steam boilers, microscopes, macrame, apples, calliopes, paintings, poems, and brandies were all on democratic but dramatic display; perambulating along the aisles, dressed in their best approximation of fashion, ladies, gentlemen, and children could attend to those things which interested them. Other than excluding the pornographic, exhibition managers made few value judgments. The best millinery, the best munitions, the best shoe buckle, the best ship design—there were awards for each; distinctions as to social value, taste, or relative merit were not made by exhibition promoters.

At the apex of these pageants of progress stood the annual American Institute of the City of New York Fair. The Institute, created by an act of the New York legislature, held its first fair in 1828 at Niblo's Garden, an indoor/outdoor performance space on Broadway below Canal Street, moved to Castle Garden in 1846, and in 1853 took up residence at the purpose-built Crystal Palace. Enclosing about four acres, the Palace was located on Sixth Avenue and Forty-second Street, extending two blocks down to Fortieth, immediately to the west of a huge reservoir that stored drinking water for the city. The main branch of the New York Public Library and Bryant Park now occupy a portion of the area where the reservoir and the Palace once stood.

The Crystal Palace, named for its extensive use of glass, was openly modelled after a similar structure erected in London for an international exhibition in 1851. The Palace had an appearance combining elements of a railway station and a greenhouse with a dome placed on top. There were three entrances, each forty-seven feet wide, leading into the building, which was built of cast iron painted buff and decorated with "the judicious use of the three positive colors, red, blue and yellow, in their several tints of vermillion, garnet, sky blue and orange, certain parts of the ornamental work being gilt." Into this color riot thronged the multitudes for a firsthand view of progress. Evening illumination was provided by gaslights, but during the day sunlight poured in through fifteen thousand panes of glass inserted into a skeleton built of three million pounds of cast iron and six hundred thousand pounds of wrought iron. These statistics were widely and proudly reported. About 750,000 board feet of lumber were also used in the grand design: "Nothing could be more instructive to the American Nation at large, or beneficial to her manufacturing and industrial interests, than an Exhibition in this country similar to that . . . on the other side of the Atlantic," asserted the sponsors to the press. Noble plans abounded.

When the Crystal Palace was opened with a parade from Castle Garden up Broadway on July 14, 1853, President Pierce spoke, bands played, and the Hallelujah Chorus was sung, "not withstanding the down-pour of a heavy rain which soaked the President and scattered the crowd," according to a *New York Herald* reporter. The Palace was seen as a monument to progress, a symbol of civic success, and a beacon to a brighter future.

A gold medal from the Crystal Palace Exhibition, such as that awarded to the Steinways, carried great psychological weight. Possession of a gold medal from the American Institute was the imprimatur of success, a certification of attainment known to nearly all and certainly to anyone who could afford to buy a piano. The gold medal detonated demand for Steinway instruments. From the 12 units produced in the closing months of 1853, to 49 units built in 1854, to 112 pianos shipped during 1855, followed by 256 in 1856, then jumping to 400 in 1857, Steinway sales traced a ballistic trajectory. This was due, at least in part, to the record of exhibition awards.

The key to Steinway success at the exhibitions was technological. When music and drama critic Charles C. Bailey Seymour recalled his 1855 encounter with a Steinway using the phrases "strange polyphonist" and "strange instrument," he might well have used other adjectives—abnormal, aberrant, or bizarre—for the early products of the Steinways were excursions into distant realms of recondite and advanced technology.

To understand the brilliance of the Steinways, it is necessary to drop back three decades from the Crystal Palace victory of October 22, 1855. Heinrich Steinway, a cabinet-maker in the mountains of northern Germany, had not yet taken up mallet or saw to make a piano; his children were still unborn. The seminal event occurred not in a European cultural capital but in Philadelphia, Pennsylvania. There, in 1825, a pianomaker named Alpheus Babcock received a patent for a one-piece iron piano frame. The problem Babcock was trying to solve with his innovation was as old as string instruments, be they pianos, violins, or guitars. A string sufficiently taut to vibrate when struck, bowed, or plucked places a force on that which holds it. The result, in a violin, may be a warped neck or a variety of other maladies, including one picturesquely named the "sunken belly." Yet a violin has but four strings pulled to moderate tension. On a nineteenth-century violin, forces might total sixty-three pounds.

In contrast, an early piano, such as those built by a Viennese firm in 1808, had cumulative tension from the strings of nine thousand pounds or four and one-half tons. With pianos, the *instrumentenmacher* by necessity became an engineer. He dealt with forces more ordinarily found in the less gentle realms of boilermaking, bridge building, and machine design. Under a four-and-one-half-ton load, the natural inclination of a piano structure was to yield to relieve the stresses brought by the strings.

Made of wood, a material which naturally expands and contracts with both temperature and humidity, the pianoforte was a nervous machine, constantly growing and shrinking with meteorological variations. At best, this meant that the piano would not long stay in tune; at worst, an expensive instrument reduced itself to uselessness in a few years, the natural by-product of the immense potential energy in the strings constantly trying to become kinetic energy. This self-induced destruction was often cited as a great difficulty with European instruments brought to America. Designed for another climate, they fared poorly in America and committed various forms of structural suicide in a few years.

Alpheus Babcock sought the solution to the inherent instability of wood with the miracle material of his age: iron. By creating a ferrous frame—vaguely resembling that of a harp—to hold the piano strings, he stabilized and tamed the pianoforte and provided it, by the standards of the time, with a more phlegmatic temperament. The value of Alpheus Babcock's innovation was not widely appreciated until he moved to Boston in 1837 and began working for Jonas Chickering. The Boston builders accounted for about one-third of the national output of pianos at the time. Babcock and Chickering created a "school" of pianomaking, and the use of unitary iron frames was conventional practice in Boston by the time the Steinways arrived in America. Another "full iron frame" was fabricated by Conrad Meyer, again at Philadelphia, in 1833.

But the iron frame was not a universally admired innovation. The New York, Albany, and Baltimore makers held the general view that iron-framed instruments sounded harsh, thin, and metallic. A frequently used adjective for their sound was "nasal." To modern ears the old Boston instruments have a delicate, some would say feeble, but sustaining quality in the upper notes not usually found in New York pianos of the same period. The high treble of New York instruments sounds like a hollow knock followed by a brief shred of tone. It is clear that tastes have changed; by contemporary standards the Boston treble is preferable to the New York.

At least part of the reason for the difference in sound was in the construction. New York builders, although their instruments used iron parts, did not employ the full iron frame. Instead they battled the implacable string tension with ever-larger, thicker, and more complex wooden structures, the dimensions of which grew to resemble church rafters in the futile search for stability. Though the application of a unitary iron frame might be deferred, physics mandated that ultimately it could not be denied, for there were other trends at work. The Steinways knew this well.

Composers and virtuosos demanded of their instruments an ever larger compass, and the keyboards grew progressively from six octaves to six and one-half, then to seven octaves or eighty-five notes. In part, this expansion was driven by the shift of musical tastes from classically restrained to romantic bravura, from the lambent precision of Haydn to the volcanic rumblings and scintillations of Liszt. With each extension of the musical range the number of strings increased and with it string tension. With the advent of the seven-and-one-quarter-octave, eighty-eight-note instrument, of which the Steinways were among the early builders, this process reached natural limits.

The first limit was anthropometric; the length of the human arm and the geometry of the seated piano player made further extension of keyboards impractical. Second, an eighty-eight-note instrument encompassed virtually the total pitch range of a large ensemble; it was literally a symphony orchestra in a box. Although unknown at the time, there was a third reason. In the extreme bass, the piano was probing the lower extent of human hearing; the frequency of its lowest note was as low as a cat's purr. Tones just a few hertz (vibrations per second) lower would be inaudible to many, no matter how loud. At the upper end of the instrument's range, at frequencies ordinarily heard in the natural world as the chirps of small birds, another limit was being reached: the ability of the human auditory system to distinguish pitch. Less than half an octave above the highest C of the piano the ear/brain of man no longer discriminates pitch and classifies sounds as simply "high-frequency." At eighty-eight notes the piano was approaching the physiological and perceptual boundaries of its creators, players, and audience.

There was a second trend as well: demand for louder instruments. Although influenced by the dramaturgics of romantic playing styles and the piano-demolishing propensities of virtuosi, there were other reasons motivating the demand for increased volume from the piano. Had artists been so inclined, their spectacular command of technique could have easily left instruments intact, but they sought, in addition to astonishing audiences with mechanical mayhem, to extract the maximum contrast—engineers call this dynamic range—during performance. One cause of the demand for power peculiar to America was the larger venues, the four-thousand-person Academy of Music and the six-thousand-person capacity of Castle Garden among them, which dwarfed the European halls that often accommodated only a few hundred people.

It may be that the demand for power in a piano was uniquely American, similar to the fascination with clipper ships and high-speed trains, an extrapolation of the postulate that if some is good, more is better. To make a piano louder required heavier strings stretched to still higher tensions, compounding the mechanical problems of the instrument. The Steinways chose to meet this challenge and attacked it resolutely, ultimately creating instruments that could be played in acoustic balance with hundred-man orchestras.

A third trend at work was succinctly described by a British civil engineer and exhibition judge, William Poole: "The constant and unreasonable rise of the pitch (of instruments), prevalent of late years, has told in a way that comes home directly to almost every family, in regard to the *price* of pianofortes. It is a well-known fact that the great cause of expense is in getting *strength* to resist the enormous tension of the stringing; and when it is considered that the effect of the modern rise in pitch has been to increase this tension by about fifteen per cent., it will be easily understood that every person who buys a piano has really to pay something considerable for the high pitch which it pleases our opera and orchestral authorities to use." The "authorities" had discovered that, for complex psychoacoustic reasons, a composition played slightly "sharp" sounded more brilliant and dramatic than before. An escalating "pitch war" ensued for much of the nineteenth century until the 1890s when the "standard" moved near the well-known "A-440," and modern concert pitch was approximated.

All these factors—larger compasses, greater volume, and rising pitch—pressed against the limits of the old concepts of design. By the 1850s some makers were employing solid wood a full five inches thick in piano bottoms to contain the forces within. The forces themselves had risen to formidable levels, twelve tons by the 1850s, and they continued to rise. String tensions of 40,000 pounds were reached in some instruments by the 1870s. This was energy equivalent to a MIG-29 Russian jet fighter on afterburner. The twenty-ton force applied to the aircraft pushes it from the ground to 20,000 feet in sixty seconds. In a piano the same force had to be contained, not for minutes or even months, but for years.

The challenges were well known to makers of all nations, and each met the problem in his own way; inventions and so-called solutions poured forth, each accompanied by claims and counterclaims. The piano trade was in technological ferment at midcentury. Pianos were strung with brass, copper, silver, and gold strings in attempts to improve tone; sounding boards were corrugated to increase the volume of tone produced; separate, foot operated bass notes were added. Pianos were augmented with "Aeolian Attachments," which gave the instruments a weird, whistling, flutelike quality that now evokes simultaneous thoughts of funeral parlors and science fiction films.

As strange as it may seem from a current perspective, the Steinways worked in the field of high-velocity technical change. The stakes were similar to more modern contests. Should an automobile be powered by steam, gasoline, or electricity? Can a video recorder be used in the home? How small and how cheap can a computer be made? Whether by analysis, hard work, luck, or some combination thereof, those who wagered correctly in these technological contests were sometimes rewarded with fortunes. The Steinways placed a technological bet beginning with their earliest known instrument, number 483. They also hedged their risks with characteristic cleverness.

Heinrich, Carl, Henry, and later William Steinway chose to work at the nexus of art, technology, and business. The interactions were multiplex because the technology was dynamic, just as it is today in the relationship between artists, composers, and computers. The anonymous *New York Times* writer commented, "In estimating the improvements . . . *in* the piano, we must also be mindful of the changes affected *by* it. A new and brilliant school of music has arisen, the professors of which attain their greatest excellency on this instrument. Composers consult it for every variety of expression. It is, indeed, doubtful whether the greatest masterpieces of the age have not derived much of their perfection from the ready capability of the piano to resolve the thoughts of their authors."

There was also a self-congratulatory sense that current levels of development could not be exceeded: "It is almost impossible to conceive anything more replete with mechanical perfection than the piano. The chronometer alone furnishes a parallel. The exactness and delicacy which characterize the latter are also essential to the former. For manipulated contrivances, the piano is superior to any piece of mechanism with which we are acquainted," wrote the same analyst. His thoughts were not unique; the same view was expressed by others, including the European master pianist Sigismond Thalberg. All were unaware that in a low-rent house on the western edge of the social swamp that was New York's Eighth Ward a few "Dutchmen" were creating with hammer, saw plane, wood, iron, and an incisive vision a very different version of "mechanical perfection."

The pianos the Steinways built were not of the forms recognized today.

They were not the once ubiquitous uprights, known in the industry as "verticals," or the elegant grand symbolic of both concert stage and sophisticated wealth. Theirs was a third type, once dominant but obsolete by 1900. This was called the "square" for unknown reasons, since it was actually of a rectangular form. Phylogenetically discrete, the square piano descended over the centuries from the clavichord while the grand was rooted in the harpsichord. While the Europeans abandoned the square in favor of the vertical form, the Americans continued to develop it. In a *New York Herald* interview, William Steinway estimated that 90 percent of American piano output in 1867 was square pianos, 5 percent was uprights, and 5 percent grands. He had also characterized grand sales as "scarce as angels' visits."

The appearance of the early Steinway instruments was entirely conventional for the square form, tending perhaps toward the restrained use of decoration, but by no means austere.

All things about 483 seem mundane until the lid is opened. Inside is bizarre mechanism, for the heart of 483 is a mutant, entirely unlike that of ordinary pianos. Shorn of technical details, Steinway & Sons number 483 can be described as treble portion of a grand piano grafted into a square instrument. Its treble strings run parallel to the sides of its case, and overlaying them at an angle are the bass strings. In a conventional piano, as built by many of the Steinway competitors, all strings lay in the same plane at an angle inside the case. After fourteen decades number 483 is not fully operable, and how it sounded cannot be known. That it probably produced a unique tonality for its times is evident, and expert opinion suggests that the instrument likely had an unusually brilliant treble, the well-known weakness in most New York instruments. In one way 483 speaks clearly through the years: the Steinways had the objective of making their square pianos in America the tonal equivalent of any concert grand; they sought to achieve parity with the vaunted Erards and Pleyels of Paris, the Streichers of Vienna and the Broadwoods of London.

This was an ambitious, but not necessarily eccentric objective, and the Steinways shared it with at least one other man, a shadowy, tragic master of piano design. "Be it known that I, Frederick Mathushek, have invented certain new and useful Improvements in the Pianoforte." So began the specifications of the letters patent No. 8470, dated October 28, 1851. The patent continued with a description of a design "for the purpose of obtaining a greater amount of power in an instrument of given size than can be obtained by the ordinary arrangement or in other words to obtain all the power of a grand pianoforte within the ordinary dimensions of a square one." Concise, even terse, for a patent, the letters conclude only one page later with a description of the string placement, "to wit, the shorter strings of the higher octaves [are arranged] across the narrower portion of the instrument and the longer strings or those of the lower octaves crossing them in the direction of the greatest length of the instrument so as to include the greatest possible size of string within the instrument." What Frederick Mathushek described in 1851 the Steinways built in 1853.

That the Steinways knew Mathushek is more than likely; not only was he a fellow German in the same trade, but in 1850 Mathushek designed a machine for making felt piano hammers, a press that held the hammer felt in place over the wooden stalk while the glue set. The Steinways, ever progressive in their use of automation, had such a machine and were enthusiastic about it. To his brother Theodore who had remained in Germany when the family emigrated, Charles Steinway wrote in December 1854, "You always maintain that felt hammers cannot be made on a machine, but I must tell you that I claim one cannot make such a firm, even and nicely formed hammer by hand as with the machine; since our machine works very well we now put felt hammers in all our pianos over the middle." Previously treble hammers had been covered with leather, in part because of the difficulty in handling the thin felt required. Charles did not mention the cost of the machine, but it was valued at thirty dollars in the 1856 inventory of Steinway & Sons. Mathushek never became a wealthy man from the sale of hammer machines, nor any of the other innovations that flowed from his fecund mind during a six-decade-long career.

Four decades later William Steinway acknowledged the importance of Frederick Mathushek's contribution: "Mathushek had invented the so-called 'sweep scale' (increasing at the same time the compass from seven to seven one-third octaves in square pianos), which greatly improved the power of the tone, but also increased the size of the instrument and weakened its durability by narrowing the soprano part of the wrest plank." What William did not write was that Steinway & Sons built about forty of these "sweep scale" pianos in 1855, roughly one-third of their total production. Steinway sweep scale manufacture ceased abruptly in early 1856, perhaps because of "durability," but not before one of the instruments took first prize at the Metropolitan Mechanics' Institute Exhibition in Washington City.

Neither Mathushek nor the Steinways were punctilious and methodical businessmen. In fact, the Steinways did not sign a formal partnership agreement among themselves until 1857. Although by then among the largest piano firms in New York City, they still did not officially register their partnership with the New York county clerk as required by law. Frederick Mathushek was likewise untroubled by formalities, "owing to that inherent carelessness common to many inventive geniuses," as his obituarist notes. Such men leave trails in time by deed, not paper, and so while there is no record of a relationship between the Steinways and Mathushek, there can be little doubt that some association existed. Whether it was distant or close, long or short, employment or joint venture, strong influence or philosophical bond cannot be told. That Steinway pianos would have been different instruments without the concepts of Frederick Mathushek is clear.

The idealism of Frederick Mathushek stood in sharp contrast to the pragmatism of the Steinways. While Mathushek sought the ultimate, the Steinways offered alternatives. Mathushek, the autocrat, sought to impose a vision of tonal perfection. The Steinways were democratic; the buyer could decide, and so they offered a cornucopia of models and types, well over a dozen in the first three years alone. There were models of six and one-quarter, six and three-quarter, seven, and seven and one-quarter octaves in at least three scale designs—common, sweep, and overstrung— all offered in a plethora of styles. Steinways were available in plain, very plain, molded, and fancy cases. They were made with rounded corners of at least three radii; there were even choices in piano legs, including one style with "Jenny Lind" legs.

If the buyer wanted advanced technology, it was available from Steinway & Sons. Sweep scales and overstrung pianos embodied the state of the art. If the buyer wanted conservative technology, that was available too. "Common scale, plain, 6¾ octave" was the entry-level Steinway. Did a piano buyer want a seven-octave instrument that had a keyboard ranging from C to C, E to E, or A to A? With Steinway this was the purchaser's decision. Heinrich, Charles, Henry, and William Steinway chose to let the buyer choose. For the time, this was radical. It was also very effective.

Gradually the Steinways coalesced on a unitary vision of the piano. This was their "overstrung" model, first sold in 1856. The overstrung square was a synthesis and a brilliant one. Combining the full iron frame of the Boston builders with overstringing used by several New York makers, these Steinways were among the first, if not the first, pianos to sound like modern instruments.

The "metallic" sound of Boston was transformed into the beginnings of the contemporary piano by what was, in reality, a step backward. Partially eschewing the exotics of Mathushek, the Steinways alloyed the best practice of the New York and Boston builders. From New York they selected heavy wood framing, overstringing, and a "French" action that gave the piano a satisfying response when played. From Boston came the iron frame, subtly but powerfully modified, probably in its connection to the case and in the attachment of the tuning pins for the strings.

The result was an instrument both stable and powerful with a tone that pleased some, but not all. To straddle the market, Steinway & Sons contin- ued to offer conventional instruments as well, all in a manifold matrix of models and styles. Frederick Mathushek and others, the long-forgotten Spencer Driggs and William Lindeman among them, probed the ethereal heights of piano design in a time of rapid change, sometimes effectively, more often disastrously. Such men followed the stereotypical course of the undercapitalized inventor/craftsmen: breakthrough . . . newspaper an- nouncement . . . silence . . . business failure.

The talent of the Steinways proved to be an astute ability to seize the essence of ideas and make them work. Driven, if not cursed, by his creative vision, Mathushek was a man who always believed his next idea was better than his last. In effect, he was self-condemned to specialize in prototypes. The Steinways converged on high-technology production and incremental but ultimately very important improvements.

There is a curious parallel to modern times. The Steinways did not "invent" overstringing; they did not "invent" iron frames; they did not "invent" hammer machines. Likewise, the Japanese did not "invent" automobiles or television, but they produce them with great success. So it was with Steinway & Sons. They played what is now the Japanese role in manufacturing, popularizing technical advances, while Mathushek and others took the role of innovators.

Newspaper advertisements told the story: buried among the help-wanteds were the musical items. Of ten pianomakers advertising on a single day in 1860, September 20, half used the words "iron frame" and "overstrung" in their advertisements. One year before, there was only Steinway & Sons. In five years four immigrants had created a revolution.

In 1865 the music critic for the *New York Daily Tribune* wrote, "There is no article of home luxury to the improvement of which such earnest attention and such costly experiments have been directed as to the pianoforte. . . . The improvements which have been really accomplished in the past twenty years are first, the enlargement of the scale; second, the increased length of the string; third, the heavier stringing; fourth, the increased area of the sounding board; fifth, the increased power of the motion; sixth, the scientific adaptation of the iron plate combining the utmost possible strength with lightness; and seventh, the system of overstringing the bass." The critic did not mention the reflexive nature of these changes, how each depended on the other in a web of complex causalities, nor did he cite Steinway & Sons. In reality, there was no need to mention them by name, for Steinway had become synonomous with virtually all the "improvements" enumerated by the critic.

The design pioneered and popularized by the Steinways became the preferred way to build a piano and ultimately the only way. Like the safety bicycle with its two equal-sized wheels and chain drive, the single-wing airplane and the first Mercedes automobile of 1901 with its engine forward driving the rear wheels, the Steinway "iron-overstrung" became an archetype. It was a conception so apt as to be obvious in retrospect, so correct that all predecessors seemed quaint, so appropriate that alternatives appeared absurd.

As powerful as this technological innovation was, it could not by itself clinch security and success for the family. With number 550 the Steinways built not simply a piano, but a small platform above the swamp of competition. It was as unlike the Steinways to remain on that platform as it was their competitors to allow respite. A long journey to wealth and fame was beginning, but not all the family would live to enjoy it.

Chapter 6

ANIMATED WITH
THE STRANGEST DELIGHTS

"From the first day of May 1856, William Steinway becomes and is partner of the Firm of Steinway & Sons, it being hereby understood and agreed, by the four partners Henry Steinway sen., Charles Steinway, Henry Steinway, Jr. and William Steinway that each of them is to receive one Fourth of the net profits of the business annually of an Inventory of the entire stock, Assets and liabilities of the business to be taken on the First day of January after the amounts drawn out by each respective partner for his own private account have been deducted therefrom and Interest at the rate of Five per Centum paid or credited to each partner for his amount of capital which he had invested in the business was ascertained and set forth in the statement or Inventory of account one year previous." Idiosyncratically capitalized and punctuated, these 142 words formed the business foundation of Steinway & Sons for two decades.

They were written in William Steinway's hand on the occasion of his admission into partnership with his father and two brothers on May 1, 1856, at age twenty-one. At the time the accounts showed that Steinway & Sons had assets of $27,903.39 and liabilities of $3,903.39, of which about one-fourth was due for rent. Other sums were due local actionmakers Stebbins and Smith, the liquidator William Wake, and the Steinway business neighbors on Walker Street, Houghton Brothers Lumber, among others. Exactly $257 was owed to the "inside hands."

58

The Steinways paid their bills faster than they were paid, for they were owed almost $8,000 by their dealers. There was $120 in cash on hand and $3,174.48 on deposit with the People's Bank on Broadway. Finished with the sums, William reckoned that the net assets of the firm were $24,000, including the eight pianos for sale in the Walker Street "wareroom." In less than six years the family had accreted a small fortune, for $24,000 represented forty-six years of labor at prevailing wages for a piano case maker.

It was a spectacular success, but only the beginning. Just seven months later when William again recorded the accounts for January 1, 1857, the value of the partnership assets had grown by 40 percent to almost $34,000. There were fourteen pianos in the showroom now, but more importantly there were pianos on loan, including one to Carl Bergmann. Formerly a principal in the critically praised Germania Orchestra, Bergmann was the conductor of the New York Philharmonic. This Steinway association was less impressive than it might appear. The Philharmonic then gave but four concerts a year, the rehearsals for them being considered optional by the musicians. Nonetheless, Bergmann, a cellist by training, was apparently the first among the New York musical establishment to recognize the qualities of Steinway & Sons pianos. This was a crucial artistic alliance for the young firm, for Carl Bergmann was a cornerstone in the city's musical elite. Bergmann was also a member of the Mason-Bergmann Musical Matinee, a chamber music group which included pianist William Mason, Bergmann, and violinist Theodore Thomas. Devoted to the "higher" musical forms, the ensemble premiered Johannes Brahms's Grand Trio in B Major, Opus 8, in 1855. To promote their concerts, the musicians themselves handed out circulars on street corners. In both scope and philosophy the Mason-Bergmann (later Mason-Thomas) ensemble shared with the Barnum-promoted extravaganzas little but the air that carried sound from players to listeners. Though Jullien could draw 24,000 to the Crystal Palace with the *Fireman's Quadrille* and Jenny Lind 6,000 to Castle Garden to hear "Comin' through the Rye," Mason-Thomas, et alia, drew audiences in the low hundreds to chamber performances of Mozart, Schubert, and Beethoven. The *Times* reviewer observed that the program was "classical in the severest sense of the word," and suggested "a slight ad-mixture of something not German would have been a relief." Nonetheless, critics took the size of the audiences as evidence of improvement in musical taste.

Whether the Steinway alliance developed by plan, chance, necessity, or some permutation is unclear, but the result was the same: from its earliest years the pianos of Steinway were conjoined with musical refinement and high aesthetic purpose. The Steinway relationships with Mason and Thomas, though not always of great fidelity (as both men endorsed other pianos), were long-lived, spanning four decades. Theodore Thomas evolved to a personage of central musical significance, pioneering the concept of municipal symphony orchestras across America. William Mason's career expanded beyond performance to renown as a music educator and critic of unusual perception. Both had pianos on loan from the Steinways as early as 1857.

The Steinway accounts show more than one peculiar entry. Five dollars is recorded as spent on "glasses and frames for Aptommas." Steinway & Sons had apparently provided the harpist, as acclaimed as he was perennially impecunious, with spectacles. For this favor and the loan of an instrument, the Steinways received a communication from the celebrated soloist of Jullien's Crystal Palace concert: "Allow me to express to you my entire satisfaction with your Pianos. . . . To me it seemed to combine the deliciously soft sounds of the harp with the peculiarly articulated tones of the flute."

Another early endorser was the pianist Gustav Satter, about whom little is known, save that he could trigger verbal fusillades from critics: "A piano player of the new school . . . which defies the mechanical distances of octaves . . . bridges the doubly elevated attics of the superstructures of sound . . . picks out the humanities and pitch of the voices divine for its themes, and wreathes the uppermost and lowermost addenda of sound thereto." Continuing, the *New York Tribune* reviewer closed on his target, "Of the new 2:40 school—in fact, the locomotive school—so fast, so strong, so fierce." Satter was also a Bergmann affiliate and performed with the New York Philharmonic; a *New York Times* critic was quick to take umbrage at the fact that "out of sixty-eight members of the orchestra, there was not one detailed to turn the leaves" for Satter. At the same concert, the *New York Tribune* grumbled about the "combination of piano solo, long and extended and mixed up and alternating with an orchestra," a form considered "unphilosophical and unsatisfactory." The work performed was Beethoven's Piano Concerto in E Flat.

Not all early Steinway endorsers were musicians, for the family quickly comprehended the sales potential of other forms of celebrity and power. The Reverend Henry Ward Beecher, a man of fame and later infamy, wrote, "I regard him as a benefactor who builds a good piano, and I am your beneficiary on that account. Having had one of your instruments for several years I can bear witness to its admirable qualities in every respect. I am more than satisfied, and if I had to buy another, I should certainly go to your rooms again. It is a pleasure to praise your work." While the Reverend Beecher was pleased with his piano, he did not pay his bill. Steinway & Sons carried his $400 account for two years.

Judges were also granted what might generously be called extended credit. The Honorable Judge Osborne took more than three years to discharge his account, and a Judge Mitchell more than a year. Another occupational class which enjoyed largesse was newspaper and magazine publishers. Frank Leslie was the owner and publisher of a weekly news magazine slanted to the sensational. Illustrations in Leslie's included a female acrobat leaping from a high wire with costume ablaze, corpses of women found floating in the Hudson, children trapped in a burning factory, and frequent train wrecks. Editorially friendly to Steinway & Sons, which was also a frequent advertiser, Frank Leslie lauded Steinway pianos in print but did not pay his bill. Mrs. James Gordon Bennett, wife of the *New York Tribune* publisher and sporadically a music and drama critic, was accorded similar treatment but to no apparent benefit.

In the convoluted world of testimonials and accommodations of accounts, there was an inherent tension. In the realm of the ideal, pianomaking as art, this was anathema; in the realm of the real, pianomaking as an economic activity, it was necessity. The Steinways proved to be masters of this duality, superb operatives who could cadge an endorsement with ease using both cash and more subtle emoluments, then appear to be both grateful and surprised upon its receipt.

There were, of course, the moral absolutists who decried the business of endorsements. Of the artists, the *New York Daily Tribune* wrote, "Their so-called testimonials become of less value than the paper on which they are written, and their motives are left open to very grave suspicion. The public begins to understand. Good wine, they say, 'needs no bush,' neither does a good piano need testimonials from professional gentlemen, four-fifths of whom are profoundly ignorant of the construction of the instrument, or of what constitutes its real merits." The realists knew otherwise, and the Steinways accreted endorsements with a dedication bordering on ferocity.

It was Charles who was in charge of sales and presumably endorsements at this time, having ceded manufacturing to brother Henry. Tall, thin, handsome, with perhaps the best command of English, and the eldest son in New York, Charles held forth in the warerooms on Walker Street, dealing with customers, piano teachers, who were offered a 15-percent commission on instruments sold to their students, and the growing network of dealers. By 1858 Charles was joined in the showroom by John F. Petri, a musician and former music dealer in Washington, D.C., who came to New York as a full-time salesman.

Working with Charles was the youngest partner, William. A man of immense strength—he was fond of demonstrating this by picking up kegs of beer with his thumb and forefinger, then holding them at arm's length—William was also gregarious, almost compulsively social. Possessed of a fine tenor voice, he often sang solos with the Liederkranz, a German singing society of amateur status but professional capability. Charles also sang quite competently.

In addition to music, Charles and William shared an interest in guns, target-shooting together at the Pythagorean Hall, Liederkranz headquarters, where Charles was president, and occasionally hunting together. Both Charles and William were members of the Hussars, a crack New York state militia regiment not unlike modern commandos. William was physically aggressive, perhaps in counterbalance to Charles's more reticent nature. Once, when hunting, William downed a duck with his shotgun, only to have the dog take the bird and swim to the opposite shore of the Milwaukee River. William promptly stripped and swam across to retrieve the fowl. William did not shrink from physical contact. His diary reveals that he once threw a disorderly drunk from a streetcar. In later years he was fond of recalling how he had bested a gang of "know-nothings" single-handedly in a brawl, and that he had once saved his brother Henry's life by pulling him from the surf at Coney Island.

Henry Steinway, Jr., was slightly walleyed, frail, witty, analytical, tubercular, and the family's technological wellspring. He was also a man who may have known his life would not be long. Described by piano parts maker Alfred Dolge as "a good musician and a splendid mixer with artists, professionals and literary men," Henry Steinway, Jr., had the quickest mind among the brothers and a powerful capacity to assimilate detail. According to Dolge he was "naturally of a highly artistic, nervous temperament" and, cryptically, "at nighttime a serious student of Bohemia."

The nature of Henry, Jr.'s evening recreations are unrecorded, but the city's diversions ranged from wagers on fights between rats and dogs to Italian opera. On Grand Street, a few feet off Broadway, was the theatrical home of the "Model Artists." Here heavily made-up young women dressed in flesh-colored tights sang "Ethiopian" songs and struck poses derived from classical statuary such as *Venus Rising from the Sea*. Such scenes were thought salacious. There was, of course, a bar; and "lewd" books were sold in the lobby. In the words of a *New York Times* reporter, the female employees of the establishment "are fit objects for Missionary attention, and they should receive it."

For those who sought pleasure beyond the scoptophilic, the city provided amply. For decades Mercer Street in Soho was one of the largest red-light districts. It was on Mercer at 89 and 91, between Prince and Spring streets, that the Steinways rented a shop beginning in 1856, and it was there that Heinrich, Charles, and Henry, Jr., had their benches and tools. Their business neighbors, according to *The Fast Men's Directory and Lover's Guide*, included Mrs. Todd at 80 Mercer, where "the women of this house race the street to pick up men and decoy them to this den where Danger awaits. Shun this resort of thieves, and if you wish the society of young ladies call at Amanda Parker's, 101 Mercer." Ms. Parker had twelve "lady boarders." There were roughly two-dozen "land ladies" operating on Mercer, ranging from Mrs. Gardner's, "a very quiet place for private couples to go to anticipate the pleasures of matrimony," to Mrs. Bennett's, "a very low place frequently filled with niggers, a rendezvous for thieves."

In general, the Germans were not perceived as clients of the fleshier diversions: "The German portion of our population have the most rational idea of evening recreation. They incline to good moral drama. . . . They make music one of their chief means of entertainment, and are strictly decent in their public pleasures. Those, on the other hand, who delight in indecent and indelicate exhibitions are chiefly the lower class of Irish, and negroes," reported the *New York Times* in 1858. "Indeed, the only place of amusement where I have seen Germans mingling largely with Americans is in the uppermost of the twenty-five-cent department of the opera, and they are, I believe, better critics of the performance, and more attentive and appreciative listeners, than the ladies and gentlemen below them in the parquet."

The brothers Henry, William, and Charles were frequenters of the opera in New York and elsewhere. Describing an opera performance he attended in Havana, Cuba, Henry, Jr., wrote to his brother William in 1863, "A local composer wrote a little opera [called] *Christopher Columbus* . . . which he managed to have performed." There were problems with "the orchestra, consisting mostly of darkies that played very badly," and the male lead, "who sounded like an old billy goat braying." Continuing with his account, Henry, Jr., commented that, "Naturally, all hell broke loose." The audience began to sing with the performers, echoing each note, en masse. Amidst the general pandemonium the ensemble segued to *Il Travatore* and finally, to quiet the crowd, an "almost completely" naked ballerina appeared. She "danced badly but had a good build . . . and this sight brought down the noise somewhat."

The audience soon began to throw canes, chairs, candelabras, glass, and other objects at the performers. "Now the public rushed onto the stage, tore down the curtain, danced madly on the stage . . . and altogether demolished everything in sight and asked for refunds of their money." The audience raged through the theater until two in the morning, but the police, fearful of igniting a general revolution, made no arrests. The incident was not reported in the newspapers. Concluding his description, Henry noted that "A scene such as this has not taken place before, although theatre riots are said to happen frequently here."

When not at the opera, Henry was the inside man; the shop was his domain and development, his specialty. He rarely visited the Walker Street salesroom. "I really know very little about the business," he wrote William, "so little that at times I don't even know how we sell our instruments. However, I console myself with the thought that I suspect that you don't know that too well either." Yet when an odd, old, or in any way interesting piano was taken in trade, it might very well have been taken to Henry's home or corner of the shop, there to be inspected, disassembled, and analyzed. It was Henry who had the power to synthesize technology or create it. Fanatically devoted to quality even as he approached death, Henry Steinway's gift to the family enterprise was a foundation of solid innovation.

Presiding, without a doubt, over his children, their lives, and the busi-

ness was Heinrich. Scarcely taller than five feet, slightly bowlegged, unable
to read or write in any language, with a physiognomy that even commissioned
portrait painters had difficulty flattering, Heinrich was a man with acute
natural intelligence, drop-forged resolve, and a willingness to take risks. He
had, by modern standards, an immense capacity for work. After working ten
to twelve hours per day, six days a week, Heinrich, in his sixth decade of
life, spent his evenings building new pianos. "Our new piano," wrote Charles,
"is ready to be strung and we think it will be completely finished by Christmas.
Father works on it every evening." Three years later Charles reported, "Father
is now working on the scale [basic design] of a grand and next year we will
try our luck with grand [pianos]." These were letters that "Father" knew
about and which were likely read to him. In other letters among the brothers,
Heinrich was the "Old Man" who had "a strange kind of generosity combined
with stubbornness and distrust."

Recreation did not loom large in the life of Heinrich, but he was known
to be very fond of lager *bier* and bowling and shared, if he did not inspire,
the family passion for eating oysters. While Heinrich never learned English
during his two-score years in New York and did not become a citizen until
1863, the last of the family to do so, he was not an insular man. He travelled
with William on business trips, visiting Colt's revolver manufactory in New
Haven, the Chickering works in Boston, and cities throughout what was
then called the West: Chicago, Detroit, Cincinnati, and Saint Louis. As
the family grew wealthier, Heinrich summered at a Sharon Springs, New
York, resort.

So far as can be known, Heinrich Steinway never retired to live a life
of opulent leisure. A year before his death at age seventy-three he was still
purchasing investment property. In his midsixties he daily supervised the
construction of the family's new piano factory: "Father is out there everyday
and every now and then quarrels with the construction workers when
things are not going to his wishes. I probably don't have to tell you that he
is entirely in his element," wrote Charles to his brother Theodore. Family
legend has it that Heinrich would climb the beams and rafters of the five-
story, block-long structure searching for knots in the timbers. Finding one,
he would demand that the beam be torn out and replaced with clear stock.
In a later letter Henry wrote, "The Old Man is done selecting material,
and since the walls of the new factory have been properly put up, he cannot
tear them down and put them up differently. . . . He is getting bored."
But soon there was more construction that Heinrich could superintend.
Business was growing.

That Heinrich was the final authority in matters of both business and
family, there is little doubt. But what portion of this dominance was attributable to the man and to the cultural context is unclear. German social
norms throughout the eighteenth and nineteenth centuries were patriarchal

in the extreme, even when calibrated by the male-dominated criteria of English-speaking peoples.

The Prussian Civil Code of 1794 specifically mandated that the father had greater authority over children than the mother, a codification maintained well into the twentieth century. For much of the nineteenth century, German women, while they might own property or businesses, were required by law to have their holdings administered by men. No matter how successful Charles, Henry, William, Theodore, and Albert Steinway became, no matter how well known, they always consulted Father . . . and ultimately asked for his consent.

Authoritarian though he may have been, Heinrich was also a man who understood the power of innovation. Though old, he was not a risk-avoiding conservative in matters business or technical. Though we cannot know what ideas—good or bad—may have been lost to his veto, those to which he assented and perhaps inspired are keystones of both the modern piano and the success of the firm. The early Steinway & Sons patents are all in the name of Henry, Jr. They begin in 1857 with a patent for a piano action, that series of levers that begins with the key, ends with the hammer, and links human to machine in musical partnership.

As always with the Steinways, the target was the best: "I obtain a more free and easy movement of the action in repeating . . . and also obtain the effect only produced in the complicated *Erard* grand action," stated the specification of Letters Patent No. 17,238 dated May 5, 1857. The Paris-built Erard was the preferred instrument of many European piano virtuosi, and Henry, Jr., had determined that he would not only improve performance but simplify the mechanism as well. This was an area of rapid development: about four of every ten piano patents granted were for actions. "I have put an action in a seven-octave grand according to Henry's instructions," wrote Theodor to Heinrich in 1857. "The only problem is that the action makes too much noise." Just thirteen months later Henry, Jr., was granted another action patent with "less friction" than his invention of 1857.

There were three later actions patents as well, but the critical innovations of Henry Steinway, Jr., were verified by the Patent Office in the closing months of 1859. The first of these was for a novel method of holding the treble strings of the instrument firmly in place. By threading the string through a small device called an "agraffe," Henry, Jr., was able to markedly improve the tone quality of the treble of his instruments. Agraffes were not new; but they had not been used in the treble portion of the piano for complex reasons related to the geometry of the string and the hammer. The solution was both elegant and arcane: the agraffes were tilted from their conventional position. "I have had a machine custom-made in order to drill the agraffes diagonally," wrote Henry to Theodore in September of

1859. "This results in a magnificently firm treble . . . it does have to be a rather good grand to rival such an instrument." One half of the signature Steinway sound—scintillating treble—was now in place. The other half—powerful bass—was also imminent.

United States Patent No. 26,532, dated December 20, 1859, described the mechanism for the powerful bass: overstringing. Though overstringing was being successfully applied by the Steinways, Mathushek, and Spencer Driggs on square pianos in New York and had been used in various ways by others in both the United States and Europe, no one had evolved a way to overstring grand pianos successfully. The concept doubtless occurred to many, but it was Henry Steinway, Jr., who actually accomplished it. In so doing, he created the modern piano. It is a conception so apt that in retrospect it is difficult to comprehend how a piano might have been designed any other way or the reasons competent men might choose to do so. The overstrung grand is to pianos as the incandescent light is to illumination. All that which precedes it is obsolete; all that subsequent is elaboration, extension, or response.

Henry, Jr., posited, then executed a fundamental change in the architecture of the piano. He raised the bass strings and rotated them over the treble strings, "whereby I am enabled not only to obtain all the results obtained in piano-fortes of other forms by overstringing; but am enabled to bring the bridges nearer to the middle of the sound board than they are in any other grand piano-forte." Henry, Jr.'s succinct words from Patent No. 26,532 understate the power of his innovation, for while they accurately describe the device, they do not mention the effect: much louder bass and, in all probability, a much louder instrument overall.

To grasp how Henry, Jr.'s innovation of 1859 works requires only a cardboard shoebox. Invert the larger part of the box and tap it lightly with the finger near any corner. A sound will be heard. Now tap the box nearer the center. With the same force a louder, deeper sound will be heard. In the language of engineering, the "compliance" of the box bottom is greater at the center than at the edges, and more of the mechanical energy imparted to the box by the finger is transformed into acoustical energy. With an intuitive grasp of the elemental dynamics of the piano as a machine, Henry Steinway, Jr., had increased the efficiency of the piano. But pianos were not then valued by the loudness of the bass alone, but by an elusive, subjective quality known as "evenness of scale," the balance *to the ear* of the relative loudness of the instrument from the lowest bass to the highest treble.

Compounding the complexity of the problem was—and is—the fact that the ear of the listener is not uniform in its sensitivity. A much louder sound is needed in the lower two octaves than in the upper two to be *perceived* as equally loud. From the standpoint of the player, still another variable is added: the tones produced, while really of different energies, must be perceived to be of the same energy and also to be produced by the same force of the finger. The "same force" concept is known as "evenness of touch" among pianists and actually subsumes another set of complex variables that involve not only the force with which the key is pressed, but the timing of the keystroke in relation to the sounding of the note. The time of sounding varies as a function of the force with which the key is hit.

Virtuoso players can develop uncanny sensitivities to these variables. A satisfactory understanding of the complex interactions between piano tone, touch, and audition still eludes physicists and acousticians; in the time of Henry Steinway, Jr., knowledge was in a still more primitive state. He was an intuitive genius who worked at the edges of perception, far beyond the conventional boundaries of craft, tradition, and so-called "scientific" knowledge. It was held by eminent European acoustics authorities, for example, that strings placed over each other, such as they were in Henry, Jr.'s Steinway & Sons overstrung designs, would interfere with the free vibration of one by another. Of course, no such phenomenon occurred.

So embedded were the theories, so imbued with tradition were the arbiters of excellence that in 1862 the judges at the prestigious London International Exhibition were able to lament that there had been no significant developments in piano technology since the last London Exhibition of 1851. Before them were the theoretically incorrect New York Steinway overstrung grands and squares, on display for all to see, hear, and play. More remarkable still were the comments of a renowned director of a French musical conservatory, one F. J. Fetis. Monsieur Fetis later complained, with some vexation, that William Steinway ceaselessly played his instruments at the London Exhibition. In fact, William Steinway had never left New York. If a Steinway were playing at the exhibition, it was Henry, Jr., indefatigably demonstrating his inventions.

Some were quicker to appreciate the potential of the new Steinway construction; among those was a twenty-one-year-old English-born and German-trained pianist, Sebastian Bach Mills. A recent immigrant to New York fresh from studies with Moscheles in Leipzig, Mills debuted in New York on March 26, 1859, to adulatory reviews: "The most remarkable player" ever heard in the United States was the verdict of the *New York Times*, but a later program was "too serious in character," according to the paper. This was a frequent critical lament for the performers who elected Steinway. There was a difference between the reviews of Sebastian Bach Mills and those of other piano virtuosi: the piano itself was lauded with nearly as much enthusiasm as the pianist.

In November 1859 the *Times* reported a concert of the Brooklyn Philharmonic: "Mr. Mills, the pianist, gave us the greatest treat of the programme, the concerto, in F minor, by Chopin, a work of exquisite beauty, and too seldom heard in the concert room. In the present day the piano-forte has a new significance as an orchestral instrument, owing to the immense improvements which have been effected in its mechanism and the volumes of tone, which is the natural result of those improvements." Then, in a statement singular for the time, the reviewer continued, "The superb Steinway instrument, on which Mr. Mills performed, imparted a character and dignity to the recitative of the Adagio movement, which was utterly unattainable in days of old, on an Erard. Under the hands of this great classical artist the piano-forte is indeed a distinct voice, full of majesty and beauty."

The critics who had described previous performances of piano concertos with words such as "ineffectual" or "unphilosophical" found what they sought: an improved balance between piano and orchestra. Nor was that all: "The Steinway pianos were again the object of admiration, for the power and brilliance of their tone, and the perfect tune in which they remained throughout the concert, notwithstanding the severe trials they were exposed to by playing of so much power," reported the *Philadelphia Evening Bulletin*.

Sebastian Bach Mills was described as a player of the "Lisztian School." Decoded, this meant that the power and pyrotechnics of "bravura" perfor- mance that had turned concerts into piano demolition derbies was a thing of the past. No longer was it necessary to have two pianos on stage in case one failed, as De Meyer had done; no longer would the "accordist" risk the wrath of the master, as when Liszt cuffed his tuner as the man attempted running repairs. Henry Steinway, Jr., had done more than simply create an instrument whose tone was one of "majesty and beauty"; he brought reliability to the instrument. In so doing, he unshackled the artists and left them free to roam new fields of expression.

Ecstatic reports continued into 1860, more than a year after the introduc- tion of the overstrung grand. At the cavernous four-thousand-seat acoustical disaster that was New York's Academy of Music, the combination of Sebas- tian Bach Mills and Steinway triumphed again: "Mr. Mills was faultlessly certain and perfect. Technical skill can scarcely be carried to greater perfec- tion . . . remarkable strength and roundness [of tone] . . . exquisite deli- cacy," rhapsodized the *New York Times* in the winter of 1860. "Under Mr. MILLS' hands a grand piano—one of Steinway's overstrung—was used. . . . [It] ceases to be a mere machine. It breathes into the soul of the audience and animates it with the strangest delights."

Sebastian Bach Mills's performance with the New York Philharmonic on Saturday, March 26, 1859, forecast the future. The place was Niblo's Garden on Broadway, where the previous attraction had been Nixon and Company's Equestrian Troupe featuring Dan Rice with his educated mules and talking horse. Niblo's was actually a theater, but the moral contempt with which many viewed dramatic entertainments led Mr. Niblo to call his facility a "garden." An architectural sop to these attitudes was provided by a series of plantings, amongst which patrons could perambulate in warm weather. Hard by Niblo's *Garden* was Niblo's *Saloon*. Gentlemen could slip from the performance space to the bar, slake their thirst, and return, telling their wives they had been admiring the flora in the garden. Niblo's was a very popular venue. There converged on a night in 1859—not far from a bar and likely for the first time—all the components in the modern concept of a "classical" musical performance: a symphony orchestra, a virtuoso of the highest caliber, a composition of refined standards and daunting difficulty, and last, but of no small importance, an overstrung grand piano. That evening at Niblo's proved to be the prototype for countless thousands of performances, some triumphs, some disasters, most merely forgettable, that continue to the current day.

There was no sense at the time that this was a seminal event. The concept of the piano virtuoso as primarily an interpreter of standard works as contrasted to a player of his own compositions was slow to take hold; it would be a dozen or more years before it became the dominant model. Ultimately the idea that a piano virtuoso must also compose, as did De Meyer, Herz, and others, was swept away. As the definition of the performance changed, so did design of the instrument, and the overstrung grands of Steinway ultimately became the de facto standard architecture of the industry.

Sebastian Bach Mills and the Steinways both benefited from the combination of forces they set in motion that night at Niblo's Garden, although in vastly different ways. Mills remained in New York for nearly four decades until his death in 1898. He taught, concertized, and retained a relationship with Steinway & Sons.

Important though Mills may have been, the Steinways were already looking east to the horizon: We are "keen on having our name well-known in Europe too," wrote Henry to Theodore in the fall of 1859. "This is absolutely necessary so we can attract the attention of visiting piano virtuosos and get our hands on them. Just as it is in Paris with Erard and Pleyel, so it is in New York with Steinway & Sons and Chickering & Sons. Lately, since we have been making the overstrung grands we have overtaken them rather clearly." Henry Steinway referred here not to the number of instruments produced, which at Steinway was about 60 percent of Chickering's output, but to the tonal and playing qualities of the instruments.

"Our overstrung grand pianos are quite fabulous. They have a fuller and stronger sound than the ordinary ones. We are no longer making any others. Other piano makers are already imitating us. Our square pianos have been copied by five or six manufacturers," Henry continued. To Theodore, struggling under a combination of heavy debt, a recalcitrant partner, and a shortage of skilled labor, this news of the success of the family in America must have been bittersweet, at best. "The Patent Office in Washington," continued Henry, "has not decided yet, but I am very hopeful that I can get a patent for the grands, since none have ever been issued before." The fundamental patent, No. 26,532, for overstringing was granted three months later.

Henry's other desire, "to get their hands on" European artists, was much longer in gestation. It was with Chickering that the most famed players allied themselves, not Steinway. While men such as Mills, Mason, and Satter were highly regarded, they lacked the éclat of international recognition. Beginning in late 1856, visiting virtuoso Sigismond Thalberg struck a tentative alliance with Chickering, performing on the instruments in Boston, perhaps to curry favor with local audiences in Chickering's "hometown." This soon expanded to include soirees in the Chickering warerooms, and it was not long before Thalberg abandoned the seven French Erard instruments he had brought with him for a logistically and perhaps financially superior arrangement.

Chickering began shipping pianos to cities where Thalberg played. After the performance Thalberg autographed the pianos, usually two, and the local dealer put them on display and sale. In at least one case an auction was held for Thalberg's instruments. There were benefits here for all. Herr Thalberg was relieved of the burden, uncertainty, and expense of freighting his Erards around the country on a demanding schedule and of paying for the transportation and lodging of a piano tuner. There were risks as well, not the least of which was that Thalberg was dependent on the skill and diligence of the local Chickering agent. In Rochester, New York, the dealer was absent from the concert and the key to the piano could not be found. After some delay, two audience members succeeded in opening the piano.

The firm of Chickering & Sons reaped powerful advantage from the arrangement. A latent sense of cultural inadequacy was swept from the minds of many Americans by Thalberg's willingness to play a domestic instrument. Combined with patriotism, a powerful impetus to the purchase of a Chickering piano was created. Since the sale of square pianos outnumbered the sale of grands by perhaps twenty to one, the chance to send *two* grands to each dealer where Thalberg played was a major sales opportunity for Chickering. In all, Thalberg performed at over three hundred paid concerts during his two seasons in the United States. Were Chickering able to ship two new grand pianos to but one-fourth of these locations, sales of 150 additional grand pianos would have resulted, likely more than doubling Chickering's sales of grand pianos during the two seasons of Thalberg's tours. The Thalberg/Chickering alliance proved, for the first time in America, that prestige, patriotism, and pianos, when combined, could yield large profits to the participants. It was a lesson the Steinways would not forget.

Thalberg was one of two artists of international stature associated with Chickering. The other was Louis Moreau Gottschalk. Born in New Orleans in 1829, Gottschalk studied in Paris for four years, toured the courts and capitals of Europe, then recrossed the Atlantic to make his New York debut in February of 1853 on his own pair of European pianos, built by Pleyel of Paris. Louis Moreau Gottschalk ultimately allied himself with Chickering. Short of funds, he sold his Pleyels and began touring with Chickering grands.

It was not long, however, before critical volleys of superficial repertoire and slovenly technique were hurled. Gottschalk's reputation for romance, his debonair manner and fashionable dress, his repertoire consisting almost exclusively of his own very popular compositions—some with titles suffused with sentimentality such as *The Dying Poet* and *The Last Hope*—were viewed as insufficiently serious. Critics slyly noted that Gottschalk's New York concerts coincided with the opening of the "fashion season," the better for the ladies to compare attire. S. B. Mills, Gustav Satter, William Mason, Carl Bergmann, Theodore Thomas, and the other partisans of the unremittingly serious, the morally uplifting, the intellectually complex in music, might seek to "educate" their audience and earnestly, if naively, labor to "improve tastes." L. M. Gottschalk seemed to take his audiences as he found them. "What will it matter in a thousand years?" he wrote in his diary.

L. M. Gottschalk knew the Steinway pianos. He judged at the Crystal Palace exhibitions when in New York and played them there. Liberal with endorsements for the pianos of Abraham Bassford, Horatio Worcester, and Spencer Driggs, the latter two technologically eccentric failures, Gottschalk did not endorse Steinway. Gottschalk was no fan of some aspects of the Teutonic musical tradition. In *Notes of a Pianist*, his diary published in 1881, twelve years after his death, Gottschalk wrote, "I was introduced to an old German musician, with uncombed hair, bushy beard, in constitution like a bear, in disposition the amenity of a boar at bay to a pack of hounds. I know this type; it is found everywhere."

In advertisements the Steinways cleverly sidestepped the lack of a Gottschalk imprimatur by noting the fact that he was a judge in competitions they had won. The same ads said nothing about the advanced technology of Steinway instruments; instead they camouflaged radical design with the phrase "Constructed with the full wooden and iron frame combined." There was no mention of improved Erard actions, overstringing, flanged plates, or other of the exotica that filled the family letters with the shared excitements of discovery and advance. To the public, Steinway & Sons made a simple offer: excellence, as shown by the gold medals won, a general claim of "moderate" prices, and reliability, as evidenced by a three-year written warranty. For the time being, the Steinways attracted no artists of international renown.

In late 1865 Gottschalk penned a testimonial to Chickering & Sons "upon the eve of my departure" from the United States. The occasion was a scandal over his seduction of a young student at the Oakland Female Seminary on a California tour. He noted that he had played over three thousand concerts in eleven years on Chickering instruments and, as evidence of their "rare solidity of construction," he had not broken a string in eleven hundred concerts. He praised the Chickerings for providing "a tuner [that] has accompanied your pianos wherever my erratic steps have been directed" and for providing "a magnificent grand Piano, transported by express at enormous expense."

About four years later, at age forty, Louis Moreau Gottschalk collapsed at his piano while playing his 1868 composition *Morte!!* in Rio de Janeiro. A few days later he died. With his death an era closed; he was, in effect, the last representative of the virtuoso tradition of piano performers/composers. His was a life of strange symmetry. The last of his tradition, he was also the first American to gain acceptance in the salons and courts of Europe. Gottschalk's apparent rejection of the overstrung Steinway was consistent with his aversion to the new definition of "serious" repertoire and pianism. The Steinways and the men who played their instruments represented the musical and technological future. Chickering and Gottschalk advocated a fading ideal.

There is a final symmetry: of the 197 million square miles that is the surface of the earth, there are, in Brooklyn, New York, a few acres known as Greenwood Cemetery. There, in an immense family mausoleum containing 250 crypts, are interred the remains of Heinrich, Theodore, Charles, Henry, and William Steinway. Also in Greenwood is the untended grave of Louis Moreau Gottschalk.

Chapter 7

BRINGING TO PERFECTION AN ART INDUSTRY

"**Y**esterday afternoon a company of invited guests, including musicians and members of the press, visited the new piano manufactory of Steinway & Sons, on Fourth Avenue. The progress of this firm from the smallest beginning to its present eminence is interesting, and is the best proof which could be given of the excellence of their work and the uprightness of their mercantile transactions," reported the *New York Tribune* on August 31, 1860. "The guests yesterday went leisurely through the building, partook of a collation, and listened with pleasure to various musical performances. These last were furnished by Messrs. Mills, Wallenhaupt [*sic*], Lasar, Fradel, and Master Denck, a lad of thirteen years." Showing uncharacteristic civility, the *Tribune* reporter demurred that, "Criticism would be out of place, in noticing an occasion of this character, and it is enough to say that the performers and the hearers seemed equally to enjoy the musical treat."

Four days later the *Sunday Times* printed its account of the factory opening: "Messrs. STEINWAY & SONS Pianos rapidly won fame for durability, and combined brilliance and softness of tone, assimilating delightfully to the human voice." Within a week the *Home Journal* announced that "The firm of Steinway & Sons has become one of the most celebrated as manufacturers of pianofortes in the country, and if industry, perseverance, and the making of the best instruments deserve to be rewarded with success, we are certain that in this instance it is not unworthily bestowed."

Charles, Henry, and William Steinway had succeeded in triggering an avalanche of attention followed by a flood of ink. This was precisely their intention, as Charles revealed in an October 1860 letter to Theodore. "As you can see from the accompanying papers, we had an opening ceremony for our new factory. And let me tell you, it was a grand affair and was immensely useful for us. Editors of about sixty to eighty newspapers were invited for refreshments, a visit to the factory and champagne. Four of our best pianists were also invited to play. After the entire group had first been treated to marinated oysters, poultry, champagne, etc., the factory was visited. The machinery was running full speed and every worker was at his place. . . . After the tour people returned to the champagne and, of course, speechmaking. Everyone was so enthusiastic that we got long laudatory reports in almost every paper. This made our name immensely well-known. This is special since most of these newspapers do not mention these private affairs."

The factory opening was the culmination of two years of intense activity. In 1858 the family began to purchase property on Fourth Avenue (now Park Avenue) between Fifty-second and Fifty-third streets in the city's Nineteenth Ward. Far uptown, the Nineteenth was essentially undeveloped, a region of squatters' shacks dotting grassy fields among hills and rocky outcroppings. By Manhattan standards, the Nineteenth was immense. With 2.4 square miles, the ward was a blanket to the handkerchief-sized political subdivisions downtown, which were about one-fifteenth the size. The ward's population, about 10 percent German, was only about 12,000 persons per square mile—compared to the Calcutta-like compaction of wards such as the Sixth, where densities approached 200,000 per square mile.

To the west in the Twenty-second Ward, farms still produced dairy products for sale downtown. To the east and west in the Nineteenth, scattered tenements housed the sparse population that found employment in the ward's fourteen breweries, a major industry. Winken's Brewery, a favorite recreational spot of William Steinway, was located not far away on Fifty-seventh and Third. Downtown service businesses had not yet found their way as far north as Fifty-second Street. The ward, reformers reported, had no brothels and a mere two hundred bars. Pigsties were a moderate local nuisance, and the slaughterhouse at Forty-fifth and Third was accompanied by the usual exposed piles of entrails and manure. Steinway & Son's nearest commercial neighbor was a cooperage and stables at Fifty-first and Fourth. Above Sixtieth, streets were still unpaved.

It was in this setting that the Steinways chose to build what Henry L. Stuart, a speaker at their opening ceremony, called a "magnificent temple, devoted to industrial art, with its hundred altars of mechanism, wheron are worked the cunning devices of manufacturing skill and artistic design."

Furbelows of Victorian elocution aside, the Steinways had, in less than a decade, grown their business from pianomaking evenings on Hester Street to the largest piano manufactory in New York.

In roughly three and one-half years the partnership's net worth increased fifteen times to over $360,000, and the annual output of pianos rose almost 700 percent. It was also an amazingly profitable business. From each piano the company made, the family retained about $100 in profit, an amount for which the most skilled and experienced piano factory worker would have labored 400 hours to earn. The retained earnings from six pianos would pay the average factory hand for a year. Had the Steinways elected to work for others, their talents would have undoubtedly allowed them to rise to the position of foreman, paying each man perhaps $1,000 per year, the equivalent of their net from 40 pianos. Building over 1000 pianos per year by 1859, profits flowed to the four partners in an amount equal to the wages of four foremen working for 250 years. This the family earned, not in two and one-half centuries, but in a single year. By any reasonable standard, the Steinways had become very wealthy very quickly.

In the cool darkness of their commercial shadow stood the veterans of the city trade: Bacon & Raven, J. B. Dunham, A. H. Gale, and all the others of the prior generation. Steinway & Sons was now, in all likelihood, the second largest maker in the nation, its annual output exceeded only by Chickering in Boston. The scope and scale of operations that Jonas Chickering had achieved over three decades the Steinways reached in less than seven years.

The press had come to stare at success, to witness the phenomenon, to assess the symbol that was the manufactory, to see what was *expected*, by the consensual myth, to happen in America: immigrants land, work hard, deal fairly, make a good product, and prosper magnificently. To explain the ascendance of the Steinways, Henry Stuart proposed "a single lesson that I wish to impress upon you, and through you, upon every family in the country." Continuing, he told the reporters, "Messrs. Steinway & Sons are a noble illustration of what a united family, with a common interest, a common purpose and common labors can do—aye, always will do. The Rothschilds in Europe, the Appletons, the Harpers and the Steinways in our own country, with a few others, have, by observing this great law of success, not only achieved fortune, but each, in their own way, have made an indelible mark upon, and moulded, the nineteenth century."

Henry Stuart's comments were, in the language of the time, "humbug." To equate the Steinways with Europe's leading bankers, whose ability to finance nations had geopolitical impact, or with the Appleton and Harper media families, whose publications influenced national attitudes, was hyperbolic at best. In the case of the Harpers there was irony: in 1846 James Harper was elected mayor of New York on the Native American ticket; his campaign was keyed to fear and hatred of immigrants and the economic threat they presented to the native-born. Heinrich Englehard Steinway and his sons were the personification of these Native American fears.

Panegyrics and encomia, interspersed with champagne toasts, continued into the evening. At length, Charles Steinway rose to address the group. Charles's words do not survive, save in a paraphrase written by Frank Leslie: "He attributed . . . their present position . . . to the progressive spirit of this country—to its free institutions which recognized the individuality of every man, and enabled him to make his mark in spite of wealthy and established opposition, and imbued him with that irresistible desire to 'go ahead' and come out first in the race for improvement." While Henry Stuart saw the family unit as the key to success, Charles cited, by implication, technology and free competition, the lessons which, as Leslie declaimed, "America teaches to those who seek her shores from the narrow despotisms of the Old World."

Charles Steinway believed these things; his comments were not simply a cynical appeal to patriotism. Of the family's fortune in America he wrote to Theodore, "Such things are possible only in America. In Germany something like this [the factory] would be impossible." It was about eight o'clock that Wednesday evening in August 1860 when the members of the press left the manufactory. Amply filled with champagne and oysters, they also carried with them a neatly printed fact sheet that described the factory and the business.

The report in the *New York Times* relied heavily on the Steinways' "fact sheet." It described a building fronting on Fourth Avenue in the "modern Italian style" for the full span between Fifty-second and Fifty-third, a distance of 201 feet with a depth of 40 feet. Five stories high plus the basement, there were over 50,000 square feet for manufacturing, offices, and showroom space in the main section. A wing ran down Fifty-third for a distance of 160 feet, adding another 38,400 square feet for a total of roughly two acres of space under the roof of the new manufactory. On Fifty-second Street three new brownstones, architecturally similar in style, were built: one for Heinrich, one for Henry, Jr., and a third that would be occupied by William and other family members from time to time. Charles later purchased a home nearby. The brownstones were cleverly located so that family members could cross between the back of the factory and their homes without being seen by their employees. The *Times* did not mention this.

There was among the Steinway workforce by 1860 a smouldering, socialist-based movement whose ambitions went beyond the modern labor issues of wages, hours, and working conditions. Some in the workforce likely aspired not only to manage the firm, but to seize it from the family. In the spring of 1859, Steinway & Sons discharged a number of workers who had joined an emerging Piano-Makers Union, a response that was not only legal but routine among employers. Under these conditions, the first ripples in what would become a maelstrom of labor conflict, the family undoubtedly found it useful to arrive and depart undetected.

The Steinways also recognized the value of quick communication among themselves and installed a telegraph between the factory and the warerooms on Walker Street. The three and one-half miles between the factory where Henry, Jr., was in charge and the showroom where Charles and William worked could be bridged in seconds by telegraph, rather than the hour needed—each way—by a messenger. Traffic in New York, then as now, moved at a rate of about three miles per hour. Nearly two decades before the commercial introduction of the telephone, the Steinway private telegraph, a galvanized iron wire strung across rooftops, was a novel symbol of technical advance, one which was mentioned in company catalogs for many years.

There was another threat to security, and that was fire, a common event in the city, usually from accidental causes but sometimes the work of "incendiaries." The family had previously met this threat, at least indirectly, by siting operations about the city on 89, 91, and 109 Mercer Street, 96 Crosby Street, and 82–84 and 113 Walker Street, plus a lumberyard on Twenty-third Street. Wood, parts, and pianos were moved about in carts by dollar-per-day Irish laborers. A fire in one of these rented facilities, save the lumberyard, would have had a minimal impact on overall operations. With manufacturing consolidated in one place, the Steinways countered the fire menace by building a masonry structure with walls up to two feet thick, iron fire doors, and equally ample party walls. No flame was allowed in the building—except for gas lamps—and heat was provided by 30,000 linear feet of steam piping. Operations that required heat, such as the drying or bending of wood and japanning (a way of applying an enamellike finish to iron that required kilns), were all done by steam heat.

"All the heavier portion of the machinery is in the basement," wrote the *Times* in a plagiarism of William's press handout, which must have delighted him. "In this room are three large planers, one of which is certainly one of the largest instruments of its class existing, planing the largest piano tops and bottoms at once. There are also four up-and-down saws, several circular saws, besides several turning lathes & c." The next sentence was edited from the newspaper account, but the fact sheet continued: "These wonderful instruments are constantly at work, shaping the rough plank ready for use in the first floor above, where the bottoms, blockings, wrest planks, and other parts of the case, are got up with the aid of moulding, jointing and other machinery." The family estimated—proudly—that their machinery replaced the labors of five hundred men.

Print reports of the opening continued for weeks. The opinion of the *Home Journal* differed from that of the others, who were principally impressed by the size of the shop: "The most interesting portion of the factory, however, to us, is a small room on the first floor, where presides the

inventive mind which plans and perfects new improvements. Here, surrounded by drawings and models, the master spirit of the establishment—
the eldest son, we believe—is to be found. It is to him the public is indebted
for many of the improvements which render Steinway & Sons pianos second
to none in the world." The writers of these words, Mr. Morris and Mr.
Willis, had seen the place, but not the man. They were peering into "Mr.
H. Steinway's Office." Unknown to the reporters, a closet within contained
the scale drawings, safely hidden from sight, which were the key to
Steinway technological supremacy. Its occupant, Henry, Jr., scarcely was
mentioned in the accounts of the opening, yet no one could leave or enter
the manufactory without passing in view of the room "occupied by the
master spirit of the establishment."

The symphony of praise continued, to near exhaustion of superlatives:
honorable, noble, extraordinary, best, huge, unprecedented, superior, and
on and on. "We presume," wrote Cornelius Mathews of the *New Yorker*,
"there is no other manufactory in the world which combines so perfectly
all the elements of creation in so simple a working order. It is this gift for
arrangement and combination which has placed Steinway senior and his
four sons at the head of an establishment so complete in the short term of
eight years. It is conceded that the Steinway piano in make, tone, sweetness
and precision is the most perfect instrument of that class to be had anywhere
in the world. It unites in itself whatever has been inherited, combined or
invented down to the present time, to make the piano they produce all that
a piano can be. In this they have succeeded."

The Steinways had discovered a potent combination of concepts which
had wide appeal: Family, Art, Music, and Excellence. The modern bureaucrat might acronymize this as FAME. The combination resonated in the
minds of the journalists touring the factory that day, a suite of themes so
powerful, so compelling, that they reverberate to the present. Whether
this occurred by design or serendipity, before the fact or after, cannot be
determined. That the family was surprised by the success of the promotional
efforts is clear. It is equally clear that the combination of themes was
susceptible to almost infinite elaboration, extension, and development. The
family, America, music, and excellence were a constellation of concepts at
once grand and abstract, so grand and so abstract that it became mirrorlike,
reflecting the needs, desires, and aspirations not of the Steinways, but of
those who reported and wrote about them and those who read the reports.
So it was on a hot August afternoon in 1860 that a family took their first step
beyond conventional classifications—Germans, immigrants, pianomakers,
citizens, businessmen—and toward myth.

Despite the accomplishment and the recognition, William Steinway
could not resist the impulse to "puff," nineteenth-century vernacular for
exaggerating claims. He claimed a total investment in the business—property, plant, equipment, and inventory—of one-half million dollars. This

was apportioned as $150,000 in property and plant and $350,000 in machinery, lumber, pianos in process, and finished instruments. In reality, the books of the partnership at year-end valued the physical plant at $108,664.07. Somehow, the value grew by 38 percent in public pronouncements. The $350,000 "investment" in lumber, machinery, and pianos was also based on generous estimates and did not, in reality, exceed $210,000.

"There are three-hundred and fifty men constantly employed, who turn out about thirty Square and five Grand Pianos every week," wrote William; this information was dutifully recorded and disseminated by the assembled reporters. While the 1,820-piano-per-year production implied by this statement may have represented the capacity of the Fifty-second Street works, actual units sold in 1860 numbered about 1,250 or about 30 percent less. Due to a recession induced by the onset of the Civil War in 1861, sales that year fell into the range of 850 pianos. All this suggests that the employment of 350 men was also overstated. In 1850 Charles had written Theodore that ten men could make one piano in one week. The employment of 350 therefore suggests a capacity of 1,800 pianos per year, a number that fits nicely with the claimed Steinway & Sons production of 1,820 units.

In the consistency of the production and employment numbers is seen the astuteness of the Steinways. Every competitive pianomaker in New York knew *exactly* the relationship between pianos built and labor hired; a Steinway claim of employment or output that violated this ratio would have been instantaneously questioned, if not repudiated, by their competitors. The family, therefore, chose a credible pair of figures in which the claimed production aligned plausibly with the claimed employment. Probable employment, based on pianos built in 1860, was about 250 men for the year. Steinway & Sons actually employed a labor force roughly equal to that of the two largest employers among the pianomakers of 1855, Lighte, Newton & Bradbury and the A. H. Gale Company, combined. Their capital investment was twice that of the city's most capital-intensive pianomaker of 1855, the pricey and prestigious Nunns & Clark, then in operation for nearly four decades. The family also sold twice as many instruments in 1860 as any maker in the city had sold just five years before.

Objective evidence indicates an amazing accomplishment, with growth in Steinway piano sales averaging 62 percent per year for five years. This was a performance that would be the envy of any Silicon Valley technology company of 120 years later, a dream enterprise for any late-twentieth-century venture capitalist. But the Steinways had no outside investors nor had they borrowed a single dollar from a bank to that time. The entire success was, as Henry L. Stuart pointed out, a family matter. The Steinways had provided the seed capital, the innovative technology, and the aggressive management on which their success was based.

That the Steinways felt the need to overstate their accomplishments with inflated numbers for production, employment, and investment was likely related to the time. P. T. Barnum and Jullien had shown compellingly and remuneratively that the press and the public responded to "monster" concerts and other large-scale events. The promoter Bernard Ullmann had lured thousands of paying customers to almost endless "Absolutely the Last" and "Final Appearance" concerts for artists he managed, such as the singer Sontag and the pianist Thalberg. If not benign, these were at least trivial subreptions.

In the case of the vaunted overstrung grands, the tone of which had transported at least some artists and critics to the outer regions of auditory ecstasy, a different circumstance pertained. The production of grands was not merely factored up by a round 50 percent as were many other "fact sheet" statistics. The implied production of grands at 250 to 260 per year was increased by a factor of six over actual production, which ran at roughly forty per year before sagging to about two dozen in 1861. Fully one-fifth of the grands built in 1860 were still in Steinway showrooms or on loan in 1861. By 1862 the ratio of unsold grands to built grands had risen to more than a third of 1861 grand production.

While an artistic and critical success among some of the cognoscenti, the Steinway grand pianos did not sell well. The thunderous bass and ringing treble, perceived desirable in later years, differed from the standard grand pianos of the time, the sound of which might be described as subdued in comparison. Hoping to create an impression of great demand, the number of grand pianos built was inflated by the Steinways. The market for these instruments, though small, was essential for success in the much larger market for "home" instruments.

In essence, there were two classes of pianos, one for professionals, the grand, and another for consumers, the square. Modern marketers would designate the grand piano of the nineteenth century as "heavy-duty, industrial strength" and classify the square as "lite." The glamour of the concert hall, the linkage to high artistic purpose, and the endorsement of virtuosi generated a prestigious glow in which the buyer of the square could bask, comforted that he or she, if not quite so skilled, was at least possessed of similar tastes and sensitivities as the virtuoso player of the grand.

This halo effect, in which buyers tender cash in return for a product endorsed by the renowned, has since catalyzed the consumption of beer, soft drinks, cigarettes, athletic shoes, and countless other consumer products. At the time the Steinways discovered the power of the principle it was rarely used and, therefore, in all likelihood, much more potent. Not all pianomakers built grands, but among those who claimed aesthetic purpose and noble goals—through which they hoped to distinguish themselves from mere makers of parlor furniture—the building of grands was almost universal. So the Steinways made grand pianos. Times changed, tastes changed, and years later preferences shifted in the direction of the Steinway conception in grand pianos. Meanwhile, there was home music and the square piano, which the Steinways built at a ratio of roughly thirty to forty for every grand.

"The state alike of civilization and education of a people must undoubtedly be measured by the degree in which it cultivates the fine arts," wrote William Steinway some years later. "If these premises be correct, the United States have attained a development of civilization which, but a few years since, would have been regarded as impossible. . . . The United States have succeeded in bringing to perfection an art industry, the inventive creations, developments and culminating results of which are devoted to the Muses. The true place of this art is at the altar of home, where it shines calm and effulgent, animating and soothing, in turn, in the form of domestic musical harmony."

The concept of home music was not a transient one. It persisted throughout the nineteenth century and well into the twentieth. "And what, of the secular style, shall this music be?" queried R. Storrs Willis in *New York Musical World*. "Simple and pure-thoughted songs and ballads," was Willis's answer to his own rhetorical question. "Pure and good poetry, well-articulated and impressively declaimed to simple music—this is what most pleases the vast majority of human beings. Poor poetry to sweet music, is an angel wedded to a clown." Home music had both limits and purpose. "Outside, entirely to this sphere, are grand operatic airs and bravura pieces: the only exception to this being in the case of exceptional talent," wrote Willis.

Music in the home was seen as having therapeutic value, "a most excellent specific for a fatherly hypochondriac or a motherly or sisterly dyspeptic." But the prime value was the beneficial effects on children: "There is nothing like teaching children mutual dependence in their home amusement, and kindly and genial ties of fellowship. . . . I knew a wise father of a family of boys in New York, who, chiefly as a means of moral suasion and the affectional and emotional training of his children, had them all trained to play stringed instruments, as an accomplishment—a family orchestra. . . . What an alluring influence from evening street roaming and dissipations!"

Putting his prescriptions and aesthetics into action, R. Storrs Willis regularly published sheet music in his *New York Musical World*. A "Gem of German Song" printed in September 1857 seems to typify the level of sophistication found in home music, the lyric for which reads,

> Friendly is thine air, Rosalie,
> Take this nose-gay fair, Culled for thee!
> Now a woman grown, Rosalie.
> 'Twere a favor shown un-to me!
> Friendly is thine air,
> Friendly is thine air, Rosalie . . .
> Think too of this heart, Rosalie.
> That with love do smart, Rosalie,

All for thee!
But a year ago, Rosalie,
Fresh my cheek did glow, Glad and free,
Think too of this heart,
Think too of this heart, Rosalie,
that loves but thee . . .
La-la-la-la-la.

The number of young men opting to render "Friendly Is Thine Air, Rosalie" as a substitute for "street roaming and dissipations" among the brothels, dramshops, and rat-fighting establishments of Manhattan is a matter of conjecture, but the anticipated benefits of simple, self-made music, whatever they may have been, triggered a boom in musical instrument sales.

In 1860 the United States Bureau of the census observed, "Our advance in wealth and refinement is attested by the rapid increase in the manufacture of pianofortes and other musical instruments." Nationally, musical instrument production had climbed for the year 1860 to $5,791,807 from $2,580,715 in 1850, an increase of 124 percent. The $5.8 million included a large but uncounted number of instruments at a time when a guitar might cost two dollars, a banjo one dollar, a fine accordion fifteen dollars, and the highest quality new violin but twenty-five dollars.

The compound annual increase in musical instrument production averaged 8.4 percent per year, a "growth industry" by modern standards, with a rate of increase more than twice that of the economy as a whole. Nearly 60 percent of the output of instruments came from New York, where 2,453 persons worked in the trade. One in seven of these men—they were all men—labored at Steinway & Sons, if William Steinway's report of 350 employees is accurate. In any case, the proportion of the city's musical instrument workers at Steinway's was not less than one in ten. Nationally, the family's investment in the business of $362,401 was about 9 percent of the total capital invested in musical instrument manufacturing in 1860. In less than a decade from the day the family stepped onto Manhattan Island, Steinway & Sons had not only rocketed to prominence; they commanded a proportionately vast share of an economically and culturally significant industry.

While the family was not even counted in the United States census of 1850, the results of their enterprise could scarcely be missed in 1860. There was only one man in the Steinway's census district personally wealthier than Henry Englehard Steinway, or who at least admitted to being so. That man was Terence Farley, native of Ireland, Tammany Hall alderman, construction contractor, and associate of a nascent political force in the city, William M. Tweed.

The Steinway ascent was as remarkable as it was rapid, particularly in the context of the national economic forces at work. At midcentury the American economy oscillated between boom and bust along a rising trendline in a manner very different from today. Economic expansions averaged roughly the same length as economic contractions, each of about twenty-four months' duration. In the years since World War II expansions have become nearly twice as long, while the durations of contractions—the recessions—has halved. The economic environment of the Steinways was haunted by regularly recurring "panics" of a social and psychological ferocity difficult to comprehend today.

"Business here is very slow and almost half the workers are either unemployed or they work only three-quarter time. I am afraid that after Christmas it is going to get worse," wrote Charles Steinway to brother Theodore in December 1854. "Our new shop has been finished for three months now. It is built very well, but of course it stands empty." Two weeks later the *New York Daily Tribune* surveyed "The Commercial Crisis," "Distress of the Working Classes," and "Depression of Industry in New York and Vicinity."

Charles was excessively pessimistic. Business did not get worse after Christmas; it rebounded and improved steadily until 1857. The Panic of 1854 was triggered by the illegal stock manipulations of the presidents of the New Haven Railroad, the New York & Harlem Railroad, and the Vermont Central in separate transactions, all of which involved the sales of phony shares. These triggered a Wall Street market crash that rapidly spread fear among the business community and the general population. With wrongdoers punished and brighter vistas on the horizon, the panic was over by mid-1855.

Two years later, with uncanny regularity, commenced the Panic of 1857. Preceded by a general decline in railway stock prices, which was caused by rising interest rates, the panic was catalyzed by the failure of a "western" insurance company, the Ohio Life and Trust Company. Ohio Life had borrowed heavily from the New York banks and had invested the borrowed money in railway securities, the same ones that had been declining rapidly. Insolvent, the firm collapsed on August 24, 1857. A few days later the Mechanics Bank of New York failed, taking with it the cash savings of several thousand craftsmen. A money-hoarding panic ensued, led by the banks themselves, who called loans to each other and to businesses as depositors stormed the tellers' cages, demanding their funds. Within two months bank deposits skidded down by one-third, to a scant sixty million dollars for the city of New York. The torrent of panic flowed from Manhattan to Philadelphia. There the Bank of Philadelphia suspended payments, and before long every other bank in the city followed. The panic flowed south, with banks in Baltimore and Washington collapsing, and spread along trade lines across the Atlantic, where the august Bank of England tottered on the brink of collapse, its reserves of gold drained to a scant three million dollars. France and Germany were soon enmeshed in the crisis.

In New York and across America merchants slashed prices, trying to raise cash to pay back the banks from whom they had borrowed before the banks liquidated their businesses. Under the conventions of the time, banks made "call loans" of no specific duration and the banks could demand payment in full at any time. This they did, and prices declined precipitously. Mass unemployment rapidly followed as demand for goods ground to a halt. Social unrest among the unemployed, some with their savings lost to failed banks, rose. A few tried to make the best of it. A formerly prosperous woman wrote to *New York Musical World* that she was pleased to be rid of her carriage and two coachmen—they were never ready when she needed them.

Madame Theresa G. Rank, a French vocalist of note, proposed "a stupendous musico-dramatic enterprise . . . half the proceeds of which she intended to devote to charity." This Victorian antecedent of late-twentieth-century efforts to relieve hunger and assist farmers through musical events was never realized, but this did not prevent Madame Rank from addressing a large assembly of the unemployed in New York's Tompkins Square, even then an assembly point of choice for the disenfranchised. Total unemployment in the city at this time might have been as high as 25 to 30 percent. Standing on a chair, Madame Rank told the crowd, "I have come here to offer you my services. I intend to give a series of concerts for men and women out of employment. I have plans which are very great, and if I can sell shares in the enterprise, I will give you half the money." The crowd applauded. "There is [sic] forty thousand soldiers ready to shoot you down like dogs, and then you would leave your wives and children in destitute condition. There is a certain process to go through for help." Madame Rank continued, "First, you must ask the government for $2,000,000 to be paid for in work, and I will pledge my word to the government that the goods made up for this money will be sold." Three cheers arose from the audience, but Ms. Rank did not explain how she would guarantee selling the goods. A suggestion that the crowd apply to the bankers for help elicited shouts of derision and hisses, but a proposal that "immense dinners" be served the poor at the Crystal Palace every day, paid for by the city, was met with more cheering. Then "Madame Rank retired amidst loud and prolonged applause," reported the *Evening Post*, "and a German, mounting the chair, pronounced a glowing eulogium upon her, and translated her speech into the language of Faderland."

In the "Faderland" Theodore Steinway was amazed by the reports of the financial carnage. "How did it happen that in Philadelphia, which had otherwise been New York's rival, all the banks went under?" Theodore asked in a letter to his brothers in New York. The letter reported good news; he had found an investor, a successful piano dealer named Grotrian, who had agreed to provide fifteen thousand thaler in capital, about eleven thousand dollars, in return for one-third of the profits, and so Theodore had plans to open a shop employing thirty men. For the moment Theodore was happy: "You may ask, where to sell them? But I don't worry about that; there are inquiries from everywhere, and with money everything can be conquered." Madame Rank and Theodore had a shared view.

Not all the Steinways were concerned with the socioeconomic devastation of the Panic of 1857 in which some 5,123 American businesses failed. Writing to his younger sister Anna, away at boarding school, William Steinway commented, "Dear Anna, I do not know what to write to you, the fact that the banks are going under is of no interest to you, and you are not interested in politics. . . . Last Thursday Thalberg came by and tried out our grands and pianos. . . . I have included $3.00. . . . Please write again soon." In these few words of an affectionate, honest, and almost trivial family letter can be found foreshadowings of the future of the family and the business. William avers, disarmingly, that outside the spheres of business and politics, he knows little of what to say to a woman. That mystification would be the source of conflict, trauma, and loss.

Chapter 8

MEN OF NEW YORK

"William is on an amorous jaunt to Buffalo where his sweetheart lives, whom he will probably marry in May, and who is supposedly very pretty and very rich. She is German, of course, and her father is the richest brewer in Buffalo. The two met during the last *Sangerfest* there and fell terribly in love with each other," wrote Henry to brother Theodore in the spring of 1861. In the same letter Charles provided his perspective: "I have to tell you that William came back from his engagement trip to Buffalo yesterday and that he will marry three weeks from now. The girl is very young and very pretty, and has $50,000. As we say here, she is a good catch."

The "good catch" was Regina Roos, the seventeen-year-old daughter of Jacob Roos, whose family holdings included not only a Buffalo brewery but a brewery in Canada and wide real estate interests. The wedding took place at the Roos home on Tuesday, April 23, 1861. The Steinway family presence was small; only William's father Heinrich and his younger sister Anna journeyed to Buffalo for the ceremony. There was no honeymoon. On Wednesday the couple visited friends of the bride, and on Thursday, in the company of his new mother-in-law, his father, sister, and sundry others, William and Regina visited Niagara Falls. After another day at the Roos home, the newlyweds returned to New York in the company of Mrs. Roos, William's father, and Anna. The bride and groom took residence at 86

Second Avenue in a home that he and brother Charles, already married, had rented for fifteen hundred dollars per year.

Why William's mother, his brother Henry, and his sister Doretta did not attend the wedding is unknown. In the case of brothers Charles and Albert, there was ample reason. On April 14, just nine days before the wedding, Fort Sumter in South Carolina had fallen. From headquarters of The Seventh Regiment, New York State Militia, came General Order Number 5: "In compliance with orders from His Excellency, the Governor, and Division Orders of this date, the Regiment will assemble at Headquarters on Friday 19th inst., at 3 O'clock P.M. in full fatigue and overcoat, with knapsack, to embark for Washington City." There was less than a total news blackout of Union mobilization, and on April 16 the *New York Times* reported that the Seventh was "ready" and that the "mostly German" Second Company was drilling in the evening at the Centre Market, just a few blocks from the old Steinway neighborhood on Hester Street.

Twenty-three-year-old Georg August Albert Steinweg, aka Albert Steinway, had been mobilized. The general order required that "the men will each take one blanket, to be rolled on top of the knapsack, suitable underclothing, an extra pair of boots (shoes are better), knife, fork, spoon, tin cup and plate, body belt, cap-pouch will be carried in the knapsack. The men will provide themselves with one day's rations." So equipped, Albert reported to the armory near Tompkins Market, one of seventy-four thousand men that President Lincoln had called to arms for three months, "unless sooner discharged."

The city was in a state of patriotic ecstasy. Yet Mayor Fernando Wood had, only four months earlier, seriously proposed that Manhattan secede from both the Union and New York State. In the annual Mayor's Message of January 1861, Wood, after a few thousand words of diffuse and prefatory rhetoric citing sundry injustices, not the least of which was the fact that the citizens of Manhattan remitted two million dollars per year to Albany in taxes, came to the nub of his proposition: "as a free city, with but nominal duties on imports, [New York's] local government could be supported without taxation on her people and have cheap goods nearly free." Wood also forecast that California and Oregon would soon secede from the Union to form a third republic. A Peace Democrat, Wood did not misread his compass of public opinion. The political bearing of the citizenry had changed.

Flags flew from every available pole. One merchant gave five thousand military caps to the war effort. P. T. Barnum personally donated one thousand dollars to the Seventh. Prominent manufacturers promised to pay the wages of clerks who enlisted and look after their families; a few firms, with grim and prescient realism, offered "pensions" to families in case of death. Cash donations poured in to forming regiments to buy equipment. Tailors were stampeded by men ordering grey uniforms; the Union colors were not yet standardized on blue. Gunsmiths and hardware merchants quickly sold their inventories of revolvers.

A special and rare Sunday edition of the *Times* described an immense rally in Union Square. The crowd of an estimated one hundred thousand persons heard speeches from dozens of politicians. Among them was the prominent German publisher of the *Staats-Zeitung*, Oswald Ottendorfer, who told the crowd, from the fourth of a half-dozen speaking platforms, that the Germans were for the Union and would put aside their differences as Republicans and Democrats for the duration. Like all the speeches, his was wildly cheered.

In April 1861, prior to Sumter, there were a scant eleven thousand men in the army, and most of those were posted in the West. Raising an armed force was the responsibility of the individual states. Commanding officers of the regiments were appointees of the state governors, usually with the rank of colonel, not necessarily possessed of military experience, but always with political credentials. A colonel, once commissioned, set about the task of recruiting up to one thousand men in a species of reverse-pyramid scheme. Appointing captains was an early step, each of whom recruited persons he knew. Through a network of personal relationships, geographic contiguities, ethnic affiliations, and political connections regiments were formed of volunteers.

The Seventh, however, was a standing regiment that had been training semimonthly. Headquartered at the armory near Tompkins Market, the Seventh assembled without notice in the months before the mobilization, but drills on the night of Wednesday, April 18, were done under the eyes of three thousand spectators, each of whom had somehow been provided with a pass to the armory. Corporal Albert Steinway was among the marching volunteers. Having fired weapons in family target practice, the young corporal likely had an advantage over many of his comrades in arms, whom many regarded as members of the "kid-gloved set." There may have been substance to this view. Not a few of the volunteers reported for duty in fashionable civilian clothing, carrying their uniforms in brown paper wrappers. Others had freshly fitted fatigues delivered directly by their tailors. They were "luxurious dogs," according to one of their number, and Delmonico's prepared the sandwiches served on the day of debarkation.

That day, Friday, April 19, 1861, was mayhem as thousands filled the streets around the armory to witness the departure. Inside brothers grasped the hands of brothers, babies bawled, and fathers beamed tragic pride. A regimental member, one J.F.O'B., wrote: "Here and there flickered spring bonnets, which enclosed charming faces, as the calyph encloses the flower; and, let me tell you, that on the face of many of those dear blossoms there hung drops of mournful dew."

At 4:00 P.M., one hour late, the Seventh Regiment with Albert Steinway emerged from the armory to tumultuous cheers, formed up, and, preceded by a phalanx of police and a military band, marched down Fourth Street to Broadway, heading south. Flags were everywhere, hanging from hastily built poles, tacked to roofs, fluttering from windows, and strung across streets like laundry. Flags were draped on horses, wrapped around hats, and were waving in the hands of babies. In the oceanic roar of the crowd on Broadway could be heard an occasional voice: "God Bless Them All." At a measured pace, some faces grim, some stern, the 992 men of the Seventh marched down Broadway. Past the warerooms of Chickering, past the emporia selling fancy silks, past Niblo's Garden, past the Walker Street rooms of Steinway & Sons, past City Hall, past Saint Paul's Church, they marched through the never-ending crowd. At Cortlandt Street, Albert Steinway with his regiment turned right to the North River. There a ferry would take them to a train waiting at Jersey City. For at least some of the Steinways, war had begun promptly.

At Jersey City the Seventh suffered its first casualty. A German medic was crushed by a freight wagon, and now there were 991 to be cheered by the crowds. After several hours' delay, the Seventh left Jersey City and chuffed south and east to Philadelphia. It was a warm spring day, and at water stops along the way the residents of New Jersey hamlets thronged to the train. More delays were encountered at Philadelphia when Colonel Marshall Lefferts, commander of the Seventh, learned that bridges around Baltimore had been burned, reportedly by Confederate sympathizers. "Great numbers of our regiment," wrote J.F.O'B., "went down to the Continental and Girard Hotels, where they campaigned on marble floors and bivouacked on velvet couches."

A steamer, the *Boston*, was somehow obtained, and the Seventh, with Albert, sailed for Baltimore. Spirits still high despite the need to sleep on decks, the Seventh's journey took on the aspect of a sea cruise on a balmy spring day. There was more singing, now of a newly and quickly composed regimental song:

> Och! We're the boys
> That hearts destroys
> With making love and fightin'.
> We take a fort,
> The girls we court,
> But most the last delight in.
> To fire a gun or raise some fun,
> To us is no endeavor.
> So let us hear one hearty cheer,
> The Seventh, lads, Forever!

The tactical mission of the Seventh was to protect Washington from attack by rebel forces. Some in the eager regiment wanted to land at Baltimore and fight through to Washington. Colonel Lefferts had a more prudent plan, and at dawn on April 22 the *Boston* hove to at Annapolis, much to the surprise of the troops. Lefferts had apparently learned of possible Confederate vessels near Baltimore, which would have made short work of the slow and ancient *Boston*. At Annapolis the Seventh of New York joined with the Eighth regiment of Massachusetts, whose ship had run aground in the harbor. Troops of the Eighth thought the grounding was an act of sedition by the ship's captain. Some of the soldiers held him at gunpoint while discussing whether or not a hanging was appropriate punishment, while others were trying to push the vessel out of shoal water. The captain's fate is unrecorded, but it may be assumed he was relieved to see the *Boston* arrive.

The *Boston* took many of the Eighth ashore, and the two regiments spent the night at the naval school near Annapolis. At Annapolis the next morning the troops of the Seventh and the Eighth found that the train to take them to Washington had been sabotaged by secession sympathizers. Eyeing the disassembled locomotive, a Yankee mechanic picked up a part, carefully examined it, and announced, "I made this engine and I can put it together again." The men of the Eighth and the Seventh fell upon the task of reassembly, mechanics and dandies together, under the supervision of the original builder. But there were not enough cars.

The troops fell in behind the engine, now pushing a car carrying a howitzer loaded with grapeshot, and began the thirty-mile march to Washington. They marched through forest and field without rest, seeing no one. The citizens of Maryland, whose government had not yet declared for the Union, fled their homes on the advance news of troops. Colonel Lefferts dispatched advance units on both flanks in the event of ambush, but the Seventh encountered no resistance. Through the night they marched in darkness, among the sounds of shuffling feet and croaking frogs and the curses of men as they tripped on rail ties. By the twenty-third of April, the Seventh was in Washington; and Corporal Albert Steinway, a citizen of the United States at age twenty-one, a soldier for the Union at twenty-three, was billeted in the chambers of the United States Senate. That same day his brother William heard Pastor Burger recite the wedding vows. After the ceremony came a "pleasant evening, dancing, singing, eating and drinking until retiring, Wedding Night," wrote William in his diary. No record of Albert's experience in the Senate that night exists.

Probably when William was at Niagara Falls on his honeymoon, brother Charles wrote; "Dear Brother Theodore—At this moment I am sitting in uniform with my sabre and cloak, balancing my accounts. Then off to Washington as the paymaster of The 5th Regiment of the New York Militia. Tomorrow at 1 o'clock we are going by the steamer *Baltic* to Annapolis and from there by foot and train to Washington. My wife is, of course, sad, but calm. I hope I will return and be able to share with you the experiences in the field and life during the war. If not, then have a good life with your sweet Johanna and remember often your ever-loving brother. Say hello to all the relatives for me." The letter was signed "Charles Steinway."

Leaving his Second Avenue home, his wife, and three young boys, ages five years, three years, and seven months, Charles made his way to the Battery on the southern tip of Manhattan, where the Fifth was forming up under Colonel Schwarzwaelder. There they remained, waiting for a steamer, huddled in tents with straw bedding, as rain poured down and canvas flapped in the cold wind. The men, reported the *New York Times*, "seemed quite content, if not positively jolly." There were no parades when the Fifth left after four days in camp. When the *Baltic* appeared on Sunday, eight hundred men boarded her. About two hundred remained behind due to a lack of equipment. Leaving his family, his fortune, and his future, Charles G. Steinway, paymaster and patriot, steamed south to war.

No law compelled Albert and Charles Steinway to undertake military service. There was no conscription, no compulsion, save their personal beliefs. Businessmen made up about 5 percent of the total rolls of the Union Army over the course of the war. Nearly half were farmers and one-fourth were mechanics, while one-sixth were laborers. The balance, about 3 percent, were professional men. This socioeconomic mix was not very different from the population.

Charles may have had some vague sense of the horrors before him; according to family legend, he was a partisan in the failed German Revolution of 1848. If so, his knowledge was more complete than the citizens of Washington, including members of Congress, who treated war as a spectator sport at Bull Run in July of 1861. Civilians and elected officials picnicked on hillsides and watched the battle, then fled at the victory of the South, creating a traffic jam of terror on the road to Washington and impeding the retreat of Northern forces.

There were in the North at any one time at least twenty-one million civilians. Among them were William and Henry Steinway, Jr. Henry, never strong, was likely tubercular by the start of the war. Newly married, William enjoyed vigorous health—his diary indicates that he had intercourse with his wife up to five times a day—but was, by the testimony of one of his sons in later years, a "Copperhead." This designation was explained in one of two ways, depending upon political sentiments. Among their political opponents, the appellation was claimed to describe the treacherous and deadly character of Peace Democrats; they were much like the poisonous snake, Ancistrodon Contortrix, which struck fatally without provocation or warning. The other view, more sympathetic, was that the name arose from the inclination of some Peace Democrats to wear a button made from a copper penny that showed the head of the Goddess Liberty.

Among the many issues raised by the Peace Democrats was the concern for civil liberties, which they felt were infringed by the actions of President

Lincoln. He had declared war, raised an army, and blockaded Southern shipping without the advice and consent of Congress, which was in recess for three months after Fort Sumter. As the war ground on and the prospects of a rapid Union victory receded, habeus corpus was suspended, military trials of civilians were permitted, and at least one newspaper, the *Chicago Times*, was closed by the government. More or less, active suppression of antiwar sentiment was undertaken, much to the alarm of some prestigious establishment politicians such as New York's Governor Seymour and the former New York mayor, Fernando Wood. Many averred that they feared for the future of freedom. Apparently William Steinway was among them.

The degree of political difference among the four Steinway brothers was likely substantial, and it also shifted over time. William noted that in the "off-year" election of 1862, Charles and he voted the Democratic ticket, while Albert and Henry voted Republican. These differences did not seriously affect the operation of Steinway & Sons in any discriminable way. While Charles was frequently away with his regiment during the war, he nonetheless collected his full share of the partnership profits, although he was clearly devoting less time to the business.

In one of New York's many parades in support of the war, a wagon carrying Steinway pianos appeared with the slogan "Our Union Forever." Given William's likely views, this was probably not a promotion of which he personally approved. Some incident or incidents, perhaps including the parade wagon, provoked Charles, who was in Germany for treatment of a chronic ear infection, to write an angry letter to the family in New York: "About the irrational reasoning of Father and Henry . . . I cannot restrain myself from expressing my fears that these useless republican outbursts may cost us dearly. . . . New York remains New York, and that means, in my mind, a city where democracy called by its true name is the rule of the mob."

Three weeks earlier William had written in his diary, "We apprehend an attack upon our factory on election day, in case of riot." The attack did not occur, but Charles's fears were far from groundless, and he had more to say: "New York is a great volcano, which in these times of increasingly despotic action and lawlessness in America, could erupt at any moment. Heaven help those who by expressing republican sentiments may provoke the rage of the mob. . . . Whether just or unjust, the New York mob does not distinguish between right or wrong, but will burn what there is to burn, will murder when given the chance. So I will once again warn not to forget the proverb that says, 'Who is among wolves has to howl with them.' "

Far away in Goslar, Charles had misread the political climate at home. In this he was not alone; Lincoln was personally certain that he would not be elected for a second term in 1864. Charles's alarm was based on "the horror of the riot days last year," vivid memories of which were evoked by brother William's description of conditions in New York. Charles was referring to the Draft Riot of 1863, when mobs seized the city from the Battery to Harlem; with total collapse of civil order came insurrection, arson, looting, and murder.

Riots were a common form of social expression in the eighteenth and nineteenth centuries. The election of 1834 precipitated major bloodshed as the Democrats repeatedly attacked the Whigs during the course of the voting, which then ran for three days. The Sixth Ward, later the site of the Steinway salesrooms on Walker Street, was the scene of the worst violence, with twenty Whig partisans killed, and events earned the ward the sobriquet "The Bloody Sixth," by which it was known until the early twentieth century.

A "bread riot" was a part of economic collapse in 1837. There were also antiabolition riots during this period. In 1849, just before Charles arrived in the United States, the infamous Astor Place riot occurred. It was brother Albert's Seventh Regiment, New York State Militia, that fired on the crowd at Astor Place. The *New York Times* commented later that, "It was mainly for their work in this riot that our famous regiment got its remarkable popularity. They, for the first time in our history, dealt properly with a mob. Roughs and rowdies have had a wholesale dread of them ever since." The Seventh also helped damp the fires of the Police Riot of 1857 in which the "old" police force of New York, made up of political appointees by city politicians, fought the "new" police force organized by a multicounty board of commissioners with, of course, the blessing of state government. Under this plan the old, corrupt, and inefficient police force was to be replaced with a new, corrupt, and inefficient police.

The police riot was rapidly followed by more civil disorder as two rival clubs, the Dead Rabbits, alias the Roach Guards, and the Atlantic Guards, or Bowery Boys, with their respective sympathizers, took advantage of the lacuna in police presence. Just a few blocks from the home and showrooms of the Steinways in the Sixth Ward, the rivals barricaded Bayard Street with peddler's carts and wagons and traded volleys of paving stones and pistol shots.

Fighting ranged up and down Mulberry and Centre streets in the area that is now Chinatown, the same area in which the Steinways had lived. The next day riots broke out in the Seventh and Thirteenth wards. By Monday disorder ran its course, and the *Brooklyn Eagle* reported that the Rabbits were in Calvary Cemetery, burying their dead: "They were a motley set. Some had on fire caps and no shoes." If not the picture of sartorial elegance, the Dead Rabbits did have pride. One Rabbit wrote a letter challenging the news reports that they were a gang of pickpockets and thieves, and offered twenty-five dollars to any reporter who could prove the allegation.

A few days later the normally phlegmatic Germans of the Seventeenth

Ward attacked a police station after one of their number was killed by a policeman. Three thousand fellow immigrants of the deceased, John Miller, marched during his funeral, during which the normal police presence at large gatherings was notably absent.

Virtually every adult New Yorker could recollect at least two or three riots, but none was prepared for the vehemence and barbarity erupting in July 1863. Events began as a protest over the Conscription Act, which provided for the draft of men into the Union Army. As written, the law provided for a "commutation fee" of three hundred dollars, which could be paid in lieu of enlistment. The amount, equal to six months' wages for a laborer, was clearly beyond reach for most workingmen. Grumblings of "Rich man's war, poor man's fight" and "$300 for a white man, $1,000 for a nigger," the latter being the perceived price of a slave, could be heard.

Through either foolishness or indifference, the federal government began the draft in working-class neighborhoods of the Nineteenth Ward, already seething with the antiwar sentiment of traditional Democrats. The indigenous attitudes had been husbanded by politicians, who claimed that free blacks would replace New York workingmen in their jobs by working for lower wages. This was plausible social analysis, for employers on the city's wharfs had sometimes hired black laborers to break strikes by Irish dockworkers.

The eruption began Monday morning, July 13, with crowds of angry men ranging up and down the city's avenues in industrial areas. Finding a working factory, they would call out to the men inside, inviting them to join the protest. Many went, forcing the closing of the manufactories. Steinway & Sons was among those closed when its workers joined the mob. This riot was different, for along the way some among the rioters chopped down telegraph poles with stolen axes, terminating communications in and out of the city. Communications inhibited, transportation was the next target, and a gang of women, reportedly Irish, tore out the railway tracks on Fourth Avenue between Fifty-third and Fifty-ninth streets, just above the Steinway & Sons factory, which led out of the city. Elsewhere, horsecar tracks were destroyed and horses killed. Later, and less successfully, attempts to burn the city's gasworks were made, only one of which was successful. This had the scent of forethought, and some felt that a Confederate plan was in place to destroy New York and simultaneously take Washington, thereby neutralizing the political and financial capitals of the Union. No conspiracy was ever proven.

At midmorning, the wheels of federal government were still turning amidst the mayhem outside the provost marshal's office in the Nineteenth Ward where the draft lottery was proceeding. On the scene arrived the firemen of Black Joke Engine Company, irate that volunteer firemen were not excluded from the federal draft as they were from service in the state militia. The Black Joke men destroyed the draft office, its lottery wheel and papers, then set the building ablaze and beat an assistant provost marshal. As the flames spread to other buildings, another fire company arrived. Choosing not to battle their fire-fighting brethren, Black Joke stood aside, but others in the crowd fought with the firemen while the entire block burned. Women and children trapped in the burning buildings screamed for help while the mob, assuming federal officials and police had escaped to the upper floors, threw rocks through the windows.

That Monday afternoon mobs roamed the city almost unimpeded, extorting what they could, looting when presented with the opportunity, and torching buildings now shuttered and devoid of ordinary activity. An armory was taken by a mob of five thousand, looted of weapons, and burned. Downtown a crowd stormed Brooks Brothers' clothing store but was repelled by police. A hotel on Forty-fourth Street was fired after its supply of food and liquor was stolen. An immense grain elevator on the North River was burned, allegedly by its employees.

About five in the evening a roving mob arrived at Steinway & Sons. Workers gone, only Heinrich, Charles, and William remained to defend their work of a lifetime. Albert was on the way to Staten Island with the Seventh Regiment, and Henry, Jr., was likely too ill to assist. As hunters, target shooters, and military men, it is probable that the Steinways were armed. The father and his two sons took up a station in the office of the now-silent works. Outside was an angry mob whose voices filled air heavy with an approaching storm and the smell of burning buildings on Third Avenue, only one block away.

It was Charles who stepped outside to meet the mob, an act of almost incalculable bravery. He was German, military, republican, and rich. That day soldiers had been beaten, the homes of rich republicans looted and burned. The Germans and Irish had long hated each other as the two groups struggled for advantage in the economic quicksand of Manhattan.

Inside the works were hundreds of gallons of varnish and spirits used to finish pianos, wood scraps, sawdust, shavings, and coal. A single match could trigger a holocaust. Behind Charles as he faced the mob on both Fifty-second and Fifty-third were the family's drying yards where hundreds of thousands of board-feet of lumber were neatly stacked, as if ready for a bonfire. A fire in these yards would not only destroy the works; it would consume the family brownstones. Later in the riot the huge lumberyard of Ogden & Company was torched, destroying a city block.

With Charles was Father McMahon, a priest from the nearby Catholic orphanage. What Charles and the priest said to the mob is unrecorded, but William wrote in his diary that Charles distributed forty dollars in cash and one bank check for thirty dollars to the "ringleaders." Whatever words were spoken, they proved palliative, and the rioters "moved off towards Yorkville where late in the evening many buildings are fired." The Steinways stood guard in their office until one the next morning, then made their way in a heavy rain to their homes across the street. They had glimpsed the darkest side of freedom.

The next day Terence Farley, alderman of the Nineteenth, ward of the Steinways and ignition point of the continuing riot, made a speech. The words were as empty as the city council chambers in which they were spoken: "The persons creating the riot, and who are responsible for it, came from New Jersey," claimed Farley. That same day President Lincoln suspended the draft in New York. The city's politicians proposed, then later passed into law with remarkable rapidity, a plan whereby "poor" men with families could have their three-hundred-dollar commutation fee paid by the Corporation, thereby exempting them from the draft. But the words, proposals, and actions of politicians did not quench the riot. The melting pot had boiled over, and the hot acids of hate, now mixed with blood, flowed in the city streets.

The most frequent and vicious attacks were upon black men. Unrecorded numbers of them, often dockworkers, were beaten and murdered. Their bodies were thrown into the rivers. One who suffered that fate was Joseph Jackson, age nineteen, who lived two blocks from Steinway & Sons on Fifty-third Street. Other blacks were beaten, then set on fire. The Steinways were aware of this activity, for William wrote in his diary, "Negroes chased away, shot and killed when caught."

The next day William continued with his terse narrative of urban pandemonium: "The 7th and 71st Regiments arrive in the city. . . . Citizens organizing for defending private property, patrolling all night. During the day I walked down to the store and back again in the evening and watch all night 'til nearly 5 O'Clock AM in the shop." William did not record what he saw on his perambulations through a city in insurrection, but he did "find to my horror that all the knapsacks of the 5th Regiment have been moved to our basement in the store. I have been unable to eat for the last 3 days except bread and drinking water for excitement." Any sign of assistance to the troops was a provocation to the mobs, and the presence of knapsacks meant that soldiers had been in the store. The Fifth was Charles's regiment and, unknown to William, he had given permission for them to bivouac on the premises.

Rumors rumbled through the city; one was that the infamous Plug-Uglies, a secessionist street gang involved in the first bloodshed of the Civil War, were in the city from Baltimore, along with another gang, the Blood Tubs. But the riot was receding; in part, this was due to the presence of troops who fired howitzers loaded with canister, a deadly antipersonnel round loaded with small bullets, down the avenues to clear crowds; in another part, news of Lee's retreat from Gettysburg implied the arrival of still more troops; in the final part was the sheer improbability that such venomous emotion and carnage could be long-sustained.

On Friday, July 17, 1863, William reported to the future: "Quiet all over the city. Mass meeting in front of Archbishop Hughes Residence cor. Mad. Ave. and 36th street. He speaks to them to desist from further riotous proceedings after which the crowd peaceably disperses." If William was there, he heard the ancient and ailing churchman address thousands.

"Men of New York: They call you rioters, and I cannot see a riotous face among you." The crowd cheered. "I call you men of New York, not gentlemen, because gentlemen is such a threadbare term. Give me men, and I know of my own knowledge, that if this city were invaded by a British or any other foreign power, the delicate ladies of New York, with infants at their breast, would look for their protection to men, not gentlemen." His Excellency's audience applauded.

It was a brief address by Victorian conventions, and Archbishop Hughes concluded with a fillip of rhetorical perfection: "If by chance, as you go thither, you should meet a police officer, or a military man, why just . . . *look at him!*" Delirious laughter was followed by thunderous applause and cheers. Then the crowd dissolved into knots of men who walked while talking, pondering the meaning of the message; some believed the archbishop condoned the riot, others that he did not. The ambiguity was essential, and the city returned to its labors.

On Monday, one week after the start of the riot, William noted that the "Irish masons" came back to work on a new addition to the factory. More construction workers were busy downtown, for there Steinway & Sons had purchased lots at the very hub of the city's cultural center near Union Square and was in the process of building a marble temple of commerce. That hot day, the masons were completing work on the first floor. Two days later, Charles and William took the ferry to Hoboken for a customary summer "swim bath." Apparently the knapsacks in the store had been forgotten. The riot did not cause the Steinways to slow or alter their plans for the business. Whatever their personal political views, the family bet on the success of the Union and invested aggressively.

As a social symbol, pianos appeared in bizarre tableaus during the riot and the war. When the home of James Gibbons, a well-known abolitionist, was attacked by the mob, pictures were slashed, furniture was smashed, and books and drapes were burned, but particular attention was paid to the piano. First set on fire, the piano was then axed to pieces and carried off by the rioters in small chunks, apparently as souvenirs. A colonel in the Union Army, occupying a plantation, asked the daughter of the owner to play. When she refused, the officer himself sat down at the instrument. The woman seized a hatchet and hacked away at the strings. "It is my piano," she declared, "and it shall not give you a moment's pleasure."

The linkage of the piano with domesticity, stability, pleasure, and culture, besides making the instrument the occasional focus of violent protest, also stimulated sales; for in the North the Civil War was accompanied by an "easy money" prosperity among the noncombatants. There were fortunes to be made in provisioning and equipping military forces. Wild oscillations in stocks, commodities, and gold, the prices of which responded in frenzied variation to the tenor of war news, gave ample opportunity for speculation. Petroleum was being exploited in Pennsylvania, and railroad building was encouraged by federal legislation. On the darker side was trade with the enemy. A barrel of flour worth three dollars in New York was worth one hundred in the South. The profit in this trade is seen in the reports of the blockade runners, who bringing medicine, shoes, or machines into Southern ports might gross $150,000 inbound and another $150,000 taking cotton out. As with modern drug trafficking, the gain offset the risk of prison and death. Entirely legally, the Mexican port of Matamoros near the Texas border became a forest of masts. The home port of many vessels calling at Matamoros was New York.

The newly wealthy were called the "shoddy," an appellation gained from the perceived quality of goods they sold during the war. Reports, perhaps even true, were circulated that in New York women used gold dust as makeup to give their cheeks a special glow. At least a few must have regretted the cosmetological fashion as gold rose to more than $280 per ounce.

It was not long before a superior financing method for the war was evolved. The solution was a basically simple one: print money. The bills printed were called "greenbacks." This was a novel currency in two ways. First, it was printed by the federal government, whereas before much legal tender was in the form of bank notes, printed by individual banks and backed by their gold reserves. While the greenbacks were originally backed by gold, meaning that one dollar in paper could be redeemed for one dollar of the metal at the originating bank, the requirement to have on hand gold to redeem greenbacks was soon removed by Congress. Shortly, the Treasury, with the concurrence of Congress, issued a command of flank speed to the steam press operators, and greenbacks gushed out of Washington. In 1861–62 there was about $97 million of this legal tender circulating in the economy. In 1862–63, the amount more than quadrupled to $388 million. Another $44 million was added in 1863–64. The flood of paper money precipitated an entirely predictable avalanche of inflation as prices rose at unprecedented rates.

On the rising tide of greenbacks, the Steinways navigated the financial seas with aplomb, adjusting prices for their pianos at any plausible opportunity, but without any discriminable effect on demand. William and Charles were in charge of Steinway & Sons' pricing policy and, once a decision was made, William communicated it to the company's agents through "Confidential Circulars," a series of irregularly published communications containing prices, piano model changes, and miscellaneous commercial tidbits.

In 1860 the cheapest Steinway square piano, one of sixteen styles then available, could be purchased at the Walker Street showrooms for $275 without haggling; for the trade, the price was $200, a discount of about 27 percent. The "richest style" square piano, with a full eighty-eight-note keyboard, three strings in each treble note, "extra" finish, fancifully ornate carving, and a full complement of the latest patented technology by Henry Steinway, Jr., was priced at $650 retail with a 30 percent discount for agents. The Steinways called this instrument a "square grand" and believed, among themselves, that it was equal or superior to their competitors' conventional grand pianos. It was also more expensive than a Steinway "parlor grand," which, while sold in minuscule quantities, could be had for $600.

A scant four years later, the prices of Steinway pianos had roughly doubled. The same basic instrument that sold in 1860 for $275 was now $550. The wholesale price had more than doubled from $200 to $412. The basic parlor grand leapt in price by 117 percent to $1,300. The war-wealthy could move still further to an ornate concert grand, distant ancestor of the instruments used for performance today, for $1,600.

The least expensive Steinway in 1860 sold for about three-fourths of the average annual earnings of a nonfarm employee, then about $363. By 1865 the wages of that average employee had risen, with wartime inflation, to $512. If that average worker aspired, although it was unlikely, to Steinway ownership, the same modest instrument was now 107 percent of his annual earnings. In reality, the piano prices of Steinway & Sons did not rise excessively compared to most consumer products. Between 1860 and 1865, all consumer prices rose about 96 percent, roughly the same as the family's pianos, yet the average annual wage climbed but 41 percent. Many, if not most, families suffered a profound decline in their standard of living.

Efforts to finance the Civil War brought more than inflation and social unrest to the North. Another innovation of the American government was the federal income tax. All businesses and families with incomes greater than six hundred dollars were required to pay a 5 percent tax on income quarterly. In these tax records can be found evidence of a commercial conflict fought and won. Steinway & Sons, with revenues of $1,001,164.42 and selling 1,944 pianos in the year 1866, was now the largest pianomaker in the reconstructed Union.

Just as significantly, Steinway was now as large as the next two makers combined, Boston's Chickering & Sons and Baltimore's William Knabe & Company. With half again the revenues of second-place Chickering and almost triple the turnover of Knabe, the competition was no longer even close. Haines Brothers, the next largest New York maker after Steinway and founded about the same time, had revenues of about $200,000. Their pianos, on average, sold for less than half of the Steinway price at $242. Older New York firms, once at the top of the trade, such as Lighte, Newton & Bradbury, had withered. Gone from the top were other powerful firms of the prior decade. Nunns & Clark, Gale & Company, and J. B. Dunham, among many others, had failed to prosper. A few early Steinway competitors such as Hazleton Brothers and Lindemann & Son had grown modestly, but their combined production was not one-fourth that of the Steinways.

The family not only made more pianos than any other American maker; they made the most expensive, averaging $515 per unit sold. Chickering, building 1,526 units in 1866, roughly the same volume as fifteen years before, was receiving an average of $427 per piano, 17 percent less than Steinway & Sons. Price, of course, was a measure of stature, and at mid-decade Steinway & Sons was not only the largest in revenues and pianos built, but likely the most prestigous pianomaker in America. That Heinrich Steinway and his sons knew these measures of their accomplishments is certain. They also knew the personal tragedies and conflicts that stained their immense success.

Chapter 9

WITII WOMANLY EYES

"The Messrs. STEINWAY, who yesterday commemorated the opening of an additional wing to their factory and of a new and magnificent marble wareroom in East Fourteenth Street, are now the largest pianomakers in the world," reported the *New York Times* in May 1864. Replaying the success of 1860, another press party was held. "Through the various departments a number of invited guests were conducted, and their surprise and gratification was unbounded. The new store is situated in East Fourteenth Street between Fourth Avenue and The Academy of Music. It is an exceedingly handsome marble building—the handsomest, in our opinion, in the City—and admirably adopted for the uses intended."

The Walker Street rooms, where Steinway & Sons sold pianos for a decade, were a thing of the past. The monthly rental payments of about $117 had been replaced by a capital investment of almost $86,000 in the lots and new building on Fourteenth Street. The cost of the custom-constructed Steinway & Sons salesrooms would have paid the rent on Walker Street for more than sixty years. The decision to move was not purely economic; it involved powerful symbols. "The response of the younger STEINWAY to the many kind references to the firm, its enterprise and deserved success, was in the best of taste, and conveyed in it the prophecy that ere long the land of their adoption would be the acknowledged land of music and song. Certainly the Steinways are contributing to that consummation," concluded the *Times*. The writer of these words, probably C. C. Bailey Seymour, was now married to the sister of another Steinway supporter, the pianist S. B. Mills. Seymour would have been even more impressed had he known that not a single dollar of bank debt was employed in this expansion. The Steinways paid cash for their factory addition and new showrooms.

They had begun both during the darkest days of the Civil War when Lee was moving briskly north of the Potomac and before the battles at Vicksburg and Gettysburg. To observers of the time this fact would have been obvious, and it implied a faith in the Union at its weakest hour that had since been confirmed by events. The family, from that contemporary perspective, was more than a group of pianomakers; they were prescient patriots who believed in the United States, with the emphasis on *United*.

The "younger Steinway," William, to whom Bailey referred, was also satisfied with his performance. "Inauguration of our new store with members of the Press and some Artists," wrote William in his diary. "Start at One O'Clock at factory with the guests, show them around. Vogel assists me, though his leg hurts very much. We then drove down to the store again, and sat down in large Room 2nd story to a fine Collation. Toasts, speeches & splendid affair in every respect. I though being alone entertain the guests handsomely."

William was alone because one older brother, Charles, was severely ill with an ear infection. Henry, Jr., the other active brother, was in Cuba where, in a therapy popular for the prosperous, he had been sent by his doctors to recover from tuberculosis. The store opening was therefore twenty-nine-year-old William's first experience as sole spokesman for the firm. Adding to his emotional satisfaction was the arrival that same day of his oldest brother, Theodore, from Germany. This was Theodore's first trip to America, and it was paid for by the family. Theodore's reaction to his first visit to the Steinway & Sons manufactory is not recorded, but he must have been astonished at the scale of operations and the obvious wealth of his father and brothers.

As with many Steinway triumphs, tragedy was not far behind. Theodore Vogel, who "assisted" William, was the factory casework superintendent and married to William's sister Wilhelmina. The problem with Vogel's leg became worse, and three days later he died. The diagnosis was "Inflammatory Rheumatism." William duly noted his attendance at the funeral and the presence of the Third Regiment, New York State Militia, in the procession, but expressed no discernible grief at the death of his brother-in-law. Three days after the interment of Vogel, William rented to a Navy man for $1,100 per year the family-owned house in which his widowed sister had lived. With the young William Steinway, business was clearly the first priority.

There was another reason that William was likely in a particularly positive frame of mind that day in May 1864, one which also explained why the store, open for two months to the public, had not been previously seen by the press. There had been a strike, and guiding reporters on a tour through an empty factory and a new but sparsely stocked showroom would only have focussed interest on the striking workers. The citywide strike by the pianomakers shut down production at Steinway and perhaps two dozen other piano shops, yet received scant coverage in the New York papers.

Organization by workers into "protective societies" already had a long history in city pianomaking. They were transient organizations, typically forming near the peaks of business cycles to demand increased wages when prices rose to intolerability, only to dissolve during the almost inevitable panic and be washed away by the oversupply of labor in the following slump.

In 1854 the Piano-forte Makers Union had met at 160 Hester Street a few doors from the Steinway home; they had collected $350, scarcely a sufficient sum to support the membership in their negotiations with Bacon & Raven. Rhetoric was freely substituted for economic power, and conduct was governed by unspoken but rigid rules of gentlemanly behavior: "That the Piano-Forte Makers do hereby discountenance and repudiate the conduct of certain unknown, over-zealous individuals, who have posted a villainous placard in various parts of the city, with the intention of bringing Messrs. BACON & RAVEN as employers needlessly into ridicule and disgrace," resolved the membership. A further resolution was adopted by the union: "We thus ever shall be opposed to all violent and improper measures in the settlement of such disputes as may arise between us and our employer."

Over the years the union men learned that the waging of what evolved into social warfare was disadvantageous under the strictures of gentlemanly behavior and high-minded appeals to a public sense of justice. Even in the 1850s there were present, if not prevalent, in the city men who advocated violence against manufacturers and merchants. "The aristocracy of New York was to be killed off, the rich merchant put to death," reported the *New York Times* in a paraphrase of an address by an anonymous speaker to the unemployed during the Panic of 1857. It was an outrage that "ladies were thronging Broadway every day to buy cheap silks while the wives and children of honest laborers are starving." This sentiment brought sympathy from a former alderman present in the crowd.

Radical views of similar type ultimately percolated into the labor organizations of the city, but that was still far in the future, unexpected by the Steinways and virtually everyone else. In 1859 the then-current incarnation of the piano worker's union censured Steinway & Sons, probably for the firing of union members or union sympathizers. There was, however, a general wage increase granted to Steinway & Sons employees in the range of 7 to 12 percent, depending upon the job. It was all the union could do, except persist. This they did, and by the early 1860s a citywide pianomaker's union had coalesced, numbering roughly one thousand members.

Membership had quadrupled in less than three years, the growth motivated by the widening chasm straddled by the workers. On one side was the rapid increase in the cost of living and on the other were constant wages. They looked to their union to bridge the gap.

Faced with a united challenge by labor, the New York piano manufacturers hastily assembled at Ittner's Hotel downtown and improvised a manufacturer's association to deal with the demands of their employees. With the strike called just two and one-half months after the draft riots, it is likely that the fear of violence chilled the assembled manufacturers, an emotional door left open to a winter's night of potential destruction. The New York makers' national position was also threatened. The relatively docile work forces of their Boston and Baltimore competitors had received no general wage increases; the Manhattan makers were at a potential price and/or profit disadvantage in the market west of the North River.

The formation of the United Piano Manufacturers by two dozen city builders was a conventional and lawful response to the challenges of labor; similar ad hoc associations had been formed in other industries in years past. A Committee of Seven manufacturers, young William Steinway among them, was appointed to deal with a Committee of Fifteen union men. The manufacturers' offer was a simple one: a 15-percent increase, against the 25 percent demanded; no other demands considered. The workmen met en masse on Saturday, October 3, 1863, and reduced their demand to a 20-percent raise while the United Piano Manufacturers hewed to their offer of 15 percent. Respecting the Sabbath, the two opposing groups met on Monday, October 5. The tensions were palpable.

"Gentlemen bosses, we, the piano makers of New York, will now assume control of the piano business. You shall no longer be permitted either to engage or dismiss any workman without our consent. You must pay us full wages irrespective of bad or good times. You must all pay the same wages, must not undersell one another, and must every Saturday afternoon submit your books to us for inspection, so that we may satisfy ourselves that you have strictly carried out our instructions. Now, gentlemen bosses, what can we report to our union as your response?" These terms of the pianomakers were recollected by William Steinway a quarter-century later. The men also demanded they be paid for the time lost to the strike.

Albert Weber, a member of the manufacturers' negotiating committee and a small but formidable Steinway rival who built generic pianos of the highest quality, broke the silence that followed the demands. He was, in William's words, "a very quick-witted man." Weber addressed the workers' representatives: "Gentlemen employees, your demands are exceedingly moderate; but in your very modesty you have omitted your most important point." "Well," inquired the spokesman for the workers, "and what might that be?" Weber spoke again. "Simply this, that every Saturday afternoon, when you have looked over the manufacturers' books, the employees shall go bowling, and that the bosses should be made to set up the tenpins for the workmen." Loud laughter followed, and so did conciliation. Within a half-hour, the union withdrew its demands for management participation and accepted the 15-percent increase offered, with a proviso that an additional 10 percent be given in the future if business conditions warranted. The pianomakers went back to work, to the relief of the manufacturers, whose orders were at a seasonal peak, and to the comfort of the union, which could not financially support a long strike.

But the additional 10 percent was not forthcoming, and five months later the union struck again, this time more selectively, but for another 25-percent raise. Steinway & Sons was the target at the top of the industry, and another was at the bottom, the fledgling firm of Decker Brothers, scarcely two years old and operating out of the old Steinway shop at 85 Varick Street. Lines were drawn for protracted conflict. The union assessed its working membership to support the strikers. In response, the United Piano Manufacturers collected from the members twenty dollars for each worker, a cash bond to be forfeited in the event that any company settled without the approval of the association. William Steinway, Albert Weber, and another "gentlemen boss," Frederick Hazleton, held the funds. "Resolve not to allow a solitary workman belonging to the workmen's association to work," wrote William in his diary. The manufacturers locked out their workers citywide, and also voted to require every worker to sign a pledge not to join any union.

The strike ground on for weeks. William, short of pianos to sell, proposed to the manufacturers that they offer a 10-percent increase to the men. He was voted down, 20 to 4. Two weeks later, the United Piano Manufacturers again refused to grant any wage increase. To destroy the union, the makers were willing to go to the brink of financial failure.

William was receiving advice from Henry, Jr., in Cuba. Henry was pleased that William was "playing it cool" with the strikers and wrote that "if this backward group of 400 carpenters and other swine don't serve the purpose any more, there are another 400 others glad to do it." This was the bravado of the initial confrontation, and, upon reflection, Henry wrote Charles that the strike could "mean ruin for the whole piano business for a while because the skilled workers will look around for other occupations."

Steinway & Sons was also plagued with quality problems, in part due to friction with the work force. Henry, Jr., asked to have an instrument shipped to him in Havana, then a cultural outpost for European builders such as Erard. When the piano arrived, the finish was "a disgrace" and a "disgusting mess. . . . Those jerks did not even remove half of the grease," which was turning a "greenish-blue hue." It was badly tuned, and with some hammers that could not reach the strings while others stuck, and with small action parts incorrectly installed; Henry Steinway, Jr., partner, had received a do-it-yourself Steinway piano kit from brother Charles, partner. With certain resignation, Henry commented that the piano "is quite a distraction and that is the most important thing." While Henry re-manufactured his Steinway in Havana, the strike continued as winter turned to spring.

Inside the silent factory, Charles was trying to finish pianos to supplement the meager inventory. Making the best of the situation, the Steinways replaced the steam boiler that drove the machinery, a job for which they would otherwise have had to shut down the works. All machinery was powered from a single engine in the standard practice of the time.

Locked out, the men had left their tools in the factory. It was the custom in all trades for a worker to supply his own hammers, chisels, saws, planes, braces, and other hand tools, as well as his own workbench. Starting with the basics, craftsmen expanded their personal kits over a lifetime, sometimes by making specialized implements. The importance of the tool kit was great, both financially and symbolically. One of the earliest functions of the workmen's associations was to provide insurance for tools in case of fire. Without their tools the men could not work, and removal of the tools from a shop was the consensus symbol for termination. When a man was fired, his tools were taken to the street; when he quit, he took them with him.

Via letter, Henry, Jr., analyzed the tactical situation, advising William, "However long it will last, don't let yourself be concerned. Even if they move everything out of the shop, that doesn't mean anything. They will move it all back again; we only know too well how it goes!" Henry had more to say: "That these fellows are completely untrustworthy and blame us for everything I can well-believe. However, I don't think it makes any difference if they hate us more or less." These words were intended as supportive, but Henry did not have complete knowledge: "Send me everything that is written about the strike. . . . You only sent me your responses this time, but I would like to know what they have to say."

While the Steinways were willing to settle with their employees for a 10-percent increase, unknown others in the United Piano Manufacturers wanted to completely destroy the union. William and Charles were not able to move their brethren bosses in the direction of a pragmatic solution. Again and again the manufacturers voted for no increase. Finally, after a "very stormy" meeting, William recorded that the manufacturers "resolve at last that each boss be allowed to settle with his own, but not to exceed 10% and not to take each other's workmen." That night, William dined with his wife and a guest at a French restaurant, perhaps in celebration. The cost of that dinner was $9.60, almost four days' wages for one of the Steinway & Sons varnishers whose work had so angered his brother Henry.

The strike of roughly two months' duration was nearly over. The Steinway workers, as well as others in the city, voted to return to work for the 10 percent offered. Without further collective action, it would take more than a year for them to earn back the wages lost to the strike from the 10-percent increase received, and their economic peril was no less than before.

With the strike settled, William wrote, "This is to inform our agents and dealers that the strike for 25 pCt. higher wages by the combined Journeymen Pianomakers of this City has been settled by a compromise of an average advance of 10 pCt . . . which result has been attained only by great sacrifices on our part, and the most determined resistance to this exorbitant demand of the workmen." A schedule of new piano prices was attached with increases in the range of 6 to 7 percent. Paving the way for still further price increases, William noted that "the enormous increase in the cost of all material, domestic as well as imported, since last fall is not at present included."

So it came to be that while the family had completed their posh new store on Fourteenth Street, they could not open it while the fires of collective action burned. With the strike settled, workers in place, pianos in production, and a presentable inventory, the press could be cultivated. What young William could not know was that his performance in the strike and for the press, his brothers in the wings, was a dress rehearsal for a future ominously near.

Two weeks after the opening of the store, Henry Steinway, Jr., returned from Cuba on the steamer *Eagle*. He had been gone for six months. The day must have been bittersweet. In a pouring rain William greeted his ailing brother at the docks, and they drove home together. Theodore, Charles, Henry, William, and Albert Steinway were reunited. "All five sons together for the first time since 1849," wrote William in his diary. It was a peculiar comment, and William may have meant *living* sons, for there was a sixth Steinway son who had come to America, Johann Heinrich Hermann Steinweg. Hermann, after returning to Germany in 1854, somehow fell from the family tree, never to be mentioned again. Any joy of the reunion was damped by the decaying health of Charles and Henry. Charles was soon operated on by a Doctor Simrock. What had begun a month before as a sore throat transmuted itself into a life-threatening ear infection accompanied by brutal pain. Charles's ear swelled "enormously" and an operation was next. Experiencing no therapeutic value from either Cuba or the sea voyage, Henry was coughing badly and seeing another doctor. "I feel very much dejected on account of Charles and Henry feeling sick," confided William to his diary.

In New York City tuberculosis was the premiere killer of the population, accounting for 13 to 15 percent of all deaths each year in the 1850s. Unlike cholera, typhoid, and dysentery, which preyed on the population sporadically, the toll from tuberculosis was as steady as it was severe. In Massachusetts in the 1860s the diagnosed death rate for consumption was in the range of 365 per 100,000 persons, a rate higher than the combined deaths from heart disease and cancer today.

Ironically, Charles had written to Theodore many years earlier that "very few Germans can stand the climate" in New York. "Almost all of them suffer chest pains" and "almost half of the people die from chest and lung diseases." The diseases, Charles thought, must be related to the climate, but he still believed New York City to be among the healthiest places in America. It was, in fact, among the deadliest. Though the family did not know it, they had placed a biological and statistical bet against death by choosing to live in Manhattan, where mortality rates were nearly two and one-half times higher than the nation as a whole.

"We plodded our way through the filthiest streets—where huge garbage-boxes offered their contents to the rays of the scorching sun—where the gutters were filled with little pools so filthy as to belie the name of water—where cabbage-stalks were by pecks decaying on the walks—where dead dogs were quietly rotting in the gutters—where there are, by actual count, eleven whisky shops to one place where bread is sold . . . where the fronts of the buildings are daubed with nastiness in long streaks . . . as if the houses had got sick at the stomach with their own filth, and had tried to vomit it forth on the street below . . . where congregate and live thieves and burglars, and garroters . . . and bullies and roughs and pickpockets . . . and those other greatest criminals of all, the men who deliberately and in sound mind play on the accordion," recorded a reporter for the *New York Times* in 1867. In the eighteen years since Charles Steinway landed in New York, little had changed, save the addition of accordion playing to the list of social problems. The Steinways did not live in such places; they lived near them and their four-hundred-plus employees nearer still, thus forming a transmission line for the biological and social pathologies of the city.

The statistics converted to case study, as the now-emaciated Henry, Jr., age 35, lay in bed with the "night sweats" and swollen ankles, pain coursing through his chest and shoulders, coughing blood in the terminal stages of consumption. "Henry very low . . . much reduced and suffering . . . very weak . . . very low . . . suffers dreadfully . . . suffers excessively . . . very low with Rheumatism," wrote William as he charted his older brother's final months.

The technological beacon of Steinway & Sons' rise to success was slowly dimming; but had Henry, Jr., lived, another affliction would have circumscribed his contribution. Henry, Jr., had become increasingly deaf, a sensory deficit as ironic as it was poignant for a man whose life centered on music and sound. Nor was he the only Steinway with hearing impairment: "I wouldn't wish this pain, ringing in the ears, knocking, stabbing and buzzing on my worst enemies, even less on my brother," wrote Henry when he learned that Charles was "suffering somewhat from what I have been struggling with for years." In addition to his hearing loss, Henry was plagued with tinnitus, the medical term for the subjective sensation of noise. He was also resigned to his condition: "Although my earaches reoccur only once every few weeks and fortunately only for a short period of time, the hammering and buzzing continues on, and I have gotten so used to it that I hardly notice any more," wrote Henry to his brothers. He sensed that his hearing became "8–10% worse." Precisely how impaired Henry, Jr.'s hearing was cannot be determined, but it is possible that the condition partly explains why he was rarely present at public events. The knowledge that the architect of Steinway & Sons' overstrung designs was "hard of hearing" might have been used in the most brutally deprecatory ways by the firm's competitors.

Henry's letters indicate that he had been told by his doctor that the "small canals and muscles in the tympanum" had become "calcified," and, in the ultimate irony, if the overall state of his health improved, his hearing would have decayed further. "My doctor is a smart fellow. . . . I talked about my ears and expressed a hope that with the general improvement of my health, my ears would get better too. He then said, on the contrary, you will become more deaf, because since your blood circulation will become stronger and faster as you get better, the pressure in your head will be stronger too . . . the stronger blood circulation will make hearing somewhat worse. The man was right."

Henry had advice for Charles on how to deal with his hearing problem: "That your ear specialist had nothing more to do than wash your ear out with warm soapy water is a sign that he understands the situation. Don't let him do anything further, because all other things can only do harm and are never any help, as I found out much to my regret." Henry's condition did not prevent him from making judgments about the sound of Steinway pianos, nor did he shrink from modifying designs or drawing new ones to improve the instruments.

In some of the same communications in which he discusses his hearing difficulties, Henry, Jr., also makes judgments on the "equality of scale" of a proposed design, that is, the evenness of tone from lowest note to highest, and talks about "sweet-toned" instruments, the desirability of a "flute-like" quality, and the need for a "clearer, singing tone." He compares Steinway's sound unfavorably to a French Erard he heard; his own piano was slightly "tubby." He also describes the instrument sent to him in Cuba as "lacking power." Though hearing-impaired and dying, Henry Steinway, Jr., had not lost his critical capacities or desire to improve the instrument.

While critical facility was still present, there can be little question that the piano sound heard by Henry Steinway was different from that experienced by persons with normal hearing. While it is impossible to determine with certainty when Henry, Jr.'s hearing started to decay, it was likely somewhat impaired during the time he developed the seminal Steinway patent for the overstrung grand with improved treble string positioning.

The general effects of Henry, Jr.'s hearing loss, though not the specifics, are determinable. Tinnitus aside, he would have experienced two separate but related effects. The first of these, known as threshold shift, results in a reduced overall sensitivity of the ear, i.e., soft sounds that could previously be heard cannot now be heard and, in general, any given sound will seem less loud subjectively than to a person with normal hearing. It is likely that *all* pianos would have seemed "less loud" to Henry, Jr., than to an unimpaired male listener of the same age. The second effect Henry likely experienced was "treble roll-off," a disproportionate decrease in the ability to hear high frequencies. Henry's experience with roll-off, in its early stages, may be crudely approximated by rotating the treble control of a stereo to its full counterclockwise position while playing a piano recording. Simultaneously reducing the volume of the stereo while cutting the treble clumsily compresses into seconds the auditory experience of the closing years of Henry Steinway's life.

More can be divined on the subject of what Henry, Jr., heard—and did not hear. A modern piano of 88 notes tuned to the "standard" concert pitch of A = 440 hertz, i.e., vibrations per second, spans a frequency range from the lowest A, the key farthest to the left, at 27.5 hertz, to the highest C, farthest to the right, at 4,186 hertz. The range is extraordinarily wide, greater than that of any combination of instruments conventionally found in an orchestra. A bass viol cannot reach the eight lowest notes of the piano, and a piccolo cannot attain the top three. Yet the pitch of a note is only one aspect of its character. A pitch alone cannot be characterized as "sweet-toned," in the way Henry described one of his pianos. Among the manifold aspects of piano tone besides pitch, one of the key determinants of character is the series of "partials" which make up the tone, their relative intensities and durations.

After being struck by the hammer a piano string vibrates at multiple frequencies, the lowest of which our ears tell is the pitch of the note. The string also, for complex mechanical reasons, vibrates at two, three, four, five, six, et cetera, times the "pitch frequency." The A above middle C— A-440—when sounded excites the air and consequently the ear at 440, 880, 1,320, 1,760, 2,200, 2,640, et cetera, vibrations per second. Up two octaves, still an octave and one-third from the last key on the piano, the fundamental is at 1,760 hertz, and the partial series continues at 3,520, 5,280, and 7,040 hertz. Henry, Jr.'s hearing loss, even if only very mild, would not have allowed him to hear the higher partials in the treble of the piano. He would have misjudged the sound as heard by a person with ordinary hearing. In all likelihood, a piano assessed by Henry Steinway, Jr., as "properly voiced" may have seemed "harsh and jangly" to a listener with unimpaired hearing.

Charles Steinway likely suffered from a similar, though probably less severe, impairment. In addition to these obvious deficits, some of the materials with which the Steinways worked were likely ototoxic substances such as lead; the absorption of lead by the body adversely affects hearing. Lead, of course, was a common ingredient in the finishes the Steinways used to decorate their instruments. To the extent the Steinways suffered from ototoxic effects, the impact would not have been very different for them than for other pianomakers of the time.

Impulse noise, for example, that of hammering, is among the most deleterious sounds to which the ear is subject. For the Steinways, and the thousands of other men in the trade, the sound of hammering was also the sound of prosperity. During their lifetimes their ears were subjected to uncountable tens of thousands of these impulses. The bare outlines of the effects of this were known in the nineteenth century. It was called Cooper's deafness, so named for its early detection among men who made barrels.

A further factor in the Steinways' hearing was their use of guns for target shooting and hunting. Firing guns without ear protection is now known to cause hearing damage, a notch effect similar to the impulse noise of hammering. While black-powder Victorian weapons have a sound different from modern arms, such noises create permanent notches in the ear's frequency response and also result in a diminution of the ear's response to high frequencies. Typically this occurs in the range at and above 4,000 hertz. Charles, William, and Albert Steinway all likely had the hearing impairments that are a by-product of the use of guns. Rifles and shotguns, held closer to the car than pistols, are greater producers of hearing loss. The brothers used all three types in hunting and target shooting. Firing weapons indoors compounds the damage due to the containment of the acoustic energy. Charles and William target-shot Colt revolvers inside the Pythagorean Hall, headquarters of the Liederkranz singing society, where there was a range. That they unknowingly damaged their hearing is virtually certain.

In the case of Heinrich, the father, there is a very high probability of hearing impairment from at least two independent sources. The first of these is related to aging, which results in an effect that audiologists call presbycusis, an essentially unavoidable consequence of time, exposure to urban and industrial noise, plus stress and other factors. The hearing differences between a thirty-year-old and a sixty-year-old today are pro- nounced, and they were likely similar in the nineteenth century. In the upper ranges of the piano, the last octave, Heinrich may have lost as much as 99 percent of his hearing compared to his sons if they were of normal hearing. Charles and Henry were, of course, *not* normal, and suffered from their own hearing impediments.

In Heinrich's case there is another likely factor that contributed to hearing impairment. Heinrich Steinweg was a heavy drinker. In part, his consumption of alcohol was cultural; some doctors felt that the German propensity to consume lager beer was a health benefit. They attributed the "better health" of the city's German population to their substitution of beer for city water. Consumption of beer was routine in daily factory life in the city. When the Decker Brothers settled a strike with their workers, they treated the men to barrels of beer. After a few drinks, everyone returned to work. Even in shops outside the piano business where drinking on the job was prohibited on penalty of dismissal, flaunting of the rule was common.

Contemporary reports indicate that children visited breweries with their parents and drank the same refreshment. Many of the breweries had outdoor gardens where bands played and food was served. The Steinways once went to a school exhibition for the children at the Achen Brewery. William, his family, and their guests frequented Winken's Brewery not far from the factory and also regularly visited the Lion Brewery. At the many German social and musical events, such as the outdoor concerts at Jones' Wood, beer was freely sold and served to all, regardless of age. Notwithstanding different public attitudes on the use of alcohol, Heinrich Steinway, though not dysfunctional, was very probably an alcoholic.

While many in the medical profession today believe that heavy alcohol consumption adversely affects hearing, auditory impacts are only one of a vast panoply of maladies attendant to alcoholism and are studied relatively little. Since alcoholics frequently experience head trauma, there is confounding of causative relationships on the direct and indirect influences of alcohol use on hearing. One of the few available studies found that hearing loss in the higher frequencies was present in a group of alcoholics. It was further found that the hearing loss increased as a function of the number of years spent drinking, relatively independent of the age of the drinker. Heinrich probably suffered from such effects, which may have accelerated the ordinary hearing loss of presbycusis.

In addition to the long-term consequences of heavy drinking, there are also short-term effects on hearing. Tragically, hearing damage can be exacerbated by drinking in noisy environments. Alcohol consumption inhibits what is known as the "acoustic reflex," a system of muscles in the ear that contract in the presence of loud sound, presumably to protect the ear. The nineteenth-century convention of drinking at work was therefore destructive of hearing in ways then unknown. While evidence on the behavior of all the family members is not available, William recorded, without knowledge of the implications, that he sometimes visited breweries and returned to the factory. The result would likely be damage to William's auditory acuity—or that of any person doing the same thing.

With routine consumption of beer or other alcoholic beverages come other immediate effects that are as strange as they are recent in discovery. Studies have indicated that alcohol consumption triggers a predilection for louder musical sound. By allowing persons to adjust the loudness of music before and after drinking, investigators have observed that, on average, there will be a rough doubling of the subjective volume when subjects' blood alcohol reaches the levels needed to be legally drunk in most jurisdictions. If the Steinways evaluated their pianos after drinking, it is likely that they found them wanting in loudness or "power," compared to the same evaluation without alcohol.

Alcohol also influences the perception of auditory time. By asking people to estimate the lengths of tones presented to them before and after drinking, again to the legal criterion of drunkenness, researchers found that a subjective acceleration of time occurs. A tone must, on average, be 1.17 seconds long to be judged as one second in duration when subjects have a blood alcohol level of 0.1. Without alcohol, most people are able to judge accurately the length of the tones. The effect of this acceleration may be best understood in another way: an inebriated person driving at sixty miles per hour would have the same subjective experience as driving at seventy miles per hour sober. For complex reasons, rate changes, such as the decay of a piano tone in time, are accelerated even more than the steady-state perception of 17 percent. To a driver, acceleration, braking, and cornering would seem more violent than they really are. To a piano listener, the note would seem to diminish much more quickly.

Considering only the short-term effects, a hypothetical pianomaker who was continuously and uniformly intoxicated would prefer an instrument that was louder and produced longer tones to his otherwise identical counterpart who was always sober. The cultural context of the Steinways encouraged the consumption of alcohol, and it is likely that they experienced these short-term effects, although to what degree cannot be known. Older and less reliable investigations done with piano tuners suggest other musical effects, including altered pitch and rhythmic perception as well as a reduced ability to learn simple melodies, occur after alcohol consumption. The likely regular use of alcohol by the Steinways may have profoundly influenced their preferences in piano sound and consequently the design of their instruments.

The sound of the early Steinway pianos was controversial; even Steinway partisan C. C. Bailey Seymour acknowledged that "a remarkably free and easy war" raged around Henry, Jr.'s overstrung grands. The reason for this may be found, in part, in the fact that the Steinways inhabited a different acoustic world. The hearing impairment likely routine in their trade, the use of weapons, the consumption of alcohol, the medical problems of Henry, Jr., and Charles, and the age of Heinrich at the time of the family's design innovations all indicate altered auditory perception.

Had only Heinrich, the patriarch, suffered hearing loss, this would have been influential enough. Beyond the common bonds of genetics, culture, family, and life experience, the Steinways had another bond: hearing impairment. In an ironical way this may have increased their cohesiveness; had the brothers not experienced hearing difficulties, they might well have disagreed not only with their father, but with other family members on what constituted an "ideal" piano sound. As it was, decisions at the largest piano manufactory in America, whose instruments and their sound was the benchmark for the future, were made by men with a unique perception of the auditory world.

It is no accident that the early Steinway instruments were known for both power and the ability to sustain tones. The by-product of that power, the "unpleasant" tone to which some objected, was produced in the upper partials of the individual notes. It is likely that Heinrich, Charles, and Henry Steinway—and probably William—did not hear these partials in the same way that others did, if the Steinways heard them at all. It is a part of the collective genius of the family that, laboring under the load of auditory deficits, they designed and built instruments that transcended their personal limitations and afflictions. The basic architecture, now found in virtually every piano built, still prevails in the din of the late twentieth century.

Henry, Jr.'s contribution ended for all time on Saturday, March 11, 1865. On Friday evening William travelled uptown to visit his dying brother. The last will and testament had been signed and the annual partnership accounts approved at Henry's bedside. They showed that the family had a net worth of almost three-quarters of a million dollars and liabilities of only fifty thousand dollars. They had drawn from the partnership an additional $209,000 in compensation. The immigrant family of one and one-half decades before was now a millionaire family.

At Greenwood Cemetery an immense stone mausoleum in which Henry Steinway, Jr.'s remains were to be placed was under construction. "Find Henry dreadfully low, feet and hands swollen. . . . Henry just got over an attack of coughing. I leave him with heavy heart at 8 P.M.," wrote William. "Henry died at 7 A.M. in the presence of my father and his wife. Factory and store are closed and despondent in making arrangements for funeral. Dr. Schnetter and Lellmann dissect him, finding a large cavity in each of his lungs, and both lungs thoroughly diseased, otherwise everything normal."

"Mr. STEINWAY had reduced the manufacture of piano-fortes to a science, and it is probable that few men ever lived who were better acquainted with the construction of the instrument," noted the *New York Times* in a ten-line obituary appearing just above a report of the arrest of a pickpocket. The Arion Society sang at the funeral, and the procession arrived at Greenwood Cemetery at 1:30 Monday afternoon. "Fair day," noted William. "Henry's remains are interred in our new plot on Chapel Hill." In the nights that followed, William walked the streets of the city alone.

As William walked and thought, he did not know that literally half a world away brother Charles had been stricken with typhoid fever. Six months before, Charles had boarded the steamer *Hansa* with his wife and children, accompanying Theodore back to Europe. He had gone, presumably, for his health. With continuing ear and throat infections, Charles visited European doctors and tried various mineral and vegetable cures. In September he wrote that he did not know when he could return; in November he resigned as an officer of a German social club, saying he would rejoin in the future. He also sent back to America salves and elixirs for his brother Henry.

In late February 1865, William, perhaps now certain that Henry would soon die, wrote to Brunswick, where Charles and his family were staying with Theodore, "begging Charles to come home at once." That letter, and the response, if any, are lost, but by mid-April, a month after Henry died, William knew that Charles was "still sick." By the time William received that April letter, Charles had, in fact, been dead for two weeks. The family learned that Charles was dead on April 25, 1865: "Letter from Theo. Steinway with the terrible news that Charles died in Brunswick of Typhoid Fever. I go up to my parents and inform them. We are all almost heartbroke. He died March 31st," wrote William to his diary. The next day William took the last will and testament of Charles Steinway to the Surrogates Court. He had been there just three weeks before, on the same grim errand, with the will of Henry, Jr.

The weeks separating the family's knowledge of the deaths of Henry and Charles were among the most turbulent in American history. On Sunday, April 9, William noted, "Surrender of Genl Lee & his army to the U.S. Army." Since the prior fall piano sales had slowed in the general economic uncertainty that anticipated the end of the war. The Steinways had invested in gold at 260, fearing, as many did, that the greenback dollar would become worthless. The metal plummeted by half to 144 in the relaxation of uncertainty of Union victory. At the factory, wages were cut by 20 percent as an alternative to closing; the men accepted the next day.

Two days later news reached the city that Lincoln had been assassinated. The president's body was taken on national tour. As five thousand New Yorkers per hour filed past Lincoln's corpse, the president's countenance slack-jawed, skin an ashen grey, collar grimy with the grit of a city draped in black, William Steinway learned that his brother Charles was dead. The governor appeared for Lincoln's ceremonies. The mayor was there, and so were the alderman and the generals and the Irish and the Germans and a man from California in a buckskin hunting outfit, carrying a rifle. The Seventh Regiment of Albert Steinway stood guard at the president's bier. A Saint Bernard named Bruno followed Lincoln's coffin during the procession. But William Steinway was not there.

"Death sweeps over the land with so swift and dark a wing, that we can hardly detect in its black shadow whose friend has fallen," wrote the obituarist for the *New York Times*. "Whilst Mr. Albert Steinway was following the body of his chief—whom we all mourned with womanly eyes—to the grave, the news came from Europe that his brother had died." As reporting, this was more emotional than accurate, for the family did not know of Charles's death for six weeks after the death of Henry, although they died but two weeks apart. "He was a good, honest and true man; a master of his business and much overwrought in it. To help his failing health he went to Europe. . . . He placed himself under physicians and patiently attended to his convalescence. Desiring to see the principal cities of his native land before returning to the country of his adoption, he ventured on a trip which exceeded his strength and he died . . . after a sickness of twenty-four days, of Typhoid Fever," continued the obituary. "The operations of the house will be circumscribed by the calamity which has overtaken it. Mr. Theodore Steinway will abandon the German branch of the establishment, and at once assume an active part in the headquarters at New York," concluded the notice. Perhaps to avoid the complete cessation of dealer orders, the family had told the reporter that Theodore was joining the business. This, however, was more hope than fact.

Beneath the national tragedies and the personal sorrows city life bubbled on. At Barnum's American Museum, crowds thronging into the city for the Lincoln obsequies could see a "Poultry, Pigeon and Rabbit Show" with the "Most Unique and Extraordinary Display of Pure-Bred Fowls Ever Witnessed in this Country." This, of course, was in addition to Bohemian glass blowing, two steam engines made of glass, and the customary fat woman, giant, and dwarf. At The Academy of Music an opera called *The Jewess* was playing, and at Dodworth's Rooms Mrs. Vandenhoff was reading her "original mortuary ode," "Treason's Masterpiece," and another work, "Our Boys Are Coming Home."

The same newspaper columns that alerted the public to the poultry show carried an advertisement for "STEINWAY & SONS—GOLD MEDAL GRAND AND SQUARE PIANOS." "The principal reason," read the copy, "why the Steinway Pianos are superior to all others is that the firm is composed of five practical pianomakers (father and four sons) who invent all their own improvements, and under whose personal supervision every part of the instrument is manufactured." Now there were three.

Chapter 10

IN MANY RESPECTS
ADMIRABLE

"I struggle every day with the idea of giving up my business here," wrote Theodore to William shortly after Charles died. "I have three times as many orders as I can fill. I am master of my own business, my home is comfortable and I am used to my routines. Thousands of times Charles told me that he envied me. He would not forgive me if I gave up an existence he envied." Theodore Steinway was speaking his mind with characteristic directness: "You are used to the idea of sacrificing yourself to the idea of big numbers on paper, from which you poor fellows will reap nothing but an early death." Theodore had seen America: New York, Washington, Boston, the massive piano works and the wealth of the family. For Theodore, the American Dream was a nightmare. His advice to William was to sell Steinway & Sons and "retire to Europe from that land of iniquity where the worst is yet to come."

But Theodore also felt a strong sense of moral obligation. He had received financial assistance from his father, about ten thousand to twelve thousand dollars, in the form of United States Government Bonds, the famous Civil War "5/20s," which paid interest at 6 percent in gold. The sum represented the sale of but twenty Steinway pianos in America, perhaps three days' output of the Fourth Avenue factory, but paternal beneficence saved Theodore's business. He felt duty bound to help when called. A man pos

117

sessed of immense personal pride, he must have felt the cold undertow of humiliation when in middle age he applied to his father for aid.

Christian Friedrich Theodore Steinweg was walking proof of the falsehood of a nineteenth-century stereotype, the stoic and coldly efficient Teutonic character. He was a man of volcanic emotion, equally capable of expressing maudlin familial love and searing rage; his sentimental currents alternated between the two states.

Why Theodore remained in Germany is uncertain. Unlike his brothers, he was medically discharged from the decades of military service then imposed on all German males and may have already met his wife, Johanna Ludemann, whom he married in 1852. Whatever motivated the separation, Theodore sensed the loss of his family profoundly. Old biographical accounts, written at the height of Steinway success and influence in the nineteenth century, probably by William himself, aver that "young Theodore was free from military service, and this was the principal reason why he was selected to carry on and finish up the father's business." Of course, there was no business to conclude; the home/workshop was sold and the inventory of pianos, if any, was minuscule. The balance of the family possessions was shipped to America in crates. Theodore likely supported himself by tuning, repairing, possibly selling used instruments, and building the occasional new one. He may have remained in Seesen, anticipating a local boom when the railroad arrived. Five years later the railroad was still incomplete.

By late 1855—the year of the Steinway triumph at the Crystal Palace in New York—Theodore and his wife had moved to Wolfenbeuttel, a few miles due south of Braunschweig. In a former post office Theodore Steinweg set up a heavily mortgaged shop and home. On Christmas day he wrote the family in New York telling them that he had two men doing repairs, presumably on any type of musical instrument, and two more building pianos. The natural output of such a shop was about ten pianos per annum. That same year the family in New York had sold 112 units; the next year they sold twice as many in an ever-widening lead. By the middle of 1858, C. F. Theodore had managed to sell only about twenty-five of his instruments, while his father and brothers had already produced more than one thousand. By this time Theodore's young daughter Anna had died, and an infant boy was born dead. There were to be no more children; Theodore's ailing wife was, he wrote, "worn-out."

But in 1855 Theodore was infused with the joy of the holiday, the excitement of prospects in a new place, and affection for kin unseen in half a decade. As a Christmas gift he had received from America a remittance ("welcome, because things got damn tight") and a six-and-one-quarter-octave New York Steinway square piano, a type that was "in much demand here." By New York standards, it was a modest and inexpensive instrument worth perhaps $250. "I am very happy about the proof of your kindly attitude. . . . I just hope you will not fail to think of us a little bit in Germany."

Wolfenbeuttel, Theodore reported, was a place of ten thousand population with perhaps eight hundred to one thousand pianos in it. Besides building pianos he was selling violins and had just ordered forty for the local teachers college where, by force of law, all teachers were required to own and play a violin. Though profits were small, Theodore was involved because he wanted to help out the government. There was a good business in replacement violin strings as well.

Theodore was in the process of remodelling his new home and planned to rent the lower two floors. His young daughter was sick for a while but now recovered, and as he wrote, was "busily taking apart what Santa Claus has brought her." Life for C.F.T. Steinweg at age thirty seemed to be one of pleasant memories, a comfortable domesticity, and an untroubled future.

"It is a mystery to me how you can neglect the bonds of the closest blood relatives," wrote Theodore on another occasion, a small part of pages of vituperation. "The guys must run out to the beerhall every night, rather than put a few sensible ideas on paper. . . . No—I know what it is— paper and stamps are too expensive." As the dimensions of the family's achievement became clearer, Theodore, struggling to keep the doors of his business open, experienced a painful admixture of emotions. Long lapses between communications to and from America meant that Theodore occasionally learned of his family's activities from European trade papers. A man of pride, he must have been mortified that he sometimes knew little more about the attainments of his father and brothers than his friends who read the music publications.

There were other times though when family correspondence crackled with the excitement of technological advance and discovery. But the transatlantic flow of ideas was primarily west to east. Theodore was apprised of the latest in Henry, Jr.'s thinking on scale designs, action making, and other innovations. Theodore, on the other hand, saw the potential of the pianino, a small upright piano then popular in Europe. Similar instruments had appeared in the United States, where they were known, peculiarly, as boudoir pianos.

Time after time, Theodore proposed that the family sell his pianinos in America. They would be wonderful in small New York apartments claimed Theodore . . . they are popular in the South . . . they sound better than an Erard grand . . . they are cheaper to make . . . exquisitely finished . . . finely carved . . . beautiful inlays. With his heightening frustration, Theodore's communications took on a faintly frenetic tone, but this was to no avail, and Theodore cut his asking price to two hundred dollars each.

Charles explained at length, and in compelling detail, why pianinos could not be sold in America, concluding with the words, "If you want to do business in America, you have to help along American tastes with low prices. Americans don't know upright pianos and therefore don't love them." Theodore had experienced the rock-hard resolve and pragmatic realism that were the footings of Steinway success in America. "If you can get those prices in Germany or Russia, you would be a fool to send the instruments to America. . . . It would please us greatly if you would send one of your best *pianinos* for our own use, at any price, so we can see what you are capable of." The partnership accounts of Steinway & Sons reveal that C. F. Theodore Steinweg did send a pianino to New York. Somewhere in America today, perhaps in a living room, perhaps in a landfill, that instrument, the object of Theodore's quenchless passions, may still exist.

"Only Germans . . . who have tasted the fruit from the tree of knowledge here . . . know Germany. Formerly, I knew nothing," wrote Theodore to the family. Perhaps unwittingly, his comments carried an implication of cultural impoverishment on the part of his brothers. This observation detonated at an emotional ground zero, for at least Henry, Jr., felt the brothers lacked "an elegance of style and expression" that "was not our good fortune to come across among the Seesen boors." There was more: "When scholars, musicians, painters and other geniuses are among my frequent guests . . . I regret that you aren't here. . . . Here in Wolfenbeuttel I have made the name Steinweg as respectable as you have over there. That was no mean task, since the prophet counts but little in his own country."

Theodore's torment seeps through the years; he was haunted by his decision to stay in Germany. Alternately he promised to join the family and to visit. In all probability, he could not afford the two-hundred-dollar roundtrip passage for a two-month trip to America by steamer. A sail voyage was precluded by both pride and the impossibility of leaving his fragile business for a half-year or more. In America both Henry and Charles were concerned that they might be inducted into the army if they came to Germany. Voyages from both sides were cancelled because of illness. Roughly a decade passed before an American Steinway saw a German Steinweg.

But the family did find a common ground: "We are now anxious to make our name well known in Europe," wrote Henry to Theodore in 1859. "This is absolutely necessary in order to interest those piano virtuosi who come here, so we'll get our hands on them." To this end, the brothers had enlisted the aid of Adele and Charles Hohnstock, a pianist and violinist, respectively. The sibling Hohnstocks had first come to America about the time of the German Revolution and had since lived the lives of peripatetic concert artists. When the Hohnstocks returned to Germany in 1859 or 1860, they took with them an overstrung Steinway grand to be stationed, presumably with them, in Braunschweig a few miles from Theodore's home in Wolfenbeuttel. The plan, it may be surmised, was to expose the culturati of Braunschweig, both indigenous and visiting, to the sound of Steinway, obtain their reactions, and transmit the intelligence gained to America via Theodore along with, hopefully, a few orders.

As Charles explained, they had sold the grand to the Hohnstocks for half-price to secure their cooperation. The assistance proved short-lived, and the Hohnstocks repaired to Blankenburg, more than a half-hundred kilometers away and one-tenth the size, taking the piano with them. The Steinway effort at offshore market research and promotion had failed; and Theodore wrote back, according to Charles, "some lengthy nonsense about your own grands, and all I can find about our grand in your letter is that it should have a stronger sound." Charles was also unhappy that Theodore had bribed the *kappelmeister* Franz Abt to comment favorably on the piano. This was not a question of ethics; Charles had wanted honest opinions to guide the family, not endorsements for publication. Charles, peeved but fair, also admitted that the instrument should have been sent directly to Theodore.

The next year Henry, Jr., hatched the idea of giving a piano to Franz Liszt and queried Theodore about such a gift: "What do you think about the following idea which I read in the paper lately. Namely, that we should ship one of our grands to Liszt in Weimar in order to show him that we are not as musically backwards over here as is commonly assumed in Europe. . . . I am convinced that such an instrument would not fail to make an impression, and that whatever is written about it would have to be incredibly useful for us and for you. In any case, it could help to make our name world-famous." If Theodore responded, the reply is lost. But not all efforts at transatlantic cooperation failed.

In 1863 Theodore lured, albeit temporarily, the renowned Hans Von Bulow into playing a Steinway publicly at a concert of the *Gesellschaft der Musikfreunde*. How Theodore accomplished this is unknown, for Bulow was intensely loyal to the Berlin pianomaker Carl Bechstein, whom he called his *beflugler*, the "man who gave him wings." The Court Pianist to His Majesty the King was a man whose talent was exceeded only by his ego and apparently a considerable capacity for treachery. Unknown to the Steinways, Bulow had not only cleared his performance on the Steinway with Bechstein, but had actually rehearsed for it in Bechstein's factory. He also prepared a public notice, which he sent to Bechstein before the performance, telling Bechstein he should make as many copies of it as he wished, which Bulow would then sign.

"The use by the undersigned of an in many respects admirable concert grand by the firm of Steinway and Son [*sic*] . . . has given the all too ardent friends of this firm an excuse to issue various advertisements which are calculated to mislead the public. . . . The more trouble I have taken to acquaint myself *instantly* with all the products of foreign industry . . . the less I am inclined to waver in my preference for the Bechstein. . . .

Nevertheless I feel it is my duty . . . to sacrifice my personal taste . . . to encourage some other praiseworthy and thorough industrial effort." Knowledge of the condescending Bulow broadside was largely contained to Germany. Theodore swallowed his pride and persisted, offering to arrange other performances for Bulow a few years later.

The Bulow debacle may have been in Theodore's mind when he wrote to Charles that he worried his letters might be a source of amusement to the family in New York. He feared that the family thought his business was ludicrous, his friends insular, and his politics appalling. No evidence exists to confirm Theodore's fears. His brothers clearly felt that he had done as well as might be expected with a business in Germany and that their success was a uniquely American one, impossible anywhere else.

Though the family gave Theodore a subscription to the New York German language newspaper, the *Staats-Zeitung*, this was insufficient to allow C. F. Theodore to comprehend the economic miracle that was the new world . . . and that he lived in the old. A socioeconomic world away, Henry, Jr., saw this more clearly: "Under the present circumstances of your business, you will never become rich. Your partner is an ass and an obstacle. You must get yourself one who is an efficient worker and supervisor . . . otherwise you will not get ahead despite all your efforts."

The partner to whom Henry referred was Georg Friedrich Carl Grotrian. Now in his fifties, G. F. C. Grotrian had owned a music store and made pianos in Russia but now lived in Schoningen. The relationship apparently extended beyond business: "Take the little Ludwig Grotrian in and help him as much as you can in Americanizing himself. He is a businessman and wants to become a millionaire," wrote Theodore to his parents when one Grotrian son immigrated to America in 1857. With some capital already invested, Theodore and Friedrich Grotrian gave legal form to their agreement on April 7, 1858.

In Wolfenbeuttel at the home of the Ducal Brunswickian notary, the principals and witnesses assembled. If there were bonds of friendship between Theodore and Friedrich Grotrian, they were placed in abeyance, for in return for a total investment of ten thousand thaler, Herr Grotrian received one-third of the profits of the business. He was also given a lien on Theodore's home and factory, his inventory, tools, and receivables; and he was made the beneficiary of an insurance policy on Theodore's life. Theodore paid for the insurance. Further, if Theodore died, Grotrian was to determine what to do with the business and real estate. Johanna, Theodore's wife, appeared to be disenfranchised. Herr Grotrian was able to extract his investment over five years with notification; Theodore could not stop working without permission.

Onerous terms not withstanding, Theodore was enthusiastic about the agreement, writing his family that he had many orders, was planning to hire thirty men, and that the Grotrian money solved all his problems. The partnership lasted for thirty-two months until Friedrich Grotrian died in December 1860. This was yet another tragedy, for in the fall of that year Theodore had moved the few kilometers north to Braunschweig, purchasing a home/shop there, mortgaging it for fourteen thousand thaler. He had not sold his property in Wolfenbeuttel before moving and still owed on that as well. Some combination of the move, Grotrian's death, and perhaps other business reversals left Theodore with massive debts and no revenue.

Grotrian's heirs, meanwhile, were contesting the valuation of the business their father had signed, predictably claiming that it was higher and that they had invested extra money not shown on the books. Theodore, equally predictably, claimed he had not received any additional money and that the assets shown on the books overstated their value because he had made many improvements in the Wolfenbeuttel property, now empty, useless for any purpose but pianomaking. His business at a standstill, loaded with debt on which just the interest was treble his annual earnings in a good year, and having lost one-fourth of the business's capital, Theodore Steinway was well down the road to financial ruin. The family in New York knew neither the grim details nor at least one principal fact: when Henry wrote that Theodore's partner was "an ass and an obstacle," Grotrian had been dead for over two years and for more than a year Theodore had been sole owner of the business in Braunschweig.

The strange agreement mixing concepts of both equity and debt that began the partnership was transformed into an ordinary debt, which Theodore had promised to pay to the Grotrian family on extended terms. Under the new terms Theodore was given more than fifteen years to pay back the Grotrian family, certain evidence of the enfeebled condition of his business. When the time came—one and one-half years later—to make the first payment, Theodore had already asked the family in New York for the financial help they had given.

The Steinways in New York had done much more than send money. Theodore also received the designs and models for a half-dozen different New York Steinway pianos, at least some of which he actually built in Braunschweig. A few instruments bearing the legend "Steinway & Sons, New York–Braunschweig" still survive, and the Steinway at which Von Bulow sneered was built by Theodore from a New York plan.

This was the setting in which played the drama of William's plea that Theodore come to America after the deaths of Charles and Henry, Jr. William offered a full partnership; it was, in fact, an extraordinarily generous offer. It meant that, as a partner, Theodore would share equally in the future profits of the firm, then a dozen years old, and he could do this without a monetary investment. Theodore, however, thought entering the New York business was like running downward on a very steep hill. "I am praying," wrote Theodore, "Lord, take this cup away from me."

Christian Friedrich Theodore Steinweg arrived in New York with his wife, Johanna, aboard the steamer *Hansa* on Thursday, October 26, 1865. After more than two months of uncertainty, William learned that Theodore would at least sip from the cup, if not drink heartily. Just a month before leaving, Theodore sold his *fabrik* to three men with the permission to operate the business under the name of C. F. Th. Steinweg's Successors. The partners were to pay twenty thousand thaler for the business, ten thousand of which was the forgiveness of debt due the Grotrian family. This was possible because one of the purchasers was twenty-two-year-old Franz Wilhelm Grotrian, one of the sons of C. F. T. 's deceased partner. Theodore received no cash from the transaction but agreed instead to permit the new owners to pay him back over ten years. The partners also received the right to build the American Steinway instruments for which Theodore had patterns, but this unusual provision was carefully circumscribed: "Mr. Steinweg permits the buyers to use these models and scales for their own production without having the right to copy or alter them without explicit consent." The buyers also agreed to place the designs "at the disposal of the seller . . . if called for and to return them" at any time. From a much stronger bargaining position, Theodore limited the compensation of the owners to five hundred thaler per year each. Perhaps most significant, Theodore did not sell his home and shop, but rented it to the partners with the proviso that he could live again on the second floor if he so chose.

Upon arriving in America, Theodore moved into his late brother Henry's brownstone near the factory. On the day of his landing, Theodore's sister, thirty-two-year-old Wilhelmina, the widow of Theodore Vogel, was remarried to William Candidus, an opera singer. "Merry wedding," was William's only comment on the day his brother joined the firm and his sister married. Even in the high-velocity world of William Steinway, the previous few weeks were remarkable for the changes they wrought. In that same month William and Regina's four-month-old son was christened George Augustus Steinway. The newborn was listless and weak, but William noted that he responded well to a few drops of brandy and soon became stronger.

Earlier that October Albert was married to Louise Kreischer, the daughter of a wealthy brick manufacturer. Albert's role in the business before 1865 is unclear. He may have intended a career in the military or politics. Before retiring from the militia in 1871, Albert served in three separate regiments, with promotions from captain to colonel and finally to brigadier general after the war. The higher promotions suggest political approval, if not influence.

Albert travelled to Albany for the ceremonies opening the state legislature in 1872 when John T. Hoffman, a Tammany Hall Democrat, was governor. He also communicated with Ezra Cornell, then a state senator, to advocate the chartering of the Uptown Savings Bank for workers. Pianomaking aside, Albert Steinway at least waded in the turgid waters of machine politics.

What Albert's original career goals were is uncertain. Records show that as an adolescent he worked in keymaking at Steinway & Sons and in 1860 was involved in the casemaking department. During the Civil War he was sometimes in New York and sometimes with his regiments. He occasionally purchased lumber for the partnership, a task considered critical and usually done by Heinrich. Albert's relationship with William does not seem close; though they would see each other at family parties, occasional target shoots, and sometimes "played music together," Albert on cornet and William at the piano, months often pass between mentions of Albert in William's diary.

Perhaps significantly, an April 1861 partnership agreement for Steinway & Sons provides that if the father Heinrich should die or withdraw, "Albert Steinweg shall be accepted as his successor by the other three or any surviving copartners." Signed just three months before Albert's twenty-first birthday, the clause appears to deny Albert participation in the "firm and trade of Steinway & Sons" before the death of his father. The grisly provision was suspended four years later when Henry and Charles died. It was that year that both Theodore and Albert replaced their brothers. That Theodore joined with the greatest reluctance is clear. Albert's views are lost. Whether he wished to join the family business in bittersweet substitution for his dead brothers or whether he feared a role in the firm, accepting the yoke of family responsibility only reluctantly, as Theodore did, is unknown. There were two deaths, two marriages, one birth, one christening, and two new partners for the family in 1865. For the nation, the Confederacy fell, a war ended, and a president was murdered. It was a year of change.

Chapter 11

NO BAD FAITH
OR EVIL INTENT

"This deponent is informed and believes that the petitioner's domestic associations and her own morals and character are such as tend to corruption and contamination." The words were William Steinway's characterization of his sister-in-law. Ernestine Hildegarde Muller Steinway, the twenty-three-year-old widow of Henry Steinway, Jr., opened the curtain on a transcontinental drama that played for three years, culminating in the Brooklyn courtroom of Judge Gilbert in what the *New York Herald* called "a singular case."

Paris-born Ernestine Muller, the daughter of a tailor, married Henry, Jr., in May of 1860. Seven and one-half months later their first child, Lillian, was born on December 26. Two other children were born during the marriage of less than five years: Anna in 1862 and Clarissa in 1864, less than a year before the death of her father. Also living with Henry and his wife in the Fifty-second Street brownstone was Marie Muller, Ernestine's mother, who took care of the three young girls while Ernestine attended to her dying husband. When Henry, Jr., went to Havana in late 1863 at the order of his doctors, Ernestine accompanied him. They were both seasick on the six-day voyage.

In Havana, a city Henry thought was populated by "the stupid, bigoted and lazy [as a result of] Spanish domination and slavery," the couple spent time sewing baby clothes. Henry wrote that he could not tolerate the boredom without his wife. He soon received a false diagnosis from a Havana doctor: Henry did not have tuberculosis but chronic bronchitis. On that hopeful news, Ernestine sailed for New York, her luggage full of smuggled cigars for the family, on the theory that she would receive better medical care in New York for the baby she was carrying. Arriving back in the city, Ernestine sent Henry a family photograph. It brought him "great pleasure," he wrote in a letter signed "Your Loving Henry." After giving birth to their third child, Clarissa, while Henry was still in Cuba, Ernestine became ill, and Henry admonished her to stay inside until she was fully recovered. A month later he left Cuba and returned to his wife and family in New York with but ten more months to live. At the funeral of Henry Steinway, Jr., Ernestine wept continuously and inconsolably, finally throwing herself on the coffin in a hysterical display of grief.

"Mrs. Ernestine Steinway—In writing you these lines I am at a loss how to begin," wrote William to Ernestine eight months after Henry's death, "for were I willing to give vent to my true feelings, I could not find words strong and emphatic enough for it. Suffice it to say that you have again most successfully contrived and managed to become the object of remark and derision of everybody by your deplorable impudence and indiscretions (to use the mildest term) during your stay this summer on Staten Island." His pen propelled by outrage, William continued: "This time it is the respected name of our family whose unworthy bearer you are upon which you have cast disgrace by your inexcusable conduct.

"It is talked all over town," continued William, "that Mrs. H. Steinway has during her stay on Staten Island kept constant company with a coachman, has taken walks with him arm-in-arm, rode out on horseback with him, that he spent the evenings with her in her house and even that said coachman did not come home until morning very often. And it is generally supposed that said coachman and Mrs. H. Steinway are married, but many others contend that they are not married, and the Mrs. St.'s sudden departure for Europe was a necessary consequence of her intimacy &c &c &c."

Ernestine Hildegarde Muller Steinway had transgressed in three ways. First, within three months of the death of her husband she had begun a romance with another man; second, that man was of much lower status, a servant; third, she had made no effort to hide the relationship with Charles J. Oaks, the twenty-three-year-old English coachman who was employed by a man named Wooster. "I was thunderstruck when I heard these rumors and instantly went to work to ascertain the origin and truth of these stories, and to my intense grief and mortification, gathered overwhelming proof. . . . I am almost heartbroken. I have not a word to say," continued William. But William had many more words, including a chilling threat.

"Now Ernestine if it is possible to awaken as yet a spark of self-respect and regard for a good name for yourself and the future good name of your children, let me beg and implore you to live as a true and respectable woman and mother ought to live." William believed his powers extended beyond moral suasion: "Unless you do so it becomes my sacred duty to deprive you of the custody of your children, over which the last will and testament [of Henry, Jr.] as well as the law gives me full power. God knows how kindly disposed I have been towards you, but if necessary I shall do my duty towards my brother's children."

There was, in fact, a clause in Henry's will that read, "I do hereby nominate and appoint my brothers Charles and William Steinway to be Guardians of my said children, who shall receive a good and liberal education, and I hereby commit the tuition and custody of my said children, for such time as they or any of them shall continue unmarried or under the age of twenty-one years, unto my said brothers." This was called a testamentary guardianship, and there were other provisions that gave financial control of Henry's assets to his brothers for the benefit of his wife and children. The will was prepared by William and his attorney, James Eschwege, then signed by Henry, Jr., with a shaking hand just one week before he died. What Henry thought the clause meant or if he could even comprehend it in his final days is unknown. That William had the advice of an attorney and believed that Ernestine could rear her daughters only with his forbearance is clear. The depth of William's convictions would soon become manifest.

Ernestine Steinway was not on Staten Island nor was she in New York at the time William wrote to her. She was in Braunschweig at the Hotel de Prusse with the three children, her mother, her brother, and a nurse for the children, named Leonore. The entourage had hastily left New York on November 4 for reasons now opaque. Theodore Steinway played some role in this, apparently advising Ernestine that she might live more cheaply in Braunschweig, and that since the Steinway name was known there, her social opportunities would be better than in Paris, which was apparently Ernestine's first choice for a European sojourn. Atlantic crossings in winter were genuinely hazardous and not lightly undertaken. Theodore moved into the house where Ernestine had lived, and she later claimed that she went to Europe to accommodate Theodore.

The thoughtful might suspect the rumors of Ernestine's summer romance were already extant that fall and that she was as eager to be gone as some of the family was to see her go, particularly if they thought her pregnant. Once guided to Braunschweig by Theodore, Ernestine would be under the surveillance of family friends, who could report on her conduct. Whatever her activities were or would be, Ernestine and any scandal would be far removed from New York and "said coachman."

William's forbidding letter was the second round, not the first. A portion of an earlier letter from Ernestine to William survives, dated three days before his letter to her. In it Ernestine confesses that she forgot to pay some bills, denies she is extravagant in her expenditures, and alludes to a limited aspect of her conduct on Staten Island: "I am sure in those 5 short but eventful years of my married life I have had very little or no recreation until the last few weeks on Staten Island when I took to riding bareback twice a week, and that I hope no one will begrudge, as it is the most innocent as well as healthy of inclinations."

With these words Ernestine stepped on an emotional tripwire in the character of William Steinway. A man who placed unyielding emphasis on the appearance of propriety and high ethical standards, he also had the capacity for nearly saintlike forgiveness. Years later when a man named Phyfe embezzled the immense sum of fifty thousand dollars from the firm through phony insurance bills, William, against the advice of his lawyer, accepted restitution and did not press charges. The key to William's forgiveness can be summarized tersely: submit to his authority and admit to guilt. Those who responded contritely when confronted with a transgression were the recipients of benevolence, albeit humiliating. Those who did not learned William was an adversary with both power and endurance.

After five years in the family, Ernestine did not understand this conundrum and chided William: "Very well, I shall show you that I know how to make ends meet. You all told me it was so cheap here? Perhaps it is if I had another name. I must pay for the name I bear." Ernestine neither admitted nor submitted.

Another letter from William steamed across the Atlantic: "Mrs. Ernestine Oaks!!!—You will probably be very much surprised at this address but certainly not more than I heard that henceforth . . . I have to thus address you." Ernestine was secretly married to Charles J. Oaks in New York, just five days before she left New York for Germany, and William had found out. Albert married on October 3, Wilhelmina on October 26, and, unknown to any in the family, Ernestine on October 30, 1865. "I do not know . . ." wrote William, "whether I shall despise you on account of your acts so utterly devoid of decency and reason, or whether I shall pity you. . . . Today I had a conversation with your present husband Chas. J. Oaks, and he was sensible enough to state everything fully to me."

The marriage was verified by the minister, Reverend H. A. Montgomery, who "found it necessary to inform me to at least partly soften the daily increasing gossip. . . . I am deeply pained by the manner of your marriage. After the conversation with Oaks I went to Dr. Montgomery and found that you were married as Miss Ernestine Miller without informing him that you were the widow of H. Steinway, Jr." William underlined the words *Therefore a fraud*. After charging that Ernestine had kept the marriage secret even from her mother, William continued his indictment: "And how can you dare yet to act here as well as in Europe as Mrs. H. Steinway whilst you are not and your name being Mrs. Oaks. Do you not know that this is a punishable fraud upon us and upon all with whom you come in contact?" Ernestine, in William's view, had not only sullied the family name but also clung to it when it was no longer hers.

After the charges came the sentence: "Under these circumstances, I cannot answer before God and mankind if I leave in your custody the children of my brother, for the physical and moral welfare of whom I have solemnly promised him to care; and I must take the children from you until you show by your behavior that their education can be entrusted to you." The date William wrote this—Tuesday, November 28, 1865—was the same date that, according to his diary, he had his first contact, an "interview," with Charles J. Oaks. Ernestine and her entourage had left for Europe only twenty-four days before. Neither letters nor persons could cross the Atlantic in less than ten days, and twelve to fourteen days was more common. While a transatlantic telegraph was operating at this time, it was used for only the tersest messages. The velocity of information interchange is significant in the context of William's next words to Ernestine Hildegarde Muller Steinway Oaks.

"I therefore demand that you deliver the children of my brother H. Steinway, Jr. forthwith to a Mr. Attorney General Koch of Braunschweig. This respectable and highly esteemed gentlemen, who is fully authorized by me as the guardian of the children, will place them for the winter in one or more respectable families in Brunswick until in April or May I come myself, and can convince myself personally that you lead such a life that the moral education of the children can be again confided to you. I hope for your sake and the sake of the children that you will comply with this demand for you rendered it necessary by your unjustifiable conduct. If not, I will find ways and means to compel you, for the law gives me not only the right but the duty to care for the welfare of the children."

The man to whom Ernestine was to deliver her three infant girls was Carl Koch, a forty-four-year-old attorney, "Solicitor to the Crown," and a friend of Theodore since 1849. Theodore wrote to Koch to enlist his assistance, but the timing of events suggests that either Theodore and William were very sure of their position and believed that they could rely on Koch to take the children or that there were previous communications. The twenty-four days between Ernestine's departure and William's letter ordering her to deliver her children to the lawyer were insufficient to set up such a complex transaction fraught with procedural, ethical, and legal implications. Whatever the case, it must have been clear to Ernestine that she had been gulled into residing in Braunschweig. A stranger in the city, she was dependent entirely on William for financial support and now learned—with what must have been stark terror—that in Braunschweig the word of a Steinway had the full force of law.

Powerless and penniless in an alien land, Ernestine Hildegarde Muller Steinway Oaks, the tailor's daughter, cried across the ocean: "William! Can you really be so heartless, as to desire to t[ake] my children from me? No you cannot, I have at least a hundred times, pictured you to myself, with your kind and benevolent features, and found that it was impossible for you to take the children from me, nay, that you certainly would not do it, without any just cause, you say you have to answer before God the welfare of my children? How can you answer for their welfare by giving them up to strangers?"

There was more: "Reflect William, how very young and tender they are? How very often they are sick? And do you think a stranger no matter how well paid will have the patience of a mother?" Even in her anguish Ernestine was unrepentant: "William! What have I done that I should forfeit my children? Was it because I had not the courage to say no to the entreaties of my present husband to become his wife?" Ernestine accused an unnamed person of telling William "dreadful things." This man could "turn like a serpent and sting after being treated cordially. . . . People . . . will always exaggerate." Ernestine then pleaded that her mother, in Braunschweig with her, be allowed to care for the children. Mother had "taken the best possible care a grandmother could take, did she not have entire charge of them during their dear father's lingering illness? . . . Why must she suffer for the offence I have committed?" queried Ernestine. "Is it because she allowed Charles to spend the evenings with us? Or because [of] taking walks with him? Is all this a crime? I may have walked the world for years and not have found one that I cared so much for as I do for him, can I help it that he was thrown in my path so prematurely? Enough of this, it is to myself alone that I have to answer." Mrs. Charles J. Oaks's anger and agony was as profound as it was impotent, and she acknowledged this in her closing words: "May God soften your heart and hear the entreaties of an almost distracted mother." She did not sign the letter.

William's response, if there was one, is lost. Most likely he ceased communicating directly with Ernestine and used Koch as the intermediary. Multiplying Ernestine's anxiety was the health of the children. "On the night of 26/27 November 1865," recalled Dr. Oswald Berkan, "I was hurriedly called to the Hotel de Prusse in this city. I found there a lady who was introduced to me as the mother of Mrs. Steinway of New York together with her three grandchildren. . . . The two oldest of the children suffered with a severe cough, the so-called *Pseudokrup* which continued for several weeks and often was accompanied by severe fits. The youngest child also coughed and was equally as sick as the rest." For the next ten days the doctor made daily visits, and Lilly, Anna, and Clarissa Steinway progressed toward health until four days before Christmas 1865 when their relapse required twice-daily visits from the doctor. The children "were very weakly, looked very pale and suffering," recollected Dr. Oswald.

Dr. Carl Knocke, a "physician and medical professor," also saw the girls and reported that they "were not free of scrofulous casualties and hindrances in the digestive functions, they were inclined to bronchial Catarrh and of weak and sickly countenance." Scrofula was the name for a form of tuberculosis of the lymph glands characterized by cheesy deposits on the neck. Dr. Knocke's regime called for "regulated diet and prudent care, not so much the use of medicines." When Carl Koch first saw the girls on December 10, they had been under the care of Dr. Berkan for two weeks. He recalled that "the throat of the two oldest children was sewn up in a piece of flannel and was often rubbed with grease. The two oldest suffered with a severe cough. The youngest, who could not yet walk properly, had a distended belly." The girls were wrapped in cloaks and shawls. That Christmas Ernestine must have wondered whether it would be William Steinway or death that would take her children. She did not give in to William.

A few days after Koch's first visit Ernestine's husband arrived in Braunschweig from New York, though on the wages of a coachman he could not afford to make this journey; William, who knew the date of his departure and wrote to Ernestine that her husband was coming, probably paid for the trip. What, if any, understanding existed between William and Charles J. Oaks is not known, but upon arriving in Braunschweig he wrote two angry letters to William. All that remains of these letters is Solicitor of the Crown Carl Koch's responses to them: "I cannot sufficiently recover from my astonishment yet, that Mr. Oaks should be so mad and so impudent as to shower upon you insults and threats, such impudence has never before been known in the history of mankind. . . . [This has] confirmed me in my opinion that it looks very suspicious in regard to the past history of Oaks. . . . Why did he not . . . get from his place of home some proof of his respectability? If the past of his life were pure, he ought to hasten to give his relations the happy news that from being a coachman he had through his amiability risen to the station of gentleman." The siege and supporting psychological operations continued.

Ernestine, entirely without funds, took to borrowing from Steinway family friends in the city. Koch was able to cut off this aid by telling the friends his version of the truth. For unclear reasons, the Grund family, which kept the hotel in which Ernestine stayed, seemed to be willing to let the bills mount up. "Only Mrs. Grund is not to be convinced by anything, not even by the letter of her sister Johanne, what kind of people she has in her house." Koch attributed this to a desire for profit—the bill was now about four hundred thaler—but it seems unlikely that Mrs. Grund had any credible assurance of payment.

Ernestine and her husband, her three sick children, her mother, her brother, and the nurse spent the Christmas of 1865 in their two rooms at the Hotel de Prusse. There were gifts for Lilly, Anna, and Clarissa. Each child received "doll rooms," three large dolls and kitchens. Unintentionally revealing the psychological state of the little girls, Carl Koch reported indignantly, "that of all the nice Christmas presents . . . not the slightest particle is in existence. Everything is not only broken but is completely smashed and gone." Who gave the gifts is unclear but Ernestine was destitute, so the probable source was William in New York. The grotesque aspect of this benevolence seemed lost on Koch, who wrote, "Three women have been with the children the whole day and they have not even chosen to pick up the playthings from the ground but have allowed them to be swept away!"

After two months of the German winter, her children ill, knowing that if she tried to flee she would be arrested, Ernestine still did not capitulate. On January 24, 1866, Koch again visited the hotel, his frustration apparent in his report to William: "I went to Mrs. Oaks, whom I found in a tender tête-à-tête with her coachman. We together read the will. I explained everything to her, she persisted in not being able to separate herself from her children, and when I was about leaving abruptly, she requested 48 hours' time to consider. . . . I have also advised with our sharpest and most clever and at the same time very honorable attorney Dr. jur. Aronheim. If Mrs. Oaks does not consent today, Aronheim will commence his proceedings tomorrow . . . and without leniency towards those foolish women and that stubborn Englishman who continually encourages his wife to resist because he does not like to lose his board. My patience has been very great but it is gone now."

Koch outlined to William what was in store for Ernestine. "Aronheim, for I must now remain in the background, will give to the police sufficient reasons for interference, false names, no money, many debts, vagrancy, forfeiture of right to educate the children on account of too early a marriage &c. Aronheim does not doubt to wind up the matter in a few days in spite of the tricks which will doubtlessly be tried." That it was within Koch's power to jail Ernestine was no idle boast. In a later letter he wrote of having several persons arrested for frauds and forgeries. Financial pressure was also applied. Carl Koch promised Mrs. Grund that Ernestine's hotel bill would be paid from America, and Ernestine herself was offered three hundred thaler per month if she would leave Braunschweig.

Ernestine somehow obtained the services of a attorney named Ropcke, and before the letter to William was mailed, she sent a note to Koch at 5:00 P.M., January 25, 1866. It said, "I have spoken to lawyer Ropcke. You shall have my children, the dearest of what I have on this earth on the consideration that I get same back as soon as I have a household of my own. I shall, however first have another conversation with lawyer Ropcke tomorrow morning." Ropcke told Ernestine that her case was without hope.

"Most honored Sir, I hasten to inform you that the children together with their nurse were placed under my charge yesterday at 1 1/2 o'clock. . . . Today or tomorrow the company will depart from here whither, I don't know yet. At the departure 300 Thaler will be paid and then again 300 Thaler on the first of March and so forth on the first day of the month if Mrs. Oaks will give me her address," wrote Koch.

Mrs. Oaks went to Luneburg "for the purpose of living cheap. I do not believe however that she will endure very long in that miserable hole," related Koch three days later. Ernestine and her mother visited the Koch home where the children were to live, saw their rooms ("warm . . . very healthful . . . facing south"), and had arranged for the nurse Leonore to stay with them. "I am glad that Mrs. Oaks has been with us, she knows the place where the children live and among whom they live. All that will add toward consoling her. . . . The children feel quite at home at our place and are very lively and gay, even the little Clara has become so attached to me that she calls me Papa. . . . Excuse me, honored Sir, if I have tired you with these children affairs . . . Something of business yet . . .," continued Koch. He had paid Ernestine her monthly stipend and received the bill from the hotel for 608 thaler. It was not extravagant in the solicitor to the Crown's judgment.

Ernestine did not go to Luneburg; she went to Hanover, about three hours away by train. During the episode Koch became a general operative for William and Theodore. He was holding in safekeeping a painting Theodore had won in a raffle, had given unspecified photographs from the Steinways in New York to a Braunschweig museum, and was arranging for the body of Charles, now dead for almost a year, to be returned to America.

Factotum Koch, amidst these trivialities, also reported that Ernestine and her husband had "secretly" left for New York, leaving behind her mother Marie and her fifteen-year-old brother Gustav. "In order to avoid scandal or interference by the police . . . I have paid Mrs. Muller 50 Thaler . . . in hopes of your ratification." After six weeks with the children in Koch's home the nurse was dismissed. She had, said Koch, tried to seduce his son: "It is fearful and exasperating that this woman has endeavored to corrupt an inexperienced young man of 16 years, the son of the house of her employers." Leonore, the nurse, was demanding free passage to America, but was sent instead to her grandparents in Waldshat. Koch concluded his communication to William with a caution: "Do not on any account enter into any conversation with Mr. Oaks. My wife fears it and sends you friendly warning! Who knows what that man is capable of."

Back in New York, William had a "conversation" with Mrs. Oaks followed by a frigidly polite letter in which he outlined her financial status: "*Oberstaatsanwalt* Koch in Braunschweig informed me that he had handed to you a statement of your account with the Estate of H. Steinway, Jr. and I will now again fully explain to you your financial condition." Ernestine's share "now that everything has been turned into money," was to be about forty-five hundred dollars per year, a sum equivalent to that earned by nine American non–farm workers in 1866.

Ernestine's response to William's letter was rapid: "Sir—It was not with the view to have my financial affairs explained that I have returned from Europe, but to hear from your own lips what you intend to do in regard to my children, whom you have taken and given to the care of strangers. I will say nothing of the means you employed to get them nor of the treatment I received at the hands of the Lawyer . . . though I sometimes think he could not have been instructed by you to treat me as he has done. All I want to know is do you intend to restore my children to me or not?" The answer was in the outcome. For thirty-three months the children remained with the *Oberstaatsanwalt* and might have remained in Braunschweig indefinitely.

The Steinways believed in German education. At the same time that the Oaks family was in Braunschweig at least two other of the family children were there as well. Young Henry W. T. Steinway, Charles's son, and Charles Ziegler, the son of William's older sister Doretta, were being privately tutored in the city. Charles's widow, Sophie, moved back to Braunschweig so that all her children could receive a German education. The Steinways were willing to endure long separations from their children and from each other for this purpose. That the separation of Mrs. Oaks from her children was involuntary seems to have been a minor, but entirely justifiable, point in the family's view.

William had strong feelings as well about the education of young Gustav Muller, Ernestine's brother. He first arranged for Gustav to be tutored in Braunschweig with the other two boys. Gustav was expelled by the tutor. William then tried to arrange for Gustav to attend Jacobson School in Seesen, where he and his brothers had been educated. Koch wrote to William: "If anything is to be made of that Gustav yet, . . . [he] must visit the Jacobson School in Seesen." The plan, as developed, was for Gustav and his mother to go to Seesen where Gustav would enroll in school and live with his mother. Mrs. Muller would then be nearby—but not too near—so that she might visit the children occasionally "and give information to her daughter."

Gustav, at age fourteen, proved uncooperative and refused to continue his education, while his mother demanded to stay in Braunschweig near the children. Mrs. Muller and Gustav also refused to live within their fifty-thaler-per-month stipend and began to incur debts. In the spring of 1867 young Gustav went on a spending spree, spending almost a thousand thaler on cigars, gold chains, dancing lessons, photographs, and clothes on credit; it was an amount more than twice that which a German worker earned in a year. "The old one complains that he mostly stays away from school and consequently learned as good as nothing," reported Koch. The bills were paid from Ernestine's estate before Marie and Gustav Muller returned to America in May 1867. Gustav Muller would appear but twice more in William Steinway's life. Fifteen years later William received a cablegram advising that Gustav Miller "would be ruined at Liverpool" if he did not remit 3,000 pounds, about $15,000. William cabled back: "Gustav Miller no relation." Two years later Gustav appeared in New York using the name Milair and tried to pass a forged five-thousand-dollar draft on Steinway & Sons. The attempt foiled, William, "after some exciting talk," induced Gustav to sign a confession. "He finally draws a revolver with which he

would have shot himself," recorded William laconically. He did not prosecute, and Gustav Muller, aka Miller, aka Milair, drifted away to an unknown end of what Carl Koch called a "reckless life."

Ernestine, however, was different. From America she tried without
success to regain her children, writing several "impudent" and "rude"
letters to the *Oberstaatsanwalt* to no avail. At Christmas in 1867 she sent
presents to the little girls, whom she had not seen in nearly two years. Koch
wrote William that the older girls had forgotten most of their English and
showed special musical talent for which he recommended they receive lessons. Their nurse taught Lilly, Anna, and Clarissa the song "Silent Night,"
and on Christmas Eve the little sisters appeared before the Koch family:
"The children sang it under the illuminated Christmas tree. In spite of the
song having three verses and a nice, but difficult melody, they sang it without mistake, and even by the shining lights and the Christmas table covered
with food, gifts, picture books and dolls . . . allowed themselves to be led
away. The solemn song of these three children was so touching that in truth
there was no dry eye in the whole company."

Papers were served on William Steinway on the eve of his departure for
Europe in May 1868. In this there was an irony: now William would have
to fight from Germany to keep the children while Ernestine was in New
York. In the reversed transatlantic battle, Ernestine had the advantage, for
she did not fear public knowledge as did the Steinways. Soon the New
York newspapers were carrying Ernestine's version of events, much to the
mortification of the Steinways. In July William wrote in his diary, "Suddenly find in *Herald* Mrs. Oaks infamous lies, much exercised. Sleepless
night."

Ernestine claimed that she had been tricked into travelling to Europe,
that her children were "predisposed to consumption," and that she had
been stranded in Europe without money by William. When she was in a
"helpless condition" a "petty magistrate" came to her, threatened to have
her ejected from Brunswick as a vagrant, and took her children. Her babies
played in the streets and lived in a tenement, said Ernestine. Beyond the
treatment of the children, there were further allegations that she had been
deprived of her inheritance by fraudulent real estate dealings and that when
she returned to America after her ordeal she found her home occupied by
Theodore Steinway, who would not leave.

High crimes against the home, motherhood, and financial frauds were
not the end of Ernestine's media indictment. "She says," reported the *New
York Herald*, "that when the Steinways came to America they were not
worth a dollar and that all the wealth of the family was gained through
the inventions of her husband, Henry, Jr." Ernestine further alleged that
William had threatened "that if she ever gave him any trouble he would
cut off her income." Beyond this publicly plausible threat, Ernestine denied
that she consented to the appointment of William as a testamentary guard-

ian. William, fearful in 1865 of the whisperings about Ernestine's conduct with a coachman, now confronted a full-blown scandal, one which struck at the heart of not only his personal reputation, but the perception of Steinway & Sons. The family's values, its ethics, its deepest secrets would be endlessly probed in court as reporters' pencils scratched and the printing presses turned.

Rapidity was the essence of nineteenth-century justice, and *Oaks* v. *Steinway* for the custody of the infants Lillian, Anna, and Clarissa Steinway was at trial in less than two months. In addition to family attorney James Eschwege, the Steinways retained legal powerhouse Judge Joshua Van Cott. Van Cott argued that since the children were in Germany, they were outside the jurisdiction of the New York courts and that the court was therefore powerless to render judgment in the matter. The argument was rejected by the Honorable Judge Gilbert, who ruled that the domicile of the children was presumed to be at the residence of their mother and the trial should proceed. Virtually the entire family took the stand to testify against Ernestine. Theodore testified that he had bought the house on Fifty-second Street at the appraised value from Ernestine with her full knowledge. Theodore also testified to the "excellent" climate of Braunschweig and that he recommended she go there "where the late Henry Steinway was well-known and she would meet with the greatest hospitality." Braunschweig was also cheaper than Paris, stated Theodore. In key testimony, Theodore averred that he had been in Braunschweig, saw where the children lived, that it was not a tenement, but a home with a garden, that the children were well dressed and "looked neat" and did not roam the streets; but he conceded that Lilly had scrofula.

The Steinway sisters, Wilhelmina and Doretta, testified as to the family's friendly relations with Ernestine and that they did not know she had married secretly. They supported the contention that Ernestine wanted to go to Europe. To their credit, neither sister impugned Ernestine's capacities as a mother. Even Heinrich testified, through an interpreter, of the circumstances surrounding the drawing and signing of his dead son's will.

Attorney Jenks, for the plaintiff, argued that the dispute was not whether Ernestine had gone to Europe voluntarily, but whether she had left her children there of her own free will. Letters and sworn statements were produced by both sides. Ernestine's mother deposed that "all insinuations or statements against the associates or morals or character [of my daughter] are wholly and entirely false." A Mr. Nicholas B. Taylor testified that as Henry, Jr., lay dying he told Taylor that he "had the best wife in the world." A Mrs. Robinson testified that "she has always found the said Mrs. Oaks to be a chaste, pure and virtuous woman, refined in her manners, and fully capable of bringing up her children in such a manner as will promote their best interests."

Judge Van Cott introduced papers showing that Ernestine had falsely used the name Steinway and a sworn statement from Koch presenting a different version of events. Ernestine's mother was "an old, weak, most silly and uneducated woman." Ernestine had abandoned her mother and brother in Europe. Her brother Gustav, save for Koch's intercession, could have "without doubt been sentenced to jail for several years for recklessly making debts." Ernestine, according to Koch, "once for nearly a year left our letters unanswered, from which I am compelled to infer that her love for the children could not have been so tender . . . and the children must be pretty indifferent to her."

The legal jostlings continued, with Van Cott arguing for the Steinways that the court had no power to compel William to return the children. Judge Gilbert was inclined to agree with this view. Attorney Jenks asked for a dissolution of the restraining order that prevented Mrs. Oaks from "interfering" with her children and also for a ruling on the issue of possession. On this equivocal note the proceedings concluded, and Judge Gilbert took the papers and reserved decision. That hot July afternoon in the city the lives of a mother and her children were placed on the scales of justice.

"There are some facts which embarrass the exercise of the discretion entrusted to me," wrote Judge Gilbert, "but after much reflection my conclusion is that it is my duty to grant the application." Ernestine, Lilly, Anna, and Clarissa were to be a family again. "The petitioner is the mother of the children. To take her children from her without cause would be an act of cruelty. The father was guardian by nature, and on his death his right as such devolved upon the mother. It is a natural and inherent right. It extends only to the custody of the person, and does not involve any power affecting the estate of the infant. The deceased father's appointment of the Respondent as testamentary guardian, without the written consent of the Petitioner was illegal, and, consequently, ineffectual." The clause in the will was apparently key to the judge's decision. What the judge did not know—and it did not matter legally—was that an earlier version of the will disinherited Ernestine if she remarried. Henry, Jr., removed the provision from his final will, and his act of decency inadvertently set the stage for the emotional carnage that shook the entire family and its business.

Judge Gilbert, though he noted that the allegations of misconduct on the part of Ernestine "lack the basis of fact which is essential for judicial action," left a legal door open on future court review of her suitability as a mother. "If future events shall show . . . that either the personal conduct of the petitioner, or the relations growing out of her second marriage shall effect the welfare of the children unfavorably, a new proceeding for their custody and tuition may be taken."

Judge Gilbert also decided that, since Ernestine, William, and the children all "domiciled" in New York, his court had jurisdiction. William received a partial exoneration, one which the *New York Herald* did not trouble itself to print: "Under the actual circumstances of the case, no bad faith or evil intent can justly be imputed to the Respondent. On the contrary, I think he acted from the best of motives. Nevertheless, he committed a legal wrong and is bound to make restitution for it." William, in Europe and seeing his nieces Lillian, Anna, and Clarissa regularly, received the news by cable. In his diary he wrote, "I feel very sad."

In August of 1868 Ernestine Hildegarde Muller Steinway Oaks crossed the ocean on the steamer *Union* to Cowes, accompanied by an attorney named Piper. Arriving there, she telegraphed William that "she will receive the children at Hotel de Prusse, Braunschweig." The symbolic choice of the hotel for the reunion with her children could not have been lost on William. William and Ernestine did not meet at the hotel that day. The girls were reintroduced to their mother by their nurse. Spending perhaps a dozen hours in the city, Ernestine and the three little girls left for Hanover; and in late November Lillian, Anna, and Clarissa Steinway were back in the land of their birth with their mother and her husband, Charles J. Oaks.

Legal reverberations regarding the valuation and handling of the estate continued for some time; these were finally settled out of court on unknown terms, but there is no suggestion of impropriety on the part of William. For the next six decades Ernestine lived, much of that with her husband, as "the chaste, pure and virtuous woman" that Mrs. Robinson swore during the trial that she was. The Oakses with the children moved to Germany in 1873. There, the two older daughters of Henry Steinway, Jr., married, in the usage of the time, "respectably." Later Ernestine and husband Charles returned to the United States with her unmarried daughter Clarissa, and they lived together in Richfield Springs, New York. Ernestine died in 1927, six years after her husband, and her daughter remained in the home. When Clarissa died at the age of 91 in 1955, she was still receiving income from the estate of Henry Steinway, Jr. Throughout her life, however, she wished to be known as Clarissa Oaks.

Chapter 12

OF A BURGLARIOUS
DISPOSITION

"The day was beautiful. . . . At 2 o'clock, the twenty-two thousand fortunate holders of tickets having long been in their places and looking with anxious expectancy for the moment of their coming, the Royal and Imperial company, heralded by the thunder of cannon, the clangor of bells, the flourish of trumpets and the shouts of more than a hundred thousand voices, entered the vestibule of the Palace. . . . They were greeted by the spontaneous uprising of the vast throng within, and universally by enthusiastic shouts of '*Vive l'Emperor!*' " The words were those of J. W. Hoyt, who published a report on the international expositions.

Among the witnesses to the spectacle that July 1, 1867, afternoon in Paris was, in all likelihood, Theodore Steinway. He would not have missed a chance to see a dozen European heads of state in procession with the emperor of France, Napoleon III. "Their Imperial and Royal highnesses being seated beneath the golden and crimson canopy, and the Inaugural Hymn of Peace—the words by Pacini, and the music by the illustrious Rossini—having been performed by a grand orchestra of 1,200 musicians," the French minister of state delivered a characteristically lengthy peroration. There were, said the minister, a grand total of 56,000 tons of objects brought by 50,226 exhibitors to the Paris Universal Exposition of 1867. On the 108 acres allocated for the fair in the Champ de Mars, the palace itself covered 32 acres. The machinery on display consumed more than 1,000 horsepower, and the water system installed on the grounds had the capacity needed for a city of 100,000 persons. Almost one million people visited the exposition.

Impressive though the statistical description might be, it was not the essence of the thing, declared the minister of state. "The International Exhibition . . . dissipates inveterate prejudices, overturns long established enmities and causes sentiments of reciprocal esteem to spring up in their stead." Perhaps this was the intent, or at least the hope, but in New York that summer different emotions were generated by the exposition. "Chickering gets cablegram. . . . Great Jubilee in their store. . . . We feel in despair," wrote William, and later, "I get sick with disappointment and rage." The source of William's torments may be seen any day on Manhattan's Fifty-seventh Street, just east of Sixth Avenue. There, atop an office building that was once the showroom and New York headquarters of Chickering & Sons, large aureate medallions glisten in the gritty light, passive beacons to achievements past. Amplified to architectural scale, the medallions are ectypes of the Cross of the Chevalier of the Legion of Honor awarded by the emperor of France to Chickering & Sons in 1867.

The award, the French equivalent of a knighthood, placed Chickering in the halcyon of industrial achievement by the standards of the time. Cyrus H. McCormick, a name still recognized in rural America, received the cross for his reaping and mowing machines. Elias Howe, "inventor of the sewing machine," received another. Further down the scale of awards was the artist Frederick E. Church; his "artist's medal" was accompanied by a cash prize of five hundred francs (one hundred dollars) in gold. Cyrus W. Field, whose Ocean Telegraph Theodore and William used to click messages to each other at one dollar per word, received a lesser award. These were but a few of the more prominent premia among the 16,766 awards dispensed.

There was ample honor for the Steinways; they received a gold medal. This was no small distinction, for among the fifty-thousand-plus exhibitors, less than 2 percent received gold medals. The competition for medals in musical instruments bordered on the gladiatorial: "There was no class in the exhibition more thoroughly represented than this," reported the United States Commission. "Every nation contributed its quota to the aggregate. That the art of music 'hath charms to soothe the savage breast' was amply demonstrated," wrote one of the commissioners.

Cultural contrast and auditory mayhem prevailed. "The wildest and strangest countries contributed their eccentric contrivances of bamboo and hide—instruments that were dulcet to native ears, but hideous to the average tympanum of civilized Europe." Clay drums, trumpets made of antelope horns or elephant tusks, and gazelle-skin violins were played by native masters wearing indigenous costumes. A few physical steps transported the visitor across chasms of time, technology, and culture amidst competitive cacophony. As Arab bagpipes keened and the tusk horns honked, "of which the sound is heard for a league," visitors to "Class 10" exhibits could also examine the latest advances in piano technology. In total there were 178 makes of pianos on display, a number exceeding the combined total of all wind and string instruments. Among the distinguished visitors to this battlefield of art and culture was Hector Berlioz. Berlioz was enthusiastic about the Steinway: "Their sonority is splendid and essentially noble; moreover, you have discovered the secret to lessen, to an imperceptible point, that unpleasant harmonic of the minor seventh . . . which heretofore made itself heard . . . to such a degree as to render some of the most simple and finest chords disagreeable. . . . [This is] progress for which all artists and amateurs gifted with delicate perception must be infinitely indebted to you." Monsieur Berlioz received a piano, and the Steinways reproduced his letter for decades in their sales brochures.

None of this was accidental. Theodore crossed the Atlantic in February to function as field commander in the European theater of operations, well before the opening of the exposition. Much needed to be done. "Send our patents via steamer. Everything allright," telegraphed Theodore in April. Letters sailed across the Atlantic detailing strategy and tactics. It was too expensive to outbid Chickering for favorable coverage in the *Musical Gazette*. Ritter could, for a thousand francs, write a letter that contradicted his previous opinion. (This was probably Alexander Ritter, a violinist and composer married to Wagner's niece and friend of Liszt and Bulow.) Not wise to play pianos in public without greasing palms.

Theodore's field orders and intelligence advices streamed in from Europe: Fetis claims Steinway learned concert promotion from Chickering. (François Joseph Fetis was head of the Brussels Conservatory, an influential music critic, teacher, composer, and an exhibition judge.) Get Rossini a piano. There are problems with Escudier, a French music journalist, and Brandus, a music publisher unfriendly to us. Avoid them. Pianos with patent numbers on them sell fast here; send some, will price at 5,500 Francs ($1,100). Tell Dachauer I want gold medal and cross. Do not split awards and give Chickering the medal and me the cross. Sending 7,000 Francs. Let me know how spent. (Dachauer was Louis Dachauer, a New York–based Catholic church organist, composer of masses, and covert operative for the Steinways.) Why Theodore felt he could order medals though Dachauer like menu items is a mystery.

At the exposition Theodore lectured on the salient points of piano design. Thousands of brochures in French, German, and English were printed and distributed with diagrams illustrating Steinway piano construction and, in William's later words, "furnishing the proof the improvements were based upon physical and acoustical laws." Demonstrations were given to members of the jury to show that "a string develops the finest tone if strained as near as possible to the limit of elasticity." Other demonstrations, with special apparatus, illustrated "that compression of the sounding board . . .

materially heightens the energy of the tone, and its ready or prompt response and development." The Steinways recognized that technical explanations were necessary but not sufficient. None of the technology was new in America; the architecture and concepts Theodore explained were pioneered by Henry, Jr., and disclosed in his patents of 1859; yet eight years later in Europe the "Steinway System" was still unconventional and exotic technology.

There was widespread skepticism based on pseudoscience; some thought placing the strings one layer above the other would interfere with their free vibration. "Fetis," observed William, "with great reserve, awaited the opinions and the judgment of celebrated physicists. . . . It became clear to this great mind that strings laying over and above each other disturb each other as little as those laying side by side." Others held, more plausibly, that overstringing in a grand piano was without material benefit but was of definite value in square pianos. The technological tempest continued, and one magazine published a cartoon of a piano labelled "Steinway System" exploding like fireworks in the Paris skies.

Perhaps most significant among Steinway partisans was exhibition judge Dr. Eduard Hanslick. Though drawn to music from childhood and a student of the piano, Hanslick completed a doctorate in law before his success with a critical article on Wagner's *Tannhauser* deflected his career. Some scholars consider Hanslick to be the first serious aesthetician and musicologist in European music; he lectured widely and pioneered the concepts of music appreciation. A portion of his power came from his ability to dispense government grants to worthy composers.

This man of formidable intellect and wide acquaintance in the world of music came to believe that the Steinway was the best way to build a piano. How this belief was formed is lost; one likely influence was the pianomaker Streicher, a fellow Viennese, whose firm's history included the favorite piano of Mozart. By the time of the Paris exhibition, Streicher was building instruments with an architectural, if not acoustical, debt to Steinway. Hanslick's aesthetic beliefs were as well developed and well known as they were intransigent, so it is unlikely that emolument could have changed his opinions on matters musical.

Hanslick's support included the recommendation that other pianomakers adopt Steinway design features. A book Hanslick wrote on musical instruments contained drawings actually provided by Steinway & Sons. Here the narrative trips on an enigma. Though the Steinways held United States patents protecting many of their innovations, they did not move to safeguard them in Europe. In Germany at least, where Theodore maintained a residence, this would have been easy to do, and the expense would not have been great. Instead they freely circulated information on their designs, in effect putting them in the public domain with the imprimatur of Hanslick and the assistance of untold numbers of journalists. Discussing this media campaign William later commented, "To the numerous reporters of every nationality, who at that time congregated at Paris, it proved a real gold-mine; its contents, with the drawings, were embodied almost unchanged in their printed reports on the Exposition."

By adopting a posture of noblesse oblige toward the family innovations, the Steinways immeasurably increased their prestige in Europe. In the United States, a nation which still looked east to the Old World for verification of culture and quality in the arts, this could be turned to commercial advantage. Steinway & Sons was, in effect, endorsed by the aesthetic powers of Europe. There was a secondary effect as well. Within a few years the fertile eggs of Steinway innovations deposited by Hanslick and another scholar, Dr. Oscar Paul of the University of Leipzig, hatched into a covey of Steinway imitators in Germany.

Since William, Theodore, Albert, and Heinrich, the surviving partners, were collectively astute—though not infallible—it can be inferred that they either made a strategic error in positioning themselves for the Paris Exhibition of 1867 or that, as a firm, they had no interest in pursuing the European market, other than through the occasional opportunistic sale. A dozen years in the future and henceforth for the next century, the decision to disseminate rather than protect haunted the firm; but as William and Theodore plotted exhibition strategy in the winter of 1867, those problems lurked unseen like icebergs in the uncharted seas of the future.

From the shorter view the Steinway return to Europe approximated triumph. Fetis was finally converted. This was crucial, for, as reporter of the jury, his words became the official record of instruments at the exhibition. The eighty-three-year-old musicologist was no less an aesthetic conservative than Hanslick. Fetis did not believe that music naturally improved or progressed with time. To illustrate his points he organized lecture-concerts on sixteenth- and seventeenth-century music and advocated renewal of the Gregorian chant. A lifelong piano player, he collaborated with Moscheles on a book about piano technique. Another Fetis project was a book on church organs, and he was himself an organist and composer of masses. These skills, shared with the shadowy Dachauer, may connect the two men in a common Continental past.

From a biographical context, Fetis's response to the American pianos was surprising. The musical conservative was a technological progressive. "The secret," he wrote in the jury report, "of the great tone of the American pianos consists in the solidity of construction, which is found as well in the square piano as in the grand piano. . . . The principle of solidity is . . . in the iron frame, cast in one solid piece, which resists the tension of the strings instead of the wooden framework of the European pianos." As yet, the Fetis report did not distinguish between the pianos of Steinway and Chickering.

Chickering was mentioned first. "In 1840, Jonas Chickering . . . took a patent for an iron wrest plank bridge. . . . He commenced to use heavier strings, the sonority of which was found to be better," wrote Fetis. "Today the strings of American pianos are a great deal heavier than those used by the German, French and English makers. To place them into vibration, the hammers required a more energetic attack . . . hence the considerable increase of the strength of tone." These were the positives. "But this advantage is balanced by the hardness of attack which renders the blow of the hammer too perceptible, an objection more offensive in the grand than in the square piano," reported Fetis.

The next words must have brought a smile to the face of William Steinway and a grimace to the countenance of Frank Chickering: "The firm of Steinway took a patent for a system in grand pianos, which in great part does away with the defect just designated. In this system the iron frame received a new disposition for the placing of the strings and the overstrung bass." As the labored Victorian prose unwound, it became clear that Theodore had entirely convinced Fetis that not only did the Steinway approach have merit, but also that Steinway developments naturally superseded the work of Chickering. Into the official record Fetis placed each major Steinway claim—almost verbatim from sales brochures—as verified fact. Next was the demolition of the prime claim of Steinway detractors, that nothing had been invented. "The system of overstringing is not new," recorded Fetis, "it has been tried several times without success, having been employed without intelligence."

Fetis followed with detailed critiques of the individual pianos, presumably speaking for the jury. "The pianos of Messrs. Chickering & Sons are powerful and magnificent instruments, which, under the hands of the virtuoso, produce great effects and strike with astonishment." Having said something positive, Fetis unsheathed his critical sword. "In a large hall, and at a certain distance, the listener is struck with the fullness of tone of these instruments. Nearer by, it must be added, there is combined with this powerful tone the impression of the blow of the hammer, which produces a nervous sensation by its frequent repetition."

Fetis wrote that a note played on a Chickering clunked, or perhaps banged, at the onset, distracting the listener. The effect Fetis noted can be experienced with some modern concert pianos today—one and one-quarter centuries later—by standing against the rear wall of a large performance space. From this position a rapid series of single notes will be sometimes accompanied by a machine gun–like rattle. This is what Fetis heard, and his opinion of it was devastating: "These orchestral pianos are adapted to concerts; but in the parlor, and principally applying them to the music of the great masters, there is wanting . . . the charm that this kind of music requires." Stripped of cushioning verbiage, Fetis held that the Chickering was unsuitable for any but virtuosi, should not be used in the home, and was defective for "classical" music under any circumstances. Long outsold in the marketplace by Steinway, Chickering & Sons now found themselves denuded of European critical approval from a cause that had little, if anything, to do with the value of the overstrung system.

"We take much pleasure to inform you, that the Official Report of the International Jury on Musical Instruments at the late Paris Exhibition has been published and received here," wrote William to his dealers in the spring of 1868. "As you will perceive from the enclosed correct translation . . . our success is complete." This, of course, was the report of Fetis. Besides the laceration of Chickering, the document contained an adoration of Steinway: "The pianos of Messrs. Steinway & Sons are equally endowed with the splendid sonority of their competitor; they also possess that seizing largeness and volume of tone, hitherto unknown, which fills the greatest space. Brilliant in the treble, singing in the middle and formidable in the bass, their sonority acts with irresistible power on the organs of hearing." This was a statement beyond the boldness of even patent medicine advertising, yet it emanated from the pen of a distinguished musicologist. Steinway was the piano for all musics and all players in all places. The Fetis endorsement of Steinway, and presumably that of the jury of the Paris Exhibition, was virtually unlimited.

It cannot be known from this distance what factors influenced Fetis, Hanslick, and the balance of the jury. Certainly there were political dimensions. Sentiment in England was avowedly anti-French, and a few months before the exhibition there was talk of war against Prussia in France. "Our neighbors do not love us, and they judge us with severity; not content with hating, they calumniate us," commented one French newspaper. An assassination attempt was made on the czar during the exhibition, reportedly by a "mad Pole." When the king of Prussia visited the fair, the population of Paris pointedly ignored him. Against this geopolitical backdrop, the microdrama of piano awards took place, and the willingness to consider distant American achievements may have been enhanced by local enmities and tensions.

The perceptions of America in Europe at midcentury were bizarre. The pianist Gottschalk noted that a Russian duchess thought Barnum a great American statesman, that an educated Frenchman assumed the New York fur trade was carried on by Indians, and that the director of the Paris Conservatory refused to meet him because "America was only a country of steam engines." American visitors to London for the exhibition of 1851 were assumed to have left their buckskin shirts and rifles at home. With such images of the nation extant—the reverse face of the coin of American cultural insecurity—the view advanced by Fetis, Hanslick, et alia, that Americans built the finest pianos in the world was probably viewed by many as just another strange possibility. In America, anything could happen and often did.

"AMERICAN PIANOS. Chickering & Sons have been awarded at the Paris Exhibition, by the Emperor Napoleon, July 1, 1867, the GOLD

MEDAL OF HONOR and the decoration of THE LEGION OF HONOR as a testimonial of the superiority of their instruments over all others at the Exposition. WAREROOMS NO. 652 BROADWAY NEW YORK." Via the Ocean Telegraph and a perfect sense of timing, the announcement appeared in the Manhattan newspapers on Independence Day 1867. Steinway & Sons had prudently withdrawn their normal newspaper ads, having nothing to report. Theodore was late in cabling New York, and William was both anxious and depressed.

Nine days lapsed before Steinway & Sons responded; devoid of definitive word from Theodore, William joined his family in Long Branch, New Jersey, for a few days' vacation. On Thursday, July 11, the cable was received from Theodore: "Victory of the Overstrung System." The Steinway announcement was prepared: "The Paris Exhibition. STEINWAY & SONS, of New York, have been awarded THE FIRST GRAND GOLD MEDAL FOR AMERICAN PIANOS. It being *distinctly classified first in order of merit and placed at the head of the list of American exhibitors by the* SUPREME INTERNATIONAL JURY. This final verdict of the *only tribunal* determining the rank of awards at the Exposition, places THE STEINWAY PIANOS *at the head and above all others*. In addition to the above the great 'Societe des Beaux Arts' of Paris have, after a careful examination and comparison of all the musical instruments . . . awarded to STEINWAY & SONS THEIR GRAND TESTIMONIAL MEDAL 'For greatest superiority and novelty of construction in Pianos.' Warerooms first floor of Steinway Hall, Nos. 71 and 73 East 14th-st. New York." Theodore, learning that Chickering had two medals, had apparently enticed the *Societe* to provide another to Steinway. The advertisement appeared, not in the normal musical classification on page eight of the *New York Times*, but in the middle of the paper among the news items.

Along with it and above was Chickering's announcement: "AMERICAN PIANOS TRIUMPHANT at the EXHIBITION OF ALL NATIONS. In addition to THE GRAND GOLD MEDAL OF HONOR, the Emperor Napoleon, in person, accompanied the presentation with the decoration of THE CROSS OF THE LEGION OF HONOR, thereby conferring to the CHICKERING MEDAL the only distinction over the four other medals awarded for Piano-fortes, all of which are exactly alike and of equal value, and thereby confirming the unanimous award of the THREE JURIES AND THE IMPERIAL COMMISSION placing the CHICKERING PIANO at the HEAD OF ALL OTHERS."

In the frenzied competition for certification the truth was stretched beyond its elastic limit on both sides. The emperor did not personally award Chickering the gold medal for the simple reason that the medals were not ready when Napoleon III made his presentations. There were three other gold medals awarded, not four, as Chickering stated. The medals were of equal value only in a monetary sense; the jury reports make clear that discriminations were made among the winners, but at this time no one in America had seen the reports, and they probably had not been written. Steinway, in its claim for "first" medal, was relying on a published telegraphic report in the *New York Times*, which, in listing American winners, did begin with Steinway & Sons for reasons entirely unknown. The official lists, published months later, listed Steinway behind Chickering. The competition between Steinway and Chickering had left the orbits of rationality, never to return.

In the larger context of advertising truthfulness, these were minor infractions when gauged by the practice of the time. Immediately below the Steinway and Chickering ads was yet another: "Honors well merited. A Legion of Honor conferred on Mme. Chevalier by the Emperor of the French. CHEVALIER'S LIFE FOR THE HAIR. This recently improved article positively restores gray hair to its original color; is a dressing which imparts life, growth and strength to the weakest hair and stops the falling out at once . . . SARAH A. CHEVALIER, M.D. No. 1,125 Broadway." Whether Dr. Chevalier was French is unknown; that she was not awarded a medal from the Legion of Honor is certain. By the ethics and standards of medicine, piano advertising was a paragon of honesty and restrained decorum.

On the question of the larger significance of the Paris confrontation, it is likely that the Cross of the Legion of Honor meant less to many Americans than to either the Chickering forces or the Steinway family. The *New York Times* held forth editorially at some length on the significance of the cross. They began by quoting Thackeray: " 'The emblem of the Order was but a piece of ribbon, more or less as broad as it was long, with a toy at the end of it.' " The *Times* continued, "The very next steamer that sweeps from the east may bring to our ears the clash of resounding toys. . . . The Common Council has voted no appropriation for kid gloves and carriages. . . . The glorious news has been received with an indifference approaching apathy. In a country where popular joy naturally overflows into noise, not a single gun has been fired, not a bell has been rung. Congress has been provokingly silent."

This was wrong, maintained the *Times*. A great moral victory had been won, "whose importance can scarcely be over-estimated. . . . The Old World does homage to the new in these bits of ribbon. . . . Let us therefore rejoice and be exceedingly glad. Let us honor those who have brought honor to us." There was no reception, no celebration, no parade. Americans remained unimpressed with ribbons granted by European crowned heads. In the official government report of the Paris Universal Exposition the Chickering cross was also ignored. The focus was on the medals awarded, and little distinction was made between the achievements of the competitors.

It was later reported—without certifiable accuracy—that Steinway and

Chickering had spent a combined $160,000 in their Paris campaigns, an amount equal to about $1.5 million today. The $160,000 roughly represented the profit on the sales of sixteen hundred pianos at Steinway. The expenditure was likely never returned, for the two companies did not sell an *additional* sixteen hundred pianos as a result of winning their gold medals. Contrary to the probable intent of both firms, sales growth of Steinway and Chickering pianos was below average for the industry. Between 1866 and 1869 Steinway revenues increased 20 percent while Chickering grew 26 percent. Meanwhile smaller firms grew more rapidly. One maker—Albert Weber—tripled in size, while many others increased by half or more. While William Steinway and C. F. Chickering fought each other in Europe and in the press, their smaller competitors were happily selling pianos to buyers less concerned with prestige than price.

Later in the nineteenth century, the proponents of holding companies and trusts talked often about the paradox of "ruinous competition" where firms would literally destroy themselves in Spenserian combat with their competitors. The monopolists argued that by eliminating such competition through common ownership, prices could actually be lowered. Not withstanding the general truth of the proposition, the trust advocates might well have cited as an example the Steinway and Chickering conflict at the Paris Exhibition of 1867. In the end there was no winner. At Steinway & Sons not even the medal remains. In 1989 the glass case holding the Paris Exhibition award, along with several others, was smashed and the medals stolen, never to be recovered.

Anomolies fall like leaves around the 1867 exhibition. Among the most peculiar is the sense of astonishment and discovery surrounding the American pianos. It was as if, somehow, the pianos were transported to Paris from the moon. Paris was actually the second time the Steinways had competed successfully in Europe. Just five years before, William wrote in his diary, "Charles, Henry & I work till 10 PM packing pianos for England, for fair." On March 8, 1862, William noted, "Ship a fancy Grand & square piano per steamer Etna to Liverpool." A week later two more instruments were sent: "To my horror find that officers of steamer 'City of New York' will not receive the two pianos for London. I immediately run to pier 44 North River where she lies, and after a good deal of trouble and giving the stevedore $5 and his men 50 cts, succeed to get the pianos on board. Henry goes to England with this steamer which departs at 12:30."

The International Exhibition at London was held in the renowned Crystal Palace, the original for which the New York structure, now burned, had been named. Attendance was nearly as large as Paris at six million persons; and 132 pianomakers competed for awards. Judging was somewhat different, as there was only one class of medal, and by the rules these were dispensed generously. One-third of the participants in class XVI, musical instruments, received medals. The judges, including two men who would serve on the Paris jury five years later, Fetis and Schiedmeyer, were forced to comment that "in making the awards for pianofortes . . . the Jury consider that they will not be exceeding their powers in placing certain makers at the head of their list, with notices more full and special than those which follow."

Then came the short list consisting principally of the famous names. From England there were Broadwood and Hopkinson. Broadwood was "without controversy, at the head of the pianoforte-makers who exhibit on the present occasion." Hopkinson was lauded for "great excellence of tone" and an "ingenious" pedal that raised each note by one octave when pressed. Herz of France was specially noticed for "excellence in every kind of piano, power and equality of tone," and Pleyel, Wolff & Company "on the same ground as to Messrs. Herz." Schiedmeyer of Stuttgart and Bechstein of Berlin were both awarded for "excellence of construction combined with cheapness." Streicher and Son of Vienna were awarded for "powerful tone and novelty of invention." There was a historical note by the jury that Beethoven composed "his famous sonata Op. 106" on a Streicher. Last among the special mentions was Steinway & Sons of New York, adjudged to have "powerful, clear and brilliant tone, with excellent workmanship." A lengthy description of the technical features followed. Steinway pianos possessed "an important peculiarity" in their iron frames and the "plan is a bold one . . . on account of its cheapness, strength and unity." Offsetting this apparent recognition was a statement at the beginning of the report that "although eleven years have passed since the last Exhibition, we have not to record the introduction of any very important novelty." The London judges looked but did not see, heard but did not listen. While the jury clearly missed the significance of the "Overstrung System," Streicher did not. Five years later his 1867 prizewinner was a copy of the New York Steinway.

While myopia was widespread at the London Exhibition, it did not affect all. The London *News of the World* said that the Steinways "are without a doubt the musical gems of the Exhibition." The *News of the World* reporter had found the piano of his dreams. So had others, suggested the *New York Times* exhibition correspondent, probably the omnipresent C. C. Bailey Seymour: "All the best players in London tried the pianos, and some of a burglarious disposition even went so far as to break the instruments open when they found them locked." Henry, Jr., was joined in London for a brief period by Theodore, whom he had not seen in over a decade. Apparently the brothers were not always present when the exhibition was open.

Rounding out the trio of national approvals was Henri Roche, a music critic for *Presse Musicale* of France. Roche was impressed by the velocity of Steinway ascendancy: "This firm, not known among the exhibitors at the first London Exhibition (of 1851), has taken in a very short time an astonishing development. . . . This firm is also the only one which distinguishes itself in the manufacture of pianos by new inventions worth being favorably considered." Roche also confirmed to the public the private boast of Henry, Jr., of three years before, saying that "a square piano of Messrs. Steinway fully possesses the tone of a grand." To the Europeans who had long ago abandoned the square in favor of the upright, this statement must have generated amazement if not incredulity.

London Musical World expanded on this theme: "By invention of an ingenious acoustical instrument they were enabled to ascertain the exact vibrations of the sounding board, and to place the bridges—two or more, as the case might require—on exactly the spots that would least interfere with same."

Twelve decades later acoustic researchers, today for practical purposes, have confirmed that the sounding board of a piano vibrates in specific modes via computerized measurements. The first of these modern papers, published in 1985 and frequently cited in scholarly studies of piano acoustics, is replete with three-dimensional drawings of a sounding board vibrating when excited at various frequencies. It becomes clear that, in the middle of the nineteenth century, Henry, Jr., not only knew about these "modes," but understood how to take advantage of them in building an instrument.

Whatever the state of his knowledge, Henry, Jr.'s efforts at London came to little. London merchants Cramer, Beale & Wood purchased the four medal-winning instruments and were appointed London agents for Steinway & Sons. The relationship did not mature, and when Henry returned to New York in the fall the Steinway presence went with him. While the European notices proved useful in America, the Continental tastemakers were quick to forget. So fugitive were the impressions that only five years later the pianos of Steinway & Sons were new and miraculous once again.

The role of innovator was an arduous one, and no better testimony to the difficulty is found than the fate of G. H. Hulskamp, the other American to win a medal at London for his pianos. A piano and violin maker, Hulskamp held a half-dozen piano patents. His award was for "singular and novel construction" in a piano of "small size, but . . . powerful tone." Hulskamp, despite his award, returned to America and the obscurity from which he came.

The European expositions occurred only every five to six years, and the competitions carried risks greater than a return to obscurity. A loss to a competitor directly—by being awarded a lesser medal or a poorer judge's report—was the most obvious penalty. Both Steinway and Chickering promoted their victories *over* European makers, thereby establishing an apparent superiority for American pianos and engaging patriotism as a sales tool. If only one of the two firms exhibited and the other did not, then there was an obvious loss of prestige for the nonexhibitor. Under this calculus, even a loss by the exhibitor could be turned into a victory by claiming valiant defense of the national honor. Should both exhibit and lose, mutual ignominy would follow, and the value of previous wins would be greatly depreciated. Should both win high honors, little was to be gained save another round of semantic conflict over which firm won the highest honors.

When the time came for the next international exhibition, William Steinway wrote in his diary, "Send regular application to Van Buren, 51 Chambers Str., for space at the Vienna Exposition." The fair was to begin in the spring of 1873 and, as a matter of routine, the papers were filed for yet another commercial combat with Chickering. Nothing happened for two weeks. On November 25, 1872, a man appeared at Steinway Hall: "E. H. Osborne, No. 1 Pemberton Square, Boston, calls and states that Chickerings would like to make an arrangement with us by which both of us will not exhibit at Vienna. Both Albert & Theodore are strongly in favor of such an arrangement," wrote William in his diary.

The next day Louis Dachauer, Steinway operative at Paris in 1867, appeared at William's office and "tells me that Frank Chickering called on him several times, offering to engage him." A family conference ensued and, wrote William, "We all consider it to be good policy to arrange with Chickering." The Steinway amenability apparently made its way back to Chickering, for four days later William received a letter from Frank Chickering and a meeting was arranged, not at the office but at William's home. Two days later the men met again at Chickering's home. After a "long conversation," an agreement not to compete at Vienna was signed.

Dated December 2, 1872, the agreement opened with a list of reasons why it was deemed inadvisable to exhibit. Austrian law provided no protection for owners of "valuable patent rights"; there was but one class of medal—copper—rather than the gold, silver, and bronze of prior exhibitions; many of the "leading Piano-Forte manufacturers" had decided not to exhibit. The agreement did not mention that the sales torrent in the boom of 1870–71 had slowed to a trickle by the winter of 1872–73. Veterans of the trade knew that slowing sales were sometimes prelude to a panic. The wiser of them would not want to be in Vienna if the New York markets crashed and the banks closed, nor would they want to spend cash to exhibit internationally with weak sales at home.

"The Messrs. Chickering & Sons and Steinway & Sons are of the opinion that, under these circumstances, it will not be worth the while of either firm to incur all the trouble, expense, and personal inconvenience of exhibiting their Piano-Fortes at said Vienna Exposition," read the agreement. The two firms agreed to withdraw their applications for exhibition space. They also agreed that they "will not send, cause or permit to be sent to the said Vienna Exposition of 1873, either directly or indirectly for competition, exhibition or any other purpose, Piano-Fortes of their own make." William Steinway and C. Frank Chickering pledged to keep this agreement "strictly confidential." There was also a penalty clause: $50,000 "lawful money of the United States," about $550,000 today, would be forfeited by either firm if it sent a piano to Vienna.

Chickering was the first to withdraw from the exposition after clearing with William his letter to Commissioner Van Buren. A discreet eleven days later the Steinway & Sons withdrawal, cleared by Chickering, was submitted to the exhibition commission. Writing of what he thought the détente accomplished in 1875, Chickering said he "looked to the avoidance of any advertising advantages which an European Exhibition would offer." The Steinways, however, took a less general view.

Theodore sailed for Europe in February and that spring and summer made himself a fixture at the Vienna Exhibition. Among the judges at Vienna that year were three old friends of the Steinways; all had been judges at the 1867 Paris Exhibition as well. Stuttgart pianomaker Julius Schiedmeyer and musicologist Eduard Hanslick were on the panel judging musical instruments; and Leipzig University professor Dr. Oscar Paul, in addition to being a judge, was the official reporter of the jury.

It may have been only the Chickerings who were surprised when an advertisement appeared in some city newspapers after the close of the exhibition: "We regret that the celebrated inaugurators of the new system in piano-making, MESSRS. STEINWAY & SONS, of New York, to whom the entire art of Piano-making is so greatly indebted, have not exhibited." This statement was signed by all fourteen of the Vienna exhibition musical instrument jurors, not just the piano jurors friendly to Steinway. Interestingly, the expression of regret did not appear in the *New York Times* that December. In the *Times*, a major Steinway promotional medium, ran a different ad promoting the gold medal from Paris in 1867, six years past. Just below the Steinway insertion was a larger Chickering advertisement, booming superiority based on the Cross of the Legion of Honor, from the same Paris Exhibition. But outside New York there was a Steinway coup; they had won at Vienna by *not* competing. Although the issue never came up, it is likely that William planned the notices which ran in Chicago, Boston, and other cities but was able to preserve deniability by claiming that they had been placed by dealers, not Steinway & Sons.

"Receive letter from Frank Chickering about the Vienna affair and threats," recorded William. Chickering had written that he was "so strongly convinced that an outside influence had been brought to bear, that I shall immediately address myself to His Excellency, Baron Schwartz Sanborn upon the subject." William was concerned and spent Christmas morning at Steinway Hall writing Theodore and making copies of three documents, the Steinway-Chickering contract, Chickering's letter, and a letter from Dr. Oscar Paul which apparently formed the basis of the announcement that inflamed Chickering.

Nothing happened. Chickering did not meet with William; William did not write Chickering back. The issue may have been mooted by the claim of a *third* pianomaker, George Steck, one of two American exhibitors at Vienna. Steck claimed that he won a gold medal. If Steck had won, the Steinway and Chickering squabble over *not* exhibiting would be preempted by a legitimate win. The transatlantic cable pulsed with piano intrigue. William cabled Theodore, querying if the Steck award was legitimate. Theodor cabled back that Steck positively did not win a government medal and that Steck was a *"schwindler."*

As this went on, there sailed from Boston an operative for Chickering whose mission was to learn what had occurred in Vienna during the summer of 1873. His job was to track down the exhibition officials and get their statements. The investigation took four months. "You will understand," wrote the agent in Vienna to Chickering, "that all the jurors left this city long ago, and I am unable . . . to find their addresses."

Ultimately the Chickering man did find the addresses he needed and trundled around Europe that winter, assembling evidence. Later Chickering wrote that the Steinway newspaper announcement was "a forgery, a tissue of impudent falsehoods . . . a preposterous fabrication" and was based upon "collusive trickery" involving the "habits of a mountebank," which debased the great American piano industry "below the level of a common country circus." As Chickering seethed and roared, there was an unusual silence from the Steinways. In his diary William commented that he had sent a man to change the wording in a new catalog about the "Vienna matter." The original translation of the jury's comment, as it first appeared in a Steinway circular bearing the date November 25, 1873, was, "We regret that the celebrated inaugurators of the new system in Piano-making, Steinway & Sons, New York, to who the entire art of piano making is so indebted, have not exhibited." The revised translation, somewhat less glowing in its prose, referred to "the pathbreaking firm" rather than "celebrated inaugurators" and completely deleted the mention of the "new system."

The only surviving record is Chickering's, and the high dudgeon of the language suggests a document designed to persuade more than objectively inform. It does appear that several of the jurors whose names were appended to the report were unaware of its existence. The Bohemian instrumentmaker Cerveny thought such an endorsement "was out of the question." Archcompetitor Bosendorfer, a Viennese pianomaker who roundly condemned most Steinway technical innovations, reported that about five judges had attended a showing of the Steinway grand at a private home.

Julius Schiedmeyer offered yet a third translation of the now-infamous endorsement: "In regard to the 'American Division,' it is to be regretted that the famous pioneer firm of Steinway & Sons, to who the entire Piano Manufacture is so much indebted, has not been represented." This resolution, Schiedmeyer stated, was passed at a section-meeting of the piano judges. Hanslick was less equivocal: "The official compliment . . . is perfectly correct and is no humbug." The new Imperial Exhibition commissioner, however, called the Steinway statement "fraudulent puffing humbug." The official position was later modulated, and the Austrian Imperial and Royal Minister of Commerce wrote Chickering that the piano jury had "the right to give . . . a private opinion on an object which has not been exhibited . . . cannot be taken away from the Jurors, nor can it be questioned." When William changed the language in the translation, removing the reference to "celebrated" and "new system," he conformed, it appears, more closely to the actual resolution of his friends, the jurors.

The newspapers of the time regularly used, to the point of cliche, the headline "PIANO WARS" when reporting the charges and countercharges of competitors. The Steinways had flanked C. Frank Chickering in Europe and returned to America victorious. Chickering knew this, the Steinways knew it, and the trade did as well. When New York's secondhand piano dealers advertised the brands they sold, the order was now Steinway first, then Chickering. C. Frank Chickering, chevalier of the Legion of Honor, had lost not just the battle but the war.

Chapter 13

CONDENSER OF
POLYPHONY

"About 12 o'clock last night, flames were discovered in the kitchen attached to the restaurant belonging to the Academy of Music. . . . When our reporter first arrived on the scene a dense and suffocating volume of smoke filled the vast interior of the building, so blinding that the firemen could not gain a permanent footing on the stage and were compelled to fall back," reported the *New York Times* on May 22, 1866. The home of the city's string of opera companies and its Philharmonic Orchestra, the Academy of Music on Fourteenth Street, burned to the ground, and two firemen lost their lives.

The flames leapt to the College of Physicians and Surgeons and soon consumed it; the building housing Ihne & Son, a minor pianomaker, was totally destroyed, and the lumber of pianomaker Horatio Worcester was also lost to the fire. The entire block of Fourteenth Street between Third Avenue and Irving Place was "a sheet of flames. Frenzied efforts saved the trained horses and mules at the Hippotheatron, a circus, but "during the progress of the fire twenty or thirty birds were fluttering in the immediate vicinity of the burning pile of buildings, and every now and then one or more of the little songsters was swallowed up in the vortex of flame."

The loss of the Academy of Music was scarcely mourned; it had a reputation for fair acoustics but even as the rubble smouldered, a reporter condemned its design: "It appeared to have been the special device of the architect to keep every spectator as far from the stage as possible." Whatever its quality, the city lost its largest performance space. Seating roughly four thousand persons, its capacity was slightly greater than Carnegie Hall today. Four days later William Steinway made an entry in his diary: "Laying cornerstone of our new Hall. Fine celebration. Mayor Hoffman lays stone." Whether the timing was a coincidence or an acceleration of an existing plan is unknown, but Heinrich and William had decided to fund personally the construction of a large auditorium as part of their Fourteenth Street warerooms.

When finished, it seated a claimed twenty-five hundred persons, although the actual seating charts suggest a capacity of nearer to two thousand for the main room. No architect was engaged, and the hall seems to have been largely designed by the family. Two weeks after laying the cornerstone William and Theodore were in Boston at Russell Music Hall, measuring the space and taking notes in a process that might be called "build first, design later." In September William was working on the seating plans for the nearly finished auditorium, and in early October the plasterers finished their work. The entire space, 9,225 square feet, was built and furnished in roughly four months. The Steinways had scaled their hall to be larger than Irving Hall, which still existed on the next block, but smaller than the burned Academy of Music, which was likely to be rebuilt. No larger auditorium—before or since—has ever been built by a musical instrument manufacturer.

The concept of performance spaces associated with piano sales was not a new one. In 1839 the French pianomaker Pleyel built a hall with a capacity of about four hundred persons in Paris. Chickering's hall in Boston, built in 1862, was noted approvingly by the pianist L. M. Gottschalk: "Chickering has just constructed, in one of his magnificent warehouses, a music hall, a perfect gem, which he graciously places at the command of artists who visit Boston. The hall contains nearly four hundred parquet seats."

Although both Chickering and Steinway claimed pioneering roles in the sponsorship of performances in America, the patent nature of the linkage meant it already had a long history. An Albany dealer for Hazleton pianos held a vocal concert—featuring a member of the Hazleton family—in April 1853. Three hundred persons reportedly attended. Similar concerts were held throughout the Northeast at other stores selling other makes of pianos. Albany-based pianomaker Myron Decker sponsored a concert at the state fair in Syracuse, New York, in 1858; there Decker received a medal for his pianos, and the performer, one Richard West, received an award for his playing.

Though small in scale and sporadic, activities of this type were common and intended to establish the pianomaker as not merely a manufacturer but as a patron of the arts. The Steinways expanded the scale, scope, frequency,

157

and prestige of patronage to achieve an unprecedented prominence. With the Academy in ruins, the new Steinway Hall was now the largest musical venue in New York City, and it was owned not by a syndicate, not by the municipality, but by two men.

Therein lies a peculiarity. At the time the hall was built, Theodore and Albert Steinway had replaced their deceased brothers Charles and Henry in the partnership. By the rules of the partnership, each partner shared equally in the profits independent of his investment. Heinrich and William drew the $90,786 it cost to build the hall from Steinway & Sons. Their investment in the partnership was reduced by that amount. Theodore and Albert, though they had sufficient funds in the partnership to cover participation, did not contribute to the construction of the hall. This suggests that Theodore and Albert may have questioned the value of building Steinway Hall. At the time all Steinway & Sons real estate—the Fifty-second Street factory, the Fourteenth Street warerooms, and miscellaneous minor properties, some taken in trade for pianos—were owned by Heinrich and William; they had purchased the real estate from the estates of Charles and Henry for cash in compliance with the partnership agreement and the wills of the brothers. For several years Heinrich and William "rented" the factory, warerooms, and hall to Steinway & Sons, the partnership, at a rate of 7 percent of its valuation. But by 1870 all four partners once again held the real estate, with Albert and Theodore each receiving a deeded one-fourth interest. Whether this was a gift, perhaps at the insistence of "Papa," or whether Theodore and Albert purchased the buildings is not clear from surviving records. One thing which is clear is that Theodore was not convinced of the value of promotion through concerts. In 1877 he proposed to William that the hall be turned into a warehouse. The suggestion was ignored, and Steinway Hall was in operation as a concert venue for more than a decade after Theodore recommended closing it.

Steinway Hall opened on Wednesday, October 31, 1866, with the Bateman Concert Troupe, a stellar aggregation of vocal and instrumental performers. "Everybody is delighted with the acoustic qualities. House filled to overflowing. Great success. Supper afterwards, jolly time til 3 A.M.," wrote William in his diary. The house, which "overflowed," did so at one dollar per ticket for open seating and $1.50 for reserved seats, suggesting that the gross reached roughly three thousand dollars for one night, with full houses continuing for the run.

Just how impressive this was can be judged from the "Receipts at Places of Amusement," which were reported for the purpose of collecting a 2-percent federal gate tax, a legacy of the Civil War. In September 1867 a rebuilt Academy of Music grossed a mere $1,154 per night from the grand opera playing there; the New York Circus averaged but $597 per night despite offering "Dashing Heroics, Bold Riders and Spectacular Gymnasts." The long-lived Niblo's Garden averaged $1,433, while several minstrel shows drew about two hundred to three hundred dollars an evening. Only Barnum's renowned museum came close at $1,661 per day, an impressive gross when it is considered that at twenty-five cents per head an average of more than six thousand persons per day trekked past the mermaids and bearded ladies.

The success of the hall was not accidental. The night before the grand opening William convened members of the press for a preview: "STEINWAY's new Music Hall was partially lighted last night in the presence of a few visitors," reported the *Times* the next morning. "It will interest our readers to know a few particulars of the edifice." There followed, in forecastable fashion, the words from one of William's press handouts. Fire was the terror of the time, particularly for theater- and concertgoers. In 1858 the famed Crystal Palace burned; in that fire the Steinways lost a half-dozen pianos to competitor Chickering's dozen. There was no loss of life. Barnum's Museum burned in 1860 and again in 1865. The Academy of Music was next in 1866. None of these fires cost the lives of patrons, but the fear was valid, and William took pains to emphasize Steinway Hall's safety.

The doors opened outward on both the Fourteenth and Fifteenth Street sides, and the whole building could be evacuated in three minutes. Construction was of stone, inherently fireproof, and almost pyramidally sound; the basement walls were of granite three feet thick. The brick walls of the upper stories were a stolid thirty-two inches, laid with cement, and had "heavy external supporting buttresses." Two walls rose from the basement to support the main floor and secure freedom from vibration. "The whole building has been constructed," wrote William, "in the most substantial manner without regard to outlay."

Steam boiler explosions were another source of mayhem; scarcely a month went by without a stationary or marine steam explosion being reported in city papers. To allay these concerns, the "generator" was placed "outside in another building." Having reduced the anxiety of patrons about being crushed or charred or scalded to the lowest possible level, William went on the extol the "elegantly cushioned iron-framed armchairs" which made Steinway Hall "the most comfortable grand music hall in the United States."

The premiere concert itself was a mix of vocal, violin, piano, and orchestral music very unlike modern performances. At 8:00 P.M. Theodore Thomas's Grand Orchestra, normally seventy strong, filled the hall with the sound of the overture from Wagner's *Tannhauser* as the last of the standing-room-only audience jostled for position. There followed Donizetti's *Maria de Rudens* romanza sung by baritone Signor Fortuna, a solo violin performance by Carl Rosa of the first movement of Lipinski's *Concerto Militaire*, tenor Signor Brignoli singing another romanza, *M'appari* by Flotow, and soprano Mademoiselle Parepa rendering Rossini's *Bel Raggio*. Sebastian Bach Mills then seated himself at the Steinway grand piano and played the first movement of Schumann's *Concerto in A minor*. Signor Ferranti, a buffo basso, sang more Rossini; and the first half of the evening's entertainment concluded with a duo by Parepa and Brignoli, Donizetti's *Da Quel Di*.

After intermission the Grand Orchestra played the overture to *Jesonda* by Spohr, violinist Rosa reappeared to perform Leonard's *Souvenir de Haydn*, followed by another vocal duo, this time Ferranti and Fortuna, singing Rossini's *Un Segreto*. As the applause receded, Brignoli stepped forward with another romanza, Donizetti's *In terra et diverso*, and Mademoiselle Parepa sang *The Nightingale's Trill* by Ganz. S. B. Mills returned with a piano solo, Liszt's *Midsummer Night's Dream*, after which, with a certain predictability, all four vocalists sang a *quatour* from Donizetti's *Don Pasquale*. Accompanying the singers was pianist J. L. Hatton. Meyerbeer's *Torch-light March* concluded the lengthy musical inaugural of Steinway Hall, ensuring that patrons received at least one dollar's worth of music.

The evening's emphasis on Italian opera was congruent with the taste of the times. In one instance the penchant for Italianate vocal music resulted in an opera, *Lurline*, written in English by William Vincent Wallace while in New York, then performed in London, being translated into Italian to be performed in New York. The second concert, similar in content, was no less successful than the first. "The attendance was excellent, representing the taste, fashion and strength of New York. It is not an easy matter to fill a hall of this capacity," remarked the *Times*, "but if Mr. Bateman meets with the success he honestly merits, the establishment—ample as it is—will be taxed to its uttermost limits." There were garlands for all. Mademoiselle Parepa's "superb rendering" was also "in largeness of style, fullness of voice and complete appreciation of a somewhat old-fashioned style of music . . . never been heard to better advantage." Mills played "faultlessly, with absolute perfection of touch and execution." This, of course, may have been the view of C. C. Bailey Seymour on his brother-in-law's talents, but Brignoli's performance was also lauded: "The gentleman is in superb voice and as an artist he has ripened immensely." More remarkable still, the H. L. Bateman concert series was launched with a one-day rehearsal.

Next into Steinway Hall was the New York Philharmonic under conductor Carl Bergmann. Burned out of the Academy of Music, the Philharmonic took up a temporary residence. There were grumblings, however. The stage was not deep enough for a large orchestra; the hall, hurriedly finished, was austerely plain—the walls were given a pearlescent wash but were otherwise devoid of decoration—and not everyone shared William Steinway's assessment of acoustic splendor.

"Steinway Hall, as last seen, was plain in all its appointments, almost to poverty—as bare as a country church. All this will be changed," commented a *Times* writer two years later. "The interior arrangements of which it will be remembered were somewhat hastily concluded to supply the public want consequent upon the burning of the Academy of Music, is about to be thoroughly overhauled, and decorated in the highest style of art. To this end a few days ago Mr. Heinrich Beck, a distinguished architect, arrived here from Vienna. . . . It may be stated that the architect named designed and superintended the decoration of the world-famous pleasure gardens of Vienna—the Prater—and that he lately completed the construction and ornamentation of a travelling car for the Empress of Austria." Steinway Hall was a smaller job; for a mere twenty-five thousand dollars the hall was to be decorated, whereas the empress's car cost fifty thousand dollars.

Decorations were to be "elaborate but chaste" in the style of Louis Quatorze. Two immense statues were installed, one representing "composition," the other "music." Busts of Beethoven and Mozart were placed over the proscenium boxes and a new proscenium installed over the stage. Above the stage was to be a "Panel of Honor" on which would be mounted a large portrait "of the artist of the occasion—composer, prima donna, or other, as the case may be, whoever is the chief attraction of the entertainment." In its use of a giant portrait, Steinway Hall anticipated, in a strange way, the late-twentieth-century practice of projecting large-screen television images of performers.

By building their new hall, the Steinways seized for themselves a central role in the city's cultural life, one which by its scale, if for no other reason, assured them of a prominence greater than any other pianomaker. Prior to building the hall there had been the occasional soiree in the warerooms. The normally docile *Times* critic complained that a performance by the Mason-Thomas Quartet held in the Steinway warerooms "seemed to have been arranged to a gradual density and dullness" and that the "room lacks size, visual ability and ventilation." This, and a few other minor performances, was the sole concert management experience of the Steinways before the construction of the hall. It is likely that the decision to build Steinway Hall was heavily influenced by several factors. The first of these was the problem of artist endorsements in general and Louis Moreau Gottschalk in particular.

Acclaimed variously as the successor to Chopin and a man of rare and refined tastes, a more basic appeal of Gottschalk was that he was an *American* who had the imprimatur of European acceptance, a living antidote to the national feelings of cultural inferiority. Of course, Gottschalk played an American piano, the Chickering, and he was immensely loyal to his chosen instrument. William Steinway's diary reveals that many pianists came to the warerooms to play new instruments. Some of these were clandestine trials by players publicly affiliated with other makers; Gottschalk's name is not among them. Gottschalk was, of course, aware of the competition between Steinway and Chickering: "A young lady amateur," he wrote, "full of pretensions, like all amateurs, after insisting upon being placed upon the posters refused to play when her turn came, on the pretext that she could only play upon her Steinway. I played in her place, and all my pieces were encored. Steinway and Chickering, Guelphs and Ghibellines of the musicians, are divided into two factions—the Germans are for Steinway." Gottschalk and Chickering were a potent commercial combination. The premier American pianist played an American piano, and Chickering was not above appealing to nativist sentiment in its advertising: "Our house is purely an American house, and is conducted upon American principles. In our factory . . . every department is directed by American skill, judgment and enterprise." This was a claim Steinway & Sons could not rejoin, and it was impossible to obtain Gottschalk's endorsement; his aesthetics and values were impermeably anti-Teutonic. The brightest light in the American pianistic firmament would never sanction Steinway.

There was also a subsidiary problem with endorsements. Most artists, save Gottschalk, were notoriously loose with them. At the height of the Christmas selling season two advertisements appeared in the city papers, one for pianos by William B. Bradbury, a conductor, composer, hymnodist, and partner in various pianomaking firms, now on his own, and another for Steinway & Sons. Of the dozen Steinway endorsers, nine also appeared in Bradbury's advertisement. Among the common endorsers were Steinway stalwarts S. B. Mills, William Mason, John Pattison, Theodore Thomas, and Henry C. Timm. Counting the endorsements, Bradbury weighed in with thirty to Steinway's dozen. To offset promiscuous piano approvals, Steinway ads carried copy along with the artist names: "We have at various times expressed our opinion regarding the pianos of various makers, but freely and unhesitatingly pronounce: MESSRS STEINWAY & SONS PIANOS, BOTH GRAND AND SQUARE, INCOMPARABLY SUPERIOR TO THEM ALL." Others could cadge endorsements, but only Steinway had the financial strength to build a vast performance space. It was a clever strategy; Steinway aligned itself not only with pianos, but with music of all types.

The musical involvement of the Steinways transcended business and was integral to their personal lives. Charles, Henry, William, and perhaps Albert were all able to play the piano at least passably. Albert played the cornet as well. William's diary recorded social events at which family and friends entertained themselves by playing and singing. William's vocal skill as a tenor was apparently outstanding; he was able to sing on parity with professionals, with whom he would sometimes perform at parties. On the issue of musical skill, the Steinways needed to be perceived as talented amateurs and appreciators of the art, but not so skilled as to threaten professionals on whom they relied for endorsements. A performance space provided a way to participate personally, a form of patronage that did not threaten artistic egos.

The Steinways had three methods of extending their influence into the distribution system. The first of these was to sell pianos at retail as they had done since 1853. Secondly, they recruited prominent allies among virtuoso-teachers; Sebastian Bach Mills, an Englishman, and William Mason, a native American, were among those who played apostolic roles for many years. "Mason is growing rather fat," wrote pianist Von Bulow to a friend. "A nice fellow, but unfortunately, it appears, wholly in the hands of Steinway." By the time this was written, Mason was teaching in a Steinway Hall studio, perhaps rent-free.

While the provision of teaching-studio space was one way of extending Steinway influence and presence into the distribution channel, the hall's auditorium was a far more powerful linkage to the mainstream culture. Functioning in the manner of a mass medium—similar to the ownership of a television station today—Steinway Hall provided the family, and William in particular, with control of a service for which there was wide demand: entertainment. That the demand was large can be seen in the statistics of revenues for New York theaters and operas: according to tax records, almost three million dollars was expended in 1869 for these entertainments; this implies that every man, woman, and child in the city went to the theater or the opera at least three times per year. Comparable national per capita attendance in the late twentieth century is on the order of 0.055 performances per person for opera and 0.034 performances per person for legitimate theater. Very roughly, a nineteenth-century Gothamite was thirty times more likely to go to the opera or the theater than an American today. Concerts, unlike theater and opera, were not taxed, and revenue data is therefore unavailable. These unrecorded concerts would add greatly, but unspecifiably, to the total performances attended by New Yorkers.

Today the theater, the opera, and "serious" concerts are considered entertainments of the educated and/or wealthy; this was not so in William Steinway's Manhattan. One 1858 analysis of entertainment expenditures concluded that 55 percent of the revenues of the "first class theaters and the opera house" were provided by the "artisans, laborers and others of the poorer classes." Intriguingly, critics sometimes commented that the balconies of New York performance spaces were filled with mechanics, bakers, gold beaters, and tailors who were more attentive, polite, and better behaved than the wealthy occupying boxes near the stage. A man who spent a day's wages to take his wife to the opera was naturally more inclined to pay attention.

The demand for entertainment was not only large; it was growing rapidly. In the ten years ending 1875, the number of professional musicians in New York State nearly doubled, while the number of music teachers almost tripled. The number of music dealers—of instruments and sheet music—grew 80 percent, while the number of pianomakers increased 55 percent. When Heinrich and William chose to build their auditorium, they positioned Steinway & Sons on the crest of a rising wave of cultural consumption.

Open from roughly September through May each year for nearly a quarter of a century, Steinway Hall was the scene of perhaps one thousand or more performances—complete records are not available—and certainly not less than one million persons trekked through its doorways to their seats inside. Each of them had the name Steinway imprinted in their memories by the experience. Each in that vast cumulative audience had been there, had listened, had been entertained, poorly or well, and would not forget Steinway. The link between performances at the hall and pianos was tighter than might be imagined in our age of radio, broadcast, cable or satellite television, videotape recorders, video discs, stereo records, compact discs, and cassette recordings, all of which compete as sources of domestic musical entertainment. It was probably C. C. Bailey Seymour who wrote that the piano was "truly a domestic orchestra, a real condenser of polyphony, the solitary muse of the parlor."

In musical entertainment there was in the nineteenth century a simple duopoly. Music could either be heard in a public space or it could be performed in the home. By building their hall, the Steinways achieved a self-reinforcing presence in both domains, firmly linking the "solitary muse of the parlor," the pianos they sold, with the manifold muses, grand scale, and glamour of professional performances.

Of the hundreds who performed at Steinway Hall over the decades, there was one man who appeared more frequently than others. That man was conductor Theodore Thomas. Born Christian Friedrich Theodor Thomas in 1835 in Germany, the son of a musician, young Thomas immigrated to America with his family in 1845. With virtually no formal training, an adolescent Thomas supported himself as an itinerant violinist, then worked as a section player in Jullien's renowned orchestra before allying with William Mason in the long-lived Mason-Thomas Quartet.

A man of immense energy and talent, he began conducting at age twenty-four and within a few years was producing, programming, and conducting orchestral concerts at Irving Hall, a Manhattan venue seating about fifteen hundred persons. The propellant behind Thomas's rise to fame was a series of summer performances of what today would be called "pops concerts." The mix of works such as Rossini's *Stabat Mater* with lager bier and German sausages apparently had a cross-cultural appeal, and within a year the Theodore Thomas Orchestra, now forty players strong, developed an audience sufficient to support a hundred concerts per summer. From his own positions within, at various times, the New York Philharmonic, the Brooklyn Philharmonic, and the house orchestra (for which he was contractor) at the Academy of Music, Theodore Thomas not only had access to the best musicians in New York—he offered these players steady work. Thomas was a one-man Manhattan music industry, concertizing more frequently than all other orchestras and bands combined.

Thomas was also active with the German choral societies, the Arion in particular, and sometimes was a judge at the *Sangerfests*. Given the common cultural background and at least equivalent drives to succeed, it is no surprise that William Steinway and Theodore Thomas allied to their mutual benefit. The most popular conductor in the city was a natural to fill the newest hall, and this he did, not merely once or twice, but hundreds of times, and his ensemble became the de facto Steinway Hall house orchestra.

Thomas knew, of course, that there was a larger national market outside New York. "We take great pleasure in informing you," wrote William Steinway to his dealers in October of 1870, "that Mr. THEODORE THOMAS with his Grand Orchestra, has commenced his Concert Tour at Boston, and will visit the larger cities of the United States, accompanied by the celebrated pianiste, Miss Anna Mehlig, and that our Piano-fortes will be used exclusively by the troupe. Mr. Thomas has agreed to notice the fact of the Steinway Piano being used exclusively at the foot of his concert programmes as well as in the advertisements of the concerts in the public newspapers in every city which he visits. A fine concert piano will be sent in time for the concerts in each city, and our Tuner, Mr. Lubker, will accompany the troupe."

Artists with international reputations were too few in number to regularly fill the hall, and, from a programmatic standpoint, William was certainly aware that there were many piano buyers whose wealth exceeded the refinement of their tastes. These factors led to uses of the hall for what might be called a broader spectrum of entertainments, both musical and nonmusical.

Among these were appearances by Blind Tom, a young mentally impaired former slave who apparently had the ability to play a melody heard once, although his white master, one Perry H. Oliver, sometimes found it necessary to motivate Blind Tom with rewards of candy and cakes. When Blind Tom appeared at Steinway Hall in 1873, the advertisement quoted a *Manchester Guardian* review: "We were quite prepared . . . to find in Blind Tom some extraordinary qualities, fortified . . . by the testimony of M. Moscheles who tested the alleged powers of this negro youth at Southsea, and publicly expressed his opinion that Tom was 'marvelously gifted by nature.' . . . The fingers fly over the keyboard and he seems like one possessed. . . . Behind that strange visage and underneath that imperfectly-organized brain what is going on? We dare not speculate." Blind Tom was heard in a series of fifty-cent concerts, presumably playing a Steinway.

William did not attend, although he did once indicate that "Theo, Albert and I . . . stop at our Hall a short time, nigger Concert there. We then walk up home." The "nigger Concert" was a group of Jubilee Singers, ensembles of black vocalists, usually former slaves, who toured the country performing spirituals. The group William saw was likely from Fisk University and consisted of eight male students whose vocal ability, according to the *New York Tribune*, was "naturally slight, . . . not equal to, or certainly not above that of an ordinary village choir." The reviewer held that the audience was there to "aid a useful charity and hear real negro melodies," and that notwithstanding "the rudeness of their music" the singers were "curiously fascinating." The Fisk singers raised twenty thousand dollars for their school that year and returned to Steinway Hall the next year as well. Other such groups also performed at Steinway's, including the Hampton Institute Singers and the Wilmington Colored Jubilee Singers, billed as "The most popular slave band of jubilee singers ever before the public."

That William directly controlled events for which Steinway Hall was used is clear. "Refused to let Hall to Mrs. Woodhull, to her agent in afternoon," noted William in his diary in December 1872. Blind Tom was acceptable, but unsuitable was Victoria Woodhull, faith healer, member of Marx's International, stockbroker, confidante of Commodore Vanderbilt, United States presidential candidate, publisher of the first American edition of *The Communist Manifesto*, and a weekly newspaper advocating short skirts, legalized prostitution, free love, children as communal property, and world government, among other things. William did not record which of Mrs. Woodhull's many social views made her unacceptable for even a brief tenancy. There was no blanket exclusion of women, for in addition to the dozens of female musicians who performed at the hall, there were also female lecturers. Just three months after the refusal to Mrs. Woodhull, Miss Emily Faithfull was addressing audiences at Steinway Hall. According to an advertisement, "The distinguished philanthropist, author and editor" presented her final lecture in America entitled "Last Words on the Woman Question."

There is little question that the most notable event in Steinway Hall's quarter-century history occurred in the fall of 1872, but planning and maneuvers began much earlier. In March of that year William noted that "during the day Strakosch urges me to try and get Rubinstein for him." The Rubinstein sought was Anton, the eminent Russian pianist. A child prodigy who gave his first concert at age ten, he was heard in early adolescence by Chopin and Liszt, who were reported to have commented favorably. Liszt, however, apparently declined to instruct Rubinstein, contributing to a singularity among pianists: a renowned player who had no famous teachers. After touring Europe with success, Rubinstein cofounded, with a member of the czar's royal family, a conservatory at Saint Petersburg. When the Steinways and impresario Jacob Grau caught up with him in late 1871, Anton Rubinstein was conducting the Philharmonic at Vienna and continuing to compose prolifically. His stature as a pianist was unsurpassed.

The actual arrangements are murky and subject to varying accounts. On

March 14, 1872, Maurice Grau, Jacob's nephew, called on William to tell him that his Uncle Jacob "would prefer to make arrangements with us," probably a veiled reference to an alternative Chickering sponsorship for Rubinstein. William's diary notes little on the Rubinstein negotiations until June. Then, on June 14, Theodore cabled from Europe that he "took $12,000, Rubinstein commences September 23rd. Von Bulow certain next year." At this time Steinway & Sons appeared to have a bearing on both of the world's most renowned pianists. About two weeks later a long letter from Theodore arrived. It contained a proposed Rubinstein contract and a notice of a draft in the amount of $13,190.68. It is unclear whether or not this was an additional amount, or simply an unrelated transfer of funds. The possibility remains, however, that Rubinstein's passage to America was smoothed with a Steinway prepayment of more than twenty-five thousand dollars, about two decades' earnings for a New York doctor.

The Graus, both Jacob in Europe and Maurice in New York, were still very much involved, and in mid-July Maurice delivered to William a revised Rubinstein contract. Ultimately the agreement stipulated that Rubinstein would receive two hundred dollars per concert for two hundred concerts and, among other quaint stipulations, that he would be protected from "savage Indians" and would not have to play in beer halls or the South. This last provision, based on the itinerary, was rescinded. Apparently aware of exchange rate volatility and skeptical of the value of "good and lawful money of the United States," Rubinstein demanded payment in gold. Legend avows that William demonstrated the physical difficulties this entailed by asking Rubinstein to pick up a large sack of gold. Thus convinced, Rubinstein accepted payment in German thalers and even became sufficiently persuaded of the safety of the American financial system that he allowed William to purchase for him five thousand dollars in federal bonds, which paid interest in gold. No permanent convert to paper money and apparently a believer in the adage "cash is trash," Rubinstein recalled that "on my return I hastened to invest in real estate."

William recorded, "To my surprise find that Rubinstein has drawn his whole money 51,000 Thalers," and later that bankers "Herig & Frantz have also paid 16,000 Thalers and that the matter is therefore settled." Combined with an earlier reference by William to a letter of credit for 35,000 thalers, it is clear that the proceeds to Anton Rubinstein were substantial, perhaps as much as 102,000 thalers, in addition to the dollar sums paid before his arrival. Since there were at least two Germanic thalers in use at the time and William did not record *which* thaler was paid, it is impossible to convert the Rubinstein amounts to dollars. At a contractual minimum, the 215 concerts Rubinstein played would have netted him $43,000, or roughly $450,000 today. Anton Rubinstein came to America a highly respected but impecunious artist and, within eight months, became comfortably wealthy. Between his arrival and departure much transpired.

"Rubinstein and Wieniawski arrive with the *Cuba*, and call on me around noon. Rubinstein is much pleased, with Steinway Hall and our grand . . . write letter to Theodore," wrote William. Henri Wieniawski, a Polish-born violinist, had also been contracted to perform on the same bill as Rubinstein. Of equal stature and skill on his instrument, Henri Wieniawski's ego was soon to be unjustifiably immersed in the cold waters of public indifference. By the end of the American tour it was reported that Rubinstein and Wieniawski, despite a long relationship in Russia, no longer spoke to each other. Arriving together, they departed on separate ships.

It was still the practice to have "assistants" at concerts, a solo piano concert being considered a risky enterprise. To further buttress the bill, two vocalists were added. These were Mlle. Louise Liebhart, "the most popular soprano of the leading London concerts," according to the advertisements, and Mlle. Louise Ormeny, "a favorite contralto from the principal opera houses of Italy." All this was supported by a "FULL GRAND ORCHESTRA" under the baton of Herr Carl Bergmann, the terminally alcoholic director of the New York Philharmonic. Why Theodore Thomas was not engaged for the initial concerts is unclear, but a Rubinstein and Thomas combination was soon forthcoming.

While prudence may have dictated a combinatorial approach with a piano, violin, and vocal mix, the three most popular musical formats of the time, the precaution soon proved superfluous. Rubinstein had likely barely recovered from the seasickness that plagued him on the voyage when the entire New York Philharmonic appeared outside the Clarendon Hotel where he was staying for a serenade, an honor only rarely bestowed and most recently more than twenty years before for Jenny Lind. "The desire to see Rubinstein," reported the *Times*, "joined to the exquisite harmonies of the Philharmonic orchestra attracted a large concourse of people . . . and between the morceaux loud cheers and calls were given for Rubinstein." Continuing shouts from the street caused Rubinstein to step onto his balcony and briefly address the crowd. "Gentlemen: I cannot find words to express my feelings or the gratitude that overpowers me; but I do assure you that I am deeply sensible of the honor you have conferred upon me and the recollection of it will be one of the happiest moments of my life." Anton Rubinstein then stepped back inside. Some reporters were moved to note the master's excellent English.

The publicity machine was already operating at full throttle under the guiding hand of William, his press liaison John Darcie, a former critic, stoking the fires with the assistance of the Graus. Two days after the serenade, the obligatory biographical pamphlet had been widely circulated. The crop of post–Civil War pianists venturing to America had been largely female, and Rubinstein's "biography" contrapuntally played on his "rugged and virile nature . . . apparent in his face and demeanor" and the "singular, indefinable likeness to Beethoven which strikes the beholder." Rumors

floated that Anton Rubinstein was the illegitimate son of Ludwig van Beethoven; palpably preposterous, Rubinstein did nothing to deny them. This
was good box office. That the man's physiognomy struck a resonance with
Victorian females is clear from the record. A letter from Lady Eastbrook
was quoted in the brochure: "I have seen a pianist who did not inspire me
with pity. It was Anton Rubinstein. They call him the Piano Emperor."
The mesomorphic Rubinstein was tall, was broad-shouldered, and had a
large head. This, in a time when phrenology still had influence, connoted
great intelligence, and Rubinstein furthered his image with a persistently
brooding facial expression. Countless women must have fantasized on their
individual abilities to transform the virile, sensitive, famous, but sad artist
into a virile, sensitive, famous, and happy one. Some, undoubtedly, paid
to see and listen . . . and dream.

Reserved seats for the debut performance were set as high as three
dollars, a record price for the time, and general admission was one and one-
half dollars. The event rapidly sold out. For Monday, September 23, 1872,
William wrote in his diary, "I am excessively busy all day. Rubinstein first
appearance, he creates an immense success. Drink beer with Ottendorfer,
Uhl and afterwards at Monument House." It was a good time to drink beer,
for the weather in New York was unusually hot with evening temperatures
in the eighties. Neither William's wife nor his brother Albert attended the
performance.

The *Times* critic the next morning was ecstatic: "The highest expectations of Mr. Rubinstein's admirers were not disappointed, and the enthusiasm his performances awakened quite dwarfed by its demonstration the
proportions of an already very flattering welcome. More remarkable piano
playing than Mr. Rubinstein's cannot be imagined." The *New York Tribune*
exclaimed that Rubinstein possessed "the strength of a giant and the delicacy of a poet." The critics paged their dictionaries for superlatives: "a
touch of inexhaustible variety," "marvelous power and delicacy," "exceeding science and taste," "executive skill which no one can excel," "difficult for Liszt to rival . . ." A portion of the *Times* review implicitly gave
credit to the piano, with encomiums usually reserved for sales catalogs. "In
the most tremendous *fortes*, in which the piano, under Rubinstein's fingers,
copes victoriously with the orchestra; and in *pianissimi*, in which the effects
generally attainable only by the use of stringed instruments are wrought,
the quality of the tone produced is of unvarying beauty." There was more.
"The runs are now brilliant as though each note were a diamond, now close
as chains formed of the finest links." Steinway & Sons also triumphed that
night.

The concert, about four hours long, left the writers time for nothing but
a "hurried allusion which can do no one justice." A few jotted words
disposed of Henri Wieniawski: "To the extent to which any artist can share
the laurels of a contest with so colossal a genius, Mr. Wieniawski divided

them with Mr. Rubinstein." One vocalist was "somewhat hoarse," the other was of "limited compass." Sharing the program with Anton Rubinstein proved a hazardous undertaking, no matter how impresarios preferred to hedge their positions. Rubinstein was recalled twenty times during the evening, but seemed "indifferent" to the cheers of the audience and "disdained, rather ungraciously, the floral tributes."

The concerts continued through the week, checkerboarded with a Strakosch production of vocalists Carlotta Patti with Signor Mario and eighteen-year-old piano virtuoso Therese Carreño. Crowds jammed the hall, scalpers prospered, and the reviews were almost incoherent with praise. Then came the fallout from the media explosion. An editorial carried the headline "Fresh Air in Public Halls," and it appeared in the *Times*, which, in most matters Steinway, was a complaisant ally. Apparently the work of an editorialist unfamiliar with Steinway & Sons' advertising expenditures and/ or possessed of an unusually acute sense of the public weal, the piece began with a general statement of the need for improved ventilation in "places of public resort." Four lines in came the specifics: "Steinway Hall is particularly unfortunate in this respect. . . . The atmosphere there . . . during the Rubinstein concert was simply murderous. Several people had to leave the hall before the end of the performance, and others who sat it out have since taken ill in consequence." The writer went on to suggest that the hall be closed if it could not be ventilated as "the owners have no business to poison the public in this way." The editorialist revealed that during the prior season "ladies were taken ill there over and over again" and the hall was "not only intolerably hot, but disgustingly foul." Perhaps amusing by modern standards, such allegations terrified nineteenth-century New Yorkers. They lived in a world where cholera, typhoid, tuberculosis, and other bacterial diseases reaped lives at will while doctors mumbled vague theories about vapors, miasmas, and atmospheric electricity.

After calling for new laws, the editorialist continued: "Certainly the gratitude of audiences and artists must have value, even in the most selfish sense, to the owners of such a building." The writer struck at the heart of the very existence of Steinway Hall, and William took action: "Scathing article in the Times about our Hall as to Ventilation. I see Geo. Jones personally and promises to insert anything we write. Darcie and I get up article and send down."

William's article appeared the next day. "We are assured that we have unintentionally been led into some grave errors," stated the *Times* in a remarkable and rare apology, "and have done the Messrs. Steinway injustice." There followed a description of the new ventilating system being installed, but not yet completed, a notice of the unusually hot weather, the heat from seven hundred gaslights in the hall, the audience of three thousand, the lack of breezes in the city, and other exculpatory factors. "We feel the Messrs. Steinway will leave no means unapplied to render their magnificent hall as perfect in every other requirement as it is in its acoustic qualities." The response was not confined to the editorial; The reviewer of the Friday night performance by Rubinstein, et alia, also took notice, probably not serendipitously: "The cooler atmosphere without had an immediate influence in the house, and there was no obstacle whatever to a thorough enjoyment of the programme." The hall's ventilation was now a problem for Anton Rubinstein who, recorded William, "is somewhat annoyed by windows slamming and dog howling in the next yard." On balance, conditions improved with the dropping temperatures; the crowds remained both huge and happy, the critics purred their approvals, the newspapers ceased grousing, and William observed that piano sales showed a marked increase.

Using New York as a base of operations—he performed fifty concerts there—Rubinstein toured the nation east of the Rockies and in Canada. Ever-proper Boston was first, and there the press gave notice to Rubinstein's disheveled clothes, untied shoelaces, and falling socks. The Rubinstein-Steinway forces probed, generally in triumph, as far west as Colorado and as far south as New Orleans. In total there were 215 performances in 239 days, sometimes at a rate of two or three cities per day. "May Heaven preserve us from such slavery!" wrote Rubinstein. "Under these conditions there is no chance for art." But audiences and critics disagreed, and the maestro did not, it appears, seriously entertain the notion of rejecting the money in favor of higher artistic standards.

The concerts were not only numerous; they were lengthy. The four-hour New York debut was one example; another was an all-Chopin solo recital in which Rubinstein played—from memory—forty-three of the composer's works for piano. The all-Chopin recital was part of a programmatically radical series of "Farewell Concerts," occurring in May 1873. The idea of a recital, in which a single artist performed unassisted by other artists, was novel, and the critics believed it risky. The term *recital* had been introduced to New York two years before by the German pianist Marie Krebs, who sustained a three-month series of weekly solo performances at, naturally enough, the smaller concert room in Steinway Hall. The modest audiences of cognoscenti were quietly pleased.

Two years before that, another obscure pianistic pioneer, Miss Alida Topp, had also performed a similar but shorter series in Steinway's smaller room. Promoted as "A Historical Survey of Classical and Modern Piano Music," Topp played Bach, Beethoven, Haydn, Handel, Chopin, Liszt, and others. In a flurry of commas, the *New York Tribune* observed: "No other lady pianist, and few artists, indeed, of either sex, with whom we are familiar, have attempted the dangerous experiment which Miss Topp tried last night of entertaining an entire evening without assistance of any kind, and with a selection of music fitted only for persons of somewhat refined and cultivated taste." The definition of a piano virtuoso as one who principally played his or her own compositions, occasionally performed the works of others as a sort of musical paprika, and who shared the program with violinists and vocalists was under probing attack.

The May 1873 *enfusillade* by Rubinstein demolished the old conventions. In a series of seven Farewell Concerts of generous, some thought tedious, length, he alone entertained the immense audiences at Steinway Hall in the recital format. Sold as a subscription series for ten dollars, or one dollar per concert, reserved seats two dollars, the first recital focussed on Bach, Handel, Scarlatti, and Mozart. The second was a half-dozen Beethoven piano sonatas; the third offered Schubert, Weber, and Mendelssohn; the fourth was all Schumann; the fifth presented Chopin expansively; while the sixth emphasized Liszt. The seventh and final recital consisted entirely of Rubinstein's own compositions; thirty-two of them were presented. While Anton Rubinstein was a man of immense musical ability, he also took note of the market. The final sounds heard in America from the Steinway under Rubinstein's hands were his Variations on Yankee Doodle. It was reported that the Rubinstein concert series grossed $350,000, about $3.7 million in today's currency, or nearly a half-million dollars per month. By today's standards a Rubinstein performance was an immense bargain; a ticket cost about twenty current dollars. In contemporary Manhattan, routine recitals by the modestly distinguished can easily cost half again as much.

In all likelihood the return to Europe was aptly timed, for the American critics, at first dazzled by Rubinstein, had become habituated to genius. Of the last recital the *Times* critic wrote, "If we make exception in favor of a few of his melodies and his 'German' waltz, we confess that his writings for piano seem to us rather unimaginative in point of thought and rather labored in treatment." "Yankee Doodle" did not escape censure. The piece was "prepared in accordance with all the canons of art and (as to selection, at least, we opine) in opposition to all canons of taste. . . . No genius can dignify 'Yankee Doodle,' and though the eminent pianist gravely set about clothing the theme in all the pomp and circumstance of a Liszt fantasia, we do not believe that for a moment he was in doubt of the result." Steinway Hall "was filled to repletion . . . and when the vast throng rose to its feet, and became animated with myriads of waving kerchiefs, the spectacle was one not soon to be out of mind." Enthusiasm had been transmuted to ennui, at least among critics, if not the public.

While young Maurice Grau was nominally the impresario, it was William Steinway who functioned as Rubinstein's business manager. On the last full day of the pianist's American sojourn William visited "Rubinstein at 9 A.M. Look over all his documents with him, at 6 P.M. go to supper with him at Cafe Brunswick, present M. Grau, Albert Schirmer and I." Unlike many of William's social encounters, the dinner with Rubinstein was not described as a "jolly time, drink beer, home 3 A.M." The next morning, a Saturday and the day of Rubinstein's departure from the New World, William wrote, "Call on Rubinstein at 8 1/2 A.M., give him all his documents and obtain a little certificate from him." The words "little certificate" carry the dull thud of chagrin 120 years later. In 125 words or less, Rubinstein tendered the obligatory endorsement of Steinway pianos, characterizing them as "unrivalled" and having the "capacity of enduring the severest trials. For during all my long and difficult journeys all over America, in a very inclement season, I used and have been enabled to use your pianos . . . with the most eminent satisfaction and effect." Liszt wrote that Steinways were a "glorious masterpiece," Berlioz called them "magnificent . . . splendid and essentially noble," while Wagner would write that he missed his "Steinway Grand as one misses a beloved wife." Rubinstein's endorsement was both tepid and brief by comparison.

Thus ended the last recorded contact between the maestro and William in America. The meeting was short; unlike most departures of his friends and associates, William did not accompany Anton Rubinstein to the Hoboken docks. By noon William and Albert were at the Morgan Ironworks inspecting the new boiler and engine for their yacht, *Mozart.* That evening William was at the Liederkranz conducting the chorus, and Anton Rubinstein, aboard the *Donau,* was eastbound through the blackness of the Atlantic night. Though he lived, performed, taught, and composed for another two decades, Anton Rubinstein never returned to America.

In the wake of the *Donau* and despite William's palpable disappointment, there was profound change. No longer was classical music the province of a small coterie of necromantically inclined connoisseurs. No longer was it necessary for piano music to be interspersed with vocal and violin performances. No longer was it required that a piano virtuoso play primarily his own compositions. Anton Rubinstein, through the power of his playing, gave a new respectability to the "executant." His performances propelled the pendulum of taste in a new arc, away from the "fashionable" music of De Meyer and Thalberg and Gottschalk and simultaneously toward the past and the future.

Twelve decades later those who listen to the sound of a Chopin nocturne on a Steinway grand in a concert hall or to a stereophonic broadcast in the night as they glide down the road at one mile per minute are, perhaps unknowingly, indebted to Anton Rubinstein and William Steinway. Those two men forever changed—during eight frenetic months in 1872 and 1873—the cultural landscape of America. They did not, however, get along particularly well.

Chapter 14

HANS IS EASILY RECOGNIZED

"In company with some ten thousand festively inclined Germans and Germano-Americans, we kept the season of Whitsuntide at Jones Wood yesterday," wrote a *New York Times* reporter in May 1866. "At 2 o'clock the districts on the east side of the city, where the Germans principally reside, were the scenes of active preparation for the carnival. . . . Half an hour later the bodies assembled in front of the German Assembly Rooms. . . . The procession was formed and proceeded to Jones Woods." Leading the parade the several miles uptown were the police, followed by a marching band. Then came, in order, the *sangerbunde* (or singing societies), another band, the sharp-shooters, another band, the gymnasts, and finally "Miscellaneous German Organizations" and another phalanx of police. The position of the singing societies was a clue to their status in the German community, and even among societies there were certain distinctions made.

Both Charles and William had leadership roles in the Liederkranz, perhaps the most prominent of the city's many *sangerbunde*, and for which the famous cheese was later named. Another well-known German singing society was the Arion, but there were dozens of these in metropolitan New York with names such as Colonia Teutona, Mozart Union, Harlem Mannerborn, Social Reform Union, Fidelia, and the Jersey City Sangerbund. Ostensibly amateur choral societies, the level of musical competence was often entirely professional, and some groups employed noted musicians as choral directors.

Leopold Damrosch, for example, was director of the Arion. The more prestigious societies limited their memberships and also had significant roles in the business and political life of the city, functioning as mediators of German political and economic power.

The Liederkranz had among its members men like Oswald Ottendorfer, a sometime-alderman and editor/proprietor of the *Staats-Zeitung*, the larger and politically more conservative of the city's two German-language daily newspapers: and John Hoffman, at one time the mayor of New York. Hoffman's membership suggests that a prime agenda of the Liederkranz may have been political. American-born, he spoke German poorly, and there is nothing to suggest he had musical talent, but only about one-third of Liederkranz members were actually members of the chorus.

The German choral societies also had a national organization. Beginning in 1857, they assembled once a year during the summer for a *sangerfest*, a multi-day competitive event in which their singing was judged. The New York Liederkranz was among the best of the choral societies, always competitive and frequently victorious among hundreds of participating organizations. The *sangerfests* were vast events. At the Philadelphia *sangerfest* of 1867, some sixty thousand persons were in attendance. The New York *sangers* assembled in the city two days before the Philadelphia event, some eighteen hundred men strong. "Having formed in a line," reported the *Times*, "with drums beating, bands playing and many colored flags flying gaily in the breeze, they marched through the Bowery and Broadway to City Hall. Here they were reviewed by Mayor Hoffman, whose appearance they hailed with enthusiastic cheers." The *sangers*, en masse, marched from City Hall to the Cortlandt Street ferry for Jersey City, there boarding special trains for Philadelphia.

William did not march in that Sunday parade; he was at a rented summer home in Long Branch, New Jersey, with his family. But on Monday he took the train to Philadelphia to join his Liederkranz brethren and later wrote in his diary, "Prize concert. L. K. sings beautifully. . . . After concert, take a bowl of Punch with Sangerbund. Very Jolly." The *Times* reported, on page one, that "the celebrated *Liederkranz* of New York sang Marsheras's well-known composition, 'Wie Kama Liebe,' and at the close they were cheered by the audience, whose enthusiasm had already become aroused by the previous efforts of the singers from Baltimore." The correspondent was not particularly pleased with the choice of repertoire: "There seems to have been committed a great mistake in the selection of pieces by some of the societies, the compositions being generally calculated to suit the German taste for the sublime and sentimental only, and anything like lighter or more pleasing music, better suited to the general taste, being set aside." While the Germans sang for the Germans, they were not exclusionary or unfriendly, and there were immense crowds of spectators. A German undertaker "actually had an arch over his door with the word '*Willkomman*' (welcome) inscribed in the center. The intention may have been good, but the invitation was too suggestive for general acceptance," commented the anonymous *Times* reporter.

The next day William learned after a picnic: "Liederkranz gets the First prize, a fine banner. Very jolly, I have to make a number of German and English speeches." Back in New York a few days later, the society held a Grand Concourse to celebrate their victory, to which seven hundred persons came. "I preside," William told the future, "and also conduct *Wasserose* and our prize song, both of which are sung most splendidly."

While Charles was president of the Liederkranz for a brief term before his death, William's involvement was long and intense. He was president of the society for more than a dozen years and raised large sums for the organization, made major donations, was a trustee, became deeply involved in the construction of the society's building, purchased Liederkranz bonds for himself and others, bought land for a summer Liederkranz resort, and sometimes organized the annual masquerade ball held each winter.

This was a bizarre event in which people appeared in elaborate costumes, apparently by the thousands. "For many years," commented the *Times*, "this festival has been held in high favor by the best of our people, the purchase of tickets being found in every circle of art and literature, bound by no national ties, confined by no hamperings of prejudice." In some years even the cavernous Academy of Music was filled with costumed revelers dressed as scorpions, dragons, apes, witches, wizards, wasps, beetles, and all manner of personages and creatures. "The intent was to give one the idea of Pandemonium, and the idea was certainly given," observed the reporter. A surviving engraving shows a Liederkranz member costumed as a giant but lifelike chicken. However strange, the event was also sufficiently wholesome that children attended, often in costume themselves, and stayed until the festivities ceased early the next morning. The purpose, of course, was to raise money for the Liederkranz, and with tickets selling for up to one hundred dollars—roughly one thousand dollars today—the Liederkranz Costume Ball was eminently successful as a fund-raiser.

The New York German community was subject to many condescending reports of their activities. At a regular spring outdoor festival in 1866 a reporter observed that "dancing, drinking, shooting, drinking, jumping, drinking, scupping, drinking, flirting, drinking, and all that sort of Teutonized merriment which so thoroughly marks the nationality of the participators" was in evidence. Ethnic distinctions were readily and publicly made by most persons, if not all; even the globe-girdling and sophisticated Gottschalk did not hesitate to record his views of Germans: "I call German the countrymen of Schiller, Goethe, Mendelssohn and Beethoven; and Dutch [an American phonetic corruption of *Deutsch*] those whose only characteristic traits of their mother country are love of beer, a cordial hatred of every person who combs his hair regularly, sometimes washes his hands and has the unpardonable weakness not to circumscribe his geographical notions by the Rhine or Danube."

One of the German social practices disapproved by some New York citizens was Sunday entertainments and accompanying beer drinking. "One of our reporters," wrote the *Times*, "has an almost romantic interest in our German immigrant population, and has studied their character and habits with the deepest interest." There followed a tour of the "German quarter" on the Sabbath, documenting many instances of "Sunday profanation." At the Odeon the investigator found that "the libations are peculiarly Americo-German, in quantity and quality. Lager-bier, and plenty of it, . . . goes down the throats of the devotees, young and old; and either the steam created by the contact of a liquid with a heated surface ascends and fills the air, or some weed of Virginia origin is burned freely, and fills the air, and sends out its odors, we can hardly tell which, so blended are the fumes of lager-bier and tabac."

Working up a lather of moral indignation, the correspondent was particularly appalled at the banner over the Volks Garten announcing *Eine grosses sacred Concert*. "But you become a little skeptical . . . when you read the programme," observed the reporter. On the bill was a comic operetta in four acts, a one-act play called *The Beautiful Milleress, or a Secret Passion*, vaudeville acts, ballet, and a grand orchestra concert. "It all looks very *grand*, but not very *sacred* . . . and none of them [the audience of 350, including children] seemed to be imbibing anything more sacred than bad lager," wrote the observer.

"Discarding all ultra views of temperance, and disavowing sympathy with extreme 'Puritan' notions of the Sabbath, we cling to the old-fashioned idea that there is a better way of spending Sunday than in tippling, theater-going and gambling. Good citizens are made of sterner stuff . . . the wholesale manner of desecrating the Sabbath, accompanied with wholesale drinking, rises into . . . the leading cause of the rampant crime and disorder which infest our city," opined the *Times* correspondent. The crescendo of moral righteousness now reached its peak with a concern for "the future of those thousands of young lads seen in a single Sunday night in places of sinful diversion. Whose sons are they? Have they mothers to weep over them? Have they homes to go to? What security has society from rowdyism and disorder if our youth are corrupted systematically and educated in vice? Is it wise to leave the nests of vipers undisturbed . . . ?" The "nests" were, in fact, left "undisturbed" as the issue of Sunday drinking and entertainment raged on for decades across a great cultural chasm. On one side were the working class "Dutchmen" numbering in the hundreds of thousands, who sought something to supplement a church service on their only day of rest. On the other were the moral reformers who saw *lagerbier* and *volksgartens* as the great incubator of vice, crime, and social decay. There was, of course, an alternative: at Steinway Hall on many Sundays there were genuine sacred concerts as the Liederkranz, the Arion, the Theodore Thomas Orchestra, and others performed the religious works of the masters. They were, of course, Germans, not Dutchmen.

Like many stereotypes, the perceptions of Germans contained the occasional molecule of truth. The statewide 1875 New York census revealed a few trace elements of veracity. The tabulations show that while persons of German origin constituted 7.8 percent of the state's population, they were heavily concentrated in certain occupations and trades. Germans comprised the largest single ethnic group making cigars; 44.1 percent of all those in the trade were born in Germany. Among wine and liquor dealers the Germans were also heavily represented, again the largest group at about 43 percent. Germans working in the brewing industry were an immense 60.6 percent of the total persons so employed. While the census is silent on the *consumption* of alcoholic beverages and tobacco by various ethnic groups, the Teutonic domination of these trades likely generated disapproval among the many who viewed beer, wine, whiskey, and tobacco as corrosive agents attacking the fabric of society.

English language reports of German gatherings invariably mention the drinking of *lagerbier*. Among the more peculiar of these festivities were the *scheutzenfests*, target-shooting contests held in Central Park or Jones Wood, usually in June. The occasional stray round that broke a window or struck a bystander seemed to be no impediment to the continuation of these annual events, nor did the firing of rifles next door to an illuminating gas works. Covering one *scheutzenfest*, a *Times* writer noted that the "Germans have an intenser national fondness for social organization than any other people. . . . There is something sensible in the way the Germans set about enjoying themselves." To some at least, large crowds of persons shooting guns and drinking beer, when amply supervised by the police, was constructive urban recreation and thoroughly German.

"Hans is easily recognized," observed one piece on German-Americans, "no matter how he may strive to look as though he had never worn short jackets with bell-buttons and a queer little tail, nearly up to his shoulders." Recognition was evidently so simple that the writer did not report the visual correlates of Teutonicity.

Adopting New York sartorial customs was not merely a matter of fashion. *New York Musical World* reported an incident with two German musicians, "one with a bugle, one with a clarinet," who were set upon by a street gang near City Hall and forced to play "Hail, Columbia." The terrified musicians were then commanded to lead an impromptu parade. "Before marching was really commenced, however, one of them made his escape. The other was then hustled about and driven up St. Mark's Place toward the house of the Mayor." The man ran into the basement, whereupon "the mob surrounded the house, and bellowed, 'Fetch out the Dutch Devil.' The occupants of the house, afraid of having it sacked, drove him out. . . .

He was again seized by the crowd . . . and dragged to the Mayoral residence. He was there stationed before the door and ordered to salute the Mayor. He attempted, but there were two reasons why he did not succeed—his instrument was ruined and his breath was exhausted for one day." This item was provided as light reading among articles on harmonic theory and a critique of the Philharmonic Society of Brooklyn.

Musicality was another element in the "native American's" perceptual matrix of German immigrants, albeit a more positive one in the sense of social benefit than the production and sale of beer and tobacco. There was a Teutonic hegemony in music as well. Of the 2,540 professional musicians in New York State in 1875, nearly 40 percent came from Germany. This was more than five times the German proportion of the general population and comprised the single largest ethnic group. Among the 1,859 pianomakers uncovered by the 1875 census, about 53 percent were of German origin, outnumbering American pianomakers by a ratio of five to three. Statistically, the Germans dominated both the production of music and musical instruments. In New York City there was probably an even greater German domination of the music trades, for it was there that the largest number of Germans lived (at least 165,000), as well as the vast majority of pianomakers (62 percent) and musicians (71 percent). For the Steinways, New York was therefore the ideal base of operations; the men with the skills to produce the instruments *and* play them shared with the family a common background of language and culture.

While the primary programmatic emphasis at Steinway Hall was musical, there were many other events. A dramatic reading was given by Edwin Forrest, one of the precipitators of the Astor Place riot of 1849; but easily the most famous to read at the hall was Charles Dickens. "Meet Charles Dickens at our Hall," wrote William in his diary on Sunday, December 8, 1867. Dickens, who had not been in America for a quarter-century, opened his tour in Boston, perhaps under the assumption that the city was, as it had been, the nation's cultural capital. New York was his second stop, and Steinway Hall the venue of choice. "Sales of tickets for Chas. Dickens, a great crowd," observed William. The scalpers were busy, the bookstores were crowded, and at least some of the city's photographers were doing well selling images of the famous author. William, despite a very bad cold, was present on opening night.

The hall was filled and even standing room was sold. Dickens, claimed the *Times*, "will take as high a place . . . in the immortal literature of the richest language now spoken or written on the earth" as Sir Walter Scott. "He has given as great delight to the world, and has moved far more deeply and touched more powerfully the deepest springs of emotion and affection in the human heart than even that great master of human nature and the English tongue." From these words it can be inferred that within a year of opening, the hall was being used by William to reach the mainstream of

179

American culture, to alloy values held in general esteem, and to extend the name Steinway beyond the boundaries of Teutonicity and even beyond music. *English tongue* was perhaps the key phrase. Whether this was intuitive or calculated cannot be known, for William Steinway was not a man who committed his strategic plans to paper.

So successful were the Dickens readings that two more groups of them were scheduled, and Dickens spent more than a month in Manhattan. He was, by report, a talented reader of his own work. At the second evening of readings with selections from *David Copperfield* and *Bob Sawyer's Party*, the reviewer commented that the audience "seemed to forget, in their enjoyment, that they were listening to a stranger. . . . Every eye was bent on the reader's expressive face, and the contagion of his mood seemed to pass directly to every individual in the room like a subtle magnetic influence." William witnessed that reading too, without his wife and children.

By the second series of readings, critics were, as was their custom, beginning to detect flaws in Charles Dickens's presentations; his "voice was neither powerful or flexible. It is heard to best advantage in purely narrative passages, where a slight emphasis impresses or illumines the onward path of the story." Dickens also had a slight lisp. But there was great drama, and the crowds continued to pour into Steinway Hall. The *Times* described the routine: "Precisely at 8 o'clock the gas is turned up and Dickens is turned on. He walks rapidly to the desk; deposits there a book, which looks like a postage stamp album; bows to the audience; looks over them for the most part, into them occasionally, turns over a few pages of the album mechanically with his long fingers and still-longer thumb, and then says in a breath, and with scarcely so much as a comma's pause, "Ladies and Gentlemen, I shall have the honor of reading to you tonight the story of . . ." So it went in that December of 1867: a famous author and a house filled nightly.

As Christmas neared, audiences continued to throng to the hall, each person trekking by the displays of glistening rosewood and ivory that were Steinway & Sons pianos. The authentically Dickensian could be found in places other than Steinway Hall that holiday season, for there were those in the city whose lives did not require injections of vicarious pathos. On Christmas Day 1867, a *Times* reporter canvassed the city, describing the celebration. At the downtown churches he heard hymns sung and organs played. On Ward's Island there were twenty-two hundred men, women, and children under the care of the Board of Emigration charities. At the Home for Little Wanderers the children were found enjoying a hearty turkey dinner. At the Five Points Charities, "dedicated to saving women and children from careers of vice and degradation," those present did not receive a dinner, although there had been a fine Thanksgiving feast. They were treated instead to "most motherly and excellent Christian counsel." At the Newsboys' Lodging House, two hundred Christmas dinners were served, and gifts of shoes, boots, and caps were donated. These were among the more fortunate of the city's nonfiction Dickensian characters. Others were in the Tombs, the city's aptly named prison. One boy there was jailed for stealing shoes, another for the theft of newspapers. Then there was "John Johnson, a bright and intelligent boy of twelve years, in custody for stealing toys, and while he hung his head at the confession of guilt, he seemed quite anxious that his parents at No. 328 Eighth Avenue should be informed of his arrest." A few blocks and a world away from the Tombs, William's cold still vexed him, and his throat became sore, but by Christmas Eve he was "quite well." On Christmas Day the tree was aglow, and William Steinway had a "very jolly time with children."

International renown was a scarce phenomenon in the nineteenth century and, after the starbursts of Dickens and Rubinstein illumined the cultural sky, Steinway Hall was largely populated with entertainments and artists whose fame was more transitory, if not less deserving. After a nine-year competitive slumber on the artistic front, perhaps resulting from the Gottschalk scandal, Chickering and Sons awakened in 1875 and brought to the United States Hans Von Bulow through the efforts of Bernard Ullmann, easily the most ruthless of New York impresarios. Although he once had a critic beaten by the New York police and threatened to shoot a competitive promoter, even Ullmann could not control Hans Von Bulow.

During a lacuna in his European bookings, Hans Von Bulow signed with Ullmann for an American tour. According to his correspondence, he was to receive compensation at a rate of six thousand francs per fortnight, or about five hundred dollars per week. Theodore wrote Von Bulow that Steinway & Sons would not take half his earnings as Ullmann did and that Ullmann and his associates were guilty of unclear wrongs against Theodore at the Paris Exhibition of 1867. This was disingenuous; when Bernard Ullmann offered William sponsorship of Von Bulow's tour, William declined without deliberation. Hans Von Bulow became a Chickering artist by default. Whether he knew that he was signed to play on Ullmann's— and America's—second choice is not known. Privately to a friend he praised Chickering's pianos highly, saying that while before he had played "like a pig," he now played "like a god" and that he was practicing four hours per day. William learned that Von Bulow's debut in Boston was a "fair success."

Hans Von Bulow's New York arrival did not inspire a serenade, as did Rubinstein's, although his reception was by no means cold. Inaugurating a new hall which Chickering & Sons built in Manhattan, his reviews were initially positive, with some preferring his measured and intellectual renderings to those of Rubinstein. William was there and wrote, ". . . with wife to the Opening of Chickering Hall, Von Bulow playing splendidly. Acoustics good. Hall very neat, entrance narrow and steps. Am at Delmonico's with wife . . . Chickering there too." William witnessed the performance through a cold fog of business and personal anxiety. When Von Bulow appeared in America, the nation was but halfway through the longest depression in its history. Economic activity contracted for sixty-five months, longer by half than the famous Crash of '29. The words "with wife" must have brought to William the most intense personal sadness, for in the margin of that same page appears the entry "Pay Hogan $50." Hogan was a private detective hired to investigate the activities of William's wife. That William and Regina attended the Von Bulow opening together was a matter of social form, not substance.

The wisdom of the Steinway decision to allow Von Bulow to represent Chickering soon became apparent. On one occasion Bulow kicked over a placard with the Chickering name on it, announcing to the audience that he was not an advertisement. He cursed a conductor for slovenly direction and an audience for insufficient appreciation. Reviews, as was the custom, became increasingly critical and audiences shrank. Hans Von Bulow cited his health and cut his tour short. Unlike the packed houses for the farewell concerts of Rubinstein, Von Bulow's last New York appearances were before embarrassingly small audiences. The *Tribune* reviewer felt compelled to note that "The better the concert, the smaller the attendance. The taste of New York's great public is yet somewhat crude." Von Bulow remained in America for a few months before sailing to Europe, acrimony and disappointment gurgling in his wake. It is probable that Hans Von Bulow did not help sell many Chickering pianos.

Unlike the sporadic efforts of C. Frank Chickering, it was William's goal to maintain a continuous Steinway presence before the public, both in New York and nationally. Many of the pianists Steinway underwrote were women: Arabella Goddard, Annette Essipoff, and Therese Carreño were among them. The tours continued in what became a standard format. Steinway provided the piano and a tuner for major artists, advertised on the back page of preprinted programs, advised their dealers of the tour dates for local promotion, and basked in the reflected glory of patronage and association. The artists invariably tendered letters of endorsement. While William did not develop this format, he did bring it to a homogenized perfection, the residuum of which remains in the cultural consciousness.

There were other events at Steinway Hall as well. For a brief time banjo contests were in vogue. Not surprisingly, the hall was the site of many charitable events for the German community: Lutheran church benefits, concerts by not only the Liederkranz, but the Arion and Oratorio societies; plus various relief and hospital charity functions were held each year. For such events the use of the hall was often free. There were also experiments in cultural uplift; Theodore Thomas produced special programs for children and also for workingmen.

While the primary emphasis of Steinway Hall events was musical, there was no shortage of lectures. Among the more prescient of these was an 1877 demonstration of the musical telephone, the invention of Elisha Gray, a formidable competitor of Alexander Graham Bell and Thomas Edison for supremacy in telephony. Bell himself was in the audience that first night. "The rush to Steinway Hall last evening was unparalleled. The stairways, previous to the hour of beginning, were blocked, so that entrance was a matter of dishevelment and ruffled temper," reported the *Times*. The crush of the "paying audience, and a very miscellaneous one," was less caused by the renderings of the Young Apollo Club, piano arias by Mademoiselle Carreño, Sauret, and sundry vocalists, than Professor Gray's exhibition of his invention. The demonstration was preceded by a musical program, about which the reporters were amiably diffuse.

Shortly after 9:00 P.M. a telegraph operator, who ambled onto the stage, was greeted with waves of applause, followed by a stagehand, who deliberately positioned two pianos, one of which had on its top an apparatus made of rectangular hollow wooden tubes, brass fastenings, and electromagnets. The device was about two and one-half feet high and nearly as long as the grand piano on which it rested, its silken wires trailing off the stage to the right. Another round of applause greeted Professor Gray.

Elisha Gray announced to the audience that he proposed to show "not a musical instrument merely, but something wonderful in electricity." Gray allowed that he did not know what the audience expected: "Some, he supposed, had come to hear a full orchestra, others nothing. Both would be disappointed." There was laughter. The professor averred that the operation of his musical telephone was complicated and could not be easily explained in the short time available; he was also undoubtedly aware of his competitor's presence in the audience. There followed, after a few clicks of a regular telegraph key and rapt stillness in the audience, the melodies of "Home, Sweet Home" and "Yankee Doodle" played by pianist Professor Friedrich Boscovitz—who was not in New York but in the Chestnut Street Western Union office in Philadelphia. The simple melodies, distinct but soft, were met with uproarious applause by the audience, although the reporter for the *New York Daily Graphic* commented that "the music was not remarkable in an aesthetic sense." *Leslie's Illustrated Newspaper* described the transmitting apparatus as "consisting of a sixteen-note keyboard, the lower or bass octaves being adjusted to the sound of the haut-boy, and the other octaves to the sound of the clarinet and flute." In Philadelphia there was naught but a whirring sound. "Further than this, it was the same as pressing down the keys of a piano detached from the key-board and the strings." The audience of Philadelphia dignitaries melted away when they found that the performance there was silent. The telegraph clicked again, and Gray's musical telephone, powered by a 300-cell battery of perhaps 400 volts, sounded the then-familiar melodies of "Come Gentil" and "You'll Remember Me."

During the applause and cheers Gray moved his mechanism to the floor from the piano to demonstrate that it did not need the piano to operate.

Becoming somewhat fainter, though still with the sound of a reed organ, the electrical recital continued through several more songs, finishing with an encore of "Yankee Doodle." "Professor Boscovitz performed nearly all the music with one hand, seldom requiring the use of both," noted *Leslie's*. The sharp-eared *Times* reporter noticed that during the "Last Rose of Summer" one note was completely absent, his intolerance not ameliorated by Elisha Gray's explanation that the recent rains would allow "electricity to escape from the wires . . . which would pass under three rivers" before arriving at the New York Western Union office, there to be transmitted to the hall. "The telephonic portion of the entertainment, which, as a novelty, was highly entertaining, though, unless an almost incredible improvement be effected, it is difficult to see how the transmission of music over the new instrument can be of any permanent or practical value, the inferiority of the reproduction in contrast with the performance being very great." Such was the assessment of the *Times*.

The audience, however, was "cheering heavy" and "getting excited," according to the telegraphic dispatches. They had witnessed, although they could not rationally extrapolate it, the birth of the electronic music synthesizer and the electromagnetic transmission of music. It was the ultimate irony that Steinway & Sons premiered a technology that marked the onset of the eclipse of the piano as the "solitary muse of the parlor," to be replaced ultimately by a plethora of devices that would one day provide passive entertainment in tens of millions of homes.

With rare precision, the onset of the age of electronic entertainment can be set as Monday, April 2, 1877, at 9:14 P.M. Philadelphia time, the address 109–11 West Fourteenth Street, New York, New York, in a place called Steinway Hall. William's diary entry read, "Dark rainy day. Business wretched for the week past. In afternoon Telephone experiments, in evening at Steinway first Telephone Concert quite successful." The next morning William busied himself with deeds and taxes, going home at noon to walk with his children. It seemed, in all detectable ways, an ordinary routine, but the night before the distant future had flickered into view, a land seen in a flash of lightning. At Steinway Hall there was the foreshadowing, removed and tentative, of music detached from its creators in space and time, encoded as signals, electrons pushed from atom to atom, musical information pulsing from Philadelphia to New York, there transduced into sound. Volta, Ampere, and Ohm met Yankee Doodle at Steinway Hall, and the crowd went wild.

Chapter 15

THE DESPICABLE
DEPRAVED CHARACTER

*N*ew Year's Eve, 1875—". . . Tretbar & wife, Dachauer & wife, Albert & wife come. Tretbar, Reck, Albert & I play Skat in which I win 50 cents, but had lost One Dollar in 66, with Reck before supper. . . . [A]t 12 we congratulate each other, then sit down to a light supper, remain up til 3 A.M. By a super human effort I contrive not to show my mental sufferings too apparently while my wife seems to enjoy herself very much, and thus pass from the year 1875, the most horrible year I have ever lived through, into the year 1876 with the settled conviction on my mind that for me all enjoyment of life is forever gone, and only praying to the Almighty God to extend my life long enough that I can put all our firm's affairs as well as my private matters into such a shape as not to distress my brothers, yet to take care of my children properly, and shield them from disgrace."

That night William was in the company of his closest associates. Tretbar was also a German immigrant whom William had hired from the Steinway agent in Canada, Nordheimer & Company. Ten years along in a four-decade career with the house, Charles F. Tretbar was already an insider. As a preparer of the firm's annual inventories, complete with arithmetic errors, and a witness to the signing of wills and other estate matters, Tretbar was the only non–family member who understood the wealth of the Steinways. Charles Tretbar also worked on behalf of the family in sensitive matters such as the Oaks case, talking to the press and delivering subpoenas.

Evidence suggests that it was he who was in charge of both sales and activities at Steinway Hall.

Henry Reck was an engineer of sorts, responsible for the planning of Steinway & Son's real estate development and various construction projects, such as the vast family mausoleum at Greenwood Cemetery. He lived in a company-owned apartment next door to Steinway Hall. Dachauer's role remains mysterious; a church organist at the still-standing Saint Ann's on Twelfth Street, a composer of masses, a sometime-owner of a music store, he emigrated to America from Switzerland before 1856 with his brother. Louis Dachauer's business role is unclear, and the connection to Steinway & Sons might be described as close friend and unofficial operative.

Albert was functionally in charge of all manufacturing operations. The pianos William promoted with passion and brilliance Albert built with profound competence, managing the militant 420-man work force, scouring the country for the finest woods, and supervising constant revision and expansion of the Steinway factories. He was by 1875 a thoroughly practical man, quiet if not shy, who preferred working on or sailing the steam yacht *Mozart* to the society of artists. Like his brothers, Albert enjoyed target shooting and hunting. No matter how celebrated the event, Albert was rarely found at Steinway Hall; he seemed to be present only when the plumbing or heating systems needed improvement. If Albert ever heard Rubinstein, Essipoff, Carreño, Nilsson, Thomas, or any of the others in performance, William, uncharacteristically, did not note it. Albert, his wife, Louisa, and children, Henriette and Ella, lived uptown in one of the family brownstones on Fifty-second Street. That New Year's Eve they had travelled the thirty blocks downtown to William and Regina's residence at 26 Gramercy Park.

The elegant facade of 26 Gramercy, the bustle of activity, the holiday gathering of close friends, and the familiar routine of the complex three-handed card game skat that William played almost every night were insufficient to shield him. The customary became empty, if not repellant. William Steinway had learned during 1875 that he was not the father of the six-year-old boy he thought was his son.

There had been Christmas gifts under the tree for the children: George, the oldest boy, received a cap gun; Paula, magnetic fish; and Alfred, a pop gun. For himself William bought a Colt revolver, and to Regina he gave one hundred dollars on Christmas Eve. Christmas morning William spent in the store, testing Theodore's new piano design commemorating the one hundredth anniversary of the nation. It was called the Centennial Grand, and there were two of them. One cased in walnut and tuned to the "French Pitch" of 435 hertz William described as "being soft"; the other, in rosewood, was "high-pitched"—probably the Steinway-standard 457 hertz—and "brilliant." That afternoon William visited the family uptown and played skat with his nephews Charles Steinway and Henry Ziegler. In the evening he went to the Liederkranz and once again played skat.

On Sunday he was back at the store, then walked the several miles uptown to visit Albert and predictably played skat. At dinner Monday night with his lawyer, George Cotterill, William opened the subject of divorce, but not with a discussion of his own problems: "Have prudent Conversation with him as to Divorce matters mentioning Steigertahl." Steigertahl was an employee to whom William had loaned money for a divorce after Mrs. Steigertahl chose to have a "carnal connection" with a coal dealer she met at the annual Steinway & Sons workmen's picnic in the summer of 1874. William testified for Albert Steigertahl during the divorce, an inadvertent preview of events to come. Whether by accident or design, at 11:30 Monday evening William saw a man in the fancy goods trade named Louis Stern. "Have a long talk with him during which I became finally convinced that the worst I feared is true. Have exciting talk at home which lasts to 3 A.M. No sleep."

The next day a cold rain fell; but William, tired and depressed, had a business to run and social obligations to meet. Orders were slow and no cash was coming in; it would be necessary to sell commercial paper soon. That evening William, Regina, Albert, and Louisa went to the Germania Theater. On Thursday a cousin from Saint Louis appeared, whom William quickly dispatched to his mother's. William's throat was sore and his voice hoarse. "I feel dreadfully downhearted, seeing no escape whatsoever from the dreadful trouble and its inevitable consequences." That night William played skat with Albert, young Charles, and Henry Steinway. "I lose 85 cents, Charles winning heavily."

On New Year's Eve day there were mortgages to be paid and deeds to be signed; money was available, for twenty thousand dollars in Steinway & Sons commercial paper had been quickly sold at 5 percent. Perhaps in preparation for what lay ahead, William began to sweep marginal activities from his life and tendered his resignations to the Palette Club and the New York Municipal Society. In the wet gloom of the final day of 1875, William Steinway made all possible efforts to conceal the truth from his friends and family. His is but one muffled voice heard through the closed door of time. What his wife, brother, nephews, and friends saw and thought and felt that New Year's Eve in Gramercy Park is forever gone.

Regina Roos Steinway appears only in low relief in William's life. There are scant clues to her personality or thoughts, save those filtered through William's responses to her. William's brothers thought her beautiful. To cope with the fractiously verbal Steinway family as an equal, Regina must have had an ample intelligence. That she possessed both social skill and cultural sophistication is a given, for she regularly accompanied William and other family members to the theater, the opera, concerts, and balls.

These were the venues through which William enhanced and extended both his business and personal prestige. She appears to have been accepted in the society of her female relatives and also visited independently with the wives of William's powerful German-American friends. But ultimately Regina Roos Steinway chose to wage open warfare on William and his family with the supreme social weapon of Victorian America: sex.

There are few clues to how this came about. That William and Regina had an active physical relationship is clear from the records William kept. Early in the marriage they made love as many as six times a day and frequently five times in the early months of marriage. The number 300 appears alongside William's running tally on day 207 of their marriage, but there are no insights into whether Regina was ardent or submissive. In the early days of 1862 William wrote that Regina "is indisposed during the night and in her sufferings pinches and kicks me," and the next day noted, "find Regina pretty well." At the close of 1866 William recorded that "my wife has nervous attack, over soon."

Regina Roos Steinway's first ordeal with childbirth occurred when she was nineteen. William's narrative begins on Wednesday, January 22, 1862: "On arriving home at 6:40 P.M. find my wife in bed with symptoms of her approaching confinement. After supper Charles and myself move the bed into my room & send for Mrs. Merkel, midwife who examines Reg. and believes that the confinement will take place. I go to bed at 11 P.M. upstairs, Mrs. Merkel & Sophie [Charles's wife] attending my wife. At 1 o'clock A.M. Sophie awakes me, Mrs. Merkel having gone home, thinking nothing will take place during the night."

William continued his unusually detailed account: "I attend my wife and lay down with her, when all at once she says 'I think the water broke, I am flowing.' I immediately examine her and find the blood trickling from her very fast. . . . Send Theresa [a servant] after Mrs. Merkel and run myself to Dr. Schnetter who both arrive with me at 1:40 A.M. Mrs. Merkel stays up with Reg. while Dr. Schnetter stays upstairs & I stay on couch which we drew into the bedroom."

At seven the next morning the doctor examined Regina and, in consultation with the midwife, forecast that they would not be needed until 10:00 A.M. At noon the doctor returned and ventured his opinion that the baby would be born in the early evening.

"At 1 P.M. my wife is seized with pains which occur regularly every four minutes, she is in labor until 2:30 P.M. when she is delivered of a dead baby boy, who evidently has been dead 24 or more hours before birth." After the birth Dr. Schnetter reappeared and "pronounces it a premature birth by at least a month. My wife feels much relieved after the birth." William telegraphed Regina's brother and wrote her parents, "acquainting them with the facts." In the evening William went to the undertaker and ordered a coffin and a carriage, then retired for the night. "Sophie stays up with my wife, who does as well as can be expected."

The next day William, Henry's wife Ernestine, Charles's wife Sophie and William's sister Doretta "proceed in a Carriage to Greenwood Cemetery to inter the dead infant. . . . The cemetery is covered with a white sheet of snow, the child is buried in the same grave where Chas. little girl was interred." From the cemetery William went to the store. When he returned home that night, he found his mother and father with Regina, who was now in fever. "I try my voice," wrote William "and find that I am a little hoarse." The day he buried his firstborn child, William Steinway then went to work and came home to sing. He also gave his wife four dollars and fifty cents.

The next day, a Saturday, Regina's mother arrived from Buffalo. William wrote that he felt "unwell during the day & am fearful that I will not be in good voice for the concert in the eve." Nonetheless, William went to the Brooklyn Philharmonic concert that evening at which the Liederkranz performed, and he sang two solos. The first was "not very good," but the second was rewarded by "tremendous applause & encore, same song repeated." After the concert William drank champagne in Brooklyn. But from there he did not go home: "Stop at Pit drink and sing a few songs. Arrive home at 12:30 A.M. Mother in law stays up with wife."

Regina's ordeal was not yet over. Five days after the birth, a servant rushed to the store to tell William that his wife was very ill. Arriving home, William was told that Regina "had been raving & Dr. Schnetter ordered a mustard plaster placed on her stomach, which is left on about one hour, when Regina can no longer stand the terrible pains and burning and it has to be taken off. . . . We are all sadly frightened by the crisis." The next day William stayed home with his wife, using a messenger to send letters to the office. "Mother and myself place towels wrung in hot water on her stomach as hot as she can possibly stand them." There was more therapy. "In the eve. we draw with hot bottles which we made hot in boiling water, apply to the nipple & cool the bottles & this way we draw several spoons full of milk. I stay up with my wife, have to get up a great many times, but towards morning Regina sleeps pretty well." Two weeks after the onset of her first childbirth Regina Roos Steinway was able to dress and leave her bed for the afternoon. That day William bought Regina a copy of *Jane Eyre*.

No reliable statistics can be found for fetal deaths in New York or the deaths of mothers during childbirth during the 1860s, the years in which Regina bore her children. Yet an infant surviving birth was exposed to risks at least as great, if not greater, than those in the womb. For the year 1865 in Massachusetts, a pioneer in the recording of social statistics, almost one in five infants died during the first year of life. In some years the proportion reached one in four. The death rate for infants was higher than that for all those over age eighty. In New York City the infant death rate may have been much higher; a computation for 1867, an ordinary year in that there were no epidemics, suggests that about one-fourth of Manhattan babies died within one year.

Dr. Elmer Harris, Registrar of Vital Statistics, commented that "during the past twenty years every summer has witnessed a fearful slaughter of infants in New-York." This was the reason that every family that was financially able, as were the Steinways, fled Manhattan each summer for Long Island, the Jersey shore, or upstate New York. There the women and children decamped until the cooler days of September when the bacterial invasion of the city ebbed. In 1867 the *Times* declaimed that "adequate means should be at once devised to check the appalling death rate which these figures present. Otherwise the deaths in this City of infants bid fair soon to run *pari passu* with the births." That did not happen, nor did matters improve for many years.

In April 1863 Regina gave birth three months prematurely to another stillborn boy, suffering, in William's words, "pain beyond description." This time there was no midwife; Dr. Schnetter and William's mother handled the birth. So it came to be that Regina Roos Steinway issued two dead sons before her twentieth birthday.

The first live birth occurred in June 1865. William had changed doctors, and the new one, a Dr. Gardner, used chloroform to ease the anguish of nearly twenty-four hours of labor. "At 7:30 A.M. the baby is born which proves to be a little boy, very weak at first, but gradually picking up . . . after an hour or two eating spoons full of milk cream with sugar and a few drops of brandy," wrote William. "My wife feels very well. Great joy in our family. The baby was not full time by about three weeks." William was apparently not certain that the child, later christened George Augustus Steinway, would survive; for it was not until the next day that he telegraphed his Buffalo in-laws. Slightly more than two weeks later, mother and child were well enough for a ride through Central Park. But the baby still faced the statistical malignance of Manhattan infancy. George Augustus was just over eighteen months of age when the "diarrhoe" struck. Three doctors were in attendance, but after a week "George is so exhausted that we fear he is about to die, we are almost heartbroke." Because of or in spite of the "constant stimulants of brandy," young George rallied and recovered.

While the young boy was running the biological gauntlet that was Manhattan, Regina gave birth to another child in December 1866. "The baby is born and proves to be a fine, healthy girl, who screams lustily as soon as she is born." William's account of the birth of his daughter is both shorter and less enthusiastic than that of his son. After the customary lapse of a few months she was christened Paula Theoda.

Two years later Regina had yet another miscarriage, but on her twenty-sixth birthday, October 11, 1869, she again entered confinement under the care of Dr. Gardner. "At a few minutes before 7 A.M. a splendid, large, healthy boy, the very image of George, is born. I come into the room a few minutes afterwards and am overjoyed. I go with Dr. Gardner to our office, general rejoicing," noted William. "I telegraph to Theodore at Braunschweig 'Splendid Boy born, all well.' In the evening our servants drink champagne. At Liederkranz I treat two kegs of beer, afterwards drink champagne and seltzer." William's pleasure at the birth of another son was shared with most of the rest of the family: ". . . Georgie and Paula very fond of their little brother, Grandfather visits his newborn Grandson and is greatly pleased with him."

What Regina thought or felt, alone in a night of pain while William and the doctor slept, is unknown. Certainly she knew that the father of the "splendid" child about to be born was *not* William, but could have been a man called by William "the Jew Stern." The servants who drank celebratory champagne may have suspected as well, for they had witnessed events of which they would not speak for many years. The next day William, flush with fatherly pride, resumed his frenetic life. There was a business to run, lawyers to visit, songs to be sung, and mortgages to be signed. This, of course, was all routine.

In June 1870 the youngest "Steinway" was baptized Alfred Theodore, and the Steinway children had a party in the afternoon. In the evening the adults gathered to celebrate the baptism, and William noted that "at table Georgie makes a little speech." The party continued until the early hours of the next morning when it began to rain. "Very nice and jolly time," wrote William. Among the two-dozen guests was the *pianiste* Anna Mehlig.

There is little to indicate the course or causes of the deterioration in the relationship between William and Regina. Analysis of William's diary for the two prior years and the year of Alfred's birth shows that, proportionally, William spent less time with his wife and children than he did in other activities. By far the dominant activity in William's life at this time was the Liederkranz. More than 22 percent of all diary mentions involve the society. William frequently spent long evenings there, sometimes socializing, sometimes rehearsing choral performances, sometimes planning for the renowned Liederkranz Ball or other events. The Liederkranz was also a part of William's daytime routine, and he would frequently interrupt his business day to deal with club activities.

In second place among the diary mentions are business matters related to Steinway Hall, strikes, piano sales, visits with dealers, and similar items. Business accounts for about 12 percent of all diary entries. William's personal health accounts for about 10 percent of diary mentions; it was during these years that he first experienced the debilitating and painful rheumatism that would later render him immobile for days. William recorded sore throats, upset stomachs, and loose bowels with a diligence that might suggest self-absorption . . . until it is remembered that in Victorian New York a loose bowel might mean death in days from cholera.

Family meant much to William, and he visited often with his father and brothers "uptown" at the Fifty-second Street factory, but he was about twice as likely to go alone as with Regina. Visits uptown, alone or with his wife, account for about 10 percent of diary mentions. The business and social life of William Steinway were tightly related in many ways, and not the least of these was his attendance at musical, operatic, and dramatic performances, These accounted for about 7.5 percent of his recorded activities.

William was also more likely to go to a performance alone than with Regina. Regina receives but 6 percent of diary mentions, a scant sixty-two times in 1,095 days, William's children are cited in about 5.5 percent of the entries. William rarely spent an evening at home, but when he did, he was often writing business letters or revising Steinway sales catalogs. Time spent at home accounts for less than 10 percent of diary activity. Later in his life William's time at home was most often occupied in playing card games, skat, 66, and occasionally whist, almost always with his brothers, nephews, and male friends.

That William Steinway lived primarily in the society of men, at the Liederkranz, at work, and often at home is clear. For his time, this was routine. In his letters to William, Theodore writes of his clubs and musical societies in Germany; they too were exclusively male. The evidence suggests that German households in New York imported the traditions and practices of *das Vaterland*. If so, families were patriarchal, the model being a father who was distant and strong, perhaps to the point of severity, a mother whose role was sharply confined to child care and household management, and children who were expected to defer to authority. Education was a Teutonic key value, and this the Steinways definitely shared. William's brothers did not believe that American education was adequate and sent their sons to Germany for a "proper" education at a young age.

Whether Regina Roos Steinway chafed under the restrictions of the Teutonic family structure or those of a society that treated women as virtually unable to make responsible decisions is simply not known. Whether her behavior was grounded in sociopolitical beliefs or was simply that of an individual will forever be a mystery. But Regina Steinway chose, it appears, to live the life of "free love" that Victoria Woodhull advocated. The decision was costly.

William transmits few clues to the present. He "talked strongly" to his wife and her niece after they arrived home at 5:00 A.M. one summer morning in 1875. He recorded that he "felt somewhat sad during the last two days thinking over the beginning of 1869." His diary for those months enigmatically reveals that after the "splendid" Liederkranz Ball at the Academy of Music, William had "a great deal of trouble and takes a fearful cold." This was followed by a week in bed, disabled by rheumatism in the knees. A week of recovery followed. It was then that "wife tells me she is ———. I tell her it cannot be." A day later William's rheumatism again worsened and he began taking sulphur baths and applying turpentine to his knees. After a few more days in bed, William recovered to resume his life of Liederkranz meetings and evenings at concerts, the theater, and the opera. In April, William and Regina commemorated an eighth anniversary with supper at a restaurant. In May 1869 William calmly reported that "my wife thinks that for several days past she has felt signs of life of the child." The "cannot be" *was*—and William accepted it—thinking perhaps that there was an error in his recordkeeping. Routine domesticity prevailed as William and Regina selected decor for their newly purchased home in Gramercy Park.

By the fall of 1875, William and Regina had come to live parallel lives from the same address. William's diary mentions activities with his wife but two or three times per month during the winter. For the summer of 1875 the family rented a home at Nanuet, but William spent much time in the city launching an immense new project: the building of a bridge across the East River at Seventy-seventh Street. The bridge, three thousand feet long, was planned to connect Manhattan with Long Island via Blackwell's Island. Though Commodore Vanderbilt approved of the plan and William was elected president of the New York and Long Island Bridge Company, the bridge itself was never built.

Domestically, a governess, one Miss Reynolds, had been retained for the children, and Regina was free to move about, spending her summer at Nanuet and at Newport, Rhode Island. As summer turned to fall, William completed negotiations for a three-month tour by the *pianiste* Arabella Goddard. Respectably and inexpensively fortified against the impending Von Bulow invasion, William repaired to Nanuet.

There William and Regina talked. "After playing Skat, the long impending explanation occurs," wrote William, "and I suffer the tortures of Hell and pass a perfectly sleepless night, the most terrible I have ever lived through, by the discovery I make." The crisis continued the next day: "Dejected beyond description, I am almost unable to eat a morsel of food, my wife sick in bed. I can barely collect my thoughts, play Skat again in evening, lose $1.08. In bed at 11 P.M." William did not mention the whereabouts of the children during the crisis.

The next day, a Monday, William returned to Manhattan and forced himself to resume work: "My mental anguish is beyond description and is telling dreadfully on me. . . . Sleep at least a few hours during the night, towards morning in dream. . . . ." The dots were William's, whose suffering ebbed and flowed, forming eddies of anguish and vortices of despair. Two weeks later, again on a Sunday in Nanuet, William wrote, "Have further conversation with my wife which elicits all the details. No language can describe my utter wretchedness." The next night William and Regina were at Steinway Hall for the premiere of Arabella Goddard and the prima donna Therese Titiens.

William thought the performance a success, but that was not the reason that William slept "fairly under the circumstances." William Steinway had a plan; and the next day, after a talk with Attorney Cotterill, he went to the office of C. V. Hogan, agent. Mr. Hogan was not in but called at 8:30 the next morning at William's home. "I give him minute instructions about L Stn. He will commence operations tomorrow morning." Hogan was a private investigator who was about to look into the activities of a young man in the fancy goods trade, apparently of considerable charm, named Louis Stern. That evening William travelled uptown to audition the latest of Theodore's designs. "The new extra large Concert grand is in playable condition and seems to be of wonderfully large tone." This was the first mention of the now-legendary instrument, the Centennial Grand. Characteristically, William had substituted action for self-pity and felt better. For her birthday Regina received the customary gift of one hundred dollars— about twelve hundred dollars today—from William, and he gave each child five dollars to give to their mother.

A few days later William wrote, "I still have spells of extreme sadness on me, and my heart is torn by conflicting doubts and hopes as to A. [Alfred]." That night William and Regina talked. They had an "earnest and long conversation in which I go over the whole ground from 1868 up to the present time and elicit all the details so that I have a perfect insight into the whole matter. Sleep well and soundly afterwards." The next day William and Regina decided that she should "immediately" go to Buffalo, and that night William consulted with Theodore and "the whole family together," presumably partially disclosing his domestic situation. "At 10:30 A.M. my wife and Alfred start for Buffalo by fast train. It rains in torrents. . . . At 1 P.M. we drive to Hoboken, and Theodore sails with the steamer *Donau*. I am deeply excited and for hours cannot master my tears. The rain falls in torrents all day. Can hardly eat my supper and shortly after fall into the wildest paroxysms of grief." Cleaving to the family that remained, William played skat with Albert and Louise in the evening.

The next day, a Sunday, William went to work at the store and walked with Georgie and Paula. In the afternoon he prowled his daily journal, looking for clues to the destruction of his marriage. Out for a walk in the evening, he passed the Belvedere House on Fourteenth Street across from Steinway Hall. "See Stn playing cards and gaze at him for about half an hour then walk to L.K. Play Skat." As he did when his brothers died, William Steinway strode the city. "Yesterday afternoon walked through West 16th street and West 22nd street with a heavy heart." He may have been searching for the houses of assignation where Louis Stern consorted with his wife.

It was not long before detective Hogan appeared with a report on Louis Stern and an unexpected bonus, Stern's "memorandum book," which, Hogan told William, "he lost while intoxicated at 11th street." When Regina returned from Buffalo, William went "through Stns Memorandum book with wife, who is horrified & suffers much anguish." Presumably, Regina learned at this time that she was not the only woman in Louis Stern's life.

Day by day, life trickled on with an external resemblance to routine. In early November William voted Republican, rare for him, but he was a part of the throng that swept Tammany Hall and its infamous Tweed Ring from office. William bought stilts for the boys and taught little Alfred to walk on them. "I am still very sad and depressed in spirits brooding constantly over the terrible misfortune, and unable to concentrate my thoughts upon any other subject."

Pages slid from the calendar. Business conditions worsened, and both orders for pianos and payments slowed; but William continued to work on the bridge plan, certain to cost millions of dollars. Another month had gone by, and William wrote that he "felt a pressure around my heart that fills me with the gloomiest forebodings." There were more "exciting" conversations with Regina, and Hogan's assistant was arrested for following Louis Stern too closely. On the Sunday after Thanksgiving William and the children visited his mother. William wrote that he could "hardly keep back my tears, as we are uptown and the children are caressed by my dear old mother." William's depression deepened as the temperature fell: "bitterly cold. . . . [B]oth my wife and myself are seized with the wildest paroxysms of grief . . . sleepless night . . . gloomy day . . . great deal of trouble . . . dreadfully downhearted."

The first snow of winter was followed by fog, then rain, and William descended into an abyss of anguish. "My terrible mental distress seems to increase constantly. There is not a moment in the day, nor in the night when I am awake that I do not brood over my terrible dispensation of fate, and feel that death would be welcome to end my sufferings, were it not that my death would be the most terrible thing which could at present happen to the entire Steinway family." Christmas was nearing, and with the holiday came increasing retail sales, but William regarded this indifferently. There were letters from Theodore; he had invented a way to improve the treble in the grands and was experimenting with bronze alloy strings. William ignored these developments.

Eight days before Christmas 1875, William had another "most exciting conversation, hold hands, wife assures me that she desires revenge above everything else. Very sleepless night." After another report from Hogan, William and Regina had a talk "respecting our future." Christmas came and went with hollow imitations of festivity. The winter wore on as William mechanically attended to the business. "I continue to feel excessively downhearted and am gradually sinking into a state of utter helplessness, my heart torn to pieces by conflicts between duty and pity." Regina did not fare better: "Wife is very nervous, suffering mental distress." By the end of January 1876 William had decided on a course of action. "Our sufferings are beyond description . . . Future of ourselves being determined . . . I hardly close my eyes . . . In the morning little Alfred comes into my room, I take him into my arms and am again seized with unspeakable anguish and cry and sob as though my heart would break. Everything appears to me as black as night with every Avenue of escape cut off from shielding my children." Later that day William learned that more commercial paper had been sold and that Chickering was preparing a pamphlet attacking Steinway & Sons. The next day William told Regina that "the children *must* be separated next spring." A bizarre telegram arrived from Theodore stating that Anton Rubinstein was *not* blind. That evening William and Regina, along with Paula and Alfred, attended a charity concert at Steinway Hall. William made a speech from the stage before the performance, which was for the benefit of widows and orphans.

Another month of misery passed, and in late February William received a letter from Theodore. "It is evident from his letter that he knows all, I almost sink into the ground with my terrible mental sufferings." William read Theodore's letter to Regina that night: "We both suffer intense anguish, in talking about our dark and bleak future. Wife signs confession." Three days later William dined with Albert and after Sunday dinner they walked through the silent factory to the privacy of the pattern room where brother Henry had invented the future of the piano. There, amid the models and templates and drawings that symbolized the success of the firm and the family, William told his brother "of the terrible discovery I made, he is dreadfully excited and grieved. . . . We afterwards play Skat."

The situation worsened in March. Regina revealed new transgressions. Whether she did so in penitence—confession usually brought forgiveness from William—or for some other purpose is unclear, as are the nature of her revelations. William's reaction may have shocked his wife: "After taking supper, have a three hour conversation in which details of herself, Seyffert [a German theater director] & Reinel [a niece of Regina's] are elicited which are the most terrible imaginable. I drop to the ground almost choking, matters which took place in 1873 and 1874 . . ." The next day, March 5, was William's forty-first birthday and, "terribly sad," he dined with Albert and had a "long and earnest consultation" with him.

The days passed as William struggled with what he called his "horrible fate." A few months before, he had sold a building he owned to the Women's Medical College, a school formed to train female doctors. In mid-March he forgave, in effect made a gift of, twenty thousand dollars in mortgage debt on the building, about a quarter-million dollars today. At one point the women organizing the school offered William a trusteeship; it is unclear if he accepted. He aided the new college during a time that business was "absolutely wretched." Medical education for women was a controversial, if not radical, concept. "God," declared a Boston doctor, "never intended women to practice medicine." Despite the fact that the Boston physician never revealed his source, women were banned from the Massachusetts Medical Society. Even a female doctor, Mary J. Jacobi, conceded that women had "organic imperfections" and acknowledged that female physicians might "upset our notion of womanhood." William's progressive views on the role of women did not shield him from personal torment.

During the night "my wife comes, shivering into bed with me," but William did not respond. The next day: "I feel as though death was welcome to me, and when I see my children my heart almost breaks. I am stiff in both feet and have to walk quite slowly. . . . I am so utterly crushed mentally that I can only stagger along under the dreadful load." When William learned of the death of the wife—after a "severe confinement"—of German-American Carl Schurz, a United States senator and Civil War general, his reaction was both potent and bitter: "I feel unspeakably sad and downhearted with the conviction that noble women like Mrs. Schurz must die, while atrocious monsters who deliberately bring eternal disgrace and infamy upon their own children will continue to live." That night William played skat with Albert and Louise, winning thirty-six cents.

It was about this time that William had a conversation with his attorney. Cotterill informed William, after checking with the proper persons, that he could expect a "decree to be immediately drawn." William Steinway had decided to divorce Regina, this at a time when there were in New York City a scant 221 divorces in 1880. In all of New York State in the year 1876—the year of William's divorce—only 629 divorces were granted among a population of about 4.7 million persons.

Commenting on what its editorialist assessed as an unusually high divorce rate in Chicago, the *Times* felt that "it shows that there is something wrong in the style of its men or in the training of its women." The Chicago situation provided "a warning to mankind which deserves to be heeded. It is no argument whatever against marriage," observed the editorialist in a veiled repudiation of women's rights radicals, "whose divine and beneficent character is seen in its perfect adaptation to the wants of human nature." Divorces were sufficiently rare and amply scandalous that they were given regular coverage in the New York daily papers with the more notorious cases receiving full treatment, including publication of testimony. William Steinway, in electing divorce, was stepping into a social mine field. He could not venture there alone.

When Theodore returned to America in the spring of 1876, the matter of divorce was the first item on the agenda: "Theodore, Albert & I drive up in carriage & the heartrending explanations take place in which I convince my brothers that terrible as it might be, divorce is the only solution of the terrible misfortune brought upon herself and children by her criminality."

That night William was at Steinway Hall for a covert visit by Hans Von Bulow, who came to play the Centennial Grands. Bulow was "very friendly" and seemed "very pleased with the tone and action." At home that night there was "terrible excitement" as William revealed that he had letters which illuminated Regina's infidelities. "She is dreadfully frightened," wrote William. The next day William received still more letters, this time from his brother Theodore. They were letters to Carl Seyffert from Regina. "I read them on my way down [from the factory to home, apparently in a carriage], and no language can describe the mental tortures I endure on reading these horribly depraved and impudent missives."

In the evening there was a silver wedding anniversary party for William's sister, Doretta Ziegler. "Everybody in high glee, and I the most miserable of human beings, in vain try to repress my sadness which is generally noticed, not withstanding my efforts to conceal it. . . . During the night my wife comes shivering into my room, she has . . . ." The dots are again William's, and the next word is in an almost indecipherable scrawl. William may have written *syphilis*. It was not long before Regina signed another confession, this time covering her relationship with Carl Seyffert.

Though attorney Cotterill was at work on the mechanics of the divorce, there was no relief for William: "I again feel unspeakably wretched constantly brooding over the Crimes of the depraved creature I loved so deeply, and about the fate of poor little Alfred. I come more and more to the terrible conviction that she is utterly devoid of decency and shame, and capable of any crime without being troubled by any sentimental feelings." Days passed glutinously; by mid-April William learned that his entire family was aware of the scandal surrounding Alfred. "I [am] the unhappiest man in the world, becoming more horrified every day as I discover daily more and more the despicable depraved character of the detestable creature, who has become the blight and curse of my family and hers and her own children. . . . I now have abundant proof that all my family know the curse of my life, even my mother." But it was not long before William climbed from the trough of self pity: "I feel very tired and dejected but am firmly resolved to be a man and act accordingly."

The next day attorney Cotterill visited Regina Roos Steinway. At the end of the three-hour call the lawyer reported to William that Regina was "utterly crushed and penitent and that she feels herself slighted by others." Slowly, like the budding trees of spring, Regina's fate unfolded, and William's diary entries became terser. "Have conversation with wife regarding her future movements," wrote William. Soon Cotterill reappeared with the necessary legal documents: a will, a power of attorney, and passport forms in the name of Bergtold, another branch of the Roos family. It was arranged that the boy would receive a new baptismal certificate as Alfred Bergtold as well. In their new identities mother and child were to leave the two other children and depart for Europe, never to return to America.

After the legal details of Regina's impending exile were fixed, William and George Cotterill worked together on another pressing matter: Steinway & Sons' certificate of incorporation. After almost a quarter-century, the firm was to be transformed from a partnership to a corporation. Shortly Regina went to Buffalo to see her family for the last time. William stayed in New York, eating salt for his rheumatism and painting his joints with iodine. He spent his fifteenth anniversary alone, in pain and barely able to walk, prowling his diary for "points for my complaint for a divorce." Regina returned and William told Hogan to "watch my wife until her departure," having learned that she had again seen Louis Stern. In time, the entire Steinway family terminated contact with Regina, and Louise, Albert's wife, refused to speak when she passed Regina on Seventeenth Street.

William continued to probe the dark corners of his wife's life. In early May he wrote, "It becomes my settled conviction the more I think over it that my wife has also been guilty of A—— with Fink, brother-in-law of Haines, and there is no doubt that it was he who sent the Valentine during February last." The Haineses were a family of New York pianomakers. The next day William learned Regina did not constrain her relationships to competitors, but had "met" his friend and employee, the engineer Reck, at the Vienna Exhibition of 1873. William recorded no reaction to these revelations, but little Alfred was another matter: "I suffer dreadfully by his presence, having the deepest sympathy for him."

On May 15, 1876, Regina Roos Steinway was served with her divorce complaint, certified by Judge Hoffman, who did not know its contents, and delivered after supper to Regina by a Morris H. Dillenbeck, a lawyer in Cotterill's office. "I introduce my wife to him in the Parlor, he hands her the complaint, and leaves, she goes upstairs, I sink upon the Sofa, utterly crushed, when suddenly my wife rushes into the parlor wild with rage and excitement because we put the Seyffert matter in, we are both dreadfully excited, the children scream." Georgie, Paula, and Albert were sent to Steinway Hall, and the lawyer Cotterill appeared, apparently by prearrangement. It was decided to remove the "German matter" from the complaint, and William talked with his wife into the night, "retiring disgusted with her terrible unfeeling character." That day Regina, in the company of Pastor Krusi's wife, had booked passage for Europe and applied for a passport, not in the name of Steinway, but as Regina Roos.

May 20, 1876, was a "lovely day." In the morning William copied his wife's new will and gave her two thousand francs in cash, about four hundred dollars. Regina signed a receipt for the money and also signed a power of attorney, giving William control of her assets, which had been loaned to Steinway & Sons. With a family inheritance, Regina was comfortably and independently wealthy, but for unknown reasons chose not to assert financial autonomy. "At 1:40 wife takes leave of the children Georgie and Paula, a most affecting scene, only little Ditz [Alfred] laughs," wrote William. Proceeding by carriage to Hoboken where the *Labrador* lay, William cried. "On the Steamer Wife gives me a little package begging me to open same, when I get home. After drinking some champagne together I kiss little Alfred with bitter tears in my eyes, and kissing wife take leave. The steamer starts at 3 P.M. precisely, I catch a glimpse of them and they of me & I see that my wife weeps bitterly. I then break down utterly, so that Fritz Steins [a servant] has to support me. I get home in car, to office, Theodore there, open package, wherein wife returns me our wedding ring with a few affectionate and penitent words. I again break down and sob as though my heart would break, Theodore consoling me . . ." In the evening William dined with the children, then played skat with Theodore and Albert. A week or so later a keg of beer arrived, a gift from Regina's brother to William and Albert.

To an observer the parting of William and Regina would have seemed unremarkable. It was common for a wealthy woman to summer in Europe without her husband, and that too was a part of the plan. Regina's departure raised no suspicions, and William recorded that "I feel a little more quiet in the consciousness of having acted like an honorable man should do, now thoughts of revenge filling my heart against the Judas who destroyed the happiness of my life & that of my wife & children, and corrupted and contaminated her forever."

William did not, however, act on his thoughts of retribution. That Louis Stern feared William is certain. Once, in a random encounter on the street, Stern saw William Steinway, hastened to the other side, and disappeared in the crowd. What William did not do, nature did. "The jury have found the said Louis Stern is a lunatic and of unsound mind so that he is incapable of the government of himself or the management of his lands, goods and chattels," intoned New York Supreme Court papers in late 1881, and Mr. Stern was remanded to the Bloomingdale Insane Asylum on 117th Street.

Stern's commitment was laden with irony, for in 1876, the year of Regina's exile, Stern had his sister committed to Bloomingdale. As her brother and "heir at law" he expected to receive about eighteen thousand dollars in jewelry; but when the safe was opened under court supervision, it contained only a few spoons and old letters. Stern became violent in the office of an attorney, who swore that Stern was insane. A woman claiming to be Stern's wife begged the attorney not to take action against Louis, saying that he was "poor and himself a lunatic." It was also alleged that Stern "procured by trick, device or fraud, $1,000 from the said lunatic," i.e., his widowed sister Caroline. Stern later petitioned the court to release his sister; apparently the request was denied, and in 1881 Stern was himself committed to Bloomingdale by the same judge, Charles Donohue, who granted William's divorce. Stern died in the asylum a few days before Christmas 1881 of "general paralysis and epileptiform convulsions," which had begun three years earlier. He was thirty-seven years old. His fate was tersely noted in William's diary. Louis Stern's estate was thirteen hundred dollars in cash, real estate worth three hundred dollars, and seventy-five dollars in office furniture.

Though Regina was gone, there were still the mechanics of divorce. William had petitioned for, apparently as required, a remedy known as *absolute divorce*. "When an absolute divorce is granted," pontificated a Department of Labor study in 1909, "the complainant may marry again during the lifetime of the defendant; but a defendant adjudged to be guilty of adultery, shall not marry again until the death of the complainant. Exception is possible if the conduct of the defendant has been absolutely good." There were no grounds for an absolute divorce except adultery; intriguingly, about 60 percent of adultery divorces were granted to husbands nationally. Women more often alleged cruelty as grounds; and of those granted, 85 percent were to women.

Under the legal system of the time, the facts were found by an appointee of the court known as a referee. In this case of *Steinway* v. *Steinway*, the referee was Richard M. Henry, who was paid $250 for his services by William. Much concern was expressed by the public on the fairness of the referee system; and the use of referees, their qualifications, and presumed pliability was subject to debate. That R. M. Henry was known to William's attorney and that he somehow agreed in general terms to the divorce prior to his appointment is clear from the record. Judge Charles Donohue, before whom William had appeared in other matters, presided, so to speak.

Charged with fact-finding, Referee Henry took the testimony of witnesses. Regina was neither present nor represented by an attorney, though in the proceeding before the court she might be ordered never to remarry and have her children George and Paula permanently taken from her; additionally she could be completely disinherited after fifteen years of marriage. No mention whatsoever was made of seven-year-old Alfred; as far as the divorce was concerned, he did not exist. None of this, however, prevented matters from going forward in an entirely legal manner. Officially and sufficiently, the reason was that the "defendant has not appeared herein nor served any answer or demurrer to the complaint in this action and is therefore in default."

A carefully scripted drama of spousal infidelity began to play in the Pine Street office of R. M. Henry, an audience of one, on July 28, 1876. True to his word, William had excised the matter of Seyffert, and there was no mention of other relationships, which William now suspected spanned almost a decade of his marriage to Regina, whose two written confessions were not entered in evidence; apparently there was no need. The day before the carefully selected cast debuted, there was a dress rehearsal: "I feel sick all day," wrote William. "At 3 P.M. to Cotterill's office, with Dillenbeck to Pastor Krusi, introduce D. to the pastor, his wife and Mrs. Roesen. We go together through the testimony of all three. Find that Pastor Krusi speaks english pretty well."

Bartholomew Krusi was pastor of the German Presbyterian Church, and it was he who provided the false baptismal certificate for young Alfred. He also had talked with Regina in his pastoral capacity during the Steinway domestic crisis, though the Steinways rarely attended church. Regina, William reported, was "disgusted with Pastor Krusi talking to her." Pastor Krusi was married to Louise Roesen, who once worked for the Steinways as a nurse/governess. It was Louise Roesen Krusi who accompanied Regina and witnessed her passport application. Mrs. Krusi's mother, Mrs. Minna Roesen, was also a nurse and/or midwife who helped deliver William's son George eleven years earlier. The players at this point consisted of the pastor, his wife, and his mother-in-law, the latter two of whom knew for nine years of Regina's liaisons but kept silent. They were mute no longer, and it is possible that a one-hundred-dollar loan by William to Pastor Krusi may have somehow stimulated both memories and tongues. On July 28, 1876, at one o'clock William called in his carriage for the Krusis and Mrs. Roesen at their home and brought them to Referee Henry's office at 38 Pine Street.

"I commenced to notice," deposed Louise Roesen Krusi, "that she flirted with Mr. Louis Stern" in late 1867. In 1869 Louise reported that "when Mr. Steinway was out of town, Mrs. Steinway would go out of the house in the evening, first having made signs to Mr. Stern." Even in a Victorian court, this was probably insufficient for divorce, but Mrs. Krusi had more to say, and described how, one night in July, she served ice cream and champagne to Mrs. Steinway, but had also seen Mr. Stern enter the home. William was in Baltimore at a Liederkranz *sangerfest*. That night Mrs. Steinway was in her nightgown and did not want to be disturbed. Later that night Louise heard the jingling of glasses and Mr. Stern's voice. At five the next morning the ever-alert Louise detected footsteps on the stairs and the sound of Louis Stern's voice as he left Regina's room.

Taking a seven-year leap, Louise Krusi swore that on April 20, 1876, Regina "confessed she had committed adultery with him [Stern] and . . . that she had been improperly intimate with him for over three years. I asked her how she could act so having such a kind husband. She replied that she did not know but it always seemed to her that she must have another man besides her husband. She told me that she used to go with him to a house of assignation in 16th street." Mysteriously, William makes no diary mention of an April 20 meeting between Louise Krusi and Regina, but the soon-to-be-former Mrs. Steinway was both an ocean away and unrepresented during the divorce. The record is therefore unmarred with petty quibbling over points of fact.

Minna Roesen had less to say but testified that she was visiting with Regina in January 1869, when about 9:30 P.M. Regina excused herself to go shopping for corsets. Apparently close enough in her relationship to the Steinways that she felt she might linger without her hostess, Mrs. Roesen testified that she observed Mrs. Steinway beckon Mr. Stern to the basement stairs and from there proceeded with him to the parlor. With the locking of the parlor door, Mrs. Roesen must have realized that her companionship was no longer required and departed the premises. William's diary shows that he was not home half the nights in January 1869, and it is likely that during one of those absences Alfred was conceived, although there is no clear evidence that Stern was the father. In her brief deposition Minna Roesen had one further item to place on the record: "I have often seen Mrs. Steinway standing in her nightdress in her window throwing kisses to Mr. Stern, which he returned." Mrs. Roesen did not explain how, why, when, or where she made these observations, nor did the referee query further into the matter.

Pastor Krusi swore that "on May 2, 1876 Mrs. Steinway came to my house and confessed to me to have committed adultery with Mr. Stern and that Mr. Steinway discovered this infidelity with other acts of infidelity." The pastor did not mention that the primary purpose of the visit was to obtain a false baptismal certificate for an illegitimate child or that Regina visited him at William's insistence. The pastor did assert, "When she made this confession she was not a member of my church. She was never such a member. It is no part of the discipline or custom of the Presbyterian Church that its members should confess their sins to their pastor." Having scrambled to these high moral grounds, Pastor Bartholomew Krusi's statement was complete.

At this point the reference concluded with evidence that was objectively less than compelling, but Pastor Krusi and his wife were still hard at work, trying to find other servants employed by the Steinways during the time of Regina's liaisons with Louis Stern. Ida, a former cook, was found, but had no direct knowledge of events. Pastor Krusi had advertised without success in the *Staats-Zeitung* for Augusta Appel, a servant fired by Regina. Through unclear means, William did locate Augusta Appel, now married and living in Brooklyn. "I immediately go up and elicit from her all the details of my wife's adultery with the Jew Stern, she promises to . . . testify. I am overjoyed in thus having found the all important witness."

A few days later Augusta Appel Krauss testified before the referee. Apparently unable to speak English, servant Krauss's statements were translated by the totally trustworthy Charles F. Tretbar, William's second-in-command at Steinway Hall. The testimony was richly detailed, and some statements were expurgated for the record. "She saw them both undressed & he put my nightshirt on, saw them go to bed, and heard the bed squeak. I feel dreadful," reported William. The signed English-language deposition omits the acoustic reference, but establishes that Augusta Appel witnessed through a keyhole the activities of the five-months-pregnant Regina and Mr. Stern. The servant added a particularly piercing detail: the events she observed occurred on June 4, 1869, the fourth birthday of William and Regina's son, George Augustus. William had left on a business trip to Buffalo earlier that day, and his wife and son accompanied him to the train. When he returned eight days later, he learned that Augusta had been fired and replaced by Louise Roesen.

The testimony of witnesses was now sufficiently complete. Next the referee heard the plaintiff, William Steinway, who concisely certified that he was married to the defendant and had a marriage certificate and at least fifty-eight witnesses to the fact. William also deposed, as required by law, that "the adultery as charged was committed without my consent, connivance, privity or procurement," and stated that he "had not voluntarily cohabited with the Defendant since the discovery of either or any of said acts of adultery, nor have I cohabited with Defendant at all since such discovery."

A day later R. M. Henry was paid his $250 fee, and to expedite the proceedings with Judge Donohue, William himself carried the papers from the referee's office to the judge's chambers. During a heavy rain the next morning Morris Dillenbeck appeared at William's office. "I give him $100 to disburse, he comes back in about one hour, has seen the Judge, who will take the papers with him, and sign decree tomorrow morning." If it seems that Judge Donohue provided speedy justice at moderate prices, it also appears that he was a careful man. "Judge Donohue wants additional proof that the complaint has been served, otherwise it is all right," noted William. Louise Krusi, the pastor's wife and former servant, was hurriedly called to testify that Regina admitted to her that she had been served, and Judge Donohue deemed this sufficient "additional proof."

It was a "very pleasant and cool" morning five days later when Morris Dillenbeck walked into Steinway Hall at ten o'clock to deliver important news: "To my unspeakable joy he informs me that Judge Donohue this morning signed the divorce decree, forever freeing me from the outcast who has consigned me to a living death and become the curse and blight of my darling innocent children," scrawled William.

With a reference outside the courthouse, a docile judge, carefully selected witnesses, and lawyers who could count on vast fees if they remained close-mouthed, William Steinway was exposed to little risk of public scandal. But now that *Steinway* v. *Steinway* was concluded, a judgment would normally be filed in the clerk's office. There and at the courthouse prowled the pressmen, always on the alert for a suitable scandal. William solved this problem through Dillenbeck, who visited with "Hardy & Duryea who will both do their best to keep secret." The payment of fifty dollars apparently increased their resolve, as the next day Hardy and Duryea "concluded not to make any entry at all of the case." First by acquiring fellow Lie-derkranz member Judge Hoffman's signature on a complaint of which Hoff-man knew nothing, then by personally carrying the papers from the referee to Judge Donohue, combined with generous payments for special services received, William accomplished his goal, which was not merely a divorce, but a *secret* divorce, *Steinway v. Steinway*, wrapped in tan paper and tied with a red ribbon, sank in the slough of paper that was the clerk's office, to remain unopened for 115 years.

The decree, with suitable judicial gravity, stated that "all the material facts alleged in the complaint herein are true and that the Defendant has been guilty of several acts of adultery. . . . It is ordered and adjudged that the marriage . . . is dissolved . . . that it shall be lawful that the said Plain-tiff William Steinway to marry again in the same manner as if the said De-fendant Regina Steinway were actually dead; but it shall not be lawful for the Defendant Regina Steinway to marry again until the plaintiff is actually dead. . . . Regina Steinway is not entitled to any right or title of dower in the Plaintiff's real estate, or to any interest or distributive share in his per-sonal property in case of his death intestate. And it is further ordered that the care and custody of George Augustus Steinway and Paula Theoda Steinway, the lawful issue of said marriage, be and the same are hereby awarded to said plaintiff William Steinway." William bundled up a copy of the decree and mailed it to his former wife about one month later.

Aftershocks continued. Regina threatened to return to America several times. In William's view, this was "reckless and impudent as ever." Regina considered herself a "persecuted woman." Now living with Louis Da-chauer's mother, she sent William a letter she received from friend and employee Reck. "Tretbar has fitted the torn letter & pieced it all up & I now have proof of the rascality of Reck fully in my hands," reported William to his diary. Reck was not a Steinway & Sons employee much longer. "Reck calls by appointment," noted William, "is utterly crushed when I read his letter to him, knows nothing of other paramours, swears that nothing ever happened between him and Madame Regina Roos. I tell him to call next morning, get his money and leave Steinway Hall forthwith." The next morning Reck appeared "utterly crushed with Remorse & Shame." Atypi-cally, this did not sway William; he gave Reck $10,036 in cash—Steinway & Sons often acted as a bank for employees and friends—and told him never to enter Steinway Hall again. Jobless and homeless, but seemingly far from poor, Reck left the orbit of the Steinways.

There were other casualties; a servant named Robert was dismissed when William became satisfied that he had been aware of one of Regina's relationships since 1871. "I tell him not to come to my house anymore to attend the fires, but that Louis will attend to them." But amidst the familial and social wreckage that was the Steinway divorce, one man stood un-scathed. That man was Louis Dachauer.

When, precisely, William learned that his wife and his friend Dachauer were also lovers is unclear, but he certainly knew of this before granting Dachauer a power of attorney to look after Steinway & Sons' interests in France. There, pianomakers Mangeot Freres had a license to build Steinway pianos, but matters were not going well. Louis Dachauer visited with Regina during the summer of 1876, shortly after her move to Europe. It seems that at this time William trusted Dachauer completely. After Louis Dachauer returned to New York, William met with him. "In eveg have interview with Dachauer until 2 A.M. I tell him the whole history, he is very much amazed and astounded never having believed that Mm. R.R. could have been so bad, and will advise her to keep perfectly quiet for her own sake." Dachauer's deceptive skills may have been extraordinary, for most collapsed into candor during one of William's "interviews." Soon Dachauer told William that Louis Stern spoke badly of his wife in 1869 and that Regina would be moving to Nancy in France. One day later, however, Mrs. Dachauer visited William and told him she planned to divorce Louis. William advised "extreme caution."

The situation developed rapidly from this point. Apparently aware that his wife might be named a correspondent in the Dachauer divorce, William had a "long talk" with Louis and Marie. The next day Marie Dachauer presented a letter from "R.R fully establishing her relations." Then William, a man of unswerving principles, if one ever lived, in matters matrimonial, made a most peculiar diary entry: "Tell Dachauer that if his wife brings suit against him for divorce on acct of his intimacy with RR I must cut his acquaintance."

Dachauer also wanted to borrow six hundred dollars and start a Steinway agency in Paris. Neither of these requests by one of Regina's consorts was rejected out of hand. Meanwhile, Mrs. Dachauer was fulminating over Regina's residence in the house of her mother-in-law. When Louis Dachauer sailed for France on December 30, 1876, he did so as a representative of Steinway & Sons. William cabled Theodore to act in a friendly manner toward Dachauer, perhaps because Louis now knew more about the Steinway domestic difficulties than anyone else outside the family. Theodore, in typically volcanic but randomly wandering prose, cautioned William about "Jesuit tricks to establish the legitimacy of the youngster [Alfred]. . . . Every piece of writing he receives is a tool in his hands. . . . As soon as he is married he will start up if we don't do what he wants." Theodore may have feared that Dachauer would begin making pianos under the Steinway name using little Alfred as the namesake. William's response to Theodore is lost, if there was one.

Marie Dachauer did file for divorce. According to the *Times*, "Mrs. Dachauer charges her husband with having had improper intercourse with one Regina Roos Steinway, the wife of William Steinway. The latter, Mrs.

Dachauer says, has since obtained a divorce from his wife on account of such improprieties. . . . Mrs. Dachauer says her husband is now living with the divorced Mrs. Steinway." While William could exercise control over the judges, referees, and others in the judicial system, he could not control an angry Marie Dachauer and the reporters to whom she talked. *Steinway v. Steinway* became public knowledge through the back door of the edifice of secrecy William had built to contain it.

In the ten months since Regina had left for Europe, many had casually asked William about his wife, among them Oswald Ottendorfer, publisher of the *Staats-Zeitung*. Now the divorce was public, but William sent the lawyer Cotterill, along with his press liaisons Darcie and Phelps, "to stop all further publications, in which they succeed. . . . I grow more quiet." Later in the day the dismissed Reck appeared, claiming that "all he had belonged to his mother. I give him $50," wrote William. A few days later a distraught Marie Dachauer called on William, showing him a letter in which her husband vowed revenge. By this time William had already used his contacts to examine the Dachauer divorce papers and found that in addition to naming Regina the complaint also alleged that Louis Dachauer had visited a "house of ill repute."

Marie Dachauer apparently saw the error of her ways and reported to William that she "withheld papers and referee report." Nine days later, after selling her furniture to Tretbar for $250, Marie sailed for Europe in search of her husband. William, though he does not say so, must have been relieved. A year had passed since Regina's departure. Later Marie reported to William that when she found Louis and Regina at Nancy, they "ran away" from her. William was spending more time with his children: Georgie killed his first pigeon with a rifle; the children enjoyed Elisha Gray's telegraph concert; a party with "many" guests was held for Georgie's twelfth birthday.

Normality prevailed at 26 Gramercy Park. A week later the Ocean Telegraph pulsed a message: "POWER TO ARREST, ANSWER, MARIE DACHAUER." The cable pulsed again: "NO ARREST FOR CHILDRENS SAKE, I BEG YOU. WM.ST." This was the last flaring of the emotional bonfire that was the Steinway divorce. Letters from Regina became less frequent, and in August 1877 a Style 3 upright piano—the fanciest grade—was sent to Regina by William, complete with "extra pedal & India Rubber Cover." In October Marie Dachauer returned from Europe, auctioned her possessions, and steamed east again with a loan from William.

Christmas 1877 had the semblance of routine domesticity. When the tree was lit on Christmas Eve, there was a velocipede under it for Georgie. William did not note Paula's gift in his journal. From his children William received the works of Schiller, and each member of the household staff received ten dollars. Christmas morning found William at work in the store.

On New Year's Eve the family gathered, and the children stayed up for the first time. "George and Paula jumped into the New Year," wrote a tranquil William.

How Regina Roos and Louis Dachauer spent the holiday season of 1877 is unknown, but it was their first and last together. "A cable dispatch received yesterday from Nancy, France announced the death there of Louis Dachauer, who was once one of the best-known organists of this city," reported the *Times* on August 18, 1878. Dachauer's musical achievements were cited: winner of first prize at the Paris Conservatory, for composition; composer of a frequently performed mass; organist at Saint Ann's Roman Catholic Church; among the best organists in the nation; once proprietor of a music store. "He returned to France about 18 months ago and has since been living at Nancy. He was about 40 years of age." The obituaries, which ran in three city papers, were written and placed at the direction of William Steinway.

A French insurance company wanted to know if Louis and Marie Dachauer were married. William telegraphed: "M.D. NOT DIVORCED IS LAWFUL WIDOW—STEINWAY. On this his word must be taken, for not even a single page remains in re *Dachauer* v. *Dachauer* in the New York County Clerk's Office. Judge Lawrence's daily log shows he heard the case, but no trace of the papers can be found. Somehow, William Steinway induced the Dachauer genie to return to the bottle, and it was not long before the newspapers referred to William as the widower Steinway.

Chapter 16

BAD BIRDS EVEN THEN

"For some time past there have been mutterings in the piano trade. J. P. Hale—he of the largest collection of stencils in the country—had girded his loins, put on his war paint, arranged his scalp-lock, polished his tomahawk and stepped out in the open to do battle for the public and kill the hideous monster, the high-toned, high-priced piano. He is sick and tired, noble fellow, of seeing the nation fleeced by a Steinway, a Chickering, a Decker, a Knabe or even a Weber." The words were those of John C. Freund, editor and publisher, at 800 Broadway, of the *Music Trade Review & Dramatic News*, a newly launched trade paper. Aggressively edited, artfully designed, and printed on good-quality stock, *Music Trade Review* was funded, at least in part, by William Steinway.

Like many new publications, *Music Trade Review* had a cause célèbre: the stencil piano and its builders. As sometimes sold, the stencil piano would today be called a counterfeit, and the largest market for them was in the "West," i.e., Ohio, Indiana, Illinois, Nebraska, and Texas. There, distant from the palatial warerooms of Steinway, Chickering, and others, lived people of modest means who, like their eastern brethren, desired to own pianos. The wives of "western" farmers and tradesmen wished to learn to play, to entertain themselves, to sing hymns, and to have their children benefit from the much-discussed uplift and discipline of musical instruction. At least a few had heard masters such as Gottschalk and Rubinstein

209

perform on national tours. So successful had been the promotional efforts of Steinway and Chickering that far from the cultural capitals of the East the desire to own a piano was kindled and now burned brightly. But the longing exceeded both sophistication and means.

A glance at the Steinway & Sons price list for January 1876 shows why. The least expensive Steinway, an unadorned square piano of seven octaves (eighty-five notes), which was made of black walnut stained to imitate rosewood, had a retail price of $550 and a wholesale cost of $330. Against this retail price was laid the average 1876 earnings for a non–farm worker of $403. Assuming the ability to save 10 percent of income per year, the average worker needed to save for a dozen years to afford the cheapest Steinway, assuming, of course, that he was also able to negotiate a 10-percent discount from retail. This was clearly impossible for most families, and Steinways were typically sold into but one of every four thousand households each year during the 1870s. Though Chickering, Knabe, Decker, and Weber, among other competitors, sold somewhat less expensive instruments, they were often priced within 10 percent of Steinway. Expressed another way, Porsche automobiles were proportionately about twice as common in the 1980s as were Steinway pianos in the 1870s.

The western demand for pianos could not be easily met by the sale of used instruments. There were few pianos of any description in these more recently settled areas. This was a market ripe for exploitation, and beginning in the mid 1860s Joseph P. Hale developed the necessary mechanisms. Having moved to New York with thirty-five thousand dollars gained in the pottery trade, Hale entered into partnership in 1861 with James H. Grovesteen, a fifteen-year veteran of New York pianomaking. "I do not now remember where their factory was," said William many years later. "They were regarded as bad birds even then, but their concern was so small that little attention was directed to them." By 1864 Hale was on his own, making, in William's words, "the very cheapest piano-fortes. Then he extended his business, after a time, to money lending and went largely into the manufacture of contract piano-fortes." By 1869 Hale's manufactory was the seventh largest in the nation.

The "contract" piano was not a Hale innovation; many small makers built what today would be called "private label" instruments, buying keys, actions, plates, cases, legs, and other necessary components from specialists who made only, for example, piano legs. In this arrangement, a dealer or agent would agree to purchase a quantity of instruments at a fixed price from such a maker, really more of an assembler. On them he would have his own brand name affixed; Thomas H. Chambers, the Broadway music dealer with whom Steinway & Sons had a relationship in the early years, sold such pianos into the 1870s and had been doing so for at least a quarter-century. Acceptable, if not outstanding, pianos were sold as stencils, and playable Chambers pianos survive a century after they were built. The buyer received a reduced price in return for eschewing the perceived security of what would now be called a "national brand." The owner's satisfaction with the "house brand" resided with the knowledge and integrity of the seller, and, predictably, not all sellers were virtuous.

It was here that problems arose and that Joseph P. Hale found an immense opportunity. Hale, it was claimed, made Steinmay, Steinman, Steinmetz, and Stanley & Sons pianos, as well as Chickring, Chickening, Becker, and Decker & Bros instruments. The brand names were executed in Old English and Teutonic typefaces so festooned with ornamentation that only a typographer or calligrapher could be expected to distinguish between the *w* in Steinway and the *m* in Steinmay. Some of Hale's instruments were, in short, counterfeits. Until 1876 there was no meaningful trademark law, and reputable makers of almost any product were subject to look-alike imitations. Importers of expensive wine and champagne also had much difficulty with forged labels, printing being a process much simpler than piano manufacture.

The pianomakers responded to the problem by casting the maker's name in the iron plate of the instrument, but this was not entirely effective. Many buyers did not understand the implied meaning of a nameless plate, and some counterfeiters took the trouble of brazing a name on a blank plate and refinishing it. A few, Hale among them apparently, actually cast counterfeit plates if an order were large enough. Counterfeits found their way into even the sophisticated eastern markets; some were sold as "slightly used," either by dealers or private parties who put them in their parlors while others were regularly sold at auctions.

J. P. Hale produced, it was claimed, more than five thousand pianos per year, selling them to anyone who wished to buy at $100 to $150 each. Much of Hale's output went west, where it was sold by transient agents who would set up in a town, hold a "piano sale," then move on. Hale also had customers in the lower reaches of the permanent trade who would buy instruments under various and ever-changing names and sell them to naive buyers under some plausible scenario such as a "manufacturer's overstock." Others trundled over the dirt roads of the nation with wagonloads of pianos, vending them to unsuspecting farmers far from any metropolitan area. Externally, the pianos were presentable; internally, William claimed that "within a year they would become the direst rattletraps imaginable." J. P. Hale was slaking his commercial thirst at the well of Steinway and Chickering brand equity. "Out West," wrote a piano tuner, "a New York piano is looked upon with as much suspicion as a member of Congress."

A dealer from Columbus, Ohio, wrote of his experiences with a Hale piano in a letter to *Music Trade Review*: "The sounding board had warped up against the strings, so that there was no possible chance of vibration. Her piano was not worth the strokes of an axe that would make it into kindling wood. She [the owner] cried very bitterly and said she had saved the money over many, many years. We were touched by her terrible grief and wrote to Mr. J. P. Hale. He replied that the piano must have been placed in a damp room, that his work was always perfect and that he was not responsible for the conduct of his pianos." A few wrote in to say that their Hale pianos had given excellent service, but the weight of printed opinion was clearly against Mr. Hale.

Hale had a different view, one which he advanced volubly in newspapers near his markets. In what may be a record for the length of a single sentence in an American newspaper, the *Cincinnati Daily Times* printed: "Some fifteen years ago Mr. J. P. Hale, an enterprising citizen of Massachusetts, of ripe experience in various departments of practical industry and of commerce, a man of uncommon judgment and discernment in affairs, a mechanical expert as well as a far-seeing, cool-headed financier, given to observation and invention and liberal views, but endowed with constitutional strength of purpose in the patient execution of business projects, conceived the idea either that the traditional system of high and purely artificial prices in the piano trade was a stupendous humbug, to which the community ought to be the folly of submission, or else that the monopoly of the piano by the upper ten thousand was a fraud upon the great industrial middle classes, the idea being that the manifest destiny of the instrument was that of a larger utility and larger beneficence, like that of the printing press, the fulfillment of which in placing it within reach of the multitude was a duty which commercial enterprise owed to society." Though almost lost in the undergrowth of verbiage, Hale was attempting to portray himself as a populist with a social mission.

Hale called this a "new revelation . . . of the larger social destiny of the piano." Its source "was the easy and simple result of the mathematical computation of the necessary outlay of production and a comparison with established market prices." The arithmetic, Hale claimed, showed the "incredible margin of profits" and "a magnificent opportunity for rendering the nation a vast service . . . by supplying . . . a national necessity for which the commerce of the age made no provision whatsoever." The only difference between his pianos and an $800 piano was "$35 on account of extra mechanical finish," while Hale's pianos sold for one-third the price. J. P. Hale's claims were credible to many, particularly in rural areas, where farmers felt the pinch of high freight rates and were ready to believe in yet another New York conspiracy to separate workingmen from their money. But however plausible, Hale's polemics were economically false.

"Am at store in evening, & finally complete our inventory, the result of which is very unsatisfactory, showing that we made no money in the year 1876, work til 11 O'clock," wrote William on March 29, 1877. When the bookkeepers completed sundry adjustments and recomputations, there was a profit, however minuscule. Steinway & Sons still employed an archaic method of accounting based on an annual inventory. Once a year in January

trusted employees counted every piano, partially completed piano, or component, every stick of wood, each nut, screw, and bolt, each can of glue or
varnish, every ounce of felt and whatever else, including stamps, blotters,
and ink, that could be found in the factories or warerooms. To this was
added the cash on hand and in banks, plus money due from dealers and
an estimate of the value of the real estate. From the grand total was
subtracted the liabilities—money Steinway & Sons owed to suppliers or
banks—and other charges, such as amounts the partners withdrew for
their own use, i.e., their "salaries." After a few more accounting steps,
there resulted a number that was the "net worth" of Steinway & Sons.
When this number went up, there was a profit; when it went down, there
was a loss. By this quaintly imprecise method of reckoning, Steinway &
Sons produced a profit of but $16.30 for each instrument sold during 1876,
or about 3 percent of the average selling price. Here was J. P. Hale's
"incredible margin of profits" that he proposed to return to the "industrial
middle classes" while providing that "national necessity," a piano.

America's centennial year of 1876 was an economic bloodbath slightly
beyond the midpoint of a long and deep depression that began in October
1873 and continued for sixty-five months until March 1879. It was and is
the longest economic contraction in the nation's history, a depression more
severe than that of the 1930s. Over nine thousand businesses failed during
1876, 17 percent more than in 1875 and triple the number of failures in
1871. That Steinway managed to sell 2,420 pianos that year and turn a
small profit was a feat approaching the miraculous. One way William
achieved it was through price cuts. A parlor grand that cost $1,250 in 1869
was slashed 20 percent to $1,000 by 1873. By 1876 a small sum had been
added—5 percent—and the same grand now retailed for $1,050.

The Steinway & Sons workmen shared the pain, with average factory
wages dropping from a high of about $966 per year in 1872 to $781 in 1876.
In the persistent and strong deflation that characterized the American
economy of the 1870s, the Steinway workers lost little in actual earning
power and were continuously employed. Millions were less fortunate. Reports came from the Pennsylvania coal fields that miners' children were
dying of starvation. A proposal was seriously considered that the city of
New York "give a few millions out of the city treasury to manufacturing
firms, so as to enable them to give employment to artisans." The proposal
was rejected on the grounds that it would "give rise to a war . . . resulting
in general ruin and anarchy" because it was unjust to aid a particular
segment of the community. William's friend and Liederkranz associate
Oswald Ottendorfer presented the report against the plan. Instead, the
Common Council recommended that the citizens develop "confidence,"
which was certain, in the opinion of the aldermen, to lead to economic
growth.

Amidst the economic agonies of the 1870s Joseph P. Hale expanded his business. On land he purchased along Tenth Avenue between Thirty-fourth and Thirty-fifth streets, a succession of ever larger buildings was built. A man who did not believe in superfluous expenditures, Hale commenced the construction of an eight-story factory, radically tall for its time, without using either an architect or engineer. One brick wall was erected to a height of more than seventy feet when a wind blew it down. The falling bricks crashed into a neighboring tenement, killing six persons. Without delay but now with the help of an architect, a new wall was soon headed skyward. In 1875, well into the depression, Hale was augmenting his manufacturing capacity with an eight-story addition of 160,000 square feet and claiming that he would soon have the capacity to manufacture seventy-five hundred pianos per year. He was quick to point out that this was "three times larger than that of any other establishment in the world." This was an unsubtle reference to Steinway & Sons, who, everyone knew, was the nation's largest manufacturer and had been for at least a decade.

Hale's genius, and he was a genius, was in cost control. While the Steinways, the Chickerings, and other traditional makers would air-dry wood for years, maintain immense inventories of hardware, use custom-made fasteners, pay high wages to the best workers, create designs of arcane complexity, apply for patents, build concert halls, promote artists, and assign dealers exclusive territories, none of this was done by Joseph P. Hale. For him the piano was a commodity to be built and sold just as he had built and sold crockery and wooden boxes in prior enterprises. Hale's marketing methods were quintessentially modern and so were his production methods, which would today be known as "just in time" manufacturing. His inventory was never more than one week's worth of production. Cases, keys, actions, plates, and everything else that could be was bought from outside suppliers. Hale's volume, ability to pay cash, and, in all likelihood, relaxed standards of quality, assured the lowest prices.

Equally radical were Hale's distribution methods. Avoiding the conventional agency system with its exclusive territories, J. P. Hale sold to anyone, anywhere. With the traditional structure this would have led to conflict, price wars, and dealer failures. Hale avoided the problem by placing different names on his instruments. If in some growing midwestern city there were four stores selling Hale pianos, they were all sold under different names, and each sold what he could with a minimum of destructive competition. Hale, of course, supplied them all, but the buyers did not know that. In an industry where the *family* name and a reputation built over decades was considered the ultimate asset, Hale's "tell us what to name it" pianos were viewed as a moral travesty. His apparent willingness to produce counterfeits or deceptively named pianos was merely a compound offense.

While those opposed to Hale such as William Steinway referred to his pianos as "rattletraps" and "kindling," it is likely that much of Hale's output was at least minimally serviceable to novice players. Were it not, men such as William Wallace Kimball—whose firm still survives—could not have sold thousands of the pianos per year as a Hale "jobber." Kimball scoured the midwestern countryside for motivated young men living in small towns. Having found one, he would supply pianos and organs on consignment, and his newly designated dealer would travel his territory with the instruments, selling them to farmers. Repeat local sales would not have been possible if the quality of the pianos was below the expectations of buyers, and Kimball operated in this way for over a decade. Kimball and others, who today would be called mass merchandisers, were soon asking a question: Why pay the freight from New York? Piano factories then began to appear in Illinois and Ohio, closer to the buyers.

J. P. Hale's strategy was therefore self-limiting, and he may have recognized this himself, for there were rumors that Mr. Hale had a $150,000 interest in Chickering & Sons and also an interest in the New York works of Albert Weber, a small, astute, amoral, and aggressive Steinway competitor. It may have been Hale's plan to form what was then called a "ring" or "combination" through which he could dominate the national market by combining his manufacturing methods with the prestige of established names. Such a combination would have been immensely threatening to Steinway & Sons. The industry was something of an oligopoly functioning under a price umbrella set by Steinway. If Hale achieved control of an established firm, he would use his manufacturing economies to compete on price.

Steinway, already operating on thin margins during the depression, would be unable to meet such price competition, and a quarter-century of effort and sacrifice by the family could be lost. If the house survived Hale's price challenge, it would be as a less prestigious and less profitable second-tier firm. The Steinways, William, Albert, and Theodore, all understood firsthand the meaning of the Hale threat; they had eclipsed Chickering, Bacon & Raven, Dunham, and dozens of other firms in their own technologically propelled ascent to supremacy. If the family and firm were to survive, Joseph P. Hale must be stopped. This was the strategic imperative.

Theodore was aware of the menace and gravely concerned about the cost of Steinway pianos, noting, for example, that in Germany a Bechstein sold for 350 marks retail while the wholesale price of a Steinway was 700 marks. C. F. Theodore proposed a solution: stop spending money on artists and advertising, then cut the dealer markups. "He who does not want it can go to Hell, but our business will benefit. . . . My boy, a piano is a piano, a little better or not does not make a difference with people." Theodore also wanted to simplify the instruments, and, in the ultimate apostasy, issued a veiled threat: he would break from the family business and contract with local makers for cheap pianos under his own name. Steinway & Sons was snared in the trap of its own success. The family's technological developments, particularly overstringing, were widely imitated. The technical benefits were now available from others, yet William continued to advertise and promote the "Steinway System," in effect advertising for their competitors. This galled Theodore.

How William responded to Theodore's ultimatum is unknown, but in the fall of 1876 Steinway & Sons was once again concertizing. With William's steady hand at the strategic helm, the Russian *pianiste* Annette Essipoff had been guaranteed half of her fifty-thousand-franc salary by Steinway, or about five thousand dollars. Voting via the bank account, William once again chose class, not mass. "In evening with children at Steinway Hall," wrote William. "Essipoff concert, she makes a glorious success. . . . My dear old Mother is also there, enjoying the performance very much. All Musicians and pianomakers pronounce her the greatest success since Rubinstein's advent.

"We should be guided by only one principle: *cheap, cheap, cheap* and fabricate simply so that we can meet every competition. The name of Steinway is strong enough to remain at the top without all this noise only if the price of our pianos is not too high, which can only happen if we get rid of all that is a burden in the business!" erupted Theodore. Soundboard compression was "humbug." Albert's newly patented sostenuto pedal was "silly humbug," and sundry other Steinway & Sons innovations came under the lash of Theodore's pen. "I will," rumbled Theodore, "find my next task in building certain cheap pianos, others, with all kinds of patents are expensive." Theodore's views remained in the family, known only to William and perhaps to brother Albert. The larger world would not learn during their lifetimes of the ideological kinship of C. F. Theodore Steinway and Joseph P. Hale.

The "burden" against which Theodore inveighed was, in fact, insufficient to place Steinway at economic parity with J. P. Hale. The guarantee paid Essipoff amounted to about two dollars per piano sold that year, a fraction of 1 percent of the wholesale price of the cheapest Steinway. If the concert space in Steinway Hall cost the partners $250,000 over its quarter-century of use, this was but ten thousand dollars per year, amounting to between three and six dollars per piano, depending on annual production. Theodore advocated turning Steinway Hall into a warehouse, but William knew, intuitively, if not in an accounting sense, that for the sum of less than ten dollars per piano he could create a powerful psychological linkage and a bond with the purchaser.

When the wife of a dentist in Des Moines acquired a Steinway, she did so with the security that she had bought the best; a link, thin but real, had been created between the buyer and Annette Essipoff, Anton Rubinstein, and a working majority in the pantheon of musical giants of the age of Romantic classicism. J. P. Hale could never achieve that linkage, and William must have understood that to relinquish it for a few dollars per unit in savings was to beckon destruction of the family's life work. Controlling about 45 percent of the company to Theodore's 27 percent, with Albert holding the balance of 28 percent, William did not have to act upon Theodore's ideas; he only needed to appear to listen. Practically speaking, Theodore could not rationally desert the partnership; to do so would have been to destroy his own financial security. The risk was that Theodore was not always rational. If he did any meaningful work on cheap pianos, no evidence remains. At the time of the Hale threat C. F. Theodore was spending most of the year in Europe. William and possibly Albert may have felt that Theodore did not understand the American mind-set with its nagging sense of cultural inadequacy. Those feelings led Americans to place high value on cultural artifacts endorsed by European artists.

Cancellation of promotional programs would not reduce the Hale threat; other means were found, beginning with a meeting on December 21, 1875, at the Fifth Avenue Hotel. Present was a group of pianomakers who later referred to themselves as "reputable." There were two challenges that the group planned to address: one was the bogus instruments of Hale and others; the second was a bizarre judicial decision that allowed landlords to seize rented or loaned pianos and sell them to satisfy rents on houses and flats. Wrote William: "I make motion to organize as a protective Society to the interest of the trade, am appointed on a Committee to employ counsel and draw up brief articles of association." The city's pianomakers had set aside their normal predatory practices to deal with Hale as a group. This was a rare event; only when confronted with citywide strikes by their workmen had the pianomakers associated, and then only for the duration of labor unrest. Depressed and anguished by his domestic situation, William still functioned in a leadership role. After the holidays the committee convened to discuss the group's constitution with attorney G. W. Cotterill.

It took Cotterill only a few days to draw the bylaws of the new association, and they were presented to the committee, which met at Chickering's warerooms on Fifth Avenue, but a second meeting was required before the group agreed to a general meeting that would officially mark the beginning of the new society.

On Monday, January 31, 1876, the pianomakers convened at Steinway Hall. William's narrative captured the essence: "At 2 P.M. in the smaller Steinway Hall 65 parties appear and to our intense disgust J. P. Hale is elected President and Weber Secretary, through having a lot of piano dealers and outside parties there packed by Weber and Hale." A ten-dollar membership fee (about $120 today) did not provide adequate protection, and J. P. Hale now controlled both the funds and the protective society. But control was not enough; humiliation was also on the agenda as J. P. Hale began to publish accounts of his victory.

The next day fifteen of the makers including Steinway met to form a new society. Wasting no time, the task was accomplished just three days after the Hale coup. "In the morning William A. Pond and Lowell Mason sign the Certificate of Incorporation," transcribed William, "and we are now ten of us." Notable in absence was C. Frank Chickering, who, like the Steinways, had sufficient prestige to be heavily plagued by appellative piracy. But a foot of freshly fallen snow did not prevent Chickering from attending the next meeting, where he and William were elected vice presidents of the new society and Lowell Mason of Mason & Hamlin, organmakers of Boston, became president. It was then that the first return salvos were fired by William in the *Staats-Zeitung* and over the wires of the Associated Press. It was probing fire.

"I suffer great mental pain both on account of our personal trouble & bad business," William wrote, but this did not preclude him from functioning as theater commander in the battle of the bogus pianos. "In afternoon with Haines and Freund to the daily Times. Show to Jones and Mr. Reed the article written by Lowell Mason, after some consultation succeed in getting the article in as an Editorial though paying for it. Order 5000 copies. In eveg. with Freund to Times Office to read proof, draw up written order to Weinhold how to send off the 500 Times to the different piano makers."

The next day William observed with satisfaction that the *New York Times* piece was "creating great sensation." On the *Times* editorial page was an item headed "MUSICAL DISCORDS." It was indistinguishable from other editorials to the reader.

Lowell Mason had artfully crafted a masterpiece of propaganda, and William had tactically placed it where it might do the most harm, or good, depending on perspective. After an introductory paragraph congratulating the citizens of the nation on their good taste and generous patronage of music and a notice of pianomaking as "one of the great industries of the country" with suitable nods to "CHICKERING, STEINWAY, and others of hardly less reputation or merit," Mr. Mason pierced to the heart of the matter. "This is that the making of 'bogus' pianos has become a business by itself. There are, it seems, men who find it profitable to put in the market instruments which bear a name so like an eminent maker that the unwary are deceived by it." The editorial went on declare that there were so many of the counterfeiters "that they were able to capture and take full possession of the very association which was organized for their destruction." There was a "large trade in spurious instruments" which will "not stand two years in one of our furnace-heated houses." It was necessary to consult an expert, advised Mason in the *Times*, just as in the case of old Italian violins, and "we are sure that honest makers and dealers will not protest."

William and his allies had created a running story, and the next day yet another article appeared in the *Times*; it was an exposé of "a few of the successful frauds" and repeated, with the vitriol diluted, the charges that appeared in *Music Trade Review* while expanding on the list of deceptive trade names: Hazeltine or Hazelman in imitation of Hazleton Brothers,

Baines or Haynes to emulate Haines Brothers, as well as Nasun and Hammin Organ Company in an impersonation of Mason and Hamlin. "Such names are bought by an unsuspecting public who do not discover that they have obtained a spurious article until it is too late.

"A few weeks since, at a meeting of the trade, it was proposed to form an association for the purpose of remedying these and other evils to which the business is subject. . . . When the votes came to be counted, however, a very unexpected result was discovered. Some of those who had been foremost in the objectionable modes of doing business . . . were found to have been elected to leading office," continued the *Times* story. Without mentioning their names, William and his allies accused J. P. Hale and Albert Weber of counterfeiting.

Strategically, this left Weber in a very uncomfortable position; unlike Hale, who saw the piano business as a target of opportunity, Albert Weber was a lifelong "pianoman." Weber was not a technological innovator, as were the Steinways. He had no patents, and his approach, it appears, was to build a generic piano of high quality using conservative methods. There was no Weber Hall, and Weber had neither the means nor inclination to build one. He once commented that running a hall added one hundred dollars to the price of every piano. An occasional participant in the artist game, Weber could cadge endorsements with the best, but he did not attract artists of the stature of Rubinstein or Von Bulow.

Albert Weber was, more or less respectably, a second-tier competitor who for a time grew quite rapidly. But after the Panic of 1873 Weber was short on cash, as were many businesses. In a typical nineteenth-century panic, depositors pulled their money from banks in fear of bank failure. Banks did not therefore have funds to lend, and Weber turned, probably involuntarily, to none other than J. P. Hale, perhaps through Hale's West Side Savings Bank. Several years later William learned that Weber owed Hale about eighteen thousand dollars, probably callable on a moment's notice. The debt meant that Joseph Hale had Albert Weber on a very short financial leash.

There were rumors that Weber was selling Hale pianos, and these can be shown to be true, rather obliquely. A piano tuner from Poughkeepsie, one F. E. Wildman, wrote *Music Trade Review:* "I tuned a piano for a lady not many miles from here. She says she bought the piano at Weber's warerooms from Weber himself, and that he told her that it was made in his own factory, although the piano had Philip Phillips' name on it! I recognized the piano as one of Hale's immediately and no part of it was made in Weber's factory." Phillips, also known as the Singing Pilgrim, was a popular religious singer and composer/publisher of hymns as well, with titles such as *Musical Leaves for Sabbath Schools* and *Methodist Episcopal Hallowed Songs for Prayer & Social Meetings.* In a lawsuit filed a few years later, the Pilgrim swore that his fame and worldwide travels made him an ideal agent for Hale's pianos and that he had helped sell many of them. The Poughkeepsie piano tuner knew a Hale piano when he saw one. The "dark ways of the makers" to which the *New York Tribune* referred were inkier and more convoluted than any editor imagined. Even Joseph P. Hale had an "artist endorsement."

At the same time that he was selling Hale pianos under Phillips's name and claiming they were his own production, Albert Weber was himself being counterfeited. A man named Robert Webber teamed with John N. Young, a small Manhattan pianomaker, to produce an instrument stenciled WEBBER, NEW YORK, which he, Robert Webber, was selling to the unwary upstate. Webber and Young had the audacity to use a cut from Albert Weber's catalog to illustrate their own catalog. Weber filed suit against Webber and Young, obtaining an injunction which prohibited the sale of Webber pianos. Robert Webber was also ordered to pay $85.83 in costs, but no damages were awarded.

Albert Weber quickly turned his peculiar position—spokesman for a group of counterfeiters—to advantage. "Your uniform love of fair play will, I trust, allow me a few words in reply to the article published," wrote Weber to the *Times*. "No one, I am sure, has done more to elevate the reputation of New York pianos than myself, and my faith in the intelligence of the people has been rewarded by a patronage second to none, and a reputation which has made the Weber piano known throughout the world, and procured for it the admiration of every great artist and competent critic." This, of course, was known as puffing, and Albert Weber now claimed that he was equal in size and stature to Steinway & Sons.

Weber went on to say that he did not believe in the pianomakers' protective society: "I had fought my way up to the top, felt secure in my position, and believed that each manufacturer would accomplish more by being un-trammeled." His competitors "got scared and magnified every little shadow one-hundred fold" and decided to form a society. After they were not elected to office, claimed Weber, "a few disappointed *outs* met in a little conclave and decided to form an *exclusive* society, where all could be officers." Mr. Weber was not quite finished deprecating those who left the Hale-dominated group: "If a little ring chooses to come together and form an insignificant coterie for mutual admiration, that is their business; but let them abstain from throwing mud on their own handiwork simply because it has gotten too unwieldy for them to handle." The Weber arguments were almost simpleminded, but they were sufficient for his purposes. Albert Weber used the pianomakers' society conflict to elevate himself from the second tier to a position alongside William as spokesman for the trade. Albert Weber did not, however, explain why he was elected secretary of the Hale society or why he, a devout believer in individual initiative, was still a member of a society of "bogus" pianomakers.

To ensure that the public understood the difference, William and his allies published yet another article in the *Times*. "Sixty to seventy thousand piano-fortes and organs are made and sold in the United States yearly. Such is the excellence attained in their manufacture that America has . . . a considerable foreign market among those who appreciate the highest excellence in such instruments, and are willing to pay the higher prices." This was a clever half-truth designed to buttress the perception of American supremacy in pianomaking while simultaneously stirring patriotic feelings. The true half had naught to do with pianos. It was American organs which the Old World desired, particularly the English, who imported over $300,000 worth in the typical year of 1880. The export piano trade to Europe was tiny; a mere eighteen thousand dollars' worth, perhaps fifty units, were sent to Germany and only sixty-nine thousand dollars' worth to England. Overall, organ exports exceeded piano exports by two to one, and the largest volume of piano trade was done not with Europe but with Canada. All musical instrument exports were scarcely one-tenth of one percent of America's total exports and were also smaller than the imports. In 1885 only fifty-five American pianos were sent to Germany, fifty-one to England, and seven to France. American pianomakers had not and would not conquer the world, but more pianos could be sold at home if buyers believed that American instruments were in wide use in Europe. "The manufacture of piano-fortes and organs is thus of great and growing importance, employing as it does large capital and a vast amount of skilled labor," concluded the *Times* propaganda piece.

"A new piano war has broken out," reported the *New York World*, "which threatens to rival in intensity the old conflicts over the Paris Exposition, and to far exceed any former war in the number and cruelty of its warriors." The *World* dispatched to the "chieftains" the "discreetest [*sic*] reporters . . . who have no ear for music and cannot be beguiled by grand pianos . . . to gain all possible knowledge of the situation." The *World* felt it necessary to explain to its sophisticated urban readership that "piano playing in our day is not confined to metropolitan parlors. Long before Von Bulow came or Pattison lectured, the homesteads, the farm-houses, the cottages, even the adobe shelters of the great West included a piano among the household utensils. But it does not appear that the great West, which wanted a genuine piano, was always disposed to pay the genuine price." So there arose, explained the *World*, "manufacturers who believed in adapting themselves to the wants no less than the tastes of the people."

Then followed two interviews, one with William Steinway and another with Albert Weber. William assumed a statesmanlike role. "You ought to make it clear that this is a matter in which the public are the chief sufferers," said William to the reporter. When baited on Weber, William demurred, "I do not desire to say one word against Mr. Weber as a businessman or maker, but his action in this matter convinced all his friends, I think, that he was under some sort of obligation to Mr. Hale."

Weber's "insignificant coterie" letter to the *Times* was "quite funny. Mr. Weber shows a great deal of humor in his advertisements, more humor than truth sometimes."

When the article appeared in the paper William noted in his diary that his interview was "most incorrectly given, and Weber's being in his usual bombastic style." The *World* reported that a "square reporter having been sent to Mr. Steinway, an upright was despatched to Mr. Weber who was quite willing to converse." Declared Weber, "Nobody had a worse time with these bogus fellows than I have." This was preface to a rambling diatribe, not against "bogus pianos," but "bogus newspapers," and most specifically the *Music Trade Review*, which Weber designated, with obvious contempt, "a Steinway sheet." The logic, to the extent it existed, in Albert Weber's argument, seemed to revolve around the notion that he was not prepared to support the manufacturers' association because Steinway supported it and *Music Trade Review*. Lurking just beneath the surface was a charge that any maker who refused to advertise in the trade paper would be smeared in its pages. "It's all a question of advertisements and the bogus piano business has very little to do with it," claimed Weber. "Bill Steinway says that Hale makes fifty Stanley & Sons pianos a week. Well, does Bill Steinway think the American people can't tell the difference between Stanley and Steinway? All I've got to say is that Mr. Steinway must make a bigger difference between the pianos himself then."

The "upright" reporter kept making efforts to rein in the rambling Albert Weber. "Yes, but about the bogus pianos?" "Oh that's an old story," claimed Weber. "A good thing will always have imitators. . . . If a farmer out in Iowa buys a Steinway piano and thinks he's got a Weber, all we can do is laugh at the ignorance of the fellow." Albert Weber, obviously relishing his new fame, could not resist the chance to attack the Steinways.

But suddenly the story died; Albert Weber had no more to say. It may be that he was silenced by Joseph Hale, whose business was certainly not benefiting from the heightened public interest. Nor did William or J. P. Hale or C. Frank Chickering or any of the other partisans have much more to say to the popular press. Only the *Music Trade Review* continued to sound its tiny trumpet of moral outrage. It may be that the combatants came to comprehend that they were corroding confidence in the entire trade, both "reputable" and "bogus" alike. The piano war was short and intense; there was no victor, and all survived to fight again . . . soon.

Chapter 17

AGGRESSIVE
AND IRREPRESSIBLE
MANUFACTURERS

Wednesday, June 7, 1876. "Depart with the 7:30 A.M. train, arrive Philadelphia at 10 A.M. Yesterday all the pianos were moved to Judge's Hall, but General Oliver being sick trial postponed to this morning, nearly all the pianomakers are in the entrance in front. After some delay Albert, Theodore and myself go in and we explain to the four jurors Kupka, Schiedmeyer, Bristow and General Oliver our points of excellence in the Grand pianos and action. We take dinner at Laubers, spend the afternoon pretty confident of victory, towards evening Albert & I walk to Schiedmeyer's house, who tells us that both Oliver and Bristow are our enemies and that Kupka makes 'Mennle.' Albert & I ride to Blasius house Spring garden str. Tell Theodore who gets into a terrible excitement, and Albert is very sick." So begins William's description of the critical days of the summer of the nation's centennial.

Though called the Centennial Exhibition, the event at Philadelphia was not a retrospective. Historical artifacts were few and far between, consisting primarily of George Washington's false teeth, a colonial kitchen, and a display of models from the United States Patent Office. When the old was shown, it was usually to create a quaint contrast to the modern. Such was the case in Group XXV, Instruments of Precision, Research, Experiment and Illustration including Telegraphy and Music, Class 327, Piano-fortes, where Chickering & Sons, in addition to a full display of modern pianos, also exhibited a reliquarian piano of 1823 in fine condition.

It was, however, the future that balanced tenuously on the outcome of the Philadelphia Centennial Exhibition. The Steinways and Chickerings had last competed directly at the Paris fair of 1867 and indirectly at Vienna in 1873. C. Frank Chickering was awarded the Legion of Honor at Paris and for nearly a decade had been promoting this "victory" over Steinway. Steinway, of course, had its antidote to Chickering in the form of the judges' expression of "regret" from the Vienna Exhibition of 1873.

But now there were more than just two credible competitors. The Decker Brothers, David and Jacob, launched operations in 1862 after working for Bacon & Raven as well as Steinway & Sons. Peculiarly, their first business address was 85 Varick Street, from which Steinway also began. George Steck, another notable adversary and holder of a handful of patents, had a reputation as a fine scale designer and builder of durable instruments. He was also an enlightened employer who offered his employees shares in the firm. In emulation of his larger competitors, Steck maintained a small concert space called, not surprisingly, Steck Hall. Steck and the Deckers together did not generate one-half of the revenue of Steinway & Sons, but they were worthy competitors. Like Steinway, Decker Brothers and George Steck & Company were members of The Piano-forte and Organ Manufacturers and Dealers Protective Association of New York, i.e., the Steinway/Chickering axis in the bogus piano wars.

Most formidable of all, though, was Albert Weber. Having scrambled to a position in the public perception of near-equality with the Steinways, the Hale-aligned Weber was soon putting to work what he had learned during the protective society battle of a few months before: journalists were less interested in truth than in wild claims. For the Steinways, there were many ways to lose. While there was little question that they would leave the Centennial Exhibition with some award, even that could be a loss. To maintain supremacy, they had to depart Philadelphia with a clearly superior award, a prize that would buttress their claims of biggest and best.

For William this was particularly important. As the developer of the Steinway & Sons' strategy of *prizes plus prestigious players plus patents equal high prices*, a loss of face at the exhibition could mean a shift to Theodore's concept of "cheap, cheap, cheap" pianos. If Hale had control of Weber and an interest in Chickering and either or both equalled or exceeded Steinway in the awards, the sluice gates could open on a flood of cheap Hale-produced pianos using the Chickering or Weber names. William knew that a prize-winning three-hundred-dollar piano would destroy Steinway & Sons; he had reduced wholesale prices by twenty to fifty dollars that winter, and in the spring a prestigious rosewood case was added to the cheapest Steinway; fancier carved legs were now used on two other models. Price cuts and model changes helped little; sales were still slack. The reason was the depression. In the first quarter of 1876 business failures increased by half to 2,806 firms, and Dun, Barlow & Company, the compilers of the data, observed that "in the struggle for business existence, the doctrine of the survival of the fittest receives fresh illustration." Another Darwinian conflict was about to begin at Philadelphia.

"We also avail ourselves of this opportunity to inform our business friends that we have just forwarded to the Centennial Fair at Philadelphia, for exhibition and competition, five Grand, three Upright and one Square Grand Piano, containing our latest patented improvements, which, with the elegant fitting up of the space alotted to us, in the Main Exhibition Hall, will make a magnificent display," wrote William to the dealers and agents on May 1, 1876. "We also exhibit in the Machinery Hall a number of our own Composite Metal Castings in their various stages of progression, also the various metal parts of Pianofortes, which we manufacture in our own establishments." Steinway & Sons, the only pianomaker casting its own metal parts, had found a way to compete for two medals, not just one.

A special car was leased to transport the pianos, components, and display to Philadelphia. There the roughly eight thousand pounds of Steinway pianos joined the fifty-seven million pounds of objects, flora, and fauna sent to the Centennial Exhibition; they were nine crates among 150,000 exhibition-bound crates, boxes, barrels, and bags, 10,084 tons destined for the Main Hall. The Pennsylvania Railway, which at one time or another handled almost every item at the Centennial, had good reason to keep accurate records. Freight was charged by the pound. "The efficiency of that great industrial corporation, directed by a single will, remained throughout the Exhibition a source of ever-fresh wonder to the intelligent visitor," wrote Francis A. Walker in a "critical account" of the fair. No statistics were kept on the proportion of the almost ten million visitors who experienced "ever-fresh wonder," but it was calculated that seventy-five tons of packing material and trash were removed in a single day before the fair opened.

Crates marked "Steinway & Sons, New York" were certainly among the rubbish, along with the containers of sixty-three other piano exhibitors, with thirty-two of those coming from Europe. Germany was most heavily represented with ten exhibitors; in total the number of pianos exhibited was "upwards of 200," according to the Judges' report. Only ninety eight of the pianos on display were actually judged and, of those, seventy-six received awards, a magnanimous 77.5 percent. At Paris in 1867 only 34 percent of exhibitors received any award and less than 2 percent merited a gold medal.

The judging system at the Centennial was a sharp departure from the traditional European system of gold, silver, and bronze medals awarded by volunteer juries, along with the occasional royal medal or special certificate thrown in for good measure. To begin, the judges were paid for their services with a stipend of six hundred dollars for American judges and one thousand dollars for foreign adjudicants, the latter reflecting the higher cost of transportation to the fair. This was generous remuneration for what amounted to no more than six weeks' work and was given for the avowed purpose of obtaining more diligent and qualified judges. Not stated was the obvious: a man well paid might be more difficult to bribe.

"The radical defect of the medal system is that it conveys no practical information," claimed F. A. Walker, and it "merely signifies that an article is good; but it does not answer the question which Socrates was wont to confound his adversaries: Good for *what?*" Under the American award system there was but one medal, a sign that the product was good. "The report," declared Walker, "tells what it is good for, where good, and how good. . . . In other words, the report is the real award." The report was to be written by a single judge and signed by him; he was, however, to obtain the concurrence of a majority of the judges. There were lengthy written instructions on judging developed by the eminent Professor J. C. Watson of the University of Michigan. The unlimited potential for strife in this report-based award system was undetected by its advocates, but the consequences reverberated for years.

Clarity, brevity, and equity were the theoretical goals of the judging system, but the theory soon met a practical challenge. In the case of the piano judges, the problem was in finding sufficiently disinterested experts. Judge Henry K. Oliver was known to be a lifelong friend of the Chickering family. George F. Bristow, a Brooklyn-based composer and teacher, was closely allied with Albert Weber and endorsed his pianos in advertisements. Julius Schiedmeyer was a German pianomaker, friend of Theodore, and had played a central role in inducing the jury to endorse the absent Steinways at Vienna in 1873. F. P. Kupka, from Austria, was described as an "amateur." Though he was not prealigned with any of the exhibitors, there were rumors that Mr. Kupka's assessments at Vienna, where he had also judged, were malleable in the presence of cash. In sum, it was widely believed that there was a Chickering judge, a Steinway judge, a Weber judge, and a judge for rent.

"Great excitement again," wrote William. "Albert has a fearful headache, calls Chickering a loony fool. . . . I send Albert and Theodore away, I explain our Square piano to the Jury." Later that same day William met with Schiedmeyer and received a report from Friedrich Boscovitz, the pianist Steinway & Sons hired to demonstrate their instruments each day during the fair. Boscovitz told William that "he had seen Kupka," and that night William "slept well."

The next morning Boscovitz reported to William again. "I send Blasius [a local Steinway dealer] to Philadelphia for $1000 which I give to Boscovitz. This is 12½." After a leisurely lunch and a visit with Charles P. Kimball, centennial commissioner of New York State ("He will do all he can for us"), William took the train back to New York City. Tretbar returned separately and in the afternoon told William that he had seen George Bristow, "who amazes T. by telling him that B. received something from Kupka which he indignantly returned. We consult about this at Theodore's house, Tretbar immediately goes to Philadelphia." Unable to find either Schiedmeyer or Kupka, Tretbar shuttled back to Manhattan.

Sunday William spent with Theodore busily drafting the Steinway & Sons judge's report, which they planned to give to Julius Schiedmeyer. Monday was cold and wet when William, hoarse and coughing with a cold, once again shuffled off to the Centennial, presumably to deliver the report to the judge. The plot thickened as Albert chanced to encounter George F. Bristow and had "a pleasant chat with him but no reference to the developments on Saturday" when Kupka gave Bristow "something." The week moved on without material developments until Thursday: "At Schiedmeyer's house at 7½ A.M. work with him like a beaver getting up written report. Eat nothing all day. Finished at 5 P.M. go to Exhibition. Meet Decker. See Schiedmeyer at Scheutzenhalle who says that both Bristow and Weber are satisfied with the latter's report."

On Friday, June 16, 1876, there were two significant developments. First, the judges had a "great dispute" over Chickering's report. It is unknown who wrote the Chickering report, but it was certainly not C. Frank Chickering. The disagreement centered around the wording. Originally the report read, "The Concert Grand was of the older (not overstrung) method of stringing, was of quite elastic touch, and of broad and clear resonance with the utmost power of utterance that its class affords, consistent with obtaining a pure, delicate and singing quality of tone." As ultimately published, the report made no mention of "older" or "not overstrung"; but an astute reader of the reports, skilled in decoding obscure messages, might conclude that the judges thought the Chickering concert grand lacked power. The many pianomen lurking near the open windows of the building certainly overheard the details of the dispute as did Frank Chickering, who spent the entire day sitting on the stairs of the Judge's Hall probably mortified by what he heard. Chickering, if not very effective, appeared to be honest.

There was another contact that Friday of greater but murkier significance: "At 11½ A.M. Geo. Cook of the Schoninger Organ Company, New Haven calls at our stand, hints that money has been handed to some of the Judges and that he can be of great advantage to us &c &c," recorded William. "Make appointment with him for Tuesday at 12 o'clock." It is here that events assume a Balkan complexity. The Schoninger company supplied organs to William Wallace Kimball; Kimball bought pianos for his Chicago-based business from Joseph P. Hale. It was therefore possible that Cook was a part of the Hale/Weber contingent, perhaps seeking to ensnare William in some admission of corruption. At their store in New Haven Schoninger also sold Weber pianos. But if William suspected Cook's allegiances, he did not record it, and he probably saw Cook as a source of intelligence on Albert Weber's activity.

George Cook and William met briefly on Tuesday morning as scheduled: ". . . arrange with him for his services," was William's cryptic entry. There are no clues to the nature of the "services" Cook was to provide, but the day's intrigue was not yet concluded. Later that Tuesday Albert Weber told William "that he last night returned to Kupka from Bristow what the former had given the latter." The possibilities here are manifold, but the most probable is that Kupka was acting as a conduit for payments by multiple parties to the judges and Bristow in particular.

William then returned to New York. There he learned that Simon D. Phelps, an advertising agent who sometimes worked for Steinway & Sons, had seen those most secret documents, the judge's reports. The reports were shown to Phelps by George Bristow, who was apparently unaware of the Steinway-Phelps connection. The jury members had failed to observe the first rule of successful corruption, that silence is essential, and they were soon found out.

When William returned to Philadelphia it was "dreadfully hot," and Julius Schiedmeyer briefed William on what judge Gen. Henry K. Oliver knew. At the Judge's Hall "I have a long and earnest conversation with General Oliver, telling him the Kupka Bristow borrowing affair." That evening half the "loaned" amount reappeared, but not from Kupka or Bristow: "Schiedmeyer gives me $500 to take care of for him," noted William. But matters were less than settled. Commissioner C. P. Kimball summoned Albert for a "long conversation." He had seen Weber as well as Bristow and wanted Albert to prepare a written statement which he would use, if needed, in the future. For some reason it was Theodore who prepared the statement in German, which William then translated into English, to be carried by Albert to Commissioner Kimball in Philadelphia. That same day F. P. Kupka's finances improved, and he returned his five-hundred-dollar "loan" to Boscovitz. Perhaps eager to avoid scandal, Centennial officials did no more, and in the first week of July Albert reported "that Matters are not forced in Phila. and may be deemed settled." He was wrong.

"The New York Herald," wrote William, "has a defamatory article of 3½ columns charging Schiedmeyer, Bristow & Kupka with corruption connecting our name with Schiedmeyer." Too many knew, and now among the knowledgeable were reporters. "WHAT'S THE PRICE OF AWARDS AND MEDALS?" howled the *Herald* headline. "Female Charms Brought to Bear on the Judges. . . . SOMETHING FOR THE COMMISSION TO INVESTIGATE. . . . If examples are made now of the comparatively few corrupt judges the evil may be stopped . . . [or] the same bargaining for and sale of awards will attend the Philadelphia Exhibition as brought odium upon those held at Paris and, notably, at Vienna," admonished the *Herald*. "Although there have been murmurings among exhibitors in the sewing machine, furniture and leather departments and discontent among manufacturers of agricultural implements and textile fabrics, the most pronounced rumors are afloat about the maneuverings for the pianoforte awards." After admitting that he did not have time to verify the rumors, the *Herald* reporter did not let the lack of confirmation inhibit his moral outrage: "Three at least of the judges of group 25 ought to be disgracefully removed and consigned to the obliquy which attaches to those who abuse public trusts imposed in them and who seek pecuniary profit at the expense of honor." The only tentative exclusion from "obliquy" was General H. K. Oliver, who was described as "a good natured old gentleman from Boston."

Schiedmeyer was the subject of the most specific charges: "He was a member of the jury at both Paris and Vienna, and on account of certain transactions at both exhibitions, he is declared to be, by reputable gentlemen of the piano trade, an utterly unfit person to serve in such a capacity. He is, in the first place, a pianomaker himself. . . . Schiedmeyer's pianos are said to be copied after the Steinways. . . . He is said to be their private agent in Europe, and is openly spoken of as 'the Steinway's man' on the jury. . . . It is believed by many that his appointment at Philadelphia was procured mainly for the purpose of taking advantage of his preferences and to render more certain a favorable report for the same pianos." It was undoubtedly these statements which William considered defamatory; in fact, the correspondent attributed power to the Steinways that they did not have. Julius Schiedmeyer, though partisan, was selected by the German government with no evidence of influence by William or Theodore. His appointment was simply a matter of good fortune for Steinway & Sons.

In a paragraph vaguely alleging "pecuniary considerations," the name of Kupka appeared: "Mr. Kupka then came in for his share of blame, and those who had watched his movements closest said they would sooner trust Mr. Schiedmeyer than him," continued the *Herald*. The reporter suggested an investigation of Mr. Kupka, who, he thought, "can probably tell more than any of the others about what a judge's report is worth."

George Bristow, renowned American composer, violinist, and church organist, did "not escape the general smirching, and whether he deserved it or not he was openly proclaimed as acting in the sole interest of one New York maker, whose interests he was prepared to advance at any cost. The published advertisements of this New York pianomaker, in which a representation of his showroom is given, actually contain a full-length portrait of Mr. Bristow, 'the judge' leaning in a picturesque attitude against a piano placed conspicuously in the foreground." Despite an apparent penchant for detail, the *Herald* correspondent failed to mention that this "New York manufacturer" was Albert Weber. The *Herald* also revealed that Bristow admitted showing copies of the judges' reports to outsiders, a gross violation of the rules.

Buried deep in the article was the reference to "female charms." According to the *Herald*, a Mr. H. W. Gray, president of an old Philadelphia firm, the Schomacher Piano-forte Company, was invited to dine with a "New York maker" and the judges one evening. The unidentified piano man whispered to Mr. Gray, "You see I got my wife here to-day. We fix the judges all right. What I cannot do, she can. You see?" Mr. Gray, who made the report, also indicated that he "indignantly" declined to accept the offer of hospitality.

Gray also claimed that a "man from Brooklyn," a less-than-opaque reference to George Bristow, had said, "I can fix it so you can write your own report and say what you please." The incorruptible Mr. Gray, even when presented with this extraordinary offer, did not accept, nor did he ask the cost. While it is clear that both Weber and Steinway did write their own reports, it is improbable that Bristow and Schiedmeyer combined in corruption, since both fought bitterly with each other for the victory of their favored firms. For some long-lost reason, H. W. Gray attempted to paint a picture of a trio of corrupt judges acting together, whereas the evidence suggests prior alliances and individual dishonesty.

There was about the whole episode a certain blatant disregard for the appearance, if not the actual existence, of propriety on the part of the judges. Weber and Bristow were seen together often at dinner, while the Steinways and Julius Schiedmeyer were frequent lunch partners. While William prepared his report with Schiedmeyer in the latter's quarters, Albert Weber was less circumspect. "One of the judges is said to have handed out of the window of the Secretary's office in Judge's Hall, to a New York piano maker, the written report upon his pianos. This person is alleged to have made alterations in the document to suit himself, and to have returned it to the office, where it was once again placed on file with the forgeries in it," reported the *Herald*. Why the paper did not report that the Weber document was handed to Albert Weber, probably by George Bristow, is unknown, but William was aware of this, as were others.

Garbled details and the unknown agenda of H. W. Gray aside, the *Herald* article was sufficiently compelling to force a response from William, which he drafted with the assistance of John C. Freund of the *Music Trade Review* and Charles Tretbar: "We read in your issue of Sunday last a communication . . . based upon the ex-parte statements of an insignificant piano manufacturing company in Philadelphia. . . . The firm of Steinway is singled out in connection with Mr. Schiedmeyer." With a tone suitable to its Olympian stature, Steinway & Sons claimed that the Schomacher firm was attempting to "force itself into notoriety by a controversy with us." The charges, "one and all, are as absurd as they are untrue." Mr. Schiedmeyer was a millionaire and a Steinway competitor in Europe and South America. He had no need of soliciting small bribes from the Schomacher company, which "he could buy up with a single year's income." William personally delivered the letter to the *Herald*. "Though our puff is left out it still reads very well," judged William. George Bristow also responded: "I repel the covert charge of having allowed either money or friendship to influence my opinion as infamously and maliciously false, and invite a thorough and most searching investigation of my actions as a judge of the Centennial Commission, Group 25," wrote Bristow to the *Herald*. The letter was a model of brief indignation. "My connection with Group 25 not having ceased I cannot now answer many of the indirect innuendoes and vague insinuations without violating my duty to the Centennial Commission," demurred Mr. Bristow.

There appeared that same day another story on the piano competition, this time in the *New York World*. William thought the *World* piece "very able, much more just than the Herald one," but he seemed more concerned with rehearsing testimony with witnesses for his pending divorce. The *World* piece was sophisticated, interpretive, and generally dismissive of the *Herald* charges of serious wrongdoing. "At all events the pianomakers here are in a state of excitement that forbodes another piano war of large dimensions. It is a singular fact that nearly every world's fair has given rise to similar conflict among these aggressive and irrepressible manufacturers. . . . In any other than a purely fanciful or a purely technical sense the instruments of these makers are probably so nearly alike that nobody but a trained expert could tell the difference." The unusually astute *World* analyst continued, "But that is of less consequence to them than popular prestige. One of them, and one only, can by official act be recognized as the pianoforte maker par excellence of America, and it is to this distinction that they have bent all their energies." The analysis was as succinct as it was correct. The *World* reporter also observed that "the accusations against the judges are too frequent and loud not to warrant the attention of the commission, and the vindication or dismissal of the subcommittee." The commission, however, was in recess.

Shortly after the articles appeared, William lunched privately with Julius Schiedmeyer and had "a long earnest talk with him," the standard phraseology William used when he was attempting to get at the truth. The next day Schiedmeyer called upon all the other credible competitors, save Chickering. Steck, Decker, and Knabe seemed to present no threat, but Schiedmeyer was "very much excited and disgusted" by Albert Weber, who was "lying to him about new juries." Schiedmeyer would soon leave America, and William presented him with a gift, his personal Stevens pocket rifle with a twenty-inch barrel, then accompanied Schiedmeyer to the docks at Hoboken to board the *Main*. Although his closest jury contact was gone, William was not devoid of resources. Pianist Friedrich Boscovitz was still playing each day on the Steinways in the exhibition main hall and was delivering regular situation reports to William. Tretbar told William that Charles P. Kimball called "and thinks everything will be allright."

Desperation was soon to provide a new ally in the form of General

Oliver. "I hurry and meet the old gentleman, with whom I have a pleasant conversation. He begs me to give him the data for the development of piano building in New York, as the task has been assigned to him to write the introduction to the Jurors' reports. Albert takes him to the factory . . . meet Genl Oliver at factory, again explain to Genl Oliver the Kupka-Boscovitz transaction, also the Jew Goldschmidt connection with Kupka, then return to store," wrote William.

All was quiet for several weeks, during which time William arranged for the entire workforce of Steinway & Sons to visit the exhibition. About eleven hundred persons took the transfer steamer *Kill Von Kull* to Jersey City and there boarded two chartered trains to Philadelphia. For employees the trip was free. At the Centennial Depot in Philadelphia the Steinway forces formed a procession nearly a mile long and, led by a band, marched into the fairgrounds. A special concert for the employees was played by Friedrich Boscovitz, after which the group dispersed to see the sights. Heavy rains did little to dampen the fun, but thirteen men missed the special return trains and William himself arranged their transportation back to New York. William remained in Philadelphia, his rheumatism making it difficult for him to walk.

Back in the city a few day later, he heard a report from Albert that "a desperate effort will be made to set aside the entire piano Awards." If William were concerned, he did not record it, and he continued to work on the piano history report for General Oliver. It was early September when George Cook of the Schoninger Organ Company reappeared to tell Albert that "Commissioner Donaldson of Idaho had moved to withhold the medal from us charging corruption & fraud &c &c.," noted William. Detective Hogan, the investigator for the divorce, was dispatched to Philadelphia to pick up letters obtained by Boscovitz that detailed the charges.

Two days later William and Albert were summoned to Brewster & Company, a New York carriagemaker, by Charles Kimball. "Kimball wants us to make a positive statement that we never paid any money to the judges which I do and send off per mail," wrote William, apparently relying on the very fine point that the thousand dollars was returned. But the psychological toll of staring into the abyss of disrepute was beginning: "Gloomy, rainy day. Business again very discouraging, and I feel very wretched over all the troubles which only seem to pile up higher everyday."

Ensnared in a thicket of corruption as brazen as it was incompetent, William saw no escape. Had he refused to "loan" money to the jurors, the certain result would have been an indifferent report that Weber and Chickering, presumably aligned with J. P. Hale, would broadcast endlessly as official certification of the fall of the house of Steinway. By making the "loans," he did not guarantee a victory, for William surely understood that a man who took one "loan" would accept others. Realistically, he had done nothing but reduce the probability of defeat. The firm was still hostage to the integrity of the corruptible. There had been no choice but to "loan"; the circumstances were more akin to blackmail than bribery. But in the binary good-bad world of public morality such pragmatism was regarded as despicable as the deed of bribery itself.

In less than two weeks the Centennial Commission was to announce the awards, and the absence of Steinway & Sons from the winner's list could trigger a frenzy among both the press and competitors. There was now real risk of exposure, and the Steinway reputation that William fought to protect and advance would be indelibly stained. Rumors of William's divorce and the reasons for it were already percolating among his acquaintances; compounding the personal moral crisis, Steinway & Sons was now potentially subject to charges of corruption and bribery in business.

"All day long now," reported the *Times*, "great sheaves of paper are flowing into the Judges Pavilion. These documents are 'The Reports of Awards,' Form 209, which have been harvested for the past few months in the vast pastures of the Exhibition. . . . Almost anything that can be grown by man, or caught or built by him, finds its place here." The fruits of the piano "harvest" had been found to be contaminated and were now in peril of rejection by the commission. To save the crop, William journeyed again to Philadelphia: "See Kimball and have a long consultation with him. I leave with 12 o'clock train. Though in sleeping car, I do not sleep a wink." William's next step, apparently with Kimball's approval, was to write two letters, content unknown but backdated almost three months to June 1876. These were soon picked up by Charles Kimball's son. Just four days before the official announcement of the awards, William received not one but three letters advising him that "after a hard fight with Beckwith [another commissioner and the designer of the award system], the Centennial Commission adopted our report without altering a word. . . . I am very much relieved."

Charles P. Kimball had not only prevailed; he succeeded spectacularly, obtaining for Steinway not merely one but two medals. The first of these was the medal for the pianos and its accompanying award, written by William and Julius Schiedmeyer, mysteriously signed by General Oliver as the official author, then duly certified by the commission. At twenty-eight lines, roughly one-half of a printed page, the Steinway & Sons piano report was at least triple the length of the Chickering award and five times the length of Weber's. The Steinway report, lathered with superlatives, evaluated not only tone, evenness of scale, elasticity of touch, and overall quality, as did all piano reports, but also listed six "improvements" patented by the firm. If the length of a report was a measure of societal significance, then Steinway was equated with Edison and Bell.

There was a second Steinway award for "Metal Ware"; at ten lines, it was more than twice as long as the typical piano report. The only pianomaker with its own foundry, Steinway succeeded in an alchemal transformation of cast iron into sales gold: "The full metal frames of cupola shape possess an unequaled degree of resistance, permitting a vastly increased tension of the strings without the slightest danger of break or crack in said metal frames, thereby considerably increasing the vibratory power and augmenting the lasting qualities of their instruments." A dealer in Detroit or Cincinnati could translate that labored prose into a powerful sales claim: "It plays loud and it won't break," might be considered the essence. William was very pleased: "Receive our Iron report from Kimball, it is magnificent & was officially added to the piano report . . . and very much strengthens our other report." Perhaps prudently, William did not attend the official awards presentation held by the Centennial Commission.

It is clear from the record that Charles P. Kimball was a prime force in the suppression of scandal and the ultimate awards to Steinway & Sons. Less clear is *why* Mr. Kimball assumed the role of Steinway advocate. Kimball may have realized that to open one case of possible corruption involving judges from Europe, now long departed, was likely to precipitate an avalanche of accusations, some perhaps justified, by disgruntled exhibitors in many classes, not merely pianos. Most of the potential American witnesses to any alleged corruption were contaminated by obvious self-interest, as in the case of Albert Weber. Foreign judges and exhibitors were completely inaccessible, shielded by oceans, viscous communications, and potentially uncooperative governments quick to take any charge of dishonesty as an insult to national honor. The price to be paid by the commission was also high; the probity of the judging was ultimately the responsibility of the commissioners who had, in fact, vetted the judges. In the case of the piano judging, the commissioners had done nothing with the early protestations about "Chickering Judge Oliver" or a "Steinway Judge Schiedmeyer" or "Weber Judge Bristow." Ultimately charges of dishonesty would reflect upon the Centennial Commission, and the commissioners appeared to lack both the will and the mechanisms to deal with such issues.

Another factor, perhaps bearing more directly on the Steinway awards, was the fact that Charles P. Kimball was a lifelong supporter of the Democratic Party, as was William. Born in Maine, Kimball had been twice nominated for the governorship of that state. A prosperous carriagemaker, he moved to New York and joined Brewster & Company. He was appointed to the Centennial Commission by Gov. Samuel J. Tilden, who harvested immense political benefit from the downfall of William Marcy Tweed. Playing a minor role in those events was one William Steinway, a reluctant member—he attempted to resign—of the Committee of Seventy, a citizens' group that sought evidence of Tweed Ring corruption. "Silk Stocking Sammy" Tilden and William were neighbors in Gramercy Park. The former New York mayors, Hoffman and Havemeyer, were well known to William through the Liederkranz. Judge Donohue, another Democrat, was the recipient of modest Steinway largesse for his expeditious justice in the divorce matter. But William's most significant political contact was likely Oswald Ottendorfer, alderman and publisher of the German-language newspaper *Staats-Zeitung*. The paper had already published, without William's intercession, a tribute to Julius Schiedmeyer, a sort of national antidote to the scandalous *Herald* article. Ottendorfer and William sometimes lunched together, but William rarely logged their conversations. It might be surmised, however, that the political powers of the Democracy calculated that the reputation of a famous, energetic, wealthy forty-one-year-old German of loyal political sentiment was worth more to them alive than dead.

Scarcely one month after the Centennial Awards the *New York Evening Post* carried an item that Mr. William Steinway might be nominated for alderman-at-large. This news William read, "much to my disgust." So it came to be that William did not save himself but was spared by men more powerful than he, men wealthier than he, men who perhaps saw the utility of a name respected in the city's Teutonic community. Of his evasion of infamy William wrote that he was relieved; he did not realize that perhaps he should have been grateful to dun and potent forces whose instrument was a Yankee from Bethel, Maine.

There was little time for introspection and analysis; another piano war flared immediately. The official but preliminary announcement of the awards were as lightning strikes in a drought-stricken forest: brief events with colossal consequences. By any rational standard what followed was bizarre.

Chapter 18

THE TRUTH AT LAST

"The excitement attending the preliminary announcements . . . does not abate but rather increases," observed the *New York Times*. "The [award] system itself being entirely novel, and totally unlike that of other great international fairs, has come in for a large share of abuse and praise. . . . The Executive Committee . . . had hoped to avoid all bickerings and complaints and issued circulars in quantities and gave such publicity to the matter that it was thought the matter was thoroughly understood by everyone. . . . It is held that a proportion of about seventy-five percent of the entire exhibitors received awards."

In the piano competition 77.5 percent of all pianos tested received medals, a proportion not very different from that of the exhibition as a whole. The theory that the report was what really counted and not the medal apparently caused the judges to loose medals on exhibitors in a metallic cascade, only to later realize that they would have to justify the medals with words that answered Walker's Socratic question, "Good for what?" The limitations and vagaries of language soon swamped subtle differences. Words became the battleground as competitors clubbed each other with adjectives, slashed with modifiers, stabbed with prepositional phrases, and gladatorially jousted in advertisements. The principal combatants were, of course, William Steinway and Albert Weber.

This was language as bloodsport. If competition between rival firms is today constrained by law and regulation of false advertising, misleading statements, libel, defamation, or industrial espionage, there were no such checks on Albert Weber and William Steinway. The only limits were those of conscience. These proved, in the main, to be remarkably elastic. At stake was perceived primacy in the industry; the waning fortunes of Chickering foreshadowed the future of the defeated in the contest.

Two men, each of extraordinary ability, were about to commit their lifeworks, their fortunes, their firms, and, most important to them, their reputations, to a contest of supremacy. It was no small irony that this commercial warfare was fought over the Centennial Awards that were in themselves corrupt; it was also inevitable, for Steinway & Sons needed to perpetuate its string of "victories" to maintain dominance while Albert Weber needed but one "victory" to assert preeminence.

Adding psychological weight to the conflict was the immense popularity of the Centennial Exhibition. Of the ten million persons who passed through its gates, over eight million were paid admissions; roughly one of every six Americans paid to visit the Centennial. Against this background of widespread public knowledge and interest, a three-year conflict began.

The first Steinway advertisement after the awards advised its readers, "No individual explanation or ingenious torturing of words into a different meaning from that intended is here necessary." The Steinway award was unanimous; it gave the firm first place, the ad claimed. Immediately below was the view of Decker Brothers: "Referring to the announcements of other manufacturers that they have obtained prizes over all competitors, we desire to inform the public that there was but one award for the highest order of excellence." There was in effect at this time a "secrecy order" by the Centennial Commission that prevented winners from publishing the text of their awards. Those not acquainted with accommodating judges did not know the contents of their own reports.

None of these formalities impressed Albert Weber, who distributed circulars on the exhibition grounds containing his report. The Weber circulars were quickly confiscated by Centennial authorities and were found to contain not merely the Weber report, but a more favorable version of it written by Weber himself but rejected by the jurors.

The report the jurors after much dispute signed referred to "sympathetic, pure and rich tone, as shown in a *grand piano of large dimensions*." The Weber-added phrase "combined with greatest power" was deleted. Skinned of the Victorian verbal furbelows, all Weber's pianos except the concert grand were well built and played smoothly, but did not have outstanding tone. Some men might have taken pride and comfort in building a concert grand piano roughly equal to Steinway's, but for Albert Weber this was not enough; he had clearly decided that as the self-designated successor, or at least joint tenant, at the pinnacle occupied by Steinway & Sons, *all* his instruments must be equal. This was a practical choice; concert grand sales were few and far between. Knowing that more than a year would pass before the official reports were printed but that public interest in the awards was then at a peak, Weber began to advertise the report *he* wrote, rather than the one bestowed on him by the judges.

This was an effective, if crude, falsification, which William took in his competitive stride. At the time he was more interested in reviewing General Oliver's draft of piano history that would preface the published jury reports and in the details of Regina's relationship with Louis Dachauer that unravelled along with the Dachauer marriage. Weber's advertisements also quoted, not mentioning the name, a portion of the Steinway award: "largest volume, purity and duration of tones," which Weber described as "mere mechanical qualities—to Weber alone are accredited the highest possible musical qualities." Albert Weber was capable of brilliant subreption, and he published an example of his best work in the *New York Times* on October 27, 1876.

Under the headline "THE PIANO WAR" came a subhead: "GEORGE F. BRISTOW, JUDGE OF THE JURY ON MUSICAL INSTRUMENTS AT THE CENTENNIAL EXHIBITION, EXPLAINS THE SITUATION." As in the earlier battles over "bogus" pianos, there were no clues to the reader that Albert Weber had paid two dollars per line to purchase a full column in the paper. The piece was signed "SPHINX," who appeared to function as an interviewer. In the piece Bristow gave the impression that the "facts" were being drawn from him only reluctantly, and there was a certain balance in his reticence. But by the end of the interview Bristow was recorded as saying, "That is *beyond a question.* Weber's pianos are *undoubtedly* the *best* in America, probably in the world." Judge George Frederick Bristow, American composer, church organist, and pedagogue had spoken, or so it seemed, and the impact was immediate. Wrote William: "Weber publishes Geo. F. Bristow Interview in Times, am excessively pestered all day."

It was likely no coincidence that the next day a gentleman named Herbert Van Dyke called on William and told him "important news about Weber and Bristow at Philadelphia." Herbert Van Dyke was a former Weber employee, probably a salesman, and was also the erstwhile manager of pianist John N. Pattison, who played Weber instruments at the Centennial.

The "important news" vouchsafed by Van Dyke was truly significant, for Mr. Van Dyke claimed knowledge of, in the language of the time, "a corrupt bargain" between Weber, Bristow and F. P. Kupka. Such an arrangement William undoubtedly believed had existed, and Van Dyke provided specifics, stating that Weber had paid Bristow $5,000 and that another $5,000 had been promised. Kupka, said Van Dyke, received $1,500 and that $3,500 further was to be paid. The aggregate sum was large, $15,000, or about $175,000 today. A part of the arrangement with George Bristow, claimed Van Dyke, was the Sphinx interview, and Bristow, used the first $5,000 to pay off the mortgage on his home. While the amounts involved may have seemed unusually ample to William, Herbert Van Dyke, for expenses and a fee to be decided by William, offered to marshal proof of the bribes.

Over the next month Van Dyke was paid a total of five hundred dollars for his services. He did not, however, succeed in proving that Bristow was corrupt; Van Dyke's own search of the courthouse records showed no mortgages on Bristow's property. He did, nonetheless, provide William with the statements of two prostitutes who saw Weber and Bristow in a house of ill repute, reports of Weber, Bristow, and Kupka dining and drinking together, and a claim that Bristow was the source of an anonymous letter to fellow judge, General Oliver, "wherein an exceedingly vile conundrum is propounded having a very evident intention to liken the General to a certain filthy and nameless thing." The letter, according to Van Dyke, was dictated by Bristow and written by a piano tuner named Jones. So went the relations between the august judges during the nation's Centennial Exhibition.

William Steinway and Herbert Van Dyke continued to meet sporadically into 1877, and a breakthrough occurred in early summer. After eight months of silence, George F. Bristow decided to condemn and renounce the Sphinx interview. What the renunciation lacked in timeliness it replaced with vigor. Bristow, according to Van Dyke, had gone to Weber's warerooms shortly after the publication of the Sphinx piece. There Weber denied knowledge of the interview and said he had not authorized it. Bristow told Van Dyke of the falsity of the Weber report, claiming that the judges' signatures on it were forgeries, and that it was always his intent to award the highest honors to Steinway. He himself had awarded all the Steinway pianos a full twenty-four points, the maximum under the judging system. Bristow also indicated to Van Dyke that he was prepared to document his assertions. Mr. Bristow and Mr. Weber had, for unspecified reasons, come to a parting of the ways, much to the benefit of Steinway.

At this point a new force entered the intrigue. A lawyer named Ernest Hall, unknown to William, called on him and said he represented George Bristow. Hall reported that Bristow would "do all he can to undo the falsehoods of Weber," wrote William. Although Bristow had refused to sign a document presented him by Van Dyke a few weeks before, he was willing to cooperate, apparently placing more trust in Mr. Hall than Mr. Van Dyke. Hall soon delivered a signed certificate from Bristow repudiating Weber. For this low-effort but essential exercise Hall received a fee of $750.

Another front had also been opened in the battle to defeat Weber and the Sphinx, who was now known to be a reporter named Wheeler who had worked for the *New York World*. Charles Tretbar, secretary of Steinway & Sons, had been corresponding with both General Oliver and Professor J. C. Watson at the University of Michigan. Watson was secretary of the

Group XXV jurors. Albert Weber was soon to be outflanked but was not yet out of maneuvering room. In an amazing display of cheek, Weber applied to the Centennial Commission for alterations to his award, and, more amazing still, his request was granted. To accomplish this, Weber either had the help of Bristow or led the Centennial Commission to believe he did. Weber's new award read precisely as had the false report. Through this bureaucratic legerdemain false became true, but only transitorily.

Albert Weber's strategic error was the publication of a fabricated set of jurors' scores in which he claimed that Weber received a total judges' score of 95 to Steinway's 91. Semantic strife over the meaning of the awards might have continued indefinitely to the enrichment of the newspapers, the amusement of reporters, and the ultimate indifference of much of the public. Arithmetic claims were markedly less ambiguous and allowed Steinway to seize the high ground. "We feel that many piano-forte manufacturers whose Exhibits at the Centennial stood as high or higher than Mr. Weber's are seriously affected by his villainous falsehoods," wrote Tretbar to James C. Watson. Tretbar thought the remedy was a certificate—of course, in the best interests of the entire piano industry—stating that Steinway received the highest average points and was therefore given the "first and highest award."

Watson was persuaded, and arranged the necessary letters of introduction and explanation so that Steinway & Sons could obtain the signatures of the *entire* Group XXV jury, not merely the musical instrument judges. "When a man's honor is at stake, he should act without hesitation, to vindicate it; or when he perceives that an injury is being done, that he should strive to remedy it," wrote Tretbar to Watson. It apparently struck neither man as ironical that "honor" was invoked by the same firm that was earlier forced to write letters denying bribery of the judges.

Tretbar was soon on his way to Europe to obtain the signature of some truly distinguished Group XXV jurors, none of whom had anything whatsoever to do with the piano judging. Among them were Emil Levasseur, the noted political economist and geographer, and Sir William Thomson, the renowned mathematician and physicist later known as Lord Kelvin. Tretbar was in Europe for more than two months and took the opportunity to visit Regina and Louis Dachauer. He also tried to locate, but could not, Mrs. Ernestine Oaks, whom William had not seen in more than a decade.

While Tretbar was soliciting signatures in Europe, S. D. Phelps was doing the same in the United States. Among the signers were Joseph Henry, a physicist who made fundamental discoveries in electromagnetism and was later director of the Smithsonian Institution, and Dr. F.A.P. Bernard, president of Columbia College. Among the musical jurors signing, F. P. Kupka's name was notably absent. General Oliver, despite William's help with piano history, apparently had misgivings. At one point he signed a certificate, then cut his signature out and returned the document. Ultimately the general, then the mayor of Salem, Massachusetts, did sign.

While Steinway agents were writing letters and traveling Europe and America in the high-stakes autograph hunt, the biggest news of all came when William received the afternoon editions on Monday, September 3, 1877. Joseph P. Hale's massive piano works burned to the ground, taking with it virtually the entire city block between Thirty-fifth and Thirty-sixth streets between Tenth and Eleventh avenues plus many surrounding buildings. "A scene of terror and confusion that has seldom been paralleled was being enacted," wrote the *Times*.

Over 250 firemen fought the blaze but soon found that hydrant pressure in the area was so low that the streams from their hoses could not reach above the second floor of the nine-story factory. The firemen laid pipe to the river. Thirteen ambulances responded to care for the burned and injured. Men were reported to be jumping from windows as high as the sixth floor. One man did jump from the eighth floor and died on impact. It took four hours to bring the blaze under control, and by then over eighty factories, tenements, homes, sheds, and stables were destroyed. Several days later the ruins were still too hot to allow a search for bodies. By elimination—no remains were ever found—it was reckoned that six men died in the fire. Hundreds of families were left homeless, and many were jobless as well since their places of work were also burned in the fire.

"Papers have scathing articles on Hale's flimsy structures," recorded William as he took the opportunity to examine the fire escapes at the factory and Steinway Hall. The story of the Hale fire ran for days, and a *New York Sun* reporter called on William: "Sun has an acct of Hale based on my information, reflecting pretty badly on his business." It was the more or less standard tale of bogus pianos, but in the telling was revealed William's dark hatred for Hale. Mr. Hale himself could not be found by reporters. There were calls for prosecution, but an investigation held Hale harmless. Undoubtedly, the city fathers did not wish to stimulate legal defenses involving city water pressure. When the rubble cooled with the loss of about $450,000, Hale began to rebuild his factory. J. P. Hale was as implacable as nature.

Undoubtedly William would have preferred to mount his attack on the Hale-Weber-Chickering forces before the embers cooled on Thirty-fifth Street. This, however, was not possible since Tretbar was still in Europe with the original documents. While Charles Tretbar kept William informed by Ocean Telegraph and he knew of the signatures as they were obtained, he perhaps also realized that it would be imprudent to act without the signed certificates securely stowed in the safe beneath the stoop next door to Steinway Hall. When the *Britannic* berthed at Hoboken on October 28, 1877, and Tretbar walked down the gangplank, William was there to meet him along with S. D. Phelps, who had gathered the signatures of the American jurors. Little time was wasted, and the next Sunday found William, Phelps, and Tretbar at work on an article for the *New York Times*, which carried the headline "THE TRUTH AT LAST."

"*THIS IS TO CERTIFY that the piano-fortes of MESSRS. STEINWAY & SONS, comprising Concert and Parlor Grand, Square and Upright, exhibited by them at the Centennial Exposition at Philadelphia in 1876, presented the greatest totality of excellent qualities and novelty of construction, and in all points of excellence they received our highest average of points, and accordingly our unanimous opinion concedes to MESSRS. STEINWAY & SONS highest degree of excellence in all their styles.*" There followed the names of ten of the Group XXV jurors from America and Europe.

William and his loyal associates had succeeded, with the unintended assistance of Weber, in eliciting from the jurors an unconditional endorsement of Steinway as the best. This was a total and unilateral revision of the operating rules for the original awards, which were to be based upon the written reports. Both the medals and the reports had been thrown aside, and the jurors now declared a single victor. Not only Weber, but Chickering, Knabe, Steck, Decker Brothers, and more than two dozen other firms were indirectly but officially designated also-rans. In the piano wars there were neither prisoners nor noncombatants.

Weber was publicly silent. A week passed, then two, then three, before a notice finally appeared in the *Times*. William observed, probably with relief, that it did not mention Steinway by name, thereby making response optional. There was, however, little doubt of the target. "Detected and defeated in their attempt by questionable means to regain a waning popularity, secured by fraudulent and impudent claims, founded upon fictitious victories, some Rip Van Winkles in the piano trade have just woke up to learn of the Centennial, which has passed into oblivion over a year ago," rumbled Weber. The reference to Rip Van Winkle had currency as a popular play of that name was then on the boards at the Broadway Theatre. If the speed of Alfred Weber's rejoinder was less than it had been, the strength was still apparent: "Several ocean voyages are made, thousands of miles are travelled, and many months of correspondence ensues. . . . What for? (*sic*) asks the innocent reader. Was it to learn to make a piano as good as the *Weber*? Oh, dear! no! no! no!" The effort was made, declaimed Mr. Weber, "to see if it was possible to make their award *equal* to Weber."

After again declaring his pianos the best, "and what is better still, sold at the most reasonable prices," Weber remarked, "Life is too short to follow these piano quarrels, which have actually become a nuisance."

Weber hammered home the next point: "An *honest* man looks for justice to the verdict of the Court—a dishonest one sneaks among the jurors, and to acknowledge having done so publicly, a man would be generally deemed an *idiot*, besides being a knave." As a propagandist, Weber was of the first rank and wrote that "it is always sad to see the decline of a once great house. . . . If, however, a few private individuals . . . of unquestioned renown in their own sphere, desire to sign a Card of *Condolence* in very *bad* English (I wonder who wrote it!) for a defeated piano maker, . . . it is perhaps best to throw the Mantle of *Charity* over it . . . New York is especially a city of progress and enterprise—hence, the Heathen Chinese so child-like and bland, who, in ways that are dark, attempts to play his tricks a year after the curtain has rung down . . . becomes an object of pity and contempt, and a fit companion for the fossils in the Smithsonian Institute." Though having much else to say, Mr. Weber was silent on the matter of judges' interviews and scores.

Likened, albeit not by name, to an idiotic heathen Chinese knave who wrote English poorly, William may have been amply provoked, but he did not respond. There was in progress another action. With the help, once again, of C. P. Kimball, ably assisted by Commissioner Beckwith whose earlier umbrage over the Steinway "loans" to jurors had apparently dissipated, the question of Weber's altered award was raised with the very influential Francis A. Walker, secretary of the Centennial Commission.

In January 1878, one and one-half years after the judging, Mr. Weber was summoned to Philadelphia by the Centennial Commission Executive Committee, and there his award was changed back to its original form. Albert Weber's genial persuasive powers proved inadequate to overcome the evidence.

"I have just returned from Philadelphia and I am pleased with the action of the Executive Committee," Weber told a reporter from the *New York Tribune*. Candidly admitting that some of the judges asked that his report be changed, Weber then said that "if a few judges can be manipulated . . . and the full Commission change their official awards, then all the official reports become a delusion and a snare." Forgetting, it seems, that his report was to be changed back to its *original* form, Weber showed his greatest concern: "This matter does not concern me alone, but everyone of the 16,000 exhibitors to whom the Centennial Commission decreed an award and gave an official report." Nonetheless, Albert Weber was demoted to pianomaker second class by the commission.

The dark force behind these events, according to Mr. Weber, was Steinway & Sons, who, for nefarious purposes, had undermined the entire system of awards. "The Steinways have singled me out . . . because in the last two or three years my business has increased to so great an extent that I have become their most serious competitor. With them it has become a matter of existence." It did not matter; the bitterest battle of the piano wars was now joined.

"There is no 'war' between Mr. Weber and Steinway & Sons, however fondly Mr. Weber clings to the hope that there may be," wrote William to the *New York Tribune* two days later. "But there is a 'war' between the judges on musical instruments . . . and Mr. Weber, growing out of the fact that Mr. Weber has been for more than a year publishing as genuine . . . a spurious report and fraudulent figures of ratings, which he knew the judges never made, signed or recommended." Weber, according to William, "has obtained for him the unenviable notoriety of an official protest from the judges of his group, and a resolution in the nature of a vote of censure from the Executive Committee."

Partially screened from public view, rougher tactics were brought to bear. "About noon," William wrote, "Tretbar introduces a man to me named J. B. Wass, representing himself as from the Tribune, stating that he had proof that Hale made pianos for Weber." Wass, if that was his real name, was in fact an agent for J. P. Hale, and William was apparently suspicious: "I tell him that such a thing seems to me absurd, for every respectable maker has his name cast into the iron frame which would fully prevent such a thing. He asks to see letters addressed to Stanley & Sons in order to connect Hale with Weber. I tell him that years ago we received letters addressed to Stanley & Sons, Piano-forte Manufacturers, 4th Avenue, New York, but I cannot see what Weber has to do with it. In afternoon Shanks of the Tribune with Phelps happens to be in for a few moments when Wass calls, tells me that Wass unknown to the Tribune and apparently a swindler who ought to be arrested." The next day Mr. Wass appeared again to say that his source for the story, a cartman, had died, and both Weber and Hale denied the relationship. Mr. Wass then disappeared.

A day later another stranger named Muldoon visited William. He "says he has facts against Hale . . . and says he supposed I had an interest in the Music Trade Review. I tell him I have not the slightest, beyond paying for our advt therein, & if he wants to put in anything into the Music Trade Review, to call on J. C. Freund, its sole editor and proprietor. No doubt this man Muldoon is a spy for Joseph P. Hale." William, of course, was still operating under the theory that Hale, Weber, and Chickering had formed a combination. He did not have to wait long to see the fruits of the attempted espionage, but first there was a further card to write against Weber.

"SIR: In a recent issue of your paper appeared another card from Mr. Albert Weber. In which, as usual, he artfully dodges the only real questions at issue." Then followed the official text of every award Steinway & Sons had gleaned at London, Paris, Vienna, and Philadelphia. Weber, apparently recognizing that his strategy only gave Steinway the opportunity to polish their medals in public, did not respond. The public phase of the war was suspended.

Scarcely a week later John C. Freund, the editor of *Music Trade Review* and a Steinway partisan to this time, was arrested and jailed, charged with libel by Hale. Under the law of the time, arrests for civil charges were permitted if it could be shown to a judge that the defendant was likely to flee. Judge Noah P. Davis was sufficiently convinced to have Freund thrown into the Tombs for the articles he had written against Hale two years before during the bogus piano war. Freund's bail was set at the immense sum of ten thousand dollars, about $120,000 today. Willing to put up half of the bail himself, William tried to get other "reputable" pianomakers to sign a bond for the other half. The Decker Brothers refused, as did Frederick Hazleton. Perhaps they did not enjoy having their Centennial Awards destroyed, collateral damage in the war against Weber. Napoleon J. Haines was travelling and could not be reached. Finally, William recognized that "there is no alternative left but to have Theodore sign the other bailbond."

Freund was freed and told William that "Hale had also made preparations to have me arrested on the plea of appropriating letters addressed to Stanley & Sons, N.Y. but that my furnishing bond . . . so promptly staggered them. Weber said to be dreadfully excited." The purpose of the strange visitors was now clear. If William had admitted an interest in the *Music Trade Review* he would have been arrested with Freund; had he shown to Wass a letter from Stanley & Sons, he would have been arrested for mail theft.

The next day William was charged by the post office with opening Hale's mail addressed to Stanley & Sons. This proved to be but a minor inconvenience, and William was able to convince the Manhattan postmaster that he had done nothing wrong. Hale, lacking the Steinway aptitude for media relations, did not take the obvious step of notifying the newspapers of the charges.

Though the charges of mail theft against William were still outstanding, this did not prevent Joseph Hale from sending a man named Wardwell to negotiate on the issue of the Freund libel suit. Apparently Hale came to be concerned about what Freund's answer to his suit might contain, Freund having promised in print to make some sensational revelations. Through his intermediary Wardwell, Hale indicated he would be satisfied with an apology. William, while disavowing any influence on Freund, indicated that he would try to "restore peace." Freund told William that he "would rather rot in jail." In a few weeks there appeared in *Music Trade Review* a long statement by Hale averring that his was an honest business delivering large numbers of pianos to those in modest circumstances. There were numerous testimonials to Hale from his dealers, as well. J. P. Hale soon began giving regular interviews to Freund, but more than one year later William could not find any evidence that the suit had been discontinued. William Steinway was not the only man who had friends at the courthouse.

William did not suffer passively through the Hale and Weber onslaughts. Using agents he obtained samples of Weber, Hale, and Chickering pianos and began suit against all three in federal court for patent infringements, usually on various technical aspects of Theodore's action designs. So as not to give the appearance of special treatment to his enemies, several minor makers were also given notice of their infringements of Steinway patents. "These infringements have been carried on to such an extent that patience ceases to be a virtue, and we are absolutely compelled in self-defence to assert and protect our rights," wrote William to the dealers, asking them to report possible patent violations they found. Steinway & Sons planned to prevent unauthorized use of their action patents, and William used the patent suits as a selling opportunity as well. Without their patented action rail, "the touch would become uneven . . . and the piano would consequently be constantly out of gear and an intolerable nuisance."

When Joseph Hale learned of the infringement charges and satisfied himself of their truth, he sent a man to William to work out a settlement. William delayed, saying he would have to consult Theodore in Germany. After a time Hale himself called at William's home. Still William made no attempt to contact J. P. Hale. When an evening meeting finally occurred, Hale agreed to pay five thousand dollars in damages. The next day the money was delivered. Hale might have easily argued that the infringement was not his, but that of a contract actionmaker. J. P. Hale, above all else, did business quickly and in cash.

Not all of Hale's business habits were as admirable as that of his record for prompt payment. Along with Weber, Hale spread rumors of Steinway & Sons' financial weakness, suggesting that Steinway was about to fail. A credit reporter from Dun, Barlow & Company, a predecessor to Dun & Bradstreet, called on William several times to inquire into the firm's finances. Credible rumors of financial stress could destroy a business. Creditors panicked and demanded payment at the same time that buyers deferred purchases, fearing that they might not get delivery. At a minimum, the ability to borrow, as Steinway & Sons did, via low-cost commercial paper could be damaged or destroyed. The company was in remarkably strong condition given that it had just survived a half-decade of depression. Assets exceeded liabilities by more than four to one, while liabilities themselves had been reduced by more than one-third in a single year. William was able to persuade the credit reporters that the house was sound, and he took pleasure in recording that fact: "To my great joy I see that as in Bradstreet's the Dun Barlow & Co. Agency has given us the highest mercantile mark."

More than three years of conflict with Albert Weber and Joseph P. Hale over bogus pianos, Centennial Awards, and patents was grinding to a close. There was no truce; there was no declared victor; there was no celebration. Survival was the reward of the fortunate. Albert Weber died on Wednesday, June 25, 1879, at 7:15 A.M. New York time. "Obituary notices of Weber rather weak," observed William. The *New York Times* wrote that "one of the most famous piano manufacturers of the world, Mr. Albert Weber, died yesterday morning. . . . He had been ailing for nearly a year. . . . Mr. Weber's career was intimately associated with the progress of New York in musical culture in late years, and was especially of that type which is marked by great energy and force of character." After a long paragraph devoted to Weber's career, the obituarist wrote, in a masterful control of his understatement, "in his contentions with rival manufacturers he was aggressive, full of resources, and most fertile in expedients."

Others with a role also fell aside. Herbert Van Dyke, the ex–Weber employee who had made the spectacular charges of bribery against Bristow, turned on William and sued him for $6,495 in fees and expenses for his claimed investigation and miscellaneous other services. William, probably not eager to have his name further associated with bribery and industrial espionage, made Van Dyke an offer: keep the four pianos Steinway had given him to sell on consignment, his notes for several hundred in loans would be forgiven, plus Van Dyke would be given three hundred dollars in cash. Van Dyke refused this offer and sued. After five years in the courts, Herbert Van Dyke not only lost but was ordered to pay over one thousand dollars in fees and costs.

John C. Freund, the *Music Trade Review* editor, went on to display a newfound journalistic independence, publishing negative articles about Steinway & Sons. A minor contretemps with Knabe of Baltimore, again on the semantics of Centennial Awards, found Freund giving full play to the Steinway opponent. Hale boasted that he would soon be making ten thousand pianos per year with a profit of ten dollars per piano, making him the world's largest maker, and Freund published the puff. This was a claim certain to make William ooze rage.

J. C. Freund, flush with advertising revenues that flowed from his more neutral position, rapidly forgot that he was launched in his new career—after a time with the *Hat, Cap & Fur Trade Review*—by William Steinway. John Freund had found a money machine based on the implied threat that those who did not advertise might find themselves the subject of unfavorable stories. Somehow, Freund was able to collect money for advertisements before they ran and spent even faster than that. He built a large home in Tarrytown, New York, and played the role of prosperous publisher . . . for a brief while. By December of 1879, Freund was begging William for money, apparently unaware that there was no greater transgression in William's view than disloyalty. At Christmas Freund sent gifts to William's children. There was a broach for Paula and a breastpin for George, "much to my disgust," commented William. This stratagem failed and, unable to borrow from any source, John C. Freund fled the city to evade his creditors, leaving the publication, now renamed *Musical and Dramatic Times and Music Trade Review*, in collapse as the sheriff seized the office furniture. The newspapers trumpeted the Freund defalcation, using it as something of a moral lesson against both profligate consumption and gullible lending.

George F. Bristow returned to the sedate existence of pedagogue and noted composer, satisfied apparently that the life of a celebrated piano endorser had debits, as well as credits. Bristow lived into the 1890s and took with him to his grave the knowledge of his true role, if any, in the infamous Sphinx interview. Bristow did not exploit his relationship with William Steinway, although he did once ask if he could attend a symphony rehearsal at Steinway Hall.

Even Joseph P. Hale seemed to lose his taste for combat after the death of Albert Weber. If there was, in fact, a triumvirate of Hale, Weber, and Chickering intent on driving Steinway & Sons to destruction by price cutting, Hale certainly realized that C. Frank Chickering lacked the pragmatic aggression, improvisatory skill, and powerful intelligence that Weber possessed. Hale had other business interests as well, not the least of which was his New York, New England and Western Investment Company, an investment banking firm and dealer in municipal bonds. In the brief time left him, Joseph P. Hale did not again engage the Steinways.

"DEATH OF JOSEPH P. HALE, A Millionaire Pianomaker Who Started Life as a Post-boy," read the page-one story in the *New York Sun* on Wednesday, October 17, 1883. "Died of heart disease . . . said to be worth ten million or more . . . born in Bernardston, Massachusetts in 1819 . . . carried the mail twice a week 75 miles . . . started as a carpenter . . . made $30,000 as a crockery merchant . . . in 1860 established a little pianoforte factory at Hudson and Canal . . . transactions all on a cash basis . . . had no clerk or bookkeeper . . . wonderfully retentive memory . . . said to have made 50,000 pianos." Uncomprehended was Hale's immense accomplishment: the transformation of the piano from class to mass. It was for this, as much as anything, that William despised Joseph P. Hale. The *New York Tribune* observed that Hale "was a conscientious business man, and his personal habits were simple to the verge of frugality. He was strictly temperate, not even indulging in tea or coffee." William Steinway, apostle of European culture and bon vivant of Gramercy Park, had met J. P. Hale, a Yankee ascetic of West Thirty-fourth Street. The two men fought each other for the supremacy of their visions; it was, in fact, a philosophical war of high quality and refined art, or pretensions to it, against volume production and popular taste. The meaning is far clearer now than it was then. For William, there was simply an inchoate loathing and a dead adversary.

Chapter 19

FINE LOOKING AND
INTELLIGENT MEN

"We have met to demonstrate that no police commissioner or his hirelings or a military force can trample us! [applause] We must win our fight. We care not whether this revolution is obtained by peaceable measures or by force! [prolonged applause] The present society of the United States is a fraud on civilization. What kind of government is it that can give employment to working men only eight months a year? We must secure this Eight Hour System to give our brothers employment, and if that is not sufficient demand six hours! [applause]. . . . The police will not protect a poor man, but would turn out in full force when Steinway called. We were not afraid of them. We could have stood our ground, and in half an hour had 50,000 men armed to the teeth at our backs. With that force we could sweep the entire city!" The speaker of these words was a Mr. McMaken; the occasion was an address to an "Indignation Meeting" at Manhattan's Cooper Institute organized by the Eight-Hour League and reported by the pro-labor *New York Sun* on June 22, 1872.

For a half-dozen weeks that summer the city was in pandemonium as strikes swept the trades, shutting down industry after industry. The first to strike were the carpenters, on Monday, May 13; the masons soon joined, as did the cabinetmakers. The *New York Herald*, also sympathetic to labor, commented, "The eight hour system is rising among the living social issues. . . . Now that half a dozen trades impose but eight hours work per day, those who contentedly labored ten hours or more in others, may change their minds as to what they choose to call their rights." Precisely that was occurring among the pianomakers, whose "protective association" variously claimed between sixteen hundred and twenty-five hundred members.

The notion of working eight hours per day, six days per week was not a new one. It first took root after the Civil War in the federal bureaucracy, even then pioneering ways to do less with more. Several states passed legislation that addressed the question of the hours of labor, New York among them. Employers generally maintained that law permitted shorter workdays but did not require them. For at least the more radical employees, the law was interpreted as creating a legal right to work no more than eight hours.

In addition to the concept of creating more jobs, it was often posited, particularly by upper-class promoters of social change, that working men would use their newly found leisure time to "improve" themselves by reading, study, and patronage of musical or dramatic events. This "mental culture," it was argued, would make them better citizens. A particularly brilliant theory was advanced by a self-educated machinist prominent in the labor movement named Ira Steward. Mr. Steward believed that more jobs for more workers would create large new markets and economic growth without loss in wages. More than a half-century later Henry Ford used similar logic to justify his decision to pay his workers five dollars per day, albeit for ten hours.

The intellectual wellspring from which flowed the sociopolitical justification for the eight-hour day was none other than Karl Marx. In *Das Kapital* Marx argued that "surplus value" was added when a man labored more hours than necessary to support himself, and that this surplus value went to his employer, rather than the worker. Therefore, "the laborers must put their heads together, and, as a class, compel the passing of a law, an all-powerful social contract that shall prevent selling . . . themselves and their families into slavery and death." The eight-hour day was a part of the agenda for the redistribution of wealth along communist principles. The connection between European radical thought and daily life in New York was closer than might be imagined. Karl Marx was for ten years a foreign correspondent at the *New York Tribune*. About 485 pieces by Marx, some ghost-written by Friedrich Engels, were published by Charles Dana, the socialist editor of the *Tribune*. One-third of these were editorials, and most of the Marx articles were unsigned. Hemispheres apart in both geography and social philosophy, Karl Marx and William Steinway would have agreed on one thing: the importance of getting the story into the newspapers.

To the employers of New York, the demand for eight-hour days was a nightmare. At Steinway & Sons, then employing about six hundred men in their Fourth Avenue plant, the arithmetic went as follows: 600 men times 60 hours per week equalled 36,000 hours of work per week. To obtain the same 36,000 hours at 48 hours per week would require 750 men, a 25-percent increase in the labor force. Since the workers were not willing to concede wages, this meant a 25-percent increase in labor expense, an amount sufficient to absorb almost all profits. One-fourth more workers would require more space as well and mandate capital outlay for an additional plant.

There was also the very practical problem of where to find the additional skilled workers. New York pianomaking then employed something more than twenty-five hundred men, implying that an additional six hundred to seven hundred skilled workers would be needed in the city if production were to be maintained with an eight-hour day. Finally, there was the problem of competition from pianomakers in Boston and Baltimore, where there had been little agitation for shorter hours and where wage rates were lower. Clearly, the demand for a 20-percent briefer workday could not be feasibly met, but in the early summer of 1872 rationality was in short supply.

A further factor complicated matters in many trades, including pianos. It was traditional that "prices" not "wages" were paid. Men worked by the piece, not by the hour, and were paid for each piano case built, each keyboard assembled, each leg turned, or each soundboard made. The *New York Times*, in a particularly foggy bit of thinking, proposed hourly pay as a solution, saying that if a man then wished to work eight hours, he would be paid for eight hours, not more, not less. The editorialist somehow failed to comprehend that there was also a relationship between time and money in the piecework system. A change to hourly wages would accomplish little, except to penalize particularly productive workers. So robust was the piecework tradition in pianomaking that it remains in use at Steinway & Sons in the 1990s, twelve decades after the Eight Hour Strike of 1872.

Workers' earnings at Steinway & Sons were high, the highest in all city manufacturing, according to the *Times*. While direct proof of that assertion does not exist, available evidence indicates that it may well have been true. As compared to the *average* earnings of America's nonfarm employees in 1872 of $1.46 per day, even the lowest-paid Steinway workers, the laborers, earned $2.00 per day or 37 percent more. Very skilled workers such as tone regulators (who adjusted the sound of the instrument) and actionmakers averaged $3.67 per day, and the best of these could easily earn over $4.00 on piecework. Soundboard makers commanded 30-percent higher wages at Steinway than at Chickering in Boston, while the tone regulators received 56 percent more at Steinway. Even the unskilled laborers were paid 40 percent more at Steinway than Chickering.

As it had for many years, Steinway & Sons also paid more than the rates for comparable skills in other industries. An average Steinway varnisher earned $2.67 per day, fully one-third higher than a varnisher who worked for Brown & Bliss, a large Manhattan furnituremaker. A Steinway topmaker who fabricated piano "lids" earned $3.33 per day in 1872 while a cabinetmaker with no less skill making table tops earned but $2.50, about 25 percent less.

There was a combination of factors at work to create these high rates. Men who made pianos were among the industrial elite. An 1870 study of pay in dozens of New York occupations from bricklaying to watchcase making showed no group better paid than the pianomen, and the Steinways seemed willing to offer a premium to obtain the best and most experienced workers. Commenting on the Steinway work force, the *New York Herald* wrote that "they were . . . , as a body, remarkably fine looking and intelligent men." A man could say with pride that he had worked at Steinway's; and many boasted of this, particularly when they started their own small piano shops.

Another factor contributing to Steinway labor rates was the cost of living in New York, which was slightly higher than in other areas. However, compensation was proportionately higher still and created for the workers a better standard of living. Another contributor to high earnings was that Steinway & Sons was invariably the first target of the "trade societies," as unions were then known. When strikes were called, they often began at Steinway, and the outcome typically set the pattern for the entire New York piano trade. It therefore becomes impossible to determine to what extent the high earnings of Steinway workers were the result of family policy, the skill of the labor force, or the activities of the trade societies. Each undoubtedly contributed to what were high rates of pay.

One factor entirely under the family's control was the policy of continuous operation. Real or suspected financial panics were dealt with at most firms by layoffs. In the recessions of 1857, 1860, 1865, and 1869 Steinway & Sons not only remained open, but it did not lay off workers. Cuts in the piece prices, typically 10 percent, were often a part of the Steinway recession response, and the workers sometimes had to strike to regain their old rates when business improved. The financial strength of the house allowed continuous employment; pianos were built and held in inventory until sales improved. In contrast, Albert Weber laid off half his work force and put the balance on half-time during the great panic of 1873. This was the more typical response, and in a time without unemployment compensation and in a place where landlords evicted instantaneously, no long study of social philosophy or political economy was needed to divine that a wage reduction was preferable to no work.

There were advantages in continuous operation for the Steinways as well. They were able to keep their best men, who would not be forced to look for other work during a layoff. More subtly, the piano inventory built during bad times was excellent protection against the strikes that were almost inevitable when conditions improved. Consistent with the practices of the time, higher piece prices were never voluntarily offered by the family.

To obtain an increase, the workers had to threaten a strike, and in most cases at least a brief strike was necessary.

It was against this background that the drama of the Eight Hour Strike of 1872 played out. Job actions for an eight-hour workday first flared in mid-May of 1872 among the carpenters, stonemasons, and others in the building trades. The first striking groups did not seek a change in their compensation but merely the right to work eight hours instead of ten. To the surprise of the tradesmen, the demand was granted, and eight hours briefly became the standard day in several of the construction crafts. Emboldened by a seemingly easy victory, other trades soon made a bigger demand: the same pay as for ten hours but only eight hours' work.

In his diary William observed that "agitation for the eight hour system commences. Meeting at 2 P.M. of the Men, our shop not represented." At that meeting of five hundred men it was resolved to send delegations to each of the city's piano shops to urge the workers to strike. "A committee of 16 attempts to get into our factory but are refused admittance," recorded William. Eight-hour optimism was running high among the workers, and even the *New York Times* adjudged that success was likely: "The manufacturers will probably accede to their demands readily, as the large stocks of pianos held by them will be advanced in value fully twenty percent." This logic proved to be as defective as its arithmetic. "Weber's men are on the rampage," noted William, and Dunham's varnishers were already on strike. All over the city the pianomakers put down their tools and walked off the job, except the men of Steinway & Sons, who continued to work. The Steinway men "were, it is alleged, very unwilling to strike," reported the *Times*.

Five days after the first pianomakers' meeting, the virus of discontent reached Steinway & Sons. Knowing full well that their strike would fail without the participation of the workers at the city's largest and most prestigious piano manufactory, strike leadership under a man named Seibert ran what William called "inflammatory" announcements in the German-language newspapers and began intercepting the Steinway men on their way to work. The tactics were successful; and on Tuesday, May 28, 1872, the Steinway workmen sent a committee to Albert Steinway, who was in charge of the factory, to demand an eight-hour day and a 20-percent increase in earnings. "Agreeable to a previous understanding with Albert," wrote William, "he tells them to assemble at 8 A.M. the next morning . . . note down eight points on which to speak to our men."

The next morning, though William "did not feel quite well," he journeyed uptown to the factory to address the employees. "What you ask us for," said William, "will increase the price of piano-fortes 33% and reduce the demand by half. . . . The result would be a decrease in business and half of you would as a consequence be unemployed." The demands would, William argued, "drive the house out of New York City," put Steinway at "the mercy of Eastern pianomakers, who even now are selling the same description of piano for $475," against Steinway's $650, and "virtually destroy much of the export trade," reported the *Times*. William asked the men if they really thought their plan for eight hours and a 20-percent increase could work. "It can, it can," shouted the men.

William then asked for a vote on whether the men "will treat with us directly or be dictated to by others." This was done by secret ballot, and of the 418 votes cast, 254, about 61 percent, were in favor of dealing directly with the Steinways. After the vote, William made his offer: a 10-percent raise or a reduction in hours from ten to nine; the men were to decide which they preferred. William also averred that he "did not wish to fight against the feeling of the age but wished the men to go gradually about this business," reported the *Times*. The meeting was adjourned until 2:00 P.M. when the workers were to reconvene and decide to accept or reject the Steinway proposition.

It did not take long for word to leak out of the factory that the Steinway men had voted to deal with their bosses directly and not through a trade association and, just as badly, might accept a compromise settlement. When the workers reassembled after lunch, "having been talked to and drinking beer," they were not alone, for outside the factory three thousand angry men surrounded the building in protest. To William and Albert, the crowd must have evoked memories of the Civil War draft riot. Only twenty policemen were available to control the demonstrators.

An employee named Henry Helling chaired the workmen's meeting, assisted by another employee, Joseph R. Rivers. Speeches, ranging from spirited to angry, were made in German and English while outside the demonstrators milled about, cheering for trade unions, the eight-hour day, and Steinway workers. "Several enthusiastic speeches were made urging the men to strike," reported the *New York Herald*. "Speakers who endeavored to propose compromise were silenced without mercy, and those urging a strike were received with applause." Violence was never far below the surface during labor conflicts, and there must have been those among the Steinway workers wondering what the crowd outside would do if they did *not* vote to strike.

When the vote came about 4:00 P.M., it was nearly unanimous in favor of the strike. A committee visited William, "and told him that they had resolved not to accept his proposal. . . . They were very courteous, and intimated in the plainest language that they had been morally persuaded by their associations against their will," wrote the *Times*. William then revealed the next part of his plan. He would, he said, write the dealers and ask them if they thought buyers would pay a higher price for Steinway pianos. If the dealers thought higher prices were feasible, "he would accede with pleasure but if their judgment was adverse, he should steadily refuse" and close the factory indefinitely. The employee committee, upon hearing this news, "bowed and withdrew," reported the *Times*. Most of the Steinway workmen left the factory and joined the crowd still milling outside; temporarily at least, they were brothers in a just cause. "I am much worn out," observed William.

That night William wrote to the dealers: "The movement is general and so formidable in its character that there is hardly a doubt that it will be successful. Its accomplishment is the greatest misfortune that could have befallen the industry of this country, and especially the piano trade, as the unreasonable and unwarrantable demands of the workmen will force the prices of pianos to a point altogether beyond the reach of people of moderate means." Nonetheless, "we are compelled to oppose the movement with all the means and perseverance in our power, no matter what the danger may be to our lives and property, and the magnitude of our losses."

True to his word, William did query the dealers as to "whether you prefer to have the strike come to an end soon by our yielding and you having to pay an addition of $60 to $120 to the wholesale price of each piano, or to have no supply of Steinway pianos for some time, and after all be finally compelled to pay the advanced prices." The sixty-dollar amount was much less than the one-third increase that William told the workmen would result from their demands; it was about a 17-percent increase in the wholesale price of the cheapest Steinway, and at retail the price would increase from $500 to $585. A $120 addition to the wholesale price of the most expensive grand would have increased its wholesale price about 12 percent. Using William's statements that about two-thirds the cost of a piano was labor, a price rise of about 16 percent would cover the demands of the eight-hour men. While still a very large increase, there is little question that the disaster forecasted in William's rhetoric was much more severe than the economic reality.

The dealers, not surprisingly, were against an immediate price increase. When the men came to the factory to collect their pay on Monday, June 3, 1872 (Monday paydays were intended to discourage workers from drinking their earnings on Sundays), they were told of the dealers' refusal to pay more. Over the weekend the city piano manufacturers met and resolved to stand united against the eight-hour day but to leave to the discretion of each manufacturer the question of price increases. The combined manufacturers' message to the men was simple: they might or might not get a raise, but the eight-hour day was impossible.

Other trades were meeting similar resistance; the twenty-three hundred employees of Singer Sewing Machine were on strike, many thousands of cabinetmakers, metal workers, foundrymen, ship builders, and carriagemakers were also out, facing adamant employers opposed to the eight-hour system. There was the occasional victory; the illuminating gas workers cut their workday from twelve to eight hours, ending citizen fears of a city without light, and the barbers seemed near a reduction in their fifteen-hour days. In the main, employer resistance was much stronger than the city's workers expected.

William received word that his men would accept a compromise of a 10-percent raise and a nine-hour day. He did not respond, and on Tuesday the Steinway men met and voted to return to work at ten hours and a 10-percent advance. "This is reported by the Spaniard Rivera (discharged by us) at the mass meeting, which makes the wildest excitement," wrote William. The *New York Sun* filled in the details: "Mr. Joseph Rivers [aka Rivera, apparently], a bronzer, who was considered one of the leaders of the strikers, and discharged yesterday morning, repeated the action of Steinway's men at the mass meeting in Germania Hall. . . . The blood of the cabinetmakers began to boil in their veins when they heard of the treachery of the Steinway men who had so meanly abandoned the common cause after pledging themselves to stand or fall with their fellow men." The plan, as it developed, was for a large body of strikers to assemble at the factory and persuade the Steinway men not to return to work. William learned of this at 10:30 in the evening.

The next morning William wrote, "I rise at 6 A.M., dress quickly and proceed to the factory . . . Find Capt. Gunner with 40 policemen there and an immense crowd in front on 53rd. street who yell at every man who enters the factory." Despite the heavy rain, the crowd, estimated at thirty-two hundred men, remained. The number of police was increased to three hundred and by 7:30 A.M. they had dispersed the crowd "without violence" but remained at the factory all day to protect the 150 men brave enough to work. The *Sun* remarked that "it was one of the grandest turnouts of the whole strike," and that "Mr. Steinway seemed to really have apprehensions in regard to the safety of his building." William had reason to be concerned, for the crowd was "yelling, hooping and hissing like madmen" and it was reported that some employers had received arson threats. The next night at a meeting, one pianoman "exclaimed that if he had his way, he would blow the factory into the air. He was," declared the *New York Sun* phlegmatically, "promptly declared out of order." Other pianomakers claimed that the Steinways had "set the police against the workingmen by treating the officers in charge to boiled spring chicken." That same day a carpenter working "overtime" in Forty-first Street watched strikers smash his tools before he was beaten and shot in the face.

The next few days were a standoff. About one-fourth of the Steinway men appeared for work while the balance remained on strike. Estimates of the total number of strikers ran as high as seventy thousand, and William recorded that "the whole city is in a blaze of excitement about the strikes." During this impasse the manufacturers did not keep their views secret. "The fact is the piano men have struck at the commencement of the dull season, and . . . have outwitted themselves," said William to the *New York*

Times. "Business will not be brisk for three months and the manufacturers would only have been making stock to keep their hands going, so that this strike is a godsend to most of us. . . . Our men have been deluded into the idea that there would be an eight-hour strike in Boston, Baltimore and Philadelphia among the pianomakers, but they have been greatly deceived. The country workmen are too glad of a good spell of brisk trade, being accustomed to dull times and half days." Albert Weber opined that if the men were "resolute, they [the owners] would look about for some other means of investing their capital," while Napoleon J. Haines said that he tried the eight-hour system for a week and it did not work. Propaganda aside, William decided to close the factory rather than risk further confrontations with mobs of angry strikers.

The Eight Hour League planned a march and demonstration, claiming that forty thousand men would turn out. Scarcely two thousand did. It was, William said, "a grand fizzle." Seeing that the strike was losing momentum, William once again opened the factory, and a small group of dissidents demonstrated before being dispersed by the police. On Friday evening, June 14, 1872, the strikers held a meeting at the Germania Assembly Rooms downtown. About seven hundred men attended to hear speeches on the tyranny of capital and the battle against moneyed monopolists. There a resolution was made, which in William's words, "advocated a move on our factory." The pianomakers, the cabinetmakers, and the iron workers would all take part. The plan was to "clear out" Steinway. "Clearing out" involved the forcible entry of a factory by a band of strikers. Once inside, they would use whatever force was necessary to persuade the men to cease working and leave the shop. Destruction of shop machinery, workers' tools, and whatever product was being made was common, and arson could not be ruled out; foremen were sometimes beaten, as were any workmen who resisted. The strikers, reported the *Times*, were "rendered desperate by desertions from their ranks and may not be easily deterred." Statistics for the furniture trade showed that of the roughly sixty-six hundred normally employed, 73 percent were back at work for ten hours; less than 10 percent had achieved the eight-hour objective. The final 17 percent were either still on strike or discharged.

Saturday morning William rose early, walked up Lexington Avenue, and watched from a distance as the strikers assembled. "There being 300–400 policemen around our factory, they do not dare to go up there," wrote William. What he did not know was that there was at the factory a braver group of strikers confronting the police at that very moment. Over five hundred Steinway men appeared for work at 7:00 A.M. They in turn were met by hundreds of strikers while 250 police guarded the factory. Another 150 police were concealed at a nearby station. Mounted officers galloped up and down the streets, reporting on the positions of the strikers. The crowd of demonstrators had been salted with plainclothes detectives, and the entire operation was personally commanded by Police Superintendent Kelso.

"Deterred by the large force of Police, the plan of attack on the building was abandoned," reported the *Times*. "The strikers contented themselves with gathering about the corners and following up Steinway's men, who were going to work, and endeavoring to dissuade them. While so engaged the Police did not interfere, but when some strikers, bolder and more excited than the rest, attempted to prevent the men from going to work, the Police charged and drove them off, and several times resorted to their batons in dispersing the crowd." It was a common belief of New York law enforcement at this time that a few blows with a club was punishment roughly equal to an arrest but was much more convenient for the officer. Undeterred by the batons, a hundred strikers charged the factory entrance. "They were beaten back, and ran in dismay toward Third Avenue where they dispersed," wrote the *Times*.

Later that day William learned from one of his many informants, probably a reporter, that Steinway & Sons "have nothing more to fear at present." The police remained at the factory and escorted the workers to "dinner," the one-hour break for a noon meal that split the ten hours into two equal five-hour work periods. Most of the police left the factory in the afternoon, and at 6:00 P.M. when the day's work was done, the men picked up their pay and "departed to their homes without molestation."

The *Times* reported the scene in the city's *biergartens* and parks the next day, a sunny Sunday: "The strikers worked zealously all day. . . . There were men with lowering brows and stern faces, who mingled with others as yet undecided and urged them to quit work and join the bands of strikers. There were Communists . . . with arguments in favor of the eight-hour movement, disseminating their ideas advocating an equal division of the wealth of the country, and attempting to spread dissatisfaction." For the men of Steinway, whether they were workers, foremen, or bosses, the strike had come to an end, and, as though a keystone was pulled from an arch of resistance, the piano strike collapsed. Men at the other shops appeared for work on Monday. Except for the 10-percent raise at Steinway, there was no gain for the workers from their three-week strike. The pianomakers were once again working ten hours per day for the same prices as before.

William, called by Police Superintendent Kelso, appeared at the investigation of the policemen charged with beating strikers: "Officers' conduct commended and complaint dismissed" was the terse diary entry. The day before William had played the stereotypical role of capitalist in a Communist newspaper cartoon as he and seven friends travelled in two carriages to the family yacht *Mozart* to spend a pleasant Sunday steaming about Bowery Bay and fishing. That evening they docked at William's summer mansion on Long

Island. There a servant cleaned and cooked the fish for the party and made a "nice coffee. . . . We amused ourselves splendidly," wrote William.

By late July the last visible signs of labor unrest evaporated in the city heat, and those willing to work labored ten hours each day. It was ninety degrees in the shade when William sent a notice to the factory "informing our men that the advance of 10 percent will be taken off" on Monday, August 12, 1872. Though he did not say so, William may have detected signs of sales weakness. In any case the three-week strike produced a raise for the men that lasted for less than two months. The workers did not protest. Perhaps they came somehow to comprehend in a collective way that their demands had been wildly visionary; It was to be a half-century before the average American worker labored forty-eight hours per week and just as long before that average worker earned the annual pay of a soundboardmaker or topmaker at Steinway & Sons in 1872.

Directly ahead lay the biblical seven bad years, which economists would later calibrate as the longest business contraction in American history. Though the depression of 1873 did not officially begin until October of that year, William was already noticing slowing sales and "tight money" during the holiday season of 1872, and national economic activity did not begin to recover until March 1879.

In his only published remarks, it was Albert who spoke for the firm at the onset of the panic in September 1873. A *New York World* reporter "visited the piano factory of Steinway & Sons to ascertain the effects of the general lock-up of currency on their trade. Rumors have been quite numerous of late that employers of large numbers of artisans had contemplated a general discharge of workmen in consequence of the general stagnation of trade and the impossibility to get funds."

Albert then gave the future a glimpse into the practical terrors of a money panic: "Orders are coming in, but very slowly, as people are afraid to contract for fear that they cannot pay. We have a sufficient margin, however, sufficient to pay our workmen something, if not all they earn, for three or four weeks to come, but that at the very furthest. The utmost difficulty is experienced in getting money. To be sure, we can obtain sums of money in large bills but these our workmen cannot use. Small bills cannot be obtained as they are all out of circulation. We cannot pay our men regularly. We are forced to pay them so much on account, when the money comes in, and while it is only disagreeable to us, it is seriously inconveniencing them. We might pay them in checks duly certified, but you see they are of no use. Their butchers and grocers would not take them, as they themselves must have currency, and that is the reason why a lock-up of currency has such a bad effect upon workmen at once. Paper they can't use and money they can't get."

Showing a grasp of business far beyond his status as a junior partner who was compensated at about one-fifth of William's earnings, Albert continued: "Our payroll amounts to about $24,000 every fourteen days, and you can see, therefore, in what manner it affects our workmen, as it is fairly impossible to raise that amount at present. Today I managed to make a raise of $6,000, which, as you can see, I am now paying to my men on account. I use every endeavor to get their money for them, but you can see how we are placed. But I do not think these matters can remain as they are at present."

Having explained why many prudent citizens kept their savings under mattresses rather than in banks, Albert went on to analyze the cause of the present difficulties: "It is the evil result of men taking their money out of the channels of legitimate business and placing it in the hands of bankers for the 4 per cent interest which it yields. This money is then speculated with, and stocks of unbuilt railroads are bought. If these same [men] had deposited in banks used for the accommodation of merchants, as either loans to them or for the purpose of discounting their paper, legitimate interests would have been advanced, to the benefit of the community. As it is, we are forced to suffer because unhealthy speculation is indulged in. And when the depreciation of values reaches the manufacturer or merchant, it creates heavy losses upon him and he suffers. We are just beginning to feel it, and I think that, judging from the present circumstances, the shock will be severe."

Albert Steinway seemed to have no less distaste for some capitalists than did his socialist employees. His analysis was also pointedly correct; the trigger for the Panic of 1873 was the failure of the Philadelphia merchant banker Jay Cooke & Company. Cooke's firm, famous for its role in the financing of the Civil War, had undertaken to sell $50 million in railroad bonds for the Northern Pacific, which was to run from Lake Superior to Puget Sound. A huge American foreign-trade deficit, plus the failure of about one in six insurance companies after the famous Chicago fire (and a less remembered Boston conflagration), plus other factors, left Cooke unable to move the bonds although construction on the road was under way. Cooke's firm closed its doors on September 18, 1873, and the public made a plausible inference: if the famous Cooke firm could fail, banks were a poor place to keep money. The runs started; gold held by New York banks plummeted 70 percent in two months, and 87 percent of the greenbacks were withdrawn. This was why Albert Steinway was unable to find money to pay his men. On September 20 the stock exchange closed for the first time in its history. Before the panic was over, one hundred railroads defaulted and the nation tipped over into a long depression despite the fact that greenbacks and gold had returned to normal levels in the banks by February 1874. Albert's forecast of a "depreciation" was also prescient: prices for general commodities—wheat, corn, oats, et cetera—fell quickly by 27 percent while iron fell 35 percent and petroleum 50 percent. Business failures in 1874 were double those of 1871 and by 1878 had nearly doubled again to about 10,500.

The first signs of panic mobilized William. A meeting with the president of the Pacific Bank extended a twenty-thousand-dollar loan the bank had called, while William watched closely the condition of the two banks in which he had invested. The German Savings Bank and Bank of the Metropolis both had small runs, but depositor confidence was apparently high enough that they were able to remain open. "I was very much excited all day, also Albert," wrote William on September 23. The Union Trust Company and Bank of the Commonwealth both suspended operations. William's small investment, along with members of the Tiffany and Vanderbilt families, in the Bank of the Metropolis paid off when, despite the worsening panic, the bank told William "that we can have all the greenbacks we want." Cash to pay the men was now available, but William met with Albert and his second-in-command, longtime employee Henry Kroeger, "to reduce stock and draw in our horns."

As often happened when William was heavily stressed, he caught a cold and his rheumatism flared, but this did not prevent decisions. A lumber shipment due in the fall was postponed until spring; the factory was closed for three days. Business, wrote William, was "perfectly dead." In the midst of the panic, Theodor arrived from Germany. "Have good talk with Theodore who fears Albert's machinery improvements more than anything else," noted William. By November, William put the Steinway Hall personnel on three-quarter time. Meanwhile, there were several attempts to obtain loans and mortgages, all unsuccessful. Steinway & Sons was short of cash, very short. To add to the problems, a group had rented Steinway Hall for a meeting advocating the invasion of Cuba. This spirited assembly broke many seats.

On November 19, 1873, with sales at a standstill during what was normally the busiest time of the year, William, Theodore, and Albert cut prices in the factory. A "great commotion" arose among the men, and the next day found the brothers making revisions, presumably upward, but still cutting earnings for the workers. After three months of effort, a mortgage was finally arranged on the factory, and Steinway & Sons, with a fresh $100,000 in cash, was more or less ready for the years ahead, but neither the family nor anyone else understood how bad those years would be.

In March 1876 the *New York Times* published a thorough analysis of commerce in the city: "The appended reports . . . show that the mechanical industries have not yet recovered from the depression caused by the financial panic of 1873. The number of hands employed seems to be gradually decreasing and the wages show a corresponding reduction. The trade unions now number only about one-third of their total strength three years ago." Combining both union and nonunion workers, unemployment in what would now be called the "manufacturing sector" stood at 34.7 percent.

But not all fared poorly. The elite of the cabinetmakers, those who made custom furniture to order, had but 15-percent unemployment in the winter of the nation's centennial. Carriage builders also did well, relatively speaking, with 85 percent of their trade at work. All of the city's two thousand musicians were employed that winter, and there was work for custom tailors, who could earn over one thousand dollars per year making bespoke garments for the wealthy. As prices fell, people with cash saw relative bargains, and they did what people always do when they see a bargain: they bought. For those provisioning the prosperous with what they needed, or at least wanted, the depression was more remote. So it was with the pianomakers.

The *Times* reporter gathering unemployment statistics in the winter of 1876 could not mask his disbelief when told that "the demand for skilled laborers . . . is ahead of the demand last year. . . . The principal makers say they are running on full time with full forces of men, and some of them claim to be doing extraordinary business." The bogus piano war was at its peak, and neither side would admit that sales had slipped since such an admission would result in a declaration of victory by the opposition. Cannily assessing reports from independent dealers, the *Times* reporter estimated that the trade was down 25 to 35 percent over the prior year in New York. The reality was worse.

In January 1876 William pruned up to 11 percent off Steinway & Sons wholesale prices. The reductions provided no stimulus: "Business very quiet. . . . Business wretchedly dull. . . . I suffer great mental pain on account of my personal trouble [the divorce] and bad business. . . . Business continues dreadfully dull. . . . No orders and little money received. . . . No doubt we are losing money fast. . . . Business prospects are wretched beyond description . . . we are daily losing money," scrawled William in his diary. The cumulative pressure of his failed marriage and dwindling business brought William to the brink. On a carriage ride with Albert he was "seized with the wildest paroxysms of despair, and sob, as though my heart would break, Albert crying with me." On his birthday William observed that the "sun shines brightly, but all is black without and within me."

While the private William wandered the involutions of personal and professional despair, the public man remained resolute and confident. There was no strike that spring, and the workmen of Steinway continued to make pianos for which there were few buyers. By borrowing money William built a paper bridge between supply and demand. The company's debt ballooned while profits decayed. Yielding a lush 12.9-percent return on assets in 1871, the rate plummeted to less than 2 percent by 1873 and stayed there. The family was earning less than two cents per hour from each workman employed. Raises were out of the question, but Steinway & Sons did not close and they did not lay off men. As much as anything, this was pride.

While the family did not gain wealth during the depression, the workers did. The socialist objective of redistributing income was subtly advancing through an improved standard of living for those working among the "working classes." The unemployed, of course, suffered severely. While the popular image of the capitalist was of men who beggared workmen and starved their children to gain extortionate profits, the actualities were quite different. Economist Edward Atkinson explored the phenomenon in the 1880s, attempting to comprehend the nature of what was by then a recognized but mysterious phenomenon: low prices and high wages.

To do this, Atkinson devised what would today be called a "market basket" of goods: a daily ration of food, clothing, and fuel needed to sustain one adult. The basket, by today's standards, was quite full. Atkinson assumed that one adult would each day eat one pound of meat, one pound of bread, two pounds of potatoes, smaller amounts of eggs and cheese, then wash it down with ten ounces of milk and several cups of coffee and tea, the entire feast sweetened by a quarter pound of sugar. This ration cost thirty-three cents in 1870. Atkinson did not add the cost of alcoholic beverages to his list of "necessaries," but gave a figure for them based on actual expenditures that would have added 10 percent to the daily cost of food. Other allowances were developed for clothing, fuel, and housing, and Atkinson was now able to compute the actual cost of living versus earnings of workingmen. What he found was a marked increase in purchasing power for all classes of workers, from the lowliest laborer to the most skilled "Boss Machinist." Dollar earnings had gone down, but prices had dropped even further. Noted Atkinson: "The value of a day's labor to him who exerted it, yielded more and more of the necessities and comforts of life as the years went by."

At Steinway's, the men had worked virtually every day during the long depression. Steinway & Sons employed roughly six hundred at the start of the slump, and there were six hundred when the recovery began. Though their "prices" had been cut, they had fared well. The real earnings of the Steinway workmen grew in almost every year during the depression, and a vast chasm opened between the fortunate few who worked regularly and the uncounted legions of the unemployed.

Near the bottom of the socioeconomic pyramid, nearly crushed by its weight, were the recipients of aid from the city's Department of Charities and Corrections; it was no coincidence that jails and charities were run from the same department. Being poor, other than temporarily, was considered indicative of moral defect. No Steinway men would be found on the welfare rolls. In the winter months of 1875, 16,806 families received aid in the form of $47,428 cash and 3,909 tons of coal. The 61,069 persons assisted comprised about 6 percent of Manhattan's population. In 1991 about 40 percent of the residents of New York City received financial assistance in the form of a governmental "transfer payment."

At the bottom of a society the communists, socialists, and anarchists thought was in terminal decay were the "bummers" or "tramps," whose unreckoned population now centered in the old Steinway neighborhood in the Fourteenth Ward. In January 1877 the *Times* trained a spotlight of journalistic indignation powered by moralistic superiority on the "bummers" in a story headlined "VILEST OF THE VILE." "The Extremity of Degradation . . . Foul to the eye, loathsome to the nostrils, revolting to the moral sense of all decent people who behold him, the tramp slouches through life, a continual reproach to the inscrutable Providence who has permitted him to exist, yet has not made him a crawling thing." The problem began, traced the *Times*, with the Civil War, where men learned in the military "how much of what they deemed the necessities of life were really its luxuries. . . . To this great army of tramps . . . there came—as the years of financial distress throughout the country rolled on—hordes of recruits from the unemployed, the bankrupt, the dissolute, and the petty criminal classes." They begged pennies during the day to buy a five-cent sleeping space on a bare floor at night; with straw, the same space cost ten cents. Some passed out in the saloons that had backrooms to which they were carried to sleep off their ration of "one-block whiskey," so named for the distance a man could walk before passing out after drinking it. One such place was known as the Morgue, another as the Velvet Room.

Food was stolen from the markets or picked from the garbage; the more energetic tramps followed the milkman on his rounds, drank the milk, and sold the pitchers. Those who could not afford liquor found employment in saloons washing glasses. Their compensation was known as "slops," the unfinished drinks of paying customers.

In the winter some tramps patronized the reading rooms of the Astor Library and the Cooper Institute, where warmth was to be found. These, observed the reporter, wore paper collars and sometimes washed their hands. Tramps were not dangerous, however. "With all their degradation," commented the *Times*, "it is seldom that a genuine tramp achieves any great crime; not that moral prejudices against felonies exist in their minds, but that they have not the energy, physical or mental, to attempt departures from the routine of their everyday lives." To the out-of-work laborer, mechanic, or pianomaker the "bummers" marked the way to the depths of an unremittingly Darwinian society. Would a man with a job strike for a raise the same day he saw a "bummer" lying on a stoop? Even the radical reformers, minds aflame with the fires of social injustice, did not ask the question.

Chapter 20

VILE FIENDS, SUCKERS, AND BLOODHOUNDS

"Aperfect pandemonium all day," wrote William. "To factory which I find partly stopped, the Casemakers, Machine Men & Blockers not working. Meet delegation of our workmen who demand 10 pr.ct. and Blockers & Machine Men 15 pr. ct." With a perfect sense of timing the workmen of Steinway & Sons had detected the end of the great depression of the 1870s. Seven years of submission had ended.

The comatose union was resuscitated, its activities "said to be conducted with all the secrecy which attends the Masonry," noted the *Times*. As before, union activity put a worker in peril of discharge, but the pianomen had also learned that meetings with reporters or outsiders present meant that the bosses would soon be fully informed. Workmen were told not to discuss union business with reporters, and so quiet was the strike that it was in progress for weeks before the press discovered it. "The leaders were men at the head of their trade, who were discreet and intelligent enough to discuss the piano business from a mercantile as well as mechanical point of view," explained the *Times*.

The city's piano trades did not walk out en masse and then storm the buildings of their bosses as they had in 1872. Instead, a sophisticated strategy of targeted strikes was used. After presenting their demands to a piano manufacturer, usually for a 15-percent increase, and usually refused, the men struck that maker and that maker only. At the small sixty-man shop of Kranich & Bach the men were out for thirteen weeks before winning the raise. During the strike, the Kranich workers were financially assisted by the union, which assessed its working membership to help support them. This refined technique was used at the Sohmer, Decker, Hazleton, Steck, and Lindemann shops as well; each time the United Pianomakers Union won increases, often in just a few days.

On Thursday, September 11, 1879, when William travelled uptown to the factory he was likely summoned by a call on the recently installed telephone. The selective strike weapon was now pointed at Steinway, and a confident union had its finger on the trigger and William in the sights. The busy season had just commenced, those last three months of the year when the majority of sales were made. It was the second example of superb timing, and William was in no position to refuse. "After lengthy conversation I agree to allow them an average advance of 10 pr. ct. to be at once deducted again if the trade cannot stand it." The Steinway strike of 1879 lasted but a few hours. The union then turned its attentions to Joseph P. Hale and Albert Weber, where, with greater difficulty, similar increases were obtained in a few weeks.

William had learned to make effective use of the militancy of his work force with the general public, many of whom considered, not incorrectly, the more extreme trade unionists to be a threat to the established social order. His newspaper interviews not only portrayed Steinway & Sons as a societal bulwark against the depredations of socialists, communists, and, later, anarchists, but further spread the fame of the firm. William's public position was progressive for his time. He acknowledged that workingmen had the right to organize in the matter of compensation; they did not have the right, however, to "dictate" on other matters, such as the hours of work, the hiring of apprentices, the quality of an employee's work, or the appointment and dismissal of management, all of which were or would be the focus of strikes. William Steinway held that these were the "freedoms" of owners and could not be infringed.

A few months lapsed, and worker unrest again stirred at Steinway & Sons. There was only one day's notice "that a strike was brewing." On Friday, February 13, 1880, William recorded that he went "uptown at 11 A.M. Strike of our Varnishers, they stop work at 12 o'clock." The workmen had learned that it was not necessary to call a strike of all hands. With a strike in a single "branch," as the various departments were known, it was possible to test the response of the bosses while the rest of the men were working and, most important, being paid. This was a new method, and evidence of the growing sophistication of union strategy.

William's response was likewise different. In the strike seven years before, he had asked the men if they would rather deal with him directly or be "dictated to" by others. The men had voted to deal directly. This time, William did not ask; he presumed, undoubtedly with good reason that the men would not separate from their union. This required different tactics, and William told "the com. of Varnishers, 3 men . . . that I will not see them unless they go to work at 7 A.M., and if not working Monday, that they are all discharged." This was a message couched in symbolic terms, but amply plain to the participants. William was saying, in effect, that the union was attempting to "dictate" how he should run his business and that he would not yield to this infringement of his freedom. Since the strike was now the weapon of the union, he would not negotiate with the men while they were on strike. William also knew well that if he conceded to the demands of the varnishers for an increase, he would soon have to raise compensation for all his workers.

The choice of the workers to have the varnishers lead the strike was strategically astute. While there were only sixty-five men in the branch, varnishing was, in effect, a valve in the production pipeline. Huge numbers of pianos sat in the varnish branch, each to be sanded and coated as many as ten times before going to final polish. Because it took a week or more for a coat of varnish to dry, vast quantities of instruments were always found in this area. After the investment in lumber, the inventory in the varnishing branch represented the largest use of Steinway & Sons capital. The union had found the perfect choke-point.

A new response was needed, and William had one at the ready; when the varnishers did not appear for work on Saturday, he placed help-wanted advertisements for varnishers in the New York *Sun, Herald,* and *Staats-Zeitung* and telegraphed his dealers in Boston, Baltimore, and Philadelphia to advertise for varnishers in those cities. From his perspective, William was justified, as he did not expect his men to work on Monday. "New hires," however, were the union's "scabs." On Monday William had an "extended talk" with a workers' committee and reiterated his precondition, "telling them that Varnishers must first return to work." The response was a factorywide walkout, and William seemed surprised when the polishers who worked at Steinway Hall joined the strike. Consulting with the Manufacturer's Society, William learned that "the sentiment among those present is not to pay any more wages at present. Am greatly pestered by reporters."

While the strike in late 1879 had been quiet, the union men decided to report their version of events first. While William did not have time to hire any scabs, the strikers quickly turned his advertisements against him, convincing the conservative *New York Times* that "Mr. Steinway . . . received a lot of tramps from Philadelphia and other cities, and when the rest of the workmen saw these strange men brought into the shop, they resolved that the entire body of working men should go on strike." The "Vilest of the Vile" were used as strike-breakers by William Steinway, if the union was to be believed, and the mere mention of the word "tramp" was calculated to elicit a shudder of revulsion from respectable citizens.

The union men showed that they had mastered more than strike strategy;

disinformation was now a part of their armamentarium, and their skills were sufficient to induce the *Times* to place its imprimatur on the worker version of events. The strikers, at a meeting in Turtle Bay Park (adjacent to the Turtle Bay Brewery), showed reporters a list of prices for Steinway & Sons. The *Times* man wrote, "A list was exhibited of the wages the men in Steinway's earn, and it was found that $12 is the average there, while in other first class shops the average is from $12–$16 per week." Cooked data was another skill the union had mastered; the actual Steinway average for varnishers was, in fact, precisely centered at about fourteen dollars per week in 1879. William noted in his diary that the *Times* was "incorrect," but with twenty years' experience in dealing with the media, he was wiser than to attempt a direct rebuttal.

The varnishers were demanding an increase of 10 to 20 percent, but another demand soon surfaced, one that attempted to limit the number of apprentices or "green hands" by increasing their starting pay from five dollars to ten dollars per week. The functional effect of this would have been to reduce the number of green hands in training, thereby cutting the number of men able to become journeymen and ultimately increasing the wages of existing journeymen. Reducing the supply of skilled labor at its source was yet another example of increased labor sophistication.

The probable source for these new techniques was the increased cooperation and communication among the union men; a pooling of ideas and experience was under way. Carl Schiff, a striking Steinway man, addressed a meeting of cabinetmakers on strike at the same time. Schiff, reported the *New York Sun*, "urged the men to be firm and united. He said the American workmen should take care that they were not reduced to the helpless condition of those in Europe." Just a few years earlier, the distinctions of craft status and earnings made such cooperation impossible, but the new emphasis was on collective action and cooperation: "Six hundred sacrificed wages to get a raise for sixty-five. This commanded the admiration of all the working men of the country," self-congratulated one orator at another union meeting. The attendance at these meetings was large; the commitment of the men aside, there was another factor which encouraged their presence. At the meetings the pianomakers' union dispensed four to seven dollars in strike pay to their "destitute brethren." The *New York Sun* revealed that a half-hundred or more of the Steinway workers owned their own homes: "Pianomakers as a body are intelligent, frugal men and a large number have property ranging from $5,000 to $20,000." The thousands of working New Yorkers who skimped to pay the twelve dollars monthly rent that three or four small rooms commanded must have read that reportage with astonishment.

The union set forth a new demand, an escalation which it delivered to William by letter. The journeymen pianomakers now called for a general 10-percent increase in all wages. News of the new union requirement moved quickly in the trade, and J. P. Hale and Albert Weber, Jr., called on William at home. A meeting of the Piano Manufacturer's Society was in order.

"NOVEL AND RADICAL METHOD OF STOPPING STRIKES," headlined the *New York Times*. The bosses were "perfectly satisfied" that the union intended to "enforce a general advance . . . and other obnoxious and arbitrary rules and regulations dictating whom we shall employ." The rate of wages had already been increased 10 to 15 percent, which "made it exceedingly difficult . . . to compete." A "splendid export trade to Europe" had been built and the demands of the men would mean that the export business "will be entirely lost." The "splendid" export business amounted to about 60 pianos to Germany, 230 to England, and none to France for the *entire* American piano industry in 1880. The cost of making pianos in New York, averred the bosses, "was from 15 to 20 per cent above that of any other city. . . . Any further rise in wages . . . would have the most disastrous effect." Last, the society claimed that it could not raise wages "without ruining the business. . . . Therefore, be it *Resolved*: That each and every piano-forte manufacturer of this city notify the workmen in his factory that unless the workmen of Messrs. Steinway & Sons return to work by Saturday, March 13, we will close our factories on the following Monday, March 15."

The gauntlet was down, and explained the *Sun*, "The piano manufacturers have resolved upon this step in case the employees of Steinway & Sons do not resume work at the old rates prior to March 13. In that event the funds of the Pianomakers' Union will be severely taxed to furnish support to the many who need aid. Others of the pianomakers are amply able to support themselves, having the savings of many years amply invested." The *Sun* reported division within union ranks: "Many of the strikers deplore the action of their comrades. They would much prefer to be quietly at work earning money." On the streets near the factory the striking workers posted observers to take down the names of any men who appeared for work. None did. All was silent within the four-story factory, except for the scratching of the pens of three clerks who went about their tasks guarded by two policemen. This was a war of waiting. The new union tacticians, unlike the old, knew the futility of storming the factory gates.

Instead they talked to reporters, telling them that the Steinways warned grocers and butchers not to sell food to the men on credit because they might not get paid. Taking a page from the Manufacturer's Society techniques, the union published a manifesto.

To the Public, to the workingmen and most especially to the pianomakers: When, after a long series of years, during which misery and deep despair have not only entered the homes of the poor but also of the rich, during which many thousands of the former have suffered a slow death for want of sufficient and proper nourishment, and many of the latter, ruined in business, have either been driven to suicide or thrown back in the ranks of the workingmen; when business begins to revive and the laboring class once again hopes to live like human beings, we see their hope dispelled by a most unjustifiable lockout of thousands of honest mechanics with families to support . . . Society as organized has at all times afforded greater protection to the employers than the working classes. It is therefore the duty of those who receive the most favor from society not to act against their fellow men at large by closing their factories and rendering them breadless.

William thought the manifesto "pretty lame."

"There were many expressions of surprise and disappointment among the piano workers yesterday on learning that the 600 strikers of Steinway & Sons had made no terms with their late employers," reported the *Sun*. The lockout was on, and the objective was clear: destroy the union. But inside the manufacturers' group there was trouble. William wrote of an "excited debate, in which the wisdom of our action is questioned." Unlike the workers who grumbled to reporters, William and his allies pro tem understood the power of apparent accord. But the manufacturers' facade of unity was already cracking.

J. P. Hale, apparently unable to take any straightforward action, closed his shop along with the rest of the makers but posted a sign saying he was closed for inventory and repairs. At their weekly meeting, the men "violently assailed Hale as not having the manliness to tell his men that he had joined the lockout," reported the *Sun*. Other workers decided it was time to open pianomaking cooperatives, and the *Sun* also carried a background story on the half-dozen cooperatives that sprang up during the 1868 lockout. None survived as long as a year.

Vituperation and invective against the bosses became a prime tool of the union, now struggling to maintain control of its membership. "Haines was accused of grinding his men down and once keeping them out on strike for four weeks. . . . It was said of the Fischers that three years ago they advertised for casemakers at $7 a week, and men joined them with $200 worth of tools for that wretched sum. . . . One man, it was said, became so disgusted he cut his throat and another blew his brains out," wrote the *New York Sun*. The workingmen heard speeches by union members from the Paterson, New Jersey, silk weavers, the cabinetmakers, and the bagmakers. The Baltimore pianomakers pledged financial support, as did the silk weavers; and the Socialist Labor Party began to take up collections around the city for the men.

The union rhetoric escalated: "We must sweep away those vile fiends, suckers, and bloodhounds . . . that haven't the feelings of a dog," declaimed one speaker. "The bosses ask us to renounce our union and they will renounce theirs," said another. "Our union will live when that gang of bloodsuckers will have gone to ————! Our union is the only friend we've got." A Mr. Frank McCarthy addressed the workingmen: "These leeches who have been sucking the lifeblood out of us and our families must go somewhere else to do such things. We are the original producers and we should be the original dividers. We are not to be bought by all the money of all the capitalists in the World. We will either win or we will all sink at once." Schiff, one of the original organizers from Steinway, made vague allusions to violence. "The workingmen," quoted the *Times*, "would soon hear an explosion such as has never been heard since America and the civilized world existed." Mr. Schiff declined to elaborate on the nature, location, or timing of the explosion. A cautionary announcement was made that only the union and Socialist Labor Party were authorized to collect donations for the strikers. In a peculiar turn, the Steinways were now praised because their actions, the men claimed, had strengthened the union.

The union men began to spread a report that "certain Capitalists representing Chinese interests" had made the bosses a proposition. They would supply the manufacturers with "Mongolians for 50 cents a day for the first year and 75 cents for the second year." Foremen were to act as instructors "to the Chinamen . . . who were adept at imitation, and would become excellent pianomakers in a very short time." The Chinese, in addition to their modest compensation, asked only that their bones be returned to "The Flowery Kingdom" if they died in America. The unnamed capitalists also offered to put up three million dollars as security, an amount adequate to cover the cost of about ten thousand pianos. While the skeptical may have originally viewed this tale as union propaganda playing to racial prejudice, it was, in fact, true.

Encountered as a group by a *Sun* reporter, the manufacturers acknowledged the proposition and set forth their views, albeit anonymously. "I don't want to bother with a lot of Chinese," said one manufacturer. "I hate 'em worse than the devil. We don't want any alien Asiatics here," said another. "I would rather pay white men more money." A third declared that "We'll be getting so many Chinamen here that the amalgamation will become serious," while a fourth said he hoped that "we shall not be driven to anything of that sort by the men's folly." The concept of Chinese labor received no further consideration from the bosses.

William was quoted on another issue at least as threatening to the interests of the men: "I may anticipate events and say to you that the present strike of the pianomakers will result in the removal of that industry from New York City and vicinity. The voice of the piano trade is unanimous on this question. You may state as a positive fact that two of the largest houses of piano manufacturers have already begun negotiations for building sites in a New England state and will remove their manufactories from New York with as little delay as possible."

This was no idle threat; William had just bought—sight unseen—the "business and factory" of L. W. Porter, a piano case maker in Leominster, Massachusetts, a small town about fifty miles northwest of Boston. Acting for the family was Charles's oldest son, Henry William Theodore. It was the first recorded instance of a major responsibility being given to the next Steinway generation. Along with Henry W. T., "a carload of stuff goes there," recorded William.

Meanwhile, the pianomakers had demanded a 10-percent increase citywide, and the lockout began to disintegrate. The first to concede was the tiny firm of Bacon & Karr. The fourteen workers had, according to the owners, said that they were not union men and so were allowed to work. The workers denied that they disavowed the union, but, after a "commemorative dinner" paid for by the firm, returned to their labors.

The lockout might have survived the loss of the smaller shops, but when Napoleon J. Haines, William's choice for vice president of the Manufacturer's Society, defected, the lockout was lost. Haines, a sophisticated builder of medium-priced pianos and president of the Dime Savings Bank, had for his men a seven-point plan that presented a surface of equity and nobility, at least from the capitalist perspective. The men were to agree that they would not "hinder or interfere with any respectable man in good standing." They were "to not be controlled by any union whatever in regard to the affairs of this shop in the future" —that they "do not desire or wish the trade of pianomaking to be driven from this city" and that they "wish to have the same good feeling and harmony prevail between men and bosses as heretofore." Haines told reporters that "this agreement was read slowly and carefully to the men" and agreed upon unanimously. The men said they had made no such agreement but were planning to return to work. Albert Weber, Jr., simply resigned from the manufacturers' group, saying it was too weak. He had learned well from his father.

Faced with these and other desertions, William told the *Times* he "approved" of the arrangements and then amplified his position: "It is my intention, so far as wages are concerned, to do what is right after my men return, but they must come to the shop first. I think the agreement between the employers and their men shows that the workingmen's organization is not very strong, as the men agreed to return without asking the consent of the union." That night the Socialist Labor Party "and other similar organizations" gave a grand ball at the Germania Assembly Rooms with half the proceeds donated to the pianomakers' union. They did not call it a victory party, but it was.

"We are willing to say squarely that we are beaten," one anonymous piano manufacturer told the *Times*. "It was impossible for the lock-out to result in anything else but our defeat, since we have shown so weak a front from the start." Most of the firms had agreed, at least tacitly, to advance pay the 10 percent demanded. The *Times* wrote that "J. P. Hale has posted a notice on his factory to the effect that as the contemplated repairs in the building have been completed, the factory will be open today." On the *Times* editorial page was a lesson in ethics and economics for both capital and labor: "It has long been the custom to condemn all attempts by trade unions to dictate to employers. . . . In this case a number of prominent manufacturers adopted the very tactics that have been the subject of so much censure, and undertook to coerce a body of workmen in one shop by locking out all those employed in a number of shops. . . . Any attempt to defeat by artificial combinations the influences which determine prices . . . must inevitably fail."

The next day William acceded to an increase of 10 percent "all around," and, cryptically, for the varnishers to "each Dollar made full and one Dollar added and the rest $2.00 each." The headline of the *Times* blared "MR. STEINWAY SURRENDERS." The Executive Committee of the union advised acceptance of the offer and diplomatically suggested that the men "simply ignore any scab or non-union man who might be at work" when they arrived. William, still rummaging for merit in the wreckage of the lockout, told a reporter "that they had shown to the public that they had made an earnest attempt to hold down wages and had failed." Higher piano prices were inevitable now.

It was in a circular to the agents that William showed, replete with eccentric punctuation, the expected vehemence following his betrayal by the other manufacturers: "It is perhaps hardly worth while now, to speak of the sudden collapse of the 'Lockout' within one week after its beginning, through the ridiculous weakness of some of the smaller manufacturers, were it not for the deplorable fact, that the Piano Manufacturers Society which triumphed completely during the great strikes of 1864 and 1872; is now practically dissolved, and there is nothing to prevent the workingmen in the piano trade from soon attempting to force wages up still further, and reducing the hours of daily work."

William's umbrage was not constrained to other makers and the workers. "The piano dealers throughout the Country however are also to blame, because large numbers of them hastened to New York . . . to buy up all the pianos they could obtain, thus creating the fictitious impression in the minds of the makers of cheap pianos, that the trade was immense." Enclosed were new price lists in which retail prices remained the same but wholesale prices were increased. William had decided to punish the dealers by reducing their profit margins.

The great strike of 1880 was almost over when a workers committee and a Mr. Bartholomew of the pianomakers' union visited William to demand that several of their fellows be fired by Steinway & Sons. These men agitated for the strike, then returned to work as scabs, claimed the union.

Such perfidy was not taken lightly by either side. William explained that he had asked some of the men to come back and he could not therefore fire them. "I refuse in the case of the first four, & consent if charges proven to discharge the two last," noted William. "Com. returns at 1½ P.M., brings four witnesses," and the balance of the story was recounted in the *Times*. A man named Flesse was sent for and "discharged on the spot. Then the committee asked that he and Steinhofer [the other man charged with inciting to strike] be permitted to remain at work, as each was over 60 years old and had a large family to support. This was agreed to by the firm, and thus matters between the firm and the workmen were finally settled to the satisfaction of all parties." William observed privately that "it was a very touching scene." Why William chose to play a leading role in this tableau of worker brotherhood is a mystery.

As a final act of celebration, the pianomakers, several thousand strong, planned a march around the city, complete with brass bands. Though cancelled because of rain, the Steinway men still marched to the factory led by a band playing "Hail, Columbia." At the gates they were greeted by Theodore, who was making one of his longer visits to America. Theodore addressed the men, and they responded with three cheers. Apparently moved by the display of cameraderie, Theodore pulled out fifty dollars, gave it to the workers, and told them to take the day off and go to the Turtle Bay Brewery.

Movement was still under way to begin production at Leominster, Massachusetts, where plans for a new three-story factory were being made. When the Massachusetts plant burned a few months later, the Leominster effort was abandoned completely. But the most significant consequence of the strike was William's acquiescence to a long-cherished plan of brother Theodore. Theodore and William had decided to make pianos in Hamburg, Germany. "To store at 9½ A.M.," wrote William. "Briefly inform Holwede of Theo. & I intending to have our own business in Hamburg & him as manager at which he is very much rejoiced." William had no way to know that this seemingly casual decision would reflect into the next century or that within his lifetime the family would once again be subject to humiliating scrutiny because of it. Hamburg production seemed to William, almost certainly, as a way of hedging, if not escaping, the demands of a militant labor force. In Germany the government jailed socialists when it did not deport them. Perhaps, just perhaps, William looked ahead to a time when he, too, could be home again, a respected, wealthy man leading a life of comfort and peace.

There were, of course, more strikes. In September 1882 the men struck to obtain the discharge of a bookkeeper named Adolph Sommer who, the *New York Times* said, had "interfered with their work, was very close about paying them, and took other actions calculated to ingratiate himself into the favor of his employers at their expense." That Mr. Sommer possessed some undesirable traits as a manager is plausible; at one point William reprimanded Sommer for attempting to cut pay without informing him. The flash point came when Sommer fired two topmakers whose work had cracked when it was shipped to Steinway Hall. The men claimed an injustice, saying that the foreman had approved their tops as good. Before long the entire shop walked out in sympathy.

After nine weeks the workmen came back, still to be held responsible for the quality of their work, but aware that Mr. Sommer and his family had gone to Germany for six weeks. Passage and expenses were paid by William. "Our victory is complete and the men are very much cowed down," noted William. Letters poured into Steinway Hall from strikers and their wives, pleading to return to work. A notice also appeared in the *Times*, carrying the italicized legend *commercial advertiser*: "Single-handed, this great piano house fought and defeated the most formidable, as well as the most unreasonable, strike that ever disturbed the piano trade, and which claimed to have the support of all the trade unions." After a quarter century of confrontations with the workmen, William, the master of media subtleties, was reduced to bombast.

Steinway & Sons, throughout William's time, was a lightning rod through which the strengthening labor movement discharged bolts of discontent. In the opening days of May 1886, the *New York Sun* chronicled the state of the city's unions as yet another eight-hour strike began. There were in the city 180,000 union men in 300 separate unions, but they were now centrally organized as well. About 160 unions were affiliated with the Central Labor Union, which was organized by an English tailor. Another 100 were a part of the nationwide Knights of Labor. The 2,500-member pianomakers' union was a part of the Central, and each Sunday five pianomakers attended the Central Labor Union's weekly meetings where eight-hour strategy was planned.

"A notable thing," said the *Sun*, "is that those occupations in which the German-American element is the most powerful have been foremost in this line. . . . The whole German population appear to be looking for short hours as a necessity of the modern industrial system." A new element had also been added to an already volatile social mix: anarchism. Anarchists believed that property rights began with theft, and it was therefore permissible, even desirable, to burn or bomb in pursuit of "just" social goals such as the redistribution of wealth. The anarchist symbol was the red flag, and those sympathetic to the movement often wore bits of red cloth or red ribbon on their lapels.

As the eight-hour strikes began nationwide, it was widely reported that the Chicago anarchist August Spies had triggered the infamous Haymarket Riot with "incendiary" speeches. Many were killed, including several workingmen shot in the back by police. The Chicago events caused New York papers to focus on the city's anarchists of whom the putative leader was a

German named John Most, publisher of *Der Freiheit* and pamphlets "teaching the use and composition of nitroglycerin, dynamite, gun cotton, bombs, torches &C. &C. Price 10 cents per copy. Every revolutionist should be in possession of this pamphlet." Most's International Working People's Association was estimated to have only one hundred members, but a reporter noted that when Most's newspaper was available "a few" pianomakers purchased it.

On Sunday, May 2, 1886, twenty thousand people turned out for an eight-hour meeting in Union Square, just a few hundred feet from Steinway & Sons. Among the speeches they heard was one by Edward Conkling: "The capitalists seem to forget that human lives were created for any other purpose than to swell the hoarded millions of those who toil not, nor do they spin." Those against the eight-hour system thought that "it will infringe a little upon the luxuries and lavish expenditures of the monopolists who are backed with all the force and power of the government." The *Times* observed "little incendiarism in the tone of the speeches," perhaps because well over one thousand police were in plain view. The reporter did notice, however, a number of people wearing red on their lapels.

A few days before the first of May, William recorded that he was called on by "Geo. H. McVey and Joseph Helback of the Exec. Com. of pianomakers who bring me official notification that our men will only work eight hours a day after May 1st. Compel them to sign that the matter of wages is to be left to the agreement of employer & employees." How William was able to "compel" the union men to sign such an agreement was not revealed, but he was now in a position to make a clear and enforceable statement that less work meant less wages.

Putting essentially this proposition before the workers resulted in a vote of two to one in favor of maintaining the ten-hour system. Among the dissenters were once again the varnishers, who wanted ten hours' pay for eight hours' work. After some grumbling and a visit by a workmen's committee on Monday, the target day for the start of the strike, all the Steinway workers were present the next morning when work started at 7 A.M. Albert Weber, Jr., had somehow come to an arrangement with his men as well, and the eight-hour strike of the pianomakers was defeated before it began; Weber and Steinway combined employed perhaps one-third of the city's pianomakers. Unlike strikes past, there was no communication whatsoever between William and Albert Weber, Jr.

It took the Grand Lodge of the Order of United Pianomakers about a week to realize that their strike was doomed before it began. The blame, of course, was placed on the Steinway and Weber men who did not strike and instead "played hide and seek with the Executive Committee." A *Sun* editorial commented that when the union "gets over its first chagrin, and stops to think more calmly about the matter, we are sure that so intelligent a body of workmen will change their minds, and come to the conclusion that those who held back took the reasonable and prudent course. When the project for making 8 hours a day's work was submitted to Mr. Steinway . . . he laid before his workmen a fresh and clear statement . . . in which he showed that it could not be carried off without harm to themselves. A reduction in the hours of labor would increase the cost of production, and make it necessary to charge higher prices . . . but home and foreign competition absolutely forbade any increase in price. . . . Production would inevitably cease and there would be no work for them." On that basis, it all seemed so rational and so obvious. Two days later William recorded in his diary that "John Most the anarchist arrested last night . . . , being pulled from under the bed of a prostitute in 188 Allen street." The great wave of social unrest that washed the eight-hour movement across Manhattan Island ebbed. Life was normal once again. With time now to visit the Liederkranz, William was showered with congratulations: "Everybody compliments me on the strike and the way we handled it."

There would, of course, be still other strikes, and they were more alike than different. Many were the lectures, monographs, and histories on the Labor Question; many were the speeches of every political gradation. But there was a man known only as E.M. who wrote to the *New York Times* a few days after the conclusion of the pianomakers' strike of 1880. E.M. was clearly a workingman, perhaps a pianomaker, and possessed of a clarity of perception rare in any calling. He began with a deferential thanks to the editors for allowing his views to be published, then: "It seems to me there is a precious deal of cant and nonsense in the eloquent sermonizing on the amicable and happy relation which should exist between capital and labor. . . . That they are mutually necessary to each other is unquestionable; but their interests are not identical—they are even opposed, and will be, I fear, until the world's end. . . . Given his undoubted right to sell his labor, as he would any other saleable commodity in his possession, to the highest advantage, the laborer finds he can best effect that object by selling it, so to speak, *en bloc*. In other words, he aims at a monopoly. . . . If we win, we 'dictate' to capital; if we lose, capital 'dictates' to us, and nothing loth. . . . Mr. Editor, the workmen hold that the rewards of industry are unequally distributed. We believe that capital gets much more than a legitimate profit. . . . The trades-union may not be wholly unobjectionable as an instrument to bring about an equalization, but there is no other." In 175 words, more or less, E.M., the working philosopher, set forth the essence of the conflicts past and future.

Chapter 21

GODFORSAKEN ASTORIA

June 6, 1870—"I start with our steam yacht from foot of 9th str. up the East river, take Tretbar to Harlem, we then proceed Ward's Island down the Bay, past Bowery Bay, Flushing Bay, College Point, Whitestone, Willet's Point to Little Neck Bay. Our Sweet Water giving out, we lose two hours time to get a supply of water. Just before reaching Hell Gate on the return a dense fog sets in and a few minutes before 11 P.M. we run aground at Astoria, opposite 86th Str. We land in our Yawl, drink beer, hire a fellow to tow us to Dulzer's Park, where we land, walk to 3d Ave. and thus get home at 12½ A.M. We had a very jolly time of it & enjoyed the trip very much. I had wet feet all day," wrote William.

This, the maiden voyage of the Steam Yacht *Mozart*, signalled a sea change in the way the Steinways viewed themselves. For reasons unclear— there was a "business depresson" in progress—William, and perhaps Albert, came to recognize that they were wealthy men. At the end of 1869 the business had built up assets of almost three-quarters of a million dollars, and the whole family had "drawn" from the partnership more than a half-million dollars over the years, roughly one-third of that in the last two.

There were but a few hundred steam yachts in all America, and in the spring of 1870 William and Albert decided to purchase one, advertising in the *New York Herald* for a suitable vessel. The craft they bought, from several offered, was taken to the Morgan Ironworks, renowned for its

Heinrich Englehard Steinway, literally the founding father, as he appeared in the lens of photographer Matthew Brady circa 1862.

Charles Steinway in what was likely his last photograph before his death in 1865. As the eldest brother, he helped guide S&S to its position as the largest American piano manufacturer in less than a decade.

William Steinway as he looked when the destiny of the house and the welfare of widows and orphans came into his control.

Henry Steinway, Jr., whose innovations formed the foundation of Steinway technological supremacy and forever altered the design and sound of the grand piano.

Albert Steinway, the youngest of the four brothers, was more comfortable with machinery than music; his natural domain was the factory where Albert's efforts to automate manufacturing caused anxiety and dread in older brother Theodore.

C. F. Theodore Steinway about 1877 and near the zenith of his formidable creative power. Theodore disliked living in America and thought the future lay in cheap pianos, a concept the Japanese and Koreans exploited a century later.

William Steinway with his wife and children on January 26, 1874, the year before William came to know his wife Regina as "a depraved creature" and the child Alfred as "unfortunate." Son George stands next to his mother, Paula stands with her father, and Alfred, nicknamed "Ditz," is seated.

William and his second family. His wife Elizabeth holds the baby Theodore E., and William R. is seated on his father's knee. Fred Steinway strikes the classic Victorian photographic pose while son George wears a bowler hat. Daughter Paula is seated. "Certain weaknesses, infirmities, and habits" of George had already manifested themselves.

William at the portals of his mansion and the apogee of his fame and power. He is wearing a writing jacket to keep clean the sleeves of his dress shirt. This informal portrait was likely taken by Fred Steinway, a talented photographer.

Henry William Theodore Steinway, eldest son of founder Charles, in his twenties. William thought H.W.T. had "insane ideas" even as a young man. This most apostatic Steinway disavowed the family and brought years of court battles and public humiliation to his Uncle Bill.

Charles H. Steinway, second son of founder Charles, as he appeared after he had steered the firm to stability. As private as William was public, Charles decoupled the name Steinway from William's celebrity and firmly attached it to pianos and only pianos.

*Frederick T. Steinway, third son of founder Charles.
"Democratic and genial," Fred looked like a nineteenth-
century man but thought like the future. Record profits and production were catalyzed by his incandescent advertising and
promotional strategem during the final years of the piano halcyon.*

Theodore E. Steinway, son of William. For more than a quarter-century he fought with increasing desperation and decreasing effect the four horsemen of the piano apocalypse: radio, depression, world war, and television: "We aren't selling soap or hot dogs, you know."

Henry Ziegler Steinway in a portrait taken by his brother John H. about 1955. Soon the future of the house would be in the hands of this fourth-generation pianoman.

fabrication of ship's machinery, to be overhauled under Albert's supervision. On this first excursion they travelled about a half-dozen statute miles up the East River, past Blackwell's Island (now Roosevelt), through Hellgate, then generally east for another seven or eight miles. The level of preparation for the trip and the "sea sense" of the Steinways may be judged by the fact that they ran out of Sweet Water—the fresh water used to generate steam in the boiler—halfway through the trip after a distance of not more than fifteen miles. This was the steam equivalent of running out of gas. On the return they chose to navigate, at night and in a fog, the infamous Hellgate, the graveyard of many competently managed vessels with its capricious currents and rocky shoals. It was, in a sense, an insight into William's character, and running aground at Astoria that summer Monday night would prove a strange and powerfully foreshadowing event.

The voyage of the yacht *Mozart* may well have been a reconnaisance expedition along the then-verdant shores of Long Island, the occasional farm or hamlet interrupting the forest and salt marshes of undeveloped land just a few miles from Manhattan. Albert and William took a second trip to the same area just six days later and encountered the ferocious tides of Hellgate on the return: "lay up about twenty minutes & then go through. Arrive at Eighth Str. about 9 P.M. having gone through agst. the tide all the way. Albert feels sick and vomits." The *Mozart* had been able to make less than two knots opposing the tide. Albert soon attended to the yacht's performance by having her run aground for a bottom painting and replacing the engine's condenser, but William was at work on matters of more long-term significance.

If one recognized symbol of wealth was a yacht, another was a mansion, and William soon found a suitable property in the area they had reconnoitered by water. "At 11 A.M. Mr. Winants, Albert and I drive via Hunter's point along the Shore Road past Ravenswood, Astoria, to Bowery Bay, view the property of the late Benjamin Pike, Jr., now Tracey, about 70 acres with 4,000 feet of Waterfront, and a magnificent Stone Mansion which cost some $80,000 to build. Afterwards drive past the shore farm of Douglass, fine beach, then by Jackson Avenue past the Bricklayer's reservation, thence to the German Cabinetmakers reservation." The "reservations" that William saw were cooperative settlements. The German cabinetmakers, section one of their association, purchased ninety-one acres for the astonishing, if true, price of $225,000 in 1869. Their purpose, not unlike that of certain counterculture groups one hundred years later, was to establish a commune of like-minded individuals where men and their families could work and live. Communal living, usually along socialist principles, was as frequently attempted as it was unsuccessful through much of the nineteenth century, which, in America at least, might be called the Age of Blind Idealism.

As matters evolved, an uncharacteristic blindness appears to have afflicted William in the matter of his Long Island real estate acquisitions. He did not take long to decide, nor did he examine any alternatives before buying "certain pieces, parcels or plots of land situate, lying and being at the Poor Bowery, in the town of Newtown, Queens County, State of New York," according to the warranty deed. William was back in the area again in a few days, looking at more property to augment the Pike farm that he had already decided to buy. On Monday, July 11, 1870, William signed the papers that made the "country seat of the late Benjamin Pike" his. "It is situate on Bowery Bay in the Rear of Astoria, splendid Chateau on the ground & about 80 Acres of Ground together with over 14 Acres of Waterfront," described William to his diary. William finally claimed to own four hundred acres in Astoria, but his use of shell companies and surrogate owners makes the claim impossible to verify.

The day after the papers for the mansion were signed, William, his father Heinrich, mother Julia, and brother Albert drove "over to view the land I bought. All are delighted with the magnificent house and place. . . . Father wants to go halves with me on the purchase. Returning we drive through the German cabinet makers reservation." Heinrich, at age seventy-three, was still thinking of the future and willing to invest in it. As the ownership ultimately evolved, the chateau and grounds were owned by Steinway & Sons, shared equally among the partners, although William retained some land for his own account.

Real estate was not a new activity for the Steinways, but the scale of the enterprise far exceeded anything they had attempted before. William had been buying and selling houses in Manhattan in a bewildering series of transactions for years and had assembled the plot from a series of small lots on which the Fourth Avenue factory sat. The family even owned land in Indiana, acquired in settlement of a debt from a midwestern piano dealer.

The investment in the Nineteenth Ward factory property proved spectacularly profitable. Within a few years of the family purchases the ward exploded with growth; in 1866, for example, nearly one-fourth of all building activity in Manhattan was in the Nineteenth Ward. Whether this was prescience or luck cannot be told, but there is little reason to doubt that William was an experienced real estate investor, one who had just placed a large wager that the city would expand, leaping across the river to the east and north. As the fowl in the salt marsh flew, "East Astoria" was roughly two miles east of 110th Street in Manhattan, and a ferry regularly steamed between Astoria and the eastern foot of Ninety-second Street on the island of Manhattan.

Characteristically, William recorded no plans for his acquisitions, and at first there may have been none, other than to park surplus capital in the way of future development and await the opportunity to sell. One clue may be found in the fact that the family did not buy the crops on the land when harvest came; this suggests that they were not interested in becoming gentlemen farmers. William's diary details many trips to the "farm" for hunting, target shooting, and hiking. After William closed on the Pike chateau in September, paying most of the $127,000 price in cash, he spent remarkably little time there. His wife, Regina, to whom he was still married, did not visit the mansion for a month after it was purchased. The yacht was docked at the mansion, and in the early period of ownership the property seemed to be a male recreational preserve.

If the purchase of the thirty-eight-room chateau with stables, outbuildings, and gardens signalled the opening of a new era for the family, it was not long before another closed. William documented the beginning of the end on December 14, 1870, just three months after the mansion and grounds became partnership property: "To my consternation, I found father, who has been ailing for several weeks, very sick & with swollen feet and legs." William's recognition of Heinrich's condition ignited a blaze of activity. The next day William consulted with Attorney Cotterill, updating his father's will and working up deeds and other property transfer documents. The activity continued for days as Heinrich's condition deteriorated. On December 20, 1870, William wrote, "Father has the dropsy," an affliction for which there was no cure. On Christmas Eve it was "piercing cold" when the family gathered at Heinrich's brownstone to sign the new articles of partnership and hear their father's will. Heinrich was "sitting in an armchair, and no better, complaining of pain in his stomach. . . . I read the will in German to father. . . . Walk down home. Feel much relieved on having now everything arranged and all fathers and the firms affairs in order." William, it seems, had accepted his father's imminent death. On New Year's Eve, William again visited his father: "He is very much swollen, and with a heavy heart we go home at 10 P.M."

A consulting physician was called shortly: "About 5 P.M. Mrs. Albert comes in a carriage and tells us to come up to father's right off as the Doctors intend to tap him. I hurry up, and find Dr. Schnetter and Professor Clark. Theodore supports father on his right side and I on the left, father standing up. Dr. Schnetter makes the incision, and a stream of water shoots out, fully a pail and a half full. Father is very much relieved, has appetite."

The incision the doctor made in Heinrich's abdomen allowed the fluid which had gathered there to be drained; it was but temporary relief, for Heinrich Steinway's liver had failed, and he was suffering from an electrolytic imbalance, one of the results of which is the retention of fluids that swell the abdomen and limbs. The condition is now known medically as ascites and more commonly as the beer drinker's disease. Heinrich Steinway, despite his life of achievement, was likely an alcoholic, although his lifelong exposure to lacquer finishes and felts made with mercury may have contributed to his liver failure. Heinrich, who was nothing if not resilient, rallied, and both the family and the doctors hoped for his recovery, but it was not to be. In mid-January William reported that "Father was slumbering when we came, but he got up from bed, on which he was laying dressed, walked to the table and signed the inventory." The inventory was the year-end accounting of the assets and liabilities of Steinway & Sons, the partnership's key financial document.

With what was obviously a guided hand, Heinrich placed his signature on the page in a large, irregular, almost childlike script. It was the last official act of the founder, and William observed, with obvious anguish, his father's final days: ". . . rapidly sinking . . . no hope . . . sits in his chair . . . lost his speech." Heinrich's dignity and pride would not let him remain in bed when his sons visited. He would insist on walking to his chair, supported by his sons on both sides.

The senior Steinway was "tapped" again by the doctors, two pails of fluids were collected, and Heinrich improved briefly; but the end came soon. As a terminal condition, ascites is considered benign; there is no great pain but merely discomfort followed by a lapse of consciousness and quiet death. Heinrich Steinway died at 2:30 A.M. February 7, 1871. Born the son of a charcoal burner living in virtual serfdom in the mountains of northern Germany, he died the owner of a mansion half a world and a lifetime away.

The obituary notices, written by William, appeared in virtually all the New York newspapers and were "splendid." Heinrich's death mask was taken, after which "Father is dissected by Dr. Schnetter at 4 P.M. They find liver entirely shrivelled up." The *instrumentenmacher* Heinrich Steinweg was then removed to the undertakers where he was begowned in a flowing white funeral robe and placed in a silver-trimmed casket. On short notice an ornate funeral ceremony was orchestrated for Steinway Hall. A nineteen-piece band, a choir, and an organist were hired, as was a pastor, and the hall was draped in black. At 10 A.M. the ceremonies began with some two thousand persons in attendance. The organist played, the choir sang, the pastor spoke, and the band repeated three marches for the forty-five minutes it took the assembled mourners to pass the casket. One and three-quarter hours after the start of the service the cemetery procession was formed outside. With the band at the head followed by the hearse, then the family members in carriages, the procession included the massed marching work force of Steinway & Sons and a total of sixty-one carriages. At the foot of Catherine Street where the ferry crossed the East River the workmen left the procession, which continued on to Greenwood Cemetery, where Heinrich's remains were placed in the seventy-thousand-dollar mausoleum near those of his sons and daughter. After the interment ceremony Theodore, William, and Albert returned in William's carriage to his home for a dinner.

During the time of his father's final illness William continued to buy property in Astoria, even asking the county clerk to determine who the adjoining property owners were, a tricky task that William could not accomplish himself. Astoria was named to honor John Jacob Astor, whom the original founders of the settlement hoped to attract as an investor. Though Mr. Astor declined, the name was retained. In 1870 Astoria, along with Ravenswood, Hunter's Point, and miscellaneous minor hamlets, plus many acres of farms, fields, forests, and swamps, the latter being prominent, were incorporated by an act of the state legislature as Long Island City. But there was both more and less to Astoria than met William's eye, or if he were aware, he did not record it.

A decade later the *New York Times* gave a righteously indignant summary: "About ten years ago a number of politicians in Hunter's Point and its vicinity, having watched with envious eyes the apparent success of the Tweed Ring in this City, thought they saw an excellent opportunity to line their own pockets at the expense of the public. It occurred to them that if they could only have a City Government to run for themselves they might profitably follow the example of Tweed . . . and enjoy the unwonted experience of helping themselves at will from a City Treasury. . . . By a united effort the scheme was successfully carried through the Legislature . . . with all the machinery of a full city Government provided for in the charter." William had invested in a quagmire of corruption.

Bribery was endemic in Manhattan. It was the time of W. M. "Boss" Tweed; and William, like any citizen, had to cope with a contaminated government. He dealt successfully with the voraciously corrupt Judge Albert Cardozo of the New York State Supreme Court. Cardozo, in less than four years on the bench, triggered the still-remembered Black Friday gold panic of 1869 when he issued in favor of Jay Gould a ruling that closed a bank. A nationwide depression ensued. Court records showed that the judge released over two hundred convicted felons from jail, each represented by the same law firm. He had received over sixty thousand dollars in cash payments from Gratz Nathan, a receiver Cardozo appointed to handle bankruptcies. Loyal to the Tweed Ring, Judge Cardozo jailed without charges an opposition candidate for Eighth Ward alderman and kept him locked up for a month after the election. An investigation by the state legislature developed evidence on all these charges, but Cardozo was never tried; he resigned and was allowed to continue private law practice. Many years later his son was appointed to the United States Supreme Court by President Franklin D. Roosevelt.

William Steinway had the sophistication and the contacts needed to deal with such urban predators. When William sued the hapless Ernestine Oaks and her three young girls to ensure that there would be no residual claim to Steinway partnership property, the matter was tried before Judge Cardozo. William's liaison with the judge was Joseph Howard, a newspaperman famous for his Civil War reporting. "I see Jos. Howard in relation to the suit, who confers with Judge Cardozo & promises that the motion will be denied," confided William to his diary. The price of justice sought in this instance appears to have been a piano sent to Cardozo's summer home in

Long Branch, New Jersey. A member of the Howard family also selected "a fine grand piano," but it is unclear if this instrument was purchased or was a gift. Joe Howard also had a relationship with Judge Barnard, who was likewise investigated but remained on the bench.

William was likely confident in his ability to deal with government if necessary, and it does not appear that he made any effort to meet the elected officials of newly incorporated Long Island City before investing there. For audacity and rapacity, if not for net proceeds, the politicians of Long Island City would soon demonstrate that they were equal if not superior to Manhattan's public servants. The impact on Steinway & Sons proved profound, but none of this was evident as William seized the bargains to be found in Astoria real estate.

The first real clue to William's intentions does not appear in his diary for more than a year after his first purchase in Long Island City's Fifth Ward. It was in November 1871 when he recorded that his friend, architect/engineer Henry Reck, the designer of the Steinway Mausoleum at Greenwood, "commenced to survey streets over our farms." A few days later William walked his property with Reck, but it was not until they drank champagne that they "hit upon a plan of laying out streets . . . that much pleases me." The difficulty may have been in accommodating the irregular shape of the property, which extended back from Bowery Bay a few feet short of a mile and was two-thirds of a mile wide, each at maximum. Streets 75 feet wide (boulevards by Manhattan standards) subdivided the property into blocks, most of which were 200 feet wide by 800 feet long, each containing 62 lots, the standardized size of which was 100 feet by 25.

When this exercise was complete, a design existed for a community in which William had the opportunity to sell well over 2,000 building lots; such a development could easily house 25,000 persons in an idyllic suburban setting. William and his family now owned a nascent subdivision four times the size of the Fourteenth Ward, the ward where they first lived after arriving in New York twenty years before. If built to the population density of the Fourteenth, *Steinway*, as it came to be known, would contain over 600,000 persons. To the extent there was a plan, it was a grand one. Reserved for the family was a waterfront ten-acre plot on which the mansion and its outbuildings stood.

Roughly thirty acres were set aside as a sort of industrial park, obviously intended as the development's engine of economic growth. Just a few hundred feet off the northerly corner of the property was Berrian's Island, now landfilled, which sat in the mouth of Berrian's Creek. Here William had dredged a quarter-mile-long canal, 150 feet wide. Nearly 2,000 feet of seawall kept the industrial area shoreline from eroding into Bowery Bay and the creek. A basin was dug in which "millions of square feet" of logs were kept in floating storage. When wet, the logs would not crack, and they were unloaded directly from ships into the basin by a derrick on the dock. The

Steinways were nothing if not passionate about the quality of wood used in their pianos. There was no detail of the development too small to escape William's attention—he personally chose the lightning rods for the foundry and sawmill, the first two manufacturing buildings finished on the site in 1873. Together with Albert and Theodore, William worked out the piping plan that brought water to the building from a spring. When the docks were finished, William measured them to make sure they were the agreed size. Alfred, of course, chose the boiler and engines and personally travelled with them from Morgan's Iron Works to Astoria on a barge.

When the foundry was finished, both William and Albert were there for the first firing. This nearly set the building's rafters ablaze, and metal sheets were quickly installed over the beams. When pilings were driven at a slight angle, William noticed. He paid close attention to the details of street construction, determining grades and levels, and when the water in the salt marshes became too high, William ordered a cut dug to drain them. There were, William noted, "Myriads of Mosquitos." While functioning as city planner, civil engineer, general contractor, construction boss, and purchasing agent, William was also orchestrating the Anton Rubinstein tour and attending to his normal "business and commercial" duties at Steinway Hall, as well as functioning as president of the Liederkranz. Throughout the pioneering period at Astoria, William was, at age thirty-seven, plagued with attacks of rheumatism that sometimes left him unable to walk for days. As if this were not enough, he and Albert were also supervising the rebuilding and refitting of the *Mozart*, adding eighteen feet to her length after she had sunk at the dock during a storm. Albert likewise discharged his normal duties as head of manufacturing at the Fourth Avenue factory. During all this William maintained the requisite social presence at concerts, operas, and the theater. Though no one ever said so, their enemies might have credibly claimed that a Steinway never slept.

In the midst of this frenetic activity Theodore sailed again for the calmer life of Germany. From there he launched critiques, presumably of the business, that William thought "a mix of jest and insult. . . . I am much grieved and so is Albert." That Theodore was no admirer of the American way of life can be seen in the fact that in the first nineteen years of his New York partnership he spent less than half his time in the United States. Apparently his wife, Joanna, was even less enthralled with the New World. On many of Theodore's visits she remained in Germany. Theodore was not the only Steinway to prefer life in *das Vaterland*. William's sister Wilhelmina, married to the opera singer William Candidus, returned to Germany, as did his sister-in-law Sophie, who, about this time, refused to let her youngest son Fred leave Germany for America, where he was born. In all likelihood she wanted Fred, then twelve, to have a German education. Even Mrs. Oaks ultimately decided to live in Germany. It was, ironically, the American success that provided the freedom of choice.

Though Theodore was absent from America and daily operations much of the time, his influence on Steinway & Sons was profound. A presence in America was not required for "invention," which today would be called "research and development." Such work was essentially solitary and a perfect use of the volcanically irascible Theodore's talents. Between 1868 and 1885 he was granted forty new United States patents, an average of one every five months. His creativity, or at least the patents that marked it, occurred in bursts. Roughly one-fourth of Theodore's letters patent were granted in a two-month period during 1878 and one-fifth more during six months in 1880.

Theodore's approach to research would today be called "whole system": no aspect of design is emphasized to the exclusion of others, and, very importantly, the interactions between design changes are recognized. Theodore's goal for his instruments can be summarized as "more": more power, more control, more tonal richness, more serviceability, more reliability. In his quest for the design beyond the design, Theodore expanded on the concepts of his brother Henry, making them his own. In the ultimate configuration he achieved a perfection that would leap from the nineteenth to the twenty-first century and stand as a criterion, a *true* benchmark against which all pianos are measured. It is fair, if not an understatement, to claim that every piano made in the twentieth century, except for reproductions of antique instruments, carries the imprint of the inventions of Theodore Steinway, protestations of competitive makers notwithstanding.

The first hairline cracks in the shell of the yet unhatched egg of the modern piano can be found in United States Patent number 93,647 granted August 10, 1869. The patent covered the "action-frame," that portion of the piano action assembly which holds and locates the hammers and the complex series of levers that send the hammer against the string when a key is depressed. "By these improvements," claimed the patent, "an action . . . is so constructed that all the parts can be readily interchanged, and each action frame can be inserted into every piano-forte of the same class without requiring any fitting." Henry Ford would have been impressed.

Combined with other patents, a new method of making actions resulted, one with important benefits. In addition to allowing interchangeability, the action could now be removed from the piano as a unit, "obviating," in William's words, "the difficulty formerly existing, that repairs to the action of a Grand Piano could not be made without the entire instrument being sent" back to the factory or a repair shop. The wheel of Theodore's revolution began to turn.

Just three years later Theodore gave that wheel a sharp push with his patent 126,848, which covered what William named the "Grand Duplex Scale." It was a fundamental advance. While Steinway & Sons was already known for the glistening treble of its instruments, Theodore found a way to improve it—by strengthening the partials—which has since been adopted by almost all the world's pianomakers.

The actual "live" length of the string sounds is attached by two "dead ends" of that same string. It was common practice for pianomakers to interweave felt in these dead ends to keep them from vibrating, which they were naturally inclined to do. In conventional practice, the dead ends introduced dissonant sounds if they were not damped by felt. Theodore's inspiration was to adjust the length of the dead ends so they produced sound consonant with the live portion of the string and then allow them to vibrate naturally. The result was a markedly enhanced—clearer and fuller—sound in the upper register of the instrument. The skeptical may test the auditory effect on most grand pianos by placing a finger on that portion of a string just forward of the tuning pin, striking a note, then removing the finger. The sound of the note will fill in, as if by magic. The effect is not magic nor is it subtle; it is a tribute to the genius of Theodore Steinway who found a way to make the unwanted useful.

While other patents intervened, Theodore's next fundamental improvement was validated by the federal government on May 21, 1878, with patent number 204,106. William called this invention "most important," and wrote that "it consists in the combination of an inside and outside rim . . . , each rim being composed of a series of strips of hard wood in one continuous length of 18–23 feet, glued together and bent into the required form." Heretofore, piano rims were made in at least two pieces joined together, usually on the left-hand corner of the nose, like a piece of furniture. Theodore's construction, which today would be recognized as a type of plywood, combined thin strips of wood in as many as sixteen layers to form the basic shape of the case. To build rims this way, it was necessary to invent special machinery, and, in due time, Theodore applied for patents on this as well.

The advantages of one-piece case construction were profound and lay in several areas. One area was mechanical strength; a one-piece rim was much less likely to crack, an embarrassingly frequent problem in cases made of two or more pieces. The additional strength in the rim was a part of Theodor's general strategy of increasing the string tension in his designs as fast as the metallurgical development in string-drawing would permit. Greater string tension tended to allow greater power in the tone of the instrument and also increased harmonic richness.

While capable of the grandest and most profound conceptions, Theodore also attended to fine details, and seemed to have had an almost limitless capacity for practical experiments. Pianist/teacher/critic/lecturer/writer Fanny Morris Smith described three large folios she saw on a visit to the factory in the early 1890s. They contained the results of Theodore's investigations into the strength of piano wire, written small in his own hand, and preserved the data from thousands of tests.

Theodore concerned himself with more than the mechanics and acoustics of his instrument. As a part of his whole-system approach, Theodore functioned as what today would be called a stylist or industrial designer. Theodore's styling exercises, though consonant with their time, show remarkably restrained use of carving and ornamentation. If this was an expression of Theodore's aesthetic sensibility, then he anticipated the twentieth century in his visual as well as sonic taste. Always concerned with what he thought were excessively high prices set by William, he may simply have been trying to reduce manufacturing costs. Carved curlicues and furbelows were expensive.

As peculiar as it may appear today, Theodore's technical advances were fuel for William's sales efforts. Brochures written by William invariably list and explain the majority of Theodore's inventions; an 1884 brochure contains thirty-one Steinway patents with explanations while an 1876 catalog contains fourteen pages of technical descriptions. The reader, it was assumed, knew the locations and functions of the wrest plank, agraffes, bridge, keybed, capo-d'astro bar, and other components of the instrument. This is not as improbable as it first appears; technological advances were the great pride of the time. The design of a new cannon, telegraph, steam engine, or ship was often page-one news, and the reports did not stint on technical details. Americans, delighting in the benefits of technologies simpler, if no less elegant, than ours in the twentieth century, had not yet abandoned the hope of understanding the machines they purchased.

Then, as now, it was not necessary to understand to use. For those disinclined to probe the arcana of acoustic dowels, ring bridges, and cupola frames there were always artist endorsements and exhibition awards. For potential customers interested in the scientific as well as the musical, William elicited—through the customary means of the gift of a grand piano—an endorsement from a man whose stature as a scientist among informed Victorians was similar to Einstein's in the twentieth century. His name was Hermann Ludwig Ferdinand von Helmholtz.

Born in Potsdam in 1821, Helmholtz studied medicine, then branched into physiology and ultimately physics, making basic contributions in all these fields as well as mathematics. His book, *Die Lehre von den Tonempfindungen*, was translated into English in 1875 under the title *Sensations of Tone as a Physiological Basis for the Theory of Music* and is perhaps the most cited work on music and hearing ever written. Helmholtz wrote to Theodore that "with such a perfect instrument as yours placed before me, I must modify many of my former expressed views regarding pianos." The statement carried immense weight, so much so that when Theodore perfected his duplex scale, another instrument was sent to Helmholtz. "I have repeatedly and carefully studied the effects of the Duplex Scale . . . and find the improvement most surprising and favorable, especially in the upper notes," wrote the scientist, "for splendid as my Grand Piano was before, the Duplex Scale has rendered its tone even more liquid, singing and harmonious.

The endorsements from von Helmholtz, as translated by William, were a part of Steinway catalogs for nearly two decades, along with the collected approbations of Liszt, Wagner, and many others. Their instruments were carried on the books as "loaned" and at zero dollar value. Liszt, according to 1885 internal records, had been lent Steinway number 49 382, Wagner was the recipient of 34 304, and von Helmholtz, a devotee of the works of Bach, then possessed 50 515, a style B grand.

In 1893, a now lionized von Helmholtz visited America. He toured Steinway Hall and the factory, but William visited with him only briefly; he did not accompany him on his factory tour and did not attend his New York lecture. William did, however, send the departing scientist a "fine souvenir of flowers." The Steinways, who themselves encouraged the notion that a relationship existed between Theodore and Hermann von Helmholtz, probably did so for reasons of reflected prestige. No evidence can be found that Helmholtz had any direct influence on Theodore's work, though Anna von Helmholtz wrote that William told her father that he learned much from his famous book. In fact, both William and Theodore seemed largely indifferent to, if not disinterested in, the developing science of acoustics. When acoustician Rudolf Koenig displayed an immense collection of his acoustical machinery at the Philadelphia Exposition, it was considered by many to be the most impressive exhibit at the Centennial. Nowhere does William record that either he or Theodore saw Koenig's machines, which, among other wonders, "synthesized" musical sounds.

There was ample reason for this: Steinway practice was so far in advance of theory that even the most erudite scientific investigators could tell Theodore only a little about what he had done and nothing about what he might do. Von Helmholtz, for example, noted in 1893 that the crown of a Steinway soundboard was interesting in that its curvature was similar to that of the human eardrum, the tympanum. Though fascinating, this was an observation devoid of utility, for Steinway soundboards possessed a similar, if not identical, crown since the time of Theodore's "Cupola Frame, Self-Compression" patent reissue of 1880. Whatever their genius, William and Theodore were, above all, practical men.

While Theodore's capacity for invention was vast, perhaps unparalleled in his field, he did not constrain himself to matters of innovation. Albert, for one, received direct instructions from Theodore, often in the form of engineering changes, the bane of any manufacturing manager's existence. Theodore would have a New York instrument shipped to his home in Braunschweig, where he would subject it to the most minute scrutiny. Human nature being what it is, we may assume that Albert shipped only the best pianos available, yet Theodore was able to find errors and room for improvement.

He was a man who valued clarity above politeness: "In the case of the calamity of the center strings not holding steady on the Centennials

[Steinway's flagship grand piano], I have expressly ordered the string position raised 2 millimeters. . . . Without a doubt it will be necessary within a few years to take back the Centennial grands . . . a very depressing thought. . . . We will lose thousands in money and reputation. . . . This has caused me many sleepless hours and much grief," wrote Theodore to Albert in an undated letter sometime in 1876 or 1877. Albert, of course, would likely have taken the view that it was Theodore's responsibility to assure that the Centennial's design was correct before, in modern terms, it was released to production.

William received similar letters from Theodore, who took exception, at one time or another, to what he thought were excessive advertising expenses, "newspaper shenanigans," Steinway Hall concerts, high prices, and extortionate demands of artists. "The damned artists treat pianomakers like cows to be milked," rumbled Theodore. A prime point of contention within the family was the best use of the Astoria property. When William decided to move the Steinway keymakers from Manhattan to Astoria without consultation, Theo was upset, claiming that the sea air of Long Island City was a poor place to do precision woodwork. Nonetheless, keymaking stayed in Astoria. "I know very well that you are a master of illusions who is plagued by a few fixed ideas against which neither warnings nor remonstrances have any effect. . . . You want to make up for the building lots at any price," wrote Theodore.

This was an eerily accurate assessment, for William had seriously overbought in Long Island City. At the time of his purchase the entire population of Queens County was but seventy-four thousand persons; most of these were concentrated along the shore of the East River opposite Manhattan, the population of which was not quite one million. If the entire development of Steinway that William laid out were to be populated at even moderate densities, the result would have been a one-third increase in the county's population. The long-term population growth rate in Queens was only about 3 percent per year, and little short of a gold strike would have attracted people to Steinway at the necessary rate.

William went about recruiting industry for the development with his customary energy, but the long depression of the 1870s made this difficult, and the only businesses which located in Steinway were those that William himself funded. A brief foray into the organ business was capitalized, yet when the organ factory burned, William did not rebuild it. The Astoria Organ Company survived, but did not prosper, for less than a year. A man named William H. Williams opened a veneer-cutting business with Steinway financial assistance. It was undoubtedly the plan to sell veneer to both Steinway & Sons and the nearby German cabinetmakers. The company persisted for many years though it never achieved great size.

Over time the slow growth of his nascent village became one of William's key concerns. William Steinway—a man accustomed to success, a man who neutralized his competitors when he did not defeat them, a man whose company survived when thousands failed, a man whose name was known throughout the Western world—at last met forces greater than himself in the brackish, mosquito-infested swamps of the place called East Astoria. Just as those forces would not yield, William would not acknowledge that he had been bested, if, in private and unrecorded moments, he realized as much. No one but Theodore had the audacity to question the huge sums William poured into Steinway Village from both his personal fortune and the resources of the company to grade roads, build stores, and construct homes for the workers. There are no records of William's personal expenditures, but the books of Steinway & Sons for the year ended 1880 showed that over $695,000 had been spent on Astoria real estate and improvements, an amount greater than the combined value of the Fifty-second Street factory and Steinway Hall and also five times greater than all the pianos then available for sale by Steinway & Sons.

All this came to remarkably little in the way of growth. A decade after purchasing the land, William's community had but 130 residences, suggesting that less than one-tenth of the more than two thousand building lots had been sold. The entire Fifth Ward of Long Island City contained only 2,370 persons, and the entire city now held but 17,257 souls. Growth for the last five years had averaged less than 2 percent per year.

While the depression certainly inhibited development—the buyers of the first homes William built at Steinway in 1873 could not get their mortgage funds from the banks due to a "money panic"—Long Island City was plagued with local problems that persisted throughout William's lifetime—and beyond. Anticipating that he could build an idyllic waterside village isolated from filth, disease, vice, and sociopolitical turbulence, William soon found that he had not fled far enough. The socialists, communists, and anarchists had no more trouble than William travelling the few miles of water and unpaved road that led to East Astoria, and they were certainly no less dedicated to their objectives than he to his. The men who worked in Astoria at the mill and foundry had worked before on Fifty-second Street, and it soon proved, in a variation of the old saying, "that you could take the man out of the city but not the city out of the man." Green fields and sylvan shores were no palliative for discontent, nor did they modulate the perpetual belief of many workers that capitalist profits were unjustly earned.

In many ways the Steinway development was an enlightened, even idealistic, effort to create an industrial community. It was not based on the authoritarian and infamous models of nineteenth-century "company towns" such as Lowell, Massachusetts, or Pullman, Illinois, where workers lived in company housing, were required to buy food and clothing at extortionate prices from company stores, and kept house, as at Pullman, in the shadow of home inspectors who might appear at any moment to certify that the floors were clean and the tables dusted. In such places a man became homeless the same day he became jobless.

The Steinway approach was remarkably laissez-faire. Though a grocery store might be owned by the family, it was operated by an independent proprietor who set his own prices. No effort was made to control the establishment of saloons, and that Teutonic essential, *lagerbier*, was available at free-market prices and in ample quantities for any thirst. The same approach was taken to other essentials, such as the butcher and the shoemaker.

The homes the family built were substantial, made of brick with metal (probably galvanized iron) roofs, and concrete brick cellars. The single-family homes for workmen had three rooms on the first floor, presumably a parlor, dining room, and kitchen, and four rooms plus a bath on the second. When sold, such a home cost three thousand to four thousand dollars, complete, in what would now be called move-in condition. The indoor bathrooms were a particularly luxurious feature; in many areas of New York City toilets were still outside behind the building. By the standards of the time, these were dream houses, but they sold slowly, very slowly, despite an equivalent price today of between thirty-six thousand and fifty-six thousand dollars.

Testifying before a United States Senate Committee on Education and Labor in 1883, William gave an insight into his nonfinancial motives: "I consider one of the greatest evils under which workingmen live, especially in the city of New York, is the horrors of the tenement houses—the terrible rents they have to pay. The average workingman's family has one room in which they cook, wash, iron and live, and one or two, possibly three, bedrooms, of which generally one or two are dark rooms, without any windows, or without admitting God's pure air. . . . The horrors of the tenement houses are having a very baneful effect upon the morals and character of the coming generation; in fact, I may say a terrible effect. But I do not see what legislation can do. Capitalists consider tenement houses a poor investment, paying poor returns. The only thing that I can imagine is to do as *we* have done, remove the very large factories requiring much room and many men from out of the city of New York into the suburbs. . . . I think every effort ought to be directed to having the large establishments go out to the suburbs of the city, in order to give the workingmen a chance to live as human beings ought to live." William's was a prescient vision; his grasp of the evolving pattern of urban geography was startlingly clear. William Steinway had perceived the shape of the future. It was, unfortunately, the distant future, and that futurity would not arrive in Long Island City during his lifetime.

The "workingmen" of which William spoke had a decidedly different view. During a strike meeting in 1880 the *New York Sun* reported that the

Steinways were "accused of having been stringent with the men who hired houses of them and who could not pay the rent. One man said the firm treats the men as the coal miners of Pennsylvania were treated. They did not keep stores and force them to buy high-priced provisions, but they banished them to God-forsaken Astoria and required them, if they wished employment, to hire houses belonging to the firm."

The reference to coal miners was well calculated to elicit the sympathies of even the ardently anti-union, for miners were a case study in exploitation and systemically enforced poverty. Even the *New York Times* observed that, in the depths of the depression, Scranton, Pennsylvania, miners were lucky to earn twenty-five dollars per month and that their diet consisted of potatoes and Indian meal with a little pork on payday. Tales of starving children and families evicted when a miner was injured and could not work abounded. It was not so at Steinway, of course, where even the laborers' annual earnings were twice that of a Scranton miner, but for the men the perception of dependence on the company was similar. If the Steinway "workingman" bought a home in the village, he *was* dependent on Steinway & Sons, for there was nowhere else to work in the area. It was also true that on at least one occasion William evicted strikers who were behind on their rent, although the number issued "dispossess warrants," or if they were enforced, is unknown.

But Astoria was not "God-forsaken" by design; if William's grand plan came to fruition, Steinway would have been a bustling industrial community with many places to work, a comfortable prosperity, and rising real estate values. The problem, at least in part, lay in the machinations and depredations of local government. As early as 1875 the scent of mismanagement wafted from the city when it was revealed that the police had not been paid in five months due to a lack of funds. An immense debt had been inherited from the town of Newtown, itself under the thrall of a "ring" whose justice of the peace had been jailed for fraud.

Then as now, New York City was inclined to export its wastes whenever possible, and the banks of Newtown Creek bordering Long Island City were the depositories for Manhattan's manure and slaughterhouse refuse with quantities measured in tons per week. The fat and bone boilers, driven from New York by law, soon took up residence across the East River. Long Island City's board of health seemed indifferent to this activity. William had noticed what he called the "Myriads of Mosquitos," and late in the summer of 1877 a malaria outbreak was recorded. "The malaria," reported the *New York Times*, "that has been created in Long Island City by the impairing of the drainage by the filling in of the low and marsh lands, and the sickening odors from the factories, and from the accumulated filth and slime that have washed upon the land adjacent to Newtown Creek, has assumed very serious proportions, and has confined several hundred persons in their homes with fever." Later that same year it was discovered that the former city treasurer, one John Horan, who had been previously tried then acquitted on a charge of embezzlement and was reelected, now had irregularities in his books in the amount of $33,000, or nearly $400,000 today. Of course, Mr. Horan had plausible explanations for the apparent shortages in his books. Seemingly chastened by the missing sums, the city fathers reined in expenditures by cutting the salaries of the city's schoolteachers.

Service industries, popular with today's city planners for their presumed rapid growth, educated work force, and lack of noxious emissions, were also found in Long Island City. One growth industry was "pool selling," and gambling parlors sprang up in the Hunter's Point section of the young metropolis. There was nothing covert about Long Island City gambling; White & Company had a large sign over its ground-floor quarters reading, "Hunter's Point Turf Exchange." When the *Times* visited the site, three hundred persons were found eagerly placing fifty-cent and one-dollar bets while the seven employees were busy taking money and posting race results on the chalkboards that covered the walls. To the rear of the main area was a partition labelled "Reading Room" where those with time to while away waiting for race results to arrive by telegraph could play faro and *rouge et noir*.

At the posh establishment of Kelly & Bliss—the minimum bet was one dollar—the *Times* reporter identified two well-known civic leaders, Assemblyman George E. Bulmer and the president of the Board of Aldermen, Steven J. Kavanagh. "Possibly they were there to learn the evils of these places," commented the reporter. In a strange turn of events, the police commissioners issued an order directing that the betting parlors be closed, after which two of them resigned. The police did not raid the gamblers, taking the position that the order had no effect since the officials who made it were no longer in power.

William, certainly aware of the nature of government in Long Island City, seemed to decide that the solution to the problems of developing Steinway Village in the context of a corrupt muncipality perpetually teetering on the brink of bankruptcy was to undertake the functions of government himself. For a brief period Steinway had its own police force of two, and William lent one of the officers his revolver. This may well have been preferable to municipal protection, for it was disclosed in the *Times* that two city police officers had been "extorting money from German residents of the Fifth Ward for permits for keeping cows, pigs, goats, poultry & c. . . . The system of blackmail . . . [has] been carried on for some time, the victims being generally Germans, are ignorant not only of the law, but the language of the land." One of the officers, a brother of the president of the Board of Aldermen, was allowed to resign while his less influential co-conspirator was discharged.

Initially at least, William was not alone in his desire to create a "settlement," as he called it, in East Astoria. Brother Albert also worked on the project, as did one of William's young nephews, Henry William Theodore Steinway, the oldest son of Charles, who joined Steinway & Sons in 1872 at the age of sixteen. To William, Theodore, and Albert, H. W. T. Steinway and his two younger brothers Charles and Frederick represented the immediate namebearers for the house, as both Henry's and Albert's children were all females while Theodore had no surviving children. William's son George was then but seven years old.

The significance of the next generation of Steinways was made plain in the spring of 1877. "Albert limps badly and tells me that he is rheumatic all over," wrote William on April 21. Albert appeared to recover and a few days later played skat with William, beating him for twenty-five cents, but the malaise had paved the way for something more malign: "Albert said to be sick in bed with chills and fever," recorded William nine days after the first entry.

"See Albert who is very sick with what we fear is Typhus fever. Dr. Schnetter there." It was not typhus, nor was it typhoid fever, said Dr. Schnetter; it was "malignant bilious gastric fever." That opinion was revised when William received a letter from the doctor, probably delivered by messenger, that Albert now had "a regular Typhoid fever." A week had gone by. Typhoid, an immensely painful and debilitating intestinal disease, was not a certain killer; in 1883 its mortality rate was estimated to be about 12 percent of those contracting the ailment, which normally had a duration of three to six weeks with a protracted recovery of several months. Nonetheless, William had "gloomy forebodings that the terrible calamity is upon us."

Albert was spending much time at Astoria, and it is there that he may have contracted typhoid. One possible route, unknown then, was through the ingestion of oysters, a taste Albert may have shared with other family members. Oyster beds were then common around Long Island, and these were easily contaminated with matter carrying the typhoid bacillus from Long Island City's sewers. The dumps and partially drained swamps of the city might have contained typhoid-bearing material that could have leeched into the area's high water table, then pumped as drinking water.

Apparently Dr. Schnetter elected to use the "German cure," which required immersing Albert in cool water to break his fever. For this two male nurses were hired. "It is claimed by the advocates of this method of treatment that it has been successful in diminishing greatly the mortality of typhoid fever, but they hold at the same time that its success depends upon its employment from an early stage of the disease," informed the *Encyclopaedia Britannica*. Albert had typhoid for ten days, at a minimum, before Dr. Schnetter and the consulting physician, Dr. Loomis, began the cold baths. "Stop at Albert's at 6 P.M. and see him for a moment," wrote William. "My heart almost breaks." Two days later: "We all feel dreadful,

Dr. S. having found Albert to perspire copiously. I leave at 11½ P.M. almost heartbroke, yet hoping still."

The next morning, May 11, 1877, William received a message: "To my horror a despatch comes at 9:30 A.M. that Albert is dying. I jump into a coupe, drive uptown and find Louise [Albert's wife], the boys, Dr. Schnetter bathed in tears. Robert Stephens [a nurse] reports that Albert at 9:15 A.M. had taken brandy and coffee, when soon after he breathed very heavily and at precisely 9:27 A.M. drew his last breath. Our excitement and anguish is indescribable. I hurry downtown again and telegraph Theodore 'Albert dies this morning. You must come soon' . . . then hurry uptown to meet J. J. Diehl, Undertaker, who has been placing Albert's corpse on ice. Find Louise and her two darling children who are weeping bitterly just having been told of their father's death. We decide to have the funeral service take place at Steinway Hall. . . . Two reporters from the *Sun* call on me. *Telegram* had notice of my death."

The funeral arrangements naturally were made by William. "The notices are alright," he observed, then: "At 6 P.M. stagger home, find a bible there with a few lines directing my attention to Matthew, Chapter 11th, verse——." The verse numbers, unrecorded by William, were plausibly twenty-eight through thirty:

> Come unto me all ye that labor
> and are heavy laden, and I will give
> you rest.
>
> Take my yoke upon you, and learn
> of me; for I am meek and lowly in heart;
> and ye shall find rest unto your souls.
>
> For my yoke is easy and my burden
> is light.

Reading these words William broke down, "sobbing as though my heart would break." That night he had "uneasy sleep and dreams," for Johann Heinrich Wilhelm Steinweg certainly realized that now, divorced, with his father and three brothers dead, he was the sole survivor in America; to him alone devolved the fate and future of Steinway & Sons, the widows, and the young.

"It is raining but soon clears up, becoming a glorious day. Our small hall is finely draped and being got into shape in the forenoon. Many flowers are sent, one beautiful tower from Albert Weber. I feel as though I were stupefied and in a trance. . . . Am seized with a paroxysm of grief of the most alarming kind, in the meanwhile the funeral services go on in the smaller hall where Albert's body lies in state very much changed in appearance." The Liederkranz sang, there was an "eloquent sermon," and eight foremen bore Albert's casket to the hearse while the orchestra played. William and Henry W. T. Steinway were in the first carriage, William's children and their nurse were in the second on the trip to Greenwood Cemetery. Where Albert's wife, Louise, and his children, Ella and Henrietta, were, William did not record, nor did he mention the presence of his mother, Julia. After a "short prayer" Albert's body was temporarily placed in a crypt reserved for William's mother. "I suffer intensely and cry and sob," wrote William. "This was one of the most terrible days of my life."

"You write that you feel very lonely," responded Theodore about one month after Albert's funeral. "This does not surprise me." Fifteen years older than Albert, Theodore averred that, as a brother, he loved Albert deeply but that Albert had unspecified faults typical of rich, young men. "Our old father died of liver disease . . . because of the irresponsible way the craziest things were done behind his back on Albert's orders that usually had to be changed three times." Theodore railed against the idea of making keyboards at Astoria, the project in which Albert was engaged at the time of his death a few days before his thirty-seventh birthday.

"How come you only mention such important matters only after they are done? Now I understand why Albert died; I prophesied this in the presence of his wife when he talked about building in Astoria. I said to him, Albert, please do not speak to me about this, it will kill you. You are not as strong as you think. . . . I still have some trepidations about whether your rheumatic condition will not affect you by your stay in the stone house. Shorten your time there, dear brother." Theodore closed his letter of condolence to William with the lines, "I will now have to finish with my wisdom which I always waste in a useless way. . . . Don't hold the latest outpouring about the caper with the keymakers against me, dear young man." And William did not, except perhaps in his mind, take umbrage with Theodore. They were, after all, the last surviving sons of their generation, and to William there was no concept more dear than that of family.

William now found himself immersed in the minutiae of piano manufacture, deciding, for example, on the location of glue pots and steam boxes in the factory in consultation with Henry Kroeger, an employee of more than twenty years and factory superintendent so valued that he received a royalty payment on each piano made and a salary as high as six thousand dollars per year. Accompanying William much more often now was Henry W. T. Steinway, who, at the age of twenty-one, was clearly in training for an enlarged role in the firm.

Charles's oldest son, Henry William Theodore, had the only education the Steinways considered proper, a German one, and he lived for several years with his mother, Sophia, and younger brothers in Braunschweig under the watchful eye of his Uncle Theodore. By the school term of 1869–70, Henry W. T., at age fourteen, was in America at the Mount

Pleasant Academy in Sing Sing, New York, where he remained through the 1870–71 term and perhaps into 1872.

During the summer of 1872 Henry W. T. was at the mansion in Astoria. Though presumably living the life of a rich adolescent, he came into the city to "nurse" his Uncle William, who was afflicted at age thirty-seven with very severe rheumatism in both knees. William was barely able to walk even with crutches, and it was probably young Henry who applied the leeches to William's knees and wrapped them in oilskin.

Shortly after he joined the firm in September 1872, Henry W. T. began taking private instruction in engineering from Columbia University professor G. S. Roberts at the impressive cost of two dollars per hour, for four hours each week. Henry W. T. worked, it may be presumed, directly under the guidance of Albert at the Fourth Avenue manufactory for roughly four and one-half years before Albert died. An early clue to his character appears in William's diary when he visited Astoria with Albert and the engineer/architect Henry Reck: "We give Henry Steinway a good talking to. Buildings making good progress." William did not record the cause of the disciplinary action, but it was the first of many he recorded. "Give H. St. a good talking to on account of his non-appearance last night," wrote William on Christmas Day 1879. H.W.T. had committed a flagrant transgression by failing to attend the family gathering on Christmas Eve. For this there was no exemption save illness or death. A Victorian biographer would likely have described Henry W. T. Steinway as a youth of intelligence and many original opinions, ferociously held. William described him as "obstinate," "discourteous," "rough," "abusive," "insulting," "pessimistic," and as having "insane ideas."

Nonetheless, Henry W. T. was family, and he was tolerated, even when rude to factory superintendent Kroeger, who worked for Steinway & Sons before H.W.T. was born. "I have quite a dispute with Henry Steinway about his actions with Kroeger," noted William. Although an employee of but twelve days' seniority, H.W.T. had picked the largest possible nonfamily target. Inadvertently, this may have been inspired by William, who, just a few weeks before, in front of his young nephew had given Henry Kroeger a "severe reprimand" for persistently making more upright pianos than he ordered. A rebuke witnessed by an adolescent, no matter what his surname, must have been a powerfully humiliating experience for Henry Kroeger and apparently gave the sixteen-year-old H.W.T. the impression that respect for Mr. Kroeger was, at best, optional.

That same day William and Henry W. T. visited Julia, William's mother, who still lived across the street from the factory and was being treated by Dr. Buchner. "She is still in bed and very weak, has a wound which is healing again," William recorded in his diary. It is likely that William did not realize that this was the last time he would speak to his mother. At Astoria two days later, August 9, 1877, the Steinway private line telegraph clacked at 7:00 A.M. "that Grandmother is dying, I hurry in buggy with Henry St. over to New York. Find Dorette & Jacob Ziegler [William's older sister and her husband, a furniture manufacturer], & Dr. Buchner with mother who has been unconscious since last night and slowly breathing her last. I hurry to store and receive intelligence that at 10:15 A.M. she drew her last breath passing gently and peacefully, without the slightest pain, out of this world."

By eleven that morning William had made arrangements for a funeral on Saturday two days hence and was able to return to work. The pressing task before him: obtain the signatures of the luminaries on the Philadelphia Exposition jury to counter Albert Weber's claims of instrumental superiority. Later that day William journeyed uptown to order the factory closed for a half-day for his mother's funeral and the flags to be flown at half-mast. In the evening he entertained his Philadelphia dealer Blasius and his wife.

Saturday, the day of his mother's funeral, William spent the morning working at the hall before travelling uptown to the funeral, which was held in the parlor of Heinrich and Julia's home. There was no band, no chorus, no assembly of two thousand mourners, but William did note that all the "family now residing in the U.S. is assembled." This was perhaps a dozen persons, including the children. "At 1:10 Pastor Krusi opens the funeral services, making an eloquent sermon closing with a prayer. . . . Many beautiful flowers on the Coffin which looks beautiful, is of wrought iron, same as my poor brother Albert's. The foremen act as pall bearers. Mother looks very natural and a peaceful expression on her face." One hour and five minutes later the mourning family once again made a trip to Greenwood Cemetery as they had just three months before. There Pastor Krusi said a prayer, and the coffin of Julianne Thiemer Steinweg (her name was never legally changed, nor did she become a citizen of the United States) was placed in the crypt alongside her husband at age seventy-three. Actuarially, her life was long.

About this woman who mothered a dynasty almost nothing is known; even the cause of her death is obscured by the hurried scrawl of the attending physician. It reads: "*Primary:* Enteric . . . [illegible] . . . Diarrhoeal . . . 12 days . . . *Immediate:* Exhaustion." The word *enteric* was often a synonym for typhoid, but the doctor felt no obligation to legibly inform the future. By 5:30 P.M. that clear August afternoon of his mother's funeral William Steinway was back at the hall receiving business callers. The next day in Astoria he decided that the letters STEINWAY should be painted in white on a large sign facing Long Island Sound.

One of the singularities of William's life after his divorce, emphasized by the paucity of emotional response to the death of his mother, was the absence of any relationships with women other than with relatives and the household staff, which numbered a half-dozen including a governess for young George and Paula. William did not seek feminine companionship for the innumerable concerts, operas, and plays he audited; when he went to the renowned balls of the Liederkranz and Arion, he did so in the company of family. At age forty-two, the year his mother died, William was active to the edge of frenzy and presented a commanding, perhaps even handsome, appearance by the criteria of his time with a full beard and a penetrating gaze topping a five-foot, seven-inch, 220-pound frame. After more than a quarter-century in America William was famous, wealthy, and powerful. If the number of soirees he attended is any criterion, often singing, playing the piano, and having, to use a frequent phrase, "a jolly time," William did not lack affability, self-assurance, or social grace. However, for roughly five years after his divorce there was not a single indication in his diary that William had even the slightest interest in any woman he met. In the first year after Regina sailed for France, the absence of a woman in William's life was understandable; he had to maintain the fiction that he was still married. But after the New York papers reported the details of *Dachauer* v. *Dachauer*, all those with an interest knew that William was divorced. Certainly any aspiring young *pianiste* in New York would have enjoyed the company of Mr. William Steinway. Still, the man who built pianos and sought to build cities did not become romantically involved. Perhaps there was not time enough.

"Clear cold day . . . Uptown in eveg, Theo writes to Ranft in Dresden by Steamer Germania, I enclose card Photograph, home at 11 P.M.," was the brief and cryptic diary entry that presaged great change. It was the day after Christmas 1879. Four months to the day passed before William wrote, "Theo with me in eveg. He received letter from R. Ranft, which will perhaps cause my trip to Germany with George."

In addition to being a man not given to hasty replies, Richard Ranft was known to many in the American piano trade as the former United States importer of German-made Weickert felt, which, among other uses such as hats, was highly esteemed for fabricating piano hammers. Otto Richard Ranft arrived in America in 1852, shortly met a German woman whom he married within a year of his arrival, and, with a loan from his father-in-law, commenced an import business in Brooklyn. The classic success story was interrupted by the defalcation of his partner, who absconded with the firm's funds after liquidating its inventory in 1860. Acquitted by the court, Ranft set about rebuilding the business. In this he was successful, and he returned to Germany as a "capitalist" in 1873. Among Richard Ranft's children were two daughters, both born in America.

After revising his will, a prudent measure before nineteenth-century sea travel, William boarded the *Main* and steamed for England on June 26, 1879, with his son George, now fifteen years old. Daughter Paula, for unknown reasons, was left in New York. It was a fast vessel; the *Main* rarely made less than 320 miles per day. On board William quickly assumed the role of entertainment director and presided over a shipboard Independence Day festival that starred William Steinway. There were speeches, one by William, of course; and two well-known pianists coincidentally on the voyage, Franz Rummel and Otto Florsheim, both played for the passengers, as did William. He also directed the ship's band in a selection. The passengers then climbed to the weather deck for fireworks accompanied by music. "Great joy at festival last night," wrote William the next day.

Ashore in London and presumably with young George in tow, William commenced a rapid round of visits. His first stop was at Steinway Hall in London, a scaled-down combination salesroom and concert hall modeled after Steinway Hall in New York. It was run by an Englishman named Maxwell, who was ultimately discovered to be an embezzler, but on this first viewing William was pleased with what he saw. Days and evenings were filled with business and social calls: there were two more visits with Franz Rummel and a loan to Rummel of two hundred pounds sterling. A meeting with grand opera impresario Colonel Mapleson, whose troupes were often sponsored by Steinway, was mandatory and accomplished by the second day.

From London William and George travelled to Brussels and from there to Germany, and he noted that "for the first time in thirty years all the Steinways of my generation are together in Germany." Perhaps this observation evoked in William's mind memories of times long past and his father and his mother and his brothers and his sister Anna and the unnamed still-born babies, encased in stone, across an ocean, a world away. And as William looked forward into the future, he saw the past and wrote in his diary, "Tel[egraph] to R.R. at Nancy." William Steinway and his son George were planning to visit Regina. After going to Seesen (where he was born) to dine with old friends, William once again telegraphed Regina. That Regina did not respond to several telegrams and a letter may be significant; in fact, it appears from the diary that Regina never answered William's telegrams and that his sister Doretta somehow made contact with "R.R."

Four days before revisiting the past in the form of his ex-wife, William reconnoitered a possible future: "Visit the Ranfts, meet them all, very nice family, living in fine style." The next day a Miss Spott called with her father and played the piano "pretty well" for William. Miss Spott was merely another in a measureless line of aspiring *pianistes* whom William auditioned in search of genuine talent. "Take dinner with the Ranft family. With him and the two daughters Ellie and Martha drive all around Dresden. Spend evening at their house. Mr. Ranft walks to hotel with me. He and I talk matters over frankly. Tell him I will come again in two weeks." Events would show that William was not in Dresden to discuss the subtleties of piano hammers or swap hunting stories with a fellow sportsman but to arrange for a marriage, his own marriage.

From Dresden William travelled with George and his sister Doretta to Strasbourg, and, after renting a carriage, "we drive out, meet Madame Roos

Roos in Hotel Ville de Paris." The next morning Doretta, George, and William met with Regina and spent three hours with her. "George," wrote William, "says he has no feeling for R.R." It was a day to close the volumes of the past, and William took the train to Baden-Baden, where he saw Ernestine Oaks, her husband, and the three girls, the children of William's brother Henry. William had not seen Ernestine or his nieces in more than a decade when, at the order of the New York Supreme Court, he had returned the girls to their mother.

William continued to rummage in time. He visited with Julius Schiedmeyer, the pianomaker and judge at the Centennnial Exhibition and the European exhibitions at which Steinway had triumphed. He called upon Dr. Oscar Paul, another European exhibition judge and a strong supporter of the "Steinway System" of pianomaking. *Pianiste* Anna Mehlig, who had successfully toured America under Steinway sponsorship in 1873, received a visit from William, as did the composer and *Kappelmeister* Franz Abt. William did not chronicle his feelings but did write an "answer to a crazy letter from R.R. who wants to go to America." Regina stayed in Nancy until her death in 1883.

Seventeen days after he left Dresden, William returned. Checking into his hotel at noon, William spent the afternoon with Ellie Ranft and her mother, then went to the theater with mother and daughter. Another day passed before William again visited the Ranfts. After dinner William played skat with Richard Ranft and, in a surprising omission, did not mark down the amount he won or lost. Two more conferences were held between Otto Richard Ranft and William Steinway. After the second William saw "Ellie Ranft, when after a brief conversation, we engage ourselves to be married in a few days. In eveg we all go to the Meistersinger, a master performance, afterward at the Hotel, where we eat and drink til 12 A.M. . . . . pass sleepless night."

After obtaining the necessary government documents including one called a "dispensation," William bought his bride-to-be an engagement ring and a watch. The wedding took place not once but twice, first in the presence of the American consul and then with a Pastor Ranft, apparently a relative, at Richard Ranft's house. "Splendid floral decorations, nice dinner, speeches, we sing . . . I cable New York to announce my marriage in Herald and Staatzeitung. . . . At 8 P.M. we start in sleeping car for Vienna."

Elizabeth Karoline Ranft, age twenty-six, and the eldest daughter of Otto Richard Ranft, was described in her official government papers as five feet four inches, brown eyes, high forehead, nose prominent, chin round, hair dark, complexion fair, face oval. William introduced his wife to his sister Doretta a few days after their marriage and was likely pleased that "the ladies call each other Du," the familiar form of address in German. Less than two weeks after the marriage, William, Ellie, and George were at the docks in Southampton boarding the *Main* again, bound for America. There another figure from the past appeared, Mrs. Louis Dachauer. "Give her five pounds," jotted William. "Find many letters, flowers, telegrams."

It was not a pleasant trip. William was "laid up with Rheumatism in my right foot" while Ellie and George were seasick. When the *Main* reached New York, William's rheumatism was so severe that he was "carried by 8 men" off the ship, and "driven to my house & carried in by our packers [piano movers] . . . am feverish, temp 101, pulse 120." Immobilized by pain and unable to get out of bed, William remained in the house at Gramercy Park. More than a month passed before he was able to walk, as he recorded, to the water closet. Nearly six weeks elapsed before William visited Steinway Hall for an hour, but the first thing William did after leaving the house was to make sure he was registered to vote. Among William's recuperative activities were games of skat with his new brother-in-law, Richard Ranft, Jr., who lived in New York.

One and one-half months after his return, William had a "bad relapse, both feet, knees, elbow and back very painful, remain in bed. Henry Steinway very much aggravating my sickness by childish talk." It was December before William could begin to move about without crutches or cane, and he gradually accelerated the velocity of his life. He had been in New York for nearly three months before he returned to the Liederkranz: "preside at meeting, am enthusiastically received." Things seemed as they were, as they had been, but the life of William Steinway, now officially recognized as one of New York's four hundred millionaires, was about to take a different heading, one that was at once old and new. William's new course would place Steinway & Sons in harm's way.

Chapter 22

WITHOUT COMMENT ON THE ANIMUS

"In the busy throbbing heart of that sorely afflicted community, Long Island City, a sleeping giant was loosed yesterday morning—loosed by the hand of criminal carelessness almost diabolical in its recklessness—and it carried death, maiming and destruction into more than a score of innocent and unsuspecting families. . . . Two women were sent without a prayer before their maker, three mangled men dying within the hour, three more sent to the very borderland of death with chances of their coming back, and something like a score bruised or cut by flying arrowheads of broken glass or crushed under masses of falling plaster." One hundred sticks of dynamite, it appeared, were accidentally detonated at a construction site of the New York & Long Island Railroad.

The *New York Herald* for Thursday, December 29, 1892, spiced its outrage with grisly detail. Killed were Mary Grayden, age 22, a dishwasher, of 29 Jackson Avenue, Long Island City, "leg torn off and horribly mangled by flying glass and rock"; John Hopkins, 23, restaurant keeper, same address, "both eyes destroyed, died in hospital after amputation of leg"; Nicolo Loadano, age 27, "Italian, in charge of the dynamite, died after amputation of arm"; Henry O'Brien, age 30, grocery clerk, "Head nearly amputated by glass, wife and two children. Died within five minutes at police station"; and Mrs. Peter Rocco, Nicolo Loadano's sister of 27 Jackson Avenue, was killed instantly when "a piece of wood was driven through her body. Left three children."

Having squeezed the last drop of blood from the details, the *Herald* summarized the events leading up to the explosion. "When the New York & Long Island Railroad Company—controlled, it is supposed, by William Steinway and George Ehret, the brewer—began to blast out a tunnel last spring under the East River, work was begun at a shaft occupying the center of a triangle bounded by Jackson and Vernon Avenues and Fourth Street."

This area of Long Island City was roughly opposite Forty-second Street in Manhattan, and the plan was to connect Long Island with Manhattan via a tunnel bored through the bedrock beneath the East River and to run electric subway trains through it and under Forty-second Street to Grand Central Station and from there, according to one account, westerly before emerging across the island between Tenth and Eleventh avenues on land owned by the New York Central Railroad. It was a visionary plan, technologically ambitious, and, at a projected cost of ten million dollars, expensive. The plan was also a forecast of the distant future, for now, a century later, a subway tunnel still follows the precise easterly path planned by William and his associates and is known as the Steinway Tube. But the tunnel to Queens would not be completed for more than a decade after William's death.

"It's murder—murder in thirty-three degrees," perorated Patrick J. Gleason, Long Island City's mayor. Gleason, a longtime enemy of William, was perhaps also hopeful that the tunnel explosion would deflect attention from another breaking news story: his removal from office by a judge. Gleason was a mayor in the great predatory tradition of Long Island City. "These people are liable not only financially but criminally. . . . They've blown up the town, simply blown it up through criminal carelessness. They've killed five citizens and wounded heaven knows how many more. The heart of the city is in ruins. And it all came about because they wouldn't do what I told them."

For a two-block radius around the blast site only a few windows were unbroken. Horses were knocked down by the explosion; a passing trolley car was blown from its tracks. The scene was familiar to twentieth-century eyes, having much the appearance of a block bombed from the air. But flying machines that dropped bombs were still unknown, and thousands of persons flocked to the site to view the novel devastation.

"The public are clamoring for some arrests," reported the *New York Times*. "It is felt that someone ought to be held responsible for the wholesale killing and maiming, and the community is growing restive and bitter. . . . It is a peculiar feature of the accident that in most of the cases of injury the eyes of the victims have suffered most." The *Times* then went on to describe the medical removal of the eyes of some of the victims. *New York Tribune* buyers were spared these details: "The real horrors, in the sense of physical affliction and bodily distortion accompanying the explosion cannot be described. They are in their details too repulsive and too sickening to justify any attempt to present the picture to refined readers."

Hearing of the explosion shortly after it happened, William quickly notified those papers that identified him as president of the New York & Long Island Railroad that they were incorrect. He was the vice president. The *Herald* quoted William as saying that "the tunnel company had nothing whatever to do with the matter. The work, he said, was leased to the Inter-Island Construction Company, and he understood that the latter had sublet the contract. A New Jersey man is believed to hold the contract." William was not about to admit that he was personally paying the three-thousand-dollar-per-month construction costs while searching for investors who had not yet been found. The combination of devastation at the tunnel site and another financial panic meant that none would be. At a depth of ninety feet and horizontally thirty feet to the west, construction was suspended. With the pumps turned off, the hole gradually filled with water, symbolically submerging William's hopes for wealth and glory as the man who linked two islands.

The dream began, innocently enough, a decade before with an entry in William's diary for April 17, 1883: "The Long Island City Shore Railroad with Steinway branch is put at auction and I buy the same for $9,000 of auctioneers, fee of $25 and the payment to the receiver of $8,496.92. I pay to the referee $5000 on account." A grand total of $17,521.92 was expended and William became, in a friendly transaction with the support of the bankrupt prior owner, the proprietor of the railroad.

Smoke-belching locomotives rumbling through the night, whistles howling plaintively, were not a part of the transaction; the L.I.C.S.R.R. was a *horse* railway, a trolley of sorts, the tracks of which began at the Thirty-fourth Street ferry landing from Manhattan, just above the dumps on the shores of the Newtown Creek, then angled up what is now Jackson Avenue in Queens, proceeding northeast before turning north toward the shore of Bowery Bay and the Steinway settlement. Control of this route had an obvious strategic value for William and Steinway & Sons; he was now able to move both people and goods from the settlement to the ferry without dependence on others or fear of extortionate freight rates.

In public documents there was no clue that William owned the renamed Steinway & Hunter's Point Railroad. Henry Ziegler, Doretta's son now being trained by Theodore to assume piano technical development, was elected president; Henry Cassebeer, another relative, was elected vice president, and the always-loyal C. F. Tretbar became secretary and treasurer. From whom, precisely, William hoped to conceal his interest in the railroads is unclear. Certainly anyone with casual knowledge of Steinway & Sons would have recognized the names of Tretbar and Ziegler and suspected some relationship to William; he was, however, able to confuse at least one public transit historian three-quarters of a century later.

It was Henry Ziegler who then applied for and received a franchise from the Long Island City Board of Aldermen for a new railroad route, and another phantom company was formed, this time with Steinway employee Philip Burkhard as president. This one was called the Broadway & Bowery Bay Railroad Company. It was clearly William's strategy to command all points of entry to Long Island City and carry traffic from the docks to his settlement, and he lost no time in doing this. The newly formed Broadway & Bowery Bay construction crews were laying track at the spectacular rate of more than two hundred feet per day and reached Steinway Avenue in less than three weeks after the franchise was granted. This frenetic activity continued, and by 1884 all horse railroads in Long Island City led to Steinway.

There was already at Steinway a church built by the residents on land donated by the firm, a fire company equipped and housed by William, and a bathing beach with fifty dressing rooms abutting a 250-by-200-foot park. "All inhabitants of 'Steinway' are accorded the privilege of bathing, free of charge," wrote William. A school was built by Long Island City but was covertly funded by Steinway & Sons. The financing mechanism was Long Island City warrants in the amount of about seventeen thousand dollars. In what was likely a prearranged transaction, the warrants, a form of municipal I.O.U., were purchased by Steinway & Sons. The school was a very substantial two-story brick structure and, according to a land sales brochure written by William, had a capacity of one thousand students. This was an exercise in optimistic planning, for a grade school of such size was sufficient for a village population greater than six thousand persons. In 1880 the entire population of Long Island City's Fifth Ward was less than half that at 2,398 souls.

The city provided two teachers as political patronage, and a third teacher of German and music was employed by Steinway & Sons. The salaries of teachers, invariably unmarried women, barely exceeded that of domestic servants, so there was minimum financial sacrifice involved. Student/teacher ratios of 125:1 would also cause a modern educator to quake. William Steinway was a man who believed in education, and so the settlement was also blessed with a free *kindergarten*. On more than one occasion he was present for the kindergarten's graduation ceremonies; apparently it was among his most favored benefactions. Later a free circulating library was built and stocked by the family. That which carried the name Steinway, be it place or piano, must be the best.

"To all residents of this place is thus secured the enjoyment of healthful country life, pure air, beauty of scenery, unsurpassed views of the East River and Bowery Bay, boating, bathing, fishing, together with all desirable features of city life, such as fine schools, churches, purest quality of water in every house, perfect sewerage and drainage, and use of excellent gas at moderate price," wrote William on the back of a map of the village. "Neat

307

Two or Three story frame or brick houses, cottages and villas with 5–15 rooms, containing all modern improvements (inclusive of the lots) range from $1700 to $4000 each. . . . The ground is high and dry at all times . . . precluding the presence of malarious diseases." Undoubtedly William was mystified when few came to share the idyllic delights of his village by the bay, but he was not a man to readily accept defeat.

"The attention of manufacturers, who are not engaged in any obnoxious or offensive trades, as well as those of persons desirous of living in comfortable and cheerful houses in a thoroughly desirable neighborhood, in the immediate vicinity of, and with easy access to, all parts of the City of New York is especially directed to the most eligible properties of Messrs. Steinway & Sons," hawked William. Manufacturers did not come either, save those enticed by William's financial blandishments, and so there was little alternative but to move still more pianomaking from Manhattan to Steinway.

Just four years before the first street railway purchase, case manufacturing had been established at the settlement. By 1884 roughly half of the company's one thousand employees worked there, although most of those did not choose to live at the settlement. That Steinway & Sons had come to Astoria to stay was shown by both the size and construction of the buildings, which were of brick. The four-story casemaking plant contained almost 60,000 square feet of space—1.4 acres under its roof—and alongside it was a powerhouse with four steam engines generating 300 horsepower. Beside the powerhouse was another four-story building of 16,000 square feet, which contained drying rooms and kilns for lumber. Heated by steam coursing through 60,000 lineal feet of pipe, one-half million square feet of wood was dried at any one time, with a typical stay in the drying rooms of about three months. The Steinway settlement and its factories was one of the few developed areas in Queens and a remote one at that.

Although difficult to imagine today when the county is almost completely covered with asphalt and cement, there were in Queens in 1880 almost 3,000 farms covering 130,000 acres. Of the sixty New York State counties, three out of four produced farm products of less value than Queens. The status of metropolitan development was such that even Manhattan still had 1,930 acres of farmland, principally at the northern end. The Manhattan farms were worth, according to the census, about $442 per acre, but just across the East River the average Queens farm was valued at $169 per acre. The four hundred acres of land bought by William in East Astoria were worth, as farmland, less than seventy thousand dollars in 1880. Deducting the cost of the mansion and its land, William had paid roughly $418 per acre in 1870 and 1871.

A decade later he almost certainly realized that he had both paid too much and bought too extensively. Selling the Astoria property in bulk would have resulted in large losses and also would have been an admission of failure; this William could not tolerate, and so there was but one alternative: continue development and make Steinway as attractive and accessible as possible. The task was immense, and it gradually assumed the major role in William's life, absorbing both his time and his share of the profits of the piano business. Perhaps out of guilt, perhaps out of belief in the ultimate success of the venture, William poured most of his personal fortune into the Steinway settlement and borrowed still more; the railways were only the beginning.

William noted with great satisfaction that his railroads took in $120 one August Sunday in 1883, a record amount. It meant that twenty-four hundred nickel fares were collected that day. If those record fares were achieved each and every day for a year, William's railroad would have grossed about forty thousand dollars per year. Had William devoted his efforts to finding a way to sell an additional fifty to sixty pianos at retail, he might easily have made more money. But William seemed now to be less interested in the piano business than in the development of the community which bore the family name; as in many things in William's life, this may have been a matter of pride.

A remarkable opportunity was foregone in 1883 and 1884. When Albert Weber, William's archrival, died in 1879, he left the operation of the business to his twenty-year-old son Albert junior and two other trustees of his estate, both longtime employees. The Weber firm did well initially, buoyed by the recovery following the long depression of the 1870s. But by the summer of 1883 another recession was under way, and the Weber firm foundered on the shores of insufficient cash flow. Creditors ultimately asked that the firm be placed in the hands of a receiver. Though not technically bankrupt—its assets far exceeded its liabilities—the company did not have enough cash to meet its current obligations.

William therefore had the opportunity to obtain control of his most vexatious competitor, but there is not a wisp of evidence to suggest that he even considered it, notwithstanding that "combinations" and "monopolies" were already coming into vogue. Another advantage would have accrued to William, and it is certain that he was aware of it. William's former ally in the battle against Weber and Hale, the defalcating John C. Freund, had founded a new publication called *Music and Drama*. The backer of the latest effort, in the amount of forty-seven thousand dollars, was Albert J. Weber. Mr. Weber even provided Freund with his own printing plant to produce circulars and catalogs for the trade. This was another revenue path for what was, at least in part, blackmail coupled to journalism. The Freund proposition was very simple: advertise in *Music and Drama* and/or use the Eagle Printing job shop for brochures and become a subject of laudatory articles. Those who failed to do so were, at a minimum, ignored, and some were subject to what William called "scurrilous attacks." By buying the Weber piano firm William would have gained control of Freund's publication and either silenced or controlled it.

Freund's bitterness toward William for refusing financial aid when his earlier journal failed combined readily with the editorial needs of his new investor, and Freund began a series of assaults on Steinway & Sons in general and William in particular. John C. Freund was a master of propaganda and an astute analyst of the psychology of his target, William Steinway. Freund hurled verbal knives with the intent to wound and to prolong suffering.

One of Freund's earliest attacks was designed to cast doubt on the accomplishments of the family. "August Belmont lent Mr. William Steinway $100,000 during December 1859 and March 1860 at the time of the fire which destroyed Lighte & Bradbury's factory. . . . The money was borrowed and loaned in order to enable the Steinways to jump in and get Lighte & Bradbury's trade," wrote Freund. "As the money was invested in the business, August Belmont has on several occasions refused to take it back, claiming that it is a definite investment which entitles him to a share in the business. It is said that he is getting an average of fifteen percent on his money." To give his report a contemporary relevance—it was nearly a quarter-century since the investment was supposedly made—Freund claimed that the Belmont interest in Steinway & Sons was being supervised by Adolph Sommer, the Astoria bookkeeper. Sommer was just then the target of a union action; the Astoria workers had demanded that he be fired, and William refused. A strike ensued, and Freund claimed that "the firm is tenaciously upholding their bookkeeper" because "he owed his appointment to the influence of the Belmonts."

This was a multipronged attack, as brilliant as it was false. Freund slashed at the very core of the Steinway legend: the story of an immigrant family prospering in America by its own hard work and talent. He brought into question William's principles and his oft-stated view that the union was resisted to preserve the right to manage the business in a way the owners thought best. This assertion of independence was well understood by all to mean resistance to "dictation by socialists." Freund was asserting that William was not free, but following the dictates of big capital, for the Belmonts were not only a powerful merchant banking force in their own right; they were aligned with the Rothschilds in Europe. While Freund did not say so, there were certain well-known similarities between William and August Belmont. Both were German, both were active in Democratic politics, and both invested in public transportation. But in terms of wealth and power there was a vast difference, and William's financial and political resources were much smaller.

"Without comment on the *animus* which prompted the article, its glaring improbabilities, not to say impossibilities, and for the purpose of squelching this, the silliest of all *canards*, I, William Steinway, now the only surviving founder of the house of Steinway & Sons, New York, do hereby make the following categorical statement, to wit: That neither I nor any member of the Steinway family ever became acquainted with Mr. A. Belmont, that not a single dollar, or any amount of money, has ever been loaned by him in the business of Steinway & Sons, or any of its members, nor were there any negotiations to that end ever thought of. That no person outside the Steinway family has or ever has had, directly or indirectly, the slightest pecuniary interest in the business of Steinway & Sons. Should the said editor or his alleged 'informant' be able to prove to the contrary, I hereby agree to pay to him or them the entire amount of capital which can be shown to have been loaned to any of the Steinways by Mr. August Belmont, together with the alleged profits, which by this time amount to the snug little sum of $430,000."

William's response, sniffed Freund, "positively bristles with temper," and he thereupon began running ads offering a $250,000 reward for proof of the Steinway-Belmont connection. Despite the reward, in effect guaranteed by William, no proof ever came into the hands of John C. Freund, and the matter was quietly dropped. Although neither Freund nor anyone else would ever be allowed access, the partnership's "Inventory Book" shows clearly that the ballistic rise of the Steinways was financed primarily by cash flow supplemented by the occasional short-term bank loan.

The panegyrics to Albert Weber in *Music and Drama* were interrupted just a few weeks later with another Steinway scandal, this one having more substance than the Belmont fabrication. William called the incident "blackmail," but there is no indication that Freund offered silence for money; it was revenge that J. C. Freund wanted most.

The tale involved a "Mrs. H." of Montreal and the longtime Steinway agent for Canada, Nordheimer & Company. As reported to *Music and Drama* by a Montreal newspaperman, Mrs. H. selected a new Steinway in Nordheimer's warerooms and paid cash. When delivered to her home, the new Steinway owner discovered that the French polish finish was marred and that the piano had no serial number. The piano was returned to Nordheimer to have its finish repaired and when a piano was returned some months later, Mrs. H. thought it to be an "old and battle-scarred instrument, varnished to pass for new" and mysteriously now carrying a serial number.

At this point *Mr.* H. took matters in hand, proceeded to the Nordheimer wareroom, and somehow succeeded in getting the salesman to sign a contract promising to deliver to Mr. H. a brand-new New York Steinway within thirty days. The salesman was to travel to New York to select the piano. A few days short of thirty, Mr. H. was notified that his piano had arrived. In the showroom was a new Steinway waiting for him. Mr. H. recorded its serial number, and, for some unknown reason, asked for the port of entry into Canada. The salesman responded that the port of entry was Toronto where Nordheimer was headquartered, as it was for all Steinways coming into Canada. Since this was a most indirect route to Montreal from New York, Mr. H.'s curiosity was aroused and he queried Canadian customs, only to find out that his New York Steinway had come from Hamburg, Germany. "As to how far the Steinways are cognizant of this unscrupulous use of a German piano bearing their name," wrote correspondent Arthur J. Graham, "and imported into this country [Canada] to take the place of genuine New York instruments, you must judge for yourself." German pianos, though widely exported in Europe, were looked on as cheap and inferior in North America. Vaunted German craftsmanship was a construct of the distant future. Here was a serious charge. Were the Steinways the victims of yet another round of bogus pianos? Were the Steinways themselves building imitations of their New York pianos with inferior materials and cheap foreign labor, foisting them on unsuspecting consumers? What was the truth? Readers of *Music and Drama* would have to wait until next week to find out.

William was forced to respond, and he did with regard to the origins of the Hamburg Steinway, but was wisely silent on Nordheimer's piano substitutions: "As one of the results of the strike in the piano trade in February and March 1880, Messrs. Steinway, in the summer of 1880, established a branch factory in Hamburg, Germany." This was news to North American piano aficionados and was probably known to only a few in the trade. While William's advertising materials to this time boomed the scale and excellence of Steinway Hall, the Fourth Avenue factory, and the new facilities at Astoria, they were silent on the Hamburg plant. There was more than one reason for this. Steinway & Sons had long promoted itself as an *American* enterprise that used American materials with American workers to build pianos that exceeded the performance of European instruments. A simpleminded, but eminently just, question then became, Why is Steinway in Europe if the best is in America? Perhaps hoping to avoid answering this question, William made scant mention of the European "branch" factory. Entirely unknown to enemies such as Freund was still another peculiar aspect of the *Steinway Pianofabrik*; it was not owned by Steinway & Sons, but was a separate company held equally by Theodore and William.

Dealing solely with the public aspect of the situation, as exposed in *Music and Drama*, William wrote that there were two reasons for the establishment of the *fabrik*: "To be perfectly independent as concerns the export trade, at least, of the oft-recurring long strikes in the United States, and for the purposes of properly preparing the Steinway Piano for the extreme humidity of the European climates. . . . All the Grand and Upright pianos produced in the Steinway factory at Hamburg are first made and brought to a certain state in the New York and Astoria factories . . . , shipped to the Hamburg factory and there finished, mostly under the personal supervision of Mr. C. F. Theodore Steinway of New York, the inventor of all the late important features which distinguish the Steinway Piano. The instruments produced in the American and Hamburg factories are thus precisely alike, of the same scale and make, and fully warranted." The Hamburg operation was a great success, "shipping weekly no less than six" pianos, averred William. "A few of them have been imported into Canada by A. & S. Nordheimer of Toronto, and have given the same perfect satisfaction that all Steinway pianos give."

William's response raised more questions than it answered. If the Hamburg factory was successful, why was it shipping pianos started in New York to Hamburg and then back to North America? What was the point of building pianos at high labor cost in the United States and shipping them to a low-labor-cost European country to be finished and sold, plus paying extra duty and shipping costs? Readers of *Music and Drama* were soon engaged in their own microeconomic analyses, submitting letters with estimates of the incremental duties and freight fees the Steinways were paying and counting the many weeks lost in transit. One correspondent pointed out, trenchantly, that if the purpose of the Hamburg plant was to shield the company from strikes, he did not understand how sending United States–built pianos there could accomplish the objective. Midway through the "sensation," Freund symbolically nailed a bill of consumer rights to the door of Steinway Hall: "Messrs. Steinway have a perfect right to manufacture pianos in Hamburg or Hong Kong, but they are bound to let their customers know this fact. . . . Now we are told that instruments made in their factory in Hamburg are as good as those made in New York. . . . A customer has the right to know whether the Steinway piano he pays a high price for is made in New York or Hamburg."

In the course of events William made two other statements which were soon subjected to scrutiny and found wanting by the readers of *Music and Drama*. In the course of explaining why Hamburg pianos were not sold in the United States, William claimed that the high United States tariffs made this unprofitable. For most of the nineteenth century American trade policy was protectionist; goods of all types were subject to duties as high as 50 percent. The duty on pianos entering America at the time was 30 percent, and a correspondent identified only as "More Light" quickly showed that Canadian tariffs were higher still at roughly 40 percent. "Mr. Steinway," wrote M. L., "has touched upon one point that is worthy of some consideration by our customs authorities. . . . How does he manage to send them [Hamburg Steinways] into Canada under a higher tariff?"

A *Music and Drama* headline answered that question: "CAUGHT—The Steinways and the Nordheimers Caught in their Own Trap. They declare that the Hamburg Steinways and the New York Steinways cost the same and are sold at the same prices. BUT they invoice the Hamburg Steinways at about one-half the price of the New York Steinways clearing through the Customs House at Toronto. Competent counsel declares this to be an attempted fraud on Her Majesty's Customs." With obvious relish John Freund wrote, "I state but the truth when I say that the House of Steinway has received a blow from which it will not easily recover." William made no public defense, but noted in his diary that "Freund out in his weekly with a blackmail article on alleged Nordheimer-Steinway customs house fraud. Canada." The word *alleged* was written above the line. If Her Majesty's Customs Service ever investigated or took any action, the results were not widely reported. There was no question, however, that Steinway & Sons held its own employees to the highest ethical standards. During the same week that the customs story filled *Music and Drama*, William, after consulting with his nephews, asked an employee in the action shop to resign. The man admitted that he "thoughtlessly" had taken molding knives. Like a summer squall, the customs scandal disappeared as quickly as it came, leaving behind the distant rumblings of Steinway discontent.

"A state of musical terrorism has been prevalent, by which anyone who dared run contrary of *that* piano house, was singled out for merciless attacks, both in public and private," wrote Emil Liebling, a second-tier concert artist and music teacher in Chicago. All knew to whom *that* referred, and *Music and Drama* seemed willing, if not positively eager, to publish any snippet which might cause Steinway & Sons enmity. William, with some surprise, wrote that "J. C. Freund has no blackmail in his weekly today about us."

This was but an intermission; "BROKEN AT LAST. The Steinway-Tretbar-Thomas Clique at an End." The headline referred to the longstanding relationship between Steinway and conductor Theodore Thomas, a first-magnitude New York celebrity, who, in his forthcoming tour with *pianiste* Mme. Rive-King, had struck an arrangement with Decker Brothers for sponsorship and use of an instrument. "So there has been quite a parrot-monkey time at Steinway Hall lately. Billy feels badly and Tretbar is a very, very sick man," jibed *Music and Drama*. William was, in fact, making diary entries such as "beautiful day" and recording the antics of the infant William R., the first son of his second marriage: "Having much fun with baby Willie, who refuses to enter his baby carriage or go back into the house." Two weeks later, in one of the many entries that suggest that William was spending much more time with his children, William wrote that "Baby Willie now says on shaking hands How-do-do." Consultations with his nephews Henry W. T., Charles, and Fred Steinway and Henry Ziegler were more frequent. "The boys," as William called them, were assuming greater responsibility for the day-to-day operations. Charles was in Steinway Hall with William, while Fred and Henry Ziegler were stationed at the Fifty-second Street factory, and Henry W. T. split his duty between Astoria and Steinway Hall, where he lived in a company-owned apartment in an adjoining building. In subtle ways William appeared to be lifting his eyes from the daily operations toward more distant horizons.

The change was visible from outside the firm. In yet another attack, J. C. Freund wrote, "The policy of the house, when William Steinway directed its affairs, was liberal, enterprising and fair-minded. Of late it has become illiberal, mean, unjust, oppressive and monopolistic under the management of Charles F. Tretbar into whose hands the firm has now fallen." This was hyperbolic. Steinway & Sons had not "fallen" into Tretbar's hands, but it was true that William was spending less time on Steinway and more time on other business activities. Though William clearly had the opportunity to seize financial control of the parlously weak Weber operation and silence Freund in the process, he made no attempt to do so. Within a few months both Albert Weber, Jr., and the Weber piano firm were in bankruptcy proceedings.

There were worlds beyond pianos to command. William snapped up the Standard Gaslight Company, which illuminated his settlement, for a price of $1,652, about a week's worth of Steinway & Sons' 1883 dividend. Having achieved control of the local distribution, William was not long in acquiring Long Island City's East River Gas Company for an astonishing $200 in cash and a note for $46,437. The purchase, William noted, was for fifty cents on the dollar. Bargains were available because yet another "money panic" percolated through the nation in the spring and summer of 1884.

The *New York Times* described the scene at the stock exchange during the height of the panic on May 15, 1884: "The hundreds of men and women who had crowded into the small galleries at either end of the board-room looked with wonder down upon the tumultuous spectacle. . . . The uproar was deafening. It was a terrible medley of noises without intelligible words. The hands on the huge electric clock indicated the hour of 11, and the wildest panic that Wall Street had known for fifteen years was under full headway, both inside and outside the Exchange building." That same day William wrote, "Feel perfectly well. Take $50,000 worth of L. Isl. C. bonds of Mayor George Petri and Fred W. Bleckwenn Treas. of Lg. Isl. C. who called at two o'clock. Introduce them at Bank of Metropolis [William was a minor stockholder] where Treas. opens an account." As banks failed and brokerages collapsed and even the piano business was in a state of suspended animation, William was still investing further in Long Island City. His equanimity verged on arrogance; he seemed to believe that Steinway & Sons was a money machine that not only would never stop, but would never miss a beat. Based on the results of 1883, this was an understandable position; Steinway & Sons achieved record earnings while 10,187 firms failed. The national financial carnage continued during 1884, accompanied by almost 11,000 failures.

In less than two years William Steinway amalgamated Long Island City's street railways in small-scale emulation of the classical nineteeth-century empire builders. New cars were added, a large terminal was built, a new stable was constructed for new horses, tracks were upgraded to steel, and roadways were graded and paved. By early 1885 William consolidated his holdings under a new corporate umbrella, the Steinway & Hunter's Point Railway Company, which applied for and received permission from New York's Railroad Commission to increase its capital to $250,000.

Simultaneously, William was systematically developing his illuminating gas holdings. Construction began on an "immense pit" for a gas storage tank. The small generating plant of the Standard Gas Works was decommissioned, and the company was merged into William's East River Gas Company. On paper, it was an immensely profitable transaction: William received $100,000 worth of stock when he turned over the company he had bought at auction for $1,652, plus a later purchase of its real estate for $8,800. The $10,452 invested in Standard magically multiplied tenfold in less than two years when William sold it to his other gas company. Solely an accounting profit, and an illusory one at that, it nonetheless aroused the enmity of the former owners, who sued William for breach of contract. When the trial was finally held in 1889, it was shown that the former owners of the gas company had, rather ineptly, forged company records in an attempt to "blackmail" William. "The two wretches . . . slink quite crushed out of the courtroom," wrote William on the day the judge dismissed the suit.

Pianomaking was slowly receding in William's life as daily operations fell into the hands of the nephews in New York and a trusted manager, A. J. Menzl, in Astoria. Strategy, however, was still in William's grip: "Several rabid socialists are being bounced from our factory" at Astoria, recorded William in the spring of 1885. "Executives of the Pianomaker's Union call together a meeting of our workmen at Stahl's, Astoria, showing that by the discharge . . . we have hit the union squarely between the eyes." A few days later: "Menzl tells me of the complete fizzle of the Socialist meeting at Stahl's . . . Ordered Menzl to allow beer into the factory between 12–1 P.M. and from 2–4 P.M." This, of course, was a reward for thirsty workers holding more acceptable social philosophies.

William considered himself—and was considered by others—to have "liberal" views on the condition and welfare of workingmen. Perhaps it was this "progressive" turn of mind that inspired the next great development at Astoria, a vast "pleasure ground" a few blocks east of the village. It was located near Sanford's Point on Flushing Bay; the physical geography of the place has since been entirely obliterated by the landfill on which LaGuardia Airport stands, but if contemporary accounts are to be believed, there were once "wooded shores and natural bluffs. . . . Along the shore there was a beautiful road for pleasure driving, but it was little used at that time owing to the great number of impudent roughs who indulged in nude bathing in the waters of the bay, to the disgust and annoyance of respectable residents." To reach the "pleasure grounds," a new horse railroad was needed, and William formed another shadow corporation, this one called the Rikers Avenue & Sanford's Point Railway, to transport visitors to the resort.

For the building of Bowery Bay Beach William teamed with another successful German who owned land in the area, brewer George Ehret. The strategic interests were clear. William could increase railway traffic and expose the visitors to the delights of life in Steinway Village while George Ehret could sell thirsty daytrippers beer. Both would gain revenue from the sale of concessions for the boat rides and carousels, shooting galleries and restaurants that ultimately grew on the site. So it was that the Bowery Bay Improvement Company came to be in May 1886 with William and George Ehret as the principal stockholders. This was not a unique concept; Coney Island was already successful, but there was one difference. Bowery Bay Beach, William repeatedly emphasized, was to cater to *respectable* people.

No time was wasted. Less than a month after the incorporation William's son George reported "heavy riding and quite a crowd of people at Bowery Bay." The bathhouse was not yet complete, and the grounds—mostly pasture and woods—were still unmanicured. Street railway revenue skyrocketed to fifteen hundred dollars per week with about half that on the Sabbath. At the rate of one nickel per ride, at least seven thousand people were visiting the beach on each summer Sunday. When Bowery Bay opened officially on June 19, 1886, William recorded that "immense crowds of respectable people are at Bowery Bay Beach and my railroad is unable to carry half the people. At 5 P.M. all the beer is gone, and people overflow Steinway Village and drink all the beer there." The man who had offered Rubinstein to America's cultural elite was now bringing Sunday revelry, lubricated with *lagerbier*, to the working people of Manhattan and Brooklyn. Under the impulse of Bowery Bay Beach's own private police force, the "impudent roughs" presumably found other places to bathe along the verdant shores of Queens.

But, as with most things seen as progress, there were negative developments as well. William's mansion was located between the village and the beach, and the regal but pastoral solitude of the place was now violated by the crowds. When some exuberant young men tried to frolic on his mansion's private beach on Independence Day, William became personally involved: "I drive them off with my revolver."

When the bathing pavilion was completed, the crowds grew even larger, and by the end of August William's railway was grossing over three thousand dollars per week, suggesting that the patronage on Sundays exceeded fifteen thousand persons. With such gatherings tragedies were inevitable, and William wrote, "Hottest day of the season, drowning of a young Jew,

Adolphus Ochs, at B.B. Bathing Pavilion." Less than two weeks later the legs of two men were crushed in separate accidents on the crowded horse-car lines. Not all holidays at the beach ended with smiles.

There were management problems as well. After the pavilion manager assaulted the head waiter, he was fired and replaced by another man who promptly absconded with thirty-two hundred dollars of the Bowery Bay Improvement Company's funds. Later that summer Steinway & Sons held its annual employee picnic at Bowery Bay Beach. Assembling over one thousand strong at the factory in Astoria and led by a brass band, they marched past the mansion. William watched his workers on parade as they stepped in synchronism with the band, marching down the dusty shore road to a picnic glen at Bowery Bay. "The picnic of our men," wrote William with obvious pride, "turns out to be a glorious affair, myself and Ehret participating, separate picnic place at Bowery Bay Beach being completely filled with men, their friends and families, the whole thing coming to an end at midnight, not marred by a single occurrence." When, at the end of August, a great fireworks display was mounted at the beach, William observed that "all of Long Island City and Steinway Village" were there. With Bowery Bay Beach William Steinway had created a social phenomenon, and there was nothing which he liked better.

The first successful season at the beach was an open invitation to further development, which began almost immediately. More land was bought, and in time a Grand Pier extending into the waters of the bay was built. At 500 feet long and 110 feet wide, with a cost of fifty thousand dollars, the word *Grand* was no misnomer. That the pier was substantial enough to dock ferryboats was certainly a part of the plan, for William bought a half-interest in the New York & College Point Ferry Company. From the ferry landing at Ninety-second Street in Manhattan to the pier at Bowery Bay was a ride of less than thirty minutes, no matter what the tides. This roughly halved the time required by the railway route. While it might seem that William the Rail Baron was competing with William the Sea King, both the railroad and the ferries continued to grow. Traffic on the street railway almost doubled between 1886 and 1891, and William saw fit to increase his fleet of ferries.

A few days after buying half the company in 1890, William set down this observation: "Have much trouble with the College Point Ferry question, everything seems run down to the lowest point." Within a few months there was a new ferry house and two new boats, their huge and shining black hulls emblazoned with the name Steinway, which now meant not only a piano but a place. Before a year passed, William owned all of the ferry company, and soon there were two more ferries, bringing the total to four boats. Along the way William also found time to invest in no less than three Long Island banks, the Queens, the Flushing, and the State Trust Company. Small though they were, they were yet another sign of the depth of his belief in the future of the village, for William Steinway was the possessor of a piercing prescience, an uncanny ability to see over the horizon of time. While he could conjure the shape of things to come and places yet to be with preternatural precision, he frequently failed to see the quagmire at his feet

"I have serious apprehensions as to monetary outlook and curse the Daimler Motor Company for draining me of money and resolve to stop it." William's declaration of March 18, 1896, was likely the supreme illustration of his prevision and its problems. William was now—and had been for eight years—a manufacturer of *gasolene* engines for boats, railcars, and that latest sensation—the horseless carriage. The French term *automobile* would not obtain wide usage for a decade. The current venture was not William's first contact with engine building. In 1865 he had invested one hundred dollars and received ten shares in The Recuperative Caloric Engine Company of New York, yet another in the legion of failed attempts to wrest from the iron grip of the laws of thermodynamics a successful "heat engine."

At least three of the brothers Steinway had a fascination with mechanism and technology. Theodore focussed on the engineering of pianos, creating his archetypical instruments by a rare combination of creativity, will, and indefatigable persistence. Albert, in contrast, was more of a "practical mechanic." The brute force, and when mishandled, fatal powers of steam held few mysteries for Albert, and he may have been more comfortable with machines than men; he was certainly more interested in machinery than music. Under his guidance, with William's assent and to Theodore's terror, Steinway & Sons was quick to adopt the latest in woodworking machinery and power plants. These, of course, were the best that money could buy.

All this may have had more to do with attitude than efficiency. In a report filed with the Census Bureau and published in 1886, Steinway & Sons commented that "there has been no perceptible change in the efficiency of labor." They also reported—enigmatically—that "numerous labor-saving machines have been introduced during the past 25 years, among them planing, boring, moistening, frazing and scraping machines." During this time Steinway employment was either stable or increasing while output remained relatively constant. Steinway manufacturing operations were working refutation of the Marxist notion that capitalists bought machines to replace labor and increase profits.

While the economic benefits of new technology were at best equivocal, William was quick to adopt the telegraph, the telephone, and the typewriter to business operations; after three decades in manufacturing, he certainly knew the limitations of steam, and after five years of involvement with horse railways, if not before, he clearly comprehended the weaknesses of animate motive power. In the 1870s, an equine epidemic halted the delivery of pianos for several weeks. The life of a horse in New York commercial service was but five years; horses needed to be fed and housed whether or not they worked. And so William Steinway chose to become a pioneer purveyor of the internal combustion engine. He had likely seen the engines of Otto & Langen on display in the German section of the Centennial Exhibition, and it is possible that his brothers—both Theodore and Henry—described the engines shown at the London and Paris fairs, the most notable of which was the Lenoir, of which hundreds were sold in Europe. These early engines intended to replace steam power but were painfully noisy, absurdly inefficient, and preposterously unreliable devices. They were fueled, not by petroleum, but by illuminating gas. This, plus their immense weight, made them essentially useless for fulfilling the ancient dream of a self-propelled vehicle.

There had been innumerable attempts to create usable self-powered carriages in both America and Europe, none of which met with material success. When in 1886 William began correspondence with Gottlieb Daimler of Canstatt, Germany, there were in America but a few small builders of internal combustion engines. One was a licensee of the German Otto & Langen firm; another was an American of German extraction, Claude Sintz, whose brilliant work in Ohio and then Michigan led—through a long string of interrupted Sunday afternoon slumbers—to the chainsaws, lawnmowers, and outboard motors of today.

Gottlieb Daimler, with the assistance of Wilhelm Maybach, had developed precisely the type of engine needed. It was relatively small, light for its power output, and ran on a liquid petroleum fuel. The fuel was very important. Untethered from gas mains, the Daimler engine could be put to use anywhere; it was a miracle of portable power. It burned benzine, the lightest of three types of refined petroleum products then available. The heaviest were used as lubricants, the intermediate weights as kerosene, and the lightest distillates—known as benzine—were waste products; too volatile and too dangerous to use, benzine was often dumped in creeks by refiners. Daimler and Maybach had found ways to combine benzine with air in chemically appropriate ratios and had also worked out a way to ignite the air/fuel blend with a glowing platinum tube. These were their first two strokes of genius. The third involved the speed at which their engine operated: turning nine hundred times per minute, it rotated two to three times faster than conventional engines. This gave it high power for its weight, which was also perhaps half that of competing units.

The Daimler engine was elegant and useful technology, a fact that William seemed to fully appreciate. It was first used in a land vehicle—a wooden-frame motorcycle with two outboard "training wheels"—in 1885, and Daimler had successfully installed the engine in a boat, a small trolley car, and a carriage. A Daimler engine had also been appended to a man-carrying balloon, a likely first in aerial navigation, but William's diary indicates that he took rides in only the boat and the railcar. Five days later, on August 22, 1888, William had "a long talk" with Daimler, the result of which was that William secured the North American rights to all Daimler's existing and future patents. They were, in a very real sense, the patents to an America of the future.

How William came to know Gottlieb Daimler is uncertain: there are two tales. One is that he was introduced to Daimler by his sister Doretta, who was then living in Germany. Another is that William met Wilhelm Maybach during the 1876 Philadelphia Exhibition when Maybach came to New York to visit a brother supposedly employed by Steinway & Sons. Neither version is supported by documentary evidence, but the record is clear on what happened next, for on February 2, 1889, William recorded that the first directors' meeting of the Daimler Motor Company was held. Engines, however, were not actually completed for more than a year. It was April 30, 1890, when William reported that "our three new motors are put up and work splendidly." The actual fabrication of the engines was farmed out to a Hartford, Connecticut, machine shop, and William sited his nascent enterprise in Astoria in a building formerly housing the defunct Astoria Ink Company. The rent paid to Steinway & Sons, with the permission of the board of trustees, was thirty dollars per month.

Trouble was not long in arising. Gottlieb Daimler sold his company to investors for 600,000 marks, somewhat less than $150,000. He regretted the decision after finding he was no longer in control, a fact which apparently came as a shock. A volatile personality, Daimler finally decided to stay with the company, a fact which must have been a relief to William, who certainly realized that without Daimler's technical knowledge his licenses were useless. William was in Germany when the sale took place, but by early fall all was well, and William took his first ride in a Daimler "motor carriage" in September 1890.

Thanksgiving day that year found William back in New York editing the new catalog of the Daimler Motor Company. William believed engines could be sold with the same techniques that worked so well for pianos. "We have started Works for the manufacture of these motors in 'Steinway,' Long Island City, opposite New York City, fitted up with the latest improved machinery. Every part of the motors being of our own manufacture, and only the highest skilled labor being employed and the very best and choicest materials used, we can guarantee the excellence of our motors to the public," declaimed the first catalog. With the word "piano" substituted for "motor," similar words sold tens of thousands of Steinway & Sons instruments. In time an engine showroom was set up next door to Steinway Hall, but sales were very slow at first.

William recognized that the Daimler engine was a general-purpose power source and that it was necessary to explain *how* it could be used. As a result, the one-cylinder, one horsepower Daimler was "especially adapted for all small industries" and could power "small dynamos, cream separating machines, sewing machines, pumps, ventilating fans, blowers, also Watchmakers' and Shoemakers' and all light wood working machinery." A two-cylinder, two-horsepower unit was useful for "Printing Presses, Elevators, Grinding Mills, Feed Cutters and many other uses too numerous to mention."

William's first Daimler catalog also included a map for parties wanting a demonstration of the boats he was now making at Steinway Village. The shop was located only "250 feet South of Steinway and Hunters Point Railroad Depot." The trip was convenient and inexpensive: from the Queens side of the Thirty-fourth Street Ferry slip the time was only thirty minutes and the "Fare 5 cents over entire Route." Of course people did not buy many boats at Christmas time, and it was not until February, the time of year when small boats were commissioned in anticipation of summer use, that William recorded in his diary for 1891 that "at last a demand seems to arise for Daimler motors."

What would be today called the "strategic fit" of Daimler into William's other enterprises was clear: the engines could be used on railways of the type he owned. When stationary, they could be powered by illuminating gas, and William owned a gas company. Though far too small to operate the machinery of Steinway & Sons—three hundred *steam* horsepower was needed in Astoria—the woodworking skills of pianomaking and the immense lumber inventory could easily be applied to boat building. William may very well have determined that select pieces of the tons of wood scrap remaining from each week's pianomaking could be used in boats as low-cost but high-quality material.

Boats, tramways, and shoemaking machinery aside, the later pages of the catalog showed a "Motor Quadricycle," a light, elegantly designed vehicle with four bicycle wheels that could carry two persons at twelve miles per hour. At the time bicycles were immensely popular since they were the first machines to provide Americans personal mobility with freedom. Neither animals nor schedules slowed or stymied the bicycle rider; this intoxicating feeling created an immense popularity, but, so far as is known, none of the elegant Daimler quadricycles were sold in the United States. William had properly placed the quadricycle and a motor carriage at the back of his catalog. There was no market for them in America, though some dozens, if not hundreds, were in use in Europe.

The reason was simple: outside of cities, roads turned to muddy rutted trails that meandered unmarked from place to place. Pavement, maps, and road signs were inventions of the future. Traversal of these trails, particularly in spring, would challenge, if not defeat, even modern four-wheel-drive vehicles. Europeans, in contrast, enjoyed an extensive network of well-maintained roads, the origin of which was the military needs of both Roman generals and Napoleon. There the automobile was beginning to enjoy a certain cachet among the wealthy, the same persons who might buy a Steinway piano. William knew all this and wisely placed the horseless carriages well back in the catalog. Nonetheless, William Steinway was likely the first in America to commercially offer automobiles for sale. He did so at least three years before the celebrated and controversial efforts of the Duryea brothers in Springfield, Massachusetts, and those of Elwood Haynes with the Appersons in Kokomo, Indiana. It would be eight years before a Detroit mechanic named Ford started his first short-lived car company.

With the slightly rising demand of 1892, William did what he did best: he expanded Daimler, increasing its capital to $100,000 and erecting new buildings. In characteristic hands-on fashion he was there to supervise the adjustment of heating, plumbing, and lighting when the structure was completed. Demand for engines was a fugitive and fragile thing, but William persisted, and by 1893 he was offering a line of Daimler-powered boats ranging in size from sixteen to fifty feet. The advertising material was complete with the latest illustrative sensation, the photograph. The least expensive boat, planked in cedar and framed in oak, was $650 and sixteen feet in length. The most expensive was $7,000, a fifty-foot-long "cabin cruising launch" with two twelve-horsepower, four-cylinder engines. William himself had one of these; it was named *Gemini*.

By late 1893 a Daimler motor carriage was chuffing up and down the streets of Steinway Village, making it one of the pioneer gasoline vehicles to run on American roads, but William was still concentrating wisely on boats. He must, however, have been mystified by the relative lack of success. His prices were competitive and his technology was superior to that of other motorboat builders but sales were less than outstanding. A large display at the Columbian Exposition in Chicago did little to sell boats, even when the newspapers carried a dramatic story of the rescue on Lake Michigan of a half-dozen persons whose sailboat had foundered. The summer of 1895 brought a Daimler victory at a French automobile race from Paris to Bordeaux. That, plus a spate of articles in *Harper's Weekly* and daily newspapers, triggered renewed interest. "Daimler Motor Company overrun with applicants for horseless carriages," wrote William, who immediately ordered a "sample to exhibit."

Ever optimistic, William expanded facilities still further and built what would today be called a marina in front of the piano factory. The bay was dredged and pilings for piers and breakwaters driven. For William, new construction was always progress, but the company was still operating at a loss. The living embodiment of the term "patient capital," William increased his investment. Taking a page from the past, he exhibited the boats at the Fair of the American Institute, just as Steinway & Sons had done forty years before. Daimler did not, however, win a medal. Articles about and advertisements for Daimler appeared in new magazines such as *Horseless Age*. A thick book of glowing paeans to the Daimler engine by satisfied owners was published, paralleling piano practice. Instead of famous musicians, it contained the endorsements of yacht club commodores, doctors, and military men. The prizes garnered and races won by Daimler-powered horseless carriages were prominently displayed.

But all this amounted to little, save the depletion of William's fortune. Ultimately William's "oil engine" would be shown to be superior to steam or electricity as a means of propulsion on land, at sea, and in the air. Steam, colossally profligate in its use of energy, always heavy for the power developed, would hiss its way to oblivion despite the brilliant efforts of the Stanley brothers and other apostles. Electricity was soon seen to be cursed, not only with weight, but with limited range, low speed, and high cost. Even the digital wizardry of the late twentieth century cannot resuscitate the electron as a mobile prime mover, despite ardent advocacy by the environmentally concerned.

The Daimler company would go on, not in America, but in Germany, to become Daimler-Benz, maker of the Mercedes-Benz and one of the world's greatest industrial corporations. William Steinway would not live to see this, nor a nation where the freedom to move at mile-per-minute speeds was considered a right by the citizen-owners of 125 million "horseless carriages." William died at the dawn of the horseless era. Had he lived to the age of his pianomaking father, the name Steinway might very well have achieved fame in a different sphere and parity with that of Henry Ford, Ransom Eli Olds, David Dunbar Buick, or Soichiro Honda. Steinways might be cruising the highways of the nation. But this was not to be.

Chapter 23

YOU ACT MOST UNWISELY

"**H**arbuckel now accuses you and I of acting dishonestly," wrote William to brother Theodore in August 1887, "by forcing S&S New York to supply goods to our private company in Hamburg far below cost price. Then we produced goods there. . . . We saddled London with our product at high prices and falsely called it S&S New York with the result that Steinway & Sons lost money every year, whereas you and I cashed the enormous profit." The charge of transnational accounting manipulation to loot Steinway & Sons was not made by a competitor, nor was it the allegation of William's personal nemeses such as publisher John Freund or Long Island City mayor Paddy Gleason. The source was within the family: "Harbuckel" was Heinrich Wilhelm Theodore Steinway, the eldest son of Charles, now with the house for fifteen contentious years.

While Henry W. T. Steinway was by far the most outspoken critic of William's management of the firm, he was not alone in his views. "I must confess that in regard to Hamburg I always felt most uncomfortable. . . . But to be accused of dishonesty by the brat towards whom I acted like a father made me dumbfounded, all the more so because the other two nephews looked at it nearly the same way," continued William. The "other" nephews were Charles and Frederick Steinway, Charles's other two sons. This was a conflict between the generations over the management and future of the firm. If shares were voted, there was no question as to who would prevail. William and Theodore controlled two-thirds of the stock. Yet control of the firm was, at best, an incomplete answer, for there was nothing to prevent the younger Steinways, individually or as a group, from starting their own pianomaking firm.

Such meiotic divisions were common in the industry. In Germany the Schiedmeyer family had bifurcated as two bitter branches in 1853. Julius Schiedmeyer, head of one branch and perennial exhibition judge, was a friend of the Steinways. In America, the Nunns brothers had parted ways to the benefit of none, and William himself had worked for one of the brothers in his youth. The Nunns family fight resulted in bankruptcy for one brother and obscurity for all three. In the future the descendants of both Jonas Chickering and Napoleon J. Haines would form competing companies amidst scandal and recrimination. In the piano business at least, the spirit of family was a weak force and no match for the divisive powers of injustice, real or imagined, intended or inadvertent, or, for that matter, ego and greed. The nephews possessed, as much as did William and Theodore, the prime ingredient for success: a famous name.

All this had begun, innocently enough, a decade before when William accepted the proposition of an Englishman named W. H. Maxwell to form a partnership to sell Steinways in London, which was then a plausible contender for the cultural capital of Europe. Maxwell's proposal was simple: if William provided pianos and capital, he would manage the operation for one-half the profits. After a series of failed efforts to sell Steinway pianos through agents, William likely felt that provision of both capital and product would allow closer control of the venture. Known in Europe for the successes at the international exhibitions and association with virtuosi such as Rubinstein and Essipoff, endorsed by Liszt, Berlioz, and shortly Wagner, it was certainly possible that Steinway & Sons might be able to market instruments in London.

Musical development still flowed from east to west; it was one thing to be heralded in the musical backwaters of America as the maker of a superb instrument and quite another to be acknowledged at the wellhead. To William and Theodore the allure of European success was likely druglike in its appeal. William himself had written that two-thirds of the pianos at the Vienna Exhibition of 1873 were copies of the Steinway instruments. A German government agency had actually purchased Steinway pianos and encouraged national makers to copy the instrument. This they did, and one of the prime export markets for German pianos was London.

"It is therefore a sin and a disgrace that we are not in a position to exploit our great reputation ourselves," wrote Theo to William in 1877. "We make less money than the people who use the system for which we spend money like hay advertising. Isn't this absurd?"

Maxwell, provisioned with a few dozen Steinway instruments and five thousand English pounds of Steinway & Sons capital—slightly less than twenty-five thousand dollars—promptly set up a wareroom and a small performance space on Seymour Street in London. It was called, of course, Steinway Hall, and notwithstanding the fact that Mr. Maxwell was rather slow to report financially, William evaluated the physical facilities of Steinway & Sons, London, as entirely satisfactory when he first visited the branch in 1880. From a man so fastidious that he had rocks whitewashed in Steinway Village, this was not a casual compliment.

By the close of 1880 the London investment had grown to about seventy-nine thousand dollars. This was a tiny sum and represented less than four percent of the total assets of the firm. It was in March of that year that William and Theodore decided to begin making pianos in Hamburg, Germany, a duty-free port. No clues remain as to the thinking behind this decision, but it is clear that it was made in the heat of combat. The lengthy and bitter strike of the keymakers in Astoria had just ended with a 10-percent increase in wages, the second such in six months. Simultaneously the company purchased the Leominster, Massachusetts, piano case factory that soon burned to the ground, and there were, as usual, plans for further expansion at Astoria.

William was making statements to the newspapers that socialist agitation might well force pianomakers to leave New York City. While Steinway & Sons, the corporation, capitalized London, purchased Leominster, and expanded Astoria, Steinway's Pianofabrik, Hamburg, was a private venture of Theodore and William, who equally shared the $140,000 investment. Probably for reasons of German law, Theo was designated the "Sole Proprietor." As set up, Hamburg purchased rough but complete instruments from New York, which were sanded, varnished, voiced, regulated, and polished, and then sold them back to the corporation for sale in London and to agents on the Continent. William later claimed publicly that Theodore and he undertook the German manufacturing venture with their own funds because it was too risky for the corporation. He never explained why it was riskier to manufacture in Europe than it was to sell there, an activity to which he was more than willing to commit the stockholders' funds.

In all likelihood, a major goal of setting up a European manufactory was the mollification of Theodore. Often in contention with William on pricing, promotion, and manufacturing methods, and a man who disliked, if he did not despise, things American, Theodore sometimes made threats, veiled and overt, that he might separate from the American partnership. Theodore held the patents that were the basis of Steinway technological success and licensed them to the firm. Absent Theodore's assent, Steinway & Sons might exist but could not build the famed Steinway instrument. Without Theodore, even if it were somehow able to build a satisfactory piano, the firm would rapidly lose its technological advantage, and the continuous flow of piano "improvements" from the United States Patent Office bore testimony to the fact that pianomaking was still a technological business.

As a European piano manufacturer fifteen years before, Theodore had experienced humiliation, if not outright failure. His temporal peers, men like Carl Bechstein and Julius Bluthner, had gone on to build eminent German firms while Theodore's research and development fed the success of an American enterprise. As a practical matter Theodore was, in all probability, wealthier than either Bechstein or Bluthner. Via William's unceasing promotion, Theodore's innovations had been accepted in the vast American market, and the result was the world's largest piano company. But Theodore was not a man who calibrated success in dollars, pounds, or marks. In his native land his prestige was likely less than that of his peers. Yes, his designs were the benchmarks in a nation of Indians, cowboys, mechanics, steam locomotives, and clipper ships, but in the nation of Bach and Beethoven and Wagner and Liszt and Heine and Schopenhauer and Kant this meant little. And so it came to be that Steinways must be built in *das Vaterland*. This was a point of honor, and to men named Steinway, there was no more important point.

In reality, Theodore and William had embarked on a most radical venture. Multinational business operations were almost unknown, and those that existed were generally traders, moving agricultural commodities, gold, and guns to places of greatest need. While a few American firms, such as Singer, the sewing machine makers, did manufacture outside the United States, the concept of partially assembling a product in one nation, shipping it across an ocean to a second for completion, and then to a third (or fourth or fifth) for sale was essentially unknown. Once again, as in his involvement with tunnels and internal combustion engines, William was anticipating the twentieth century. And again the clarity of vision far exceeded the execution.

Hamburg manufacturing operations were placed in the hands of Arthur von Holwede, a piano tuner who had come to America from Braunschweig with Theodore in 1865. As Steinway & Sons' chief tuner, von Holwede travelled with *pianiste* Annette Essipoff on her Steinway tour of America. It was also von Holwede who maintained the pianos at the crucial and contentious Philadelphia Exposition in 1876. By what criterion von Holwede was selected to manage the German venture is unknown, but William wrote in his diary one Sunday, "To store at 9½ A.M. Briefly inform Holwede of Theo & I intending to have our own business in Hamburg & him as manager at which he is very much rejoiced." Von Holwede, like William, was a man who worked on Sundays. After fifteen years with Steinways in America, Arthur von Holwede returned to Germany to work for the house for another forty years and did not retire until 1920.

Little remains of the records of William and Theodore's "private company." William noted that it did not pay a dividend for seven years and then yielded a scant fifty-five hundred dollars. This was, after eighty-four months, about the same as the dividend yield from nine *days* of American operations. By 1888 the Steinway *fabrik* was building about 550 pianos a year and profiting at roughly fifty dollars per piano, about one-third the per-piano net in America, which, in a good year, often exceeded $150 per instrument and rarely fell below one hundred dollars.

The London sales operation was even less profitable, in part because it was discovered that partner Maxwell had "been in town for several weeks and had misapplied funds, so that a probable separation would take place," recorded Secretary Tretbar in the minutes of the corporation. The board of trustees "resolved to give the President full authority to act in the matter and settle the same as could be done to best avoid litigation." In 1884 Mr. Maxwell was demoted and later fired. Maxwell's depredations were minor; the London operation was small and the sums that might be diverted from it insignificant. At the same trustees' meeting that disposed of the Maxwell affair, it was reported that Steinway & Sons "showed a surplus of $314,379.98" for the year 1883. This was a record profit, and William and the family could well afford to be phlegmatic if not forgiving of Mr. Maxwell.

Embezzlers, forgers, and sundry impostors were perpetually nibbling at the family fortune. Within a few years, the manager of William's horse railways sold seven of the animals and pocketed the proceeds, while a foreman in the keyboard department collected the pay envelopes of fictitious employees. An insurance agent made off with thousands of dollars in bogus premiums. The scale or specific nature of Mr. Maxwell's alleged transgressions was not recorded, perhaps because they were deemed more or less routine.

In many instances the renown of the Steinways made them unwilling accomplices in chicanery. From a friend who happened to see the item in a Saint Louis newspaper, William learned that a woman claiming to be a relative had charged a Missouri man with rape. William promptly informed authorities; and the woman, not the man, was jailed. In another instance a man appeared at Steinway Hall with an apparent interest in buying a piano. His real purpose was to purloin Steinway letterhead so that he could write fake letters of introduction to Steinway dealers, who would then cash forged checks through their local banks. As another example, a New York merchant actually named Steinway began claiming a relationship to the family in his business transactions. A call by nephew Charles stopped the pretense of kinship. Just a few steps from the hall, and in a remarkable display of boldness, the Steinway Restaurant was opened. William did not wait until lunchtime to pay the daring entrepreneurs a visit.

In time William learned to turn the actions of the name expropriators to his advantage. When a confidence man used the Steinway name to bilk hotels and merchants, William personally asked the papers to publish a warning. The rogue was soon captured, which generated still more publicity. William was portrayed as a man of great rectitude and public spiritedness, while subtly underlining the fame and the magic of the name. That

William was a man of great stature, one worthy of impersonation, was the implied message. A mountebank might claim to be a Belmont or a Vanderbilt or a Steinway but not a Chickering or a Weber. William's celebrity transcended pianomaking.

The nips of minor predators did no harm; real damage could only be inflicted by the family itself. By the middle of 1887 the conflict between generations, or more precisely between "Harbuckel" and his "Uncle Bill," had been festering for fifteen years. William's diary documented the first difficulties with sixteen-year-old Henry W. T. in 1872 when William and Albert gave "Henry Steinway a good talking to" over some unspecified transgression.

Henry W. T. had scarcely reached his majority when he came into repeated conflict with factory manager Henry Kroeger, who had been with the firm since its earliest days. Albert had died a few months before, and William began to take young Henry with him on his peregrinations between Steinway Hall, the factory, and Astoria. H.W.T was clearly the heir apparent, a role suited for the eldest son of founder Charles. "Kroeger tells me that Henry Steinway acts very discourteously to him," recorded William, but he was not quick to reprimand. Three months later: "I have quite a dispute with Henry Steinway about his actions with Kroeger." That same year Kroeger's salary was cut from six thousand to five thousand dollars by Albert, who did not consult William. William privately arranged to pay Kroeger an additional five hundred dollars out of his own pocket, but by 1879 Henry Kroeger left Steinway & Sons, likely as a result of further conflicts with Henry W. T., to whom he now reported. At age fifty-four Henry Kroeger opened his own piano repair business after William refused to award him a Steinway dealership outside New York City. William did help Kroeger find a store to rent.

It was not long before Henry Kroeger began making his own pianos, and these were close copies of Steinway & Sons' instruments. After examining the Kroeger & Son pianos, William decided that they infringed on Steinway patents, but he did not, as was his frequent custom with infringers, bring suit in federal court against Kroeger. Whether this stemmed from respect for the man who contributed much to the firm's success or concern over what court proceedings might reveal about the source of Steinway innovations can never be known. Amazingly, Henry Kroeger asked William for a loan after making public claims that he was the real designer of the renowned Steinway pianos. This was refused, and Henry Kroeger staggered along as a small maker of faux Steinways until his death in 1895. "Pass Kroeger on the street," wrote William in 1887, "who looks old and decrepid [sic]." Though they worked together for a quarter-century the two men did not speak.

Having driven away one factory manager, Henry W. T. soon skirmished with another, this time a man named Luther, who ran the expanding Astoria operations. "Have a scene with H. Steinway, after talking to Luther, they standing on bad terms," wrote William in late 1879. More than a year later the feud between the men still smouldered. "Reprimand both," snapped William

There followed a relatively quiescent series of years. By 1885 Henry renewed combat with William and was not working very hard: "Have a fatherly talk with Henry W. T. Steinway as to his excessively long sleeping in the forenoon," documented William. Still trying to bridge the gap, William again offered a trusteeship to Henry: "H.W.T Steinway refusing to act as one of the trustees, unwilling to promise that he would abide by the majority." Behind H.W.T.'s truculence were principles, though William viewed them as "insane ideas."

The renegade views and rude behavior of Henry W. T. must have seemed to William inexplicable, if not actually insane. The house was doing very well; it was invariably and sometimes spectacularly profitable. Henry W. T.'s stock paid him dividends of from $5,000 to $20,000 per year, and in good years there were bonuses of up to $2,000 on his base salary of $3,000. The $25,000 in a favorable year might easily equal a half million dollars or more in Manhattan today, given the course of taxes and inflation. Henry (who never married) also lived rent-free in a flat next door to Steinway Hall and kept thoroughbred horses and carriage without cost in the company stables; he had, as did all the family, the use of the mansion and its grounds. For a man barely forty years old and able to sleep in mornings, his circumstances were objectively beyond comfortable. To his credit and wisdom, William paid all his nephews the same salary and bonus regardless of their responsibilities or behavior.

In the spring of 1887 conflict flared again: "Have the most exciting time with H.W.T. Steinway who has the most insane ideas on valuations and wants the expense of Steinway Hall not included in the cost of pianos." So we learn that Henry W. T. and Theodore agreed on the superfluity of the concert hall. The matter of "valuations" was more subtle.

William decided to charge against earnings some of the Astoria land carried on the company's books. In an accounting sense he was admitting that the real estate was worth less now than it had been. Had he not done this, the dividends paid to the stockholders would have been closer to 25 percent than the 15 percent paid. Of course, the impact was the same for all stockholders, including William, but Henry took matters less gracefully and was acting in an "insulting manner to me and everybody" and causing William "much anxiety."

William was probably relieved to grant Henry's request for a "furlough" to make a trip to the Northwest and Sitka, Alaska, on which he was joined by William's confidential secretary, Harry Low. An ardent fisherman and outdoorsman, Henry, in his trip to northern frontiers, probably combined business with pleasure; Sitka spruce was an alternative to the Adirondack spruce then used in Steinway soundboards.

Two months in the northern wilderness did little for Henry W. T.'s equanimity. On his return he began "bitterly denouncing London and Hamburg business. I give him a piece of my mind." Henry W. T. was not the only member of the family's next generation to give William trouble. Henry A. Cassebeer, husband of Doretta's daughter Louisa, was appointed manager of William's horse railways. This Mr. Cassebeer took to mean absolute control, and he commenced the construction of a new water tower. When William saw the tower, he ordered it stopped and also found that Cassebeer—without permission from the railway commission or the town— had begun laying additional track. A judge ordered the track torn out and the street repaired, to William's mortification. Paying closer attention now, William noticed that a new office had been built by Cassebeer at the railway stables. "Stand more and more aghast at the way in which H. A. Cassebeer, Jr. has mismanaged my R.R. and run it most fearfully into debt," William scrawled, and also "Cassebeer has the good sense to offer to retire from the management of the R.R." William's nephew by marriage was replaced by a Long Island City alderman named Delahanty, who began his new job with "a good talking to" by William. In the seething swamp of Long Island City politics, it was prudent indeed to have an elected official on the payroll.

At the same time that he was putting his railroad back on track, William was dealing again with H.W.T.: "Compel Henry Steinway to take his entire deposit with interest," William wrote. This was a reference to the firm's practice of taking "deposits" from family members and key employees. For more than a decade William had been accepting cash from individuals on behalf of the firm and paying the depositor interest, usually six percent. The deposits—really loans—were sometimes very substantial, as when the Kreischer family placed twenty-five thousand dollars with Steinway & Sons. There were advantages for both sides. For the firm, deposits were a source of cash outside banking channels, where there was always the peril of a call on the loan during panics. For the depositor there was a good interest rate and, compared to at least some banks, greater safety. To Henry W. T. the return of his deposit should have been an ominous warning; William had last done such a thing in the case of Henry Reck, whom he fired upon learning of Reck's affair with his wife. But H.W.T. did not modulate his critiques of William's management.

"It will be inevitable for us to dismiss Harbuckel very soon from his position with Steinway & Sons and to beseech or finally force him to bless somebody else with his company, for it is pure pestilence to have to deal with him on business matters," wrote William to Theodore. "Unfortunately he is quite right in regard to the unhappy Hamburg-London affair and holds a moral and legal weapon which will not only be recognized by the law but will also win him the sympathy of all outsiders." William proposed either withdrawing his capital from Hamburg or selling the *fabrik* to Steinway & Sons. "You see," wrote William, "Harbuckel does not believe in your consolation regarding sacrifices for the European Reputation. Try to consider the matter coolly and find a solution."

Theodore, who resorted only rarely to dispassionate analysis, roared back: "Henry Steinway is out of the question. Should he make a row, we would liquidate the present corporation, pay young Henry in cash for his shares and found a new company including Hamburg. For such purposes I would place my securities at your disposal." Theodore was oblivious to William's major concern: the possibility for scandal inherent in charges of financial fraud. "I would like to come over at once, but I am too worm-eaten so that I dare not travel in my present condition. . . . Therefore take it easy and do not let your good humor be spoilt by intrigues."

Only one day later, Theodore wrote again: "In regard to Harbuckel's important remarks, everyone may calm down. As soon as the C grands have become good pianos and all improvements have been made, I shall resign as a director." Theodore proposed quitting the firm, but did not explain how this was a solution to the crisis. "I only wonder that you attach any importance to Henry Steinway's remarks. . . . Besides, he should realize that he can neither make a piano or sell it and that he has no idea why Steinway & Sons hold the first position in the world." In but one day, Theodore reversed himself on the idea of buying H.W.T.'s shares: "If we paid him out, the brat would be capable of making pianos under the name of Henry Steinway or to have them made, and this would be even more of a disaster for you."

From his home in Braunschweig, Theodore analyzed both the first cause and the solution: "I can only tell you to follow my counsel and to let these young people manage for themselves for a while. Strictly separate your private matters from the cash of the firm, for I have found that this is the source of the troubles, together with your remarks that you will not let anybody share your work and that you tell all who want to hear it that the young people are quite incapable subjects. This is at the core of all the discontent and discord, and unfortunately you act most unwisely. . . . We must see to it that the Steinways do not separate, otherwise farewell to prosperity."

It was Frederick T. Steinway, the youngest nephew, who stepped forward to placate Theodore, William, and his brother Henry W. T. In a letter to Theodore with a copy to William, "Fritz" played the peacemaker. Theodore's threat of resignation "can only have been said in a moment of ill humor. . . . All of us . . . know what a valuable worker you are in our business and that your splendid improvements and inventions in the field of pianomaking have resulted in the huge success and outstanding position of our company among all other pianomakers. All of us see that clearly, also

Henry Steinway, who often mentioned that in our conversations, and he only complained about what he called mismanagement at Steinway Hall."

Frederick was for the merger of New York and Hamburg and was willing to travel to Braunschweig where Theodore lived to help with the mechanics of the merger, all supervised, of course, by William and Theodore. To assuage his brother Henry, Fred offered to undertake the expenses of Steinway Hall, London, and manage it himself. "I look at it as training for the future, when heavier duties will be imposed on me, when Uncle Bill retires and when fate has taken him away." Fred's concern for the unity of the family and the future of the firm banked the fires of crisis. William did not withdraw from Hamburg, Theodore did not resign, and Henry W. T. temporarily muted direct criticism of William. For this, Fred paid a price. At dinner with William late one night Fred told him that Henry "embitters his [Fred's] life very much through his pessimistic ideas."

The dark view was unwarranted, for Steinway & Sons once again paid a fifteen-percent dividend after further reductions in the property values, enriching William by almost ninety-four thousand dollars, Theodore by sixty thousand, and Henry W. T. by fifteen thousand. All the Steinways also received two-thousand-dollar bonuses on salaries. At the annual stockholders' meeting in 1888 Henry W. T. once again made his views on management known. "I go for Henry baldheaded and tell him that unless he ceases to be abusive and insulting, we will separate."

That summer William sailed to Europe and discussed with Theodore the future of the Hamburg *fabrik*. "Unite upon proposition to increase capital stock and amalgamate Hamburg business with New York," wrote William, "which is the only thing Theodore will assent to." In effect, the plan was to sell the German operation to Steinway & Sons, New York. A cable from Manhattan stated the position of the nephews: "We are unalterably opposed to raising capital—Henry, Charles, Fred." None of the brothers wanted to pay cash for the Hamburg business, and while William and Theodore held more than two-thirds of the shares, they did not impose their will on the younger generation.

Despite this concession by William, there was no question that he was still completely in charge. "Can we use Mexican Mahogany on special cases for dealers. It reduces costs $35," cabled the brothers to William. William responded: "Don't know Mexican Mahogany. . . . Buy only best obtainable Mahogany. Charge dealers accordingly." On Steinway quality there could be no compromise.

"The year 1888 in a business point of view was good but was otherwise one of the saddest of my life, throwing heavy pecuniary losses upon me solely through my great kindness to those I helped and through the misdeeds of others," observed William in retrospect. William was likely referring to the performance of his railroad, the losses at his amusement park, and his large loans to F. Grote & Company. This firm sold ivory objects from a store on Fourteenth Street near Steinway Hall and had failed with losses likely exceeding $100,000. "Unspeakable mental suffering and many sleepless nights were the result."

That year William's children from his first marriage had themselves married. In the spring son George exchanged vows with Ottilie Roesler, whom William described as "not handsome but a good well-educated and highly musical girl . . . 17 years old September next." In the fall daughter Paula married. "I conduct Paula to the altar and place her hand into that of Louis von Bernuth" in a church "crowded with very fine people," reminisced William. But the marriages "do not lessen my poignant grief." On a more positive note, William observed that "the internal dissension which threatened our family business by the enmity of my Steinway Nephews to the Hamburg and London business have all disappeared."

Theodore, however, was disturbed by the failure of the American house to take in the *fabrik*, and in the early days of 1889 William was called on by one of his many acquaintances in the New York judiciary, one Judge Brady, who brought an offer from an English syndicate for the purchase of Steinway & Sons. While Theodore was in favor of selling the firm, the family in New York decided against it. "We agree on the opinion that we had better not sell out to anybody, therefore not to entertain any offers from the English Syndicate," was William's diary entry. Informed of this, Theo wrote that he would "sell at 200 to family members and not so cheap to strangers." He could, of course, sell his shares without permission to anyone he chose, and so Steinway & Sons was once again in peril of division. Theodore's price of $800,000 for a one-fourth interest in the firm was something of a bargain. A buyer would have earned between seven and ten percent on this investment, a much higher return than was available from most stocks or bonds.

It was death that ended the threat of sale scarcely one month later. On March 26, 1889, William wrote, "Go to store early to write Theo a nice long letter when cablegrams come in which I open with a trembling hand. . . . 'Have left for Braunschweig, shall stay there until day after funeral of my good papa Theodore who died suddenly last night. Cast 100 N plates. Holwede.' My heart almost stands still with horror. . . . My head swims with terror, I instantly summon the nephews, my son and cable Doretta [William's sister living in Germany] that we are grief stricken, to tell us when the funeral is, to let Prof. Echtemeyer take Theodore's Todten mask and to take care of Theodore's shares of stock in St. & Sons. An immense throng of people crowd me all day, and I have all I can do to give information to the press. . . . My wife and I are so excited that I pass a sleepless night." William ordered the store and all factories closed in Theodore's memory the next day.

Three days after Theodore's death William learned by cablegram that Theodore's will was not legal in Germany and that Theodore's 26.7-percent interest in the company was frozen by the Braunschweig authorities. "My many years anticipation of trouble have therefore been proved correct, as to the sad consequences of Theodore's living in Braunschweig," recriminated William. A nightmarish combination of the German government, distant relatives, and complete strangers now gazed with envy on Theodore's shares. "See to my horror that all the people at Braunschweig think Theodore has appointed no executor, evidently having gotten hold of some old, cancelled will," lamented William. Steinway & Sons was again in peril, this time by the threat of unwanted partners who might inherit or purchase Theodore's shares. The tentative truce between William and his nephews and the nephews among themselves could easily be set asunder by the introduction of new stockholders; and the disposition of Hamburg, which William inherited, was still unsolved.

William, the last of his generation surviving in America, now stood alone facing the prospect that four decades of effort by him, his father, and his brothers might be destroyed in a German court. There was, of course, an immense irony in this: the success which the Steinways sought and gained in America could be undone in the land they left in 1850. A surviving document showed the mine field of minutiae to be negotiated. In it a Hamburg lawyer explained that the authorities levied an additional four thousand marks' tax on Theodore's estate because he bequeathed to William two adjoining lots in two separate sentences rather than one.

"Brunswick authorities claim Theodore as *Inlander*, he having in 1880 declared to the magistrate that he would remain in Braunschweig," recorded William six months after Theodore's death. Theodore had applied for and received United States citizenship in 1872, and it may have been some arcane aspect of the dual citizenship that led to a letter to von Holwede from one of William's agents in Germany: "It has actually come to pass that the peaceful rest of the two deceased, Theodore and Johanna, is to be disrupted by the transfer of their remains to New York. . . . Under the circumstances, it is unquestionably best that you take on this task which you can do with love and interest. . . . I am carrying out Mr. William's wishes with the greatest reluctance." William had arranged through his old friend and ally in the case of the Oaks children, Attorney General Koch, to have shipped to New York Theodore's remains, along with those of his wife Johanna, who had died several years before.

When the coffins arrived months later, there was no memorial service, but somehow, whether by cause or coincidence, the estate problems with the Braunschweig authorities melted away. The fate of Steinway & Sons was once again safely in the hands of the living in America.

This left William with but one task, and that was to convince his nephews that Steinway's Pianofabrik should be owned by New York. The only plausible alternative was to close the German business, for William knew that the existing arrangement had endless potential for real or imagined conflicts of interest. Closing Hamburg would be a public embarrassment for Steinway & Sons, tantamount to an admission that they were not accepted by pianists and composers in the cultural capitals of Europe. Just such acceptance was an essential premise of Steinway's American success, and William had widely advertised the royal warrants obtained in London, the medals bestowed by learned societies, the triumphs at international fairs and the endorsement of the instruments by Wagner, Liszt, Berlioz, and many others. He had also claimed, endlessly and publicly, that "an immense trade" existed in export of Steinway pianos, not only to Europe but to South America. All this, refracted through American pride and patriotism, sold pianos in America, and William's nephews would have been extraordinarily dense not to understand the strategy and the implications of abandoning Hamburg. Though Theodore and William built the Hamburg *fabrik* on a foundation of pride, its maintenance was bulwarked by necessity.

It was Christmas Eve day 1889 when William tendered a memorandum offering the *fabrik* for sale to the trustees. While William had mastered the craft of larding his formal writing with legal pomposities, the offer was generous at its core. He proposed to sell the business, now his, for 600,000 reichsmarks, just a little less than $144,000 at the rate of exchange Steinway & Sons then used. This was its inventory value. He also offered a money-back guarantee, saying that Steinway & Sons could sell the business back to him for the same price at any time for up to three years. If William were to die, his son George would then buy back the firm. To make matters simpler still, William would hold the factory and rent it to Steinway & Sons at six percent of the value per year. This could not have amounted to more than a few thousand dollars. Cash was not required to buy the *fabrik*; a simple credit on the books would suffice. To further sweeten the deal, William threw in all the patent rights he held. Theodore and William paid themselves patent license and directors' fees of twenty-five thousand dollars per year, so this was yet a further saving to Steinway & Sons, which by itself would pay for the *fabrik* in less than six years. In the year 1889 Steinway's Pianofabrik had sold 603 pianos and returned about 16 percent on its capital. Through William's generous terms, this was pushed above 20 percent, roughly comparable to the American operation. In effect, the nephews were being asked to invest but $238 per piano produced in Hamburg. That same year, the American investment per piano produced was nearly four times higher at $937.

Two years before, William had written to Theodore about Hamburg: "I myself am now so sure as the sun rises and sets that matters cannot continue as before. I do not wish to spend my old age being harassed with troubles, vexations and excitements, and I have definitely made up my mind to end this disgraceful situation." William's offer was certainly intended to be that end. The day after Christmas the trustees met to consider William's proposal. He relinquished the chair to Charles and, after a "lengthy discussion," the nephews decided to buy the *fabrik* for New York. This portion of the meeting went "fairly well," thought William; there was no sign of the spirit of the holidays in the transaction, no hint of recognition of William's largesse. None in the family were astute financial analysts, and it is entirely possible that the nephews did not comprehend William's generosity. It is more likely, in fact, that they felt that it was simply necessary to buy the European albatross from Uncle Bill at the lowest possible price per pound.

Henry W. T. Steinway, though not a trustee, was present for the meeting at William's Gramercy Park home and "he makes no objection nor does he approve." Henry's silence did not continue: "After a hot fight between him and Fred T. St., viz a wordy war, the buying of veneers was given to Fred and all the figuring, charging and disposition as to charging is allotted to Henry W. T. St.," wrote William with palpable dismay. Dissension had once again boiled to the surface, but William seemed almost perennially hopeful when he noted a few days later that "Henry W. T. Steinway's brutish insulting ways caused us all much trouble and anxiety, and we are all determined to oust him from our employ unless he behaves like a gentleman. Our last lecture to him Decbr 26th however seems to have done him some good."

With the *fabrik* safely enveloped in Steinway & Sons, and the carpings of Henry W. T. reduced to a pianissimo, William launched what was effectively a new career: public service. By accepting an appointment from Manhattan's Mayor Grant to a newly constituted and purportedly nonpartisan Rapid Transit Commission to be headed by August Belmont, William propelled himself to a fame rarely equalled, save by the most notorious and/or renowned elected officials. Though difficult to comprehend now, public transportation was a glamorous issue around which revolved not only the convenience of millions of persons, but patterns of urban growth, vast fortunes in real estate, and immense existing investments in elevated lines and street railways. The latter were controlled by some whose names still reverberate a century later, men like Jay Gould and J. P. Morgan.

By simply deciding to build a stop at one location and not another, transit men could bestow vast fortunes on one group of landowners while beggaring those a few blocks away. A radical notion that the city itself might own and operate transit facilities was slowly percolating into public consciousness, and it was aided by the socialist concepts that governments were benign and capitalists evil. With municipal ownership there would be no need for profits, and legions of voters believed that profits were as vile as the men who made them. More than one politician encouraged the fantasy that a ride the length of the island at the astonishing speed of forty miles per hour would cost but a penny or two without the burden of profits, which were but the unjust exactions of the rapacious.

William sailed quickly into these roiling waters, convinced, it seems, that there was safe passage through the shoal waters and rocky cliffs represented by the public, real estate interests, railway men, the City of Manhattan, and the State of New York. Above all, William was a man of supreme self-confidence and inextinguishable optimism; and that he was appointed by Mayor Grant was no accident, for William had long been an underground pipeline for political power and influence within the German community. The Germans were perhaps more cohesive than members of other ethnic groups. This likely rendered them politically potent beyond their numbers, about one-sixth the city's population. New York's citizens of Teutonic origin were a minority too large and unified to be ignored, except at political peril, not only in the city but also at the state and national levels.

As early as 1870 the *New York Journal* reported that William, then but thirty-five years old, was to be nominated as a Democratic candidate for alderman. "Ottendorfer in evening tells me same thing. I decline positively," wrote William. Ottendorfer was an active member of the Committee of Seventy, which set about the investigation and reform of the Tweed Ring. William was also a reluctant member of the committee. Oswald Ottendorfer was even then a longtime friend of William and his companion in countless evening card games of skat. After a few years in America, Ottendorfer had obtained a job in the counting room of the German-language newspaper the *New Yorker Staats-Zeitung*. In 1858 he became editor in chief of the paper and the next year married the widow of the owner.

With the ability to shape the political perspectives of tens of thousands of New York's Germans in a time when the constraining concept of journalistic objectivity had not yet evolved very far, Oswald Ottendorfer was a man of great power. William could rely on Ottendorfer for favorable coverage during his confrontations with the labor unions, and the *Staats-Zeitung* generally ignored potentially embarrassing Steinway matters such as William's divorce and the Centennial Exhibition allegations. Germans desiring a socialist perspective on events could read the smaller *Volkszeitung*.

It is likely though that common sociopolitical outlooks were the foundation of friendship between the two men and that these were formed by similarities of experience and station. Ottendorfer was a president of the Liederkranz, a position William held for fourteen years. Both men were active in the German Society. As a benefaction the Steinways built a library at their Astoria settlement. Oswald Ottendorfer built one on Second Avenue. Ottendorfer, like William, was involved in progressive women's causes. While William donated to female medical facilities, Ottendorfer established a Home for Aged Women. It was located at Astoria. The two men were actively involved in German Hospital charities in the city, and both sought recognition and remembrance in the towns of their birth by benefactions there.

Ottendorfer's $300,000 gift to the town of his birth exceeded William's by at least an order of magnitude, while his $800,000 endowment (about $11 million now) of a home for chronic invalids dwarfed any of William's gifts. The relative political influence of the two men was likely in similar proportion, but the utility of their close relationship was not lost on elected officials. Oswald Ottendorfer was William Steinway's key to the portals of political power and the maze that lay behind them.

William's diary entry for October 15, 1885, showed how things worked at the highest level of American government: "Park Com. McLean takes me to Democratic Headquarters at Hoffmann House, Judge Alston B. Parker, William L. Muller, Robert A. Maxwell receive me and urge me to go to Washington and see Pres. Cleveland and Secr. Manning on the Ottendorfer imbroglio who opposes the nomination of David B. Hill" for governor of the state of New York. "I promise to go tomorrow." At eight the next evening William was in Washington and called at the White House, only to find that President Cleveland was out. Visiting Secretary Manning at home, William learned that "he fully approves of Hill's nomination and desires to consult Ottendorfer. We then drive back to President Cleveland with whom I have a full hour's consultation, at once being recognized by him as having met him in Buffalo many years ago. He gives me a letter to Ottendorfer, fully approves of Hill's nomination. I am charmed at the heartiness of his reception." Apparently a consummate politician, Grover Cleveland either remembered (or was reminded) that in 1869 he had met William when, as a Buffalo, New York, lawyer, he was handling the estate of William's mother-in-law.

Taking a sleeper coach for the seven-hour journey, William arrived in Manhattan the next morning and delivered the presidential communication to his friend Ottendorfer, along with a verbal report of what transpired. Rushing between Ottendorfer's home and Democratic Headquarters, it was William who made the arrangements for Ottendorfer's trip to Washington, even providing a train schedule. When Oswald Ottendorfer returned from Washington on Monday, it was William who arranged a peace conference between the publisher and Governor Hill. That accomplished, William went to a Liederkranz music committee meeting where he treated the members to two and one-half kegs of imported beer and had "a jolly time."

The next day Maxwell, the New York State treasurer, reported that Ottendorfer and Hill had met for two hours. The truce was successful, and two weeks later William wrote that "to my great joy find that Gov. Hill and the entire state Democratic ticket is elected, as well as nearly all my friends for whom I was interested in New York and Long Island City."

Among these were Manhattan judges Van Brunt and Barrett, who had sought William's support for Barrett's election in the spring. William's relationships with the judiciary were particularly amicable, and none more so than with Van Brunt. The day after a ruling in William's interest in a small matter, Judge Van Brunt appeared at Steinway Hall to select a piano. In another case, dinner with Van Brunt was followed by a ruling that moved the case of a man who severed a leg on William's street railway from Manhattan to Queens. Present for the trial, William noted that the victim "was there with his leg sawed off," surrounded by his family. Influence could not overcome the sentiments of the jury, and William lost the case despite Van Brunt's accommodation. The five-thousand-dollar award to the unwilling amputee was upheld on appeal.

William's services in the Ottendorfer-Hill conflict were important enough to warrant direct reward. In a meeting with the governor, Hill offered the post of State Inspector General to William's son George, who was then a few months short of his majority: "I have a long private talk, refuse my consent to the appointment of my George . . . urge him to appoint Emil Schaeffer which he finally does. . . . Schaeffer is overjoyed." Who Schaefer was or why William wanted him appointed is a mystery.

President Cleveland also felt the need to reward William for his services and offered him an appointment as head of the sub-treasury at New York, a critical post with impact on the nation's money supply. William declined and also arranged that the newspapers learn of the offer. His prestige and influence were thereby enhanced, while at the same time he portrayed himself as above political favors. William wanted it known that his motivation was public spiritedness and not from a desire for personal appointments.

Appointments for others were another matter, and William used his influence to secure other Germans jobs in government. President Cleveland consulted William again on the matter of an Internal Revenue Service commissioner for the Manhattan district, but this was not William's decision alone. It brought him into contact with the omnipotent Richard Croker, boss of Tammany Hall. William also pushed for the appointment of Germans as school commissioners and docks commissioners through relationships with Democratic city mayors.

Contrary to the practice of the time, and perhaps of all times, William Steinway did not generally use his political access for personal financial gain, nor did he engage in the direct corruption of elected officials, with the possible exception of a judge or two. His role seems to have been as a conduit and peacemaker between the various party factions, including those of Governor Hill, who aspired to a presidential nomination, and Grover Cleveland, who sought a second but nonconsecutive term as the nation's chief executive. The acceptability of William to both blocs—neither could safely alienate or ignore a renowned German-American with media access—brought a brief appointment to the Democratic National Committee, a task that he undertook reluctantly.

These political activities reflected back on the piano company in a peculiar but prestigious way. When the Piano and Organ Manufacturers Association met for their annual meeting in the spring of 1890, it was William

Steinway who led into the banquet room of the Hotel Brunswick the line of 250 industry luminaries past a life-size upright piano made of carnations, lilacs, roses, and violets as a band played a processional. On William's left was the former and future president of the United States, Grover Cleveland. In addition to Cleveland, William was joined by New York's Mayor Grant and former mayor William R. Grace. Also at the head table was Carl Schurz, who, in addition to being the first German-American senator, held posts as Secretary of the Interior, Union Army general, *Harper's Weekly* and *New York Post* editor, and author of biographies of Lincoln and Henry Clay. A Republican for decades, Schurz bolted the party of Lincoln in 1884 and supported Cleveland, who promised civil service reform. Carl Schurz was therefore politically acceptable at a head table whose luminaries were primarily Democrats.

After dinner came the speeches, the first of which was by William, who addressed the development of the American piano industry. "I rise and make a speech which is greeted with immense enthusiasm. . . . Several others speak all in turn introduced by me in different style and with witty remarks which are much applauded." The Cleveland speech resonated strangely with national concerns one hundred years later, dealing as it did with the issues of foreign ownership of American industries, the advancement of domestic manufactures, and issues of free trade. In 1890 the concern was with "British gold" coopting American assets and "tariff reform," which referred to William McKinley's raising of duties on imported goods with the hypothesis that this would increase employment and wages at home. "The claim is made by the political parties," orated Cleveland, "that the furtherance of industry is the first object of their efforts. . . . This has come to be almost a symbol of combat between those ready to fly at each other in wordy warfare over the subject of tariff reform."

After assuring the audience that he would not regale them with his personal tariff views, Cleveland moved on to the requisite praise for American industry, progress, and invention. "Some of our industries seem to suit the foreigners so well that they desire to own them, and every day we hear of English syndicates purchasing our manufacturing establishments." The audience roared with laughter. "I am glad to speak to one industry that has not been affected by British gold, and which includes only manufacturers honestly and fairly American." There were more cheers, and Grover Cleveland segued seamlessly into his emotive finale: "Throughout our land in every home the piano has gathered about it the most sacred and tender associations. The Christmas that brought it to the household is a red letter day in the family annals. With its music and with simple songs the daughters in turn touch with love the hearts of their future husbands. With it the sacred songs and family prayer are joined in chastened memory. With it we associate the tenderly remembered hours, the time of sickness, the time of death, the funeral's solemn rights. When the family is severed, happy is the one who can place among his household goods the old piano." Tumultuous applause and cheers greeted this conclusion of the Cleveland peroration. "Papers all have fine reports and I am heartily congratulated on speech," wrote William the next day. He had engineered the recognition of his industry by politicians, a president, and a statesman while simultaneously enlarging his own growing celebrity. It was via such means that William demonstrated his political utility, and this resulted in his appointment and later reappointment as a Rapid Transit Commissioner by New York Mayor Hugh J. Grant. To ensure that all were aware of William's role in shaping the future of the city, his acceptance letter was sent not only to the mayor but to the newspapers; and it was not long before the Rapid Transit Commission became known as the *Steinway Commission*, for William quickly ascended to its presidency, the elder Belmont having died.

Arrayed against the Steinway Commission was the Manhattan Elevated Railway Company. The Manhattan carried about 186 million riders per year in 1890, roughly 56 percent of all transit traffic in a city of 1.5 million persons. Collecting over nine million dollars per year one nickel at a time, the "L-Road" paid an average 16 percent of its revenues to stockholders as dividends. The investment was threatened by the prospect of new facilities as envisioned by the Steinway Commission, and the Manhattan was not about to relinquish its position. "Its officers have heretofore declared that there will be no rapid transit in New-York City which it will not control," reported the *Times*.

Undeterred by the pecuniary and political muscle of the Manhattan, William had already made up his mind as to the future of New York public transportation: it would be by subway. "This system consists, said Mr. Steinway, of a lofty tunnel, from 50 to 100 feet below the surface of the earth, clear of the foundations of even the largest structures. It is made large enough to contain a four-track, trunkline railway with necessary side tracks and stations, and high enough to give ample space for the circulation of air," wrote the *Times*. William's vision verged on the miraculous: "It is made light as day with electric lights, and . . . access to the stations is secured by a system of elevators capable of accommodating as many as 200 persons at a time."

There was, in fact, such a subway operating in London, but on a smaller scale with a route length of but three and one-half miles. Known as the Greathead System of tunnelling after its inventor, the London subway had two tubes, each ten and one-half feet in diameter for a total of seven miles of track on which trains ran at sixteen miles per hour. William envisioned a four-track system, four times as long, on which trains would move more than twice as fast at speeds up to forty miles an hour. It was a grand vision, very much in the Steinway tradition.

But before Greathead's hydraulic tunneling machine could start burrowing under Manhattan to realize William's grand concept in cast iron and concrete, there was a need to provide at least the appearance of a democratic proceeding, and the public was invited to submit plans. This resulted in an avalanche of schemes, and a massive crowd of promoters, newspapermen, politicians, and spectators materialized for the Steinway Commission's hearings, which were held, of course, at Steinway Hall. "There was such a resurrection of impossible schemes as nearly to swamp the one or two practical and feasible schemes presented," judged the *Times*.

There were, without doubt, at least as many opinions on rapid transit as there were riders, and these were born of experience, for each man, woman, and child in the city averaged about two hundred rides per year. That the future of transportation was the future of the city was axiomatic, and for years newspapers spanning the political spectrum were filled with the proceedings of the Steinway Commission and the pronouncements of William.

Through endless hearings and meetings he remained a staunch proponent of the subway plan, and after more than two years' work William's Rapid Transit Commission had developed a citywide transportation plan. Its benefits were indefatigably sold by William to any reporter who would listen, and dozens did. "Our plans call for a four-track road of steel rails from the Battery to the upper part of Manhattan island. The two middle tracks are for express trains, to run at forty miles per hour and to stop not nearer than one mile of each other. When this is accomplished merchants and store clerks, who now stand and sit about downtown restaurants for their lunches, will jump aboard these cars and get home in five, ten, or fifteen minutes for luncheon with their families." As always, the family was important.

By the preset procedures of the commission the franchise to build and operate this system was to be auctioned in public to the highest bidder. "President William Steinway said there was certainly great interest in the plans of the commission, and an equal thirst for detailed information concerning them on the part of all classes of people," reported the *Times*. Always selling, William claimed that he had "little doubt that the investment would be a paying one in a few years" and that in ten years "20 per cent would be a certain dividend." But the same article reported that another anonymous commissioner predicted that the city's existing transportation companies would not bid: "They already had millions of dollars invested in railroads, which investments were very profitable."

At noon on December 29, 1892, the rotunda of City Hall overflowed with spectators when William ascended the north stairway to preside at the rapid transit franchise auction. The mayor was there, as was the mayor-elect, the parks commissioner, the corporation counsel, and a large assemblage of politicians and bureaucrats. All the city's rapid transit lines sent representatives, and the crowd was increased by delegations of property owners, real estate men, reporters, and the idly interested. At precisely twelve o'clock William called the proceedings to order and directed that the specifications be read. The commission's clerk and engineer alternated in reading the forty-three-page specifications aloud over the course of the next hour. Lawyer and commission secretary Eugene Bushe then stepped forward to conduct the actual auction. Mr. Bushe's call for bids reverberated through the rotunda and was followed by silence. He called again, and again there was no response. A third solicitation was uttered, then a fourth. A voice was heard, and the crowd shuffled as a man worked his way forward until he stood before the commission and the assembled dignitaries. The lone bidder was prepared to pay five hundred dollars cash and one-half of one percent of transit revenues to the city for a 999-year lease. A whispered conference among the commissioners and the mayor followed; the result was a statement that the bid did not meet requirements. The sole bidder then made another bid: one thousand dollars in cash for the franchise. After a fruitless attempt to draw other bids from the silent crowd, the commissioners retired to the mayor's office to consider the fate of the subway.

President Steinway had been publicly humiliated by the transit interests; Gould, Morgan, Vanderbilt, and Russell Sage, among others, had decided that there would be no subway, that the citizens would not move about Manhattan in electric-lighted luxury at a rate of forty miles per hour. William's grand vision was dashed on the rocks of economic reality. They were large rocks, indeed, for a quick computation revealed the planned subway, if as profitable per rider as the existing elevated roads, would have needed 850 million riders per year to reach William's projected 20-percent dividend. In terms of the city's population, each man, woman, and child would have to ride the subway 567 times per year, almost triple the use of all existing New York public transit in 1891. William's plan was actually a utopian vision, so grand that it exceeded feasibility. It was also ultimately correct, but decades passed before the implacable forces of population, politics, technology, and economics ultimately molded the city's transit system into a form resembling that envisioned by William Steinway in 1892.

There was in all this an irony so immense that no fiction writer would attempt it. The day before the franchise auction William's tunnel under the East River exploded. Ultimately that tunnel, still known by some as the Steinway Tube, would become a main artery in the city's transportation system and be joined with the other subways that William both fought for and foresaw. But this would not happen in his lifetime.

The day after the auction J. Pierpont Morgan, Russell Sage, and George Gould called on William at his office to discuss plans for expanding the elevated railways. William had no choice but to capitulate. "To my dismay I see I stand alone in my stand to guard the city from being further disfigured in its streets," wrote William two weeks later. "I feel dreadful."

Neither before nor after the transit debacle did William limit his public role to the New York rapid transit. As his celebrity grew, he became publicly

345

political and spoke out on a range of controversial issues. There is no evidence that he considered that millions disagreed with his views or that his advocacies might reduce the sale of Steinway pianos. Late in 1895 the *Times* interviewed William on the recent vigorous enforcement of "Sunday Laws" that effectively proscribed any activity but church-going: "It is an exceedingly difficult task," said William, "to suggest a liberal Sunday clause which will uphold the sanctity of the American Sabbath and yet permit the opening of saloons and gardens where good music and light beverages may be dispensed in an English-speaking country. For it is a sad fact that disorderly persons, inclined to personal violence and ruffianism, are more prevalent in English-speaking countries than in any others that I know of."

The "blue laws," as William called them, forced "the average working-man who has neither the room nor the means to keep an icebox or to keep it filled with ice" to buy food on Saturday "and keep it in the sultry atmo-sphere of the living and sleeping room of his family." With Sunday closing the only beverage available to workers was "warm Croton water. Instead of being able to go to some garden, where he and his family could listen to good music and take a glass of light, cool beer or light wine mixed with seltzer water," continued William, "the family is compelled to remain in the dingy tenement house rooms in rainy weather or walk the streets in good weather."

"This whole thing is not a drinking question," averred William. "It is entirely a question of personal liberty. . . . Tastes and views of life differ. I, however, believe that Frederick the Great's immortal expression . . . applies with equal force in the great City of New York: 'In meinem Reiche kann jeder nach seiner eigenen Facon Selig werden.' A literal translation is: 'In my domain everyone may go to eternity in his own style.' "

The issue of Sunday closings was a potent one in the German-American community; twenty-five thousand Germans marched in protest against the laws in New York. William's statesmanly opposition was consistent with his position of leadership among German-Americans. But prohibitionist sentiment was both strong and growing, particularly among women. How many piano sales William's liberal advocacy cost cannot be determined, but the number was not small. To certain piano buyers, William's espousal of tolerance would have been heard as the voice of depravity issuing from a great sinkhole of corruption, beckoning millions to their doom in drink. In some social attitudes, as in transportation and suburban development, William was, in fact, anticipating the future.

No less shocking than Sunday drink to a substantial portion of New York's population was William's endorsement of Tammany Hall candidates for city posts in the fall of 1894. After noting that his only personal connec-tion to Tammany "was to fight it tooth and nail as a member of the Commit-tee of Seventy in 1870 and 1871," William remarked that "no Democrat in this city can be elected without the support of Tammany." The idea of not voting for men endorsed by Tammany was "silly" and the notion of an independent candidate disastrous to the city's interests. An independent would split the Democratic vote and allow a Republican win.

It was natural that the reporter inquire into William's views on mayoral qualifications, and he did. "He should be an independent businessman," responded William, "allied with no faction of the local Democracy, as matters now stand. He should have a record of thirty-five or forty years before the people, not in a political position, but as a citizen and businessman. There are scores of such men." The reporter, aware that William had just described himself as the ideal candidate, responded, "You, yourself have been spoken of, Mr. Steinway, as the man of all others who could unite the Democratic factions in this city, and secure the support of reformers if you would run for Mayor."

William handed the reporter a copy of *Musical Courier*. The *Courier* was not widely read for its political reporting, but William had an excellent relationship with its editor, combined with an aptitude for dramatic timing. In the trade paper was another interview with William: "It seems to me that the time has come when those unsought honors should not be thrust upon me. I have on many occasions specifically and explicitly refused to stand as a candidate. . . . My name has come up since 1882 in connection with the Mayoralty, and I have taken occasion to decline nominations from that time to this." The reasons William could not serve were simple: it was that "the burden of my private business affairs, as well as the conduct of the business of Steinway & Sons, occupies my entire time, and I have not a moment to spare to devote to outside affairs, however much I may feel complimented by the presentation of the opportunities."

William's diary confirms that his public posture was generally one of an unconditional refusal to seek public office and that he had actually refused the blandishments of Federal appointment. Yet the New York mayoralty may well have been sincerely offered *and* seriously considered. "In evening at 7 P.M. to Ottendorfer, play Skat, we laugh a great deal, promise Ottendorfer under no circumstances to run for Mayor, lose 74 cents in Skat," wrote William in a small, stiffly rheumatic hand on May 16, 1894. Such a pledge to his old friend and political ally would have been superfluous if William was not seriously considering the mayoralty. The reason or reasons Oswald Ottendorfer solicited this promise from William are forever lost. Manhattan politics were not conducted by memorandum.

William did not limit himself to the orbits of mayors, governors, and presidents. When in Europe, there were kings to be charmed, and he knew that one way to gain royal audience and the prestige it conferred was through that universal lubricator, money. William spent much of the summer of 1892 at the baths in Weisbaden, Germany, vainly seeking a palliative for his worsening rheumatism and gout. It was there that he made a diary entry recording a donation of twenty thousand marks to the Kaiser Wilhelm church. While William was generous with both individuals, sometimes to a fault, and institutions, the nearly five-thousand-dollar contribution to a foreign church was unusually beneficent. The strategy became clear on Sunday, September 11, 1892, when William wrote, "Lovely weather. Get shaved in my room . . . try to buy gloves, but in vain. We take 11 A.M. train . . . drive to Marble Palais . . . Am received by the Emperor in the most charming and courteous manner, he giving me his hand, I tell him things in answer to his many questions. . . . The last 10 minutes we are joined by the Empress thanking me for my interest, giving me her hand. . . . I am also introduced to a number of high officials." In addition to his donation to the church to be built called Kaiser Wilhelm Memorial Church, and another two-thousand-mark donation to the Empress Augusta Church, William also gave the royal couple a Steinway grand piano.

For the investment of roughly sixty-one hundred dollars William created a massive international media event. The story of his interview with the emperor moved first on the wires of the Associated Press. The German newsmen flocked to William's lodgings, and the foreign correspondents quickly followed. The *New York Sun* reporter filed a long story by steamer, and William did not seem the least annoyed "when the Herald correspondent gets me out of bed near midnight to interview me." Among the cable traffic the next day was William's own report to his nephews: "Steinway New York. Had one hour's delightful audience with Emperor and Empress Potsdam yesterday. Both highly praised Steinway grand. Emperor presented me with beautiful picture of himself containing his autograph signature."

A few days later, William called on a different type of royalty in Dresden, the pianist Anton Rubinstein. Retired from the St. Petersburg Conservatory, Rubinstein was then beginning what was to be the final phase of his life: private instruction and a series of historical concerts. William hoped to entice the maestro to once again tour America for Steinway as he had in the season of 1872/73. One idea likely proposed was to join Anton Rubinstein with the newest super nova of the pianistic firmament, Ignace J. Paderewski, for a combined tour of America. "He receives me in the most friendly manner. I have an hour's talk with him . . . is in splendid health, will never come to America." Though still capable of feats of pianistic endurance—he soon gave thirty-two consecutive and different weekly concerts for the illumination of his students—Rubinstein could not be lured to the New World. William accepted this, and told one of his continental operatives "not to trouble himself about Rubinstein."

When William returned to New York, he was again surrounded by reporters from the *Herald*, *World*, and the *Times*, eager for details of his royal audience. After the international intelligence, William self-reported his church contributions, as well as a visit to his birthplace of "Lessen" (actually Seesen), where, as an "honorary citizen," he made donations to the poor and to schoolchildren. Via his audience with the emperor, if not before, William Steinway achieved the status of a celebrity, a person whose activities are newsworthy simply because they are his activities. William the man eclipsed the fame of Steinway the piano, but it was not in his character to distinguish between the two. It was sufficient that "the facts of this [royal] interview had been telegraphed all over the civilized world and had been commented on by all the Newspapers," as was duly noted in the minute books of Steinway & Sons.

Notwithstanding his expanding renown and political activism, William remained near the center of power but always outside it. On one occasion he wrote that he "saw Jay Gould, Belmont, many other notables" at City Hall. There was no conversation. When William and his wife were invited to the Grover Cleveland residence at 816 Madison Avenue, she was "almost overwhelmed by the commanding beauty and amiability of Mrs. Cleveland." However prepotent in his own domain, William somehow seemed the spectator, if not a wide-eyed schoolboy, when in the presence of greater political or financial power.

In part, this was a product of the social stratification of the time. Though he owned a yacht, William was never invited to join the New York Yacht Club. The Union Club, a center of economic power, tendered him no application, though some of its members were certainly less wealthy. The Century Club, home to many with interests in literature and culture, had few, if any, obviously German names on its rolls. William's assets with the powers that were were based on his Teutonicity; this, however, was also a liability.

Through the Rapid Transit Commission he held potentially great influence over the activities of men like Gould, Belmont, or even J. P. Morgan, and it is notable that there does not appear even once in William's diary the slightest suggestion that any of these men, or their proxies, ever said to the very affable William Steinway, "Bill, let's get together for dinner some night." Nor, for that matter, did he invite them. The walls of ethnicity were so high that even William Steinway could not scale them.

William's fame, which continued to grow under his careful cultivation, reached its full measure with a report of "the sixtieth mile stone in his active and useful career," which appeared in the *New York Times* on March 6, 1896. This was, in fact, William's sixty-*first* birthday but at least two decades earlier he had, for some purpose, changed his year of birth from 1835 to 1836. "All day he was the recipient of congratulatory messages from his hemisphere and Europe, and a profusion of floral tributes and presents were showered upon him from early morning until late at night," recorded the *Times*. To William's floral-bedecked office trekked streams of employees, delegations from the German singing societies presenting "engrossed testimonials," and noted personages such as the conductor Walter Damrosch and pianist Rafael Joseffy. A baron presented a testimonial from the king of Austria, perhaps for some unrecorded benefaction. "Callers, letters, telegrams, flowers arrive and keep me hopping until 8 P.M.," wrote William.

That evening during a routine meeting of the Liederkranz directors, the doors swung open, and a chorus of one hundred began to sing a song composed especially for the occasion. It was called "Steinway, William Steinway." The assembly then adjourned to the regular meeting room for a "delightful entertainment" during which William was multiply cheered whenever he arose to express his thanks. From the meeting room the group moved to the assembly hall for what the *Times* called "a general jollification, with a bountiful supply of viands and beverages." Having learned that beer aggravated his chronic rheumatism and gout, William restrained himself to a socially acceptable minimum of three glasses, but one-sixth the amount he sometimes drank. A quartet appeared to sing William's favorite song, "Ave Maria," amidst many speeches and tributes. "I am presented with a large bouquet and a lyre of flowers . . . have a glorious time, I making a fine stirring speech . . . Home midnight greatly pleased."

This was the world of the public William in the closing years of a complex life—one of an amiable but powerful leader, a man of great wealth and generosity, a man who had actually lived the immigrant dream, a man who was known to all and admired by many. But the life of the private man was heavy with pain and sorrow and disappointment. "I do not wish to spend my old age being harassed with troubles, vexations and excitements" were William's words that had been written to brother Theodore, now dead for seven years. The wish was not granted.

Chapter 24

THE AIRY FABRIC
OF A NAME

I

Ah, yes, if notes were stars, each star a different hue,
Trembling to earth in dew;
Or if the boreal pulsings, rose and white,
Made a majestic music in the night;
If all the orbs lost in the light of day
In the deep, silent blue began their harps to play;
   And when in frightening skies the lightning flashed
And storm-clouds crashed,
If every stroke of light and sound were but excess of beauty;
If human syllables could e'er refashion
That fierce electric passion;
If other art could match (as were the poet's duty)
The grieving, and the rapture, and the thunder
Of that keen hour of wonder,
That light as if of heaven, that blackness as of hell,
How Paderewski plays then I might dare to tell.

II

How Paderewski plays! And was it he
Or some disembodied spirit that had rushed

351

From silence into singing; that had crushed
Into one startled hour a life's felicity,
And highest bliss of knowledge—that all life, grief, wrong
Turns at last to beauty and to song.

The poem of R. W. Gilder appearing in the March 1892 number of *The Century Magazine* was one view of the social phenomenon that was Ignace Jan Paderewski; there was another at Steinway & Sons. "No pianist has ever done the business so much good, nor displayed our Grand Piano to such advantage as I. J. Paderewski, who has acted in every way loyal to the Steinway interest," recorded the board minutes for April 2, 1892. The occasion was a decision by William and his nephews to pay Paderewski an additional $3,526.91 so that his bonus payment came to an even $10,000. During the 1891–92 concert season, the thirty-one-year-old pianist from Russian-occupied Poland performed to sold-out houses, transporting both audiences and critics to ecstasy, and, in at least one case, poetry. Paderewski's reputation as a player of merit in Europe was, of course, the reason that he was brought to America to tour for Steinway. But nothing in his continental performances for the pianomaker Erard forecast the effusion of American enthusiasm.

When in London during the summer of 1890 William was approached by an agent, one Daniel Mayer, who tried to interest him in two pianists, "I. J. Paderewski, a Pole, and Wassily Sapellnikoff, a Russian from Odessa." The national identifiers accompanying the names suggest that William was unfamiliar with these men. Thinking the price too high, he demurred on a contract with Mayer and instead negotiated with Steinway regular Franz Rummel to play fifty concerts for six thousand dollars, about the going rate for quality pianism. Mayer, excellent agent that he was, did not give up and soon offered William the composer and conductor Tchaikovsky at what William thought were "enormous prices." This too was refused.

William was likely risk-aversive in matters artistic at this time, for the prior season Steinway & Sons had engaged a child prodigy, Otto Hegner. The young German boy, whom William probably viewed as an offset to another prodigy, Josef Hofmann, who played for Weber before becoming embroiled in a child labor scandal, did not fare well in America: "Poor little Hegner does not draw at all, improvises before an empty house," wrote William. By the end of the season, Otto Hegner was sharing the bill with an assortment of instrumentalists and vocalists. Even the critics had reservations about savaging a child, preferring instead the tepid endorsement: "The advent of this gifted boy has not been without its beneficial influence," wrote the *Times*.

As matters evolved, Otto Hegner was among the last artists to play in Steinway Hall, for the decision was made to close the venue after more than two decades at the axis of the Manhattan wheel of culture. Nothing remains to illuminate the reasons for the closing. Even after some remodeling, the twenty-four-year-old facility must have seemed dated in an age that valued the new as much, if not more, than our own. Perhaps William simply looked at the accounts and decided, silently, that Theodore and Henry W. T. Steinway were right: Steinway Hall was an investment with a diminishing return. Without comment and with as little notice as possible, the great concert space was remodeled into a final finish area where Steinways were regulated and polished before being shipped across the nation.

The failure of the Hegner engagement, the closing of the hall, the medium-price contract with Franz Rummel, plus the early refusals of Paderewski and Tchaikovsky affiliations all suggested that the future portended a different relationship between Steinway & Sons and the artists that previously had been pivotal in its success. All this changed when Daniel Mayer stepped ashore in the United States. "Mayer arrived Monday, had a long talk with him then and yesterday & finally arranged terms for Tretbar under our guarantee to engage Paderewski from November 16, 1891 to April 30th 1892 at £6000 for 80 concerts," wrote William. Something, perhaps Mayer's salesmanship, had induced William to pay the then unprecedented sum of $29,280 or $366 per concert. He was, so to speak, buying a pianist in a poke, for neither he nor any member of the family had heard I. J. Paderewski play.

At a hastily called meeting of the board of trustees, William asked for a vote on the contract he had negotiated with Mayer. It was approved, but not unanimously, for nephew Fred Steinway voted against engaging Paderewski. For obscure reasons, the arrangement called for Steinway & Sons to guarantee the performance of a contract that was made between the Polish pianist and the longtime loyal Charles F. Tretbar, who was still employed by the company. At the same meeting William, his son George, and the nephews approved a more typical arrangement when they authorized a $125 fee for each of thirty concerts by Rafael Joseffy with the Theodore Thomas Orchestra.

The first hint that something extraordinary might have been wrought came about three weeks later with a telegram to William: "Chas H. St. cables from London that Paderewski played immense." Meanwhile, Franz Rummel was giving afternoon recitals in the city's newest venue. These musical holding actions took place in the basement of the "new Music Hall at Fifty-Seventh Street and Seventh Avenue." The *Times* reviewer suggested that "it might have been advisable to defer the opening of the place until the pounding of many hammers in other parts of the building had ceased."

The "Music Hall" is now known as Carnegie Hall, and its erection was greeted with enthusiasm and civic pride: "That a musical city like New-York needs a hall which shall centralize its musical life is a proposition which admits of little discussion. It is no secret that heretofore the piano trade governed the location of concerts," observed the *Times*. Seating three thousand with standing room for another thousand, the Music Hall accommodated a 60-percent larger audience than the old Steinway Hall, which was filled to capacity at twenty-five hundred persons. The Music Hall officially opened on May 5, 1891, with an immense music festival, the centerpiece of which was the conducting of Piotr Ilyich Tchaikovsky. William was there and called the hall "glorious." It was promptly booked for Paderewski's fall concerts, for there was no choice but to use the vast space of the Music Hall. The Metropolitan Opera House was generally deemed acoustically unsatisfactory for instrumental music, and the city's other venues were too small.

There was little to do now but wait, and William recorded in July that he had "dinner with Tretbar on his activity next season." While dinners and social events with Tretbar had been common in the past, the relationship between William and his staunch employee had changed over nearly thirty years. It is likely that Tretbar's role became less crucial as the nephews took on larger responsibilities. No foggy aesthete, Charles Tretbar was a tough-minded manager more careful with Steinway & Sons' funds than William himself. With long experience in operating the now-closed Steinway Hall, Mr. Tretbar knew the ways of artists, managers, agents, audiences, and the press.

However, when Paderewski and his manager Goerlitz arrived in New York in early November 1891, Charles Tretbar put them up in the decaying Union Square Hotel. According to a later account of the maestro, his lodgings were shared by rats and cockroaches, and after some complaining, he was allowed to move to a different hotel. Expenses of the trip were, of course, to be borne by Steinway & Sons. Paderewski also enjoyed recounting how he was forced to practice by candlelight in a deserted warehouse surrounded by pianos. If true, these tales suggest that neither Tretbar nor the family anticipated the magnitude of Paderewski's success. There was a simple reason for this: Paderewski's triumph was unprecedented, and within a few months of his arrival, he surpassed the status of virtuoso performer to become a social phenomenon. On Thursday, November 12, 1891, William confirmed Charles's critical judgment: "Paderewski tries our grands, he is an immense player." Taking no chances with the New York public's discriminating powers, Tretbar advertised heavily and gave away large numbers of tickets to Paderewski's American premiere. Whether or not Hugo Goerlitz used the method on November 17, 1891, is unknown, but Paderewski's manager later became known for providing free tickets to young girls with instructions to mob the stage after a performance or, at a minimum, faint or swoon prominently at some propitious point during it.

Prudent preparations though these might have been, Ignace Jan Paderewski rendered them superfluous. Even William, by then a wizened, four-decade veteran of the trade who had heard a thousand performers if he had heard one, remarked to himself that Paderewski was "a most wonderful player," before leaving the new Music Hall for the more familiar surroundings of the Liederkranz.

Music and Drama limned the scene that night after Walter Damrosch's Symphony Orchestra began the concert at 8:15 P.M. with Goldmark's overture *In Springtime*: "He came upon the platform with a quiet, self-possessed air, and, amid welcoming plaudits took his seat at the Steinway grand. A glance at the conductor, a run of the fingers over the piano keys, and he was ready. . . . Each moment revealed the fact that a player of infinite grace and marvelous execution was at the instrument. . . . Paderewski has a habit of drawing back his hands some distance from the keys and letting them fall at seeming random, yet they invariably drop in the right place. . . . He is a player who believes in climaxes."

The elegaic tone continued paragraph after paragraph until it reached the words that must have made William Steinway smile, for the *Music and Drama* writer touched upon the *raison d'être*: "It must be admitted that if this Paganini of the Piano won a splendid triumph, he did so under favorable auspices. He was heard in the finest music hall on the continent, if not the world; he was supported by a noble orchestra efficiently led; and he had a piano-forte which responded cleverly to his slightest as well as his most powerful touch, and seemed to be gifted with almost a self-intelligence in interpreting every phase of his musical intent. The most delicate tones were exquisitely distinct, and seemed gifted with a poetic individuality; the most powerful notes were sonorous and grand. Everyone remarked the splendor of the instrument; and though the name of the manufacturer was not conspicuously displayed upon it, the musical instinct of the cultured audience present told them it could only be a Steinway."

New York's fractious daily press, a group which could not normally agree among themselves if a given day was sunny or cloudy, was united in the opinion of Paderewski's talent and competed largely through attempts to heap encomia upon the artist at ever increasing rates. "Is he the greatest of all?" queried the *New York Sun*. "As of course he would choose to have it, the reply comes to us in the affirmative." The *Sun* also gave the best physical description of the artist: "A slender young man of about thirty years, with a clear-cut, poetical, dreamy face, with tawny hair lying in masses of curls about his well-shaped head, stepped upon the stage and made a modest, quiet salutation to the large audience which welcomed him warmly. . . . There was no trace of nervousness about him, He is too well-poised, too sensible, or, to speak more subtly, too unconscious, too objective to be unstrung by even a new public in a strange land." A parallel was drawn: "He, like the grand old Russian, Rubinstein, looks down from the standpoint of perfect musical understanding, and interprets clearly the divine language as such, not as a mere exhibition of mechanical skill or legerdemain."

There were other reviews as well of the debut performance, and the concerts of the following two nights fueled further the enthusiasm. Ink flowed in warm oceans of praise for both Paderewski *and* his piano. The eighty-concert tour was soon expanded to 107 performances across the nation, and in city after city the audiences were large and the critics ecstatic. The programs were substantive; in Chicago alone he played five different Beethoven piano concertos, plus his own works, and also delivered the expected portions of Liszt, Chopin, and Bach. His New York concerts each included *two* piano concertos.

The schedule of 107 performances in but 130 days took its toll, and by the time Paderewski reached Rochester, New York, the tendons in his right arm were inflamed. Local doctors massaged and bandaged the wounded artist, and Paderewski refingered pieces so that he could continue performing. Returning to Manhattan in March for the customary series of farewell concerts, the Paderewski phenomenon reached the proportions of what soon was labelled "Paddymania" by a *Musical Courier* writer, and William recorded that a matinee performance on March 26, 1892, had the "immense receipts of $6,580."

"A perfect pandemonium all day" was William's description of March 28, 1892. "Settlement with Paderewski, who behaves most nobly giving even our porters $100. He invests $22,000 in Steinway Railway Company bonds and takes $40,706 in drafts on Paris, and $4,500 cash." The maestro's total earnings for his sojourn in the United States amounted to $67,206 or $628 per concert versus a guarantee of $366. Paderewski's total proceeds amounted to more than one million of today's dollars, and when he sailed for Europe the next morning, he did so as a newly wealthy man.

No records remain of Steinway & Sons' proceeds from the concert series, but if the assumption is made that the average attendance was but 1,500 persons per concert at $1.50 per head across the 107 concerts, the total approaches $250,000 in gross receipts, or roughly $3 million today. Even after deducting the costs of advertising, halls, orchestras, lodging, travel, and miscellaneous expenses such as the four hundred dollars William spent on "diamond studs" as a Christmas present for the maestro, it is difficult to see how Steinway & Sons could have lost money. A predictable, but indirect, benefit of the Paderewski tour was record sales of Steinways. "Biggest retail trade ever done, sold 30 old and new pianos in one day," enthused William just two days before Christmas 1892, and at year-end: "We by far had the best year of our business existence for we shipped from our warerooms no less than 822 grands and 1657 uprights." Combined with Hamburg, where sales were down 13.5 percent to 540 pianos, Steinway & Sons sold a total of 3,019 pianos in 1891, the first time ever that the house shipped more than three thousand pianos in a single year. Virulent "Paddymania" was as profitable as it was widespread, and William declared a $200,000 dividend for the shareholders of which he received about $80,000.

As the pianos moved out and the money poured in, the scintillating star of Steinway fame moved ever higher and shined still brighter in the American cultural firmament, fueled by the personality, presentation, and performances of Ignace J. Paderewski. But far from public view a bitter family conflict moved inexorably toward crisis. At the center was Charles's oldest son and William's nephew Henry W. T. Steinway.

The renegade actions of Henry W. T. Steinway ceased for roughly a year after Theodore died and the *fabrik* was folded into Steinway & Sons, but the disagreements over management of the company did not disappear; they were simply not discussed. Henry, however, was not the only source of difficulty for William. In late 1890 he discovered that Henry and his brother Charles together had withdrawn from the company about $132,000—about $1.5 million today—for their own use; of this, about one-fifth had been drawn by Charles. The sum was equal to twenty-five years' salary for either of the brothers, and the cash withdrawals could not have come at a poorer time for the firm. "The financial situation and the scarcity of money all over the country beggars description," wrote William only two weeks later. The "money panic" was, as usual, accompanied by a sharp recession, but the house still had ample resources and reputation. How or when the huge borrowings of the brothers were repaid William did not record.

William seemed much more concerned with the behavior of his nephew than he was with finances, and in early 1891 matters took a turn for the worse. "Have a hard tussle with Henry W. T. St. and tell him that he will instantly be suspended and discharged if he is again ungentlemanly and uses foul language," wrote William. The rift was growing wider; by this time Henry was no longer speaking to his brother Fred, and the trustees ordered Henry to produce the "cost figures" that he had computed. These showed the expenses of producing each part in a piano. The question of costs was an enduring one. In 1887 Henry and Fred had been directed to investigate piano production costs and report to the trustees. If such a report was made, it was not entered in the record. Two years later the trustees issued another resolution, this time declaring that all calculations made on company time were the property of the company. It seems, however, that the data William sought on piano costs were not forthcoming, and in January 1891 the trustees passed a motion ordering Henry to produce his cipherings. "Resolved, that the Vice President Mr. Fred. T. Steinway," read the minutes, "be hereby empowered and directed to forthwith obtain possession of any and all figures, detailed or otherwise, pertaining to the calculation of the cost of any and all parts of pianofortes manufactured or to be manufactured by this company, from any employee or stockholder, and that two clean and detailed copies be at once made of such figures and calculations, one of which to remain in the New York factory of Steinway & Sons, and the other to be kept in the vault in front of the Steinway Hall building." Still no figures were produced.

The pace of the conflict accelerated, and at the next trustees' meeting Henry was ordered to pay rent for the company-owned apartment he had occupied gratis for many years. For unknown reasons, Henry W. T. offered to lease to Steinway & Sons two houses he owned in Steinway Village as a home for the Astoria bookkeeper. Instead, William decided to build a new home for bookkeeper A. J. Menzl.

Two weeks later Henry W. T. was called to appear before the trustees at another meeting, for he had not only refused to provide the calculations but had actually destroyed them. The minutes tell the story in a language strangely formal for what was in essence a family conflict: "Mr. Fred T. Steinway testified as to the nature of the data, calculations and figures which he said had been gotten up by years of patient labor and work. . . . Mr. Brand [a bookkeeper] also testified to the character and nature of such data."

Then came the renegade nephew's turn: "Mr. Henry W. T. Steinway, on being called upon to explain his action in destroying such data, admitted that he had been furnished a Copy of the resolution" that ordered him to give the calculations to his brother Fred. Henry W. T. admitted as well that he had destroyed the data after he received the order. "In response to the President's question, why he had done so, [Henry W. T. stated] that he had regarded such data as of no value, which he stated was all the explanation he would make." Faced with open mutiny, William was, at least on the record, both remarkably forbearing and rigorously parliamentary: "Resolved, that Henry W. T. Steinway be ordered with the help of Mr. Julius Brand and Mr. A. J. Menzl, to forthwith again make up all detailed data and tabular statements [of] the cost of manufacturing the Steinway pianos." Henry W. T. was also "reprimanded for having intentionally disobeyed the order of the Board." Off the record, William wrote that "I give him a scathing rebuke and tell him I will prosecute him if he defames me."

Henry W. T. Steinway had inherited the family iron will and would not be dissuaded, no matter the consequences. After moving from his rooms next door to Steinway Hall to the Florence Hotel, he continued his guerrilla warfare as traced by William: "We are again having much trouble with H.W.T. Steinway who has written me an insolent letter, and it becomes more and more apparent that we shall soon have to discharge him entirely from our employ." It was no small step to fire Henry; in addition to violating William's lifelong belief in the importance of family unity per se, there was an obvious business risk: Henry William Theodore Steinway might easily sell pianos under his own name, capitalized, in a supreme irony, by the dividends he was paid and would continue to be paid as a Steinway & Sons stockholder. H.W.T. received more than $140,000 in dividends—about $2 million now—between 1880 when the *fabrik* he detested was founded and the summer of 1891 when William finally came to accept the inevitability of separation.

On a Saturday six days before Christmas 1891 at 3:00 P.M. William and his nephews gathered in the pattern room of the Fourth Avenue factory. Henry W. T. was also there, "having been cited to appear before the Board," as the minutes of the meeting ominously noted. Present to record the proceedings was sales manager Nahum Stetson as secretary, pro tem: "A thorough investigation was then held into the conduct of Mr. Henry W. T. Steinway," wrote Stetson in a neatly rounded and deliberate hand, "who had nearly one year ago destroyed valuable detailed memorandums and compiled data, the work of many years regarding the cost of the various styles of Steinway pianofortes, more especially that of the various styles of cases in the different woods, in direct violation of & disobedience to the orders of the Board of Trustees. . . . In the Meeting of said Board of Febr. 28th, 1891, Mr. Henry W. T. Steinway had been severely reprimanded by the President and ordered by the Board of Trustees to forthwith . . . get up such data. . . . President William Steinway several times had to call to order and reprimand Mr. Henry W. T. Steinway for making offensive and insulting remarks and to notify him that he would be ejected from the premises if he did not behave like a gentleman."

Bookkeepers Menzl and Brand were called to testify, and "it became evident, and was admitted by Mr. Henry W. T. Steinway, that he had not only not made the slightest attempt to get up such data, but . . . had actually prevented Mr. Julius Brand to get up his portion of the work. . . . In the further progress of the investigation it was brought out that . . . the original detailed cipherings [were] simply destroyed or thrown into the wastebasket, thus showing that in the entire department entrusted for many years past to the sole guidance & care of Henry W. T. Steinway, no record whatsoever had been preserved of these detailed calculations, data and figures."

After asking the bookkeepers to "withdraw from the room," William read "several letters" written by Henry W. T. that "were full of vile insults and insinuations" and which personally attacked William, the trustees, and "even C. F. Theodore Steinway, deceased. Every point of these letters was discussed and the utter absurdity and groundlessness of these insinuations shown, as Mr. Henry W. T. Steinway was unable to substantiate a single one of them."

Whether or not William expected his nephew to recant or show contrition is uncertain, but the renegade Steinway was given the opportunity, and Stetson reported that H.W.T. was asked "whether or not he would hereafter act properly and express his regrets for having maligned and insulted in words & letters himself and other individual members of the Board of Trustees." Henry W. T. "then stated that he would not take back a single word of what he had said or written," and William advised his nephew that if he did not resign by January 1, 1892, he would be fired. "All the members of the Board upheld the action of the President," related the secretary, pro tem, and "upon motion duly made, seconded and unanimously carried, the meeting then adjourned at 5:15 P.M."

"We are all much relieved that at last we will get rid of this brute," wrote William in his diary that evening. On the last day of 1891 William received his nephew's resignation. It was as bland as it was terse: "Dear Sir: Wishing to withdraw from active participation in our business, I herewith tender my resignation, to take effect after this date. Respectfully, H.W.T. Steinway." William summarized the year 1891 that New Year's Eve: "We had the most brilliant year for the first time exceeding 3,000 pianos in any one year. I myself suffered badly from the gout in my hands last Octbr. and the most fearful cold of my life, and Henry W. T. Steinway's brutality and insulting behavior, ending as it did in his enforced resignation this day, caused us all untold grief and sorrow."

There followed an interchange of frigidly polite letters in which the resignation was acknowledged and a request for a forwarding address made. In response Henry W. T. asked to maintain office space at the factory and to continue to keep his horses at the Steinway & Sons stables. With both sides behaving as if the pattern room paroxysm had never occurred, the requests were denied. Several months of silence intervened until Henry W. T. asked to inspect the books in April 1892. The request was granted, and a few days later Henry and an accountant made their appearance at Steinway Hall and remained, uneventfully, to prowl the accounts for a number of days.

It was midsummer and William was at the baths in Wiesbaden, Germany, when a letter arrived: "Chas. H. St. writes that H.W.T. St. came in and wanted to look at our inventory book which they refused, that he then transferred 4 shares to his lawyer, W. N. Cromwell, which had to be issued to the latter," wrote William. The inventory book was the master business record of Steinway & Sons into which all the firm's transactions flowed. Listing all the assets and liabilities of the house, literally down to the scraps of wood, the inventory book was used to compute both annual profits and the net value of the enterprise. Charles's refusal to allow his brother to examine the inventory triggered a lawsuit, and the family disagreements soon became a matter of public knowledge. While William thought the suit contained "the most absurd allegations," the newspapers took a different view.

"Henry Sues His Uncle William and Says the Business is Wrongly Managed," read a flippant headline in the *New York World*. "Henry W. T. Steinway has brought an action in the Supreme Court . . . to compel his uncle to restore to the firm money alleged to have been indirectly diverted to the firm Steinway Piano Fabrik. . . . It is alleged . . . that William

Steinway has directed a large part of the foreign business of Steinway & Sons to the Hamburg concern." Other newspaper accounts were less liberally sprinkled with the word "alleged," but all contained the key charge: Steinway, New York, sold to Steinway, Hamburg, piano parts at artificially low prices. As a result, large profits that rightfully belonged to the New York company were realized instead by the Hamburg company, to William and Theodore's advantage and to the disadvantage of the other New York stockholders such as William's nephews and Henry W. T. Steinway in particular.

Subtleties of intercompany transfer accounts and exchange rates aside, the superficially intriguing theory of H.W.T. and his attorneys avoided a powerfully significant fact: it was Henry W. T. himself who was in charge of the pricing and billing for pianos and parts to Hamburg. Although it was never developed in the court by *either* side, the billings to Hamburg were based on the computations Henry W. T. destroyed and refused to reproduce. Still more amazing, William did not come to comprehend the circumstances until nearly three years after the resignation of his nephew. Just a few days before the trial began in late 1894, William held a meeting at the factory with the bookkeepers: "I am surprised what a strong case we have against him [H.W.T.], he having overcharged the Hamburg factory most unmercifully." Thus it became clear to William, ever trusting of family, that his nephew's destruction of records was not simply an act of rebellion but one of perfidy. For more than a decade Henry W. T. Steinway had been overcharging William and Theodore's Hamburg factory in the hope that it would founder and be abandoned in a sea of red ink. Had Henry W. T. not destroyed the cost computations, his sabotage would have been exposed.

The reality of the situation—that William had been cozened for a decade by his nephew—did not intrude upon the legal proceedings. At the trial William wrote that his nephew "squirms and tries to deny all responsibility but has to admit that he fixed nearly all prices."

After three days at trial the requisite briefs were filed, each loaded with recondite citations of law, and Justice M. L. Stover pondered the matter, but not for long: "This action having been tried by the Court without a jury, it is decided, That the complaint herein be dismissed upon the merits, with costs. The grounds of this decision are that the evidence does not establish any improper or unlawful acts of the defendant . . . or that any acts of the said defendant were detrimental to the interests of Steinway & Sons." William, with clear delight, wrote that "all afternoon papers mention Stover decision," and Henry W. T., being a Steinway, appealed.

Before the *fabrik* matter came to trial in 1894, Henry W. T. also launched two other legal missiles at his family. In one of these he made the claim that his Uncle Theodore's will was invalid. In letters testamentary of mind-numbing length and Byzantine complexity, C. F. Theodore had set up a trust for his four thousand shares of stock in Steinway & Sons. It is likely that Theodore designed the trust to create a monetary inducement for his nephews to perpetuate the business and remain together. The situation was rife with irony, for if Henry were successful, his Uncle William would have received a further one thousand shares, and each of his brothers (to whom he no longer spoke) would have also inherited additional shares, about 111 each, in the same proportion that he did. The havoc was wrought with other relatives, nine of whom would be stripped of all the shares Theodore intended for them.

Subtleties of estate law do not build newspaper circulation, so the case was largely ignored, but William, Charles, and Fred—notwithstanding that they would personally be enriched if Henry W. T. prevailed—deployed attorney Cotterill to defend the estate. Working alone, his fee for the defense was forty thousand dollars if he won and twenty thousand if he lost. In yet another twist as rare as it was ironic, Cotterill did lose the case in the New York Supreme Court, and an interlocutory decree was entered that destroyed the trust. Henry W. T. had legally beggared his cousins, including some with whom he had gone to school when a child. William did not live to see the end of this legal battle, which was still being waged a decade after his death. Theodore's trust, created to weld the family together with a common economic interest, ruptured it, and into the fissures flowed anxiety and fear for all thirty of Theodore's heirs.

"I am pained to see that my son Henry has not lost his inclinations to start legal proceedings," wrote Sophie Millinet Steinway Fricke to a niece from her home in Germany in 1899. The mother of Henry W. T., Charles, and Fred went on: "I was already prepared for the fact that I would receive no income for a longer time from the estate of my dear husband deceased [Charles Steinway, the father of the warring brothers, who died in 1865] and had prepared myself accordingly. . . . I have not given my son Henry the slightest authority to represent my affairs . . . as he personally several years ago broke off every friendly relationship and [has had no] correspondence with me." The mother of the succeeding generation of Steinways went on to express her hope that if a new executor was appointed, it would not be her son Henry: "I would not care now, as you may very easily imagine, to be dependent on Henry. . . . How deeply this matter affects me I cannot express." Moving to a lighter topic, Sophie went on to discuss the weather.

The mother of Henry William Theodore Steinway did not live to the end of the will war, nor did William. In 1900 the New York Court of Appeals, the last resort for the case, sustained the trust. Eleven years had passed since Theodore died and, as matters turned out, H.W.T. Steinway did not get the extra 111 shares of the company he had left at the close of 1891. Undaunted, H.W.T. began another suit, this time disputing who should pay Cotterill's forty-thousand-dollar fee. By the time that action was resolved, attorney Cotterill himself had died, but the court decided that

Henry W. T. Steinway was responsible for one-fourth of the defense fees in the case he brought and lost against his relatives.

While the will war was fought in legal jungles far from public view, the combat over yet another action brought by Henry W. T. Steinway was widely covered in the city newspapers. The case was not only much easier to understand, but it involved names both famous and infamous. Leading the list in the famous column was Ignace J. Paderewski, and first among the infamous was the notoriously corrupt mayor of Long Island City, Patrick J. Gleason. The essence of the plaintiff's allegations was that Steinway & Sons had engaged in business activities not permitted by their incorporation documents, which, it was contended, limited the firm to the manufacture and sale of pianos and other musical instruments. Henry W. T. claimed that a wide range of activities, including the Astoria real estate development, were conducted outside the charter.

Such actions were known as *ultra vires*, an arcane legalism then meaning acts transcending the expressed or implied powers of a corporation, including acts contrary to public policy or proscribed by statute. The remedy asked for the abundant alleged *ultra vires* was that the defendants—Henry's Uncle William, his two brothers, and the other directors—be enjoined against committing further similar acts, account for the moneys expended in such acts, and personally pay back to Steinway & Sons the money shown by the accounting. There was a certain peculiar circularity about Henry's claims. Since the trustees were also the majority stockholders, it is difficult to understand how their supposedly damaging actions as trustees hurt other stockholders more than they hurt themselves. This tautology did not, however, prevent the case from coming to trial.

Characterizing Steinway Village property as "useless wasteland" and "salt marshes," Henry W. T., through his attorneys, claimed that Steinway & Sons "squandered large sums" in developing the settlement and that they were "practically conducting the business of speculative builders." The "enormous sum" of $756,722.05 had been spent on the development, while only $330,895.44 had been realized through property sales. Further claims were made that the land had been capitalized at $500,000 when the corporation was formed, that this was wildly excessive, and that Henry W. T. Steinway had been forced by his Uncle William, when still a boy under his guardianship, to pay cash for shares while William obtained his Steinway shares in exchange for the Astoria swamps.

William, in his testimony, admitted that the Astoria development *was* less profitable than the piano business but averred that the current value of the property was about $1.7 million and had therefore been profitable. But no plausible computation, no matter how generous, suggests that the return on the Astoria investment could have exceeded 3 percent per year, and in many years—particularly during the protracted depression from 1873 through early 1879—there were clearly losses. Compared to the piano business, where, in a bad year, dividends on capital were 6 percent and in good years exceeded 15 percent, Steinway Village was, in a business sense, a poor investment. But the legal issue did not turn on the profitability of the expenditures, but whether or not they were *ultra vires*, an actuality most fortunate for all but Henry.

The complaint next specified that Steinway & Sons was illegally running a bank under the guise of a piano company and that, by 1891, over one million dollars in loans were being discounted by Steinway & Sons through what was called the "accommodation account." William and nephew Charles testified that the loans were made to piano dealers who needed financial assistance in the "dull season" and that the amounts loaned were actually much smaller because many of the loans were simply extensions of earlier loans. It was therefore incorrect simply to add up all the loan entries.

William's assertion that loans were made primarily to piano dealers was quickly demolished by Henry's attorneys, who showed that most loans were made to William's friends, Astoria business associates, and companies in which William himself was interested such as his East River Gas Light Company; the pitifully unsuccessful ivory dealer, F. Grote and Company, in which William invested heavily; the Bowery Bay Building and Improvement Company that developed the North Beach amusement park owned by William and brewer George Ehret; William's street railways and ferry; plus a long list of other firms, most of which had failed. The claim was made by William and others for the defense that the loans were profitable to Steinway & Sons because the firm was able, through its financial strength, to borrow money at lower rates than it lent to the various businesses. Another defense claim was that William himself guaranteed the loans, ensuring that the piano company would not take a loss but would profit from the interest rate spread. To modern sensibilities, the transactions do seem to be of a banking nature, but the remaining records are insufficient to assess if the greater truth lay with William or the defecting Henry W. T.

But the claims of the nephew-errant soon left the realm of the plausible and descended to the absurd. A close look at the nooks and crannies of the books revealed that Steinway & Sons had paid William's fines when he did not appear for jury duty. Amounting to less than two hundred dollars over ten years, according to the plaintiff these were "diversions of funds belonging to the company." Exception was also taken to a twelve-dollar floral bouquet for President Cleveland, the purchase of several books that contained paeans to William, and other small items, including a ten-dollar annual membership in the New York Historical Society. Also the subject of complaint were political donations to New York and Long Island City election campaigns. "That a manufacturing company should pay its President's jury fines and election expenses; that it should contribute to campaign funds; that it should buy autographs and flowers, and should take boxes at masked balls, is something so preposterous as to make comment not only superfluous but impossible. To let such things pass would be to hold that the moneys of a corporation are to be expended at the caprice and fancy of its directors, and that there are no rules governing the conduct of such officers in their management of its affairs," rumbled the brief for the plaintiff. Understandably, Henry W. T.'s lawyers did not provide a sum total for these transgressions. They amounted to $5,334.80 over a period of sixteen years or an average of about $333 per year. The alleged frivolities had cost Henry W. T. Steinway about twenty dollars per year between 1876 and 1891, during which period he had collected almost $200,000 in dividends.

Having worked themselves into an appropriate state of indignation, Henry's counselors then sank their legal teeth into yet another Steinway & Sons account, charities and donations, and with remarkable tenacity set forth page after page of Steinway & Sons' charitable contributions. "We assert," claimed the attorneys, "that in the first place Steinway & Sons have no right to contribute to this great extent to charities. . . . If this be allowed, there is no limit to the expenditures that may be made by careless or reckless trustees, and the only safe and proper course is to declare that contributions for public purposes must be made by individuals if they desire to contribute, and must not be made out of the corporate funds. . . . It is as dishonest for them as it is easy to obtain a reputation for liberality by subscribing generously to various public and charitable purposes moneys which are not theirs to give."

Apparently convinced that the sum of Steinway charitable donations was sufficient to appall the court with its mindless profligacy, the total contributions cited were given as $16,954.41, or an average of about $1,060 per year for sixteen years. Computed on the same basis as the objections to the "special expenses account," Henry W. T. had been deprived of about sixty-four dollars per year based on his roughly 6-percent ownership in the firm. The actual items showed a wide range of what would then have been called "noble" causes. There were donations to yellow fever sufferers, survivors of the Johnstown flood, school fairs, kindergartens, various monument committees, orphanages, medical causes, the Steinway Hose Company, the Steinway Union Church, and an absolutely ecumenical assemblage of faiths including Hebrew, Catholic, Lutheran, Presbyterian, Evangelical, and others. "Argument cannot be needed to show the grossly improper character of such conduct on the part of the trustees," claimed Henry's lawyers, who demanded that the trustees refund the charitable donations to the company. When Henry W. T. Steinway declared legal war on his family, neither widows nor orphans nor Men of God were to be shielded from the consequences.

The court was likewise asked to pass upon the propriety of other expenditures; there was, for example, the matter of $4.02 spent to repair a billiard table at the Steinway mansion, $2.00 for coachman's gloves, $46.00 for his livery, a whip, presumably for the coachman, and several other livery outfits. Besides suggesting that the official Steinway & Sons coachman was both well equipped and fashionably turned out and the admission of Henry's attorneys that the items were "almost ludicrous in their pettiness," they also served to "show a very serious fact, namely, that the moneys of Steinway & Sons were appropriated to the use of its President as if they had been his own private funds." The reaction of the Manhattan judge, used to dealing with murder, sundry mayhem, and miscellaneous defalcations involving millions of dollars, when confronted with these facts, is unknown. Addition in the time before electronic calculators being more arduous, the lawyers did not provide the total sum, which was $3,765.34, or an average of $235.33 per year allegedly diverted by William, who in the course thereof deprived his nephew of $14.35 per year. For most of those years young Henry W. T. Steinway lived at the mansion each summer season, enjoyed the services of the servants paid for by Uncle Bill, ate his meals and drank his beer, cruised on William's yacht, and otherwise enjoyed the baronial life style attendant with his name and position. These facts were not mentioned in the brief for the plaintiff.

After excoriating with particular severity the construction of a church, school, fire station, and kindergarten at Steinway, the brief went on to cite the "doubtful claims" on the books of Steinway & Sons. Here were found more "bad loans" to conductor Theodore Thomas, to pianist Franz Rummel and his wife, to pianist Rafael Joseffy, and to impressarios J. H. Mapleson, Abbey, Schoeffel and Grau, and theater manager Gustav Amberg. Involving famous names, many of these transactions and others like them received press notice during the trial.

During that trial William displayed both his talent for dealing with the media and considerable wit. Attorney Wheeler H. Peckham, chief counsel for the plaintiff, was reduced to the role of straight man in his examination of William. Zeroing in on the matter of campaign contributions, Peckham said to William, "I find an item here 'for campaign purposes.' What does that stand for?" Answered William, "We gave that in the cause of good government. We are as interested in good government as everybody else is." Sensing an opportunity, Peckham queried, "Ever give anything to Tammany Hall?" "That has nothing to do with the case," said William. "I want to know whether Steinway & Sons ever contributed to a Tammany Hall campaign fund," insisted Henry W. T.'s counsel. "I gave $200 when I was an Elector." "How about the Hewitt campaign?" "We gave the use of Steinway Hall and charged it to Steinway & Sons," said William. Unable to elicit any staggering admissions from his witness on Manhattan politics, Peckham shifted to Long Island City: "Did you contribute to the Long Island Campaign?" "Yes, we gave something." "Did you contribute on both sides?" William responded, "We were very much interested on both sides." The entire courtroom howled with laughter and, after a moment, William smiled as well, then said, "I guess I did not make myself clear, I didn't mean that we were interested on both sides in the Long Island City campaign, but on both sides of the East River."

Probing for something which William could not reduce to either triviality or hilarity, Peckham seized on a large cash disbursement of $1,450 listed as charity. "What does this mean?" demanded the lawyer. "That's a mistake," was William's answer. "That was money paid to Joseffy and was for 29 concerts at $50 each, at which he was to play the Steinway piano exclusively, and the programme was to state that these pianos were used at these concerts. That's the usual custom." "Do you always pay $50 when your pianos are used at concerts?" inquired Wheeler H. Peckham. "That depends," parried William, "on the persons using them. We wouldn't pay the greatest lawyer that ever lived five cents for using them." Even Judge Beekman joined in the general laughter that followed William's riposte, while Peckham forged forward grimly in search of something, anything, in the accounts that William Steinway could not blithely explain away.

The public posture of William was one thing and his private concerns another: "Papers have absurd and shameful reports of the suit, only the World has my declaration as to our dividends and nature of our business." On the stand William's nephew portrayed him as a manipulative martinet: "Harbuckle attacks the correctness of the minutes, saying that I dominated and designated generally a trustee to put a motion over. . . . The worst part is the sensational newspaper reporters who pick up items and without explanation publish them." The citizens of New York were receiving confirmation of that which even the least sophisticated undoubtedly suspected: artists did not select a piano *purely* on its merits. Loans, advances, gifts, astonishingly large fees—the fifty-dollar-per-concert fee verified by William was still an ample month's wages for many—were mandatory, as was a never-ending stream of emoluments. The shining visage that was the public face of Steinway & Sons was now revealed as blemished, if not grotesquely scarred, by crass commerce.

"The science of piano building," wrote pianist/teacher/critic Fanny Morris Smith in 1892, "has always seemed to me like a castle, a castle full of secret chambers to which no mortal has found the key. Over its door are chiseled mottos: Goethe's 'In every work of art all, even the smallest detail, depends on the conception.'. . ." Now lawyers using sledgehammers, not keys, demolished the doors to those chambers and portrayed them, when not empty, as warerooms for statues of Mammon.

"People are not wanting," continued Fanny Morris Smith, "who deny that such a castle exists. They aver that I saw only a monstrous factory upon whose grimy door was scrawled, 'No admission here except on business'; that the sages were a fat manufacturer, bedizened with diamonds the size of marrow-fat peas; an anxious salesman, and a glib advertising agent; that the manufacturer beckoned me aside and said, 'The foundation of the piano trade is the ignorance and helplessness of the public'; that the salesman whispered in my ear, 'The actual cost of manufacture is not the moiety of the price I ask; the large and profitable fraction depends but on the airy fabric of a name'; that the advertising agent gave me a handbill, upon which I read, 'The cheapest materials have the most money in them; the cheapest material for the manufacture of a first-class instrument is printer's ink.' Nonetheless, my castle exists."

Against Smith's exalted concepts were now set headlines such as "Cigarettes for Paderewski" in which it was revealed that Steinway & Sons had paid the amazing amount of $41.50 in support of the maestro's nicotine habit and had given a number of five- and ten-dollar payments to an Officer Callahan. "Judge Beekman said it was a matter of common knowledge that the artist who endorsed certain pianos did not do so for nothing," reported the *New York Times*. In the view of the plaintiff's attorney, avarice and corruption, not art, ruled the piano world, and the citizens of New York where one-fourth of all Steinways were sold could read in the daily papers the base details; William, ever sensitive to the slightest postural change in the social corpus, knew this was not good.

"William Steinway made a record yesterday as a witness," reported the *Times* on January 31, 1895. "Mr. Steinway showed the most wonderful memory for every event connected with his business during the last thirty-five years. He not only remembered the year and date, but the day, and in some instances could even tell the hour of certain events. Judge Beekman himself was astonished, and commented on the matter. Mr. Steinway smiled, saying: 'Yes, they used to call me the walking dictionary.' " Clearly, William had spent much time reviewing his diary, but this he did not reveal, even to that diary: "Judge and spectators are astounded at my marvelous memory," was the entry for that day. William's specific remembrances were the perfect offset to his nephew's testimony. "Harbuckle helps himself out of the scrape by constantly saying I cannot recollect, that may be," wrote William. Attorney Cotterill labored hard to neutralize the acids of the picayune and pecuniary poured on the Steinway legend by his adversaries: "This is a most remarkable case. It is insincerely brought on the part of the plaintiff, because there has not been shown one instance where the investments of the Trustees has not been beneficial and productive of large dividends." For Cotterill, the case was also productive of large legal fees; he was to be paid twenty-five thousand dollars for his defense, and his remarks helped him earn it: "Compare these persons, the plaintiff and the principal defendant here, Mr. William Steinway, the one is an obstructionist and the other sacrificing his health for the good of the business he founded, and which he has made the most successful in the world." William's generosity was officially entered into the record, and George Cotterill claimed that in the last three years William had "expended $100,000 of his own money for the good of the business, and none of this large sum was ever charged to the corporation." He had also, Cotterill noted, given twenty thousand dollars of his own funds to help the World's Fair at Chicago. Cotterill and William then delved into the minutiae of the Steinway & Sons accounts, justifying expenses, dollar by dollar and penny by penny. The next day the case was declared closed, and Judge Beekman called for briefs.

Fifteen months passed before Judge Beekman rendered his decision. In the interim an appeal was decided on Henry's first suit alleging improprieties in the conduct of the *fabrik*. The word came one day after William's triumphant celebration of his spurious sixtieth birthday: "Glorious news that Appellate Division of Supreme Court (all five judges concurring) dismissed Harbuckle appeal with costs. . . . Everybody seems glad that the black sheep of the family has been downed so effectively," enthused William to the diary.

Judge Beekman also dismissed Henry W. T.'s suit with costs, and William observed that the judge "bashes him fearfully." The opinion, however, was a model of dispassionate jurisprudence that systematically disassembled and demolished the plaintiff's claims. "It is proper to state at the outset," wrote Judge Beekman, "that the issues in this action do not involve any charge of fraud," thereby immediately restoring William's reputation. The Astoria development gave to the employees of Steinway & Sons "conditions and influences of exceptional advantage to them and their families . . . thus promoting better and more permanent service on their part." The church, school, library, and bath were useful "in the development of the best industrial results." The policy of the company was "a wise one, and apart from its moral aspects has contributed materially to the resources of the corporation." There were no *ultra vires* to be found in Astoria, and the judge was apparently unwilling to outlaw company towns in New York State since "a policy such as this, intelligently and liberally executed, might reasonably be expected to insure the continued and faithful services of a skilled and contented body of operatives."

On the variety of protested expenditures and accounts, the judge wrote, "I think the plaintiff expressly or tacitly approved of or acquiesced in them and has thereby made them his own." Henry W. T. had supervised the laying of streets, had contributed to the library, and had served as a church trustee. Such acts disqualified him from complaining of these matters at a later date. "The plaintiff is not in the position of an ordinary stockholder. He was . . . intimately acquainted with everything which was done," opined the judge. Beekman also noted that Henry W. T. showed "his confidence in the management of the company" when he purchased more stock in 1891 just a few months before his resignation. As to William and the other trustees, "there is not a single scintilla of evidence showing that they have ever abused the confidence reposed in them or that they have used their position as majority shareholders to oppress, defraud or impose upon the minority.

"We are entitled to consider results as evidence of the success of policies and methods. What the results have been in this case is shown by the great and profitable expansion of business which has marked the history of this corporation from its inception," wrote the Supreme Court Justice. Not even deigning to mention the mean-spirited exceptions taken to Steinway charity donations, Judge Beekman swept to a devastating observation: "If it had not been for a rupture of the friendly relations . . . growing out of circumstances not connected with the matters in this suit . . . it may well be doubted whether this action would ever have been brought. . . . The defendants are entitled to judgment dismissing the complaint on the merits, with costs." William's management was vetted by the law and found to be not merely adequate, but laudatory.

Henry W. T. Steinway appealed, of course, and the matter remained in the higher courts for several years. Ultimately, the appeal was withdrawn and, in the language of the law, "judgment was entered for the defendants." But by that time the defendant William Steinway was dead. Henry W. T. Steinway outlived his Uncle Bill and both his brothers, Charles and Fred, by decades. He never returned to the piano business and led a life of leisure far from public view funded by his Steinway & Sons dividends. His home was on 118th Street in Manhattan, but his passion was fishing, and Henry W. T. had ample time to pursue it. In his eighty-third year he died of pneumonia while on a fishing trip at Henderson Harbor, New York, a hamlet on the shores of Lake Ontario. He had been going to that place for four decades, and a waitress remembered that Henry W. T. Steinway was a difficult man who would send his morning toast back if it were not properly burnt. And so it is seen that, like other Steinways, Henry W. T. was a man who demanded that things be done as they should be.

The "black sheep" had no contact with his family and he never married. In the early 1920s Henry sold his Steinway & Sons shares to his brothers. He did not attend family funerals, nor weddings, and the family did not appear at Henry's funeral. Young Steinways born after his departure from the firm did not even know of "Uncle Henry's" existence. Henry W. T. left an estate valued at about two million dollars. Of that, only ten thousand went to a Steinway; William's son by his second marriage, William R., was the honored legatee. The majority of the estate was bequeathed to two male friends who received a "life interest." After their deaths, the trust fund created was to pass to Lenox Hill Hospital. But the old-timers who read that news in the *Staats-Zeitung* in July 1939 likely still knew Lenox Hill by its original name: The German Hospital.

Four years and four decades earlier, Harbuckle had smashed his Uncle Bill's hopes of a pacific later life free, in William's words, of "troubles, vexations and excitements." But his trials at law would prove, in perspective, to be but minor annoyances. For William, the real tragedies were elsewhere in his beloved family.

Chapter 25

THE PECCANT PIANOMAKER OF NEW YORK

"It is well known that the professional pursuit of music stirs up all the basest passions of our nature," pronounced a *New York Times* editorialist in 1893, "and that the discordant and inharmonious tempers of musicians extend themselves to practitioners of the music trades as well as of the musical art. There has never been a World's Fair yet that was not followed by a 'piano war.' The Columbian Exposition seems likely to prove an exception, but that will be because the war is fought before the fair begins, and because there will be no pianos worth talking about at the exhibition."

A Victorian world's fair without the pianos of Steinway, Chickering, Weber, and Knabe, et alia, was as inconceivable as a fair lacking steam engines, but this was precisely the condition which was emerging, much to the consternation of editorial writers in many major cities. The World's Columbian Exhibition commemorating the quadricentennial of the discovery of America was scheduled to open on May 1, 1893, the tardiness being caused by congressional fumbling of the designation of a site for the fair. At the conclusion of the deliberations of that great body, Chicago was selected over New York, and to show his liberal spirit, William, who was chairman of the finance committee for the New York site, donated twenty-five thousand dollars to the Chicago fair. In recognition of his beneficence, he was given a testimonial dinner and a tour of the Chicago rapid transit system. The good will between New York and Chicago soon proved transient.

Some months before the fair opened a fair official named John Thacher announced a scheme for judging exhibits, which he, at least, considered far superior to the venerable practice of gathering from distant reaches of the civilized world leading experts of stellar and unsullied reputation and then bribing them. In Mr. Thacher's scheme there would be but *one* judge. This was proposed on the theory that a single individual would be more accountable and there would be no dissembling by committees. The one brave man nominated to decide the commercial future of American pianomakers at the fair was Dr. Florenz Ziegfeld, head of the Chicago Musical College, whose son would later become famous for his Broadway productions. As a folly, few events would exceed the impending piano war.

To understand the loathing with which the one-judge proposal was regarded by eastern pianomakers, Steinway among them, it is necessary to delve into the commercial history of the industry. Joseph P. Hale's demonstration of the existence of a vast market for inexpensive pianos in the West led, particularly after Hale died, to the growth of indigenous manufacturing capacity in Illinois, Ohio, Michigan, and elsewhere. Such manufacturers had the advantage of lower freight charges, easier access to their markets due to proximity, and, in many areas, a labor force that was both less costly and less rebellious than in New York.

In Cincinnati there was the D. H. Baldwin Company, founded by Dwight Hamilton Baldwin, who started a music store there at age forty-two after a peripatetic career as Presbyterian Sunday school and music teacher. After opening music stores in several cities, Baldwin became a jobber for New York pianomakers including Decker, Steck, Steinway, and the inexpensive and not entirely reputable products of the Fischer Brothers. Baldwin's retail empire was as much financial as it was musical. He was a pioneer in "hire-purchase," a form of installment buying pioneered by Singer to sell sewing machines. With a modest amount down, the buyer signed a contract to make monthly payments by mail to Baldwin headquarters; the title was held by Baldwin until the instrument was completely paid off, and the dealer was remitted each month some 25 to 35 percent of the payment. Dealers were provided stock on consignment, giving Baldwin an extraordinary control over both dealers and buyers. In 1887 William removed Baldwin as a Steinway distributor and gave his territory to another agent. Before long Baldwin was in the pianomaking business with a line of instruments at various price points, as well as manufacturing several lines of reed organs.

Baldwin was only one of many who mined the western markets. In Richmond, Indiana, was located the Starr company; in New Castle, Indiana, was French & Sons; while Story & Clark operated from Grand Haven, Michigan. The Schiller Piano Company, so named by its organizer Frederick Lane to impart a suitably Germanic flavor to the product, produced sizeable numbers of instruments in Oregon, Illinois. But the new western trade had its center of gravity in Chicago, where cheap pianos by the thousands poured from the works of John V. Steger, who adopted the stencil methods of Hale and, most significantly, William Wallace Kimball. Kimball, after many years of distributing Hale's pianos, took up manufacturing in 1882, and by the time of the World's Fair was among the largest, if not the largest, of the Chicago makers. While the quality of Kimball's output may be disputed, there is no question that his pianos were cheap and intended to be sold in the largest possible volume. In the trade terms of the time, Kimball made "commercial" pianos. These were distinguished from "artistic" pianos from Steinway, Decker, Steck, Weber, Chickering, and Knabe. When issuing from the lips of a proponent of "artistic" pianos, the word *commercial* was the most withering of condemnations. Of course, commercial manufacturers mimicked, to the extent possible, the sales techniques and pretensions of their artistic brethren. Kimball had a small hall in Chicago in which recitals were given, and a few endorsements were cadged from time to time. One notable Kimball endorser was the vocalist Adelina Patti, who had earlier endorsed Steinway. Patti was promiscuous in her approvals and later earned the sobriquet Testimonial Patti. To buyers this mattered not.

For William, the prospect of competing for medals in a world's fair against cheap pianos made by the erstwhile distributor of Hale's despised instruments must have been a distasteful one indeed, but the fact soon emerged that Dr. Ziegfield's Chicago Musical College had on its board of directors one W.W. Kimball. The implied relationship between Ziegfeld and Kimball, and Ziegfeld's long residency in Chicago, gave rise to further fears of regional parochialism, and they were not William's alone.

"All the piano manufacturers in the East are disgusted with the management of the World's Fair," reported the *Times*. "Steinway & Co. yesterday sent a letter to the World's Fair authorities stating that their application for space was withdrawn and that they would not make any exhibit. This action was rather surprising to the piano trade, because William Steinway had been very friendly to the fair. He gave $25,000 as a subscription to aid it." Nahum Stetson spoke for the house: "We are not unpatriotic, nor do we wish to do anything that would put ourselves in a position unfriendly to the fair . . . but we felt that we could not make the exhibit we would like to make in view of the small allotment of space to us. Then, too, we object to the manner of making awards which will be pursued by the fair authorities."

Just three days later, with both Steinway and Chickering already announced, another fifteen firms withdrew from the fair after a meeting of the Piano Manufacturers of New York was held at Steinway Hall. Decker Brothers, Weber, George Steck, Mathushek & Son, Hazleton Brothers, and Lindeman & Sons were among the venerable makers boycotting the exposition. All this was, of course, purely coincidental, averred Stetson, who told the *Times* that "each firm acted individually. You understand.

The association has no business and no desire to dictate to the World's Fair managers in any way. . . . We don't want to hurt the fair or seem opposed to it, or anything of that kind."

The *Times* imperiously predicted the outcome: "The pianos of Peoria and Keokuk and Oshkosh will sound much better when they are not compared with the pianos of Boston, Baltimore and New York. In the absence of these effete instruments the wild and wooly pianos of the West will take all the prizes, and its makers may persuade the farmers' daughters of the Northwest that it is 'equally as good' as the instruments preferred by pianists. It is true that what ought to be one of the most attractive departments of the exhibition will lose its interest. But what is that to a lively Western pianomaker or to a committeeman of awards with a fixed idea?" Ultimately, the eastern boycott remained firm, and W. W. Kimball won the high awards, not only for pianos but for reed organs and portable pipe organs. These were bestowed not by Dr. Ziegfeld alone, but by a four-man committee of judges to which the director general had ultimately capitulated. Predictably, the traditional allegations of bribery erupted and caused several more exhibitors to attempt unsuccessfully to withdraw.

The actual competition was a flaccid anticlimax to the maelstrom of conflict that engulfed East and West before the fair opened. Into its vortex were drawn the two most prominent names in American music, known even to the farmers' daughters mocked by the *Times*. One was Theodore Thomas, the renowned former conductor of the New York Philharmonic, whose relationship with Steinway began nearly three decades before when the struggling Mason-Thomas Quartet played at the new Steinway warerooms on Fourteenth Street. It continued for many years during which the Theodore Thomas Orchestra challenged the Philharmonic for hegemony over Manhattan high culture and was also the resident symphony at Steinway Hall with national tours underwritten by Steinway & Sons. William also endured Thomas's abortive efforts to promote the construction of a competing music hall, tolerated his occasional defections to Chickering's venue, and lent the maestro large sums of money—roughly $125,000 in today's currency—that were never repaid. Whether William's enduring forbearance and largesse influenced the maestro to take a position in support of the artist's right to choose his own instrument, including a Steinway, will never be known, for Theodore Thomas was capable of what might be charitably described as independent action and frequently demonstrated a pointed disdain for commercial realities.

While Thomas's star had long glowed in the cultural sky, the other actor drawn into the conflict was that luminescent nova, Ignace Jan Paderewski. At Thomas's request Paderewski had agreed to perform at the opening concerts of the exhibition without charge. When word of this musical gift to America reached the western pianomen, they found in it precisely the weapon they needed to punish the eastern boycotters. A decree issued from exposition management that performance on a piano not exhibited was prohibited. Under this rule, if Paderewski were to perform, he would have to do so on a western piano.

Thomas, in ardent support of artistic freedom, argued that a performer had the right to play the instrument of his choosing. There was a certain practical sensibility to this, for many members of his orchestra would have been forced to change personal instruments were the rule extended beyond pianos. For his position Thomas was calumniated, the *Chicago Herald* snarling that "he should have been the leader of a barrack band in a mountainous camp in North Germany," and that Thomas was "a small despot by nature. . . . He is rough-shod; that with hood of hussar he tries to ride down all that is opposed to his vanity, his selfishness and his caprices." Attacks on Thomas were not confined to the West. In New York the *Musical Courier*, normally friendly to Steinway interests due to extensive advertising, howled that "there are some men interested in music who refuse to enter into any possible contact with Theodore Thomas, simply as a matter of taste and self-respect."

The blowtorch of defamation soon pointed in Paderewski's direction, and the *New York World*, a mass-circulation daily specializing in lively illustrated accounts of mayhem and murder, accused the "human chrysanthemum" of cravenly selling himself to a piano company. The charge of pianistic prostitution shattered Paderewski's silence, and he wrote the *World* that he did not understand "why I should be forced to play an instrument of manufacturer strange to me and untried by me, which might jeopardize my artistic success." Paderewski's plea for enlightenment was accompanied by a short message from Steinway & Sons stating that they had no contract of any kind and Mr. Paderewski was "at liberty to follow his artistic inclinations" in choice of an instrument.

In the strictest legal sense, there was no contract between Steinway and Paderewski. The agreement was betwixt *Charles Tretbar* and the pianist and was merely guaranteed financially by the corporation. The regulating document plainly stated that I. J. Paderewski would play no other instrument but a Steinway. Such a clause was usually interpreted as an ironclad prohibition covering not only public performances but rehearsals, hotel practice pianos, and even pianos in private homes. Prior piano wars with Weber and Knabe had confirmed the need for such a construction, for even a chord idly struck on a competitive piano in a hotel lobby could trigger tales of defection and preference. The words from the master, though disingenuous at best, placated many.

As the opening day of the Columbian Exposition drew near, there was still no resolution of the issue of Paderewski's piano. The maestro sat in his private railway car in Chicago, his needs well tended by a staff consisting of several secretaries, a chef, and a piano tuner. The great Paderewski piano question oozed through the exhibition bureaucracy, a no-man's-land of paid and volunteer committees with conflicting and overlapping jurisdictions and uncertain hierarchy, each with its own agenda. The day before the scheduled concert "the Council of Administration of the World's Columbian Exhibition held a meeting. . . . It was determined that pending a final decision in the matter Paderewski should be permitted to use his favorite instrument at tomorrow's concert," said a wire service report. As the words pulsed east across the wires, the insurgent Steinway was already in the exposition's music hall.

The next day 175,000 persons stood in the mud of the unfinished fairgrounds to see Grover Cleveland officially open the exhibition. The five thousand voices and 120 instruments massed by Theodore Thomas for the opening ceremonies could scarcely be heard above the din of a crowd so tightly packed that women who fainted were passed overhead to the assembly's edges where police or soldiers revived them or trundled them away to a first-aid station. That night Paderewski played his concerto with the Thomas Orchestra despite an infected finger. The unfinished and unheated hall had the acoustic of a tunnel and the temperature of a meat locker. Under such conditions there were no artistic triumphs, but there was a clear commercial victor.

The *Times*, striving mightily to turn the beacon of rationality on events, summarized the four-month piano battle of 1893 in a column-long editorial entitled "Art and Hustlers," as if there were some ready distinction between the two. "Though undoubtedly a hustler, the Western businessman . . . does not seem to be a sage. If he were, he would consider that by his, the hustler's own hysterical action, the peccant pianomaker of New-York has already got more advertising out of the exhibition than all the pianomakers who are represented in it, and has indeed produced the far more valuable impression that his piano is the only one upon which a pianist of the first rank will consent to perform. . . . If the hustler had kept quiet, comparatively few people would have known or cared what piano Paderewski played."

The editorialist carefully, sometimes awkwardly, avoided mentioning Steinway by name; but in the spring of 1893 any person in America who read the newspapers *knew* what piano Paderewski preferred. Any ordinarily sentient American knew that Paderewski played a Steinway as well as he or she knew that Grover Cleveland was president of the United States. The implantation of this fact deep in the public consciousness was William Steinway's greatest triumph. In so doing he rebalanced the artistic equation and added a third and crucial variable.

When William was young, a piano virtuoso was one who played his own compositions. This was the time of De Meyer and Herz and Gottschalk. In the slow sweep of time, virtuosity was redefined, and the *executant* who could powerfully interpret the works of other masters as well as his own became the operating norm. Though there were antecedents, the Steinway-sponsored tour of Anton Rubinstein marked the emergence of this definition of virtuosity in America. But these were dyads; an artist and a composer were all that were necessary. The Battle of the Columbian Exposition transformed the dyad into triad: virtuosity was now redefined as artist, composer, and piano. The *instrumentenmacher* was propelled from the wings to a coequal position on the stage, an integral part of the virtuosic equation.

There were foreshadowings of this. Fanny Morris Smith wrote of Stradivarius and Steinway, weaving in the mind a linkage between two legends. Rhapsodically invoking science through the names of Huygens, Chladni, Laplace, and Helmholtz, she firmly fastened Steinway to the empirical and its ultimate test, progress. That which had gone before was less: "The Boston school [e.g., Chickering] could not satisfy a nation that worshipped the lusty genius of Beethoven and Wagner," wrote Smith. There was more: *"Every true piano springs from an ideal of beauty, is a revelation of natural laws, and as such embodies and expresses the personality of its creator,"* italicized the essayist. A Steinway was not merely a piano; as a *"true piano"* it was the supreme convergence of artistic perception, scientific knowledge, and the noble labor of man. Fanny Morris Smith draped the *instrumentenmacher* with the noblest ideals of her time and pushed him into the spotlight. She had done unknowingly and guilelessly what twentieth-century marketeers dream of doing but accomplish only rarely: she had invested a *product* with ideals and aspirations shared by millions. A Steinway was not a piano; it was a symbolic object, a totem, an icon of culture.

But without a player this icon was mute, so the new piano needed a new virtuoso, one whose excellence was also unparalleled. That role was to be filled by Paderewski. William Mason, the wizened dean of American pianists and pedagogues, invoked his conversations with Moscheles and Liszt about Beethoven in a learned essay about Paderewski that implied a player of unprecedented virtuosity. Mason was but one of many critics who composed paeans to the Polish master. He wrote, "It seems to me that in this matter of touch Paderewski is as near perfection as any pianist I have ever heard, while in other respects he stands more nearly on the plane of Liszt." After riffling through a long list of pianistic luminaries, both European and American, Mason continued, "While fully recognizing the high artistic merit of all these . . . it may be said without invidious distinction that an artist of such a distinctly pronounced individuality as Paderewski is an exceedingly rare occurrence—indeed phenomenal." The opinions of the connoisseurs on Paderewski, his piano, and his music were positive; missing were the means to transmit to the many the recondite views of the cognoscenti—the notion that the virtuosic dyad had become a triad.

Beneath Steinway a plethora of piano producers in the West had grown like a pyramid emerging from the earth. At its top there was still Steinway & Sons. In terms undreamt then, a "product differentiation" took place. The Columbian Exhibition piano war provided proof for all to see that a "true virtuoso" would only play a "true piano," and, because there could only be one truth, that piano was a Steinway. So Steinway & Sons rose above the pyramid, a part of it, yet distinct, like the eye above the pyramid on a dollar bill. The many now knew what only a few had believed just four months earlier. For the millions who did not ponder the subtleties of such things, the *Times* summarized for William Steinway: "His piano is the only one upon which a pianist of the first rank will consent to perform." Thus the dyad became triad.

These events cannot be apportioned between design and serendipity, the stochastic and the causal, the opportunistic and the strategic. William himself did not go to Chicago; he dispatched his proxies. First it was Charles Tretbar, who travelled west after William received a telegram from Theodore Thomas, contents now unknown. On the scene for the opening of the exposition, and presumably supervising the final hours of the ultimately successful Steinway insurgency, were nephew Charles and Nahum Stetson. William, in fact, did not leave his Gramercy Park home. This was not a matter of choice, for from February 1893 through August that year William Steinway could not walk and could not even leave his bed for many weeks; he was immobilized by "inflammatory rheumatism upon chronic gout."

William, who had been suffering with the malady for more than twenty years, consumed a pharmacopoeia of oils, elixirs, analgesics, and miscellaneous liquids, solids, and powders in the search for relief, all to no avail. In later years he spent summers at European and American spas, soaking in springs and seeking relief. A succession of doctors applied the latest medical technology, including electrical stimulation of his legs and Roentgen's newly discovered X rays, all to no avail.

While gout was correctly known in William's time to be causally related to an excess of uric acid in the body, the condition was thought to be a consequence of lifestyle. "If inadequate exercise be combined with a luxurious manner of living, with habitual overindulgence in animal food and rich dishes, and especially in alcoholic beverages, undoubtedly the chief factors in the production of the disease are present," intoned the authoritative ninth edition of the *Encyclopaedia Britannica*. At 225 pounds and a height of five feet, six inches according to his consular papers, and five feet, seven inches by William's own measurement, he might have reasonably been suspected of "habitual overindulgence," at least by modern standards. In later years William modulated his prodigious appetite for *lagerbier*; as a younger Liederkranzer he wrote that he drank twenty glasses in one evening and on another occasion drained two kegs in the undoubtedly jolly company of a few friends. Fellowship, song, and beer were the essentials at Liederkranz gatherings, and for many years William was at the club almost every night. In so doing, he was likely ignoring medical advice, as he did in another aspect, discounting "the depressing consequences of overwork, either physical or intellectual," which were believed by Victorian authorities to contribute to the disease. William's habit of "working like a beaver," as he put it, and laboring Sundays and holidays, including Christmas and New Year's Day, would have been frowned on by his many doctors.

"My hand swells and pains, Jones' medicine don't seem to help me," wrote William on January 19, 1893, and the next day, "I suffer great pain. My left elbow affected in addition to my badly swollen left hand." The world's most renowned pianomaker was entering an epoch of agony and nearly total debilitation. The pain slithered into his shoulders, and his back muscles cramped. By the fourth day sleep was impossible, and in the second week a fever appeared, consuming William's appetite. "Unable to move," wrote William on February 9, 1893. Though Paderewski had visited earlier, William's visitors now ebbed to the essential. The next day Stetson appeared, and they discussed the fair's "obnoxious award system to be forced on exhibitors." That same day Steinway & Sons withdrew from the exhibition by letter, and both the trade and general press bubbled with reports and comment. In his 105-degree fevered anguish William was oblivious to this, his feet, knees, hands, and shoulders shiny red, dry, and hot with the external signals of gout. More than two weeks of sleepless suffering passed before he noted the "great excitement in the trade about our withdrawal from the Chicago fair." By then, at least sixteen other eastern pianomakers had also withdrawn.

It was the end of February before William was lifted from his bed by the two nurses in twenty-four-hour attendance: "Sat up in a chair for an hour & suffer great pain in the knees."

"At 3 A.M. today my wife came to my bed, seriously ill. She was out yesterday in Carriage making many Visits, getting wet feet & taking a cold bath in evg.," wrote William from his bed on the first of March. William sent his nurse for the family physician, a Dr. Satterlee. With his wife clearly very sick the next day, three doctors were called, as was Richard Ranft, William's brother-in-law, who also lived in the city. There was, the doctors said, no hope, and William became "almost crazy with excitement and grief" at the prospect of Ellie's now certain death. On March fourth William "passed a sleepless night. Doctors tell me that my wife's kidneys have not acted for two days and that she will die within a few hours. At noon she becomes unconscious, and at 3 P.M. dies, peacefully, without once having realized her danger, without pain. I am almost stupefied by this terrible misfortune, and cry together with Rd. Ranft jr. her brother."

The next day was William's birthday, and as the congratulatory cables poured in, William lay supine under the triple blankets of irony, pain, and grief when "my Willie, Theodore and Maud with bouquets of flowers come with Fraulein to my bed. I am seized with so terrible an attack of despair on seeing my beloved, now motherless children, that I feel my blood stop in my veins, and am carried to the brink of death. Nurse Brooks at once gives me stimulants, when at last I am able to weep and sob for quite awhile. The shock has literally lamed my body and limbs."

The doctors performed an autopsy on Elizabeth Ranft Steinway and found that at age thirty-nine she "had Bright's disease of the kidneys, her heart fatty degeneration, her liver affected and gallstones in her gall bladder," recorded her husband, "so that Ellie, who was never sick a day in her life, could not possibly have lived two months longer under the most favorable circumstances." William took solace in the medical facts: "This quiets me somewhat, and the fact that she died without pain, and as it were with a smile on her face, rather than a lingering painful illness consoles me to a certain extent."

At 3:00 P.M. the day after William's birthday the funeral was held at the Gramercy Park home. By request there were no flowers. Only family members were admitted, and Pastor Krusi, who spoke at Steinway funerals over a span of nearly three decades, addressed the survivors of the deceased. For William, this summoned sorrows past, and he "suffered dreadfully on hearing his voice." The remains of Elizabeth Ranft Steinway were transported to the family mausoleum at Greenwood Cemetery, and there the Liederkranz sang; but it is likely that William did not witness his wife's interment, for the next day he wrote that he was "still quite prostrated and dare not see my children for fear of breaking down."

The children of the second marriage, the oldest, William R., less than twelve, were soon under the care of Paula, William's daughter from his first marriage. She, her husband Louis von Bernuth, and the grandchildren moved into William's home to "assume the conducting & management of the house." William Steinway then did what was expected of him: one week after his wife's death he presided over a Rapid Transit Commission meeting from his bed and passed "an important resolution" regulating route extensions of the city's elevated railways. This required the assent of all the commissioners, and for the occasion William's bedroom was filled with newsmen.

A *Times* reporter described the scene: "The visiting commissioners found Mr. Steinway propped up in bed. He welcomed them warmly. . . . After about an hour he called upon his attendants to remove his props and let him down flat upon the bed. In this new position he manifested as much interest in the proceedings as before." The next day William noted that all the English-language papers "have long articles" on the meeting. Evidence that he had not lost either his power or the ability to make news was apparently therapeutic. The day after, William was able to sit in the reception room for two hours using what he called his "invalid wagon," and two weeks after Ellie's death he was well enough to have "a number of visitors."

But William Steinway was not yet a well man. It was two more weeks before he could raise his feet, and that basic move precipitated great pain.

A week later William fell from his invalid wagon, and the extent of his disability became clear: "Wagon tips over to front, throwing me heavily forwards, badly wrenching and straining my knees and feet. Paula, L.v.B. and Mr. Burke replace me in the wagon with much difficulty." The effort to lift 225 inert pounds the one and one-half feet to the wagon by two men and one woman, as well as the agony for William, were left unstated.

A masseur was added to the staff of two nurses, and William received not only injections and pills but regular massage. After a month of this therapy, or perhaps despite it, he began to practice walking with crutches, and after five days he was able to take a few steps. Just as William struggled to his feet, the American economy crashed in another panic. In early June 1893, one month after he had started to use his crutches, William was able to travel into the next room. By this time commercial activity in the nation was nearly as crippled as William Steinway.

Following the typical pattern, the Panic of 1893 was marked in the public consciousness by the failure of a large firm, this time the National Cordage Company in New Jersey, then a haven for trusts due to its very accommodating corporation laws. The cordage trust was caught in a tight money market and was unable to refinance its short-term loans. Supposedly capitalized at $25,000,000, the trust was unable to satisfy a $50,000 loan. Trading as high as $147 per share just six months before, Cordage closed at $18 the day it announced receivership and triggered another Wall Street panic.

There was other bad news on the front pages that day as well. Paderewski, almost totally depleted by his World's Fair experience, played another concert in New York. There the chain-smoking maestro was pelted with hundreds of handkerchiefs and bouquets from admirers, the more aggressive of whom climbed upon the stage in a display of affection. When he fled the lights after three encores, another clutch of admiring females ambushed the master in his dressing room. Bolting that group, he was again intercepted at his carriage. Life as prey for the gentler sex took its toll that day, and Paderweski was heard to exclaim that he would shoot himself before he played again. "The performer was in a state bordering nervous hysteria," commented the *Times*, which then reported that Paderewski "had broken down under the strain to which he has been subjected of late." Thursday, May 4, 1893, was the day that both the New York worlds of art and commerce were shaken to their foundations.

Of the two events, the "Industrial Panic" on Wall Street was perhaps the more serious, and financial commentators called the crash the worst since 1873. Any adult in middle age knew well that the Panic of 1873 was followed by almost seven years of "business depression" with business and bank failures numbering in the tens of thousands. The spiral of fear had begun, and by midsummer William noted that short-term interest rates had reached an astonishing 50 percent. Runs on banks were not long in developing, and money became even tighter. The business cycle had actually peaked in January of 1893, and there were great concerns over the effects of what was known as "bimetallism." Under the Sherman Compromise Silver Act of 1890, Congress ordered the Treasury to buy and circulate over four million ounces of new silver each month to placate western populist and agrarian interests who felt they were starved of both cash and credit by eastern financial interests popularly known as "Goldbugs." By 1893 faith in the soundness of the dollar was badly shaken, and William, who was an ardent advocate of "sound money" and against "free silver," ruefully witnessed the financial debacle from the confines of 26 Gramercy Park. Debilitating illness and the death of his wife were now compounded by a cold fear of the future.

For the Steinways, this panic seemed somehow different; economic paroxysms had always elicited concern during their forty years in business, but the Panic of 1893 precipitated stark terror. When the trustees met at William's home that summer, the minutes reflected an almost desolate fear: "Mr. Chas. H. Steinway explained that the financial crisis and severe stringency of money for several months past prevailing all over the United States had also greatly affected Steinway & Sons. That sales were reduced to almost nothing, that many of our largest dealers were not able to meet their maturing obligations to us, compelling us to not only grant them renewals, but they actually had to be helped with loans in order to enable them to avoid failure, and thereby inflicting heavy losses on us." In sum, Steinway was selling no pianos but was still continuing to make more. Its dealers were not only unable to pay for the pianos they already had, but they were asking the family for cash so that they could keep their doors open. There was, however, a solution. Mortgages were taken on the New York factory and on Steinway Hall. The cash was used for payrolls and aid to dealers, not the least of which were the Steinway-owned stores such as Lyon, Potter & Company in Chicago, and others in Saint Louis and Philadelphia.

It was a brave act. Most of the New York trade had laid off its men and closed the factory doors to wait out the financial storm. Chickering was at the abyss, and a number of smaller firms had failed. Nationwide, assets of firms failing in the first six months of the year were nearly quadruple those of the year before, and the actual dollar value of failures was half-again higher than at the same time in the last major panic in 1884.

Borrowing to continue production was no sure bet, nor was lending as the borrower of last resort to weak dealers, and by the end of the year 1893 Steinway & Sons held as inventory a full year's worth of piano production. "President Cleveland's message calls for free silver repeal," wrote William. Cleveland convened a special session of Congress to deliver his message, but the psychological effect was as short-lived as Congress's action was dilatory. "Financial situation simply dreadful," wrote William, the same day in August that he left his home for the first time since January. In a heavy rain he rode in his carriage through Central Park, and William felt that he "could stand it quite well."

But financial pressures soon kept William in the house. In a conference with Charles, Stetson, and Potter from Chicago about how to keep Lyon, Potter & Company afloat, William became "so nervous and excited that I cannot drive out to Central Park." Just two days later he chanced across a photograph of Ellie; ironically, it was their wedding anniversary, and William began "vividly thinking of my wife's sudden death. . . . Feel quite sad." He was soon contemplating how his wife "had quite literally sacrificed herself in nursing me day and night."

Not a man to sink for long into torpid despair, William mounted his first excursion to Astoria in nine months. By carriage he went through the park to Ninety-second Street, crossed on the Steinway ferry, and continued to the mansion. The motivation for the journey was the annual Steinway & Sons employee picnic, an institution for nearly three decades. To William, these events must have had great meaning. Few among the employees had seen William in three seasons, and he recorded that he "was received with immense enthusiasm." Energized by his employees, he worked all day Sunday for the first time since January, only to sink into a swamp of anxiety a few days later: "I worry very much over the [financial] situation and the fact that my mistaken liberality to other people has so denuded me of ready cash."

Physically, William was recuperating. He had discarded the invalid wagon and was soon to trade his crutches for two canes with which he found that he could walk slowly on level surfaces. By Christmas he was able to take joy in the fact that his infant grandson, William Steinway von Bernuth, would grab the crutch William still sometimes used and walk alongside his grandfather.

In his annual New Year's Eve summary of the twelve months past, William called the year 1893 "a most terrible one. . . . Our withdrawal from the Chicago Columbian Fair kept me in constant excitement . . . fearful [financial] losses . . . all of which I had to make good in cash." Business conditions were still "dreadfully depressed," but William took pride in the fact that Steinway & Sons results, though poor, were "far beyond and above any record for 1893 which any of our competitors in the United States could show." The house had not only survived but was, "in fact, the only Establishment which kept open and worked every day." Against the death of his wife, his continuing disability, and the personal financial losses, these were small things, but William listed them with seeming satisfaction.

Though William could not know it, the peaks in both his own life and the business in his lifetime were behind him. The 2,513 American pianos sold in 1892 would not be exceeded until the turn of the century. Vanishing with the sales records were the immense profits and dividends. The family would never again keep as profits three of every ten dollars in sales as they did in 1891 while paying themselves almost another dollar in salaries and bonuses. Though Paderewski would return to America to play Steinways almost every year, he did not reignite the sales explosion of his premiere. William, brilliant as he was at auguries of the distant future, did not recognize this, and he continued not only to spend but to borrow immense sums to support his reticulum of investments.

The "deposits" of family members that H.W.T. Steinway forced off the books of the corporation in his lawsuits alleging mismanagement were apparently assumed by William; it is unknown if the "depositors," mostly women in the extended family, knew or cared precisely where their money was. Was not William the apotheosis of all things Steinway? That he himself thought so is beyond doubt. Wall Street crashed, trusts collapsed, banks failed, and insurance companies were consumed in conflagrations of worthless paper. Steinway & Sons, now an American legend and a money machine for four decades, had, in fact, survived a string of panics in remarkably strong condition. In that worst of years, 1893, a dividend of 10 percent was declared, and the stockholders received another $200,000, about $3 million today. William believed, based on four decades of experience, that business conditions would soon improve.

But they did not, and Steinway & Sons sales recovered only slightly from the year 1893. This did not apparently trouble William, for he had experienced the Great Depression of the 1870s and knew that even in the poorest of times Americans bought pianos, large numbers of pianos. And so William did what he had done before; he continued to invest for the future as he saw it, confident that today's losses would become the road to tomorrow's greater wealth paved by the cash of the piano company.

In the spring of 1892 William had sold his East River Gas Company for about $130,000 and a few weeks later sold the building on Fourteenth Street that housed the Grote ivory company for $175,000. The purpose of these sales was probably to raise cash for the ill-fated tunnel under the East River, but little is clear in William's fragmentary financial record keeping. A few months later he sold 85 percent of the equity in his Steinway Railroad and 90 percent of the debt to a man named R. T. McCabe. Whether these sales yielded a profit is unclear. Although he bought the pieces of the gas company cheaply, William, ever a believer in capital improvements, spent heavily on the company.

The case of the street railroad is even more obscure. Again William had invested extensively in improving and extending the lines; horses, cars, stables, and the terminal at the village with a separate waiting room for ladies were all upgraded. The year before he sold the road, a program for replacing all horsecars with electric units was begun and a large generating plant was being constructed. The sale to McCabe was, in reality, something of an equivocal event. The seventeen thousand shares had a nominal value of about $1.7 million and the bonds another $570,000. Against this $2.27 million face value, William received but $650,000, or less than twenty-nine cents on the dollar. Within a few months the Panic of 1893 erupted, and it is not certain that William was ever paid the full amount due.

William undoubtedly felt himself to be a wealthy man, and in a sense he was. But he was also a man who had many obligations, some of them costly. As things evolved, among the more expensive of William's liabilities proved to be his son and heir apparent, George Augustus Steinway.

"George A. Steinway becomes 21 years old today," wrote William on June 4, 1886. "Give him $1,000 in Cash, $2,000 for Bowery Bay Building & Improvement Company shares and his Liederkranz $100 bond. George developing finely, and brings me a fine certificate from Packard's business college." An inch or two shorter than his father and thin at 140 pounds, George started working in the factory at age eighteen; at age sixteen he had been admitted to the Columbia School of Mines, but it is unknown how long he attended. At seventeen, his father proposed him for membership in the Liederkranz.

George Augustus Steinway was first a boy and then a man who seemed blinded by the brilliance of his father. Theirs was not a close relationship, but by the custom of the place and period, the bringing up of children was a task assigned more to mothers, nurses, and governesses than fathers. He was, in the phrase of the time, a "sickly child." The piano company was naturally a part of this young life, and William set down George's attendance at a company picnic in 1869 where he watched his father and Uncle Theodore address the workers. When William brought his son a toy donkey, the child tore it "to pieces in a few hours." On another occasion George shot several holes in a portrait of Beethoven that William believed was an original painted from life; if these acts contained any symbolic significance for William, he did not indicate it.

In general, George appears as a loved but faintly drawn figure in William's world. It may be surmised that an overriding event in the lives of both George and his sister Paula was their separation from their mother and "brother" Albert when William divorced Regina secretly in 1876. In all likelihood the children were told, initially at least, that Regina's departure was simply another trip to Europe.

"Georgie asked me where his mama was," wrote William one and one-half years later, but he did not record his answer. George was twelve at the time, and a year passed when William again wrote: "Am somewhat uneasy by the repeated questions of my children after their mama." Nine more months slid by—Regina and Alfred were gone for forty months now—before William told George what had happened: "Go home and reveal to George in brief lines that I am divorced from his mother, and what she did. He expresses no surprise, having come to nearly the same conclusion. Quite a load off my mind."

The next year George saw his mother for the first time in more than four years on a trip to Europe with William. After the visit of a few hours, son told father that he had "no feelings" for his mother. That summer William married Ellie. One and one-half years later, in January 1882, William received a cable telling him that his ex-wife succumbed to typhoid at Nancy. In the evening William told George and Paula that their mother had died; they received "the news quite composedly. My wife is quite relieved."

The details of nature and nurture are only sparsely sketched in the instance of George, but it is likely that he became at a young age a very heavy drinker. Researchers now write of the role of genetics based on studies showing that the sons of alcoholic fathers are at greater risk of developing alcoholism than sons of nonalcoholic fathers. This, however, is not science with a Newtonian determinism, and the operative word is *propensity*. Generational skips are common, a fact particularly germane to the fate of George A. Steinway, whose grandfather Heinrich was almost certainly an alcoholic. Biochemical and neurophysiological markers of a tendency to alcoholism in families have also been found; one of the more intriguing of these from the standpoint of the Steinways are differences in the brainwaves evoked by *sounds* in "normal" individuals and those who are alcoholics or children of alcoholics. Though this might suggest that the genius of the family and its curse were opposite sides of the same genetic coin, such a view is largely conjectural.

For William, George, and other family members in their time, the matter was much simpler: excessive drinking was a moral defect, not a disease or genetically influenced behavior. Other studies suggest that depression and hypochondria are more pronounced in the personalities of young alcoholics than nonalcoholics, and George, with his history of "sickliness," may very well have fit this pattern. Whether or not he did will never be known, for William carried the heavy burdens of contemporary moral judgments and described his son's condition in terms both terse and vague. He wrote guardedly of George's "strange malady," his "nervous prostration," and his "foolishness." For George Steinway life held dark terrors that were not illuminated by wealth, and while both his privileges and potential were great, they offered no protection against the afflictions that ravaged his mind and body.

That William intended that his son become a part of not only the piano business but the entire range of his enterprises is clear. For a time George was both an officer and a director of William's development companies, his railroad, and his gas company. With a gift from William of 330 shares in Steinway & Sons he ascended to that board as well. For a time George reported to William on the ebb and flow of the crowds at North Beach, but whether his role was one of active management or simply observer is unclear. George had an office in Steinway Hall, but again the nature of his job and his relationship with his cousin Charles, also at the hall and second-in-command to William on "business" matters, is unknown.

George's part as William's protégé ended in early 1891 when William placed his son-in-law Louis von Bernuth in "command" of his "various enterprises." Von Bernuth was given an office next door to Steinway Hall and the services of a bookkeeper. George resigned as president of the railroad, and von Bernuth assumed that position, as well as leadership of the Astoria Homestead Company and the job of treasurer of the Daimler Motor Company. In addition to whatever operating responsibility he may have had, George also relinquished his positions on the boards of William's businesses.

Von Bernuth's operations of William's companies were all ultimately disastrous, but William never lost faith in his son-in-law. George was given an official leave of absence from Steinway & Sons, and, along with his wife and young daughters, took a trip south. William wrote, "I worked hard to accomplish all so he could go." Whether the separation from William's businesses was cause or effect in George's illness is unclear, but two weeks later William learned that George was "ill in bed."

Three weeks following there was "bad news as to the health of my son George who is quite low and despondent at Washington," and George's sister Paula and another female relative visited him there. When George returned to New York, William was "deeply grieved to find him so weak and nervous." Before long George and his family were off to Europe for a stay of several months, presumably for further recuperation. In the fall of 1891, George, still in Europe, resigned as a trustee of Steinway & Sons for "reasons of impaired health." George's illness did not prevent him from spending immense amounts of money, however, and William had to make good almost thirty-two thousand dollars in amounts overdrawn by his son. Combined with George's Steinway & Sons dividends, he spent over one-half million dollars in today's currency in 1891 alone and an even greater amount in 1892. Living rent-free in a home built for his family by his wife's father, George continued to spend huge sums he did not have, and in March 1893 William "had to again make good his account in an enormous amount." Just two days later William received a letter from George's wife, Ottilie, that "George is in bed with nervous prostration and worry for the past 5 days."

In the fall of 1894 George's "nervous prostration" became acute, and Ottilie came to Steinway Hall for a conference with William and, according to William's diary, told him "a long tale of woe as to the sickness of my son George. Notwithstanding all my caution George's account is again heavily overdrawn, and she is also far too extravagant for their means which I plainly tell her." The next day George's wife again called on William "for help and advice," and five days after that meeting William wrote that "my son George is taken in a tug from Great Neck to Mamaroneck and enters

the sanatorium 'Waldemere' Mamaroneck, Westchester county." Waldemere, in the language of the time, was an insane asylum, and there George
Augustus Steinway spent the next nine months of his life.

Mental illness, like drinking, was considered to have a moral component.
"About twenty-four per cent. of all cases of insanity are ascribed to moral
causes," pronounced two medical authorities, Doctors Peterson and
Church, in an 1899 tome entitled *Nervous and Mental Diseases*. The best-
informed medical opinion would have attributed George's condition to a combination of moral weakness *and* "tainted" heredity, thereby casting a dark shadow
of suspicion over not only George but William and the entire family. George's
institutionalization was therefore another potential scandal which had to be
suppressed. Since George was not committed by New York's Commissioners
in Lunacy, there was no public record to catch the eye of a reporter, and the
fate of George Augustus Steinway remained a very private affair.

What might have happened, had not George's condition been well
shielded, can be seen in the example of Albert J. Weber, son of William's
arch competitor, who led a more visible life with tragic parallels to George's.
Page one of the *New York Times*, just below the masthead, bleated the
news: "ALBERT WEBER'S FALL—Once a Millionaire, He Goes Insane
to a Sanitarium." Weber, then thirty-eight, had lived his youth in a "luxurious home and in the cultivation of an intellect that was unusually bright"
but had "abandoned nearly everything to his life of dissipation." Perhaps
most scandalously young Weber was married and divorced not once but
twice, and the *Times* could not resist noting that even during his second
marriage "his revelry did not cease."

Just two weeks before in the firm's Fifth Avenue showrooms, Albert
Weber "white with rage, took a revolver from his hip pocket and declared
he would kill" Leo Engel, foreman of the Weber Piano Company. Smiling
during his hearing before a magistrate, Albert J. Weber denied that he
used obscenities during the confrontation, but the justice was not persuaded. "You have no right to call this man names," said a Magistrate
Cornell, "and you had no right to flourish a loaded revolver in that dangerous
a manner. I fine you $5." But Albert Weber, millionaire pianoman, did
not have five dollars and spent the night incarcerated.

The firm itself was no longer under the control of Albert. In 1884 Albert
J. Weber was sued by his mother, who, the court apparently believed, had
been cheated of a portion of her inheritance by her son. In the course of
these proceedings it developed almost incidentally that Albert had "peculated" about $100,000 from the firm; but there were limits to a mother's
wrath and Martha Weber seemed legally content when the court took the
firm from the hands of her son and placed it with a series of trustees who
spent more time explaining to the court what talented managers they were
than actually making and selling pianos.

"Through all his dissipations and riotous publicity," wrote the *Times*, "his mother has clung to him as protector and refuge, and today she will take him to the retreat where, doctors say, the rest of his life may be spent." The grounds for the finding of insanity were carefully described: "At times since his confinement he has sat, in imagination, at the card table and shuffled, cut, and dealt the cards. He talked of great stakes at the race tracks, rambled on about the women who helped him to spend his money, talked of big investments, and declared he was immensely wealthy." This, the doctors concluded, was sufficient evidence of insanity, and one physician quoted Albert J. Weber as saying "I'll make three millions this month easily." One of the Commissioners in Lunacy, Dr. H. V. Wildman, the surname undoubtedly a mere unfortunate coincidence, summarized the case of Albert J.: "Weber has been insane for some time. He has many kinds of delusions, but we can't yet tell the exact nature of his insanity." It was boasts about gambling, women, and money that earned Albert J. Weber both his commitment order and page-one prominence, and it was precisely this type of public notice that William avoided in the matter of George.

"My son George does not seem to improve any at Mamaroneck and I am deeply grieved in consequence," wrote William after George had been at the sanitarium for about a week. The dimmed prospect of a quick recovery caused William to remove George as an authorized signer of Steinway & Sons checks and to cancel the powers of attorney George had used to conduct business while William was confined by his own illness. William received advice on his son's condition about every two weeks, and three months passed before William heard from a Dr. Langman, who visited George, that he was "still in bed, weak, but greatly improved." The good news came two days before Christmas 1894. Two months before, Ottilie closed the country home at Great Neck and moved to the city with her three little girls, but they did not spend Christmas 1894 with William. William's holiday spanned perhaps an hour while his children opened their gifts and the servants received the customary cash gratuities. Late into Christmas Eve and all day Christmas, William worked on his correspondence.

George's holiday at Waldemere can only be conjectured, but it was, in all likelihood, a day like all his days of the past few months; he would have spent it in bed, well covered, in a warm semidarkened room, his only contact the nurses who padded in and out bringing three meals per day. George suffered from the "American disease," less perjoratively, neurasthenia, and more commonly, nervous prostration. Brought to the attention of physicians in 1869 by George Miller Beard, a pioneer in psychosomatic medicine and psychotherapy, neurasthenia was first thought to be a product of modern American life but was soon found in other nations. The essential idea was that emotions influenced the body directly by exhausting the nerves and that emotions might be the sole factor in the appearance or disappearance of disease. Initially greeted with derision by physicians, the idea of neurasthenia was gradually accepted, and by the time of George's disability neurasthenia was generally recognized as a "morbid state." It also became a diagnostic grab bag of unexplainable maladies.

"Neurasthenia is essentially a *chronic* malady. . . . Once established, neurasthenia tends to persist indefinitely. . . . Frequently remissions are presented, but the patient relapses under any unusual demands. . . . Even after long periods of improvement there is a tendency to ready recurrence under the influence of any exciting cause," bleakly intoned the authors of *Nervous and Mental Diseases.* George Augustus Steinway would never command his father's piano company, and William certainly knew this after consulting with the doctors. He removed George as an executor of his estate and provided him with a lifetime income in the spring of 1894. By this time George was able to "dress himself alone and walk outside, but his memory is still badly affected," wrote William.

The therapeutic regime for neurasthenia was bed rest, "an unstimulating diet," and "large quantities of drinking water" followed by travel: "In the *severer male cases* an absolute separation from business and family is usually required, and a long sea voyage with a pleasant companion often works wonders. As a rule the more outdoor air and recreation that does not entail effort, the better, but to put a neurasthenic on a bicycle or on long walks adds fuel to the flames," pronounced Peterson and Church.

By May of 1894 preparations were under way for George's therapeutic sea voyage, and William interviewed a man sent by Dr. Langman as a candidate for the position of George's "pleasant companion." Ultimately chosen for the job was Howard A. Burk, a former Steinway & Sons employee, probably a clerk or salesman. During George's nine-month interlude at Waldemere, William did not visit him, nor did he write for most of that time; this may have been at the direction of the doctors. In April William received a letter from George asking to return to New York, and William responded with a "long letter," but it was to be three more months before George was released.

The medical admonition to separate neurasthenics from their families took a new turn while George was still institutionalized. Ottilie recalled events a few years later: "I first consulted a lawyer in the spring of 1895 in regard to procuring a divorce from Mr. [George] Steinway. That lawyer was Judge William N. Cohen. . . . I told him that I could get a divorce in New York State for infidelity, and he suggested shadowing George Steinway, to which I wouldn't agree, and then he suggested going out—he suggested different states I could go to get a divorce—and finally North Dakota was decided upon." Both North Dakota and South Dakota were then providing divorces with easy grounds and convenient residency requirements, not always enforced. Divorce "colonies" sprang up at Fargo, North Dakota, and Sioux Falls, South Dakota.

"I told him [William] that I couldn't live with his son anymore," recollected Ottilie, "and I wanted to get a divorce. . . . I told him that I could get a divorce in the State of New York on the ground of infidelity, and he acknowledged that but told me that he wished me not to bring a suit in New York because it would bring up his own divorce suit, which happened some time ago, and that he would thank me very much for not bringing it in New York." William, of course, was at risk of a multigenerational scandal involving not only his divorce but his son's "insanity," alleged adultery, and "habitual intemperance." Coupled with the widely broadcast charges of incompetent management by renegade nephew Henry W. T. still in the courts, the potential for public disgrace and derision was large; and William knew that the press, already nettled by its exploitation in the Columbian Exposition affair, would discharge its duty to inform the public with venomous relish. Sales lost to a scandal, combined with sagging piano demand caused by the new bicycle craze, might push Steinway & Sons to the edge, from which it could topple to join the wreckage of its erstwhile competitors, Weber and Chickering.

Fortunately, Ottilie proved more tractable than either Henry W. T. or William's first wife, Regina, and William showed both gratitude and generosity as a result. William's desire to keep George's condition confidential may be judged from the fact that he signed a contract only three days later without consulting his own attorney; it was one of the few instances in thirty years when William did not consult George Cotterill on a matter of importance. "WHEREAS the said George A. Steinway, owing to certain weaknesses, infirmities, and habits, is unable to support and maintain the said Ottilie C. Steinway, and to support, maintain and educate the said children; and WHEREAS the said William Steinway is desirous of maintaining and supporting the said Ottilie C. Steinway and of supporting, maintaining and educating the said children in a manner comporting with their position . . ." began the document by way of premises. For three years William would pay the sum of six thousand dollars per year and thereafter seventy-five hundred per year until the last child surviving reached age twenty-one. Ottilie was not required to account for the funds or how she spent them, but she could not collect alimony from George. William or George could "see the said children at least once each month at their home for a reasonable time and at hours convenient . . . and conducive to the welfare of said children." The support payments would continue in the full amount if William, George, Ottilie, or any of the children died as long as one child remained alive. In today's dollars, William had committed nearly two million dollars to the welfare of his grandchildren and daughter-in-law.

With a presumably secure financial future, Ottilie and her oldest daughter, Ottilie Marie, then six, boarded the train for Fargo the next day to begin meeting North Dakota residency requirements. If George saw his soon-to-be-former wife again, William did not know of it, but about three weeks after Ottilie journeyed west, George, now released from Waldemere, visited with his two youngest children. On July 13, 1895, George Augustus Steinway boarded the steamer *Orinoco* outbound, New York for Halifax, in the company of Howard Burk.

Just two weeks after he left for Halifax, George and Burk materialized in Mount Clemens, Michigan, where William was undergoing yet another rheumatism cure, his condition having "relapsed" under the stress of George's illness and divorce. "To my pleasant surprise, my son George and Howard R. Burk come in, both looking exceedingly well and bronzed. After lunch we drive out together and they depart by Grand Trunk Railroad. . . . I give George 7 checks of $200 each." Before long George cabled for and received permission to go to Japan; this was a voyage that would last sixteen months and would take George and his companion to Australia, Egypt, China, and India as well. William was receiving "sensible" letters now and was truly heartened when George wrote that he could remember the combination to a small safe that his father owned.

George was eastbound on the *Coptic* when Ottilie obtained her Dakota divorce on the grounds of "habitual intemperance" and was awarded custody of the children in late September. William paid the legal fee of $515, which must have seemed like pocket change to a man used to five-digit invoices, immense as they were vague, from attorney Cotterill. Unlike Cotterill's bills, William paid that one immediately. Only one day after the divorce was granted, a *New York World* reporter called on William and showed him a dispatch the paper had received on the divorce. "I am deeply pained at the publicity but explain matters to him. He also interviewed me on politics." The reporter, named Roeder, was apparently a man with a heart, and the news appeared "in quite unobjectionable form" while the city's German-language press ignored the story, much to William's relief.

A scant thirty-four days after the divorce of George, now en route from Yokohama to Hong Kong, William's daughter Paula told him that Ottilie was engaged to be married again to a man named Recknagel. This did not seem to bother William in the slightest, and thus passed the last family crisis of William Steinway's life. Via cables William remitted funds and directed his son's travels through the eastern and southern hemispheres for the next year.

By October 1896 George was sufficiently recovered that he could travel on his own, and his companion left London for America while George went on to Hamburg. After arriving in New York, Howard R. Burk met with William and Paula, telling them "a great deal about my son George, who is now quite well again," chronicled William. None could know that father and son had seen each other for the last time.

Chapter 26

FORGIVE ME, I LOVED HIM

"**H**e had been ill with typhoid fever," reported the *New York Herald* on Tuesday, December 1, 1896, in a long page-one story. "A week ago he was convalescent, but he counted too much upon his strength; a chill came and relapse followed. Doctors Jacobi and Janeway were called into consultation, but his herculean physique, weakened by the ravages of the first attack of typhoid, could not withstand the strain of a relapse. On Sunday afternoon the physicians warned the family that they must abandon hope. Death came without pain and he passed away with his family at his bedside." Three months and five days short of his sixty-second year, William Steinway was dead.

"The mayor early in the day ordered the flag on City Hall at half mast," recorded the *New York World*, "and within a comparatively short period the great business and financial buildings in the lower part of the city displayed the same token of sorrow. German clubs lowered flags, and all of the great piano warehouses along Fifth Avenue and in Union Square showed their respect in the same manner."

"William Steinway died at 3:30 yesterday morning at his home, 26 Gramercy Park," detailed the *New York Times* on page one, column one. "A little after midnight Mr. Steinway awoke and looked around him. Then he sank into an uneasy slumber from which he did not awake. Beside him when he died were his son-in-law and daughter, Mr. and Mrs. Louis von

Bernuth; his nephews Charles H. and Frederick T. Steinway, and Henry Ziegler and Mrs. Ziegler, Harry D. Low, his confidential secretary, and Nahum Stetson, Secretary of the Steinway & Sons corporation. His younger children, Theodore E. and Maud S. Steinway, had bidden him good-bye early in the day. William R., a student at St. Paul's school, Garden City, arrived at the house too late to see him in life. George Steinway, the eldest son, who was travelling in Europe for his health . . . is now on his way home. He is a passenger on the steamship *Trave*, which is due in port on Friday."

There was, of course, the routine obituarist review of a renowned life: "As his fortune increased his activities as a public-spirited citizen increased," noted the *Times*. William was "a relentless foe of political chicanery," and "proud of his American citizenship." His efforts in social matters "were earnest and liberal," but "he had no taste for public office." The *Herald* observed that "the history of Steinway Hall under Mr. Steinway's control is the history of the development of musical appreciation in America." The tale of the development of Steinway Village was retold, with emphasis on its "endowment" with a church and school by the piano company.

The same papers which derided his subway advocacies on the Rapid Transit Commission now praised his dedication and pointed out that William gave his commissioner's salary to charities. William's enterprises were listed: one of the founders of the Bank of the Metropolis, vice president of the German Savings Bank and Queens County Bank, director of the Steinway Railway Company, director of the New York and College Point Ferry company, and on went the list. "His financial standing was of the highest character," opined the *Times*, and "Mr. Steinway's business interests . . . involved the management of enterprises in which more than $20,000,000 was invested." A model life for American and German alike had ended, and New York's newspapers had much to say about it by way of lesson and illustration.

There was little in the closing months of William's life different from that which had gone before. In Long Island City, Mayor Paddy Gleason was stirring anticapitalist sentiment for political ends. Another recession was ravaging the national economy, and loans were again unobtainable; but William continued to invest, particularly in his Daimler Motor Company, which was "working with a heavy loss." Ever the optimist, William toured some of his Queens County lands with an architect, apparently planning further development. Paderewski was back in America, and William noted with amazement that the gate for one of his matinees was over seven thousand dollars, exceeding that of a Metropolitan Opera performance.

Just as routinely, predators were nibbling at Steinway & Sons; a racetrack operator named Carl Lohmann had convinced "old Koven," a Steinway bookkeeper, that he was due nine thousand dollars. William took this as an embezzlement, and when looking into the matter he was "greatly grieved and excited as to further discoveries of heavy slate arrearages & racetrack frequenting by some of my family connections and clerks." The "slate" was the private accounting of the partners, against which they drew their salaries and dividends and sometimes borrowed additional sums from the company. Betting on horses was scandalous behavior, and Mr. Lohmann undoubtedly knew that William would not involve the police; the matter simply sat.

The biggest slate "arrearages," however, were William's own. "My dear Uncle William," wrote nephew Fred Steinway on May 21, 1896. "This morning while passing through Steinway Hall I had occasion to look at Mr. Koven's slate and found the remarkable amount $164,833.35 [more than two and one-quarter million dollars now] jotted down against you." After circumspectly pointing out that the loan drew no interest and that it was expected that the sum would be covered earlier by William's own Steinway dividends, Fred wrote, "I deem it my duty to call your attention to this anomalous condition."

At the time William was engaged in another mission of public service. Abbey, Schoeffel & Grau, impresarios, had a contract with the Metropolitan Opera and Real Estate Company to produce grand opera in New York. When the partnership became insolvent, it filed for bankruptcy, leaving the city with the almost unthinkable prospect of a season without grand opera. Into the breach stepped William as chairman of the Reorganization Committee, and by July he was able to quell the creditors and arrange for what was essentially a debt for equity swap in which creditors agreed to take shares in a newly formed corporation as payment for a portion of their debts.

William was elected president of the new company, and there was to be a strict separation between the production functions of Messrs. Abbey, Schoeffel, and Grau, who were paid twenty thousand dollars per year for their services, and the financial management of the new firm, which would be under the control of William and two other trustees. "Mr. Steinway's presentation of the affairs of the reorganized firm created a most favorable impression among the Directors [of the Metropolitan]," commented the *Times* on page one, "and it was decided without argument to grant his request." William himself was less equivocal a few days later: "Not since grand opera was first introduced in this country by Garcia in 1825 has its production been organized upon so solid a footing."

The "footing" of which William spoke was solid largely because of his own investment of nearly fifty thousand dollars in stock and debt of Abbey, Schoeffel & Grau. "Mr. Steinway," said an anonymous source to the *Times*, "has done more financially toward giving grand opera to New York than any other man. He has answered every financial request, and but for him there might be no grand opera this season." The word "giving" proved to be a forecast, for less than a year and one-half after his death William's investment in the opera enterprise was declared worthless by a court-appointed appraiser.

Through public benefactions such as the opera company, William's reputation as a philanthropist was widely broadcast, and it brought to Steinway Hall "a perfect pandemonium of callers, borrowers, howlers and mendicants" seeking William's largesse and influence. The success of Paderewski triggered a similar avalanche of demands by artists, and William noted that "we are pestered with Applications of Artists and would-be artists from all parts of the world." Strangely, William did not isolate himself, but personally received many, if not all, of his callers, heard their tales of travail, and often dispensed both sympathy and money.

Around the House of Steinway the trade was in collapse. Weber failed and took with it the Wheelock and Stuyvesant firms. Gildemeister & Kroeger closed its doors; in Boston the old firm of Hallet & Davis, once Steinway competitors, went into receivership; while Chickering staggered along in emaciated imitation of its former vigor. Through all this William showed little sign of personal concern and was busily planning to open a new dealership in Cincinnati while loaning Alfred Dolge money to keep open his lumber, felt, and piano hardware empire. In the closing months of William's life financial panic and frenzied activity had become routine.

Personalities from times past appeared in his final days, returning almost as harbingers of the end. "Poor old Max Maretzek came wanting to be my private secretary for the opera," wrote William. Maretzek, once a wealthy and powerful impresario who promoted national tours with the leading stars of Europe, was turned away. Marie Dachauer, William's friend of thirty years and jilted spouse of Regina's paramour Louis Dachauer, cabled William from Europe, and he paid her passage to America. Landing in New York, she made her way to Steinway Hall: "Old Mrs. Dachauer caps the climax in unreasonableness, and I finally settle with her for $500 all her claims against St. & S for alleged services during the last ten years at Paris," wrote William scarcely a month before his death. If things were as they had always been, though perhaps more so, William also showed that he was capable of change: "This is the first time in my life I vote anything but the democratic ticket, but this year the danger of the democratic candidature of Wm. J. Bryant and the unlimited free coinage of silver is so great, that no true democrat can act otherwise than to vote for McKinley and sound money."

This was William's final expression of his political philosophy, and on November 6, 1896, he recorded that "I still feel quite ill and jaded partly by the weather and partly by the Colcichium drops that I took yesterday." Just a week before he felt "remarkably well and light in my feet." On November 7: "I still feel quite ill, have no appetite, have eaten no meal for three days, and today only took bean soup and Oyster patties." But William did not slow down: "Work til 9 P.M. then drive home. I still eat little, having no appetite." That entry for November 8, 1896, proved to be the final words in the thirty-five-year journal of the life of William Steinway.

The doctors certainly informed William that he had typhoid fever, and he knew what suffering lay before him; he had seen his brother Albert die of the disease ("Albert raves," wrote William), and the enteric fevers had taken his brother Charles in Europe, his mother, and his first wife Regina. There was no epidemic, as when Charles succumbed in 1865. Typhoid was statistically about one-fourth as common as it had been three decades before, and the odds of a fatal attack were only about one in eight. In this instance the probabilities provided no protection.

"The announcement of the death of William Steinway has brought to his family an avalanche of letters, telegrams and cablegrams and cards of condolence from every direction," reported the *Times*. At the Liederkranz men worked late into the night covering with black drapes and crepe bunting the brightly colored walls of the two-thousand-seat concert hall. Florists in endless procession delivered palms, wreaths, and columns of flowers. From the pianomakers of Boston came a life-size grand piano, "in German ivy and white roses, with a keyboard of violets and white carnations." The Liederkranz floral tribute was a immense arrangement in the shape of a lyre, which loomed over the head of the casket. A life-size portrait of William was placed just inside the entrance to the hall and festooned with hyacinths and violets.

The morning of William's interment, December 2, 1896, began with private services in the Gramercy Park home. "The simple Unitarian ritual was read by the Rev. Dr. Charles H. Eaton of the Church of the Divine Paternity, who made a brief address in eulogy of his dead friend." After the private service William's casket was transported to the Liederkranz Hall on Fifty-eighth Street under the supervision of four former presidents of the society. When placed on the catafalque it was ready for view by the employees of Steinway & Sons, who filed past for more than an hour in silent procession.

A squadron of police kept all from attending the ceremonies who did not have invitations, and after the employees left, the invited were ushered by the Bachelor's Circle of the Liederkranz, thirty strong, to seats prearranged by organization and status. On the left was the Liederkranz and on the right was the Arion Society, and behind was the orchestra and chorus. William's family and friends were assigned to the balcony. There was an honor guard of Kriegerbund, decorated veterans of the Franco-Prussian War of 1870; William had made Steinway Hall available for rallies during that war, and these men with long memories now stood in geometric pattern about the bier holding American flags shrouded in crepe. The pallbearers included New York's Mayor Strong, German Counsel General Feigel, William's attorney George Cotterill, and friend Oswald Ottendorfer, the latter so weak that he had to be helped to his feet. All twelve pallbearers wore white sashes of silk with rosettes of black crepe. The members of the Rapid Transit Commission were in attendance, as were other political notables including former New York mayor Abraham Hewitt and Long Island City mayor Paddy Gleason. A special section was reserved for Steinway dealers, who travelled to the funeral from Saint Louis, Chicago, Cincinnati, Rochester, Syracuse, Boston, Philadelphia, and New Haven. German societies from Boston, Philadelphia, and Troy, New York, sent delegations, as did the Boston pianomakers.

The majestically plaintive strains of the funeral march from Beethoven's *Eroica* signalled the beginning of the ceremonies. The air, heavy with the scent of thousands of flowers, was silent as Carl Schurz arose and stepped to the side of the casket. "He spoke in German in low yet distinct tones that could be heard throughout the hall," reported the *Times*, "but his voice faltered. . . . He told of Mr. Steinway's career from his early days as an apprentice to his manhood as the head of a vast business. . . . As he spoke sobs were heard from all parts of the hall. Women wept aloud and men pressed handkerchiefs to their eyes. Suddenly, after several ineffectual attempts to control himself, Mr. Schurz broke down. His voice failed and then stopped. 'Forgive me,' he said. 'I loved him.' "

There was a long silence punctuated by sobs from the audience. Regaining his composure, Carl Schurz declared that "nothing beyond what was written in the hearts of his friends could be said of Mr. Steinway." As he made his way to his seat, the orchestra and chorus began *The Hero's Requiem*, which had been written for the ceremonies. Julius Hoffman, William's friend and now acting Liederkranz president, arose and stepped to the bier. Placing his hand on the coffin, Hoffman addressed the silent form within: "We thank you for the love you have shown us. At all times but once you have given us happiness. The once you brought us sorrow was when you left us."

"Overcome by his feeling, Mr. Hoffman was unable to continue," said the *Times*. "All around him women were crying and men were coughing in a vain desire to hide their emotion. . . . After a distinctly painful pause the opening strains of a violin obligato by Mr. Richard Arnold broke the tension." The obligato introduced William Steinway's favorite song, Gounod's *Ave Maria*, "gloriously sung by Mme. Eames-Story." There were two more songs, one a German hymn, before a prayer by Dr. Eaton was delivered. Chopin's *Funeral March* concluded the ceremonies, and then the ushers of the Bachelor's Circle formed lines to guide the mourners past the coffin.

Outside on Fifty-eighth Street the cortege had already formed, led by Steinway & Sons employees in rows eight men wide. Behind the hearse one hundred carriages stood, the breath of the horses and the coachmen condensing in the December cold. The pallbearers bore William's casket to the waiting hearse, and the procession made its way through the Manhattan streets to the Twenty-third Street ferry, bound for Greenwood Cemetery and the Steinway mausoleum. As the body of William Steinway was placed in its crypt, the chorus of the Liederkranz sang. The man was dead but a legend lived.

Whether by chance or intent William labored for a lifetime to burnish a name to an aureate glow that would shine through the fogs of time and transcend the lives of men. He did this with a prescient intuition and a galvanic sensitivity to those ideals which resonated in his time. For William Steinway there was family, there was art, there was music, and there was excellence.

These were noble concepts, and if they did not describe what was, they mandated what ought to be. The family was not one of unfaithful wives, neurasthenic sons, and schismatic nephews; it was the family of harmony and loving bonds, constant in time and across the generations. Art was not the transient or the chimerical or the consumable; it was classical, severe, demanding, and ultimately, transcendentally beautiful . . . as was the music. William's world was a moral one; there were standards.

Men, music, machines, indeed all acts and things, could be assessed. In this severe universe good and bad were unambiguous, high and low easily seen. Progress could not only be measured, but it was expected. In this place and time of tyrannical optimism—all men and all things could and *must* be made better—the keystone of William's life was his capacity to endow a device and a commercial transaction with cultural meaning. Therein lay its special value; William's customers did not buy an oddly shaped black box stuffed with wood, iron, and hair from dead animals made shiny by slathering with the ground-up wings of insects. They did not buy a piano, although they acquired one, almost incidentally. What they truly received—and valued—was a palpable symbol of membership in a cultural order with the highest ideals.

Reality was tens of thousands of young Victorian ladies playing halting, mindless songs to snare young Victorian gentlemen. They stood, these gentlemen, close to the ladies to signal appreciation of the sonance which fell upon their ears and to glimpse, perchance, some hint of forbidden flesh. But in their minds, at least sometimes, she was Essipoff and he was Liszt, and they had left the earthly plane to frolic in skies of billowing sound.

William Steinway understood that all had hopes and dreams. All, or almost all, wished to be more than they were, and if they were not, this was a sadness which could be succored, in some small way, by an icon. If one could not make sounds like Rubinstein or Mehlig or Joseffy or Paderewski, one could at least make contact with art through symbol.

In this land of mind-mirrors William Steinway was king. His ultimate genius was a telescopic perception that saw over the horizon of time, far beyond the suburbs and the subways and the motorcars that he sought unsuccessfully to pioneer. William discovered and conquered the dominion of image more than a half-hundred years before others gave to that shadowy domain its name.

William's jurisdiction, however, was not one of cynical manipulation in which superficial wants are turned to evanescent needs on a Möbius loop of conspicuous consumption. Excellence was not a slogan; it was real. Certainly William, his brothers and nephews knew that not one in one thousand buyers of their instruments was able to comprehend, much less use, the full power of the piano that sat in the parlor. This did not mean that such persons should be gulled or somehow deserved less. Less was not available at Steinway & Sons, and the result was a transaction fundamentally fair. Those stepping from the din of Union Square into the pacific elegance of Steinway Hall (a knave, a lady, a renowned artist—the city housed each in countless numbers) knew these things but dimly and therefore powerfully. William was a pilot with preternatural skill in this realm of hopes and dreams. Into the penumbral zone where object and aspiration softly melded he guided millions, both during his lifetime and after. If this was deception, it was also benign, for in this land of percept, to believe was to become.

Perhaps other men could have done what William Steinway did, but if the deeds were not bound to the man, they were tethered to the time. So epic are the names and so renowned the creations it is difficult now to apprehend that Liszt and Wagner and others in the pantheon were sensate beings once alive and not mere words on concert programs or authors of mellifluous sounds heard on the way to work. William gathered about him this panoply of giants. This was not riskless. The works of these men were controversial and sometimes reviled. It was yet another prescience, but as he died, they too were dying, and there remains only a shadow as veiled as the epoch from which it flowed. Petrified in panegyric, congealed and made sensible if not authentic as legend, it is easier to see the outline now than the truth. Perhaps this is preferable.

As the door to the Steinway mausoleum closed on the corpus of William Steinway, more than his remains were entombed. William, the public man and the copious documentor of his life, was gone. His nephews Charles and Fred had seen both the power and the tyranny of fame and elected to avoid it. A cloak of secrecy was drawn about the family; business records, voluminous in William's time, were destroyed by his survivors. Letters and personal papers were burned. No further Steinway lives were carefully archived and presented to the future. In a sense this was a modest loss, for those that came after were custodians, not architects. On the surviving family fell an ironic burden: though they did not create the legend, it was within their means to destroy it. This they avoided, but sometimes only barely, and on some the freight of deeds long done weighed heavily.

RITORNELLO

Monday, January 23, 1991, 655 West 155th Street, New York 10045. *Dawn in Harlem. A winter sun probes the bricks of 155th Street between Broadway and Riverside Drive, tentatively lighting the textures of their faces, the ripples, the cracks, the potholes, the asphalt patches. Black Mylar garbage bags assume organic forms in the nascent light, silent sentinels huddling in the cold. To the west, the iceless waters of the Hudson flow in shadow while the buildings on its shore are plated in transmutant shades of gold.*

A single gull flies reconnaissance over Trinity Cemetery, searching for a thermal it cannot find. On the ground a white Ford van moves slowly through the cemetery and stops beside a beige Toyota. The drivers are not there to pay homage to the dead at dawn. Money and dope change hands. The van crunches slowly through Sunday's unplowed snow toward Broadway; the Toyota retreats reciprocally to Riverside Drive. The gull banks right and vectors west, wings flapping hard to gain height, a diminishing dot on a fractal field of cumulonimbus clouds.

Electronic eyes have sensed the dawn. Within the granite walls a relay clicks, unseen and unheard. Sodium vapor security lights retire. The words can be read clearly now: ALL ARTS ARE ONE   ALL BRANCHES ON ONE TREE. *The epigram is cast in concrete on the beaux arts facade of the American Academy and Institute of Arts and Letters.*

401

On the left of the academy a double door frames the entrance to a minelike tunnel where grey paint is losing a contest of adhesion to moist bricks. Dampness has joined a warmer cold in the tunnel. At its lower end a tan door has a hand-lettered sign: "Close Careful Door slams two noisy." There is another door, then a right turn and a final door which opens into a dark vastness of tropical tempera-ture and sepulchral silence.

It is the stage of the American Academy, a trapezoid 51 feet 4 inches by 43 feet 3 inches by 21 feet 5 inches deep, the area of 1002.1 square feet covered with 1¾-inch oak. Well laid by men long since dead, the boards do not creak. A single, penumbral forty-watt bulb casts a yellow aura.

On that stage are four hulking black masses, two shiny, two buff, like giant, three-legged beasts hibernating in a cavern. They are of a species, these beasts: concert grand pianos, none much less than nine feet long, each weighing about half a ton. One journeyed from an island in the eastern hemisphere, Hamamatsu, Japan, the second from Vienna, Austria. The third was born in a nest of sawdust in Truman, Arkansas, and the fourth emerged from a red Victorian rock pile scarcely three miles away (as the gull flies) in Long Island City, New York.

Time skips like a rock on a pond. Baltimore, 1857: in the apologetically tendered opinion of the judges, a Steinway grand triumphed over the locally built Knabe in a seven-way competition. The Crystal Palace, 1855: a Steinway square piano was awarded a gold medal over the venerable Chickering. Paris, 1862: First Gold Premium, Steinway, in a field of four hundred, yes, four hundred, pianos. Philadelphia, 1876: Steinway, gold medal. On the stage is a photocopied page from the book of time. In one place are the instruments of what remains of the great piano manufacturers still providing concert pianos in America. There has not been such an aggregation during the twentieth century. In a very real sense, it has never happened before, for the nineteenth century has been welded to the twenty-first. There will be no human judges: machines will listen, translating local variations in molecular pressures to microvoltaic modulations. The analog flows of electrons are to be converted to digital bits, streams of zeros and ones, eighty million zeros and ones for each minute of piano sound. The ciphers will be stored when three million solid-state junctions, opening and closing at nanosecond intervals, have done their job. The fugitive sounds of art and craft will be forever imprisoned in a Gaussian cage, condemned to rotate in perpetuity at thirty-six hundred revolutions per minute in mass storage, eight-bit bytes and track numbers and ASCII files, not sounds and not music. Engineers will summon them for interrogation, recreating with the clatter of a few computer keys an eerily eidetic representation of this space, this place, this moment and its sounds.

This is a technology of which Christian Friedrich Theodore Steinweg could not even dream as he placed his ear against a large glass ball—called a Helmholtz resonator—to listen to the discrete components, the overtones, of the sound of his instruments. On the computer screen will appear a three-dimensional graph, *functionally the equivalent of tens of thousands of glass ball experiments, its ragged peaks and valleys representing the life of a sound in space and time. The graph, glowing phosphorescent squiggles of green and blue and yellow and red, is as unique as a human signature. The graphs and their cryptic quanta—dB, dB(A), Acums, SoneG, Aspers, delta T, kHz—will reveal, some say, what it is that makes a Steinway sound like a Steinway.*

Chapter 27

IMPECUNIOUS PEOPLE

*M*ay 19, 1898. "William Steinway, world renowned piano manufacturer and reputed multi-millionaire, is now said to have left an estate so seriously encumbered that there is doubt whether it will suffice to satisfy all the claims against it. Not very long before Mr. Steinway's death . . . he boasted that he believed himself to be worth in the neighborhood of $13,000,000. Now his creditors are scrambling for the wreck of that vast estate, which, according to general belief, will lack much of satisfying all the claims against it," reported the *New York Herald*.

So the world learned, eighteen months after his death, that William had died bankrupt, a scandalous materiality of which he himself may not have been fully aware. During life William's prestige, power, and force of personality were a sea anchor to windward, keeping the man and the firm off the rocks of financial destruction and scandal that claimed Chickering and Weber. In death, Steinway & Sons, bereft of that anchor, pitched and rolled perilously, unable to gain sea room.

This was not a question of competence. Nephew Charles had developed into the quintessential businessman and was now president, just as William had intended. No less energetic than his uncle, Charles was also a master of details and, unlike William, understood the value of good recordkeeping. Direct to the edge of abruptness and sometimes beyond, intolerant of that which he considered foolish or vague, constantly vigilant for superfluous expenditures, Charles was the prototypical operating executive.

Nephew Fred, now with the title vice president, was in complete charge of manufacturing for at least the six years since the forced departure of his brother Henry W. T. Mild mannered, gentle, a man who liked to read books and talk about them, Fred enjoyed the company of other family members and nights at the theater and opera. Though William might be suspected of going to the theater not to see the play but to be seen, Fred cultivated his critical senses and filled his personal daybook with plot synopses and notes on the quality of performance.

While William was peripatetically active, Fred was just as pleased to spend an evening home alone, playing the works of Schumann, his favorite composer, on the piano in his parlor. A man with a strong aesthetic sense, Fred was also an accomplished photographer whose images soon embellished Steinway & Sons catalogs. He had, through inheritance and training, manifested the family fascination with wood and carried on the Steinway practice of personal selection of stock that went into the instruments. To men named Steinway, there was no more important responsibility in pianomaking.

In the years after William's death both Charles and Fred spent little time on outside activities such as the Liederkranz and none whatsoever on public works or politics. If Uncle Bill's crown of philanthropic and public activity was available to them by inheritance, they chose to abdicate. So it also was with the newspapers; whatever views Charles and Fred had on the great public issues of the day—tariff reform, free coinage of silver, and Sunday beer sales—they kept to themselves. Newspapermen no longer rushed out of Steinway Hall with eminently quotable quotations, real or imagined, and the new generation of the family felt no compulsion to speak for German-Americans in New York, the pianomaking industry, Steinway & Sons, or even for themselves. Further still from public view, almost to the vanishing point, was William's third nephew, Henry Ziegler, who seemed entirely content to very quietly and very competently supervise the Inventions Department, a role for which he had been chosen and trained by his Uncle Theodore. While "Boss William," as even his nephew Fred sometimes referred to him, was the ultimate decision maker for decades, the operating style was now more collegial; in 1896, for example, Charles decided to pay himself a large bonus and was definitively checked by his relatives.

When the *Herald* ran its story on William's postmortem insolvency, it was Charles Tretbar, now with the house for thirty-three years, who spoke for the family and the firm. "When I saw Charles F. Tretbar," wrote the *Herald* reporter, "he was unwilling to say anything about Mr. Steinway's estate except that it had suffered depreciation owing to business depression. The corporation, he said, was in no way affected by the condition of the estate, which held a certain number of shares." The statement was as disingenuous as it was predictable, but Tretbar gamely continued to patch the crumbling edifice of William's prestige. "There is wide diversity of opinion as to the causes for this disappearance of a vast fortune," murmured the *Herald*. "On the part of those who make no secret of their lack of respect for the memory of William Steinway, it is openly alleged that he alone was to blame. It is even charged that during the latter years of his life he was beset by requests for assistance made for the most part by women of the musical and theatrical world." This was a thinly veiled slander that William had squandered millions on females then only infrequently distinguished from harlots.

"That Mr. Steinway had during his life been prodigally generous in the cause of musical art, Mr. Tretbar said, there could be no doubt," confided the *Herald* to its hundreds of thousands of readers. "Whatever Mr. Steinway gave to artists, he gave from motives of pure generosity and philanthropy. No artist ever appealed to him in vain. He was absolutely devoted to the cause of music," averred Tretbar with now unassessable credibility. Undisclosed sources "who knew William Steinway well" told the *Herald* man that "a great-hearted generosity that forbade him to refuse an appeal for assistance was the true cause of his financial disaster," while others claimed that "with all his experience Steinway was never a thorough businessman, and that while his intentions were of the purest and best, his designs often failed of execution." There was a wisp of truth in both these views, and one did not exclude the other.

But the core problem lay elsewhere. William relied on the money machine that was Steinway & Sons for the cash to service his outside investments. The recession that began in December 1895 continued well into 1897 and was followed into 1898 by a weak recovery. The result was seriously depressed piano sales, which at Steinway slid almost 29 percent between 1892 and 1896. Worse yet, sales did not rebound as they had after prior panics but stayed at levels more than 20 percent below the 1892 peak until the turn of the century. The cash spigot that was the Steinway & Sons dividend and once gushed dollars now dribbled. In the record year of 1892 William received over $140,000 in dividends and another $25,000 in salaries and bonuses, the equivalent of roughly $5 million in today's heavily taxed and depreciated New York dollars. He spent or invested all that sum, and, ever the optimist, continued to spend as dividends were crushed under the immense economic pressures of the time. By 1896 the Steinway dividends had fallen to but 5 percent, the lowest since the great depression of the 1870s, and William's income from it had slipped by three-fourths to but $40,000.

Fragmentary records show that William's response to his current income account deficit was to borrow, and this he did in large sums, usually in the names of employees. At the Bank of the Metropolis, where William was a small stockholder for more than twenty-five years, he borrowed $180,000 in the names of Nahum Stetson and Charles Tretbar. The German-American, Yorkville, and Pacific banks provided another $110,000 in loans. Adam Weber, William's longtime fire brick manufacturing friend, loaned $26,000, while brewer and partner in the North Beach amusement park George Ehret advanced $85,000 to William. A business associate of Oswald Ottendorfer at the *Staats-Zeitung*, Herman Ridder, lent $45,000, and William was even indebted to his star attraction, Paderewski, in the amount of $51,250, of which at least $10,000 was intended to endow a musical scholarship. Yet this borrowed $497,250 was only a minor portion of William's total obligations. Almost a decade after "the great philanthropist" died more than two million dollars was still owed.

William's management of his own wealth or lack thereof was only a portion of the problem, and soon other family members were drawn into the vortex of his estate. As the sole survivor of the original founders, William was also the executor of the estates of his brothers Henry and Charles, who had died in 1865. As executor he had a fiduciary responsibility not only to the widows, most of whom were comfortably remarried, but also to their children. A similar situation applied to the relatives of William's brother Albert.

All three brothers had intended for William to invest the incomes from their Steinway & Sons stock in conservative ways such as bonds and first mortgages on real estate. A clear record of William's management of his brothers' estates does not exist; in part this was due to the fact that until 1881 the records were maintained by Charles Tretbar, but as Tretbar testified in court, William took this responsibility from him and did not reassign it. The result was a small fortune—at least $500,000 that literally belonged to women and children—that was now in peril. Some of these funds which were "invested" in loans to characters such as Paddy Gleason, while they may have extended William's political influence in Long Island City, were probably not of the investment quality that his brothers had in mind when they named him executor and protector of their families. Gleason did pay his loan back before he went bankrupt, however. It appears that William also used his position as executor to channel family monies into his own real estate development and transportation projects.

"Strictly separate your private matters from the cash of the firm," admonished Theodore in a letter to William dated September 13, 1887. William had not only failed to heed this advice; he treated the wealth entrusted to him as his own. In one sense, and undoubtedly the way William viewed it, no distinction was made between his own fortune and the wealth of his family. Investments good for William Steinway were good for his family. There was a fundamental, if naive, fairness in this view.

William's financial management practices were not illegal. Many of his transactions were actually approved by the courts, a by-product of Henry

W. T.'s lawsuits against the family and the firm. While legal, they were not, at least retrospectively, always prudent. In the fifteen years through 1895 William received over a one and one-quarter million dollars in dividends and another $300,000 or more in salary and bonuses, yet an accounting of the estate showed that he had only $3,900 in cash.

Where the immense sums went was the key question, and the answer reveals another aspect of William's personality, for William Steinway willingly gave away and loaned, with no reasonable expectation of repayment, hundreds of thousands of dollars during his lifetime. There were the well-publicized benefactions: the donations to the Chicago World's Fair, the Kaiser Wilhelm church, his native village of Seesen, the annual grant to charity of his five-thousand-dollar salary as a Rapid Transit Commissioner, as well as his secret but massive injection of cash into the Metropolitan Opera production company. Since there were virtually no taxes on William's wealth, there were no deductions for charitable donations. The benefits William received from his benefactions to hundreds, if not thousands, of persons were not economic.

"Calls on me for money are fearful, everybody seems to be at his wits end," wrote William on June 1, 1884, one of the earliest indicators—midway in a recession that lasted from March 1882 through May 1885—that at least some unspecified persons looked on him as a lender of last resort. By the 1890s the tempo of William's beneficence increased, and there is the occasional insight into its nature: "Theodor Lemke arrested. His wife calls with Ringler and Co's lawyer, Davidson, and I help the poor heart-broken woman by paying $300 and giving her $20 so she has something," wrote William on May 22, 1891. There is no clue as to who Lemke was or why his wife came to William for help; the Lemkes played no prominent role in William's life. The sum William willingly and casually gave was equivalent to about $4,500 today.

"I am pestered badly by impecunious people all day," wrote William in August 1891, in only one of the abundantly similar diary entries. By the end of 1891 William had "a lattice door affixed to my anteroom to prevent being overrun." This proved inadequate, for nine days later William was "having dreadful trouble with people trying to borrow money of me, as general business is very bad here and in Europe." Less than a month after the door was installed William wrote that he "was almost ground to powder from the immense number of callers appealing for help."

Due to "the attempts personally and by letter of a multitude of alms solicitors from morning til night, I was compelled to print in English and German my answer to begging letters," remarked William to himself. The *Musical Courier* carried William's announcement in December, and that Christmas, while his cards "were chiefly from old maids," he was still "pestered all day by beggars and begging letters."

Among these was the strange case of William von Meyerinck, the man hired to assist William's son-in-law in the management of the nonpiano businesses. In January 1892 von Meyerinck signed a confession admitting that he embezzled $1,579 from Daimler Motor Company, the Astoria Homestead Company, and other of William's enterprises. Von Meyerinck was dismissed, and a few days later Anna von Meyerinck, the confessed embezzler's wife, appeared at Steinway Hall and, wrote William, "again plagues me with her troubles." William gave at least two cash gifts to the woman, "they being penniless," plus a loan of three hundred dollars for which her furniture was used as collateral. William von Meyerinck went to San Francisco while Anna sailed east to Europe, but Mrs. von Meyerinck returned to America, repaid her three-hundred-dollar debt to William, retrieved her furniture, and joined her husband in the west.

There were, of course, loans and subsidies to artists. On December 7, 1892, William had "a long talk with Rafael Joseffy in the afternoon, he having borrowed nearly $12,000, not played for three years nor given us a testimonial. He promises to do the latter soon." Apparently the accounts with pianists were examined once a year, for William wrote the next December that "Joseffy has not worked in 4 years and drawn some $18,000." At the going rates, Joseffy was in arrears for 150 to 200 concerts. His debts did not prevent Joseffy from the exercise of his artistic prerogatives, and in 1895 the pianist refused to play at the opening of the new Steinway Hall at the Lyon & Potter store in Chicago.

Throughout his life William seemed unusually tolerant, if not absolutely indulgent, of such displays of anticommercial behavior. He may, in fact, have felt a close affinity with the artists from his own experiences as a young and talented tenor. Though he did not sing publicly in his later years, he remembered with a luminescent fondness the performances of his youth: "This day 37 years ago I made a great success as tenor in the Liederkranz Concert of December 1, 1858 at the City Assembly Rooms," wrote William in 1895.

One consequence was that William spent much time and at least some money assisting the careers of young performers. Besides giving money to some, William listened attentively at auditions and gave advice to a procession of young female pianists, vocalists, and the occasional actress. Almost invariably these hearings occurred in the presence of the artist's mother, and in a copiously documented life, there is not the slightest evidence to suggest that William violated even the severest constructions of Victorian moral conduct in his relationships.

Not all William's assistance was ephemeral; when appeared the destitute son of Thomas H. Chambers, the dealer who had first sold Steinway pianos on Broadway more than four decades before, William gave him thirty dollars. Thomas H. was seriously ill and in the German Hospital, and it is likely that William, who had endowed a bed there, paid for Chambers' medical treatment as well. One did not have to be a successful business associate to receive charity. A man named Kraemer, once involved in the failed piano-stool works at Astoria, appeared one day in the summer of 1895: ". . . loaned $500 to go to Carlsbad to restore his health, he having liver troubles and dropsy. He looks a perfect wreck." The dying Kraemer was not alone in receipt of aid, and about a month later William wrote, "I remain until 9 P.M. being completely exhausted by the interminable stream of beggars and mendicants. I give away and loan out many hundreds of dollars. Arrive at mansion at 10:30 P.M. almost dead with exhaustion." For William Steinway, charity was not a matter of placing an envelope in the plate on Sunday morning.

How much money William gave and loaned cannot be known, but surviving records show over four hundred loans totaling more than $250,000. The vastness of the sum may be better appreciated when it is realized that the average total capital of a *national* bank was then but $178,772. Of the 405 recorded loans, nearly one-third were made in the final eleven months of his life. During those final months William earned about sixty-five thousand dollars in salary and dividends but loaned out nearly ninety thousand, an amount almost 40 percent greater than his income.

It was the ultimate irony that William's generosity nearly destroyed both the business and the family that he loved. No inside knowledge was needed to see the corrosive effects of the estate's impairment only a few months after his death. The *Times*, page one, in August 1897 carried the headline: "GAMBLING AT NORTH BEACH—Many Kinds of Fraudulent Games Operated Under the Very Eyes of the Police." Scarcely a year before, William's influence elicited a huge *Times* story promoting the wholesome family resort at Steinway, Long Island. The new *Times* piece reminded readers that the place "was originally intended as a quiet family resort for Germans," was "one of the prettiest places in the vicinity," and was "near the Steinway Piano Works."

The "legitimate means of diversion" had been supplemented by roulette, rouge et noir, and dozens of other games "where men, boys, and a few women struggled like demons . . . and tore each other's clothes for a chance to lose their money." Augmenting the conventional games of chance were booths "where baseballs were thrown at the heads of negroes, and here the competition was so great that one sign conspicuously informed the passer-by that he would get $100 in gold if he hit 'the coon' three times in succession." The result, said the report, was "that the Klondike itself could not in the same time give a richer harvest than North Beach did yesterday to the gamblers."

There were, of course, benefits from allowing gambling at North Beach. The reported crowds of seventy-five thousand pleasure seekers far surpassed attendance under William's management, and sales of beer, trolley tickets, and ferry rides would have increased proportionately. Many in the growing throng might have gone to Coney Island, which was known for the "Turkish sirens" dancing at establishments with names such as the Congress of All Nations and the Streets of Cairo. The 1893 Chicago Columbian Exposition, with its exhibitions of bare-breasted Amazon warriors and Turkish belly dancers on the Midway Plaisance, reminded showmen that Americans, at least the males, were eager consumers of multicultural experiences, if attractively presented. North Beach gambling was likely a response to competitive pressures of the "couchee-couchee" dances and "vulgar songs" at Coney Island, but one which William would not have tolerated as a possibility, much less a fact.

Whether or not Fred and other executors of William's estate knew of the gambling is unclear. It is certain, however, that the Steinway mansion was even nearer North Beach than the piano manufactory, that there were regular telephone communications between managers at Astoria and Steinway Hall, and that Louis von Bernuth, William's son-in-law, was still in charge of William's outside interests. But William's estate owed George Ehret immense sums, and it is likely that even if they wished to control them, the Steinways had no power over events at North Beach.

One man who likely did not know of the gaming was Charles Steinway. The reason: Charles was in London that summer secretly trying to sell Steinway & Sons to British investors. Selling the company was, Charles wrote brother Fred from London, the family's "last and only chance" to avoid "the dread calamity of the collapse of the estate and the consequent scandal on the name Steinway." To avoid such ignominy, William's nephews were willing to relinquish ownership but remain both as employees and directors of a new company to be known as Steinway & Sons, Limited, which would nominally be based in London.

The rationale behind the decision to sell the firm in London rather than New York is less clear. London was arguably still the world's principal financial center, and there was long interest there in American investments. Britain itself was America's largest trading partner; in 1898 the *London Statist*, a British financial publication, observed: "We need the United States for the supply of a great part of our food supplies, as one of the largest fields for the employment of our capital. . . . In the same manner the United Kingdom is essential to the States as the greatest customer for its produce, and as the source from which it obtains unlimited capital for the development of its industries."

It was, perhaps, with the notion of "unlimited capital" in mind that the family turned east for the ocean voyage to London; why they did not turn south for a trolley ride to Wall Street is a mystery. It was not a question of the size of the firm. The proposed six-million-dollar sale of Steinway & Sons shares was respectable, if not immense, by the standards of the time. The New York Stock Exchange listed the shares of Edison Electrical Illuminating of New York at a total value of about eight million dollars, Brooklyn Union Gas at fifteen million, and the Consolidated Ice Company at six million. The outstanding worth of the common shares of Proctor and Gamble was $1.25 million.

"Dear Boys," wrote Charles on July 30, 1897, ". . . when I struck London everything was in the dumps and the whole matter looked busted higher than a kite. . . . I can assure you I was mad as hops and actually regretted that I came. . . . Here I had come 3,000 miles full of hope and enthusiasm bound to put the matter through, and at the critical moment I got a bath of cold water thrown over me." A telegram sent the day Charles left saying that the deal was dead had missed him.

Charles set about resuscitation with the help of Edwin Eshelby, Steinway & Sons' London manager. The financial performance of Steinway in William's last years was not attractive to English investors. The trend in profits was distinctly down, and in 1896 the prospectus for the stock offering revealed that it had fallen 44 percent from the peak of 1891. "The reduction in the American profits of 1896 was entirely due to the financial depression," intoned the offering documents. Potential buyers were apparently unpersuaded, and their concern was simple: Steinway would be unable to pay the dividends they expected. On the face, the proposed dividend of about $376,000 per year to stockholders simply did not look feasible, for in three of the last five years the company had not earned enough to cover such a payment.

It was Eshelby who hit upon a solution of sorts. He suggested that a portion of the proceeds be set aside to cover the required dividend if Steinway did not earn enough to pay them out of profits. Clearheaded thought might have revealed that this was tantamount to paying the investors back with their own funds, but Charles's usual cogency was apparently overwhelmed by his desire to close the deal and save the family's reputation. "Everything at present," wrote Charles, "points to a success. . . . Of course the public is a funny animal to deal with and I can never figure out absolutely what they will take up or refuse. But in my mind this guarantee will absolutely remove any doubts in the mind of the most skeptical and makes both classes of stock an absolute safe investment for the next three years at least."

The hope was that United Kingdom buyers would pay about $2.3 million to William's estate and more than $1 million to Theodore's, while providing the nephews with roughly a half million dollars each and George Steinway about $150,000. The $6 million sought was, by modern standards, a steep price, equivalent to $323 per share for the old company or about twenty-two times 1896 earnings. Nearly a century later, Intel, America's premier maker of microprocessors, would also sell for twenty-two times earnings the day after it announced that its profits had grown 30 percent in a single year and were at record levels.

"Dear Boys. Long before this reaches you my cables will have informed you of the utter failure of my English plan," wrote Charles on August 13,

1897. "I have no excuses to make and can only tell you that we are all dumbfounded at the result. If only half the shares had been taken one might have put it to the impropitious time, rich people being away on vacation, but this is no excuse for the pitiful showing of less than half a million dollars subscribed. We amongst ourselves knew the main reason why we wanted to sell the W. St. Estate shares, but of course I could not even breathe a word of this to the people over here and hence had to keep that dread secret to myself. I cannot picture to you, but with the absolute failure staring me in the face, I wonder once in a while why I don't collapse and go crazy."

"Just at the present time Europe is not buying our stocks, nor are the foreign investors showing much a disposition to do so. . . . Our currency seems to be the specter that frightens off the European buyer. He has been made nervous by our silver threats. Perhaps that is only natural," said Mr. Benjamin Graham, a noted Wall Street figure, in analysis of the securities markets one week before the Steinway initial public offering. Blinded by hope or ignorant of the facts or both, Charles met defeat in London and wrote that for the sake of appearances he could not leave the city immediately.

During Charles's self-imposed exile a bizarre event transpired. As a page-one story the *Times* reported the syndication of Steinway & Sons as accomplished a week *after* the offering failed. That Charles had cabled the facts to New York is certain, so the appearance of two stories on two separate days is mysterious. "It was reported last night that the present members of the firm . . . had consummated a deal whereby the extensive business of the firm passes into the hands of an English syndicate. The price paid was $6,000,000. For some time after the death of William Steinway a report of the sale of the property to an English syndicate was circulated."

The next day's front-page story made it clear that a *Times* reporter had somehow obtained a copy of the prospectus circulated in England. "As announced exclusively in the *NEW YORK TIMES* yesterday, the great business and plant of the piano manufacturing firm of Steinway & Sons has passed into the hands of English capitalists." Almost incidentally, the reporter quoted Nahum Stetson, "Secretary of the Steinway Corporation," as saying, "We have not been advised of any deal having been consummated, though we do not want to say that one may not be concluded." Undoubtedly the report temporarily placated William's creditors, and there was no newspaper account of the collapse of the offering, the embarrassment of the *Times* being at least as great as the mortification of the family itself.

While general business conditions may have been improving, Steinway piano sales languished at but 1,928 instruments in the United States in 1897, almost one-fourth fewer than the peak year of 1892. Sales of Hamburg instruments held and then increased moderately, but a European Steinway brought but $372 on average while American pianos were sold for almost twice as much. Not only were the Hamburg instruments much cheaper, but they were also much less profitable, yielding only $52 each compared to $125 profit on American-built instruments. It all meant that Steinway & Sons could not pay enough in dividends to satisfy the claims of William's creditors, unless, of course, some of those owed were willing to wait twenty years to be satisfied.

One who was not willing to wait was William's attorney, George F. Cotterill, who sent the family a bill for five years of legal services in March 1898 for the staggering total of $153,000 or about $2.2 million today. This was as much blackmail as a bill, for Cotterill knew in intimate detail all the family secrets over a span of more than three decades. Cotterill's billings so incensed Charles Steinway that he threatened to resign as president of Steinway & Sons rather than pay them. The other nephews took a more temperate approach and began negotiating with Cotterill, William's erstwhile friend and counselor who, with a few strokes of his pen, became the estate's largest single obligation.

Not long after the conflict with Cotterill erupted and under the pressure of creditors, the surrogate court stepped in, and an official appraisal of William's holdings was conducted. The "in all respects just and true" 1898 accounting revealed that William's watch and spectacles had a value of $62, that he owned five Steinway pianos worth a total of $1,350, that he had sixteen other pianos worth $1,390, that he possessed carriages and horses with a value of $1,505 with three cows and a calf included, and that his eleven shares of the Deutscher Club of Hoboken, purchased for $110 in 1864, were now worth $55. This was the good news, or much of it.

William's $600,000 equity investment in the Astoria Homestead Company, his land development company for the Steinway Village and surrounds, was considered to be of "nominal" value. The $214,000 principal in the bonds of Astoria Homestead was thought "doubtful." The $119,000 investment in the Bowery Bay Improvement Company had only "nominal" value, and $87,000 in Bowery Bay bonds had depreciated 65 percent to but $30,450. In essence, William's North Beach property was considered to be worth about fifteen cents on the dollar; apparently the appraisers could not assign an economic value to the concept of wholesome family recreation as envisioned by William.

The New York & College Point Ferry Company, whose boats plied the waters of the East River, proudly bearing the name Steinway, fared no better in the gimlet eyes of the appraisers: $45,000 spent for stock was valued as "nominal" while $17,000 in 6-percent bonds were worth but $5,050 for a total of about eight cents on the dollar. William's East River tunnel project—$42,500 in stock—was charitably valued as "nominal"; all that remained of the tunnel was a hole full of water, a few drawings, and unpaid bills. The Ravenswood Improvement Company, William's other real estate development on Long Island into which another $100,000 was sunk, was also assessed as essentially valueless.

The shares in Daimler Motor Company, the embodiment of William's vision of a petroleum-propelled America, had cost $181,800 and perhaps another $100,000 in operating losses not shown in the accounting. The surrogate's appraisers declared Daimler "worthless"; though the record is not clear, it is likely that at its peak Daimler, with nearly one hundred employees building engines, boats, and the occasional horseless carriage, closed entirely when denied William's cash transfusions. The warren of machine shops fell silent; and the boat basin, dock, and showrooms behind Steinway & Sons were of no use to the family. In August 1898 a new company was formed called the Daimler Manufacturing Company. Its principal was Frederick Kuebler, who had managed, so to speak, the business for William.

The incorporation documents tell the story: the new firm began with a capital of five thousand dollars and all the rights to Gottlieb Daimler's patents once held by William. His investment was now valued at less than three cents on the dollar. Before long the new investors bought from Steinway & Sons much of the real estate occupied by Daimler for forty-eight thousand dollars. This, however, did not help the estate as the property was owned by the piano company, not William.

Though Kuebler did not long survive an infusion of Wall Street capital, Daimler, with a succession of managers, staggered into the twentieth century to build the "American Mercedes," a close copy of the German Mercedes-Benz. This was done under the terms of William's licenses with Daimler, now Daimler-Benz, but the parent company in Germany also helped independent distributors import the German-made cars. American buyers justifiably saw European automobiles as superior in the general case, and the money that could be saved on import tariffs by buying an Astoria-built Mercedes mattered less than cachet to the elite who could afford ten-thousand-dollar motor toys. Daimler stumbled through the years, wounded by poor management and buyer attitudes, until the works were consumed by fire about a decade after William died. A brutal recession in 1907–08 ensured that William's dream did not arise from the ashes of the factory. In a strange example of economic irony, if not justice, the importers of the German Mercedes failed in the same recession, and nearly a half century passed before the name Mercedes credibly returned to the roads of America.

Other of William's enterprises were also sold. Brewer George Ehret assumed ownership, probably in satisfaction of debts, of both the ferry and the North Beach amusement park, the latter surviving for another quarter-century until Prohibition dried up beer sales and a primary motivation to attend. The property ultimately came under municipal control, and the place where millions whiled summer Sundays away is now La Guardia Airport. William's Gramercy Park home was sold, and his daughter Paula, still caring for the younger children of William's second marriage in addition to her own, moved to a more modest apartment far uptown.

But the readily liquidatable was insufficient to cover the grim financial reality exposed by the surrogate accounting of 1898. Two million dollars in loans and investments were now valued at about thirteen cents on the dollar overall, or about one-quarter million dollars. The value of William's shares in Steinway & Sons was set at $1.2 million for a total of about $1.45 million; arrayed against this were about $2 million in claims.

Public pressures ascended. *Town Topics*, a Victorian predecessor of today's supermarket tabloids, wrote of William "that discoveries made since his death have shattered the reputation of a New Yorker who had posed for years as a millionaire, patron of the arts, a financier, a philanthropist, a public official and the head of a great manufacturing company. . . . Never a day passed but that the name Steinway was mentioned in some newspaper. No name was more respected in business circles." *Town Topics* vaguely alleged financial wrongdoing, and there were rumors that William subverted funds from Paderewski and mortgaged Steinway Hall to ballast his unstable empire. Plausible explanations did not silence the rumor hawkers. Media vultures circled the carrion of William's works, and it was not long before one swept from the sky to peck at the remains.

The *Musical Courier*, a trade paper, observed, "The corporation of Steinway & Sons . . . has been effected by the rumors of the involved condition of William Steinway's estate, but it assumes the lofty position of maintaining inviolate its own affairs. . . . This decision must also signify a radical departure from the late Mr. Steinway's system, which always aimed at making his house a semi-public institution." The observation was as correct as its exposition was awkward.

Editor Marc Blumenberg then questioned the very survival of his long-time advertiser, Steinway & Sons: "Events may show that he [William] was wrong; his whole theory may prove itself a monumental blunder. History subsequent to his death may illustrate that his judgment, his views of life, his personal conduct, his public activity, may all have been egregious blunders and subverted conceptions of the relations of thoughts and ideas to facts and things. It is difficult for those who for a quarter of a century stood near to his supposed prophetic personality to conceive that all this delphic wisdom was a cumulative fiction, and yet it may prove to be so. How defective then must be the education drawn from such a source." Of course, Editor Blumenberg knew well that none had stood closer to the "prophetic personality" than William's nephews, and that, by implication, he was raising questions about the future of the firm. Was it not possible, Blumenberg implied, that if the man was capable of "subverted conceptions," the instruments themselves were also somehow wrong? Marc Blumenberg was a man frequently sued for libel, and he had learned how to protect himself. This he did with a few words: "On the other hand, his [William's] genius may exist in the foundations of his works, and before long those who have charge of his affairs may be able to . . . demonstrate that the published statements were . . . unworthy of consideration."

The family was forced to issue a public statement, signed by Charles Steinway and Louis von Bernuth, denying, as best they could, the regnant rumors of William's insolvency and the implied imminent failure of Steinway & Sons. The statement said that William had many businesses, that he had not planned to die, "else his estate would have been left in far different shape," and that "there seems now no chance of realizing, immediately, on the assets on account of the war." Details on the relationship of William's holdings to the Spanish-American War were not given, and it was again claimed that the estate bore no relationship to the firm other than that William had held eight thousand shares of Steinway & Sons stock.

The governing document in the wreckage of the estate was the testamentary letters. According to William's will, his shares and other assets, after the payment of about seventy-five thousand dollars in bequests to various persons and charities, were to be divided five ways, with one-fifth to his daughter Paula, one-fifth each to the three children of his second marriage, William R., Theodore E., and Maud, and one-fifth to the grandchildren of his son George. George himself was largely disinherited and denied ownership of shares, although William provided him with the sum of six thousand dollars per year; the source of this income was to be from the one-fifth share willed to George's children. At the rate Steinway & Sons had been paying dividends, each of William's children except George would have received between $12,000 and $24,000 per year for the rest of their lives, or at least $180,000 per year in today's dollars for each and every child. It was the ultimate irony that William's financial management now threatened to impoverish his own children.

How well the family understood the situation is unclear, although there is no doubt that basics were known by the nephews. Many transactions of the estate were handled by attorney Cotterill, who refused at one point to provide Charles and Fred with the accounts, saying he would not do so until he was paid. After a series of tense and angry meetings, a deal was struck whereby the lawyer was given Steinway & Sons shares to hold, pending payment of a greatly reduced bill, Cotterill's view that he had "saved the family's honor" notwithstanding. By means unclear, the banks William owed were persuaded to wait, despite the fact that interest payments on the loans were suspended.

Problems continued to mount: at one point in early 1899 the entire European business of Steinway was threatened by a court-forced sale of the Hamburg factory to satisfy German creditors. Contingency plans were developed to build a new plant, but Charles, on a trip to Germany, somehow succeeded in buying the works in a "private" sale. The fact that he assumed personal responsibility for the transaction suggests that the other nephews may have been willing to sacrifice the German business that was once so important to William and Theodore.

Small creditors filed lawsuits, but the most significant and potentially damaging suit was launched in early 1899 by Ottilie C. Recknagel, George Steinway's former wife. The life of George Augustus Steinway ended on September 14, 1898, in his thirty-third year, when he died onboard a steamer bound for Europe on what was apparently another recuperative trip abroad. The cause of his death is unknown.

After returning to America just after his father's funeral in late 1896, George rejoined the board of Steinway & Sons for a few months, then resigned for reasons of "illness." George was suspicious of what he called "the Steinway Hall crowd," but was, according to a relative, "satisfied" with his six-thousand-dollar annuity, "although my father took away from me everything that I had." To what George was alluding in this statement will never be known; perhaps it was a reference to the stock given to his children, perhaps not. George lived the final months of his life at the Gramercy Park mansion under the care of his sister Paula with her husband, children, and his young half-brothers and sister in what was called "reduced circumstances." This, however, was relative, as George's annual stipend equaled the wages of a baker's dozen of American workers.

Whether George ever saw his children or his ex-wife again is unknown, but Ottilie was now a frequent correspondent with the executors of William's estate, including William's daughter Paula. Among the topics were the child-support payments William agreed upon for the grandchildren in the secret divorce arrangements for his son. Paid regularly during his lifetime, the money stopped when William died.

"I have just now received your letter," wrote Paula to her former sister-in-law Ottilie in late 1897. "Your children are in the same *boat* as *we* are, namely they are heirs, and in the settling up of the estate the heirs come last. First come the *creditors*, next the *legatees* and finally the *heirs*. We are not allowed to draw anything from the estate," wrote Paula, underlining as she went, "and are now living on what Louis and I have; in other words Louis' salary. . . . As for using my influence with the other executors, that is out of the question entirely; the thing is a matter of business and not personal feeling." Ottilie's later pleas, including one that she had to dismiss the governess, were essentially ignored. Finally taking to heart Paula's view that "the thing is a matter of business," Ottilie Steinway Recknagel sued in Brooklyn Supreme Court.

In reality, the family likely could not afford to remit the full support payments, but such a public admission was out of the question, and once again a Steinway scandal boiled over onto the pages of the newspapers. The underlying attitudes went beyond the ability to pay, at least according to Ottilie, who testified that Paula "remarked it was entirely unfair that my children [Ottilie's] should receive so much more than they were receiving or that they would receive; that my children should receive the money under the contract with Mr. [William] Steinway and also the money left them by their father [George]." George's three little girls did, in fact, stand to inherit over sixteen hundred shares of stock from William and another five hundred from George and two hundred more from their great-uncle Theodore, plus over $125,000 in support payments contracted by William. The income from all this could easily exceed thirty thousand dollars per year—the earnings of sixty-three average Americans—and make the three little girls among the more comfortable of Brooklyn's citizens.

"STEINWAY SECRETS OUT," read a *New York Times* headline; "Wife of George Divorced and Remarried Before His Death," continued the article before it alluded to "certain weaknesses, infirmities and habits" of George Steinway. That two of the principals, George and William, were both dead permitted Charles, Paula, and Louis von Bernuth a certain latitude in their testimony. It was claimed, for example, that William had made the support agreement with Ottilie thinking that George "had no property out of which their support could be derived." In reality, William had all of George's documents and knew exactly what he owned. Charles claimed in the papers that he did not "know whom she married or when or where she obtained her divorce from George." To believe this statement it must also be believed that William never talked to Charles, his nephew and second-in-command, about family matters, and that George himself never told Charles he was divorced. Louis von Bernuth averred that he thought George was married to Ottilie until the day he died; apparently his wife, Paula, who told William about Ottilie's remarriage, forgot to tell her husband about both the divorce and the second marriage to Carl Recknagel. It was also claimed to the *Times* reporter that the family "knew nothing of her [Ottilie's] movements . . . until she instituted the present action." This claim was belied by a large stack of correspondence between Ottilie and Louis von Bernuth on the matter of payments, in addition to the occasional exchange of gifts.

The presiding Justice Russell said, "With the wisdom of family arrangements the court can do nothing. William Steinway knew best the situation of his son, the wife, his grandchildren, and his own means to provide for the exigencies apparent," and remanded the case to trial. At that trial it was claimed by the family that the divorce of which they had no knowledge was "collusively and fraudulently obtained" by George and Ottilie, apparently in an attempt to bilk William out of $130,000, "on grounds . . . in violation of the laws of the State of New York," that the divorce was a "fraud upon the court," and that the remarriage was "concealed from William Steinway." William did, of course, know of the marriage, and he was told by his daughter Paula.

The issue of who knew what when was never definitively explored at the trial. This was perhaps fortunate for the defendants, for the judges on appeal held that "nothing was alleged that would justify a finding that the contract was void for fraud" and that the facts "have no possible relation to the plaintiff's right to recover." Ottilie and her children became, with costs, about $134,000 richer by order of the court.

This, however, was not the end of the conflict. The family now claimed that the five hundred shares of Steinway & Sons stock which had been carried on the books in George's name were really William's shares, and were not a part of George's estate to be inherited by his children. The facts are murky and complicated by a series of bookkeeping transactions, and it may be that William did take back the shares he had given his son or intended to do so and simply failed to sign the necessary paperwork. But the Steinway family was unable to prove satisfactorily to the court either William's actions or intent, and it was held that the shares belonged to George's three little girls, albeit with less publicity than accompanied the child support and divorce scandal.

As the drama of the grandchildren unfolded in the courts, Henry W. T. Steinway still lurked in the legal bushes, a sort of Steinway sniper who loosed the occasional round to harass his brothers. In 1899 New York's highest court, the Court of Appeals, decided that H.W.T. did indeed have a right to inspect the books of the company "at a proper place and time and for a proper purpose." That suit was initiated when Henry was not allowed to look at the books at the time of the failed English syndication. Another suit revisited the technicalities of Theodore's will, and H.W.T.'s legal skirmishes continued, without important result, for decades after the death of "Uncle Bill."

By the end of 1900, four years after William's death, many of his Steinway shares had been distributed to satisfy his debts and the obligations to the family estates he controlled. What had once been a very closely held firm with ten or fewer stockholders now burgeoned to more than half a hundred, with William's shares divided in small lots at a price of $200 to $250 each to satisfy claims. One result of this was that William's direct heirs—his children and grandchildren—received less than one-fourth of the stock that they might have, had his estate been debt-free.

Reality refracted William's design to leave his children secure in the proceeds of his lifework. That this was inadvertent there can be no doubt, and William's wishes were in sharp contrast to those of another pianoman, Dwight Hamilton Baldwin, who died just two and one-half years later. Baldwin, whose estate was a much smaller but solvent $550,000, left his wife a pittance, his children but $30,000, and $68,000 in marked envelopes to a few key employees. The mass of the estate and the company went to the Presbyterian Church, which fought to keep it from the widow and her children in court. Widow Baldwin won $181,000 from the church, and the Presbyterians finally settled with the children out of court. William and his former distributor were very different men.

More than seven years lapsed after William's death before Charles was able to announce—in February 1904—that the "appreciation of properties may result in a valuation of $1,000,000." More details were revealed on what was liquidated. William's East River tunnel franchise had been sold to the Belmont interests for $100,000, and a tunnel under the river and west below Forty-second Street was actually built a few years later. It is still used today, but the thousands who are daily jolted on the subway ride between Manhattan and Queens do not know that their commute was once but a failed dream of a visionary pianomaker.

At the time of Charles's announcement every New Yorker knew of the Blackwell's Island Bridge, William's prescient and stillborn plan of the 1870s. That dream too rose from the swamp of city politics to become stone and concrete and steel, though not precisely at the location he foresaw. The existence of the bridge, Charles said, would cause William's Long Island real estate "to amount to a large fortune in itself" in just a few years. Time had provided the repudiation to the *Musical Courier*'s assertion that William's "delphic wisdom" was "a cumulative fiction." William's map of the future was eerily correct; the brilliance and the tragedy of it were polar and inseparable. William's map was drawn, by decades, too soon.

Chapter 28

MEMBERS OF THE BLOOD

"Anyone who has passed along Fourteenth Street in the neighborhood of Fourth Avenue has doubtless come in contact with the iron-faced, clean-shaven, frowsy-dressed army of cheap actors that infest the thoroughfare. Their numbers make the street near to impassable," wrote *Music Trade Review* in the spring of 1900. Fourteenth Street in the vicinity of Union Square Park had, in the decades since Steinway & Sons moved there, become New York's main retail area for the piano trade. The area had a second retail magnet of no small power, Tiffany's; and the combination of music, diamonds, and gold brought to the street a disproportionately large number of young ladies who, it appears with biological inevitability, attracted young men. "The proprietors of the establishments nearby have complained bitterly to the police to no avail of the way their business has been injured by these persons," reported the trade paper. Neither the police on the beat nor the captain of the precinct took action to restore order.

This was yet another change from William's time. He would have swiftly and surely used his political power to cleanse the streets of the "mashers" who "congregate about the entrances of the establishments, expectorate in the street, use foul language and insult ladies, all of which is detrimental to business interests." The means, if a few well-deployed dollars at the station house did not provide relief, would have involved a call to the superintendent of police, who would have listened closely and acted quickly so as not to invoke the displeasure of a powerful and famous German-American.

Charles Steinway, however, had no power beyond that of citizen and was forced to write a formal letter of complaint which was reviewed in due course. An order was then issued to arrest any man "standing in one place for more than a minute or two." Explaining the need for order on Fourteenth Street, Charles told *Music Trade Review* that "something had to be done. . . . It got so bad that it was almost worth a woman's life to pass along the north side of the street. I am no enemy of the theatrical profession, but the men who called themselves actors out of work . . . seemed to think that they owned the street. They were an entirely different class from the legitimate actors I am acquainted with. I have repeatedly tried to have these vocalists and vaudeville fellows find other quarters, but they would not go." Thus the styles of uncle and nephew were clarified. William spoke to the press of his audiences with royalty, reminisced about Rubinstein, and communicated his visions for the betterment of the city and the nation. Charles, in marked contrast, whimpered about street rowdies.

If Charles projected an image of less than dazzling luminescence to the world at large, when he cast one at all, inside the milieu he knew he was commanding to the point of autocracy and sometimes beyond. "The chair, addressing the meeting, stated that he considered it a pleasant duty to make a few remarks about the business of the corporation in the year 1902, and to point to the profit and loss account and balance sheet of December 31," reported the minutes of the stockholders' meeting, now typed rather than handwritten as in the time of William.

"The house, Mr. [Charles] Steinway said, had again beaten the preceding business year considerably in all respects. A dividend of 12% had been declared and paid November 15th and another one of 15% had been declared on March 26, . . . making a total of 27%. . . . Thus for the past three years dividends of 23%, 25% and 27% or a total of 75%, had been declared, making the great sum of $1,500,000 in that comparatively short period of time." Between the lines can be read another message from Charles: even those who took Steinway stock in settlement of William's debt should be pleased. The shares, under his management, were an outstanding value and now earned far more than most investments. Charles drove that point home, saying that "not many business houses, in his opinion, could show such results, and the directors and shareholders should be well-satisfied thereat."

The tincture of arrogance in Charles's remarks aside, difficult decisions had been made, and their effects could now be seen. None could have been more trying than the decision by 1899 to slash the prices of Steinway instruments. In his thirty-one years at the helm William had reduced prices only once, and that was in response to the economic debacle of the 1870s. The cost of a parlor grand was trimmed 12.5 percent in 1871 and the concert grand was shaved about 6.5 percent. The next year, 1872, saw a further 5-percent lowering of prices, but by 1876 they were again raised slightly. Since the purchasing power of a dollar was generally growing in a deflationary epoch, the net effect was that the real price of a Steinway piano was steadily increasing throughout William's years in command.

The nephews put an end to this trend. The price of a big concert grand was slashed by more than one-fifth, from $1,800 to $1,400, by 1900 and the smaller parlor grands were unmercifully cut by more than one-third, from $1,150 to $750. The huge cut on the smaller instruments was made possible by the introduction of a new piano in 1902, the Model O, which had been designed by Henry Ziegler. While the Model O is now highly esteemed by piano cognoscenti, Fred Steinway regarded the O as a capitulation to the "cheap trade" and viewed it with contempt.

The prices of upright pianos were also lowered, in part by the introduction of a new model known as a Vertegrand. The radical overhaul of the pricing and product structure positioned the upright pianos at prices generally much lower than grands, an immense departure from William's time. The Steinway buyer of 1885 had a choice of grand, square, and upright Steinway pianos for the home at roughly the same price, generally between $700 and $1,200 at "New York Retail" and before the commencement of negotiations. By 1890 Steinway & Sons built its last batch of five square pianos, and the instruments on which the house built its fame four decades earlier were gone. Squares were viewed as old-fashioned by customers, and they occupied much more floor space in the parlor than an upright. Theodore's visionary advocacy of upright instruments a quarter-century before was finally and unambiguously verified in the marketplace.

The conventional wisdom in the trade by the turn of the century was that the hundreds of thousands of totally serviceable square pianos in American parlors were inhibiting the sale of new pianos, and schemes were hatched to rid the business of the residue of its previous successes which, it was now felt, had been built all too well. A piano manufacturers group proposed to show their contempt for the square piano by holding an immense piano bonfire at Atlantic City. Despite letters of protest from church groups, teachers, poverty-stricken music students, and advocates for the poor who begged for donations of the candidates for conflagration, the bonfire was held anyway. The result was an industry scorched not by fire but by public indignation.

Other plans appeared to solve the perceived problem of the surfeit of squares. The *Music Trade* ran multiple feature stories, complete with illustrations, showing how easily even one-hundred-year-old pianos could be converted into attractive tables, desks, and chairs. Among the many examples shown of the piano recycling was an instrument, now reincarnated as a table, tenuously related to George Washington.

The dramatic devastation of the squares seemed almost a fixation in some sectors of the trade. A plan was floated, so to speak, which envisioned a large barge loaded with square pianos being towed to sea and dumped like garbage in vivid demonstration of the "commercial uselessness of ancient instruments." This proposal was found defective by a nautically inclined writer at *Music Trades* who noted that the "enormous amount of well-seasoned and varnished wood" in the old pianos meant that they would float, not sink. "The chances are they would go floating around the ocean for some time. Solidly built, they could stove a hole at or below the waterline of smaller or weaker vessels." This was undesirable, thought the apostle of Archimedes, since it would attract the attention of the federal government to the piano industry.

The industry's problem, to the extent it had one, was one of irrational expectations, if not unalloyed greed. Between 1899 and 1904, the nation's Gross National Product (GNP) grew at a very strong average annual rate of 3.7 percent per year while piano sales in units increased more than twice as fast at 8.7 percent annually. There were many new entrants in the business, in part because the making of pianos had been greatly simplified by a components industry that made available from catalogs virtually every portion of the instrument; keyboards, actions, iron plates, cases, and every other necessary item could be ordered in any desired quantity and quality.

The minimum requirements for entering piano manufacturing were not much more than a shed, hand tools, sandpaper, and varnish. With little more than this, and a modicum of care, it was possible to build a sufficient generic piano. Against the tide of commodity pianos Steinway & Sons claimed that they were "the only Manufacturers who make all component parts of their Pianofortes, exterior and interior (including the casting of the full metal frames) in their own factories." That claim was as powerful as the language was dynamic.

By the turn of the century most of the key patents held by Henry and Theodore had expired, and critical innovations such as overstringing and the one-piece bent rim were not only in the public domain but widely used by competitors. Many found ways to emulate, if not duplicate, the sonic effects of Theodore's iron-frame designs, his wood framing, hammers, and duplex scale inventions. Steinway technological hegemony, buttressed by patents, was an advantage lost in the sands of time. The house that began with the innovations of Henry Steinway as a technology-based enterprise was transformed by William and Theodore into a firm that combined brilliant promotion and revolutionary technology. Steinway & Sons was now entering a third and final permutation under Charles: the house became a marketing concern, that quintessentially twentieth-century business form.

This was not due to lapse of application or impoverishment of ideas; Steinways deceased had done their work so well that there was little of significance left to invent, save differences that made little difference. They had forever transmuted the architecture of the instrument, refining it to a state pending perfection, work-hardening the piano to a rigid and robust penultimate form. William and Charles before him created a towering edifice of perception, its foundations drilled into the very bedrock of the culture that shadowed all that had come before and much that came after.

With growing numbers of competent imitators and the time of technological leadership forever foreclosed, there was little to do but cut prices and search for a larger market. In 1891 Steinway production accounted for 2.71 percent of all pianos produced in the United States; by 1899 this ultimate criterion of the marketing age known as "share" had plummeted to but 1.2 percent. While industry output climbed 88 percent to 172,000 units in those years of economic turmoil, Steinway production had fallen 17 percent to a scant 2,061 pianos. Whether or not the family knew these ratios is uncertain, but they certainly saw the effects and, all hopes of selling the house gone, acted.

By 1900 Steinway Model N uprights were offered for $550, and the Model K Vertegrand was available in 1904 for $500. They were the least expensive Steinways offered in decades but were by no means cheap, as the average annual earnings of nonfarm workers was $483 in 1900 while the average new home cost $2,300 to build. Cutting prices at the top and adding new, cheaper models at the bottom triggered a classical effect: Steinway sales increased, roughly doubling in the decade after William's death.

The risk, and it was a deadly one, was that sales would not respond sufficiently to the reduced prices and that the house would be condemned to selling cheaper pianos at lower total profits. The dozens of new stockholders would not look kindly on such a development. There was the further problem that Steinway instruments might diminish in prestige in proportion to their lowered prices.

The revised strategy brought an immediate response from the trade, as shown in a Lyon & Healy advertisement, the firm then holding the Steinway Chicago territory after the dissolution of Lyon & Potter. Believing the homily that the best defense was a good offense, an unknown copywriter crafted a minor advertising masterpiece, purportedly based on the observations of a "perceptive and intelligent lady" seeking, as millions of them did, to buy an upright piano. Making the rounds of the Chicago dealers, this prototypical consumer observed that salesmen for competing makes always mentioned Steinway. Having heard so much about Steinways from their competitors, the advertisement reported, the "perceptive and intelligent lady" bought one, and she presumably lived happily ever after. While Steinway had lost share of market, it had not yet lost share of mind, either with the customers or the trade.

In a speech on the history of the grand piano to the employees of a Norwalk, Ohio, pianomaker, the A. B. Chase Company, an executive of the firm said of Steinway: "To this enterprising family the piano industry owes a great deal. They have made the grand piano what it is today and have given the modern artist a chance to exhibit his techniques, pyrotechnics, and gymnastics without a whimper on the part of the piano." The speaker, a Mr. Wagner, also indirectly acknowledged that the technology developed by the Steinways had reached its apex. "What the twentieth century will bring in the line of improvements is mere speculation. I hardly look for anything startling . . . unless some new process or natural forces are discovered. We have probably reached a point of perfection, just as the violin makers seemed to have arrived at their pinnacle 150 years ago." Whatever gratitude was felt by executives of the Chase firm, it did not prevent them from badgering Steinway & Sons in the marketplace: "When you buy an A. B. Chase piano your money, less a legitimate profit, goes entirely into the instrument itself instead of to artists employed to make a reputation for the piano."

The effective solution to the challenges posed by generic instruments and withering technological supremacy was found in a chapter of William's well-worn compendium of marketing methodologies: *artist promotion*. While Mr. Wagner may have appreciated the technical contribution of the Steinways, he did not understand that prestige, glamour, and stardom attracted money with an almost gravitational certainty. The nephews, having learned well at the feet of a master, understood this intangible force and applied their knowledge with unprecedented vigor. In this they were assisted by a new cohort of virtuosi eager to shake the money trees on the concert tours.

This was a revision of the practice in the last years of William's reign when efforts centered almost exclusively on Paderewski; the new approach was shaped around the concept of a diversified portfolio of *executants* at much lower prices, although the crown jewel in the artist holdings was still "Paddy." The new direction snared a veritable "Who's Who" of pianism. There was, however, one player who had an extraordinarily powerful impact on both audiences and critics.

His name was Josef Hofmann. Touring as a child prodigy in 1887 for Weber, young Hofmann became the vortex of a child labor scandal. When the eleven-year-old genius's father, himself a conductor, opined that he was unable to pay for lessons for his son, a fund was established by a businessman to pay for the boy's support. Thus amply rewarded for a tour not made, Hofmann repaired to Germany and several years of musical tutelage. Young Josef became the pupil of Anton Rubinstein; and when Rubinstein died in 1894, Hofmann, now two years past his majority, returned to the concert stage. After accreting the requisite raves on the eastern edges of the Atlantic, Josef Hofmann ventured to America. The *New York World* distilled the Gotham reappearance of the young maestro: "The 'Child Pianist' Who Created a Furore in New York Ten Years Ago is Heard Again. SCORES GREATER SUCCESS. Musicians Find a Virtu-

oso, the Ladies Discover Another Pianistic Idol to Worship. SO EVERY-
BODY IS HAPPY."

Whether the result of clever press agentry or lack of arithmetical ability,
the *New York Sun* shaved four years off Hofmann's age and wrote that now
"at 18" Hofmann was "a man of earnest purpose, unflagging industry and
wise judgment." The unknown *Sun* critic continued: "His interpretations
are wonderful. He has immense power, real concentrated force; he has also
remarkable tenderness. There is an honesty and frankness and simplicity
about his manner and permeating all that he renders that is the surest
mark of genius, because it shows true love and reverence for his art." Then
came the crucial comparison, and young Josef Hofmann fared well: "No
pianist except Paderewski has ever given us such varied and poetic interpretations. . . . And this young artist is in one sense a truer exponent, since
he is absolutely free of all affectation and from every thought of influencing
his audience." Though many reviewers were now too sophisticated to mention routinely the piano used, Hofmann's "talking" instrument was a
Steinway, a fact plainly noted in both the advertisements for his concerts
and their programs.

As the critics cooed and the ladies swooned, a more objective auditor
visited the venue on Fifty-seventh Street. "Josef Hofmann recital Carnegie
Hall," wrote Fred Steinway in his daybook. "Still a sprained wrist, pounded,
blurred and used too much loud pedal. Great success." The triumph of
Josef Hofmann approached that of Paderewski, and poets were once again
catalyzed:

> I heard him play! My being filled
> With rapture at a bound.
> And ev'ry pulsing current thrilled
> In ecstasy of sound.
>
> His wizard fingers rose and dipped
> In waves along the keys,
> Like rhythmic billows, silver-lipped
> On bright melodic seas . . .
>
> I hear e'en now the thrilling cries
> His fingers uttered then.
> And all the gates of paradise
> Are oped to me again.

Such were the powers of the pianist in the closing years of Victoria's
reign, at least to those with lyricist predisposition or affliction as in the
case of Samuel M. Gaines, the author of the Hofmann verse. Some portion
of Hofmann's success was due to the fact that he stepped on American soil

with excellent timing between waves of "Paddymania," whose presence still brought smiles to the faces of ink salesmen everywhere.

In anticipation of the 1900 musical season, the *Times* musical editor updated his readers on the maestro's life: "The fact that he is married will in the opinion of the present writer not make any difference to the lotus eating dames who dream away the sweetest moments of their lives under the magic spell of his personality. . . . It makes little difference whether the famous Polish player plays as well as he used to or not, the women will go just as mad over him. There is something in the magnetism of the man that is quite irresistible." Continuing with his analysis, the critic commented that "there must be in this town somewhere in the neighborhood of a million young women studying the art of striking the keys of the piano. . . . When they go to hear a pianist of distinction play on the instrument the thing that astonishes them most is the speed with which he plays the pieces which they have to play slowly. . . . When Paderewski plays, the speed is the last thing which comes forcibly to my attention, for as a matter of fact he seldom plays at an amazing tempo. . . . He is accused of having less technic than some of his rivals. But the end of piano technic is not speed. The end of piano technic is tone. To preserve the pure singing tone, no matter how intricate the passage under the fingers, that is the end of good technic."

The views of the *Times* critic notwithstanding, Paderewski, like Hofmann, had taken up pounding on the piano. Lunching at Luchow's on Fourteenth Street a few days before Christmas 1899, Fred Steinway saw the editor of the *Musical Courier*, Marc A. Blumenberg. "Mark [*sic*] came over, tried to inveigle us into giving our opinion of pounding of Paderewski," wrote Fred. "Mark tries to make capital out of it to show Paderewski public success only a fad. . . . He fell flat." Later that same day Fred conferred with Charles, who had talked with Paddy's secretary Goerlitz and Fred learned that "Mark wants to create trouble between him [Paderewski] and us." Charles also mentioned that "Tretbar dissatisfied with Paddy's new departure of pounding and wants to mulct Paddy 10% of his total receipts." The perceptions of the aesthetes mattered little to the general population. "Today's Paddy recital a phenomenal success. Crowded house. 12 recalls," wrote Fred.

After an absence of four years, it was, said the *Times*, "as if he had never gone away. There was the same apparently slight figure seated alone at the piano on the half-dark stage. There was the same pale, thoughtful face with the nimbus of orange hair floating around it. There were the same graceful, sinewy hands and the same broad, powerful shoulders. There were the same manifestations of public absorption in the playing of this remarkable man." Two-thirds down the column, it was revealed that there actually was a performance. Paderewski "dropped some notes, but there was the usual loveliness of color and clarity" while "the octave repetitions were enough to drive an ordinary pianist to despair," and "there was always that marvelous singing tone to send the composer's thoughts into every heart." There was no mention of the "banging" that disturbed Tretbar; and Marc Blumenberg, sensing that the time was not right to editorially desecrate the musical idol of millions and his favorite piano, maintained a more or less respectful silence.

This could not last, and by 1908 Ignace Jan Paderewski was the locus of critical derision. After fifteen years with Steinway, Paderewski pledged allegiance to Weber. For reasons unclear, but likely stemming from dissatisfaction with the pianos available in California and Charles's refusal to alter them, the world's most renowned pianist switched brands. The occasional shard suggests that Charles H. Steinway and Ignace J. Paderewski had a history of conflict even in William's time when Charles tried to limit the maestro's expenditures on his debut tour. William went so far as to make humorous allusions to Charles's views of Paderewski's habits at a party for the virtuoso.

Charles F. Tretbar provided the lubrication between the surfaces of business and art, but Tretbar retired to Germany after forty years with the house in 1905. Less than two years passed before the friction between Charles and Paddy reached white heat, and the mutually useful promotional mechanism that had run for a decade and one-half failed. Weber was now a part of a "piano trust" formed in 1903 and called the Aeolian Company. Capitalized at $10 million and producing many thousands of instruments per year under the Weber, Steck, Wheelock, and Stuyvesant names for pianos, Votey organs, and Vocalion phonographs, the firm was well able to make a remunerative deal with Paderewski, as evidenced by their seventy-thousand-dollar season guarantee to a less famous pianist, Moritz Rosenthal.

The primary Aeolian thrust was with a device invented by E. S. Votey called the Pianola, an "automatic" piano mechanism. The early versions of these were called "piano players" and were large boxes that were pushed up to conventional pianos. The box contained the mechanism, had foot pedals, held the rolls, and had levers jutting out of the back that tapped on the keys. Absent of dynamics, tempo variations, or other inflection, the early players were musical machine guns, belching sound instead of bullets. They were aggressively promoted to the millions of households in which an instrument was found, but where no one could competently play.

Paderewski, ever alert to opportunities to earn cash, endorsed the Aeolian Pianola in 1900: "It is astonishing," wrote the maestro, "to see this little device at work executing the masterpieces of the pianoforte literature with a dexterity, clearness and velocity which no player, however great, can approach. Everyone who wishes to hear absolutely faultless, free of any kind of nervousness, piano playing should buy a Pianola. It is perfect."

Automatic instruments soon began to replace musicians in hotels, bars, restaurants, and brothels throughout the nation, and composers were also beggared by "automatic music." The copyright laws did not comprehend the creation of "mechanical music," and the United States Supreme Court, in all its collective wisdom, could not see the parallels among sheet music, melody, and piano rolls and therefore saw no reason why vendors of rolls should pay royalties to composers. Steinway & Sons held itself majestically aloof from the player conflicts: "For a long time the Steinway house have maintained the position that they did not propose to go into the player piano business, but could not prevent a purchaser from putting whatever mechanism he desired in a Steinway piano," reported *Music Trades*.

The firm "desired to maintain their position as the great artistic piano manufacturer of the world, and so preferred a position of absolute independence in the matter of players." Given the eruption of vituperation, some on aesthetic grounds, some on economic, and most an admixture of the two on the part of players and composers, this was a wise decision, but one which Mr. Paderewski did not share.

Paderewski's endorsement of the automatic piano did not endear him to his fellow musicians, and combined with his continuing immense commercial success, it made him the ideal mark for those with artistic discrimination or pretensions to it. By the concert season of 1907–08 the Polish pianist had become a touring target of opportunity for the nation's critics. Whether through planning or luck, Steinway & Sons evaded being boiled in the same pot of critical oil. Their erstwhile paramount virtuoso now played a Weber.

"The significance of Paderewski's exclusive use of the Weber piano is plainly evident," wrote a reviewer for the Portland, Oregon, *Daily Journal* in 1908 under the head "Paderewski Concert a Somber Wet Blanket of Musicless Bangs and Nerve-Wracking Crashes. . . . Yes, we may well take off our hats to the piano and its sturdy make. . . . The public likes a big noise and would probably have applauded him more wildly if he got both feet on the keyboard as some feared he might. It is players of this type that have created the cartoons of that kind and have given the world the mistaken idea of the exaggeration and lack of sanity of all great pianists."

Paderewski, it seems, had founded, or perhaps reestablished if the dress and behavior of Liszt was recollected, a school of piano pyrotechnics. In a time before the advent of laser light shows, onstage smoke effects, and speakers stacked twelve feet high, the maestro's gentler theatricalities and mannerisms could still incense critics, as did the behavior of his audiences. "There is another phase of this Paderewski business which deserves severe condemnation," editorialized the *Oakland Enquirer*. "That is the silly, almost disgusting demonstrations made at his concerts by a crowd of emotionally overwrought women . . . that almost resulted in injury to the pianist. Such exhibitions of bad taste, not to say vulgarity, are disgusting to any right-minded person who has some regard for the dignity of music. . . . It is not to be wondered that so many practical men of the world look upon music as a profession suitable only for the milksop, and consider the average man who makes a calling of the art a weak-minded, sentimental sort of creature, devoid of manly qualities, and chiefly fit for the admiration of a lot of light-headed women."

The Western press soon expanded the attacks to include the Weber piano: "I never heard a piano sound as 'tin-panny' in my life," wrote a *Los Angeles Herald* reporter, continuing that "after Paderewski's first solo a little boy was heard to say, 'I don't like him, mamma; he pounded all the tune out of the piano.' " The *Los Angeles Times* reported that the Polish virtuoso travelled with seven pianos, then wryly observed that "about two out of seven grand pianos are out of commission most of the time, for Paderewski is the Thor of the keyboard, and after every few concerts he wreaks damage enough to cause a general over-hauling of the instrument."

The crowds still came, sometimes as many as five thousand persons and at prices as high as three dollars per head. The maestro's agents hawked programs and photos in the aisles before, during, and after the concert. "Let us say nothing," commented the *Oregon Sunday Journal*, "of the bad taste of selling these things with a 'hollering' up and down the aisles in the midst of an artist's performance." The programs were "elaborate little pamphlets with the whole program made simple—a sort of 'twenty questions in philosophy' proposition, resembling the get rich quick schemes and patent cure-all remedies." Paderewski's activities in the name of his art may well have generated relief, if not smiles, at Steinway Hall, now safely severed from the activities of the maestro errant. It may be safely assumed that more than one Steinway salesman patiently explained to prospects that the so-called "pounding" was actually caused by faults in the Weber instrument itself.

But it was not long until Steinway & Sons itself was dragged into the conflict by the trade press. Sensing a sure circulation-builder, *Musical Courier* editor Marc Blumenberg scrambled to the forefront of the growing phalanx of Paddy malevolents and reprinted negative local reviews for the national audience, capping them with his own minor masterpiece of cavil entitled "Locks and Lambasting." Wrote Blumenberg: "The shock-headed poseur who flaunted in the breeze a pomaded hirsute mop, and dressed himself like a figure in a Hogarth caricature, now meets with the ridicule he deserves, and makes people wonder how a former generation could have considered such a freak anything but a pitiful guy, ripe for the country circus or dime museum." The piece did not mention Paderewski by name, nor was there a need.

A rumor soon circulated, possibly placed by Blumenberg himself, that it was Steinway & Sons which was behind the attacks on Paderewski. The source of this intelligence was William's and, later, Albert J. Weber's journalistic consort, John C. Freund, now editor of *Music Trades*. According to Freund, who was fully familiar with the Byzantine machinations of the piano business, the persecutions of Paderewski were a blackmail plot by Blumenberg, who had been rejected in his attempt to obtain twenty thousand dollars in advertising from the Aeolian Company, the sponsors of the Paderewski tour and makers of the Weber. Rebuffed in this putative extortion plot, the remarkably resourceful Blumenberg then began conspicuously visiting Steinway Hall. His purpose in this, claimed Freund, was to persuade the Steinways to pay him ten thousand dollars to *stop* harassing Paderewski since the trade already assumed they were paying him to smear the artist.

A person signing only as C.M. commented, "It seems to me that if there is any general impression that the house of Steinway is, whether directly or indirectly, connected with these attacks, the cause of this impression is not to be traced to any hints which may have been dropped by Mr. Blumenberg himself, but rather to the experience of the trade that, in times past, such attacks were generally inspired by the leading pianomakers themselves. The trade still has lively remembrance of the Great Steinway-Chickering controversy over awards at the Paris Exhibition and of the Steinway-Weber controversy at the Philadelphia Exhibition and the great scandals that resulted therefrom." How "lively" the memory was of events three and four decades past may be questioned, but the results closely followed what might be called William's Iron Law: controversy generates publicity and publicity generates piano sales. It was no accident that the next year, 1909, saw an all-time high in American piano sales with 365,545 instruments sold, about triple the number of automobiles produced that same year and a quantity greater than all the cars then on the road. Though none could know it, this was to be a production record never exceeded.

Steinway & Sons had risen with the tide but not higher, producing roughly the same proportion of the industry's output as it had ten years earlier. The market share lost during the last years of William's reign was not recovered. Had it been, Steinway would have been building twice the thirty-seven hundred pianos per year that it was in 1909. The evidence shows an almost perfect relationship between the growth of Steinway production and the national economy, which surged upward in the first decade of the century.

These facts did not prevent Charles from frequently congratulating himself on his profitable management. "All stockholders like statistics, and I will conclude my remarks with the interesting statement that Steinway & Sons for the past six years declared dividends to the amount of $2,720,000 or 236% on their entire capital," said Charles to the stockholders in April 1905. Though the arithmetic was defective—the amount was 136 percent—the accomplishment was impressive and represented an average annual return to the stockholder of 22.67 percent per year. The profits came, almost directly, from the increased volume of piano production at reduced prices. Per-piano profits in both America and Europe were a decade later roughly half the levels of 1900–01, sliding from about $150 to about $75 in 1911 in the United States, which itself accounted for about two-thirds of the contribution to the happiness and prosperity of the house's stockholders.

In the manner of managers since the dawn of time, Charles attributed good results to his own probity and that of his fellow executives while pointing to the economy as the source of difficulty in weak years. In 1908, for example, the still remarkable but reduced dividend of 15 percent was "in line with the policy of conservatism and retrenchment adopted by all the leading businesses in the United States." A recession began in May 1907 and was punctuated by a financial panic in October with the failure of the Knickerbocker Trust Company, the receivership of Westinghouse, and the suspension of trading on the Pittsburgh Stock Exchange, followed by a general stock market collapse. So severe was the panic that the city's savings banks invoked a little used rule that allowed them to limit savings withdrawals to one hundred dollars or less. "There are sure to be people, particularly among the foreigners . . . who will be howling at us for their money tomorrow. The savings banks of this city are simply attempting to protect the people from themselves," said a bank officer. It was the worst panic since 1893, and reverberations continued through the first half of 1908. The events must have reminded the family of the dark times of William's final years and the aftermath. The Paderewski troubles continued as well, though Marc Blumenberg became less obviously hostile, and the avalanche of negative reviews ceased with the close of the season.

Blumenberg now claimed that Paderewski "is merely following a destiny and cannot avoid what he is doing because of the tremendous impact of correlated forces, such, for instance, as an attractive personality operating upon a susceptible and nonreflecting people who are fed and who live upon sensationalism." This was comparatively temperate, but the impression that Paderewski was more a personality than a pianist had been tattooed in the minds of those claiming artistic standards. The maestro's obligatory statement to Weber upon sailing from America read like a patent medicine blurb: "For the first time I have not felt tired of piano playing after a long concert tour. My fingers are not sore, my arms not aching, my nerves and muscles are as strong and fresh as the day of my arrival. This is entirely due to the supreme quality of your instrument." Even this tepid testimonial to Weber as the elixir of pianos was quickly expropriated by Weber's actionmaker, Schwander, who claimed that this "supreme quality" was due to the use of their components.

The odor of the material had invaded the domain of art, and the promotional techniques developed by William were now not only blatantly copied but executed without finesse. "Steinway & Sons are through with it," wrote the *Musical Courier*. "No more will that house interfere with the business of the music bureaus by engaging pianists in Europe or by becoming musical agents. If pianists coming here to play wish to play Steinway pianos they can, through their agents, make arrangements for the use of a Steinway, provided the firm is of the opinion that the artist has the caliber to do justice to the instrument." The retrenchment was not limited to Steinway: "Chickering . . . will not even furnish their grands for any extended tour unless paid for," while Knabe only considered artists who had "not been on sale in this country before," reported the *Courier*.

The underlying forces, as usual, were hidden and were both economic and technological. Caught in the sales slump following the panic, manufacturers naturally averred promotional expenditures. More significant, however, was the impact of automatic pianos. The boxes called *piano* players, which just a few years earlier were willingly pushed up against conventional instruments, were now superseded by integrated mechanisms called *player* pianos. While attempting to build a hardware monopoly through patents and a software corner through music licensing for piano rolls, the Aeolian Company was also aggressively promoting its Pianola with multipage, multicolor magazine advertisements. Ardent advocates of what would later be called the "long-copy" approach, Aeolian marketeers embarked on a strategic campaign to convince the nation that the piano was, in *Musical Courier*'s words, "a superannuated instrument now superseded by the Pianola; that the piano is useless."

An Aeolian advertisement from 1902 set forth the basic appeals used for decades: "The Pianola solves the problem of music in the home," exulted the copywriter. "Its production was the crowning achievement of musical activity in the century just closed." Having disposed of a virtual army of nineteenth-century composers, musicians, and instrumentmakers in a mere fourteen words, the key benefit was advanced: "Within the home, where there is a Pianola, music reigns supreme, and every member of the household may be a performer. The piano is available to all. In its rhythmic tones the busy man forgets his cares. The hostess finds relief from thoughts concerning entertainments for guests; and happy young folks respond with feet or voice and in dance or song find wholesome recreation underneath the family roof."

Like the piano before it, the Pianola could succor husbands, amaze guests, and keep the kids out of the bar or the barn, but mother's effort was reduced; she did not have to learn to play; and so, like the sewing machine before it and the dishwasher after, the piano was transformed into a labor-saving appliance. Automatic piano sales rose at an increasing velocity. The scratchy honk of the equally easy-to-use "talking machine" provided little competition, and the "wireless" none at all. Radio was still a means of moving Morse-coded buzzes between shore and ship.

There were other rattlings of the future. A nineteen-year-old Cleveland man named Melville Holmes "intends to combine the advantages of the telephone and the phonograph," reported *Music Trade Review*, and he had applied for a patent on his invention. The device built by Holmes was an

435

answering machine. There was the Ackerman Grand Opera Piano that "both plays and sings," announced *Music Trade*. "This instrument not only renders all the best music of the world in an artistic manner but also reproduces with exact fidelity the human voice. A person owning one of these can in his own home listen to any of the operas. . . . A separate attachment will be furnished when desired which will reproduce the stages of the Manhattan and Metropolitan opera houses of New York showing the artists in each scene and act of the famous operas." The Ackerman, a conceptual precursor to projection television with videodisc and surround sound, was not a success.

As the twentieth century coalesced around Steinway & Sons, the industry continued to combine. The year 1908 brought the formation of the American Piano Company, which, capitalized at $12 million, was even larger than Aeolian. Into the new company went two former competitors: Chickering, which had abandoned its New York hall in favor of selling through Wanamaker's department store; and a house even older than Steinway, Knabe of Baltimore. Haines Brothers, wounded by family fights, purported embezzlement, receivership, and the death of its founder, staggered into the shelter of Ampico, as did a number of long-forgotten brands. The new firm, said *Music Trade*, "will be able to market a piano product from the most expensive to the cheapest." The key word was undoubtedly *product*.

Against the encroachments of the modern, Steinway gave the public impression of remaining resolutely mid-Victorian. When the *New York World* visited the expanded Astoria works, the reporter saw that wood and its quality remained a family fixation, just as it was in the time of Heinrich Steinweg a half century before. There were six million board-feet in the yards, enough to cover 137 acres with lumber if laid out flat. Twenty different species were neatly stacked, and each plank was stamped with the date of purchase and the name of the buyer, the crosscut ends tacked with another piece of wood to prevent checking. "The care taken with Steinway lumber may be compared with that of a mother for a child," opined the reporter. Though the reporter did not know it, some of the wood he saw was likely also seen by William, dead now for more than a decade.

Theodore and Albert's foundry was still in operation, and, like reporters for the next half century, the *World* man observed that there was an "entire absence of hurry on the part of the workmen. . . . They are not urged to make haste, and would probably rebel if they were required to relinquish their work before they, and not the foreman, were satisfied with it." The age and experience of the work force also impressed the reporter: "It is not uncommon to meet men who have been there thirty or forty years, and some have spent a half century there. As one old gentleman put it: 'We never think of leaving. We live and die right here.'" To prove the point, the *World* writer was introduced to Otto Koch, who at age seventy-five was foreman of the finishing floor and had worked at Steinway for more than fifty years.

If tradition, craftsmanship, and quality were important, so was their origin, and that was the family: "Henry E. Steinway compelled every one of his sons to go into the factory and learn how to build a Steinway piano. They in turn compelled their sons to work at the bench until they were capable of turning out the perfect Steinway. In this manner the great house has continued to develop members of the blood and consequently the pianos are made according to the precepts of the originators." There were references as well to artists and Steinway Hall. The formula developed by William had proven not only durable but at least as powerful in the new century as in the old.

In a business publication called *Systems* Charles boldly sketched his management philosophy in an article entitled "Making Every Man a Producer." Experience came first. "In our establishment we consider a man almost a newcomer who has not been with us fifteen or twenty years. It is our strict policy never to take a man from outside the business to fill a good position. Our men are producers because they know that if they exert themselves they not only have life positions, but positions that will grow better and better."

Participatory democracy was key, thought Charles. "My desk is in their midst. . . . There is no atmosphere of exclusiveness in our office, and no attitude of awe toward the men high up. . . . Here I believe is the preventive for the growth of the unproductive element that often clogs a business." This system, claimed Charles, was not confined to the offices: "The heads of the departments mingle with the workers on the basis of equality." Charles thought that "modern cost-keeping methods" made determining the productivity of a "wage-earner" uncomplicated; salesmen were likewise easy to track. For those not meeting the standards, there was a straightforward remedy. "If a man is a drone by nature, incapable of enthusiasm, get rid of him." In a business where wood had to sit for years, men could not, Charles seemed to be saying. The severity of the admonition was softened slightly by the next pithy point: "Treat men fairly in the first place. Then give them hope of gain—personal gain."

By the standards of the time, this was a modern management philosophy, and there were other signs of change as well. By 1911 Steinway & Sons was in the player piano business. In a mode that would now be called a "strategic partnering," an arrangement was made with Aeolian in 1909. In this agreement Steinway & Sons was to provide pianos lengthened about ten inches to accommodate the player mechanism. These were sent to Aeolian in Garwood, New Jersey, where the players were installed. So equipped, the instruments were to be sold by Aeolian dealers, not Steinway dealers. With a single scratch of his pen, Charles multiplied the number of stores able to sell Steinways and vastly increased his effective advertising budget. While the press reports coolly proclaimed that "there was no connection between the two companies except in this agreement," there were other provisions powerfully advantageous to Steinway.

Easily the most important of these was a clause that read, "The Aeolian companies agree to officially relegate their Weber Pianola to second place under the Steinway Pianola; and they further agree to withdraw from the artistic piano concert field and that they will exploit the Weber piano in public only through such minor pianists as Steinway & Sons may permit." Charles achieved behind the scenes what William had been unable to do in years of public battle and controversy: eliminate the Weber name as a pretender to the crown of American pianomaking. Thus was the errant Paderewski also unhorsed, and not long after he returned to Steinway. His popular appeal continued, as did the critical disdain.

No longer the production and financial mammoth of the industry, Steinway & Sons now functioned as a fulcrum, balancing the market power of Aeolian and Ampico while tilting the balance arm to its own advantage. Though no records exist to substantiate the dynamics, it was likely fear of a Steinway alliance with Ampico that brought Aeolian to tender such favorable terms.

The agreement specified that Aeolian was to buy no less than six hundred pianos per year, equal to a 15-percent increase in Steinway production. The contract was to last for twenty-five years and called for a minimum of fifteen thousand pianos to be equipped as players. Ultimately less than half that number were sold, but Charles's accomplishment was as unparalleled as it was secret. He not only vanquished Weber permanently but caused a principal competitor to acknowledge Steinway supremacy: "Enter almost any drawing-room where refinement and elegance prevail," purred an Aeolian advertisement in 1912. "Before even its lid is raised, you know the name of the piano, whose graceful presence lends so much to its surroundings. Steinway! Another name might raise a question—this one does not." So broadcast the maker of Weber, Steck, Wheelock, and Stuyvesant pianos, finally reminding the public that "these superb instruments can be seen and heard only at Aeolian Hall" and "may be purchased on moderate monthly payments."

Starting at $1,250, 60 percent more than a small Steinway grand and more than twice that of an upright, the "monthly payments" were "moderate" enough to stimulate the sale of but 125 instruments that first year. Aeolian, though selling few Steinway Pianolas, continued to advertise heavily. However prestigious the association may have been, the Aeolian executives apparently never considered that the additional cost of their player mechanism would pay for hundreds of piano lessons. Charles, however, had seen the future and made it work to reaffirm the perceptual supremacy of Steinway & Sons in the new age of the automatic piano.

Of that new age there were other indicia. In 1910 the block-long factory on Park Avenue was sold for $650,000, and all pianomaking was moved to Astoria, giving final form to William's four-decade-old plan. The cause was change in the city itself. The Harlem railroad that chuffed below the Fourth Avenue grade spewing soot and cinders into the air soon would be covered. Park Avenue in midtown, still the site of gritty industry, tenements, and saloons, would therefore experience what was later called gentrification. It was finally time for Steinway & Sons to move to Queens completely, and the family brownstones on Fifty-third Street and the factory itself, now in the way of progress, soon were razed. The intersection of Park and Fifty-third, where Charles's father Charles and a priest held drunken rioters at bay during the Civil War, where William watched mounted police club strikers as they stormed the works, and where Theodore offered to buy beers for one thousand men, was now a corner where very respectable pedestrians looked each way before crossing.

Manhattan demography mutated, and one of those changes was the movement of the population center uptown. The Fourteenth Street showroom, once at the center of Manhattan wealth and glamour, was now a monument to grandeurs past among lesser retail establishments; retailing panache migrated to Fifth Avenue. "Charles H. Steinway said last night that Steinway & Sons are to abandon their quarters on East Fourteenth Street in a short time. They will take their retail salerooms to Fifth Avenue above Thirty-fourth Street," reported the *New York Sun*. "This removal of the retail salesroom is due to the progress of business northward, the Steinway customer, Mr. Steinway said, seldom coming below Twenty-third Street, except to visit Steinway and Tiffany's." That 1901 recognition of obsolescence was not quickly acted upon. It was not until 1916, an uncharacteristically long lapse for Charles, that lots were purchased uptown on Fifty-seventh Street, not far from Carnegie Hall. But even then the house did not join the northerly migration in Manhattan.

The reasons were clearly financial, and the root cause was World War I. The output of the Hamburg factory tripled from 730 pianos in 1896, the year William died, to 2,203 in 1913, the year before the outbreak of hostilities. It was yet another confirmation of William Steinway's vision, and multinational operations were now routine for many in the music industry, including the most modern and aggressive firms such as Aeolian.

But no one could forecast that a Bosnian student named Prinzip, with three blasts from a Browning, would assassinate the heir to the throne of the Hapsburgs and his wife on June 28, 1914. The act catalyzed conflict of unprecedented scale, and within two months there were fourteen declarations of war among the nations of Europe. With the onset of war, production plummeted and profits became losses. Among the last things the English or French were likely to buy in 1914 was a German piano, and Hamburg production fell that year by 50 percent. As the scope of the conflict widened, the building of pianos became nearly pointless, and production in 1915 fell by half again to but 551 units, most of which were presumably sold in Germany. By 1917 and the entry of America into the war, German policy forbade the export of funds, and while Steinway & Sons still theoretically owned Hamburg, almost all contact was lost. In February 1917 a report was received "by radio" that piano production in Hamburg had been 1,346 units in 1916, and a small profit was repatriated. The more than one million dollars invested in the Hamburg factory was stranded for the duration and for many years thereafter; the ledgers of Steinway & Sons showed no entries for the German business until 1923.

Meanwhile, the American money machine carefully repaired by Charles once again stalled, then nearly halted, as the grit of external events clogged its wheels. The years 1913 and 1914 were recessionary, and the last half of 1914 was further chilled by the onset of war in Europe. In America there was a change in the attitudes toward Germans, and in a few years general tolerance, if not admiration, was transmogrified into widespread hate. The new Teutonophobia was a politically useful phenomenon for those wishing to engage America in the war, and since fear created uncertainty that sold newspapers, columns were filled with tales of German plots and German companies operating as nests for spies.

By 1917 New York City schools were purged of texts with positive references to Germany, and teaching the German language was forbidden. German books were to be removed from libraries throughout the nation, and a bureau was proposed to teach Germans "Americanism." There were, claimed some earnestly, two types of Germans: those favoring democracy whose fathers were a part of the German Revolution of 1848 and the others who did not. For those who believed this theory, the Steinways would have been considered "good" Germans. There was other evidence of loyalty as well. Steinway's treasury now bristled with Liberty Bonds, and hundreds of thousands of dollars were paid in wartime "excess profits" taxes. Nor was the Steinway contribution to the war solely financial: Frederick Vietor, a grandson of Albert and member of the elite Squadron A, First Cavalry, New York National Guard, served in France. As in the Civil War fifty-five years before, a "member of the blood" was voluntarily near, if not in, harm's way.

The effect of the Great War on German-related business in New York could be seen in a flurry of name changes. The German Savings Bank of Brooklyn became the Lincoln Savings Bank, while the Germania Savings Bank of Brooklyn took the name Fulton Savings Bank. Banks that did not seek the safe haven of American heroes still repudiated their ethnic origins with nondescript names. Manhattan's Germania Bank became the Commonwealth Bank and the German Savings Bank, once a proud investment of William, changed its identity, if not its depositors, by adopting the new name Central Savings Bank.

There can be little doubt that competitive piano salesmen asked customers whether or not they really wanted a *German* piano. The answer, among some buyers, must have been negative, for by 1919 Steinway piano sales slipped to the levels of 1911, and with the sales went the profits and dividends. The firm was trapped by geopolitics and social attitudes in its ancestral home on Fourteenth Street, now over half a century old, but this did not mean that it was either moribund or helpless.

To offset, or at least attenuate, the association with a now-defeated Germany, an aggressive and contemporary advertising campaign was launched in 1919. That year trade and consumer magazines carried revitalized, high-frequency messages: "Steinway, the Highest Expression of Musical Arts and Manufactures," read one lead in early 1919. "Away in the dim past, Micheal Angelo [*sic*] hit upon a great truth and the words he used to express this truth, 'Trifles make perfection; but perfection is no trifle,' find echo in the world of today." Alongside a portrait of Michelangelo, the copy continued, "Were we to give a single reason for Steinway supremacy we would choose this phrase of ancient coinage. A great many things Steinway designers, engineers and artisans do *seem* to be trifles, and they are so regarded by others. But the making of a Steinway is a business of taking care of trifles and Steinway perfection has taken care of itself. For both the man of genius and the product of surpassing merit the Star of Ascendancy shines high." William's concept of excellence was now blended with the new ideas of engineers and designers. The standards were enduring, but the methods were modern, claimed these ads.

Steinway was not a captive of the nineteenth century, and change, claimed the new advertising, was necessary: "Business statistics demonstrate that the eclipse of strong commercial names is brought about chiefly through a belief that prestige, once attained, is everlasting, regardless of how the product may be subsequently handled," read a trade display ad in the spring of 1919. Where once William had spoken individually through the nation's newspapers, the family now spoke corporately through advertising, but this was no less a reflection of personal belief.

The advantages were multiple. Advertising could be directly controlled; it was deliberatively created and its messages could be approved in advance. The natural vagary of the news process, its spontaneity, and the need for relationships with reporters were eliminated. Cash-on-the-barrelhead communications superseded the web of associations and the fame of a single man. Most important, men had finite lives; corporations, if not theoretically immortal, could survive for generations. And so the legend evolved.

In addition to introducing the then-novel notions of engineers and designers into the Steinway mythology, there was another transformation. The Steinway workers, privately viewed as "carpenters" in the time of Heinrich and "workmen" in the time of William, were now called *artisans*, at least publicly. "A Little Better Than Seems Necessary," began another advertisement. "Every Steinway artisan engaged in building the Steinway piano knows that the above phrase is a Steinway law." Employees were now recognized as a part of the process of pianomaking. This too was a change, but some things remained the same.

"Gentlemen: In accordance with the present living conditions, soaring rents and necessities of life which are accomplished by non-patriots, who are getting rich on the working class, we are compelled to be united and demand an increase of wages of 25% for all workers in your factories," wrote the "Steinway Employees" to Charles in April 1919. "The working class won the war of democracy, but not for themselves; it is only slavery and misery that we receive. We trust that you gentlemen will not be like the moneymaking sharks who do not care enough for the lives of their workers. Kindly give an answer to our Mr. Peterson, Committee Representative, by Tuesday, April 22, 1919, 11 A.M. United we stand. Very Truly Yours, The Steinway Employees."

The artisans had spoken, and the Steinways replied: "We will absolutely refuse this demand for the following reasons. 1. We do not believe that the majority of our loyal and faithful employees wish to threaten us in this manner. 2. During the past two years we have granted all your demands for increase in wages, we have granted the eight-hour day and time and one-half for overtime. 3. We know that if our employees work a full eight-hour day under the present price scale their wages are higher than any other piano factory in the U.S.A. We are now, as we always have been, willing to listen to any individual or department regarding adjustment of inequalities of wages. [signed] Steinway & Sons."

The direct impetus for the strike, which began just a few days later, was the explosive inflation of the war years. Between 1917 and 1919 the price of a dozen eggs rose 39 percent to 67 cents per dozen, milk increased 38 percent to 31 cents per gallon, and round steak jumped 35 percent to 39 cents per pound. But unlike the great inflation of the Civil War, manufacturing wages more than kept pace nationally, growing 46 percent between 1917 and 1919 to an average of $21.84 per week. The reason was an unprecedented level of strikes, which trebled between 1915 and 1917 and continued, only somewhat attenuated, through the war and into 1919. At Steinway Hall in 1919, a piano polisher was making $25.73 per week, and Fred Steinway, ever the conciliator, proposed a raise to $28, almost 30 percent higher than the national average wage. His offer was rejected, and the union responded with another demand for a 25 percent wage hike.

As in times past Steinway was the first target, but by fall the strike of the International Piano, Organ and Instrument Workers Union spread citywide, and some ten thousand pianomen were out of work. In late September that year, with the troubles at Steinway now five months old, the union escalated its demands. The new labor proposal called for a four-hour reduction to a forty-four-hour week, double time for overtime, no Sunday work, and minimum pay of $36 per week for "daywork" and $42 for piecework. Under this proposal, a journeyman pianomaker would earn more than $2,100 per year. The refractory nature of the demand can be seen in the fact that actual wages did not reach the $42-per-week level for nearly a quarter of a century. A wage of $42 was 80 percent above the average paid by all New York manufacturers. The union also called for a "closed shop"; all employees were to be members of the union. Questions of practicality aside, the men believed deeply in their cause and remained on strike for months. So it came to be that the family confronted a work force as implacable as any in the times of "Boss William."

"BOLSHEVISM NOT NEW," headlined the *New York Times* in a review of the labor unrest boiling over, not only at Steinway, but across the nation. With the menace of the Hun defeated, this new dark force was threatening, but not, according to the *Times*, with the strength of previous incarnations under the labels of socialism and anarchism. "The disease we now call Bolshevism, with the theories and purposes it represents, is less virulent and formidable than it was fifty years ago. . . . The tendency to violence, disorder and rebellion against constituted authority is weaker than it was fifty years ago."

If this was change, the methods of combat were nonetheless still the same, and the piano manufacturers coalesced again as an association. The response to the strike might easily have been drafted by the wraith of William Steinway: "We will oppose to the end, any attempt to force us to the 'closed shop.' We will never allow any outside agency to interfere in our dealings with each other. All employees who obey shop rules and do their work properly will be assured of continuous employment and protection against any outside agency whatever which seeks in any way to interfere with them in their work," wrote Steinway & Sons to its employees. Meanwhile a hiring agency was set up by the manufacturers association to vet new workers to replace the strikers, and the usual pronouncements of a refusal to be "dictated to" were issued.

The management of the 1919 strike was in the hands of Fred Steinway and thirty-six-year-old Theodore E. Steinway, William's son from his second marriage, whose career with the house began in 1900 as an apprentice. Fred and Theodore E. attended the strike meetings of the New York Pianomakers Association, not as the dominant voice as William had, but as equals among a dozen or more manufacturers. Charles, in poor health for more than a year, had not been at his desk "in their midst" at Steinway Hall for more than six months.

One month into the full strike Charles H. Steinway died of "intestinal trouble." There was a symmetry in this, for sixty-two years before when Charles was born on Hester Street, Manhattan seethed with social unrest, and when Charles died in his Fifth Avenue hotel suite, the city was once again seized with fear. Though Charles's address had changed, some things had not.

Chapter 29

A DEMOCRATIC AND GENIAL CHARACTER

"In the death of Mr. Steinway the music world has suffered an irreparable loss, for in his business and personal life he represented a distinct power for good and contributed materially to the uplift of music and business," testified the *Music Trade Review*. "Those who knew Chas. H. Steinway intimately will cherish his memory. He was a man of parts, of a lovable disposition, and he hated sham. He was always democratic and approachable and a host of friends will miss him."

The funeral was "most impressive," reported *MTR* in its next weekly edition. "Seldom have members of the music trade and profession witnessed more impressive funeral ceremonies than those conducted over the body of Charles H. Steinway . . . and seldom has so sincere a tribute been paid to the memory of a man who had sought so little of the limelight during his life." Spectacular funerals were a Steinway tradition in America, beginning with the death of Henry Steinway in 1865 and continuing through the interments of Heinrich, Albert, and William. But the standards for fashionable funerals had metamorphosed in the twenty-three years, almost to the day, since the last burial of a pianomaking Steinway. Charles's funeral drew no crowds to Steinway Hall, nor was there a wake in the home. No brass bands played, no chorus sang in German, and no great procession of employees filed past his coffin or marched through the streets in front of the hearse.

The services were held at the Campbell Funeral Church, uptown at Sixty-sixth and Broadway.

There was music, of course, and an organist named H. Everett Hall—no hint of the Germanic in that surname—played one of Charles's own compositions, *Lamentation*. "Mr. Steinway was a talented pianist and musician," explained the *Music Trade Review*, "and wrote a number of compositions for the piano." Charles's musical abilities were apparently not well known to the trade. Substituting for the massed one hundred voices of the Liederkranz, of which Charles was still a member, was the Clyric Quartet singing hymns in English. An Episcopal priest eulogized Charles before two dozen members of the trade from as far away as Kansas City and Toronto, a few artists, friends, and the members of the family. "A wealth of floral tributes turned the chapel and the adjoining hall into a bower of roses, chrysanthemums and lilies," noted the reporter. Innumerable flowers and Charles's burial in the Greenwood mausoleum were the only visible links to funerals past.

The great contraction of Steinway celebrity engineered by Charles was best measured by his own obituaries in the daily press. Where William's death had received page-one coverage in the *Times*, the passing of Charles warranted ten lines in the back of the paper. The death of Charles's father a half century before had received much wider notice. But pianomen in general and Charles in particular were not celebrities anymore; the pianoman was no longer a keeper of the flame of American Musical Culture. He was a businessman and was therefore no less or more interesting to the editors of the dailies than a banker or accountant.

This, too, was change, and Marc Blumenberg presaged the perceptual shift a decade before Charles's death. "Even if all the piano business would cease and no more pianos were made and all stores where pianos were sold were to close up or down, it would not create a ripple in the industrial, commercial or financial worlds—why not? Because the piano business is . . . only a small part of the industrial establishment." By the time of Charles's death in 1919, the federal government was assembling relatively competent data on the nation's manufacturing, and it was tabulated that the total value of all pianos produced in that year was $95,823,444.

Of that almost $96 million, Steinway that year of the great strike accumulated about 2.9 percent of the total. Ten years before in 1909 the house had 3.7 percent, so Charles, the silent Steinway who avoided the "limelight" but was privately proud of his business acumen, had actually presided over a declining company. In the last year of William's life Steinway & Sons revenues were about 5.5 percent of the output of the entire music industry, making it a major force in its segment. In the last year of Charles's life Steinway was but 1.15 percent of its industry's total sales. Musical instrumentmaking in America had grown more than ten times while Steinway

& Sons had barely tripled in size. Charles's pride in management techniques, his ability to measure the productivity of his employees, and his pioneering work in impersonal advertising as a substitute for personal fame had succeeded only moderately.

Charles H. Steinway was a hostage to the legacy of Uncle Bill. While William had been intuitive, he was analytical. Private versus public, deliberate versus impulsive, apolitical versus political; the adjectival pairs describing the two men were many, and they were poles apart on psychological inventories not yet invented. But in death it became clear that they shared personal and poignant similarities. One mimesis was the profound affection for music; each was, in a sense, an unfulfilled artist. But while William tolerated the eccentricities and demands of performers based on a personal understanding, Charles rejected those demands and eccentricities from the same comprehension.

"STEINWAY FORTUNE PUT AT $5,000,000" headlined the *Times* less than one month after Charles' death. Where the estimate of the estate originated cannot be determined; it may have been a planted item designed to quell the latent anxieties of those who remembered the aftermath of William's decease, finally settled only a few years before. The story's key was no leak: "Although Charles F. M. Steinway, son, of Mountain Lakes, N.J., receives a trust fund of one-third the residuary estate and shares a third left to his mother Marie A. Steinway, upon her death, his father directs that the income paid to him be limited to $100 per week and says 'I make this provision for my son because I am of the opinion that he is lacking in business ability, and is not competent to take charge of and prudently use, manage, and dispose of money and property.' " Charles's daughter Marie, already married, was allowed to receive one-half the principal of her share when she reached the age of twenty-one. It was in this way that the world came to know that Charles did not believe his son to be competent, a conclusion to which he came when his only male child was twenty-two years old. Charles F. M., according to family sources, suffered from the same affliction as William's son George—alcoholism.

There was another family parallel as well: an unhappy marriage. This the *Times* left its readers to divine, reporting that "Mrs. Marie A. Steinway, the widow, lives at Pasadena, Cal." Charles and his wife had lived apart for some time, and soon after their 1885 marriage they were separated for long periods with Marie in Europe and Charles in New York. Family members recollect that each had other romantic relationships. Having seen the fruits of scandal in William's life—the seizure of Henry's children, the divorce from Regina, the internecine legal warfare with his brother Henry W. T., the aftermath of George's divorce and death—Charles may well have decided that interposing the width of the continent was preferable to a public refresher course in Steinway personal history conducted by the press if he himself should divorce.

446

"The will cuts off Mr. Steinway's brother, Henry W. T. Steinway, from any participation in the estate, but gives no reason," reported the *Times*. A young and probably harried reporter on the courthouse beat, to the family's good luck, had not checked his paper's morgue for the decade-long saga of the errant H.W.T., and the will had only said, "excepting and excluding my brother HENRY W. T. STEINWAY, and his issue from the benefit of this provision." There was a cold finality in this sibling enmity: at age sixty-three the never-married Henry W. T. was unlikely to produce any "issue."

Years later, the surrogate court concluded its deliberations and supervision, and the estate of Charles Herman Steinway was distributed. It amounted to about $650,000, not five million. During his forty-five years as a working "member of the blood," Charles had received in salary, bonuses, and dividends not less than 1.5 million and perhaps nearer to 2 million essentially untaxed dollars; but, like William, he did not die a millionaire. It was yet another parallel.

Within a few days of the death of Charles H., Steinway & Sons announced, predictably, that Frederick T. was to lead the house. Head of manufacturing for more than three decades, Fred now took the central desk in the counting room, where, as his brother before him, he could both see and be seen. With his round, metal-rimmed glasses, trimmed but full grey beard, and an archaic starched-collar style, Fred Steinway looked like a nineteenth-century man but thought like the future. In the less than eight years of his command, the house soared to renown, profitability, and production levels unseen before or since.

It was Charles's good fortune to rule the house during what was, quantitatively at least, an American cultural halcyon. In 1904 fully 7 percent of the value of consumer durables produced—items for the home intended to last three or more years, such as furniture, jewelry, and china—were musical instruments. Another 6.5 percent of the value was for books. Roughly one dollar in every seven was spent on these "cultural" products; today equivalent expenditures are about one dollar in sixty. The ratios remained relatively constant as the nation grew in the first decade of the century, and in 1909 a record 364,545 pianos were produced. One in fifty families bought a piano that year, more than three times the number that bought automobiles. Twice as many pianos were sold as bicycles, and piano sales also exceeded phonograph sales by about 10 percent. Musicians and music teachers outnumbered lawyers, doctors, bankers, accountants, and even clergymen by varying but material proportions.

The social balance would shift with the accumulating weight of the century, but in the lifetime of Charles the movement was small, except for the explosive growth of the automobile. Of these there were about 7.5 million in use in 1919, each one a mobile confirmation of William's foresight; one-sixth the size of the music instrument business when the family sold

William's moribund Daimler holdings, automobile production revenues were sixteen times larger than pianos by the time Charles died. The rapid growth of that new consumer product, the motorcar, had scant impact on the national interest in music, at least as measured by the proportion of spending. The reason was simple: the American economy had grown by nearly two and one-half times and per capita gross national product was 62 percent higher.

In this general prosperity music and the new mobility could coexist. The younger generation of Steinways themselves took up motoring as a hobby. Besides spectating at popular races such as the Vanderbilt Cup on Long Island, Theodore E. and William R. actually built themselves a car. They called their sporty yet slightly ungainly runabout the SAJI, standing for Société Anonyme de Junk Shop Internationale. This droll acronym was similar to fashionable European marques such as Fabbricattori Internazionale Automobili Turin, or FIAT, which then built ferociously fast and flagrantly expensive racing behemoths for the growing market of wealthy young men who thought themselves immortal. When William R. went to Europe for the firm in 1909, SAJI went along. Though altered occasionally to keep up with changing fashion, the car was his personal and slightly eccentric transportation for the next quarter-century as he advanced to head the European operations of Steinway & Sons.

The rise of the automobile, essentially without consequence for the piano business, may have imbued the industry with a false sense of invulnerability. A 1927 survey by *Literary Digest* was, commented *Music Trade Review*, "an extremely valuable record of the modern American home, its possessions and the degree of comfort and culture which exists therein." Focusing on Zanesville, Ohio, on the theory that it was somehow quintessentially American but supplemented by surveys taken in thirty-six other cities, the researchers found that 43.3 percent of the families owning or renting homes owned pianos and 54 percent owned phonographs. The data for the three dozen other cities showed piano ownership at 50.8 percent and phonographs in 58.9 percent of the households. Tabulating family hobbies, music was the second most popular recreation in Zanesville with 25 percent rating it as their "greatest interest." Nationally music ranked fifth with 16.7 percent preferring it over other recreations.

The recreations superseding music were distinctly twentieth century: motoring was the favorite of 25 percent; going to the movies was the first choice of 17.4 percent, and that phenomenon of the decade, radio, was the hobby of choice for 16.9 percent. In Zanesville only 10 percent preferred radio; the reason was simple: only 16 percent of the homes had one, about half of the national average in the study. The *Literary Digest* survey was a snapshot of the ongoing collapse of the piano industry. Player pianos had reached their peak of popularity in 1923 when more than 200,000 were produced. By 1927 sales were less than half that; Charles's decision to participate only indirectly in the player piano business had been prescient; though perhaps two million players had been sold in a national bacchanal of mechanical music, the automatic pianos were born by the technological sword and were about to die by it.

The beginning of the end for the piano as a cultural center of gravity can be marked with a rare historical certainty. The date was August 31, 1920, and the agent, perhaps fittingly, was identified by a number not a name: 8MK. That was the night that a radio station in Detroit broadcast the returns for a local primary election. "In the four hours that the apparatus, set up in an out of the way corner of the *News* building, was hissing and whirring its message into space, few realized that a dream and a prediction had come true. The news of the world was being given forth through this invisible trumpet to the unseen crowds in the unseen marketplace," reported the *Detroit News* in aggrandizing coverage of itself.

Publisher William E. Scripps had spent fifteen hundred dollars, less than the cost of a fancy Steinway Duoart, on a surplus navy transmitter, a microphone, and an Edison phonograph. The apparatus was operated by a sixteen-year-old office boy, Elton Plant, who hoped that his uncompensated after-hours help would one day result in a job as a *News* reporter. Plant ran from the teletype room, snatched the election returns from the teletype, then trotted back to the morgue and waiting microphone. Outside on the steps of the *News* building another man announced the election returns by megaphone to the waiting crowd. That night, for the last time, the man with the megaphone had a larger audience.

Scripps was by no means a lonely pioneer, but simply among the first to begin broadcasting, which was by then a decades-old idea. In 1906 a visionary named Thaddeus Cahill constructed a vast electrical music machine that was part pipe organ, part generating plant. The huge apparatus filled ten boxcars when moved from city to city; and Cahill traversed the eastern seaboard promoting telephone concerts in Washington, Boston, New York, and New Haven. Telephone subscribers asked the operator to connect them with the Telharmonium and were billed by the minute spent listening. With a sound called "aetherially pure," the sheer power of the instrument overloaded the telephone network, making regular calls impossible. The Telharmonium disappeared, taking millions of dollars of investors' money with it to a junkyard.

Thaddeus Cahill maintained that the economic and political power of The American Telephone and Telegraph Company had crushed his Telharmonium. That same power was now promoting broadcasting. After a few years of conflict, AT&T combined with General Electric and Westinghouse to form a patent pool for radio technology. Along with the behemoth United Fruit Company, a pioneer in using shipboard radio on South American routes, the four formed a new company, The Radio Corporation of America. Its ultimate mission: sell "Radio Music Boxes" to the public for seventy-five dollars. With a precision as rare as it was correct, the plan forecast the sale of 300,000 "Radiolas" in the second year of production; in 1923 that was exactly the number sold by RCA. Added to the 200,000 sets built by tiny firms that the Radio Corporation of America harassed as patent infringers, total output was a half-million radios. In 1920 not a single radio was factory-made, and only one licensed station broadcast sporadically; but in 1925 there were 571 stations in operation and two million sets sold. In five years four and one-half million households bought radios; one of every six families owned one. It had taken the piano generations to achieve such wide distribution.

The growth did not abate. By 1930 almost fourteen million homes had radios, surpassing the number with telephones. Seemingly overnight, the piano was being literally pushed from the parlor to the spare bedroom, the basement, or the garage, its place of honor on an inside wall usurped by a box that not only played music but brought news and ball scores from Cleveland, Fort Wayne, Chicago, Detroit, Buffalo, Schenectady, Nashville, or New York into the living room. The advertising would come later.

Unable to compete, piano production plummeted from 348,000 instruments in 1923 to 131,000 in 1929, a decline of 62 percent. Carnage followed; some companies frantically solicited mergers or buyouts while others collapsed as the national economy boomed. One firm began installing radios in their pianos; another claimed that pianos were unexcelled as radio antennae. A piano roll company started to sell radio tubes. But at Steinway & Sons the 4,120 American instruments built in 1921 grew 53 percent to 6,294 in 1926. The reason was apparent to anyone who saw the two-page color spreads that sometimes appeared in the *Saturday Evening Post*. A Steinway was not merely a piano; it was *art*.

Fred Steinway, the quiet man who looked like he had just stepped from a nineteenth-century painting, the man who spent thirty-eight years in a factory office while his brother and his uncle ran the business from Steinway Hall, the man who read books and sometimes played the piano alone, was now showing all who cared to notice that he was no less the genius than Uncle Bill and no less the businessman than brother Charles. Though born before the Civil War, Frederick Theodore Steinway understood the ways of the twentieth century, and above all he understood the power of words and pictures. That he was a highly competent photographer may have contributed to his grasp of media, but the sources of his mastery will forever remain unclear. After Fred died his wife destroyed all his papers; only a turn-of-the-century daybook forgotten at the factory survived the spousal purge.

The roots of the new Steinway strategy can be traced to a decision made at the turn of the century. It began, according to legend, with an observation by N. W. Ayer, whose firm already handled the accounts of Proctor & Gamble, Montgomery-Ward, Singer sewing machines, and Ferry seeds.

Ayer argued that existing Steinway promotion—concerts and ads in music journals—reached only those actively participating in music. Neglected were millions of prospective Steinway buyers who did not yet have strong musical interests.

Ayer's proposition intrigued the family. They began conservatively, perhaps with small newspaper ads for the captive N. Stetson and Company in Philadelphia. With large graphics of musical notation, the 1900 one-column-wide insertions are arresting today. Over a large drawing of the whole note, the musically illiterate were included by the explanatory headline: "One Whole Note." The brief selling copy queried, then answered, "How long can a whole note last? Much longer on a STEINWAY PIANO than on any other. Duration of tone is the result of fine workmanship. Steinway pianos sing the best because they are made the best."

The quality of the copy and the sophistication of the appeals improved with time. The Steinway ads often stressed owning a piano but rarely mentioned playing it. They worked subtly on the buyers' confusion in a marketplace with hundreds of brands: "The name Steinway on a piano means more than the word 'Sterling' on silver, because there are different grades of Sterling, but there is only one Steinway, and that is the best." Rarely did an advertisement appear without the word "best." In another ad, "There is no such thing as a 'better' Steinway. Each and every Steinway is *the best Steinway*." One did not "buy" a Steinway, one "invested." Amidst the word magic and ever-changing incantations to the god of sales, the copywriters never missed an opportunity to mention the brand. Some sentences contained the word "Steinway" as many as four times.

So successful were the concepts and constructs of Steinway advertising that they became the gateway to a generation of marketing. Propagating first into the realm of luxury automobiles where Packard, Peerless, Pierce-Arrow, and others crafted cognate arguments of semantic supremacy, they soon percolated into lesser classes of consumer goods where coffee, cereal, and cheap watches mimicked the look of Steinway advertising, aspiring to, if not always achieving, the patina and panache of excellence and luxury.

By 1919 the phrase "Instrument of the Immortals" was in regular use. Ayer and Steinway soon embarked on a campaign that would today be called "high-concept"; its purpose was to ineluctably join the ideals of perfection, piano, art, music, family, and, of course, Steinway in the public perception. Variations on the grand theme, really the quadrature of Family, Art, Music, Excellence, played for a decade, accompanied by a crescendo of sales.

The visual keystone of the campaign was oil paintings by well-known artists. Depicted at their Steinways were Brahms, his skyward eyes seeking or receiving inspiration; an introspective Rachmaninoff, his huge hands bathed in the yellow light of a summer afternoon; a sternly Beethovenesque Rubinstein instructing the young Josef Hofmann; Paderewski evoking period-costumed dancing apparitions as he played his minuet. Composers were not as prominent, but they too appeared. N. C. Wyeth rendered Beethoven contemplating a stream; Harry Townsend painted Handel at a harpsichord; while Charles E. Chambers portrayed the death of Mozart as musicians played. Dozens of works were commissioned.

Beneath the illustrations appeared brief copy: "His moving fingers touch the Steinway into life—the master and his instrument are one—a sense of beauty fills the air—there is a hush of breathing while the listener drinks the beauty from each fleeting note. Perhaps the master is Hofmann, perhaps Rachmaninoff. Yesterday it might have been Paderewski. Half a century ago Franz Liszt and Anton Rubinstein were kings. But whenever the time and whichever the master, the piano remains the same—Steinway, Instrument of the Immortals."

Thematic elaborations were almost endless, as were the inevitable midcourse corrections. "The reputation of the Steinway has caused many people to believe that it is necessarily beyond their means. We offer remarkably convenient terms." During the sharp recession of 1921, a Steinway ad noted that many of their instruments were found in "ordinary homes." Some years later Arthur Rubinstein, after seeing his name near the bottom of an alphabetical list of "immortals," peevishly wrote to the Concert and Artists Department, "Whenever we talk about Baldwin, Bechstein, Bluthner, Bosendorfer, etc., I will never forget to mention Steinway." Later ads did not contain lists of Steinway artists.

A memorable concept, exquisite illustration, and artful copy were necessary but not sufficient. Under Fred Steinway the house spent immense sums on advertising, rising from the already high 4 to 5 percent of new piano sales in Charles's time to as much as 9 percent of new piano revenues. Steinway became a heavily promoted consumer brand with advertising expense proportionately *triple* that spent on luxury automobiles today. With rapidly rising sales, the actual dollars spent on advertising quadrupled during the boom years of the 1920s compared to the teens.

Promotion through artist concert appearances nearly doubled as the twenties roared on and might have increased further had not both Aeolian and Ampico abandoned the concert stage with their Chickering, Knabe, and Mason & Hamlin lines in a futile attempt to control expenses as the market for their player pianos was buried under the radio avalanche. In William's time there had usually been less than three artists receiving the house's largesse at any one time, and Charles rarely supported more than a half-dozen simultaneously. Under Fred, artists by the dozens received free pianos for their homes and other blandishments. At the peak over six hundred pianos were deployed for artist use around the nation, all owned and maintained at Steinway expense and free to the dealers and halls that housed them.

"Service," as it was known, was allocated by classification. In Class A, the performers chose their own special pianos, which were transported across the country at Steinway expense, complete with travelling tuner. A fee of one hundred dollars, a remnant of the "advertising allowance" from William's time, was paid for each performance. Four artists received Class A service in the 1920s. Paderewski and Hofmann were among them, as were two others: Yolanda Mero and Mischa Levitzki, whose reputations are today less luminescent. Mero was the wife of Steinway New York executive Hermann Irion, which may explain her privileged status, but the record is silent on the case of Levitzki. Perhaps it was hope.

In Class B were Sergei Rachmaninoff, a young Vladimir Horowitz, Dame Myra Hess, Rudolph Ganz, Alfred Cortot, and Olga Samaroff. These artists received the same treatment as Class A—selected special pianos and a travelling tuner—but no one-hundred-dollar-per-concert fee. In the broader population of Class C were not only artists such as George Gershwin, Sergei Prokofiev, Percy Grainger, Wanda Landowska, and Alexander Siloti, but a host of vocalists and violinists, including Efrem Zimbalist, Jascha Heifetz, and Fritz Kreisler. This lower-status group was merely provided a free piano anywhere they performed. If a Class C artist happened to be appearing in a city where there was no Steinway dealer and where the hall somehow did not contain a proper piano, one was shipped there.

Many artists received practice pianos for their hotel rooms, free of charge. These were occasionally put to expedient use. Alexander Greiner, manager of the Concert and Artists activity beginning in the late twenties, told the story of how a hotel piano was returned with a long water spot on its top by a pianist named Alexander Brailowsky. Brailowsky saw that his pants needed pressing and found that the piano in his room was an ideal place for this. Theodore E. Steinway suggested to Greiner that he write the artist and ask for a testimonial reading, "The Steinway is the finest piano on which to press my pants."

The apparent largesse of the artist program, when considered from the standpoint of its expense of about twenty-five dollars per new piano sold, was actually a bargain. Uncountable tens of millions of concertgoers at an unreckonable tens of thousands of performances were left with the lasting impression that there was but one "artistic" piano and its name was Steinway. Three-quarters of a century before, Fred's long-dead uncle Henry Steinway had mingled with the artists of his time, introducing forgotten masters like Mills and Wohlenhaupt to the musical powers of his novel overstrung concert grands and subsidizing them in modest ways, i.e., reading glasses for the harpist Aptommas.

Those methods were essential to the achievements of the house, for without the cooperation of the artists there could only be less success. Like his Uncle Henry, Fred's relationship to the players was not simply a matter of business. As Henry and later William had socialized with musicians, so did Fred. He and his wife, Julia Cassebeer Steinway, a distant cousin, became renowned for their hospitality to artists. For many, dinner with the Steinways was an event to be anticipated. The family, the pianos, and the artists were, as they always had been, bound together in a common destiny. If William's practice of loans, advice, and career management were no longer a part of the way business was done, mutually beneficial services could still be rendered. And, as in William's time, if the accounts of expenditures and receipts did not always balance, that too was acceptable. There was, three decades after his death, still a personal dimension to the relationships. A gimlet-eyed accountant may very well have disapproved, but Steinway & Sons was a family business and one that grew as the industry shrivelled.

"I think they should get rid of the long-haired geezers. The public would be more interested in Rudy Vallee or Mary Pickford." This was one advertising man's diagnosis of the piano industry's sales sickness. Some listened to the advice and recruited celebrities: "The Baldwin is the best piano that I ever leaned on," testified Will Rogers. "Boy, you ain't heard nothing yet until you hear the Baldwin," enthused Al Jolson in full black-face stage makeup. "There is something about the Baldwin tone that I have never heard in any other instrument," demurred Mrs. Calvin Coolidge. The Baldwin Company, one of the few remaining credible competitors, was schizophrenically scratching barren ground for a new sales strategy, using the slogan "Choose Your Piano as the Artists Do" while paying Billy Sunday to plug pianos from the pulpit.

The "geezers" had, like lodestones to magnetic north, aligned almost totally with Steinway. To men and women who bet their reputations each evening, performing while thousands watched and listened, crossing mine-fields of shifting taste while critics lurked like snipers in the treetops, the walk from wings to center stage was perhaps eased by the now-familiar sight on the fallboard of the gold-leafed lyre above the words *Steinway & Sons*. In the jungle of uncertainties that now included radio, cars, jazz, mustard gas, and bathtub gin, the golden lyre logotype radiated the reassuring glow of a campfire in the woods. This, of course, was the Steinway intent for both its artists and its customers, for many were uncomfortable with the pace of social change.

Automobiles and jazz were believed by some to be agents of societal decay. The *Etude* informed its readership of musicians that jazz was "an unforgivable orgy of noise, a riot of discord, usually perpetrated by players of scant musical training who believe their random whoops, blasts, crashes and tom-toming is something akin to genius . . . and is often associated with vile surroundings, filthy words, unmentionable devices and obscene plays." This music was "naturally to blame for the whole fearful caravan of vice and near-vice" then rumbling across the nation. This view of changing times was not limited to musicians. James T. Knox, a Harvard University football coach, told the Boston Chamber of Commerce, "Any of you who have sons please keep them out of automobiles and jazz parties until they are at least 21 years of age. As I look about college campuses these days, I see boys with spindle legs and hollow chests who have replaced the sturdy youths of a few years ago. The younger generation thinks that only the frivolous things of life are worthwhile."

Responding to these attitudes, perhaps intuitively, Steinway presented itself as the nurturer, and sometimes as the repository, of a great cultural tradition. In this fondly remembered world, it was forgotten that the critics excoriated Wagner and Berlioz; the tensions of the relationship between Rubinstein and William were lost; the dislike, if not contempt, for America felt by C. F. Theodore was unrecollected, and pictures were not hawked during Paderewski concerts. In this hazy world of greatness gone, men did not die of typhoid nor babies of starvation, and the streets were not littered with horse carcasses. The police did not beat strikers and the judges were not corrupt. In this distinguished past the world was inhabited by men of gigantic talent and noble motive.

"We listen to Bach much as we stand in a ship's engine room and gaze at the moving machinery," wrote W. J. Turner for *The New Statesman* in 1925. "We are fascinated by the complexity and efficiency displayed before us." In England, where Turner wrote these words, J. S. Bach was experiencing "a new and hitherto unexplained liking." The nostalgia was not apparently constrained to America, and continental and English Steinway sales climbed even as Turner wrote that "more pianofortes have rusted away in the British Isles than have ever been worn out with practice. It would not surprise me if in another fifty years the pianoforte were an extinct instrument."

Extinction, other than Steinway, seemed a real possibility in the United States when the National Music Industries Chamber of Commerce gathered in New York one thousand strong during the summer of 1926. Their purpose was to "repopularize the piano, the backbone of the music industry." To do this, the assembled multitude nominated Benjamin Franklin as the patron saint of the music industry because he was a composer, inventor, and musician. This had no discernible effect on piano sales, which slumped 40 percent from 1927 levels by 1929. Much of this loss was in player pianos, which skidded 62 percent in the same two years amid substantial, if not always glittering, prosperity. A speaker from the National Bureau for the Advancement of Music diagnosed the current situation. "In former years the piano was regarded in most homes as a piece of beautiful furniture and as a token of social prestige. This attitude no longer exists, and pianos are in general purchased today only by those who have an inherent love of music." An accurate view or not, Steinway & Sons with its advertising and concert promotions appealed to all three of the identified motives of prestige, beauty, and love of music.

The result of the reconnection of Steinway with the traditional values of the twenties was more than a doubling of the house's American new piano sales from about $2.7 million the year Charles died to $5.8 million six years later. Steinway had not grown at such a rate in half a century or more; nothing from the time of William or Charles was comparable. It took Charles roughly a dozen years to add two thousand pianos to the annual production figures; Fred accomplished that feat in half the time, accompanied by a gusher of earnings. Per-piano profits rose to the lush levels of William's time, $150 per piano, then went higher still. Dividends in cash and stock reached more than $1 million per year. Steinway & Sons seemed immune to radio.

"Your trustees are of the opinion," Fred told the stockholders in early 1926, "that it is still of the utmost importance to strengthen the financial structure of the company by passing a large portion of the earnings to the surplus account, rather than disburse them as dividends." The ever-prudent trustees, all of whom remembered at least a half-dozen panics and crashes, created the company equivalent of a savings account rather than pay themselves larger dividends. The year Fred made that statement, a deposit, so to speak, was made in the amount of $812,000. By the time the surplus account reached its peak in 1929, it contained a sum roughly equal to the profits on the manufacture of twenty-eight thousand pianos.

While the house was unqualifiedly successful in America, the results in Europe were mixed. As in the United States an all-time sales record was achieved in the mid-twenties. It was 1928 when Hamburg production reached a high of 2,602 pianos. Profits, however, were a dismal $38.76 per unit, and when the loss on the London salesrooms was considered, they sank still further to but $30.49 per piano. Throughout the 1920s Fred poured money into both the Hamburg factory and the London Steinway Hall. The London hall lost money in seven of the ten years of the decade, and for years the political situation in Germany prevented the repatriation of profits. Clearly, the money might have been better placed in a bank account. This, however, would not have yielded the intangible returns in prestige and pride that came from more than four decades of international operation.

In addition to dividends, surpluses, and European subsidies, there were also investments for the future made by Fred. From the perspective of the 1920s that future was manifestly bright, and Fred built new factories in Queens, which brought the total capacity to about ten thousand pianos per year. But photographs of these factories—plumes of smoke coursing from skyscraping chimneys—were no longer fashionable symbols of progress and did not appear in brochures.

At last demand arose for William's Astoria real estate purchased on behalf of the company a half century before, and building lots began to sell. In 1925 a public auction was held, and hundreds of undeveloped lots in the vicinity of the factory and mansion were sold. Homes soon appeared on some of the last pasture in New York City, but it was not until 1947, three-quarters of a century after its purchase, that Steinway & Sons disposed of the last of William's undeveloped land. The most visionary of Steinways had been dead for fifty-one years, but at last Astoria vaguely resembled his dream.

William had, in effect, made Steinway & Sons a hybrid company, part pianomaker and part real estate developer, and despite the Astoria experience, Fred continued with the policy. The new vehicle for the creation of wealth through real estate was not in the suburbs, but centrally located on Fifty-seventh Street in Manhattan not far from Carnegie Hall. In the spring of 1923 the firm of Warren & Wetmore, architects, was engaged to design a new Steinway Hall to be located at 109–111–113 West Fifty-seventh Street. The fifteen stories of the building, respectably towering for its time, was to be topped by a penthouse in which Fred and his wife, Julia, planned to live. When it was learned that New York City building regulations allowed only janitors to live in commercial structures, Fred decided that, rather than assume a new title, he would remain in his Park Avenue apartment, and the penthouse was converted into the latest symbol of modern technology, a radio studio.

Planned to cost about $2.5 million, construction started in 1924. A churchlike main salesroom, rare wood panelling, a gigantic chandelier, faux antique furniture, bronze busts and portraits of the family members, sculpture, and paintings of renowned artists combined to create an impression of imposing serenity and dynastic endurance in the public rooms. Steinway Hall was a cathedral of commerce and a monument to the arts. There was also a marketing tie-in; many of the paintings displayed were the originals of those used in the advertising campaigns. Several months before the opening Fred reported to the stockholders that "based on the drawings" the new building was 50 percent rented. The old Fourteenth Street hall was quietly closed and later became a clothing store, its customers likely unaware that they were buying cheap dresses in the very place where Madame Parepa-Rosa once sang, Theodore Thomas conducted, and Rubinstein played. It was so long ago.

"THRONG AT OPENING OF STEINWAY HALL," headlined the New York Times in October 1925. "More persons of note in society and music, perhaps, than New York's greatest concert halls often shelter in a day thronged the little recital salon and adjoining hallways of the new Steinway building . . . last evening for its formal dedication." It was probably no coincidence that the new opening occurred fifty-nine years, almost to the day, after William dedicated the concert space on Fourteenth Street. Rather than Theodore Thomas's symphony, a more modest aggregation of thirty-five Philharmonic players performed and were named for this occasion and later broadcasts as the Steinway String Orchestra. Josef Hofmann was among the soloists. The concert was broadcast on WJZ, New York, WGY, Schenectady, and WRC, Washington, plus "associates" of the Radio

457

Corporation of America. Any American with a crystal set east of the Rockies might have snatched the program from the ether, but there was a peculiar, almost quaint linkage with the century past. A poem was recited:

> What heart too proudly temperate and cold
> Feels not the warmth and splendor of this hour?
> What memory would not this moment hold
> A precious gift from out sweet Fortune's dower?
> For here the voice of music shall be heard,
> And never will the strings be mute,
> And never will the notes be blurred,
> And never will the sounding of the lute
> Fall upon ears untuned to harmonies.
> O Gentle Goddess, make thy dwelling here!
> O Dulcet Maid, forever here abide!
> And may thy lovely presence, year by year,
> Make us sweet Fortune's minion and her pride.

Penned by yet another of the nation's forgotten poets, S. W. Gerhart, the verse was read by Ernest Urchs, the head of Steinway's Concert and Artists Department. The response of the thousands now twisting radio knobs in the perpetual search for entertainment was not reported, but the writer did note the presence, alphabetically, of names such as Belmont, Carnegie, Eastman, Field, Fish, Guggenheim, Harriman, Juilliard, and Rockefeller. This was certain certification of an otherwise unrecorded transition; the Steinways were no longer "Dutchmen."

There were artists as well at this glittering convocation of three hundred. Among the "early arrivals" were Sergei Rachmaninoff and Mrs. Rachmaninoff, as well as Frank Damrosch. The predictable passel of politicians included New York mayor Hylan; and Calvin Coolidge, though invited, did not attend. In tactically brilliant execution of what was then becoming known as "public relations," a man named Charles Pike Sawyer was present. Mr. Sawyer "had attended the old hall's dedication" in 1866 and recollected for the reporter the performances of Brignoli, Parepa-Rosa, and Thomas. In the last paragraph of the column-long story, the Steinways were mentioned. None of the nine family members attending the dedication was interviewed by the *Times*. A comment from a living Steinway was superfluous; everyone knew the legend.

As William had before him, Fred chose to invest in real estate development at a highwater of national prosperity, and the investment was at similar level, roughly one-fourth the assets of Steinway & Sons. The building intended to be erected and furnished for $2.5 million entered the books at more than $3.1 million, a 25 percent cost-overrun. Perhaps the added expense was justified by the award of a gold medal. Just as Fred's grandfather Heinrich had won an aureate emblem of excellence at the Crystal Palace in 1855, Steinway & Sons was now so honored in 1925. The medal was not for pianomaking, however, but for architecture, and it was bestowed by the Fifth Avenue Association for the finest new building in Manhattan. Second place in the annual contest was awarded to Macmillan, the publishers.

At the annual stockholders' meeting in April 1927, Fred displayed his usual financial prudence, despite the fact that a new sales record had been set. Worldwide, 8,356 Steinway pianos were sold in 1926, and nearly all of the new hall was rented. "Your trustees still consider it most important to conserve a large part of the corporation's earnings for the financing of capital expenditures made necessary by the growth of the business." While there was still thought of expansion, there was also a cautionary note: "Since the beginning of November [1926] . . . reports which come to us from nearly every section of the country indicate we seem to be in the midst of a distinct depression," observed Fred. He was correct, for economists ascertained years later that a recession began in October 1926 and did not end until November 1927. It was a mere shiver of the economic corpus that signalled to remarkably few the paroxysm to come in 1929.

Frederick Theodore Steinway "succumbed to a heart attack at the Kimbal House, Northeast Harbor, Maine, where he had been spending the Summer with his wife, who was Miss Julia Cassebeer, and their daughter, Florence," reported *Music Trade Review* in July 1927. The daughter was adopted by Julia, but not by Fred, and there were no biological children. The *Times* provided further detail: "Mr. Steinway had attended a bridge party until late in the evening before the stroke. He was stricken about 6:30 o'clock in the morning and died shortly thereafter." The *Times* also wrote of "the finest radio concerts ever given in America," and *Music Trade Review* called Frederick T. Steinway "one of the leading patrons of musical arts in America," whose "democratic and genial character was almost a by-word. . . . Even in the elaborately furnished headquarters in the new Steinway Hall the president refused a private sanctum of his own and insisted that a place be found for his desk on the open floor."

The last man to guide Steinway who knew Heinrich and Henry and Charles and Albert and C. F. Theodore and learned the trade under William was interred in the family mausoleum at Greenwood with his grandfather, father, brother, and uncles. Time had stretched and finally snapped the strands of living memory that bind the future to the past. Frederick T. deftly and intuitively shaped a modern myth for modern times. This was his legacy, and its merit was soon to be measured, for within five years the factories designed to produce ten thousand pianos per year would be closed.

Chapter 30

THE ROAD TO DESTRUCTION

"At a meeting of the board of directors of Steinway & Sons, New York, on Monday, July 25, Theodore E. Steinway was elected president of the company to succeed the late Frederick T. Steinway who died last week," reported *Music Trade Review*. The genealogy of a Steinway was important, and *MTR* reported that forty-three-year-old Theodore was a "first cousin to the late president and both were grandsons of Henry Englehard Steinway, founder of the house of Steinway." This was true, but it was also true that Theodore never knew his grandfather Heinrich who died a dozen years before he was born. In printing verbatim what was obviously a press release, the trade paper did not cite the most significant of Theodore E.'s family relationships: he was the son of William, who died when Theo was thirteen. There were many still in the trade who witnessed the debacle of William's estate and some remembered the scandals of his lifetime, so it seems there was a conscious decision to leave the connection to William unmade.

Spending much of his adolescence in the care of his older sister Paula after the deaths of both his mother and father, Theodore E. entered the customary apprenticeship at the age of seventeen. "For five years he worked at the bench, according to the traditions of all Steinway heirs, in order to acquaint himself with all branches of piano construction," parroted *Music Trade Review*. "He even put in several seasons in the tuning department, following which he advanced to a factory position. . . . Throughout his connection with the company Mr. Steinway has worked in close association with Henry Ziegler. . . . He thus brings to his work as president . . . an unusually sound scientific knowledge of piano construction."

The mention of the almost reclusive Henry Ziegler, son of Doretta Steinway, now in his fifty-second year with the house, made yet another connection to the past. Thoroughly instructed in the occult arts of piano design as well as its science by C. F. Theodore himself, Henry Ziegler was the last witness to that epoch long past when C. F. Theodore invented the modern piano. Perhaps contentedly, perhaps not, Ziegler worked for more than half a century with an ironic handicap; born of a sister rather than a brother, he had the blood but not the name, and Henry Ziegler spent his life in long shot as the reels of the Steinway drama rattled through the projector of time. Such a supporting role, circumstantial evidence suggests, would have been the choice of Theodore E.

Though not educated beyond Saint Paul's School in Garden City, Long Island, where he was a sometimes-troublesome student, Theodore E. was a scholarly man with antiquarian interests: books, Indian relics, and whaling were subjects of engrossment at times, but a lifelong interest was stamp collecting. He had, according to *Music Trade Review*, "one of the finest stamp collections in the United States." Later in life, Theo E.'s likeness appeared on a commemorative issue from Liechtenstein "in recognition of his service to philately." The world of theater meant much to the new Steinway president, and he was a consummate amateur actor as well.

Reserved in public and always immaculately dressed, Theodore E. was not "democratic" or "approachable" or "genial." Yet there was another dimension to the man; during his tenure the board meetings were, when weather permitted, removed from the confines of Steinway Hall and transformed into picnics. To settle a friendly question over the presidential prospects of Al Smith and Calvin Coolidge, Theodore proposed a postcard race. His card, bearing the likeness of Smith, was sent west around the world back to New York. The Coolidge card was sent east on the reverse route. Fifty-five days later and separated by six hours, the cards arrived back in New York at the stamp collectors' club, of which Theodore was president from time to time, as his father had been of the Liederkranz. The Smith card arrived first, and Theodore collected five hundred dollars from Coolidge's backer, who was, however, later vindicated by Coolidge's election.

Theodore E. Steinway was not, even by the assessment of one who admired him, a manager or entrepreneur. A former president of N. W. Ayer who knew Theodore well in the 1930s and had ample experience with captains of industry viewed Theodore as "more like a musician or artist. He wasn't a businessman." By family tradition, the oldest of the male generation bearing the name Steinway should have ascended to lead the house. The calendar would have mandated the succession of William R., then managing the European operations. But the life of William R. was tinctured with scandal. He had, according to family sources, been introduced to a prostitute by Charles while in Germany and had fallen in love with the woman, who enjoyed telling stories about her seagoing adventures aboard Kaiser Wilhelm's yacht.

A separation of the pair was negotiated and a trust fund established to support the woman in anticipation of William R.'s return to America. At something near the final hour, William R. decided his love was greater than his need for power, and he married Marie. The social status of William R.'s lifemate so outraged Julia Steinway, Fred's wife and a woman of influence in the family, that it would have been impossible for him to become president of Steinway & Sons during her lifetime. From 1909 to 1939 William R. remained almost continuously on the eastern side of the Atlantic, amply distanced from Julia. The evidence on whether the house suffered from this is equivocal, but when judged by the numbers appearing in the confidential accounts of Steinway & Sons, William R.'s business abilities were not impressive. He did, however, share with his father and uncles the Steinway geniality, the intangible contribution of which might have been great. As it had so often in the time of William, the imperative of appearance once again shaped the actions of the family, and it was Theodore E., not William R., who would lead the defense against the four horsemen of the piano apocalypse: radio, depression, war, and television.

"During the year 1927 the entire piano industry suffered a very noticeable setback, and the player and reproduction piano industry a very serious one," commented Theodore E. to the stockholders in April 1928. "The excellence of our modern talking machine and its constantly growing catalog, and the immense radio sales are chiefly responsible for this condition." That year another million dollars was pumped into the expansion of the Queens factories. This was not improvident, for in 1927 Steinway actually sold thirteen more straight pianos than in 1926. Theodore reported a drop in player sales to Aeolian, but even this was modest, declining but 327 instruments. The view was undoubtedly that Steinway buyers could afford both radios and pianos. "Many player manufacturers report an almost entire falling off of their business, especially among the cheaper lines, and many dealers report the inability to market the cheaper grades of pianos as well." The problem, Theodore must have believed, was with the old nemesis, the "commercial" piano, and not with "artistic" pianos. This was a reasonable view, and even into 1929 orders by Aeolian for players did not drop much from 1928 levels.

Believing, perhaps correctly, that he was immune to the bacillus of radio or perhaps that the vaccine was advertising and concerts, Theodore spent on promotion as never before. By 1929 advertising expenses reached almost $107 per piano, more than 10 percent of the average selling price. The level was double that of Fred's early years and quadruple that of Charles's time. Profits slid predictably, but Theodore E. was still able to add nearly one million dollars to the surplus account. The crescendo of apparent success masked the creaking sounds in the walls of a house about to collapse.

Had Theodore E. or the other trustees been analytically inclined, they might have detected an ominous sign. Used-piano sales were increasing rapidly in the late 1920s, and the growing purchase of old pianos was almost always followed by economic crisis. The cumulative behavior of the customers who entered the palatial rotunda of Steinway Hall could foretell the future, but this was an oracle that spoke softly, and its voice was not heard. Men in a better position to gauge events detected little but increasing prosperity. In early 1929 President Coolidge pronounced the economy "absolutely sound" and stocks "cheap at current prices." Millionaire banker Andrew Mellon believed that "the high tide of prosperity will continue," and the chairman of the Democratic National Committee, John J. Raskob, wrote a 1929 article for the *Ladies' Home Journal* titled "Everybody Ought to Be Rich." Raskob prescribed stock investments for housewives. In mid-1929 the august financier Bernard Baruch commented that "the economic condition of the world seems on the verge of a great forward movement," while Yale economist Irving Fisher stated that "stock prices have reached what looks like a permanently high plateau."

By the middle of 1930 there were at least as many theories on the cause of the business slump as there were persons able to persuade newspaper reporters to communicate their views. Economic problems were attributed to, variously, the lack of diplomatic relations with Russia, a general moral collapse, tariff bills, and psychology. Henry Ford thought the cause was laziness, and that "it will take as long to get rid of the depression as it took to accumulate it." Ford's solution mandated a return of workers to the farm. "Too many people have believed that Santa Claus lives in the city," said the automaker. "One of the greatest evils" was "contentedness. . . . When people become too contented there's usually trouble ahead." Regarding "trouble" at least, Mr. Ford was correct.

The Great Depression became the second longest economic downturn on record, exceeded only by the slump beginning in 1873. The hardships and severities are not so easily compared, for as Ford had observed, America was no longer a nation of farmers who could, if nothing else, at least feed themselves. For those employed—and up to one in four were not—earnings fell from an average of $1,405 in 1929 to $1,080 in 1933, a decline of 23 percent. Between 1930 and 1933 over nine thousand banks suspended—closed to the public either temporarily or permanently. To make up the savings lost, Americans would have had to work for four million man-years. Wages would not reach 1929 levels for a dozen years. Housing prices dropped 25 percent; automobile sales sagged by 75 percent, not to surpass 1929 levels for twenty years. Even radio sales declined 70 percent.

Already enfeebled by social changes of the 1920s, piano manufacturing nearly ceased. Hundreds of firms failed within three years. The survivors desperately turned to the manufacture of tennis rackets, bowling pins, chairs, and boats; almost anything made of wood was considered an avenue of economic escape from the 85 percent sales slide. Those building player pianos saw sales recede to the vanishing point. Once there had been an output of 200,000 instruments per year, but by 1935 only 418 player pianos were produced. Soon there were none, and an industry died.

Initially Theodore E., like most Americans, did not comprehend the depth of the crevasse before him. In 1930 he continued to advertise at only moderately reduced levels and was rewarded with sales of less than half those of 1929, a mere 2,423 pianos in America. "It is hardly worthwhile to quote the usual statistics as to the number of units manufactured during the year," said Theodore E. about 1931 production, "as we found our accumulated stock of finished goods so large that we ceased work in our factories toward the end of the year." The optimistic plan was to reopen in August for the seasonal rush of fall orders. With the announcement of the factory closings, a Steinway tradition of more than a half century lapsed. William's promise of continuous work for the men could no longer be kept. A thousand or more left the factories on an uncertain date before Christmas 1931 not knowing when, if ever, they would return. Through the financial downdrafts of the decades they had always been at work; William Steinway had so decreed, and it was done. "We live and die right here," said an old pianomaker to the *New York World* in 1909. As these grey-haired men shuffled from the shops, some certainly feared that it was Steinway & Sons that might soon die.

Only fifty or so foremen were left to slowly complete the work in process and build the occasional special order. Grand pianos were stored vertically in the time of the Steinways, keyboard down, so that the weight of gravity would not disturb the action and hammer felts. Hundreds, perhaps thousands, of grands stood on their "noses" this way, waiting years for buyers. The remaining factorymen had wages cut about 30 percent; the clerks' salaries were reduced 40 percent. The biggest reductions were reserved for department heads and executives. These salaries were slashed by two-thirds, and bonuses became a thing of the past. Executive salaries were set, in Theodore E.'s words, "to a 1901 basis." The president of Steinway & Sons now drove a Dodge.

By 1932 Steinway Hall took on the look of a cultural mausoleum. Dispirited salesmen arrived each morning, switched on the Bohemian crystal chandeliers, and sat down at their mahogany desks to read the *Times* or *Music Trade Review*. There was little good news in either. Elegant ebony and walnut grands sat silently in the same spots, month upon month, monuments to prosperity past. The tuners passed slowly among these economic casualties, ministering to their needs, checking their condition as nuns might walk the wards of a battlefield hospital. The likenesses of

William and Theodore and Albert and Henry gazed from the walls. The errant octave or the perfect fifth might be heard as the tuners made their rounds. There were almost no customers. In New York and across America only nine hundred new Steinway pianos were sold in 1932. A total of 888 sanguine and very wealthy persons bought grands, and but a dozen purchased uprights. For every seven Steinways sold in America in 1926, only one was sold in 1932. Production in Hamburg suffered even more, a result probably due to politics as well as economics; output dropped to a mere 216 pianos.

Even with the factories closed Steinway & Sons was hemorrhaging money. The overhead of shuttered plants, the heat, light, taxes, and insurance, the operating expenses of Steinway Hall, where the tenants who did not leave were months behind in their rent, all consumed cash. Only the millions held in the "surplus" account, the gleanings of Charles Herman and Frederick Theodore Steinway's prudence during the good years, kept the house from liquidation. But by 1933 no accounting degree was needed to see that at the rate the surplus was consumed not more than two years were left before the last glow of the legend was forever extinguished. On some unknown day in his life, Theodore Edwin Steinway wrote a few words on a memo pad. "Fred came in on the road to glory," read the slip of paper written in a precise, unwavering hand. "I came in on the road to destruction."

What other truths and sorrows, what might-have-beens, never-weres, and never-to-bes crossed the mind of the stamp-collecting Steinway are unknown. The humiliations are only hinted in the terse language of the minutes of the board: "Paderewski declines his subsidy of $8,000 from Steinway & Sons on account of the present depressed state of business." The kindness of the offer, which was accepted, must have blended bitterly with chagrin. The grim responsibility fell to Theodore E. to tell Paderewski, Hofmann, and Rachmaninoff of still other forced economies in the artists' program. The venerable practice of paying one hundred dollars per concert was eliminated. Next to fall was the free travelling tuner; Steinway would still pay the tuner's salary, but the artist would contribute travelling expenses. Ultimately the cost of transporting the pianos was also borne by the artists. By 1935 concert expenditures were slashed to about one-fourth the 1929 level, yet both advertising and concert expenses were, on a per-piano-sold basis, higher than in the time of Charles. Theodore E. Steinway was a man who truly believed in promotion.

Theodore E. had staggered into a dark world in which social change was compounded by financial chaos. The Victorian request, "Play us a tune, sis," was rarely heard now in the living rooms of America, the same rooms that were once called parlors. The whine of a vacuum cleaner competed with the chatter of the radio as Sis groomed the carpet before an evening at the movies. Waffle irons, toasters, mixers, refrigerators, and electric ranges became, with almost terminal success, the new symbols of a modern household. There was nothing "labor-saving" about a piano, and its entertainment function was superseded by radio and records. To the entertainment alternatives was added yet another option, one which proved spectacularly popular: talking motion pictures. With the introduction of sound, attendance rapidly doubled. In 1930 paid attendance at the movies was ninety million persons per *week*. At that rate every man, woman, and child in the nation viewed an average of thirty-eight movies per year. Americans were in training for their future as a society of spectators.

There was more than a little wishful thinking about these phenomena as the age of passive consumption dawned. In 1930 music retailer Lyon & Healy, Steinway, and the Aeolian Company commissioned a "survey" by a consultant, yet another new concept. Robert R. Updegraaf limned with a vague desperation the tectonic cultural shifts: "Following the World War, the public was so restless and unsettled that it wanted to be constantly on the go. For a time homelife was terribly upset. The young folks dashed home to eat and sleep (briefly) and then dashed out again. And the grown-ups were not much better."

Updegraaf thought that radio had a calming effect on this frenetic activity. "Radio is beginning to have a considerable influence in keeping people at home by entertaining them as well as they could be entertained elsewhere." Mr. Updegraaf was apparently unaware of the lines at the local movie houses. Continuing with the social analysis, Updegraaf opined that "probably the greatest indictment which has been brought against radio is that it is making us *lazy*. It is making us a nation of lifeless listeners. . . . Perhaps this will develop into a chronic condition, to be improved somewhat when home television is developed and the eye as well as the ear are employed. But possibly, also, the well-known principle of action and reaction will operate in this situation. Possibly as a nation we shall presently get tired of sitting around and being entertained. The American public has a way of getting tired of doing the same old thing—whether it is bobbing its hair or exposing its knees or playing Mah-Jongg or wearing beards or reading detective stories. . . . The laziness brought on by radio may one of these days turn into restlessness—a feeling of desire to *participate* in things more, and this may extend to music."

Theodore E. was in no position simply to wait as the waves of technological and social change washed across society. He did what his father William had done when confronting the last immense depression six decades before. Prices were slashed. Pianos that sold for $1,700 in 1929 were cut 24 percent to $1,300, but sales remained viscous. A Model D concert grand that had cost two-thirds the price of a house in 1929 cost 88 percent of the price of a house in 1933, for prices were not cut fast enough or far enough to keep pace with deflation. In a sense it did not matter; few houses were being sold either.

The Road to Destruction

In the December 1934 issue of *Fortune* magazine, illustrated with the striking photographs of Margaret Bourke White, an article appeared, titled "Here Are the Steinways and How They Grew." No mention was made of the grim facts that Steinway & Sons was now one-sixth the size of 1926 and had revenues of less than one million dollars, that it produced fewer than one thousand pianos in 1934, a smaller volume than in the days before the Civil War, or that it had lost $3.7 million in five years.

The story for *Fortune* was one of a great family tradition. The accomplishments of Heinrich, Henry, Charles, C. F. Theodore, and, of course, William were replayed once again in a reprise of the American dream. The tale was told of how Charles came to America, then persuaded his father and brothers to emigrate. "From Heinrich's day on, the company has been a family institution, owned by Steinways and operated by Steinways," wrote *Fortune*. William, it was claimed, "shocked other pianomakers by advertising the Steinway," while his vision in founding the Hamburg factory and planning the Forty-second Street tunnel were duly noted. Theodore E. was characterized as "tense and dynamic," but the writer also saw couplings to the past in "the high, oldtime bookkeepers desks and the whitehaired workmen who grow poinsettias in the shop." There was the foundry, "a dark earthy place where molders spend infinite care and skill impressing the metal patterns into beds of sand" and the lumberyard that held "7,000,000 feet of spruce, maple, poplar, mahogany and walnut." These sights always stirred writers.

The enterprise was never about volume production, averred the magazine; "Steinway history has been one of quality and example," claimed *Fortune*. This fragment of revisionism entirely omitted William's boasts that Steinway & Sons was the world's largest pianomaker. Of prime importance now was The Name. The family, it was reported, turned down an offer of one million dollars to put The Name on a radio and another million for its use on a refrigerator. "The sons will learn from their elders that The Name must never be commercialized, that it must stand for pianos and pianos alone." Along with the recital of an embellished legend came some acknowledgment of the depression; it was revealed that of the one thousand men thrown out of work when the factories closed in 1932 only 560 had been called back to work. Officially, the factory reopened on August 7, 1933, after being closed for twenty months. Also claimed was a 1934 Astoria output of two thousand pianos; this was more than double the actual production, and it was further reported that the company's assets exceeded fourteen million dollars, high by nearly half.

A positive spin was put on certain necessities, such as the fact that Steinway no longer provided free pianos to artists. Payments by virtuosos to use the instruments were now cast as a tribute to the pianos' supremacy. "Safe to say," declaimed *Fortune*, "The Name will be carried on." This imparted an institutional permanence to Steinway & Sons that was scarcely warranted by the facts, but was certain confirmation of another family capacity: the ability to beguile reporters. William's FAME formula still lived, but so tenuous was the house's existence that the *Fortune* piece might well have become an epitaph.

Believing as an article of faith that somehow the business would continue, Theodore was developing a successor in the person of Frederick A. Vietor, the grandson of Albert Steinway and the son of Henrietta Steinway Vietor. According to *Fortune* Vietor was the "inventor" in the family, and though less prolific than his predecessors Henry Ziegler and C. F. Theodore, he did have two patents for "accelerated" piano actions. The essence of these inventions is still used in some American Steinways.

As the carnage continued, a decision was made, apparently at Vietor's urging, to develop new models. The first was a small, five-foot one-inch grand piano known as the Model S, and it is no overstatement to say that the little grand saved Steinway, albeit temporarily. "Baby" grands were scarcely new; they had been offered as medium-priced pianos for roughly two decades. Perhaps believing that the renowned Steinway sound could not be produced by such a small instrument—the technical challenges were formidable—the family avoided building one despite its popularity.

The public story was different: "Perhaps no announcement ever made in the piano industry was so dramatic, so well-timed and so welcomed by leading piano dealers of the United States," gushed *Piano Trade Magazine*. Employing his knowledge of drama, Theodore E. sent telegrams to his 207 North American dealers inviting them to New York for a major but unspecified announcement. Fully three-fourths appeared in Manhattan a few days later. Among the absentees was the Honolulu Steinway agent whose *China Clipper* flight to the mainland was cancelled due to mechanical difficulties. The assembled retailers, suitably wined and dined, were conveyed to the Astoria factory where a large room had been cleared of unsaleable Steinways. In the space were a dozen of the new Model S's, literally gleaming in the spotlights. Speeches and flourishes completed, the price was announced and the dealers were invited to try the instruments. This they did, and an avalanche of orders followed. "It is our opinion that Steinway timed the announcement with great business acumen," wrote *Piano Trade Magazine*. "Instead of announcing it in the depths of the depression when buying power was low, and thereby possibly creating the impression that the new Style S was a necessity of hard times, the management waited until all business was growing . . . and steadily rising." The new model was originally designed back in 1924, but with the "usual Steinway reticence" plus the need for refinement, it was not released for a dozen years; so went the claim.

There was, despite the hyperventilation of the trade press, legitimate reason for enthusiasm. Not merely five inches shorter than the next smallest Steinway, the S was also one-sixth cheaper and sold for only $885, about the price of a Ford, Chevrolet, or Plymouth sedan, but almost 50 percent more than a Knabe of the same size. Dealers could buy the S grand for as little as $503, and they did so in recordbreaking quantities. In the first year more than twenty-one hundred Model S's were sold. This was about one-third the claimed volume of orders, but for the next few years Model S's comprised roughly half of all the Steinway grands built; had it not been for the new "baby," production would have once again sunk to the levels of 1932 or 1935 when less than one thousand pianos were made. Without the S the last of Charles's and Fred's surplus fund would have been consumed, and in a matter of months Steinway & Sons would have joined the more than one hundred other pianomakers who failed during the Great Depression.

While Theodore E. was slow to offer a baby grand, the response to another industry trend was more timely. The manufacture of upright pianos at Steinway had slowed to a trickle during the golden years of Fred's reign. Less expensive, less chic, and much less profitable than grands, the cratelike, towering uprights, some taller than the women who played them, had been sacrificed on the altar of grand production capacity. By the mid-1930s Steinway & Sons was building no upright pianos at all.

In 1935 when but one Steinway upright piano was built, the Haddorff Piano Company of Rockford, Illinois, came to the annual trade show with a new model, one which would quickly resuscitate the remains of the industry. The firm, like most, was a feeble shadow when it announced a new "studio console" piano in 1935 designed by Carl Haddorff. A scant forty-five inches high, the Haddorf Vertichord Grand occupied only ten square feet of floor space. A number of tricks minimized the instrument's visual mass, not the least of which was adding two legs to the back of the piano. Four-legged pianos had not been sold since the death of the square four decades earlier. With a large wood lyre stuck above its pedals and various carvings that screamed Sheraton or Colonial at even the most fashion-deaf, Haddorff presented itself for approval to the new world of style.

The notion of "styling" as a discrete activity in the design of consumer goods was still a relatively new one; even the automobile makers, where calendarized technical change was long established as the annual model year, did not fully recognize the selling power of fashion until General Motors set up its Art and Color Department in the late twenties. There evolved during the thirties a new discipline, that of the industrial designer, whose task it was to make products attractive. Streamlining was a main aesthetic mode, and it evolved from a national fascination with aeronautical forms, the latest symbol of progress. The plausibility of streamlined toasters, waffle irons, or even refrigerators was not a part of the calculus of industrial design, but an aerodynamic piano was an absurdity too great for even the most ardent and talented to execute. C. F. Theodore Steinway, dead for a half century, had left as his legacy an immutably elegant and truculently minimal final form for the grand piano, but this did not inhibit attempts at modernization. Among the more bizarre was a grand piano designed by Wurlitzer, a company more renowned for the aesthetics of its jukeboxes. This piano had no top and its sides were cut off below the plate, leaving the strings entirely exposed. The body of the piano sat on a large S-shaped piece of Plexiglas, imparting the impression that a chopped-down piano was flying through the air.

At Steinway a more moderate approach to styling was taken, and the renowned industrial designer Walter Dorwin Teague was engaged. Teague's portfolio included the elegant but unsuccessful Marmon automobiles of the early 1930s, and his Art Moderne Steinways were offered in bleached mahogany, bleached walnut, American walnut, mahogany, or the traditional ebony. They sold no better than Marmons had. Meanwhile, many makers took to offering ever smaller pianos, some of which were disguised as desks and cabinets and given names like the "Mini-Piano." Pianos sprouted drawers in which books and liquor could be stored. Clever folding tops converted into writing desks, and radios were installed in piano benches. Radio manufacturer Zenith saw these trends and designed a radio that looked like a piano. The survivors of William's "art industry," who once built majestic monuments to American musical culture that towered in the parlor, now labored to make their instruments look like desks, buffets, or cabinets and to disguise or enhance, to the extent possible, their basic function.

The industrywide repudiation of its heritage and the introduction of the fashionable worked, more or less, and aided by the secular increase in sales of consumer goods, piano sales leapt upward. In 1935, the last year before the industry stumbled into styling, the sales of uprights were but 38,283 units. By 1937 volume almost doubled to 75,222. In 1939 the "new" pianos, now called "verticals" to distinguish them from the "uprights" that nearly became the coffin in which the business went to its grave, sold at a rate of 95,205 per year. The introduction of style opened the windows of the trade to the winds of volatility; fashion meant fast change, a variable with which Steinway & Sons had never been forced to cope in the eighty-seven years of its existence.

Theodore E. and his wizened executive group of men, with the house since the time of William and Charles, likely never knew they were performing remarkably well in a capricious market. In 1939 Steinway was the name on one in every eight grand pianos sold in America. The problem was that less than one-third as many grands were being bought compared to 1927. The new dwarf console designs pioneered by Haddorff and others were quickly copied by Steinway. There was no choice.

The first of the micro-Steinways appeared in 1938; a Model K originally designed by Henry Ziegler at the turn of the century was expediently chopped to measure forty-five inches tall. The year after saw a forty-inch

The Manhattan Steinway & Sons works on Fourth (Park) Avenue between Fifty-second and Fifty-third streets in the mid-1880s. The train is headed uptown on Fourth, and the artist has obligingly cleared the clutter of the other buildings.

Steinway Hall on Fourteenth Street. Designed largely by William and his father Heinrich E. with no sign of assistance by architects, the venue was at the axis of Manhattan culture for more than twenty-five years. Events included not only concerts but demonstrations of electrical machinery and nitrous oxide, as well as innumerable political meetings, lectures, and literary readings.

William's vision of a suburban future had the Steinway works at Astoria in Queens as the centerpiece. Some of the buildings shown in this mid-1880s illustration are still in use more than a century later. Note the large raft of logs at the lower left, the then-standard transportation method for products of the nation's forests.

The lumber basin at Astoria; logs floated in the dredged basin until picked by the sawyers. This prevented cracking of the wood. After the stock was cut, it was carefully stacked outdoors and left to season for several years. In the perpetual quest for quality, no technique was too costly or complex for the family.

The "fine looking and intelligent men" of the S&S foundry with the tools of their trade. Proprietary alloys specified by C. F. Theodore were sandcast as piano plates at Astoria. Plates were shipped to the Manhattan works and finished and bronzed, then installed in the piano, that pre-electronic home entertainment center.

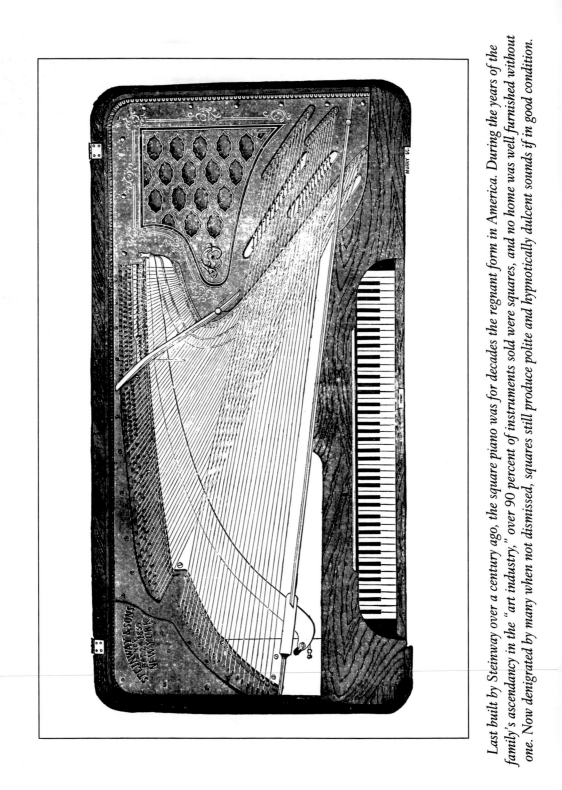

Last built by Steinway over a century ago, the square piano was for decades the regnant form in America. During the years of the family's ascendancy in the "art industry," over 90 percent of instruments sold were squares, and no home was well furnished without one. Now denigrated by many when not dismissed, squares still produce polite and hypnotically dulcent sounds if in good condition.

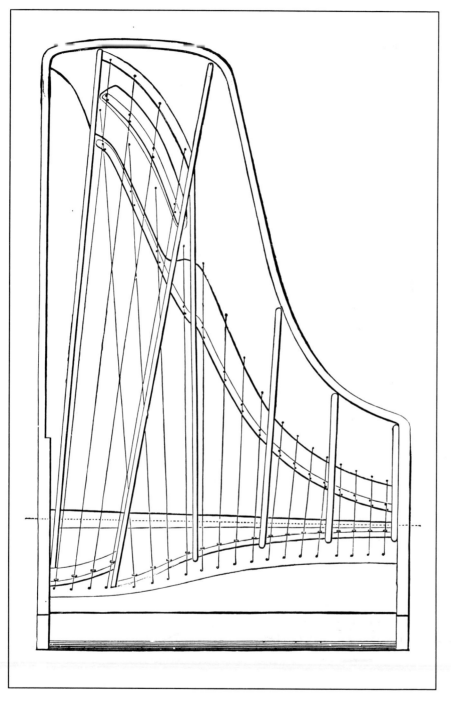

The first spoke in the wheel of the Steinway technological revolution is found in this 1859 patent drawing for Henry Steinway, Jr.'s overstrung grand. The innovation was controversial in part because it was so easy for the buyer to see. Save for arch-competitor Chickering, the entire industry adopted the technique when the patent expired.

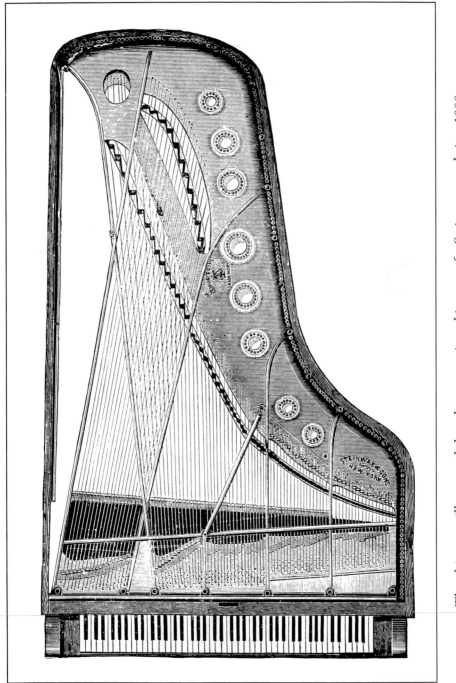

The ultimate, still unexceeded, and now generic architecture of a Steinway grand circa 1888 as developed by C. F. Theodore. The immense power and still inscrutable subtlety of this design has resisted hundreds of imitators and has defied physical explanations beyond the obvious.

model for $495; cheap for a Steinway, the retail asking price was still two-thirds higher than the average for pianos that size. The most popular of the "40's," as they were known at the now busier factory, was one styled with fluted legs and labelled Hepplewhite. It did not matter to its thousands of buyers that this little spinet which snuggled inconspicuously along the wall in the living room was as authentic as a Louis XV locomotive; it did not matter that the bland little box represented a terminal surrender of the concept "art industry." Steinway & Sons now made "commercial" pianos, instruments built to a size and a price point, albeit high. No one rhapsodized over the sound and touch of the consoles; the bass did not rumble, the tenor did not sing, the treble did not shimmer. They were appliancelike in competence.

Frederick Theodore Steinway's despised "cheap trade" had finally overwhelmed the house's patrician reserve, and in 1939 a total of 2,135 little consoles were made, as were nineteen Model D concert grands. The nineteenth century seemed at long last dead, but the new verticals were really an echo in the vaults of time. Eighty years before, C. F. Theodore, struggling in Germany, tried vainly to convince his brothers in New York to offer his new small upright pianos in America. They rightfully refused; European "boudoir" pianos, as they were then known, had a reputation in America for being cheap and unreliable, and tariffs were high. C. F. Theodore called his beloved miniature piano the Pianino, and Theodore E. revived the appellation. The new small Steinways were also called Pianinos. To most the name meant nothing more than the ephemeral coinages Vertichord, Musette, or Orgatron, but to the namesake Theodore Steinway, a man now hostage to his heritage, the choice was likely both poignant and apt.

Invocations of the past through word magic did nothing to solve a fundamental problem: Steinway & Sons did not really know how to build inexpensive pianos, and while the number of pianos built each year roughly quadrupled from 1935 to 1939, money was still being lost. The life preserver that was the surplus fund continued to deflate. In 1939 Theodore E. did what William had done in crises long past; he mortgaged Steinway Hall and used the $900,000 obtained to patch the crumbling foundations of the house. This did not change the hard fact that Steinway now received about five hundred dollars for each piano it sold when in 1929 it received one thousand dollars. The new "economy" models—the baby grand and the Pianinos—comprised three-fourths of the 4,088 instruments built in 1939, and the firm was being strangled by its own survival strategy. Almost twenty-one dollars was lost on each piano sold that year. Four thousand pianos in the time of Charles brought dividends of a half-million dollars; now that same number pushed the house closer to oblivion. Four thousand pianos for William were a dream, for Charles a prideful accomplishment, for Fred a stepping-stone, and for Theodore E. a grim foreboding of the end.

Many doors to the past closed in 1939; it was that year that Ignace Jan Paderewski made his twentieth and final tour of America. Now seventy-nine, just seven years younger than Steinway & Sons, the maestro arrived with plans for a twenty-city tour and his first nationwide radio broadcast. Alexander Greiner, head of Steinway & Sons Concert & Artists Department, wrote in a memoir, "I shall never forget meeting him in 1939 to start his last concert tour. . . . Paderewski arrived in New York aboard a small steamer, a combination of freighter and passenger boat. I went aboard ship to greet him. There was Paderewski in a tiny cabin. To my horror there was rouge on his face! He looked like a corpse, 'beautifully prepared' for the curious person to see a famous person 'lie in state.' A living corpse." The pianist and former prime minister of Poland was now nearly destitute, a casualty of bad investments, the depression, and his own impulsive generosity. An American tour was a financial life raft for his final years.

The tour began, astutely, with a performance on the networks of the National Broadcasting Corporation. The clock on the studio wall silently swung past 1400 EST as 1,450 persons sat pensively holding programs printed on silk. Silk, unlike paper, would not rustle or crackle. "Only the black, mute microphones, always hungry for sound, hung down from the ceiling ready to link Paderewski's piano with a countless audience." Silent seconds slid away; these were eons in the new world of network broadcasting, which abhorred nothing as much as "dead air," and therefore ran with a precision that humbled railroads. Paderewski, always and foremost the showman, appeared, a "tall figure, white-haired and stooped, slowly moving across the shadowless stage to the piano while the studio audience rose in admiration to applaud the entrance." The *Times* kindly omitted the usual critical summary of the performance, but Alexander Greiner reconstructed it later: "To have seen the glamorous Ignace J. Paderewski enter the stage, barely moving his tired old legs towards the piano; hearing the 'million dollar hands'—as Paderewski's hands had been described in thousands of articles during his triumphal years—feebly strike the first chords; hearing him play all those familiar pieces in a pathetically dreary, faltering manner, [I] will never forget its utter sadness." Like his pianomaker of nearly half a century, the powers of the maestro were now nearly spent.

The planned tour began but was soon truncated by illness. Paderewski performances in Cleveland and Newark were cancelled, and the entourage returned to Manhattan for what was to be a final triumph—a concert at Madison Square Garden on May 25, 1939. "Paderewski Collapses at Garden as 15,000 Gather for Concert—Suffers Slight Heart Attack in Dressing Room Shortly Before Scheduled Appearance—Other Engagements Are Cancelled," was the page-one, column-two summary of the *Times*. "When it was announced over the Garden's loudspeakers that the concert would have to be cancelled many burst into tears. Some were still weeping as they left the auditorium."

A few days later Olin Downes, veteran critic of the *New York Times*, distilled meaning from Paderewski's aborted tour in a way as wise as it was gentle. His art still resonated, though "on a reduced scale of sonority." There was "lordly magnificence . . . heroic proportion . . . laden with a spirit, a breadth, and splendor almost absent from contemporaneous thought." I. J. Paderewski was the last towering redwood in a forest filled with scrub pine, and Downes wrote that now "the tendency is to miniature." Alexander Greiner was less reflective but no less moved: "I was backstage in Madison Square Garden and witnessed the haggard man, sitting with bent head, staring vacantly into space. . . . It was quite obvious that Paderewski could not possibly play. Yes, there was Ignace J. Paderewski, world-famous pianist and statesman, but in reality it was only his shadow." The epitaphs had been written while the man was still alive, and on June 29, 1941, Ignace Paderewski died of pneumonia at the Buckingham Hotel, 101 West Fifty-seventh Street. Theodore E. delivered the broadcast eulogy.

In the fall of 1939 William R. Steinway returned to America from Hamburg. His was not a voluntary repatriation; Theodore E., concerned for both his brother's safety and the appearance of a connection to the Nazis, ordered him to return. After three decades on the continent William R. and his wife, Marie, took up "temporary" quarters in a two-room apartment on Columbus Circle, expecting to return to Germany in a matter of months.

Steinway in Europe fared worse during the depression than the American branch. American production, off about 85 percent at the bottom, was marginally stronger than Hamburg, which plummeted 92 percent. By the mid-thirties consideration was given to closing the European business. "Continue Hamburg and London operations. stop. Proceed with ess. stop. Inform London. stop. Letter follows. stop.," was the cable William R. received in early 1936 that reprieved William and C. F. Theodore's grand plan of 1881. The letter which followed was stern and formal, not at all like the relationship between the two brothers. "We have, for some time past, had the feeling that world economic conditions had changed so decisively within the last few years that the profitability of our European Branches in the coming years was more than doubtful. . . . For you to reach a turnover sufficiently large at present sales prices to make a profit seems entirely out of the question."

But there was pride and tradition to weigh, and so William R. was told by the directors to continue and to build the new baby grand as well. The implied forecast for Europe was in fact too bearish, and before long William R. was somehow managing to produce a profit of a few dollars per piano. Economic risks were daunting, but the political consequences of German Social Democratic policies were potentially and literally fatal. When the Third Reich was told, probably by a competitor, that the Steinways were Jewish, the house was faced with seizure of its Hamburg properties. The requisite family history was given to the authorities who were convinced that the makers of the Instrument of the Immortals were genetically acceptable. By 1939 and William R.'s return to America, the annual statement of Steinway & Sons no longer carried the usual red ink alongside the entry "Hamburg." Numbers did not appear, and instead there were the words "Final result undetermined."

Publicly undaunted by the wreckage of Steinway, Europe, on the rocks of geopolitics, William R. became a peripatetic goodwill ambassador, embarking on a two-month national tour of Steinway dealers. The fame of his name, an immense capacity for food and drink, and a prodigious geniality combined to produce a flood of local press clippings and the general impression that all was well with Steinway & Sons. If not, then why was this rotund and jovial Steinway handing out expensive cigars and hosting elegant dinners? The son had mastered the methods of the father but, as a half century before, the image and reality were very different.

"Mr. Theodore E. Steinway announced that the name of our new phonograph, radio and record department is Steinway & Sons Record Shop," noted the directors' minutes on October 19, 1939. Located in the basement of Steinway Hall, the new department sold Philco radios as well as classical and popular records; the new retail activity was a minor capitulation to the twentieth century. The official record, however, made no mention whatsoever of a major change: Steinway & Sons was now a union shop.

Though some labor conflicts of the 1930s were violent, there was none of this at Steinway & Sons. With the passage of the National Labor Relations Act in July 1935 the federal government effectively demolished the old principle that labor-management relations were largely a matter between employers and employees. The new law not only interposed a role for government, but it set up procedures under which "collective bargaining" would occur and created a quasi-judicial agency, the National Labor Relations Board, to enforce the regulations. While the new law severely proscribed the actions of employers and mandated that they bargain, it left unions largely unfettered. "By preventing practices which tend to destroy the independence of labor, it seeks, for every worker within its scope, that freedom of action which is justly his," declaimed President Roosevelt.

The result was predictable; union membership soared nationally by 141 percent between 1935 and 1939, and the percentage of the work force that was organized more than doubled from 6.7 percent to 15.8 percent. While one in six workers was a member of a union in 1939, the proportion was one in twenty in 1933. For Theodore E. the unionization of the family business carried multiple ironies. Representing the piano industry, he had worked hard through 1935 on a now-failed New Deal program called the National Recovery Administration. The NRA—which came to be popularly known as the "National Run Around"—began in 1933 as a program to aid economic recovery by establishing "fair" pricing, production, sales, and labor practices on an industry-by-industry basis.

Among the general provisions was one that guaranteed workers a minimum of forty cents per hour and prohibited more than forty hours of work per week. Working with Lucien Wulsin, president of Baldwin, other industry executives, and NRA bureauocrats, a code for the piano industry was hammered out; key provisions prohibited inflated pricing, false advertising, bait-and-switch techniques, and a list of evils endemic to the business since the time of John Jacob Astor. Though some of the names had changed, the piano business had not lost its fundamental fractiousness, and C. N. Kimball, son of William Wallace and an ardent conservative, refused to tolerate governmental invasion of his business. The piano code foundered, and the NRA itself was declared unconstitutional by the Supreme Court. With the NRA on the verge of dissolution, President Roosevelt embraced the Wagner Act, and three years later Theodore E. Steinway found that the New Deal he supported had given him not prosperity but the Upholsterers International Union and their piano-making affiliate, Local 102.

There was another irony. The Model S baby grand intended to resuscitate Steinway & Sons was a prime factor in the emergence of the union. In a way reminiscent of the time of William, Fritz Vietor "cut prices" for the men building the Model S. And, as in the time of William, the economic necessity of the move was explained to the men. Vietor told the workers that to sell the Model S for less than one thousand dollars, a key marketing benefit, economies were necessary and they would be paid 10 percent less to build Model S's than they were to make Model M's, which were almost identical in labor content. The men did not go out on strike; instead they voted in a union.

Perhaps to the benefit of all, bargaining and grievance committees meeting behind closed doors replaced ultimatums, mobs in the streets, and volleys of invective and counterinvective in the press. C. F. Theodore had once rumbled in the *Times* that he would "not be dictated to by socialists." Six decades later his relatives sat across the table from the intellectual progeny of C. F. Theodore's adversaries, pushed together by the twin forces of time and government. This was not a singular event, except, possibly, for its participants. Between 1935 and 1945 roughly twenty-four thousand union elections were held across America under the auspices of the National Labor Relations Board. In eighty-four of each hundred elections unions won. With or without an organized work force, Steinway & Sons still was what it had always been: a mirror held up to the face of America.

Chapter 31

SLIGHTLY LONGER THAN
A BOXCAR

"**M**r. William R. Steinway—A second time I try to get a connection with you. . . . I prefer to write in English (it is only simple) but I believe this letter will pass the censor sooner. . . . I repeat something from my first letter I mailed—now your old factory belongs to the history of S&S Hamburg. In July 1943 the factory is total damaged. Burned up for lack of water." The letter, addressed to Steinway & Sons, New York, was from Walter Petersen, a former Steinway & Sons, Hamburg, salesman who was drafted into the German army, spent two and one-half years in Russia, and was writing from a prisoner-of-war camp in Britain. He hoped his former employer could send him, among other things, a copy of Beethoven's *Appassionata* and a Steinway catalog. "I cannot say that I have been a passionate soldier but I could not change the situation," wrote Mr. Peterson in July 1945. "I hope that you, Mr. Steinway, are well."

William R. was, but Steinway & Sons was not. Since 1930 the house had lost money in moderate to massive amounts in twelve of the sixteen years. Its survival owed more to will than rationality, and its condition, due largely to the vicissitudes of war, was parlous. At the end of 1944 there was money enough to support only seven weeks of operation. It was during the war, some say, that Theodore E. Steinway began to drink heavily, a manifestation of both the burden and family propensities.

In 1941 Theodore E. had anticipated relief. Steinway sales were buoyed by a 16-percent surge in the nation's economic activity and a freshet in demand for the new verticals, so the time was right for a change of men at the helm. Frederick Vietor was to become general manager and take over day-to-day operations. Before the change, "efficiency experts" were called in and spent several months studying the firm.

"Wages are equal or higher than those of the piano industry," intoned the consultants in an attack on William's seventy-year-old strategy of paying for the best and expecting it. There was no point in C. F. Theodore's foundry; it was cheaper to buy plates from a supplier. Keymaking was superfluous on the same basis. If the experts knew or understood the concept of quality, discipline, and independence from outside sources or the sales value of the claim that "all parts of a Steinway are made by Steinway," they did not show it. The "operating management and the board of directors are the same" and this, they claimed, was a "violation of sound business practice." It mattered not a bit that for eighty-eight years, seventy-seven of them spectacularly successful, the family ran the family business. In the modern world directors were intended to be objective, and the family was advised to "always represent a minority" on the board. The board of trustees, so named when Steinway & Sons was transmuted from a partnership to a corporation in May 1876, was now to be called the board of directors.

The consultants said the house needed "strong men" and a "closely knit and aggressive sales organization." Retire senior men. Improve accounting. Hire a controller, a factory manager, an industrial engineer. Improve the plant layout, streamline the flow of materials, and update manufacturing methods. Install a wage incentive plan and initiate production control procedures. Sales departments must be reorganized; take Charles's son Charles F. M. off salary and put him on commission; assign a sales territory to William R. Steinway. Remedy "styling deficiencies" in the pianos. Sell a factory; there is excess capacity. On and on went the litany of inadequacies, consuming more than twenty single-spaced typed pages.

A holding action against the expert invasion was undertaken by Paul Bilhuber, now in charge of "inventions" and the architect of the Model S and Pianino. The foundry, wrote Bilhuber in a memo, had a "loss rate" of but 1 percent compared to the average of 4 to 7 percent for foundries nationwide. Unspoken was the fear that Steinways might soon be breaking in half, the result of invisible flaws in castings bought outside. Bilhuber took strong exception to the finding of antiquated manufacturing methods. Among other innovations, Steinway was the first to use lacquer instead of varnish and the first to use special compressed-air tools. The "failure to keep up was solely due to a lack of funds." The consultants also recommended buying cheaper grades of lumber to cut costs. "We would counsel against the use of inferior stock," wrote Bilhuber. "Each time it has been tried, the waste has, together with the time consumed, exceeded the cost of the better grade of lumber." Notwithstanding the objections, most of the report stood. After a decade of keeping the house and its traditions alive through an economic ice age, Theodore Edwin Steinway was indicted, then tried by consultants from Cleveland. The verdict: guilty of failure to yield to the twentieth century.

The record is silent on Theodore E.'s thoughts or feelings about the efficiency experts. Their arrival was catalyzed by Vietor. Soon the trade papers carried the news of Steinway retirements: Hermann Irion, formerly a manager and with Steinway & Sons for forty-six years; Frederick Reidemeister, forty-nine years of service, accountant and close associate of Fred Steinway; Albert Sturcke, fifty-two years, a multilingual stenographer hired by William in 1889. A few months later A. J. Menzl, the Astoria works manager who testified during the lawsuits of Henry W. T. in the 1890s, retired. And there were others who resigned in 1941, including two grandsons of Doretta Steinway, factory manager Theodore Cassebeer and Paul Schmidt, assistant to the president. In the space of a few months, 275 years of pianomaking experience exited Steinway for the last time.

To lower the raised eyebrows of the trade, photographs were released of Theodore E.'s sons, Henry Ziegler Steinway and John H. Steinway, voicing and regulating grands in the factory, presumably as young family members had done for generations. The message was continuity, but the names of the recently hired factory manager and the new controller had no Teutonic sound, nor did they come from the piano industry. On March 12, 1941, "Theodore E. Steinway, president of Steinway & Sons, announced the appointment of F. A. Vietor as general manager of Steinway & Sons. Mr. Vietor is a great-grandson of Henry Englehard Steinway and has been with the firm since he came out of college in 1913," reported *Piano Trade Magazine*. "Mr. Vietor is also a deep student of business management in the broadest sense." Ninety-eight days later, at age fifty, Frederick A. Vietor was dead of leukemia.

With the Hamburg factory in the hands of the Nazis, the Battle of Britain raging in the skies over Steinway Hall, London, his managers and friends of forty years gone and the heir apparent dead, Theodore E. now faced another crisis: World War II. For months before America's entry into the war the nation's mobilization was accelerating, and brass and iron were becoming difficult to obtain. A "judicious investigation" was ordered of the "possibility of obtaining war work due to possible curtailment of production" noted the new "directors'" minutes.

Ten days after the Japanese attack on Pearl Harbor the first sign of the war appeared in the annals of the house. The directors met and decided to modify the words of the Steinway warranty, basically unchanged since the time of William. It was resolved to strike the phrase "best and thoroughly seasoned material" and replace it with "best material obtainable." Soon that was no material. "Manufacturers of musical instruments will feel the pinch of government curtailment starting tomorrow, when sharp restrictions on the use of critical materials in the manufacture of all types of musical instruments will go into effect," reported the *New York Times* on March 1, 1942. A few days later the National Piano Manufacturers Association revealed that the industry had been cut to one eighth of its 1940 use of critical materials and that "manufacturers will actively seek war work on plywood parts for airplanes and other war equipment, a task for which they are already equipped."

As if to show publicly that Steinway & Sons possessed a pyramidal permanency, sponsored hour-long radio broadcasts were continued on WQXR in New York; and in March 1942, less than three weeks after the curtailment order by the War Production Board, a celebration was held at Steinway Hall. "More than 700 guests attended the party honoring the centennial of the New York Philharmonic Symphony Orchestra . . . given by Mr. and Mrs. Theodore E. Steinway. A huge birthday cake was cut," reported the *Times*, just above an item announcing that a daughter was born to Fred Astaire.

But behind the glossy commemoration of the Philharmonic centennial, attended by Leopold Stokowski, Bruno Walter, Walter Damrosch, Fritz Kreisler, and the entire orchestra was a family in crisis. At least some of the members were ready, perhaps reluctantly, to abandon the heritage of "only one name and only the best." The outline of the dilemma exists in only the tersest form. In May 1942 it was resolved to "seek post-war product diversification." If this was an extraordinary turn for a family that not long ago claimed to *Fortune* that the business was "never about volume production," that "The Name must never be commercialized," and that it turned down a million dollars to use the Steinway name on a radio, it was perhaps due to the times. A proposal was made to buy "some well-known piano name as a second line for Steinway." An offer to acquire Vose & Sons, a minor but venerable Boston pianomaking name, was voted down with William R. and Paul Bilhuber dissenting.

The Vose vote was peculiar in view of the circumstances: just two weeks earlier the War Production Board, one of the Washington agencies set up to direct the wartime economy as a part of what soon became known as the "Arsenal of Bureaucracy," ordered that "no critical materials may be processed for the manufacture of prohibited instruments." The ban covered not only new pianos built from existing stocks of material, but repair parts for old pianos, as well as virtually every other instrument using more than a few ounces of metal. By government order the acres of lumber in the yards of Steinway & Sons aged for the duration. Steinway's woods, absent the proper rubber stamp of a government inspector, were deemed inadequate for defense work.

With production completely shut down, the industry and Steinway scratched in earnest for war work. "The plants, machinery, facilities, administrative and operating personnel of Wm. Knabe & Co., Chickering & Sons and the Mason & Hamlin Company . . . have been leased for the duration of the war emergency," reported the *Times* in June 1942. By mid-August Steinway, too, had found a defense project. A newly formed firm called the General Aircraft Corporation obtained a government contract but had no factory. Though not destined to become one of the great names in aviation history, General leased one of the Steinway factories and awarded the house a subcontract to make wooden parts for a craft called the CG-4A.

"CG," in the bubbling alphabet soup of war, stood for "combat glider." Roughly forty-eight feet long with a wingspan of eighty-four feet, the CG-4A had the appearance of a giant, mutant flying insect. Its envisioned mission was to be towed over hostile territory and released, then to glide to earth carrying fifteen combat-ready troops, including the pilot and copilot. Alternatively, CG-4As could carry a jeep or light artillery piece, and it was theorized that squadrons of gliders could quickly transport large complements of fully equipped light infantry to otherwise inaccessible points, often behind enemy lines.

The man-carrying fuselage of the CG-4A was fabricated of welded tubes that were covered with cotton, then "doped" in the manner conventional for light aircraft since airframes were first covered in the years before World War I. At such a task Steinway had no plausible competence. But the wings, ailerons, and empennage of the combat glider were made of a material whose wonders had once again been recognized in a time of metal shortage: plywood. Plywood was made and worked by the same process by which C. F. Theodore Steinway fabricated his pioneering one-piece grand piano rims generations before. Modern aero and marine engineers, under pressure of war, discovered what had long been known in the sleepy backwaters of pianomaking. Plywood was an elegant structural solution, and where once they bent and cut plies of maple into the shape of grand pianos, the workers of Steinway now bent and cut plywood into the shape of wings.

By Christmas 1942 more than eleven hundred persons on two shifts were building glider components in the Astoria shops, and there appeared on the house's letterhead the slogan "Wings for Victory" along with an illustration of a glider flying over a piano. The glider program was short-lived; in total about thirty-six hundred of them were actually used in combat operations in the European and Pacific-China theaters, although almost fourteen thousand were built. They were called "flak bait" by the men ordered to fly in them, and the glider pilots were known as "suicide jockeys." Operational experience was a series of disasters punctuated by catastrophes. When a 137-glider operation was mounted as a component of the invasion of Sicily, more than half crashed into the ocean while only 10 percent reached the designated landing zone. By the summer of 1944 the military realized that, with roughly ten thousand new gliders stored in fifty thousand crates, the inventory was ample for any contingency.

It was D-day plus eight—June 14, 1944—when the announcement was made that the "wooden aircraft program" was suspended. George Stapely, president of the National Piano Manufacturers Association, claimed that firms such as Steinway "gave themselves unselfishly to war production," and the gliders they made "spearheaded the invasion and outwitted the Nips in Burma. . . ." They were "fabricated by the same expert craftsmen who normally devoted their efforts to the advancement of the musical art."

Steinway, meanwhile, was still looking for ways to diversify its postwar business. By means unclear, a connection was made with the developers of the Operadio, a public address and music system for use in factories. The Operadio was installed in the Astoria shops; and plans, ultimately stillborn, were laid to commercialize the product after the war. A plan to buy the Estey Orgatron electronic organ business was evaluated and rejected. In the interim the house obtained a contract to build Victory Verticals; the olive-drab versions of the Pianino, complete with a tuning kit and heavy-duty shipping case for the military, flowed from the factory. Ultimately more than two thousand Victory Verticals were built.

As glidermaking tapered off, layoffs were necessary once again, and the company turned to making an item that was still in great demand: caskets. The stock of select wood once destined for the concert stages and living rooms of America was now drawn upon to fill orders from the National Casket Company. Employment slipped below five hundred persons, and coffinmaking was unprofitable. In 1944 Steinway & Sons lost more money than any year since 1933, the nadir of the depression. More than the future of the house was at risk; all four of Theodore E.'s sons were in the service. They served in Africa, Australia, the Philippines, and, in one case, on Governor's Island off the foot of Manhattan.

When the war was over, Theodore E. was officially able to tell his long-suffering stockholders—there had been only one small dividend of less than one dollar per share in sixteen years—that "the old [Hamburg] factory is completely destroyed together with all our books and records. The new factory is not too badly damaged, but needs all new windows and a roof." Miraculously, about six hundred incomplete pianos had survived Allied bombing according to the British government, which was responsible for occupied Hamburg. With a peculiar pride Theodore said that "of all the U.S. industrial interests on the continent, Steinway & Sons was the only one not a foreign or partly foreign corporation."

The results of the war and the preceding depression were devastating. A dollar of assets in 1927 became fifty-five very depreciated cents by 1945. Allied occupation of Germany soon proved more disastrous for Steinway production there than had the Nazis. While the house had somehow managed to sell a few hundred pianos per year during the war, besides turning out packing crates and rifle stocks from prime piano wood, postwar production slipped to only ten units in 1947. "As to our Branch House in Hamburg," wrote Theodore E. in 1948, "it is still under British–U.S. Allied Military Command. . . . Permission has been given to complete and manufacture a limited number of pianos. We have also been allotted the necessary coal and materials for these operations. The pianos we manufacture there are, of course, all for export as the Command must obtain the necessary foreign exchange to continue the operations under their control."

In 1948 Hamburg managed to produce a grand total of twenty-nine pianos for "export." In postwar Europe the products of Germany were simply unwelcome, no matter their merit, reputation, or the fact of American ownership. It was not until 1955—a decade after the war ended—that Hamburg was able to produce pianos at the level of 1930, the first year of the depression; that output, about twelve hundred, was half that of 1912. When William R. visited Hamburg shortly after the war, he saw the site on the Schanzenstrasse that had once been the works bought in 1881 by his father and uncle C. F. Theodore. Amidst the rubble a single structure stood on the spot where once C. F. Theodore's laboratory had been. The office that once held his papers, instruments, and the notebooks documenting his revolutions in piano design was gone. In its place stood an outhouse.

What the depredations of war and depression did not destroy were left to time, which slowly covered the embers of nineteenth-century fires. No case was more tragic than that of Josef Hofmann, who, like Paderewski before him, stayed too long on stage. Alexander Greiner recollected the morning in February 1945 when he received a call from Bruno Zirato, manager of the New York Philharmonic. Hofmann had failed to appear for a rehearsal with the orchestra. Rushing to the St. Moritz Hotel, Greiner found Hofmann in his underwear, unwilling to rehearse. Later that day Greiner dragged the reluctant but now-dressed Hofmann to the apartment of the Philharmonic's conductor, Artur Rodzinski, "to discuss tempos."

Hofmann sat at the piano, a Steinway, of course, and commenced to play. "And what kind of playing was this?" wrote Greiner. "He played as if he were in a trance. . . . A pupil without any talent whatever played infinitely better! All the notes were there, but it was without any expression, without any dynamics, completely lifeless!" The conductor's wife and another woman present both began to cry as they listened to Hofmann literally execute Chopin. The concert was cancelled. A year later Hofmann appeared in Philadelphia, and members of the audience demanded refunds. Some were convinced that it was not Josef Hofmann on the stage. The pianist sent Greiner a telegram: "Philadelphia recital greatest triumph of my career." It was his last public performance.

Against the larger tragedies were set small ironies: "We sold a house and several empty lots in Long Island and have only eight vacant lots left," reported Theodore E. in a recap of 1947. More than three-quarters of a century after William bought the land, Steinway & Sons was nearly divested of Long Island residential property; the company was still overcommitted in real estate. It owned three factories with a capacity of ten thousand pianos per year but was producing less than one-third that number. The monumental Steinway Hall building had not proven, by any standard but prestige, to be a sound investment.

After two decades in the crucible of depression and war, Theodore Edwin Steinway seemed now to believe principally in the maintenance of appearances. He resolutely refused to consider selling the unused factories, although he did allow the rental of one; his son Henry Z. Steinway's 1947 recommendation that the hall be sold was tabled. "The suggestion was made that Steinway & Sons sell a second line, in order to earn a little extra money," recorded the minutes of a directors' meeting. "President Theodore E. Steinway took a firm stand against it on the grounds of policy." Raised again at another meeting, Theodore E. "vigorously objected on the grounds of policy and prestige" to the second line. Clearly, Theodore, son of William, believed—or desperately wanted to believe—that once again Steinway would build nine thousand pianos per year as it had twenty years before. He could not bring himself to dismantle that which his father and uncles built, nor could he compromise the now nearly century-old practice; the only new piano in a Steinway salesroom was a Steinway.

With a reverence for tradition, if not rigidity, the house faced the next technological onslaught: television. Technically feasible since the early thirties, television was delayed first by the Depression and then by war. Postwar parts shortages and a regulatory dogfight between RCA, which favored black-and-white television, and CBS, an apostle of its own proprietary color system, delayed commercialization until 1947 when the Federal Communications Commission opted for black and white as the national standard.

"The Radio Corporation of America will introduce its first post-war console television," reported the *New York Times* on March 27, 1947. "No list price has been agreed on but it will be in the neighborhood of $1,000. . . . It will have a ten-inch direct-view screen with a fifty-four-square-inch image, as well as AM-FM radio reception and an automatic record changer." This was, by the standards of the time, an aggressive price, for Dumont Laboratories was selling a $795 table model and two consoles at $1,795 and $2,495. The least expensive Steinway, the little forty-inch spinet, then sold for $1,180, while the most popular grand, the Model M, had a New York retail price of $2,185.

By October 1947, CBS researchers estimated that there were fifty thousand television sets in use in New York City, about 15 percent of them in bars. It took seventy years—from 1876 to 1946—for half the homes in the nation to install telephones. For television, the 50-percent mark was reached in slightly over six years. Neither before nor since has any product been taken into American homes at such a rate. In less than three weeks in 1953, more television sets were manufactured than the total number of Steinway pianos made in the first century of the house's existence. The year 1953 was the centennial of Steinway & Sons, and its American output for that year was 2,236 pianos. Had those pianos been built at the rate of television sets that same year, they would have been produced in only thirty-seven minutes of a single workday.

Change percolated through the nation with unprecedented velocity. In a Gallup Poll conducted in 1938, "reading" was designated by 21 percent as a favorite leisure activity. Seventeen percent polled stated that attending the movies was their favorite, and there was still 9 percent of the adult population that spent its leisure listening to records or the radio. Other now quaint activities still possessed considerable popularity. Dancing was preferred by 12 percent, and William Steinway's select pastime, playing cards, was the choice recreation for 9 percent. By 1960 less than half as many persons preferred reading, about one-fourth as many nominated dancing, and card playing was the choice of a third fewer than in 1938. Listening to radio and records evaporated as a preferred leisure activity; it was chosen by less than 1 percent. In 1960 television was listed as the favorite leisure activity of 28 percent, a proportion that would climb to nearly half in a few more years.

The effects of television on the piano industry were differential. Despite some probable losses, the sales of inexpensive vertical pianos trundled along essentially trendless, save for the sharp drops during recession in the years while television swept across the land. There was still social force in the obsolescent notion that pianos belonged in homes and that children were to take lessons on them. In 1949, on what was perhaps a slow day for geopolitical events, the *New York Times* could still editorialize: "One of the worst things to have in any home is a new piano. . . . Such a piano brings out the worst in everyone. It uncovers not only the neighborhood's known and recognized musicians, but tutored and untutored amateurs as well. . . . The new piano brings everyone within hearing, as well as some who, by telephone, have been summoned from considerable distances." Piano buying itself was difficult, except for those "few who can walk into the Steinway office and order—charged to the first of the month—merchandise slightly longer than a boxcar."

The "few" who wanted "boxcar" pianos were becoming fewer; for social status, imposing grandeur, ease of use, and general entertainment, a console television-radio-phonograph was now the consumer durable of choice. In the demobilization-driven recovery before World War II, grand piano sales had soared to as many as twenty-three thousand per year. By 1950 American grand sales had plummeted to six thousand, and in two more years they would decline another third to only four thousand nationwide. What radio, depression, and war had not accomplished—the extinction of the grand piano—television nearly did. Within the world in which he operated, Theodore E. had not done poorly. Steinway & Sons was making roughly 30 percent of all the grand pianos sold in America, about the same as the other two remaining major makers of grands, Aeolian and Baldwin, but that world was now much reduced. The flickering star of the grand piano as cultural symbol was imploding; like the square piano six decades before, the grand was approaching commercial denouement, as was Steinway & Sons.

For more than thirty-seven thousand days the family had made pianos in America; a rational analysis could only indicate that the final sunset might soon occur. With little in sight to brighten the future, Theodore E. determined to celebrate the past: the centennial of the family business. Planning began roughly three years before the official centennial date, which was taken as William's eighteenth birthday, March 5, 1853. There were weekly meetings of the executive staff to plan the immense logistics of the events; meanwhile Steinway sales continued to erode. Theodore E. himself created the slogan "A Century of Service to Music" and personally wrote a genial and romantic history of the house. About fifteen thousand copies were printed, and many found their way into libraries around the nation. Describing his family's arrival in New York in 1850, Theodore E. wrote, "The city of New York held out its arms in welcome, gave them a new home, fresh hope, and the blessed privilege of doing their work, thinking their thoughts, and living their lives in peace, security, and service to music." The book was called *People and Pianos*, and "it seemed to be a good propaganda item," Theodore E. told the stockholders.

The house history was only one component in a massive public relations campaign. During 1953 over two hundred commemorative concerts were given across the nation, arising more or less spontaneously with the guidance of the firm and its dealers. About one-fifth of the concerts were attended by family members.

Hundreds of Steinway stories appeared in magazines and local newspapers. That same year the Ford Motor Company was celebrating its fiftieth anniversary, and this provided a convenient lead for Associated Press feature writer Hal Boyle: "The Steinway piano is exactly twice as old as the Ford car. Both . . . have become famous name brands in America. Theodore E. Steinway, 69, head of the House of Steinway, looks with rather tolerant condescension on the Ford family's celebration. 'How time flies,' he mused at lunch the other day. 'Why it seems only yesterday that young Henry came out of his bicycle repair shop.' The Steinways have succeeded for 100 years," wrote Boyle, "by creating a tradition and sticking to it. . . . Old Theodore says pridefully:—We aren't selling soap or hot dogs, you know. We are selling something that has to do with the spirit, the soul." That year nearly three times more money was spent advertising soap than

Steinway received in total revenues; and about three thousand cars, a fourth of them built by Ford Motor Company, were sold for each Steinway piano. Demand for products of "the spirit, the soul," was weak and still falling.

This did not prevent—in fact it may have encouraged—Theodore E. to press on. Weakened by a colostomy operation, drinking heavily, and likely suffering from the cancer that would take his life in a few years, Theodore E. presided over an almost endless list of projects invented by the N. W. Ayer advertising agency and a public relations firm. A two-thousand-dollar piano scholarship fund was set up, a film was produced, a rose was named for the piano, and a commemorative vase was designed. Special fabrics with images of pianos were created; in all there were more than a hundred projects.

The largest and most complex of these was a centennial concert at Carnegie Hall, Monday, October 19, 1953, in which thirty-four pianists appeared in conjunction with the New York Philharmonic. The proceeds were given to musical charities. Thirty of the pianists appeared in three groups of ten. To avoid injury to artistic egos, the piano dectets were formed by drawing names from a hat. The hat was a fireman's headpiece from the Steinway Hose Company, a relic of William's time. The piano dectets were an evasion of the problems of both status and length posed by the serial presentation of many soloists.

Seeking wider exposure for the event, representatives of the cultural demon television were invited into Steinway Hall. Negotiations were joined with the Firestone Tire and Rubber Company, sponsors of the "Voice of Firestone," a Monday night half-hour of classical and semiclassical music on NBC. The "Voice" was also simulcast on radio, where it began in 1928. With opera singers, pleas for highway safety, and school speech contest winners among the show's staples, it was, at two million viewers, among the lowest-rated prime-time programs. Negotiations broke down over what might be called aesthetic differences. Firestone demanded that a composition by Mrs. Harvey Firestone be performed by the Philharmonic. In a program to include works by Chopin, Prokofiev, and Wagner, this was judged inappropriate by Steinway and negotiations ceased.

Via some unclear instrumentality, no less a celebrity than Ed Sullivan, host of the enduringly popular Sunday night CBS television show "Toast of the Town," offered to broadcast a dress rehearsal of a portion of the concert featuring one of the three piano dectets. Sullivan also contributed five thousand dollars to the musical charities. Thus it came to be that ten pianists played Steinways on national television on Sunday, October 18, 1953. After the performance of Chopin's *Polonaise in A Major, op. 40*, with the virtuosic ensemble more or less coordinated by Rudolf Ganz, Theodore E. was introduced from the audience in typical Sullivan style. "You wouldn't want to take your Chopin in this inflated form as a regular thing, but if Steinway wants to celebrate its next centenary in this fashion, there will be people to relish it," wrote Howard Taubman in the *Times* of the duplicate performance the next night.

On the actual "gala concert" at Carnegie the evening after the network broadcast, critic Taubman was generally charitable. The program began with another group of ten pianists playing Josef Hofmann's arrangement of the "Star-Spangled Banner." The program proceeded, in a manner that might now be called "multicultural," through Wagner's prelude to *Die Meistersinger von Nurnberg*, Edward MacDowell's *Orchestral Suite* dedicated to the American Indian, and the finale of Prokofiev's Number Three piano concerto with Dimitri Mitropoulos playing a special Steinway grand with a transparent Plexiglas lid, built so he could conduct the orchestra while simultaneously playing the piano.

After an intermission and a specially commissioned work by Morton Gould for four pianos, five tons of pianos were again pushed onto the stage for the Chopin rendering; Rudolf Ganz "faced his colleagues and gave them the beat. . . . Occasionally he sat down for some chords." A Philharmonic-only performance of Manuel De Falla's *El Sombrero de Tres Picos* (The Three-Cornered Hat) set up the conclusion of the event: a Morton Gould arrangement of Sousa's *Stars and Stripes Forever* for orchestra combined with ten pianos. This brought the concert to "a tumultuous close." Afterward there was a dinner hosted by Mr. and Mrs. Theodore E. Steinway at the Waldorf-Astoria's Grand Ballroom. The guests, reported as numbering twenty-two hundred persons, more than half the capacity of Carnegie Hall, refreshed themselves, ate, listened to speeches, and witnessed the cutting of a giant birthday cake by another Steinway named William, Theodore's seven-year-old grandson.

The oceans of ink flowing from the "Century of Service to Music" campaign did not increase Steinway sales, whatever their therapeutic benefits to Theodore E. In December of the centennial year 1953 the work force was put on half-time; this was followed by a complete shutdown for five weeks in the summer. After the expenditure of a claimed half-million dollars by the house and its dealers, Steinway sold ninety-four fewer pianos in 1954 than 1953. Each incremental piano sale lost in recessionary 1954 cost more than five thousand dollars. Theodore E. knew from costly experience during the depression that it was impossible to activate piano sales absent of underlying demand. The new and distressing lesson was that even in the robust consumer economy of the 1950s there was no demand to stimulate. Press coverage, airtime, concerts, and advertising expenditures, no matter how lavish, could not force Americans to buy what they did not want, and once again Steinway grand sales sank below one thousand pianos per year.

Sales improved only slightly in 1955, and it was Theodore's son Henry Z. who told the board of directors that summer that "piano manufacturing is the core of our business and must be made profitable." William R. Steinway wrote in the minutes, "He pointed out two methods commonly used by manufacturers to improve themselves: call in consultants, or diagnose, prescribe and take your own medicine. It is his opinion based on experience with the Heller organization and others during the war years, that we should cure ourselves, or at least attempt to, before bringing in consultants." Although he did not know it, Henry Z. was soon to be appointed principal physician.

After exactly 9,584 days as chief executive, Theodore Edwin Steinway announced at a routine meeting of the directors that "Steinway & Sons needs a healthy president," then silently left the room. He had consulted no one; he had told none of his decision. More remarkably, Theodore Edwin Steinway resigned during a strike; the call by the union was for a 15-percent increase in wages, an amount echoing a century of demands. On October 11, 1955, Theodore E. became the first president of the house who did not die in command; an office of chairman was quickly improvised, and Theodore was promoted to it by acclamation.

After breaking for lunch and "considerable discussion," the astonished directors made a relatively obvious choice for president of the house, but not before they gently told a still-hopeful William R. that he was too old for the job. "Kinsman of Founder is Steinway President," read the *Times* story ten days later. Henry Ziegler Steinway "is a great-grandson of the founder of the company, which he joined in 1937. He served as a manufacturing apprentice and as assistant factories manager until 1943 when he entered military service. After the war he became factories manager and was elected a vice president in 1946." Henry Z. had been the heir apparent to the crumbling throne for nine years.

Theodore's three other sons also worked for the house; Theodore D. was in charge of engineering, John H. supervised advertising, and Frederick was involved in sales and Concert and Artists work before leaving to join Arthur Judson, the Philharmonic manager, in a talent agency; Leonard Bernstein was the first client of that short-lived venture. "Walking through the main offices of the Steinway company," wrote reporter Robert Fetridge, "one gets a little confused with the introductions to the many members of the family. The whole organization breathes of informality. . . . Everything is calm."

The informal organization did not remain long under Henry Z. Steinway. Managers were assigned specific responsibilities, a business basic that had somehow slipped away in the darkness of the years. Regular meetings were held; these now emphasized collaboration and consultation rather than reporting and order-taking. An aloof and ill leader was replaced by one who was accessible and healthy. For Theodore E. in his later years the public emphasis was music, a life raft over which the seas of change crashed. Even in his self-written invitations to the centenary concert there was a siegelike desperation with reference to "steadfast adherence to the cause of good music" and the "furtherance of all that is fine and great in Music in America." He once said, to the amazement of a *Times* reporter, that every piano artist was his "child."

Henry Z. firmly assigned responsibility for the Concert and Artists function to Alexander Greiner and personally disavowed any special aesthetic insights. Mindful of a saying of his maternal grandmother—"Fools' names and fools' faces are always seen in public places"—Henry Z. returned to the prototypically corporate style of Charles. The house was to be promoted; personalities were not. There were other reverberations of Charles as well, although he had died before his great-nephew Henry was four years of age. "Democratic and approachable" was the archaic description applied to Charles, and it was relevant once again to a Steinway & Sons president.

The tasks that confronted Charles and Henry Z. were at once alike and startlingly different. Each first faced the task of saving the house; in Charles's case the threat was largely from within, the backwave from the collapse of William's estate. In Henry Z.'s case, the hazard was from without. American grand piano sales, awash in an ocean of consumer goods and passive entertainment alternatives, remained below four thousand instruments per year while the company still had the capacity to produce ten thousand. Industry sales of verticals rattled erratically around 150,000 per year, but Steinway was no force in that arena; the broad market was in cheap pianos, and no one in Astoria knew how to build those, even assuming an unlikely willingness.

The solution, to the extent there was one, was to cut expenses, and the primary means for that was to eliminate the immense excess manufacturing capacity in Queens. The suggestion to cut back had first been made by the "efficiency experts" in 1941, but World War II and the burst of postwar demand for pianos both intervened. By 1950 Henry Ziegler Steinway was openly advocating "factory consolidation."

In a telling memo to his father and the board while still "factories manager," he had written that there were only three reasons *not* to cut manufacturing space. The first reason was "if Steinway intends in the future to give up manufacturing and concentrate on Real Estate, Retailing or the wholesaling of products made by others." Second, consolidation was pointless "if Steinway intends to purchase or merge with another manufacturer with a better production facility." This possibility was occasionally considered. The third contingency was "if Steinway intends to abandon our current quality standards and enter the medium or low-priced field." The memo and its heretical alternatives never left the boardroom, nor did the notion of consolidation, which was "studied" for several more years.

By 1958 a revitalized and reduced factory was operating on the site originally bought by William in 1871. More was involved than bricks, mortars, and machinery; the change brought a fresh focus on the basic business: pianomaking. For nearly nine decades, Steinway & Sons had been a peculiar hybrid of pianomaker and landlord, first with the "settlement" in Astoria and then with Steinway Hall, twelve floors of which were occupied by tenants.

"The Steinway Building, one of the landmarks of Fifty-seventh Street, has been sold . . . to the Manhattan Life Insurance Company. . . . The sixteen-story building houses a number of tenants . . . including the Philharmonic Symphony Society, Columbia Artists Management, and Musical America, a magazine," reported the *Times* on April 22, 1958. Almost exactly one year before the sale, Theodore Edwin Steinway died; he had known of the plan to sell the hall and did not approve. A long lease on the basement, first floor, and mezzanine—space still occupied by the firm today—ensured that the family business would not soon be homeless. The three million dollars in proceeds from the sale helped finance the rebuilding of the consolidated factory. The building cost $3.2 million more than thirty years before, proving, if more evidence were needed, that the family was better at pianomaking than real estate.

With the sale of the hall came another shift: all executives were moved to Astoria. Steel desks and low partitions replaced palatial elegance; leisurely lunches at the New York Athletic Club and visits to the Century and the Lotos clubs were traditions gone, and the whine of machinery could now be heard by managerial ears where once the sound of Chopin wafted in the air. "It is my thought that the manufacturing and selling wholesale of pianos is the most important part of Steinway's business," wrote Henry Z. in 1950. "Therefore, if all major executives are physically located at the factory, there is bound to be more and better thinking on this main problem, rather than, as now, on other lesser problems such as New York retail, Concert & Artists, Real Estate, and so forth." Eight years later it was accomplished.

The new attention to pianomaking soon extended to piano selling at Steinway Hall. In the 1950s under Theodore E. the sale of Hammond organs, whose mewling was heard on radio soap operas and in roller rinks across the nation, had been a profitable sideline. The record is silent on how the Hammond aesthetic was reconciled with the Instrument of the Immortals, but in the lean postwar years it was common for Steinway Hall electric organ sales to reach 40 percent of new Steinway sales. When policies of the Hammond company caused sales to slip, it was not long before only the sound of pianos was heard in the hall. Under Henry Ziegler Steinway, the house acquired what would now be called "strategic focus," although he referred to it as "sticking to the knitting."

A Harvard-educated history and literature major who liked to plot his own graphs of the rising Steinway sales, Henry Z. and the slimmer Steinway were aided by a long-term trend. After bottoming out in 1958 at only 3,370 grand pianos built by all makers in the entire nation, grand piano production jumped 12 percent in 1959 and 15 percent in 1960. An 8-percent rise was seen in 1961. It had been decades since the sales of grand pianos increased in three consecutive years. Scarcely a boom—unit sales were still a trivial 4,729 American-built instruments in 1961 compared to 17 million radios— it was enough for the recrudescent firm to more than double its dividend in one year to the highest level since the Depression. The 1961 dividend of $23.71 per piano was minute by the standards of William's time when the family routinely paid themselves 150 much more valuable dollars for each instrument made, but it was also six times higher than the mournful centenary year.

Seven decades before, William was able to combine his tax payments with maintenance expenses such as painting rocks in Astoria, and they still amounted to a trivial sum. During the struggles of the Depression, Theodore E. often pointed out to the suffering stockholders that the various taxes paid left nothing for dividends. By the time of Henry Z. other circumstances pertained. There were payroll taxes, workmen's compensation payments, employee benefits, and pensions to be paid in addition to United States, German, English, and "other" income taxes. The sum of these—an arithmetic fact notwithstanding their social desirability—was about 60 percent of the house's profits. When the taxes and payments were taken into account, the result was clear: Henry Ziegler Steinway restored the family firm to the financial strength it had during the days of his grandfather William and great uncles Charles and Fred.

Among the strangest of the government-required levies was one in Germany called the *Lastenausgleichsgesetz*. By law the Hamburg factory was required, as were all German manufacturers, to pay a portion of annual proceeds to cover war damages. After having its factory effectively confiscated by the National Socialists and then controlled by the British occupation forces for another half-decade, the family was required to pay damages. It did not matter that for more than a dozen years they neither made a penny nor had a word to say about how the Hamburg business was run. Practically, however, this was a minor irritation, for beginning in the 1950s William and C. F. Theodore's *fabrik* finally fulfilled the hopes of its founders. Under the management of Walter Gunther, Hamburg production rose in synchrony with the postwar German "economic miracle," and the business became highly profitable, more profitable, in fact, than Steinway in America. Three-quarters of a century and two world wars later the vision of C. F. Theodore, the faith of Charles, and the dogged pride of Theodore E. were finally vindicated. The London salesrooms, another and even older residuum of William's international expansion, was also showing signs of economic health as vivid memories of the Luftwaffe and buzz bombs were bleached by time.

The new era of Henry Z. was accompanied by a modest piano redux and, some claimed, a new era for national culture. The sixties brought a book by Alvin Toffler called *The Culture Consumers* and loose talk of a "cultural explosion"; if measured by the number of performances by symphony orchestras across the nation, "cultural seepage" was more apt. Total attendance increased roughly with the population, averaging about 2.7 percent per year, while the average attendance per concert was virtually identical in 1955 and 1965. It was also tallied that about 40 percent of the amount spent on classical music performance was spent in New York. If the definition of "culture" was accepted as sitting in concert halls listening to the compositions of deceased Europeans, then Manhattan remained, as in William's time when Wagner, Berlioz, Rubinstein, et alia, still walked the earth, the cultural axis of the nation.

Presence in the American cultural capital, however, was now more loosely coupled to the renewed vigor of Steinway & Sons. Though sales of pianos were ascending in the sixties, the number of performances in New York in which Steinway pianos were used was not much greater in 1965— 1,040 concerts—than it had been in 1956 when the instruments were used at 905 concerts. The modest 15-percent increase in concert use was contrasted to a 45-percent leap in grand sales. One of William's cardinal concepts—the truism that Saturday night performances led directly to Monday morning sales—had been interposed by another phenomenon. Its power had been felt before as it crushed sales of grand pianos, and now television was once again affecting Steinway. Each year a few hundred more of the video-satiated turned off their televisions and opened the lids of newly acquired grand pianos. The ebony icon of Victorian culture was creeping, ever so tentatively, back into the American home, but this had less to do with piano virtuosi than in times past.

Despite this decoupling, Henry Z. recognized that, even if reduced, the association of the house with the masters of the instrument was still important. Hundreds of Steinway-owned instruments were still stationed at dealers around the nation and in Europe. The Concert and Artists function which oversaw this vast inventory of concert pianos was put on a more businesslike basis. The 116-year-old practice of "loaning" free pianos for indefinite periods to artists and influentials was discontinued in 1969, and the "borrowers" were given the alternatives of buying the instruments, renting, or returning them. The majority bought the pianos, and about one-third returned them. Four artists, names unknown, defected to other pianomakers who were still presumably willing to provide free instruments.

There were other signs of reduced noblesse oblige in the Steinway artist relations. Even as renowned a player as Artur Rubinstein was asked to pay for repairs to his personal instrument. Such a policy, shocking though it may have been to those who viewed Steinway as a patron of their art, undoubtedly reduced requests for service to a number nearer that actually necessary. This did not prevent the occasional bizarre request, such as the case of a pianist playing in London who wanted to borrow a tuning fork from Steinway to tune a Bosendorfer.

One of the strangest incidents in the recorded annals of Steinway artist relations erupted in late 1960: "Glenn Gould, brilliant Canadian pianist, filed a $300,000 damage suit yesterday against Steinway & Sons," reported the *Times* on December 7, 1960. "Mr. Gould said that . . . he was sitting in the office of a Steinway executive when Mr. Hupfer (the chief piano technician) approached him from behind and 'recklessly or negligently let both forearms down with considerable force on the plaintiff's neck and left shoulder.' " Others thought that William Hupfer had simply grasped Gould's shoulders in demonstrative greeting. Gould claimed that Steinway had failed earlier to "protect" him from the "unduly strong handshakes" of Mr. Hupfer. As a result of his injuries Gould, the suit claimed, was unable to record or perform. "Mr. Gould's idiosyncracies have earned him almost as much attention as his concert work. He wears gloves, scarves and overcoats in the summer lest he catch cold," commented the *Times*.

Through a strange combination of misreadings, errors, and delays, the house's insurance company refused to cover the incident, and Henry Z. faced the prospect of paying a huge court award and more negative publicity. The matter languished until a sultry night in August. A meeting was arranged by an executive of Gould's record company at a New York hotel. There Henry Z. found Glenn Gould in a room with the air-conditioning off and the windows closed. True to his press, he was wearing an overcoat. A discussion ensued, and Gould agreed to settle the suit if Steinway would pay his medical expenses. This was done, and the case of the demonstrative tuner was quietly closed. Separately, Glenn Gould continued his journey along the edges of eccentricity and Steinway continued to grow.

In a 1965 memorandum to his directors, Henry Z. presented some data on the growth phenomenon, which, he said, "shows some curious things, such as the fact that we are apparently outpacing the industry, a happy reversal of the usual pattern." Although he did not present it, Steinway & Sons' share of the grand piano market had risen from 24 percent in recessionary 1958 to 28 percent by 1963. There was more that Henry Ziegler did not say; he had not only increased production and market share, that golden idol of marketing men, but he had also improved the quality of the piano as evidenced by a halving of the proportionate expenses of warranty work. Steinway in the late 1960s was producing pianos with better quality than fifteen years before. Warranty expense, always minuscule at less than one-half percent of revenues, had been cut to less than half that.

With rising sales, growing profits, high quality, an advertising program that continuously hummed a message of traditional excellence, all combined with a renewed but modestly growing acceptance of the piano, Henry Z. Steinway guided the family business back onto Fred's "Road to Glory." Then he sold it.

Chapter 32

SUCH, I AM AFRAID, IS LIFE

"The Columbia Broadcasting System, Inc. yesterday announced plans to broaden its interest in the musical instrument field by acquiring Steinway & Sons, the New York piano manufacturer," reported the *New York Times* on February 10, 1972. "Under terms of the proposed transaction, shareholders would receive 375,000 shares of C.B.S. stock. . . . The transaction is valued at $20,437,750." The Columbia Broadcasting System, known then as a "glamour stock" on Wall Street, was about to add Steinway to its roster of the renowned that already included, alphabetically, Blood, Sweat and Tears, Walter Cronkite, Miles Davis, Mary Tyler Moore, the New York Yankees, Simon & Garfunkel, and Dick Van Dyke.

There was, of course, a high concept at work. Americans, the grand theory went, would have more leisure time as the 1970s unfolded, the result of increased economic productivity. The work week was expected to fall to four days while prosperity increased. As the new age of leisure bloomed, citizens would turn to artistic and recreational activities in unprecedented numbers. The argument had been heard before, a century before, when socialist advocates of the eight-hour day claimed that working men would use the extra two hours to "improve" themselves by reading and attending cultural events such as theater and opera. William Steinway, like almost every other "capitalist" of his time, opposed the notion of reduced work hours with his customary and formidable force. Generations later, the idea was reborn, suitably swathed in the cloth of social science and presented as the latest major trend.

In the new world of leisure CBS had deeded to itself the loosely bordered domain of communications, presumably based on another fashionable concept, "synergy." A corporate conglomerate, the conventional wisdom held, could be more than the sum of its parts. If, for example, a company held both the New York Yankees and the facilities on which games were broadcast, greater profits would accrue than if the company did not own both. Extrapolated across books, magazines, recordings, toys, musical instruments, television, radio, and greeting cards, strategic thinking forecast almost boundless synergy, growth, and profits. What little merit the leisure theory possessed dried up with the Arab oil embargo, inflation, and the industrial stagnation that followed. The notion of synergy also fell into disrepute as conglomerate after conglomerate foundered on the rocks of practicality; managing diverse enterprises was anything but simple.

Such an outcome was unknown on the day in December 1971 when Henry Ziegler Steinway met with Harvey Schein, president of CBS's Columbia Group, a major limb on the organizational tree of CBS on which grew the twig of Columbia Musical Properties. CMP, as it was known in the corporate alphabet, consisted of Fender, a maker of electric basses and guitar amplifiers, Rogers Drums, string manufacturer V. C. Squier, and Electro Music, a company that made the "Leslies" for electric organs. Leslies were large wood boxes that introduced phase shifts and frequency modulation into electric organ sound by means of mechanically spinning loudspeakers inside a cabinet.

The topic of the lunch was the addition of Steinway to what was essentially a collection of rock and roll companies. Perhaps unknown to Mr. Schein, Henry Z. was a more-than-willing seller. Before the appearance of CBS, Steinway & Sons had discreetly commissioned the investment banking firm of Dillon, Read and Company to evaluate the house, establish a price, and prepare a memorandum. The value of the family firm was set at $19 million by the bankers. In the parlance of finance, this was about twenty-one times 1971 earnings, eerily close to the valuation that Charles had tried and failed to achieve in London three-quarters of a century before. "Now we have the chance of a lifetime," wrote Charles in 1896.

As in the time of Charles, the trademark *Steinway & Sons* was carried on the books valued at one dollar, pianos were made in Astoria and Hamburg, and the legend still glowed. Occasional natterings were heard from piano technicians about an arcane, tiny, yet crucial part in the piano's action known as the Permafree bushing. In one of its few flirtations with late-twentieth-century technology, the house had, at the urging of Henry Z.'s brother, Theodore D., introduced Teflon into these bushings. Teflon replaced the tiny bits of felt lubricated with whale oil at four places in the action. The result, sometimes, was a clicking sound and sticking keys that could not always be reliably repaired. This was a terrifying phenomenon for those who believed that a Steinway, unlike amplifiers, airplanes, blenders, and bridges, was a perfect machine.

Ironically, the pianos built under Henry Z. were scarcely less perfect than those of his ancestors. Adjusted by the price of the instrument, the house's warranty costs—a measure of the problems a buyer experiences with a piano or other product—were immaterially different in the 1960s from those of the halcyon years of the "piano boom" in the 1920s, and they were scarcely higher than in the sunset years of the immigrant German craftsmen who experienced shop discipline so severe that workers could be fired for talking. But insistence on perfection in the late 1960s had costs. One of these was a more militant work force; the Astoria strike of 1970 was among the longest in the firm's history. Compounded by another strike in 1967, one result was a rapid rise in labor costs. These leapt 48 percent per piano in only five years. During this same time hourly wages for the entire musical instruments industry grew about 25 percent, putting Steinway & Sons at a disadvantage with their competitors elsewhere in the nation.

There were other external forces at work as well. Long Island's defense industry, under impetus of the Vietnam War, developed a large appetite for labor, and the jobs paid well. Based on national averages, a man could give himself a 36-percent raise by choosing to make the instruments of war rather than music. Some did, and this contributed to a high turnover among the Steinway workers. During the first six months of 1969 alone more than one-fifth of the Astoria work force was replaced. Attempts were made to recruit trainees from local high schools, but only four persons applied for the twelve available jobs. In the Psychedelic Sixties learning how to build the Instrument of the Immortals held little appeal.

All this had an impact, and it could be seen in an item labelled "rework," the cost of fixing substandard parts and pianos before they left the factory. In just five years rework costs per piano, previously stable, rocketed up to two and one-half times earlier levels. To the credit of Henry Z., the problems were largely kept within the factory, and warranty expense rose much less steeply. Serious consideration was given to leaving New York, as William once threatened, and moving pianomaking, in the words of Henry Z., "down where they appreciate manufacturers." As a practical matter, the cost of moving was probably prohibitive, notwithstanding the likely damage of severing the twelve-decade-long Steinway symbiotic relationship with the city that was home to 40 percent of the nation's classical music performances.

At least an equal challenge appeared in the form of a new global competitor. When once William had been able to boast that his American "art industry" of pianomaking had expunged imported instruments from the nation's parlors, he and other manufacturers were aided by a national policy of allowing free entry of people and restricted imports of goods. In the nineteenth century imported pianos were thought socially less desirable than opium or guns; the instruments carried a tariff of 30 percent while the drug was tariffed at 9 percent and rifles 25 percent. Abraham Lincoln expressed the national position succinctly: "I do not know much about the tariff, but I know this much. When we buy manufacturer's goods abroad we get the goods and the foreigner gets the money. When we buy the manufactured goods at home we get both the goods and the money." A century later Lincoln's apothegm was forgotten, and Henry Z. had only a minimal 8-percent tariff protection from imported grands, a result of the gradual inversion of national policy that now facilitated the import of goods and constricted the immigration of people.

The imported pianos arriving in America were coming from Japan and most, specifically, from the Nippon Gakki Company, Hamamatsu-shi, Dai Nippon. Founded by T. Yamaha in 1887 to build Western-style reed organs, Yamaha was already making pianos by the turn of the century, and one somehow turned up at a fair in Saint Louis, where it won a prize. For the next six decades little was seen of Japanese pianos in America, although for a few months in the 1930s the trade was alarmed by reports of a fifty-dollar "Jap piano" to be sold in department stores. The instrument was of abysmal quality and also proved unsalable as a child's toy.

Even in the early 1960s it was easy for Americans to dismiss the consumer products of Japan; its automobiles were tiny sheet-metal boxes perched on roller skate wheels, as attractive as warts to the drivers of Rocket Eighty-eights, Rancheros, and Roadmasters. In electronics the Japanese sold the lesser grades of tinny-sounding transistor radios and plastic-cased black-and-white televisions. It was perhaps ironical that the Japanese, later known for their prowess in "high technology," had an early success in the brackish Victorian backwaters of pianomaking, but there were parallel phenomena in steelmaking and shipbuilding, two other "low technology" industries. The domestic Japanese piano market grew rapidly after World War II. In 1950 the entire sector produced a scant 3,770 instruments, but by 1960 this had reached 48,557 pianos, averaging an astonishing growth rate of 29 percent per year. Very few of these pianos were exported, and fewer still came to the United States.

In 1960 Japan exported less than 2 percent of its production to America, but the Japanese proved to be prodigious domestic purchasers of pianos. By 1967 the Japanese piano industry exceeded the American industry in total instruments produced, and by 1969 the Japanese were selling more pianos domestically than the United States, notwithstanding that the population was roughly half that of America and the total domestic economy was about one-fifth the size. That same year more than sixty-three hundred Japanese grand pianos were shipped to America, more than triple the number of grands built in Astoria. Whatever the merits of these instruments, there was one uncontroversial fact: they were dirt-cheap, landing on West Coast docks at only $535, less than one-fourth the *wholesale* price of a Model L Steinway. Cost proved compelling, and again by 1969 the Japanese makers, principally Yamaha, held almost half the American market for grands. In less than a decade the Japanese went from insignificance to dominance in grand pianos. As the immigrant Steinways had seized prominence in New York one hundred and ten years before, to the alarm and dismay of "native" pianomakers, now the new commercial "immigrants" from the Far East did the same.

The means, however, were very different. The Steinway strategy of the nineteenth century was essentially technological, and profound improvements were made in the instrument. The approach of the Japanese and Yamaha in particular was more expedient: make copies of Steinways and sell them cheaply by whatever means were feasible. This resulted, among other things, in Yamaha motorcycle dealers in South America briefly going into the piano business.

The president of Yamaha publicly announced that it was the specific objective of his company to "overtake Steinway." Selling 200,000 pianos per year worldwide by the early 1970s, forty times the number of Steinways, the question was not volume; it was status and, undoubtedly, personal and national pride. Yamaha yearned, it seemed, to become a twenty-first century Instrument of the Immortals, but ambulatory immortals were in short supply. Berlioz, Hofmann, Liszt, Paderewski, Rachmaninoff, Anton Rubinstein, and Wagner were unavailable for Yamaha testimonials. The ethos of romantic classicism was forever inaccessible, and pianos that shared their names with the motorcycles contemptuously known in America as "ring-dings" and "rice-burners" were unlikely to be regarded with devotional reverence. While Japanese makers could not co-opt the legend or truly reproduce the instrument—attempts at both had been ongoing for a century—they could crush the house under an avalanche of good but inexpensive pianos.

In the psycho-economics of this strategy, a buyer is presented with a perceived good-quality product at a low price competitive with a perceived excellent-quality product at a high price. The calculus forced on the potential purchaser, presuming rationality, is one of determining the value of the intangibles in the second offering. In effect, Yamaha asked buyers what they would pay for the name Steinway & Sons on a piano. In Germany, where both instruments sat side by side on showroom floors, two Yamaha grands could be bought in 1967 for the price of one Steinway.

This was a stratagem as brilliant as it was potentially deadly, and though designed primarily to capture the higher-volume realm of medium-priced pianos unprotected by fame, the threat was real. For Henry Z., less than one thousand pianos per year was the difference between good profits and losses; a few consecutive years of red ink would demolish the house that stood for more than a century. Economically trivial Steinway & Sons, the Yamaha standard for quality, tone, and prestige, could easily become a casualty in what was the economic equivalent of the saturation bombing that destroyed the *Schanzenstrasse* factory in Hamburg during World War II.

The family firm was enfilladed by a vast international trading company that made motorcycles, outboard motors, furniture, electronics, and musical instruments from behind a wall of protected markets, friendly banks, and cheap money, all buttressed by Japanese national policy. From Hamburg came a report by a visitor that a Steinway grand was seen disassembled in the Yamaha factory. A check of the serial number showed that it had originally been bought by the president of Sony. Steinway protests of Yamaha's attempts to patent old and well-known pianomaking techniques were ignored, and at one point Yamaha advertised that they developed an improvement—a bar on the plate—that had been used for a century or more by Steinway. In Germany Yamaha "pirated three of our young voicer-tuners, whom we trained from apprentices," reported Henry Z. to his board of directors. The purpose of hiring Steinway personnel was "to learn the secret of the Steinway tone." A protest to the Hamburg Chamber of Commerce followed, and via arbitration it was agreed "that there will be no pirating either way." Steinway had not hired any Japanese piano technicians, however.

By 1971 Yamaha was showing full concert grands at the international Frankfurt, Germany, trade show. When Henry Ziegler Steinway heard the instrument, he reported that it "had a shockingly good sound." A technician named Ingo Ludemann, trained by Steinway in Hamburg, "claimed credit for the concert grand." Once apparently content to make uprights and small grands, Yamaha now took direct aim at Steinway's most renowned—and profitable—instruments.

A truculent and mobile work force, rising costs, newly imposed government price controls designed to stem inflation, and transpacific economic aggression comprised the external challenges. There were internal ones as well. For Henry Z. Steinway the cliche "generation gap" had palpable meaning. The next generation of Steinways aspired to careers in art and architecture; some dropped out of college or travelled to Europe, but no "member of the blood" wanted to spend twenty years learning how to make and sell pianos in Queens. The successional lacuna was a missing bridge on the foggy road to the future, and the fourth generation of pianomaking Steinways was clearly the last.

There was another and more immediate problem: Henry Z. had not developed a plausible successor. His death or disability would have left the house headless; while two of Henry Z.'s brothers—John H. and Theodore D.—still worked for the firm, their experiences were in the narrow areas of, respectively, advertising and engineering. Despite their surname and many years of experience, they were not viewed by influential stockholders as credible candidates to guide Steinway & Sons into an increasingly uncertain future.

The matter of stockholders proved key. In the time of William, he and three of his nephews were an invulnerable majority, and one which only Henry W. T. had the temerity to challenge. At Steinway Hall or across the street at Luchow's Restaurant, four, and only four, men were needed to decide the direction of the house. After William's death and the debacle of his estate, Steinway stock was more widely distributed, but there was never a serious challenge to the authority of Charles, Fred, or even Theodore Edwin. While Steinway was never listed on a stock exchange, beginning in the 1920s shares were available to the public through brokers. Sales were infrequent, volumes were vanishingly small, and the shares were traded in odd lots, most often when a legatee of the legatee of the founders died. The bottom was reached in 1946 when two Steinway shares changed hands for two dollars each.

That no one ever got rich trading Steinway stock is certain. In the mid-1950s when Henry Z. Steinway became president, shares sold for as little as seventeen dollars, about fourteen cents on the dollar of the firm's book value. At that price, all of Steinway was worth one-third less than it had been when William incorporated the house nearly eighty years before. The long-term performance of Steinway did not arouse the pecuniary lusts of investors, but the limited availability of its shares allowed an occasional purchase by the public, often by persons fond of music and the legend of the house. One such was William Rosenwald, a Jewish philanthropist whose immense fortune was based on Sears, Roebuck and Company. It was to prove a portentous transaction.

Rosenwald owned the American Securities Corporation, the vehicle for his investment holdings. At American the Steinway shares came to the attention of Helmut Friedlaender. Characterized by Henry Steinway as "one of the smartest men I have known," Friedlaender decided Steinway & Sons was undervalued and began to quietly accumulate Steinway shares, keeping them in what is known as "street name" to conceal the true ownership. Ultimately the Rosenwald interests owned about 15 percent of Steinway, making them the largest single stockholder. Having accumulated their position, Rosenwald and Friedlaender asked for a meeting to discuss the future of the firm. The initial Steinway response was to try to buy out the American Securities interests, and an offer was made in the spring of 1966. The offer, $120 per share, was smilingly declined by Helmut Friedlaender as "ridiculous." In that assessment he was correct, for just six years later CBS would pay triple the sum. Though he declined a seat on the Steinway board, Friedlaender met with Henry Z. often over the next few years, and in discussing the future of the house Henry Z. came to believe "upon mature reflection," in William's phrase, that "a sale was the answer for the stockholders, employees and the future." This meant, in effect, that the family firm would have to take refuge from the storms of change in the shelter of some giant corporation.

Though Henry Z. had done a spectacular job of returning Steinway to prosperity and productivity—profits in his best years achieved parity with the halcyons of Charles and William when adjusted for the exactions of government—some family members, notably the Ziegler branch, which owned 12 percent, were eager "to get the money out" that had been invested in Steinway for more than 110 years. Quintessentially patient, even forbearing, capital had become impatient in an age that deified rapid growth, and for Steinway there had not been such growth in half a century, nor could there be. Dividends reduced by recession and strikes undoubtedly added to the pressure to divest in 1969 and 1970.

Through the years there was no shortage of interest in acquiring Steinway. Over two dozen inquiries were made between 1955 and 1968 by potential purchasers, some quite unlikely. The legendary firm had fallen under the gaze of Beatrice Foods; Teledyne, an electronics conglomerate; Avnet, a defense electronics supplier; Congoleum, the flooring company; Royal-McBee, office machines; as well as Magnavox, the television manufacturer. That none of these suitors succeeded meant, perhaps, that the future was spared a Steinway breakfast food, guided missile, floor tile, typewriter, or television, but it also verified the magic of the name. In July 1970 Helmut Friedlaender arranged for Henry Steinway to meet secretly with representatives of the Japanese pianomaker Kawai. Nothing happened after the initial meeting.

With "anxious" Ziegler family members and Helmut Friedlaender "leaning" on Henry Z. to "make something" of Steinway's $14 million in assets, the stage was set for a meeting with Harvey Schein of CBS on Thursday, December 2, 1971. At that lunch there was likely little surprise in Schein's asking if Steinway & Sons might be acquired by CBS; CBS had, in fact, considered purchasing Steinway in 1965 and, through CBS/Sony in Japan, held an interest in Kawai. The next day Henry Z. met with the Dillon, Read dealmakers, and after the lapse of only a week, negotiations began with CBS. In only sixty-two days, including the Christmas and New Year holidays, a deal was struck.

CBS would exchange 375,000 of its shares for Steinway's 55,448.6 shares. For each share, CBS seemed eager to pay about $367, roughly triple what the thinly traded Steinway shares had been selling for over-the-counter, and a premium of nearly one-half for the company's name over the book value of the assets. The roughly $6.4 million premium could be considered the cost of the name *Steinway & Sons*, which was carried on the books at a value of one dollar. If so, the price of the legend must have seemed modest.

All of this was reckoned not in cash but stock, a form of exchange which has its own peculiar rules. Steinway was actually slightly more profitable than CBS. As long as CBS did not pay more for Steinway than each dollar of its own earnings were valued on Wall Street, the transaction was, by the calculations of financial analysts, an acceptable one. In the terms of that trade, the transaction was "non-dilutive." As a practical matter, it was also trivial, for the entire revenues of the makers of "The Standard Piano of the World" routinely flowed into CBS coffers every 4.4 days.

Though there is no evidence that many bothered to congratulate him for it, Henry Ziegler Steinway had during the sixteen years of his stewardship of the house increased its value almost 17 percent per year on average for each and every year. Long-term investors in the American stock market, suitably diversified, may, also on average, expect only a little more than half that appreciation. By any logical standard it was an extraordinary performance, but Steinway was not merely a financial entity. It had always been about family as well, and not all family members were eager for the embrace of a conglomerate, no matter how glamorous. "My own feelings on the CBS acquisition," wrote John H. Steinway to a young nephew in early 1972, "are that it is a bloody shame, but apparently unavoidable. . . . Some . . . are more interested in making a fast buck than on the preservation of a tradition of four generations. I feel a little like an unwilling funeral director. Such, I am afraid, is life."

Up to the moment of the actual vote of the stockholders on April 27, 1972, Henry Z. did not know if his mother, Ruth, would vote for or against the sale to CBS. She had helped her husband, Theodore E., endure the trials of radio, depression, war, and television, and fifteen years before, Alexander Greiner wrote that Ruth Gardner Steinway reminded him of "the heroines of Greek drama." At the stockholders' meeting convened to vote on the sale to CBS—held in an industrially plain room in the Astoria factory, not Steinway Hall—Mrs. Steinway addressed her son: "Some of us . . . were not born to Steinway blood but in sixty years absorbed it. . . . The basis of our interest has been the quality of the Steinway piano, to make the finest damn Steinway piano that can be made and if you will continue we will be proud of you." As a symbol this mattered; as reality it did not. Most shares were voted by proxy and the sale was virtually certain, Those who came to the meeting were there to witness history, not change it.

Consistent with the protocols of such occasions, Henry Ziegler Steinway rose to explain the reasons for the sale. The house's management was aging, "none are getting any younger," said Henry Z., then fifty-six. It was implied that the number of stockholders, now 228, made decision making unwieldy. New York City was now "hostile to manufacturing" and "if we ever move, we will need lots of capital." Hamburg, supplying the major share of profits, was also in the "inner city" and may need to relocate. The Japanese were "an opportunity and a menace," commented Henry Z. Now the world's largest market for pianos, Steinway might sell pianos in Japan with the aid of CBS. There was also a diaphonously covered reference to Yamaha as "one huge company [that] has the avowed purpose of overcoming Steinway." Last was a reference to the new regulatory climate, principally price controls and occupational safety standards. These were matters best dealt with from within a large company with a phalanx of lawyers and expert staff. "We think," said Henry Z., "that CBS can handle our product in the right way." When the votes were counted all but a handful of shares owned by a retired piano tuner were voted in favor of the acquisition. "We are looking forward to the new challenge," said Henry Z. Then the meeting was adjourned. Exactly 44,878 days after *instrumentenmacher* Christian Karl Gottlieb Steinweg stepped ashore from the bark *England's Queen* onto the streets of Manhattan, the end of the family business could be clearly seen. It became publicly official when the tombstone appeared in the *Wall Street Journal* four days later on May 1, 1972: "Columbia Broadcasting System, Inc. has acquired Steinway & Sons," read the announcement.

The real powers of CBS, William S. Paley and Frank Stanton, invited Henry Z. Steinway to lunch shortly after the acquisition. He had not met them before, and he would not see them again. Steinway, with Henry Z. as president, was tucked away in a corner of the maze that was the conglomerate CBS in recognition of its lack of economic significance. Harvey Schein, the architect of the deal, soon left CBS for Sony, and Henry Z. reported to Robert G. Campbell, president of the Music Division. Surrounded by an army of staff, Campbell worked from Chicago and reported back to New York to the Columbia Group, which held the toy and greeting card operations and a forever-changing list of miscellaneous other enterprises. With five levels of "management" above, the predictable soon happened.

"I continue to be concerned by the endless chain of paper and the degree of concentration on its production at CBS," wrote Henry Z. to the Music Division president less than six months after the buyout. "We hoped the merger would bring efficiency, not bureaucracy." Before long the powers at CBS were pressuring Henry Z. to grow the business. It was "made clear during our merger negotiations . . . that the piano market has not had and in my opinion cannot have any drastic growth," commented Henry Z., who usually documented his assertions with charts and tables. Quantitative data did not change minds at CBS.

Based on his decade of experience with them in both America and Europe, Henry Z. knew that the real competitive challenge was the Japanese. "The Japs are here now. Yamaha has acquired the Everett Piano Company." In an early version of what became known as the "transplant" strategy later used by Honda, Kawasaki, Matsushita, Nissan, Sony, and Toyota, Yamaha bought Michigan based Everett. There they planned to build pianos under both the Everett and Yamaha names. The threat to

Steinway was great, for roughly 90 percent of Steinway dealers sold Everetts, and it took little imagination to envision 25-percent cheaper Yamaha grands flanking Steinways throughout the national dealer network.

The hazards of toe-to-toe competition did not impress CBS executives, who responded by raising prices on Steinways while flirting briefly with a "cooperative" arrangement with Kawai, the distant second-place pianomaker of Nippon. CBS and Steinway were ultimately saved from that pianistic Dunkirk by Yamaha itself, which quietly discontinued its first transplant experiment after a few years' experience with the attitudes of Michiganders toward their jobs.

Meanwhile, the thinking at CBS had evolved along other lines, and there were demands to simultaneously increase production, slash inventories, and cut personnel. Any appearance of collegiality disappeared, and Henry Z. received "instructions" from Robert Campbell to execute such a plan. "I find these instructions illogical. I further believe, that if carried out, these instructions will destroy Steinway," wrote Henry Z. in his characteristically direct way.

No effort by Henry Ziegler Steinway could change the corporate mind, no amount of patiently repeated explanation that wood must be aged, that the best must be purchased when available, that most bought parts were made by single suppliers whose cooperation was essential, that time was a fundamental factor in high-quality pianos. The men who managed from afar by the numbers knew that sliced inventories and shed personnel would emerge immediately as profits, much to the pleasure of *their* bosses. Quality was vague and immeasurable; money was not.

A bizarre, but typically corporate, anomaly was lurking in these demands. The information needed to control inventories and costs was not available. The CBS data processing department never wrote the software needed and claimed at one point that meeting even the payroll reporting needs of Steinway & Sons was impossible. Almost four years after the acquisition basic management reports were still unreliable. While Steinway could not get information back from the company, the bureaucracy was insatiable: "Maybe I will live long enough to see us add enough competent staff to keep up with CBS bookkeeping requirements," observed Henry Z.

In this exotic world, staff was to be cut at the same time it needed to be increased, material stocks were to be reduced while production was increased, and all the while Steinway prices were being raised like Arab oil. Above Henry Z., presidents and vice presidents came and went with the frequency of subway trains. The belief at Black Rock, Columbia Broadcasting System headquarters in New York, was now that "people will pay any price for a Steinway." When Henry Z. took exception to this view in late 1975, he was stripped of the power to set Steinway prices, which was taken by his boss.

Blissfully but inexplicably unaware of the implications of the Japanese strategy of delivering value (good quality at reasonable prices) in its products, CBS continued to jack piano prices ever higher in a search for larger profits. This proved to be a strategic error of the first degree. As prices were raised, market share fell in virtual lockstep. Because the market for grand pianos continued to grow, Steinway production dithered around an essentially flat and trendless line, undoubtedly mystifying the ever-growing executive staff of the CBS/Columbia Group Music Division. Economists explain this phenomenon as the "demand elasticity of price" and plainspoken manufacturing men know that "if you sell more, you make more, and you sell more at a lower price." Both the arcane and obvious versions of this basic truth eluded the management of the corporation, and market share atrophied to less than half what it had been during the trying times of Theodore E. when the house teetered on the abyss.

Having clearly lost the price conflict while fighting the inventory battle to an uneasy standoff, Henry Z. continued to advocate improvements in quality; the pleadings were so frequent that it is difficult not to infer a deterioration of excellence, although no direct evidence exists. There was, Henry Z. reported, increasing talk about "good, old pianos" with the words "pre-CBS coming in more and more." Citing plans for the year 1975, Henry Z. advised that "the most important mission for the coming year is the improvement of quality in the New York factory."

A few months later Henry Z. admonished, "Let us not forget, *as we do not*, Chairman Paley's injunction to put quality first." In 1976 it was more of the same: "I ask that quality improvement be our most important objective next year—more important than meeting production schedules and inventory levels." In most American corporations of the 1970s this was heresy, but Henry Z. continued: "We will rise or fall on the good opinion, and the ability to buy of the serious [musical] amateur. . . . CBS wants to believe that everything should go up 10% per year." It was essential, continued the oldest pianomaking Steinway, "to improve quality, which in the last analysis is all we have to sell. . . . We must look inward and see that we do, in fact, produce the best piano in the world, and build the organization that can engineer, control and manufacture it." That year Henry Steinway delivered to the Music Division profits 6 percent below budget.

"JOB CHANGES: Robert P. Bull, 50, has been named president of Steinway & Sons, succeeding Henry Z. Steinway, who will become chairman of the piano company that is now a component of the CBS musical instruments division," read an eight-line item in the *New York Times*. In Henry Z.'s words, he was "unfrocked" and the title of chairman, though impressive, carried neither defined duties nor responsibilities. CBS was sufficiently astute not to throw a Steinway into the street, as was its general custom with unwanted senior managers, but for the first time in 124 years a Steinway was not in direct command of the destiny of Steinway & Sons.

Robert Bull, a member of the Story & Clark pianomaking family, had most recently run the Fender guitar and amplifier operation of CBS. The staple sound source for innumerable "killer grooves" and "smokin' riffs" in rock, soul, and the blues, Fender electric basses, guitars, and guitar amplifiers, particularly the Twin Reverb, were already commanding a premium in the *used* market when pre-CBS. From a corporate perspective, Robert Bull had increased profitability at Fender and was therefore an excellent candidate to manage Steinway. "According to insiders," reported the *Times*, Mr. Bull "had an abrasive manner and rarely consulted with Steinway family members and senior employees. . . . 'He imposed his own way of doing things, without any consideration for the more than a century's worth of experience at his fingertips,' said one longtime Steinway executive." Robert Bull's firing of William T. Steinway, Henry Z's son who had joined the firm in research and development, did little to endear him to the surviving family members.

Robert Bull lasted for about one and one-half years, the first in a succession of CBS appointments to the Steinway presidency. The next, on January 1, 1979, was Peter M. Perez. When profiled in the *Times*, which after 120 years still doted on Steinway as a Manhattan cultural totem to a degree exceeding its empirical significance, Peter Perez was described as a forty-year-old executive who wore pinstripe suits, French cuffs on a monogrammed shirt, and Gucci shoes. A Yale graduate with an MBA, "at age 34 he became the youngest president of C. G. Conn, Ltd., a music instrument manufacturer [of brass winds such as trumpets and trombones] in Oak Brook, Illinois."

Perez described his job as "the practice of craft management in the Twentieth Century," which the reporter interpreted as "a delicate balancing act between the requirements of the hand craftsmen on the shop floor and the demands of the financial overseers at corporate headquarters." The *Times* writer got the tour which had impressed reporters for at least three generations, beginning, as it always did, in the lumberyard with the "1.5 million board feet of wood—Brazilian Rosewood, African Mahogany, Alaskan spruce . . . [which] undergoes as much as four years of indoor and outdoor weathering," dutifully noting, as reporters usually did, that half of it would be thrown away as unsuitable for a Steinway. The craftsmen worked at an "unhurried pace," and the routine sights were shown of a man carving legs for Louis Quinze grands, as well as the plinks, pokings, plonks, and rubbings of tone regulation. Peter Perez displayed an apparent and devout regard for tradition and craftsmanship.

To some this was reassuring, for just a few months before, Steinway experienced the yield of Henry Z.'s unheeded warnings about quality in the form of what can only be called an "artist's rebellion." The virtuosi who verified the Steinway legend in concert halls across the nation and, when contractual obligations allowed, around the world, began to defect.

Arrau, Ashkenazy, Barenboim, Gutierres, Pollini, Peter Serkin, and others began to avoid the Queens-built instruments, but they did not flee to Baldwin or Bosendorfer or Yamaha. In a convolution worthy of a Lewis Carroll tale, the maestros chose the *Hamburg* Steinway.

Buffered not only by an ocean, but the natural corporate reluctance to molest enterprises remitting large profits, the *fabrik* made pianos more or less as it always had. This independence was not new; for forty-five years Hamburg had not submitted to the Astoria innovations of the Diaphragmatic Soundboard and the Accelerated Action. The models built were also different: the ancient A and C grands, as well as environmentally incorrect ivory keys, were still offered, and there was not a single molecule of the dreaded Teflon in a Hamburg grand.

Whatever the merits of the claim—and they ranged from vehement declarations of Astoria decay to strong assertions of improved Astoria quality—the fires of rebellion were soon spent. *Spielart*, the totally subjective combination of touch and tone which an individual piano presents to each player, was not ultimately a factor. A few Hamburg Steinways were brought to New York and San Francisco through grey-market channels, those lines of commerce by which goods move between nations without the authorization or approval of their manufacturers. The grey market would also plague Mercedes-Benz, Porsche, Nikon, Yamaha, and a shipload of consumer electronics manufacturers, all of whom legally tried to exclude certain products from specific markets for reasons of price or competitive strategy. Chairman Henry Z. Steinway made one of his direct pronouncements along these lines: "We have two factories with two markets and they shouldn't be mixed up." This, however, had less effect than an entirely practical consideration.

Outside a major city or two, there were no Hamburg Steinways available, but there were hundreds of Astoria Steinways owned by the Concert and Artists Department and maintained by Steinway dealers; the strategic power of this legacy of William now emerged. To play a Steinway in performance in Indianapolis or Denver or Dallas or Phoenix meant to play an Astoria Steinway held by a dealer or use a house instrument. A half century before, artists were given Steinways or even paid to play them by the Concert and Artists Department. Now the C&A function was basically a piano rental business deriving revenues from fees paid by the artists. Economics snuffed the fires of discontent; faced with the daunting logistics and high costs of moving Hamburg Steinways across the nation for tours, the virtuosi collectively, if not necessarily individually, decided that ample musical merit could be coaxed from the Astoria grands already conveniently located in major cities.

"Like all great debates, this one has died out," commented John H. Steinway some years later. The immediate response inside CBS to the contretemps is undocumented, but if a warning were needed that the verbal triad of Steinway/Artist/Quality possessed a power undiminished after more than a century, the Hamburg insurrection was precisely such a signal.

Peter Perez survived for another two years; his departure was accompanied by a brief CBS statement that he "left to direct his family's business and investment holdings." Perez, taking his dismissal public in the *Times*, claimed he had no such interests and owned only a few stocks. A new president of the CBS musical instruments group refused to reveal the reasons for Perez's departure, but Peter Perez claimed that CBS was about to commingle Steinway & Sons with Gulbransen, another musical acquisition in the CBS ditty bag. This act, tantamount to corporate miscegenation, Mr. Perez had opposed. A firm once associated with player pianos, Gulbransen now made electric organs and was apparently in trouble, the result of obsolete products in a market that changed with what was literally electronic speed.

Leaving the foundering Gulbransen ship was the next president of Steinway, Lloyd Meyer, whose prior experience was with another electric organ company, Lowrey. At Gulbransen, Meyer "devoted much of his time to Gulbransen's Equinox music computer." This device was reported to perform a number of musical feats; for example, "a banjo might be added to Dixieland music. . . . The machine determines the harmony and adds an arrangement," reported the *Times*. The connection, if any, between robotic banjos and the heritage of Rachmaninoff, Hofmann, and other of the revered immortals was not stated.

After departing Steinway, Peter Perez acquired the remains of the Aeolian company, which still owned the Chickering and Knabe names, hoping, it may be surmised, to rekindle the fires of that ancient competition. In little more than two years Citicorp, the lender, seized the residue of Aeolian assets. Out of cash, the company was already closed; five hundred workers in Tennessee lost their jobs. Despite the efforts of Tennessee senator Albert Gore to resuscitate Aeolian by funneling government funds to it in the name of saving jobs, Aeolian was sold to Wurlitzer, another once-potent maker of commercial pianos, organs, and jukeboxes. Before long, Wurlitzer was bought by Baldwin, itself the survivor of a financial failure a few years earlier. The American piano industry, beset by overcapacity and falling final demand, was eating the carrion of its own long-dead glory while diversifying into grandfather clocks, circuit boards, and office furniture.

By the numbers, the results of CBS management of Steinway & Sons were less disastrous than elsewhere in the American piano business. The 1976 postwar production high reached by Henry Z. Steinway of 5,442 pianos had not been exceeded by any of his successors; in fact, by the close of 1982 the number of Steinways produced worldwide was down 20 percent. The continuing emphasis on profits resulted not in their rise but a decline. The pre-tax margin—the percentage that was profit before paying income taxes—was down more than 11 percent from the rates achieved in the last five years of family ownership and radically below the peak margins achieved by Henry Z. in the mid-1960s. The CBS policy of unremittingly raising prices had failed to produce profits. Manufacturing productivity in Astoria fell precipitously; more people were doing less work. In the last years of family ownership, one production employee was needed to produce about ten pianos per year, on average. By the early 1980s under CBS this slid to an average of 7.2 pianos per worker, and the quality of those instruments, rightly or wrongly, was now the subject of artist grumbling and newspaper inquiries.

It was easy to blame the Japanese imports for the condition of Steinway, and perhaps some did, but industry data reveals a notable phenomenon. Between 1971 and 1979, Steinway's share of the slowly expanding grand piano market dropped from about one in six to one in eleven grand pianos based on the sales of only American and Japanese instruments. Over the same period the Japanese share, after approaching half of American grand pianos, later *fell* by about 9 percent. By this reckoning, the share of other American makers increased as Steinway waned. While imported pianos were a serious threat from without, there was also a menace within. "Each one of these music companies represented a labor-intensive manufacturing business we knew nothing about. . . . We were totally out of our element in the music business," commented an anonymous CBS executive later. CBS solved the decay produced through its own decisions by, at last, following an example set by a Steinway. It put the company up for sale.

Chapter 33

MY GREAT, GREAT
WHATEVER

"**W**e're bleeding down here. The people are really hurting," pleaded Bill Youse, business manager of Steinway's union to a *New York Daily News* reporter. "It's been a long, hot and unhappy summer at Steinway & Sons 100-year-old factory in Astoria, where workers labor for nine months or more to create the world's most famous grand piano," continued the *News* story of August 20, 1985. "The company is about to be sold, and the workers are wondering if their old-fashioned way of doing business will be able to stand up against the siren call of New York real estate developers. . . . Sales have slumped, and most of the employees blame the uncertainty created by CBS' plans to sell the factory."

Eight months earlier CBS announced in the *Wall Street Journal* that it intended to sell its music division, much to the relief of securities analysts who followed the stock. Fender was quickly parsed to its management, a part of a package that included Rhodes, a maker of electric pianos, and drum manufacturer Rogers. Known in the trade as "combo products," these formed a natural grouping, and their expeditious sale ensured that the nation could rock on, safe from interruption in the supply of electric guitars. Organ builder Gulbransen was shortly bought by a Southern California dealer in those instruments.

Left was a distinctly ad hoc and unhip residuum of prior invocations to the unyielding goddess of synergy. There was a harp maker, Lyon & Healy, a shard of the formerly dominant Chicago music retailer that once helped William make the Columbian Exposition safe for Paderewski and his piano. There was an Elkhart, Indiana flute manufacturer, Gemeinhardt, that specialized in student instruments. In Hillsboro, Oregon, was the Rodgers Organ Company, whose specialty was "institutional" organs for churches, auditoria, and concert halls. Founded in 1958 to commercialize technology developed by Tektronix, a company best known for its oscilloscopes, Rodgers was a troubled entity that lost money, customers, and personnel, the latter falling by 40 percent in less than four years. Rodgers planned to gain new business by building pipe organs, the traditional instruments on which the young Heinrich Steinweg worked sixteen decades past. The final firm in the corporate orphanage on which CBS nailed a for-sale sign was an old Queens pianomaker, one of the last of its breed in New York; once there had been dozens of pianomakers in Manhattan alone, employing up to ten thousand men. Now the entire American musical instrument industry gave jobs to about the same number.

The announcement was buried in a press release that dealt mostly with CBS plans to borrow money in Europe to pay for some magazines it was acquiring. Handling the sale of Steinway and the other musical waifs was the firm of James D. Wolfensohn, an investment banker, friend of violinist Isaac Stern, chairman of the board of Carnegie Hall, and an adviser to the Metropolitan Opera. Despite this, the notice generated an almost instantaneous and dark anxiety. Scarcely a month after the press release, critic Samuel Lipman assessed the divestiture in *The New Criterion*. The companies CBS was jettisoning were mostly "little more than the flotsam and jetsam of the band and pop worlds," but Steinway was "a commercial and artistic horse of a different color." A condensed version of the legend was recited, and it was concluded that the "slogan, 'The Instrument of the Immortals,' seems justifiable hyperbole."

The profile of possible buyers was explored. An Asian pianomaker in search of prestige, a practitioner of brand extension who would use the name on a range of consumer goods, the corporate equivalent of a junk dealer who might sell the real estate and the name separately, and "a star-studded group of musicians and notables" desiring to "save a national treasure" were among the possibilities. What was needed, thought Lipman, was a buyer with "the commitment to build the best piano in the world, nothing more, nothing less."

As these words were written, the potential buyers were already beginning to visit the factory, tapping the chest of the legend, examining its teeth and checking its ears. By one count, seventeen qualified buyers examined the collection of companies, but few liked what they saw. Weeks became months, and Steinway stood exposed, like some forlorn whore under a streetlight, while CBS tended to more important matters: its survival.

"Senator Jesse Helms is helping to organize an effort by conservative investors to buy sufficient stock in CBS to change what the North Carolina Republican says is the 'liberal bias' in coverage by CBS news of 'political events, personages and views,' " reported the *Times* on January 11, 1985, five weeks after the plan to sell Steinway was announced. This was tantamount to a hostile takeover attempt, and CBS was soon, in the jargon of Wall Street, "in play."

As global finance was done in the 1980s, it was possible for small groups or companies to seize control of much larger companies through a network of banks, brokerages, bond dealers, and other financial intermediaries that loaned the funds to purchase the target company's stock. Known as the "leveraged buyout" or LBO, the technique was not normally applied for sociopolitical purposes as it was initially in the case of CBS. The common motive was purely financial. Barracudas cruising the waters of corporate finance in search of an economic snack would find some fat, slow-moving company that was "underperforming." This meant that its stock was relatively cheap. Such companies, as in the case of CBS, were often made up of various businesses, which could be cut along the corporate dotted line and sold. Essentially, players of the LBO game bought companies wholesale and sold their pieces retail, perhaps retaining a portion of the company as a profitable souvenir.

In the middle 1980s there was a boom in this "mergers and acquisitions" activity. By 1988 LBO financings reached $77 billion, quadruple the level of 1983. Immense fees, salaries, and commissions for dealmakers, banks, syndicators, and lawyers made this arena the place to be. Only the "underperforming" were uncomfortable, and much effort was spent by practitioners of this particular paper shuffle to show that it was socially desirable because it made companies more competitive and managements more responsive.

For CBS the threat of living dismemberment was real, and its executives responded with a volley of lawsuits, meetings with potential "white knights," borrowings to buy its own stock, sale of its publishing division, layoffs, reorganizations, and other techniques designed to fend off the unwanted, which now focussed on an offer by cable network operator Ted Turner to buy the company. A much-changed and chastened, almost self-mutilated, CBS ultimately survived the turmoil, but in this context the disposition of a Queens pianomaker was a minor issue.

Steinway, whatever was to be its fate, was still good for the occasional light feature on a slow news day, and the *Times* carried yet another one when the house had been for sale for roughly five months. Although the focus was on the views of piano movers and technicians, pianist Eugene Istomin sounded a diminished chord: "We are excruciatingly concerned. Steinway Hall is the center of the piano playing universe. We cringe at the thought that the company could be liquidated, could disappear forever, for the amount of money Michael Jackson makes in a year." Steinway managers were putting on a brave face for the trade: "We are already back-ordered on a number of models for the upcoming year," said executive David Rubin to *The Music Trades* in March 1985 at a company sales seminar. "And consequently we are working to assist our dealer family in effectively selling all Steinway models." Whatever the situation in March, the results for the year 1985 showed but 1,387 grands sold, down by 35 percent from 1983. Sales of verticals were off by 40 percent. Dealer orders had been swept away by the winds of uncertainty.

New York's Steinway devotees called on the city to mount a rescue of the house similar to the one which saved Carnegie Hall from demolition. They were gently rebuffed: "My family owns two Steinways," said Bess Myerson, Mayor Koch's commissioner of cultural affairs, "but this is a very different situation. . . . Steinway is a company that sells pianos. It could exist anywhere. Still, I can't imagine anyone taking it out of town. Long Island City is a company town—a community of craftsmen. Moving it would be foolish." Apparently Ms. Myerson had not visited Long Island City in some time. A decaying urban polyglot of about 200,000 persons, less than four hundred of whom worked at Steinway, Long Island City, was scarcely the pastoral village of Astoria nestled on the glistening waters of Bowery Bay where grey-bearded Germans in leather aprons sang songs, sipped *lagerbier*, and puffed on their meerschaums. The grip of the legend was still strong, even among the sophisticated. The "community of crafts-men" was more likely to drive to work crabbing aging deuce-and-a-quarters along clogged expressways than amble from nearby cottage to workbench when the five-minute whistle blew.

The same vague images invested the idea of selling the factory to a real estate developer with a terror it did not have. A condominium rising on the site of William's lifework was improbable indeed, for Steinway & Sons' factory was now merely a red brick pile in an industrial ghetto. There was talk of valuable "waterfront" property. The waterfront actually consisted of a weedy and silted ditch that was once William's canal. The Steinway waterfront had long been filled, and on it stood a tank farm. The view from these imaginary condos would have also encompassed the Riker's Island prison, a sewage plant, and the stacks of a Consolidated Edison generating plant, scarcely the entrancing scenes of sales brochures. Attempting to muffle the poignant sobs of the premature mourners of Steinway as cultural artifact, CBS said that it would not liquidate the firm. There was good reason for this. Steinway was worth more alive than dead; the value of the plant was but a few million dollars. A CBS spokesperson said that the buyer, still unfound, would have to "offer a good home . . . have a managerial philosophy consistent with the product" and pay a price that was "right. . . . If we do not find a suitable buyer we will take Steinway off the market."

By August, eight hundred unsold pianos were stored at the factory and layoffs had already occurred. "Artists tell me we're building the best pianos in 20 to 30 years," said president Lloyd Meyer, but the word on the shop floor was that Meyer would soon be gone. "Price isn't an object. You either build a Steinway or you don't," continued Meyer. "It's the piano music is written on, performed on. It's what everything is judged against. If Steinway were to cease to exist—it would be just awful."

Fully aware that negotiations were nearly complete with anonymous new owners and he was out of a job, Lloyd Meyer still made his emotional plea for continuity. That year 56,822 pianos were imported into America from the East. Of these 41 percent—23,141—were grand pianos. They outnumbered Steinways built by almost seven to one. The year before, the Japanese makers alone built about 300,000 pianos, or 150 for every American Steinway. They also managed to produce 503,582 electric pianos, 287,012 electronic organs, 214,000 music synthesizers, and about 1,000,000 portable keyboards. The grand total, 2,375,224 instruments of one genus or another, but all with the familiar black and white keys, was perhaps the most compelling evidence of profound change. In this flood of keyboards Steinway had not yet drowned.

On Friday, September 13, 1985, a "media advisory" was scheduled at Steinway Hall, and Steinway & Sons' 286-day public purgatory was terminated. Whether the outcome was ascent or descent became a subject of diverse opinion. "This is an exciting day," declaimed new Steinway president Bruce Stevens to the press. "It marks the beginning of a very important journey. For the Gemeinhardt Company, Lyon and Healy Harps, Rodgers Organ Company and Steinway & Sons it provides the opportunity to continue making and selling the finest quality musical instruments in a close-knit and responsive environment."

Stevens continued with his speech: "Let me assure you that these fine companies are in good hands. There is a great deal of musical interest, business expertise and a very high energy level represented by the four of us. Our business backgrounds, which cover law, marketing, management and finance, are extensive. For the past year and one-half I have been president of Robert Williams, Inc., a manufacturing company which converts films for the packing industry. . . . We all feel a particular sensitivity to the attention we must pay to quality and the audience to which we sell. . . . Our longer term objective will be to shed 'new perspective' on how to market and sell these products more effectively." This was a historic speech in the annals of the firm; never before, so far as can be determined, had anyone ever called the Instrument of the Immortals a "product."

Among those present that Friday were two "members of the blood," Henry Ziegler Steinway, forty-eight years with the house, and his brother John Howland, forty-six years. The holding company that bought Steinway and the others was to be known as Steinway Musical Properties, and SMP had decided to retain the Steinways as "consultants." SMP's public relations counsel had guidance for Henry Ziegler as to what he should say to reporters and other influentials present at the "advisory" in the event his genetics and experience proved inadequate to the task. Bruce Stevens sent Henry Z. a note saying that "you might find useful" the enclosed "talking points." According to the document from the Boston communicators, Henry Z. was to talk about Heinrich E. Steinway, "my great, great whatever," Theodore E. Steinway, "Henry's whatever and my whatever," and to quote from the book by Theodore E., *People & Pianos*. He was also to say, "In these swift-moving, fast-changing times roots can be lost sight of very easily. Yet roots . . . and traditions do matter."

For those seeking further information on the quartet that now owned the 132-year-old legend, lock, stock, and tuning fork, less a few dozen million dollars owed a syndicate of banks, the press kit advised that Robert P. Birmingham, age forty, was formerly "the chief executive officer of General Automatic Heating, a large Boston area retailer of fuel supplies." His brother John P., age forty-three, was an attorney who once "concentrated in the trial of securities cases." James F. Stone, forty-five, was earlier a senior vice president at the Boston Company, whose specialty was pension fund management. Bruce Stevens, forty-three, was previously an international marketing director for Polaroid. For anyone confused by what the Robert Williams company, also owned by the Birminghams, really made, the press kit explained more fully: "The company supplies a broad spectrum of markets in the envelope, packaging, consumer goods, and graphics arts industries." Decoded, the principal Williams product was apparently the windows used in envelopes for bills.

Two heirs to a heating oil fortune, one manager from an instant camera company, and a pension fund expert now controlled Steinway. This was made possible by the same financial methods that nearly demolished CBS. According to a later report in the *Wall Street Journal*, the price paid for Steinway and the other three was $53.5 million. The transaction was an LBO led by the Bank of New England, which, in just a few years, would lose billions as a result of its intemperate lending practices and would be liquidated. John Birmingham was quick to disavow financial buccaneering, declaring to *The Music Trades*, "This is not a high-risk leveraged buy-out. Steinway Musical Properties rests on a very solid foundation and is backed by considerable resources." But it was a leveraged buyout, or so Salomon Brothers believed, when they announced the purchase in the obligatory tombstone in the financial press, recording that they had "acted as a financial advisor to Steinway Musical Properties and assisted in the negotiations."

SMP is not a public company, and there is no requirement that it reveal any aspect of its finances. Persons close to the transaction aver, however, that SMP put up 10 to 20 percent of the purchase price and borrowed the rest. Some aspects of the purchase looked favorable; it is clear that Steinway's assets were bought at a discount, and by the standards of 1985

LBOs, the purchase price was probably not excessive in terms of two vital financial measures, earnings and cash flow. But another aspect of the "deal," the interest payments due on the money borrowed, was burdensome, at best. Steinway and the three other companies had not grown materially for at least five years; these were static businesses. Payments on interest alone, assuming ordinary terms, were a much greater percentage of earnings than was normal for the time, and a dip in sales could have easily left SMP with an inability to meet its obligations to the bank. In this scenario, one of two conditions may have pertained: either the buyers of Steinway were able to convince their bankers that they had a plausible plan to boost profits or the bankers failed to investigate, an almost unimaginable oversight. As a practical matter, the novice owners of the crown jewel of America's "art industry" would be forced, almost immediately, to "improve" the performance of Steinway to meet interest payments and pay back more than forty million borrowed dollars.

Publicly and initially, things did not go badly. Employees were relieved; for a while, at least, they would have jobs and were assured that Steinway was not leaving New York. Also assuaged were those who had feared that the company would be liquidated. Even Henry Ziegler Steinway pronounced himself pleased: "I believe that it's good to go into private hands again, because conglomerates don't seem to work very well."

Neither employees nor devotees were destined to live happily ever after, nor were the Birminghams or Bruce Stevens. Before long, James F. Stone left and the Boston quartet became a trio. In a 1991 interview John Birmingham described how in January 1985 his group had made the highest bid for Steinway but that the deal had been slow to close. Meanwhile, sales for both Rodgers and Steinway had collapsed due to dealer uncertainty. The bid, claimed Birmingham, was based on a "very rigorous analysis" by Salomon Brothers, and he and his partners decided they could "add value." According to Birmingham, Steinway was "neglecting its dealers," and many of the 150 dealers had "no knowledge" of how to sell pianos; the list of dealers was soon pruned to ninety-five. Additionally, Steinway & Sons' management was "not very good," and Birmingham vividly specified the shortcomings of senior executives in finance, marketing, and production. What Steinway & Sons had needed, in the opinion of John Birmingham, was "an infusion of management." This was the "valued-added" to be provided by SMP.

Some in the trade at the time were openly skeptical. John McLaren, long with Yamaha before joining CBS as executive of the music group, thought that the new owners of Steinway "face a formidable challenge. They will have a new, untried management team at Steinway, New York, a seriously weakened company, dealer and worker uncertainty and low morale, increasingly powerful competition and a soft market for pianos world-wide. . . . After a few months the Birminghams will surely feel that they are dealing with a much more complicated challenge than they at first anticipated. Though they seem confident at present, there is nothing visible in their experience to indicate they have the necessary operating experience to manage these firms."

In the first full year of Birmingham ownership Steinway sales climbed about 34 percent from the depressed levels of 1985 to 1,858 American-built instruments, but this was still well below the average production during the CBS years. An internal document reveals warranty expenses for this period, and they average about $184 per piano. This was fifty-seven times higher than twenty years before when Henry Z. still managed the family-owned firm. Rework expenses were almost eight times higher. Some of the rise was certainly due to inflation, but the most popular grand, the Model M, had increased in price by a factor of about 4.5 times. Thus there was probably a basis in fact for the widely reported claims of reduced quality during the years of CBS ownership. When scrap costs were added to the rework and warranty expense, losses amounted to about $584 per instrument. On this basis about one dollar in fourteen of the wholesale cost of a Model M was spent replacing ruined work, fixing pianos at the factory or, worst of all, repairing pianos already in the hands of customers.

The situation demanded action, and the Birminghams took it in 1987, removing the old factory manager and bringing in a new one, Daniel T. Koenig. He had spent twenty-one years with General Electric, where he worked on steam turbines and electric motors. "His remarkable qualifications and accomplishments in the field of manufacturing will only enhance Steinway's already exacting standards of quality manufacturing in design, materials and workmanship," opined Bruce Stevens to *The Music Trades*.

Soon the factory was undergoing a complete revision in its layout, which had been made by Henry Z. Steinway and his staff many years before. More than the physical layout was changed. The organization was also completely revised. New foremen were named, and a number of experienced but uncooperative senior men were pulled from the shop floor and given the job of rebuilding old pianos. Quality experts were hired from the medical and other industries; they set about the task of "documenting and improving" production methods. A former member of the group recalled that the quality men developed manufacturing standards for hundreds of jobs and inserted these in loose-leaf binders for use by the work force. By mid-1992 the entire quality assurance group, which at one time numbered about nine employees, was gone. According to one of the quality engineers, their work was never fully used due to resistance to the methods by the "operators," i.e., the men whom the Steinway family once called "artisans" and "craftsmen."

A May 1988 memorandum by Daniel Koenig to other executives revealed the General Electric man's view of the internal situation. The company was at a "turning point" in its management philosophy. In the year Koenig had been there, Steinway & Sons "evolved from an organization dedicated to day-to-day survival to one groping with defining its mission and reason for being." Production workers had only "foggy information as to how pianos are built," wrote Koenig, and "we now build pianos by folklore rather than skills." The result of this was a "gradual rise in annoying quality defects over the years getting out into the market place." There was a need to "improve quality (in reality, to match the marketplace perception)." The root cause, thought Koenig, was in the decay of the "guild hall" method of manufacturing employed by the Steinways, itself a result of the fact that "the cultural make up of the work force has changed, particularly there is no longer a reverence or even a concept of the apprentice system." Steinway, Koenig seemed to be saying, had institutional amnesia; it had forgotten how to build the Instrument of the Immortals.

"We have a problem," wrote Koenig. The solution was to "evolve into a documented methods driven and controlled manufacturing operation as quickly as possible in order to meet our goals." The goals, revealed earlier in the memo, were "highest possible quality, fair price, market share and profit levels." As measured by scrap and rework expenses, some improvement may have been made in manufacturing during Koenig's first year. These declined about 23 percent in 1988 versus 1987, but they were still 46 percent higher than in the last year of CBS ownership and the "infusion of management" that John Birmingham felt would "add value" to Steinway.

Steinway had not only drunk of the waters of the river Lethe but engineering, thought Koenig, was "retrograded," and the "status quo in construction and materials usage has become revered." This was "illogical." Koenig feared that competitors would develop "superior pianos, build them, and market them. If that happens and we can't respond, we're out of business. The probability of that happening is reasonably high." Piano design, thought Mr. Koenig, was a matter of "differential equations" solvable by computers "to come up with better scales."

This internal view of manufacturing in disarray and fatal competitive threat, whatever its merits, was soon reflected in a public statement by Steinway Musical Properties president Bruce Stevens. In an interview with other industry executives appearing in *Keyboard* magazine, a publication normally covering the volatile world of electronic keyboards, signal processors, and software, Stevens accused Yamaha of "probably dumping" pianos in America at less than they were sold in Japan; Yamaha's new concert grands were verbally flagellated: "What they're merchandising is the damndest thing I've ever seen," said Stevens. "The consumer is supposed to perceive that what you see on stage is what you're buying in the store, and it's not true. With Steinway, it is true; each of our products is made with exactly the same standards and specifics." Next, Stevens questioned the "ethics and morality of the process" used by Yamaha in selling their pianos and concluded, "After buying one of these P.S.O.s—piano-shaped objects—they realize what a good piano should sound like, and come to us and do what they should have done in the first place." The year before 2,162 "consumers" bought the Steinway grand "product" in America. That was a scant 7 percent of all grands sold. In the time of family ownership when instruments were purchased by artists, musicians, and the aspirants to such status, the market share was four times as high.

It was not long before persons who thought of Steinway in terms of artists and music rather than consumers and products took note of the situation. One of the first to write about the effects of the ownership change was music critic Edward Rothstein in the *Smithsonian* magazine. On this occasion it was Robert Birmingham who spoke for SMP: "I was looking for a business and we heard Steinway was for sale. The attraction was a tremendous trade name with a product equal to it, which is a very rare thing. I can't say we bought it for musical reasons, but once we got in we began to smell the flowers." Daniel Koenig added his views as well, although they were somewhat different from those of his memorandum: "The methodology of building a piano is very well documented. It can be learned in a textbook manner. Continuity is insured by doing the best we can to debrief the older people in the factory."

Rothstein later reported on Steinway under its new owners in *The New Republic*, and this time the piece, entitled "Don't Shoot the Piano," was markedly less reverential and more revealing. Robert Birmingham's comments were expanded: "It's really different from selling oil; it's black, but that's about it"; as were Daniel Koenig's: "I get uptight about advertising hand craftsmanship and things like that. To me, it doesn't indicate quality, but a stubbornness, holding on to the past." For those who revered Steinway as a link to romantic classicism, Koenig uttered what may have been an ultimate apostasy: "The design of the piano has been too damn stable. It hasn't changed since 1920 or so, and neither have the manufacturing operations." To many, this perceived stability was the source of their affection for Steinway pianos. On this point two classes of ignorance collided. In reality, many hundreds, if not thousands, of design changes have taken place in the instruments over the years, and while most believe that there are but a few Steinway models, there are, in fact, more than two hundred that have been enumerated. Design changes were made even through the years of CBS ownership. But reality means less than perception in such matters. Clearly, Edward Rothstein and the executives of Steinway Musical Properties spoke to each other from opposite sides of the doctrinal schism between art and commerce.

"For the first time in its history, the company is entirely guided by a philosophy alien to a century of piano invention and craft," wrote Rothstein in *The New Republic*. SMP was "unburdened by historical precedent or historical knowledge"; it was "injuring the remnants of the artisan culture upon which Steinway's virtues depend." There was, reported Rothstein, evidence of "cut corners" and "complaints about quality control. . . . The most knowledgeable practitioners are leaving the company or being dismissed." A stress crack had appeared in the wall of the legend.

At roughly the same time that Rothstein was writing on his fears for Steinway's future, another piece appeared in a data-processing trade publication, *Computer World*. Ironically, it seemed to confirm the quality problems of which Rothstein wrote, and the source was none other than John Birmingham. " 'When the market starts to turn off a little, there's got to be a reason for it,' Birmingham said. One such reason, he noted, was inconsistency in quality, a symptom of an antiquated manufacturing process," wrote *Computer World* staffer Richard Pastore. The remedy, according to Birmingham, was to "add a little science to the art of piano making." This took the form of a new Computer Integrated Manufacturing (CIM) system and studies of the acoustics of Vladimir Horowitz's grand. The reported purpose was to compare the sound of Horowitz's instrument to "ordinary pianos in hopes of finding clues to consistency in sound quality." While this was the story for *Computer World*, one and one-half years later Steinway Research and Development manager Bill Strong denied that Steinway had ever made acoustic tests on *any* piano.

Concerns expressed by music critics in magazines for the intellectual elite and oblique admissions in trade newspapers were merely an overture to the media events which followed. "Sour Notes. In Clash Between Art And Efficiency, Did Steinway Pianos Lose? New Business-Minded Owners Modernized Production. Forced Out Old Managers. Firm Calls Criticism 'Hokum'," was the page-one story in the *Wall Street Journal* in March 1991. With a circulation of millions, many of whom could afford to purchase a Steinway, the piece was easily the most devastating in the history of the firm. There were, of course, the obligatory interviews with artists, some on each side of the quality issue. John Birmingham defended his company's products, saying that millions had been spent to improve quality, that they now had computer data bases of engineering drawings and had automated their inventory systems.

Just a few months earlier a new general manager had been recruited. Sandford G. Woodard had the requisite masters of business administration, a background in quality control, and experience in strategic planning at General Electric and the manufacture of induction furnaces. When asked by the *Journal* about the practice of hiring executives without music experience, John Birmingham responded: "The music industry is made up largely of people enamored of music and the instruments they make, but they don't necessarily have great management skills. We thought it was important to have people in there with good solid business experience. There's a romance on the part of the people in this industry who think they're the only ones who can do anything." Once again the message was clear: business first, music second.

This was a direct assault before millions on the image of Steinway so carefully nurtured by the family for generations. Charles and Henry, Jr., had planted the seeds in the days before the Civil War, carefully building relationships between the young firm and artists; pianos were loaned and critics cultivated. It was William who brought the seeds to full flower. Under his guidance Steinway Hall became the seat of musical culture in New York and by extension throughout America. Rubinstein and Paderewski were recruited for roles in the great Steinway drama of immigrant struggles and success. Charles H. and then Fred refined the Steinway mythos and propagated it through artful advertising. Theodore E. struggled to keep it alive and talked poignantly of a "Century of Service to Music." Henry Z. revitalized a dying legend. All these men knew they were running a business, but they also knew that Americans did not love their business; they loved their pianos. And if they did not love the piano for itself, they loved it for what it represented: the Family, the Art, the Music, the Excellence. Using precisely sixty-two words John Birmingham ripped the gown from the goddess and exposed the scars of commercialism.

The next day an article appeared in the *New York Times*. Gentler, perhaps, than the *Journal* piece, it nonetheless contained a compendium of troubles. The *Times* cited "changes in two of the main ingredients of pianos: labor and materials." A piano technician was quoted as saying, "They're living off their name." A piano teacher and a former employee both said they preferred old Steinways to new ones. Lloyd Meyer, the former Steinway president ejected by the Birminghams, was given an opportunity to assess them: "I don't think these guys wanted to screw it up, but they know nothing about the piano business, and there are ways to go wrong." Meyer had since gone on to head a company which bought the discontinued Mason and Hamlin name and put it back into production. As surely as the family was gone from the company, doting paeans to Steinway & Sons were gone from the *Times*.

Both the *Times* and the *Journal* articles made mention of a new malady in the growing public list of perceived Steinway pathologies: cracked soundboards. Judith Valente, the *Journal* reporter, wrote, "In early 1989, problems began cropping up in the soundboards of the Steinway pianos at a store in Waterford, Conn. J. Michael Yaeger, the store's owner, began finding cracks in soundboards. . . . In all, Mr. Yaeger and his customers reported 112 cracked soundboards. . . . The Birminghams say there isn't any evidence of a widespread soundboard problem. . . . They point out that Mr. Yaeger was in a contract dispute with Steinway at the time. (Steinway had sought to terminate his dealership contract because he was selling his Steinways for less than the company's recommended price. Mr. Yaeger maintained he had the right to sell the pianos at any price he chose. He no longer sells Steinways.)"

In May 1991 a long feature on the soundboard controversy ran in the

Philadelphia Inquirer. The *Inquirer* is owned by the Knight-Ridder chain, which, in one of those peculiar loops in time, began more than a century and one-quarter ago with New York's German-language *Staats-Zeitung* edited by William's lifelong friend and political ally Oswald Ottendorfer. In that era the Steinway scandals were often ignored by both Ottendorfer and Ridder, who had come to work for the paper. That was then, this was now.

The *Inquirer* piece was complete with a photo of a cracked Steinway soundboard, in addition to the routine journalistic snaps of pianos and protagonists. The story radiated an emotional heat that made the brutal battle between William, Weber, and J. P. Hale in the 1870s seem like a skat game. "Garbage," was Michael Yaeger's characterization of modern Steinways. "Madman" on a "vendetta," was Robert Birmingham's view of Michael Yaeger. "Steinway officials, who once lauded Yaeger's salesmanship, are saying he is 'nuttier than a fruitcake.' They're thinking of suing him. . . . Yaeger's campaign, Birmingham says, already has been 'very damaging,' and he vows that Steinway will fight back, possibly in court: 'The gloves are coming off now for this guy.'" Two years later, the Birminghams had not yet sued Michael Yaeger.

Some unknown millions of readers of the Knight-Ridder papers could inspect for themselves excerpts from Daniel Koenig's 1987 memorandum on Steinway's problems and perils, as well as a lengthy quotation from a February 1989 memo by Steinway sales vice president Frank Mazurco to Bruce Stevens "pointing out a 'deluge' of 'major warranty problems' at a Boston dealership in the previous six to eight months." This was Steinert's, a store where Bostonians had been buying Steinways since the days of William.

"This particular dealer, who is our best dealer overall, has really been experiencing some of our shortcomings in product quality," transcribed the *Inquirer* from Mazurco's memo. "Notice this piano, #503678, with a cracked soundboard. In addition, I have raised concerns in the recent past about the numerous cracked soundboard reports and arms (authorizations to return merchandise). We must look more carefully into this matter. I believe we have never had this many cracked soundboard problems in the past. I believe our own records would provide proof of this." Yaeger called the memo a "40 megaton bomb" while Koenig averred that "Frank has to be manufacturing's severest critic. Every time he sees a speck of dust on a piano, he's got to complain about it. And that's the way we want him to be."

Robert Birmingham, apparently taking a view different from his brother, said that "this company is about music, not manufacturing," while claiming that manufacturing methods had not been "compromised," according to the *Inquirer.* Birmingham also asserted that "fewer than 1 percent of all consumer complaints—other than those from Yaeger's customers—concern the soundboard."

Whatever customers may have been complaining about, if anything, another Steinway document shows that of the ninety-three instruments in the Astoria factory for warranty work at the end of April 1990, 42 percent were diagnosed, apparently by factory personnel, as having soundboard problems. Removing Yaeger's instruments left seventy-five pianos and of those, 29 percent were listed as requiring some type of soundboard work. Of non-Yaeger instruments with soundboard problems at the factory for repair, more than one-fourth had been sent there from Steinway Hall. Of that half-dozen, four were from Steinway's Concert and Artists Department. Soundboard problems were twice as common as the next most frequent need for warranty service, which was veneer. Finish problems were a distant third, accounting for about 5 percent of needed repairs. The three leading problems were followed by a long list of miscellaneous and proportionately infrequent difficulties. The data suggests that soundboard problems were perhaps more common proportionately than Steinway executives either knew or wished to acknowledge.

Reduced to its essence, discontinued dealer Yaeger's contention was that the Birminghams had in their search for profits abandoned quality. "In his view nothing was more compromised than the way spruce was dried and treated for soundboards," reported the *Inquirer*. By 1992 Michael Yaeger marshalled what he considered statistical evidence of the decline in Steinway soundboard quality. He divided the more than four hundred Steinways sold by him into two groups, those bought during the CBS years and those purchased during ownership by the Birminghams. Many of the pianos had been inspected by Yaeger or other persons. By this analysis, 25.6 percent of the pre-LBO pianos had imperfect soundboards while 64.6 percent of the pianos purchased after the Birminghams took over were imperfect. With the computed defect rate leaping two and one-half times under Birmingham ownership, the case seemed as clear as it was arithmetically correct.

But it was not, for Yaeger and the piano technicians reporting to him had not inspected equal proportions of pre- and post-LBO instruments; in fact, they had examined nearly twice the proportion of Birmingham-built pianos as CBS-built. There were many other problems with Yaeger's data, such as the fact that the selection of pianos was not random and that there were no apparent controls over the more than one dozen persons doing the inspections; but if accepted at face value, there was no meaningful difference in the soundboard "defect" rate between CBS and Birmingham pianos. Of the pianos actually inspected, 87.9 percent of CBS instruments reportedly showed anomalies in their soundboards, while 93.7 percent of the Birmingham pianos were so classified.

The rate seems astonishingly high when compared to the perception of Steinway pianos as objects of perfection. The question ultimately becomes one of defining a "defect." This is no simple matter, for pianos are not like light bulbs, which either illuminate or do not. The piano is not a device of binary states and clean causality. For that, too, there is a reason, and it lies in the nature of wood, of which soundboards and many other piano parts are made.

If movement is life, then wood never dies. Consider a thin slice of spruce forty-eight inches wide. The cells of the wood absorb and expire water to and from the air, seeking a state of equilibrium with its humidity. As the moisture in the air increases, the wood literally grows as it takes on water. The forty-eight-inch spruce slice can easily change dimension by one-tenth of an inch. Anyone who has struggled with a sticking drawer in August knows the phenomenon. The soundboard of a piano, by the nature of its task, must be firmly affixed to the case of the instrument. Its movement is further constrained by the ribs underneath it, whose job is to help resist a force from above, that of the strings, which, in a Steinway, bear against the board through the bridge with a nominal force of nine hundred pounds. Constrained from above, below, and sides, the question arises as to how the wood can expand as it takes on moisture, and the answer is largely by crushing itself, much as a sponge can be squeezed in the hand.

Within a certain range, known by materials engineers as the proportional limit, the cells of the wood expand and contract without damage to themselves, much as the sponge does. Outside this range, wood cells are crushed, and they will not return to their original shape. Since the tree grows fastest in the spring, these cells are largest and have the weakest walls; they crush first, and in a soundboard the broken cells appear as a ridge on the smooth face of the board. To slow the intake and exhaust of moisture, pianomakers coat the board with varnish. When the cells crush, they may damage the coating, and the wood at that point is now freer to follow its natural inclinations. A cycle of destruction begins, and after some entirely unpredictable number of cycles and lapse of time, the cells break down completely and a crack appears in the board. The crack is more likely to be seen in winter when humidity is very low than in summer when it is high.

The point of controversy is the effects of all this on the performance of the piano. Theoretically, a "damp" piano would have a louder, shorter tone while a "dry" one would sound softer but longer; yet piano players, even the most sensitive, do not generally perceive such differences. All this has been known since the time of the founding Steinways. Their fastidious and costly wood-seasoning practices and huge lumber inventories were rooted in their experiences with the unstable dimensionality of their main material and were their method of controlling it.

William, 107 years before Michael Yaeger met the *Inquirer* reporter, wrote that "Continued dampness . . . will also swell and raise the soft fibers of the sounding-board, thereby forming ridges, which by the inexperienced observer are mistaken for cracks, while in reality affording the best proof of excellent, well-seasoned material." Using these words, it becomes possible to construct an inferential chain. The founding Steinways certainly knew that ridges could ultimately turn into cracks, but they chose to take the risk. In this, they were likely compelled by the design philosophy of C. F. Theodore, who took piano strings and plates to their mechanical frontiers in his quest for the criterion piano tone. If plates and strings, why not soundboards? Perhaps the sound of a Steinway is the sound of an instrument at its physical limits, perpetually hanging on the cliff of self-destruction.

Steinways are not the only pianos that can display anomalies in their soundboards. At a 1990 industry convention, Michael Yaeger found "flaws" in the boards of thirteen of fourteen manufacturers showing instruments. Irregularities of one sort or another were present in the boards of pianos from America, Japan, and Europe. But what neither Yaeger nor the Birminghams likely knew was that an old derogation of Steinways had found new life. Santayana's dictum that "Those who do not know the past are condemned to repeat it" was being confirmed in the pages of the *Wall Street Journal*, *New York Times*, and *Philadelphia Inquirer*.

Fortune magazine in its 1934 article on the Steinways recounted the tale of a Mrs. Southworth in search of a piano: "I am told your soundboard cracks easily," said the woman to a salesman at Steinway Hall. "The salesman seemed neither affronted nor surprised," reported *Fortune*. "He led her to one of the pianos, made her try it, and when she confessed she liked it he told her that for experimental purposes that particular piano had been built with a cracked soundboard." Company records confirm the existence of such an instrument, #252 316, built in 1927 and apparently resident in the hall for many years.

Fortune had more to say about this: "The Steinways have chosen to build into their instruments the driest soundboard in pianomaking. The dry wood gives a clarity and life to the tone. It also introduces a hazard; the drier the board, the nearer the cracking point— a fact Steinway's competitors delight in pointing out. But when they are whole, dry sounding boards are unequaled for brilliance and they rarely split fatally."

A 1931 company memorandum from Paul Bilhuber to quell the concerns of another sales prospect revealed that of "the warranty repairs of whatever kind made on pianos over a period from April to September 1930, only 8 percent had anything to do with soundboards. . . . No manufacturer can truly say that he has insured his soundboard against cracks and checks forever. . . . I think Mr. Aiken can explain to his prospect that the risk she is running on this score in buying a Steinway is very slight indeed and whatever risk there is, is amply offset by the superior tone quality of the instrument." In that different time no one called a Steinway "garbage" or rejoined with assertions of mental derangement.

Some even believed that cracks in a soundboard were beneficial. In the *Musical Courier* for May 31, 1930, a tuner from Tiffin, Ohio, wrote that "in the greatest number of cases it is an unintended blessing in that it provides means for some expansion and contraction that does not affect compression or downbearing of the strings. . . . I am entirely out of sympathy with the sales person who will and does condemn the product of the New York maker . . . because his soundboards split, for they know not whereof they speak."

It is difficult not to conclude from the diverse evidence that Steinway soundboards sometimes cracked. They may or may not have cracked more frequently than those of other makers; if they did, it was perhaps a result of a design decision by the master himself, C. F. Theodore, who made what today's engineers would call a "tradeoff," choosing some ineffable aspect of tonality over an imperfection that was often cosmetic when it appeared at all. Rather than fight the battle in public, the family adopted a policy of quietly replacing cracked pianos, some up to a decade old, when they were brought to their attention.

Undoubtedly, there are hundreds of thousands, if not millions, of pianos of all makes in living rooms around the world with cracked soundboards. The uprights are pushed against walls and moved only when the room is painted. Even then, there is no compulsion to inspect them. Countless grands sit with their lids down for decades, and no one looks or feels compelled to inspect. Tuners, many believing that ridges and cracks make no difference if they do not cause the instrument to buzz or become difficult to tune, ignore the imperfections if they note them at all.

An American icon was under assault; Yaeger's assertions combined with the vehement response of Steinway management detonated a blast at the base of the legend; the emotional denials and *ad hominem* attacks could easily have convinced the casually interested that there was merit in the charges since most Americans are fully accustomed to tales of exploding gas tanks, rancid meat, poisoned medicine, crashing bridges, and other events at least potentially the result of incompetence and irresponsibility.

Steinway's new owners had been dragged by reporters into the kingdom of percept where once the Steinways had ruled. Curricula in law, engineering, and business administration do not include courses in legend management, and when tested by the media, they flunked. The brute power of myth turned on its new keepers and clawed them. Everyone *knew* a Steinway had been a perfect machine.

Yaeger's assault on the legend was not the only one. For several years SMP had been developing a new "second line" of pianos to be sold by Steinway dealers. Not sharing proportionally in the growth of the grand piano market and beset by much cheaper grands from Japan and Korea—

the "piano-shaped objects" to which Bruce Stevens referred—the strategy was to enter what would once have been called the "commercial" piano business. To do this, SMP arranged with a noted maker of "P.S.O.s" in Japan, the Kawai Musical Instrument Company, to build a piano for SMP. The new piano designed by "Steinway & Sons" was to be called the Boston. When queried on the identity of the designers, Bruce Stevens stated that they were the engineers in Astoria; that none of these engineers had ever designed a piano before was candidly admitted. They had, however, taken a one-day scale design seminar from an outside consultant and were adept in the use of computers.

The design completed and prototypes sent down the Kawai line along with their regular production, an announcement and a press conference were planned to introduce the *Boston* piano. Before the press conference, a *Los Angeles Times* reporter somehow gained the impression that Steinways would soon be made in Japan, perhaps from a Kawai representative. This was news, and it was printed. As a result SMP spent most of its media space explaining why the Boston was *not* a Steinway, rather than the more useful promotion of the features of the new piano, which included a wide tail much like some Hamburg Steinway models, a different diamond-shaped hammer and the words *Designed by Steinway & Sons* cast in its plate. Virtually all Steinway dealers already sold a line of Asian pianos and some refused to carry the Boston, most notably the immense California-based chain of music stores called Sherman-Clay. This name, once again, dated back to the time of William.

At the press conference introducing the Boston, Bob Dove, the general manager of the Boston Piano Company, described the Boston as "designed by Steinway & Sons engineers, drawing upon 139 years of expertise and tradition, and these designs, while not the *same* as Steinway's, do share some of the same attributes and are what set the Boston piano apart from other pianos in its class." The Boston "is manufactured in a state-of-the-art plant, benefitting from the latest computer controlled equipment and exacting quality control." No mention was made of Kawai or Japan in the prepared remarks. But it was not long before all who cared knew, and the question was soon asked, "Can't Steinway build a piano better than the Japanese?" The answer seemed obvious, and there were reports that the workers in Astoria feared that all Steinway production would ultimately be moved to Japan.

Boston pianos, it soon became clear, were expensive compared to the Kawais built in the same Japanese plant by the same workers. A five-foot ten-inch Boston had a list price of $13,900. A few blocks away from Steinway Hall, the same-sized Kawai was advertised as on sale for about $6,000. The wholesale price of the Boston was $7,590, about 26 percent higher than the "street" price of the Kawai. Here was the explanation of the lack of enthusiasm by many dealers: to make even a modest profit on a Boston, it would have to be sold for thousands of dollars more than a Kawai. The words *Designed by Steinway & Sons* carried a steep price. SMP had also provided a talking point for competitors who wished to trigger concern about Steinway quality. It warranted Bostons for ten years; Steinways still had a five-year warranty.

Music critic Edward Rothstein, now with the *Times*, found his anxiety over Steinway's future increased by the Boston piano. "A venerable piano maker is in major transition, and here's proof: a Japanese 'Steinway,' " wrote the critic in the *Sunday Times*'s widely read "Classical View" column. "The Boston would never have been made by the old family firm of Steinway & Sons. . . . The Steinway was just too important," claimed Rothstein, who also reprised the management changes and cracked soundboard complaints. "Steinway & Sons is caught between two cultures—the old culture of the family factory and the modern culture of industrial engineering in a troubled marketplace."

Not totally insensate to the perceptions of them by artists and critics, the Birminghams had hired Schuyler G. Chapin, a former dean of the Columbia University School of Arts, as head of the Concert and Artists Department. It was Chapin who responded for the firm in a rejoinder to Rothstein's column. "The company has made enormous strides in quality control. . . . As to the inferred manufacturing inferiorities, I think Mr. Rothstein feels a wistful nostalgia for a quieter, simpler time. The Steinway miracle is that craftsmen still dominate in an age when modern engineering is called upon to aid their processes, not thwart them." Replied Edward Rothstein: "Modern engineering practices can make a perfectly good violin, but they have not been able to produce a Stradivarius. I hope they can, in an injured tradition, still make a Steinway." A century after pianist/scholar Fanny Morris Smith had first likened a Steinway piano to a Stradivarius violin, the analogy now haunted Steinway Musical Properties.

SMP made other efforts to connect with the aesthetic besides hiring Mr. Chapin, whose tenure was brief. When a celebration was held for the production of the five hundred thousandth Steinway in 1988, furniture designer Wendell Castle was commissioned to create a special instrument in simulation of Steinway celebrations past. Described as "visually arresting" by a trade magazine, this half-millionth Steinway was autographed, like a baseball, by hundreds of "living Steinway artists." Striped in light wood and with huge, abstractly reptilian feet, only a pair of eyes staring from the fall-board were needed to complete the caricature of a mutant frog. In this there was a peculiar fidelity to tradition; pianomakers for more than a century, including Steinway, often birthed the grotesque when trying to make a special instrument.

Tearing another page from the book of time, SMP held a concert at Carnegie Hall. It was, commented *Times* critic Michael Kimmelman, "the longest set of encores ever staged. After nearly four hours had passed and some 20 artists had crisscrossed the platform performing mostly tidbits from the Romantic repertory, Steinway's commemorative grand was finally unveiled—a hulking, big-footed post-modernist concoction." Notable in his absence, just as at the Centennial Celebration thirty-five years before, was Vladimir Horowitz. Present, in a rare public appearance, was Van Cliburn, and it was rumored that he might play. He did not, but instead accepted an award from the Steinway Foundation. Though less grandiloquent than in the times of Paderewski and Liszt, testimonials could still be made and Cliburn declared, "The Steinway piano is probably, without question, the universal piano."

The Steinway Foundation was another attempt to lasso aesthetic admiration by the Birminghams, this time by commissioning new piano works for public performance. The perception of Steinway & Sons as a patron of music was an ancient one brought to its peak by William and continued by Charles, Fred, and Theodore E., who had close relationships with artists and could be found in the audience at performances throughout the New York season. In the Birmingham version, however, Steinway emerged not as a patron of the arts but, as in William's word, a "mendicant." Donations to the foundation were publicly solicited.

In what became known as the 21st Century Piano Project, three composers were commissioned to write new concertos, and these were performed in June 1992, not in New York, but in Washington, D. C., at the Kennedy Center for the Performing Arts. "If last night's music was a metaphor for Steinway's plans for the 2000's, then it carried an ominous message indeed," declaimed *Times* critic Bernard Holland after reminding his readers of "inconsistent workmanship," the Boston piano, and "some wonderful instruments." The composers chosen were described by Holland as a "maker of background music for Hollywood thrillers, . . . [a] top bureaucrat in the oppressive old Soviet composers union," and a "member of a new and opportunistic American merchant class eagerly marketing its brave new world of nostalgia." The works themselves were not spared, but there were a few approving words for two of the artists who performed them, nineteen words to be exact, before the reviewer concluded: "A company in need of new glories seemed to be paying an awful lot of attention to old and irretrievable ones." To be sure, this was the opinion of one man, but it appeared in the newspaper of record in the city where historically one-fourth of all Steinways were sold. Trying to elicit a smile from the muse, the Birminghams were slapped in the face before a large crowd.

All this has had its effect om SMP management. "What are you writing? Barbarians at the Keyboards?" growled John Birmingham with a trial lawyer's bellicosity during an interview. "I'm gonna change my name to Steinway." No query elicited these remarks; they boiled over, heated by frustration. There is little doubt that the Birminghams and the balance of management have done the best that they can, given what they know. New

York is no longer a reservoir of talented pianomen; there are only two other makers of any size left in the nation. Both have diversified into markets such as grandfather clocks, hospital furniture, and electronic circuit boards, and there cannot be more than a dozen executives competent to run a piano company among them. It is no surprise that SMP has hired outside its industry; there is almost no industry left.

More difficult to comprehend are the statements of Daniel T. Koenig, who after four and one-half years at Steinway seemed to take specific delight in savaging the family's pianos. Walking through the almost empty Astoria factory, he came upon an ancient, fancy-legged Steinway grand in the repair area. The instrument was gutted. The top, action, strings, and pins had been removed. Blotches of corrosion oozed through the bronze of the plate, and the case was mottled and alligatored by the sun and perhaps rain. Examining the soundboard, Koenig declaimed, "Look at that, it's terrible. It's not color matched. We use more grains per inch now." Clearly, Daniel Koenig had heard what some had said of new Steinway soundboards, and this was part of his defense. "Look at that. They put every patent number they had on it," sneered Koenig while pointing to the patent numbers cast in the old instrument's plate. He did not seem to know that the numbers were displayed as required by law.

Back in the office, he talked of 170-point checklists to ensure "landed quality," motivation plans for "operators," the "industrial chaos" in which he found Steinway that included "zero quality control" and "archaic inventory and production control." The G.E. engineer volunteered further opinions on the founders. "Theodore Steinway was just feeling his way, cut and try." Belligerently now: "We've done our computer studies. We know just as much about this as Theodore Steinway. There are a whole bunch of letters from Helmholtz to Theodore; Helmholtz showed him how to do it." These letters, claimed Koenig, were deposited at a Queens junior college, yet no such letters have been found. Daniel Koenig continued to demystify the legend, claiming that "everything about pianos has been studied, there are guys out there who have studied it." Queried on the nature of the studies he may have done, he responded, "Everybody in the industry thinks we're lightweights. We want to keep it that way." Combat with ghosts may make men speak strangely.

Some critiques of SMP have charged that there were plans to increase production 50 percent, as if this was some crime certain to defile the quality of the product; such a charge is historically baseless. In its roller coaster ride through history, Steinway & Sons has *doubled* its production in just a few years more than once. Between 1900 and 1906 Charles H. doubled grand output to about 2,200 units, a volume no different than the CBS epoch. By 1926 Fred Steinway nearly tripled that and brought production to more than 6,000 grand pianos a year. From a diminished base, Henry Z. Steinway more than doubled Steinway production again between 1958 and 1964 to 1,701 grands. No one took any note of these accomplishments, and the record is uncontroversially clear that the quality of the instrument did not suffer, nor for that matter did it improve when production fell. The difference, and it was a large one, was that the Steinways did not discuss business with the press, even to the trade. They straddled the chasm between art and industry and understood, profoundly, that their success was based on this peculiar, perhaps singular, posture. A step to the side of industry meant rejection by the aesthetes, those whom an economist named Gramp described as having minds "befogged by the anti-market virus."

The virtuosi with whom the firm dealt understood the economic reality; they negotiated for pianos, cash payments, advertising exposure, and they counted the gate. Rubinstein, Paderewski, and Rachmaninoff were all realists; so were most of the rest, save when there was a tactical advantage to be gained from appearing otherwise. The deals were done behind closed doors and were inviolately private. This was in the interest of all, and the press was invited to the cocktail party afterwards where everyone smiled for the camera.

Paderewski was excoriated by the critics for what, in their estimation, was craven supplication to Mammon. Selling pictures and programs violated expectations. How well he did or did not play became peripheral to the controversy of his conduct. But Paderewski was shielded by fame. The SMP management trod on expectancy by speaking of Steinway in unabashedly commercial terms: the piano was a "product," the name was a "trademark." Though obviously correct denotatively, such references, in the coded language and beliefs of many, was a connotative abomination. So the controversy began and grew with an inadvertent effect. Those genuinely concerned with Steinway as *objet d'art* damaged that which they hoped to preserve through their publicly expressed reports and critiques of business practices.

Beginning in late 1991 a few months after the media meltdown, workdays were reduced in Astoria, first to four days per week. In the piano business fall is a busy time, and this was an ominous sign, but one which was plausibly attributed to economic factors. "Short time," as hourly workers sometimes refer to it, continued intermittently throughout 1992, and by mid-1993 the work schedule was two weeks on and two off. In 1989, Astoria was producing ten pianos a day, or roughly twenty-four hundred per year. By the fall of 1992 this was said to be seven to eight pianos per day. Taking the midpoint, Steinway production had dropped by 25 percent based on management's public statements. The industry as a whole produced roughly the same number of grand pianos in 1992 as 1989; the problem was with Steinway, and it was severe.

Using the number of pianos produced per day and multiplying them by the days *worked* reveals that in mid-1993 Astoria was building grands at an estimated rate of less than one thousand per year, or roughly the same output as during the great Panic of 1893, the depression year of 1932, or the recession of 1958, the effects of which were compounded by the onslaught of television. Steinway Hamburg, far from the storms of the American controversy and largely inoculated from change by its profitability and distance, also turned down as the result of recession in Europe.

There were other large factors at work. One of them was the price of a Steinway. In the case of large, discretionary purchases, price can be awesomely powerful. Porsche, the German manufacturer of sports cars, saw American sales plunge 86 percent, from 30,471 cars to 4,115, as it raised its prices rapidly between 1986 and 1992. At the time SMP acquired Steinway and the other music companies, all of which have since been sold, the traditionally most popular Model M grand had a New York retail price of $15,900. In early 1993 this was $27,400, an increase of more than 72 percent. Under SMP Steinway prices rose an average of 7.6 percent per year compounded, almost twice the consumer inflation rate. Since dealers buy Steinways at about half the New York retail price, there is ample margin to discount, and it is possible that buyers would not have experienced the full impact of the price increases if dealers had conceded larger discounts to, vernacularly, "move some units."

With a policy of regular price increases, SMP claimed in advertisements that Steinways were "the world's most notable investment," and "have a legendary history of price appreciation, outperforming such prized possessions as rare vintage wines, classic automobiles, and luxury yachts." The pleasures of music seemed second to the pecuniary, and there was certain distorting selectivity in the examples given in a little brochure that supposedly documented the "investment" performance of the piano. In the larger world of collector cars, a buyer of a Duesenberg in 1929 might have paid $10,000 for it, and sixty years later $1,000,000 would have been a bargain price. The Duesenberg appreciated more than one hundred times. On that basis a Steinway Model D would have been worth $300,000 or more. A new one cost $62,300 in 1993, and used ones were commonly offered at roughly $20,000. Lower on the automotive totem was the Corvette, and for roughly the same price in 1957 a buyer might, however implausibly, have chosen a black Model L Steinway or a red fuel-injection convertible. The Corvette was worth $50,000 or more thirty-five years later, the Steinway perhaps one-fourth that. Oddly, the Steinway advertisements, though confabulating about investment potential, did not carry the usual disclaimer that past results are no indicator of future investment performance.

Other sales techniques tried by SMP included offering Steinway buyers free zero-coupon bonds, 6.9 percent financing, free piano benches, free piano tunings, and other incentives. They also offered baseball caps, T-shirts, and coffee cups emblazoned *Steinway & Sons*. Once Steinways were sold with copy that read, "His moving fingers touch the Steinway into life—

the instrument and the master are one—there comes a gorgeous shower of sound. . . ." In 1993 the appeal was a free "anniversary Gift Package: a $1400 value." The power and effects of advertising are controversial and often subtle, but that a major change in appeals has occurred seems clear.

Also abandoned since family ownership was the policy of regular advertising, irrespective of content. The theory behind this, and one considered valid by many marketers, is that the advantages of the product must be continuously communicated or the customer will buy on price. In what remains of the piano business, this means the buyer will purchase a Japanese or Korean instrument because it is cheaper. Marketing men have a term for the modern Steinway advertising strategy: "milking the brand." Brand milking usually involves marked price increases combined with short-term promotional events. The result is a diminution of the power of a name to command a premium price and a consequent loss of market share to cheaper competitors. Over the more than two decades since the family sold the business, this is what has happened to Steinway & Sons. For the Steinways advertising was important enough to have a family member in direct control of it; for many years that was John H. Steinway. Now advertising is handled by a middle-level manager, and a common message is "Buy a piano now before we raise the prices."

What SMP may have done to Steinway by its management policies and what others may have done to Steinway in response to those policies are only a portion of the forces at work. There is a secular decline, some think, in the market power of all brand names. One study by an advertising agency found that in 1977, 77 percent of "consumers" bought brand names exclusively. By 1990 this proportion declined to 62 percent.

Forbes reported that across a wide variety of consumer goods loyalty to leading brands slumped markedly between 1985 and 1990. In some categories the top three brands lost 30 percent to 40 percent of their 1985 market share by 1990. It is no minor irony that the "name" the family labored to build and polish for nearly twelve decades has had its power reduced by a general decline in the perceived value of all names.

There is a particularly deadly ramification in this for Steinway. A person might buy detergent every few weeks; a sale lost to a competitor can be quickly recovered on the next trip to the market. That same person might purchase a new car every three to five years, last time a Honda, this time a Ford. But most of the tiny number of families buying pianos (less than twenty-nine thousand purchasing grands in 1992) buy it once and keep it for a lifetime. A piano sale lost to a competitor is lost for decades, if not forever.

But the past is SMP's most menacing threat. Each year for more than a century the family built pianos by the thousands. To the Steinways quality and excellence were not mere slogans or brochure copy. The words did not describe ideals or goals. There was no vagary about them, and the standards were absolute. Longevity of the instruments was a prime objective, and it was achieved. In the words of Henry Z. Steinway, the instruments were "built to stand," and hundreds of thousands of them do just that in living rooms and halls throughout the world. In Astoria between 1891 and 1977, the first year reliable production data are available and the last year a Steinway controlled the firm, about 175,000 grand pianos were built. Roughly another 100,000 were made in Hamburg. To this might be added a further 125,000 upright pianos, but uprights have never been preferred, except by C. F. Theodore himself. To the family-built American grands can be added another 25,000 made since CBS bought the house.

There have been roughly 200,000 American Steinway grands made in a century, the vast majority of which still "stand." The result is an immense inventory of used Steinway pianos, most of which either do, or can be restored to, perform at least as well as a new one. From the standpoint of new piano sales, the Steinways built too well. It is as if all cars manufactured by the Ford Motor Company since its founding in 1903 were still in operation *and* a 1909 Model T was indistinguishable in its performance, comfort, and safety from a new Lincoln Continental.

In the early 1960s entrepreneurial craftsmen began to leave Steinway and set up rebuilding shops. In New York one shop among many rebuilds three hundred Steinways per year; while precise numbers are not available, the sum of Steinways rebuilt in the city each year, either well or not so well, far exceeds the quantity of new ones sold at Steinway Hall. All that is needed to rebuild an instrument, besides knowledge, is Theodore's bent-rim case and his cupola plate. The rest can be made or bought, so even the most abused hulk can be returned to concert condition. A total rebuild of a Model M at a major New York shop costs about ninety-five hundred dollars before negotiation, or about one-third the retail price of a new one. Here resides the real threat, for in a good year the production of new instruments is only about 1 percent of those that have been built. SMP executives may talk about "motivating" and "training" the "operators." The best of them *are* motivated and trained; they moonlight for the rebuilders, and the result is dampened demand for new Steinways.

Enigmas are intertwined with anomalies in the Steinway saga, and here a paradox rises from the mist. At the same time that moonlighting operators are sapping demand for new instruments, they are also ensuring that there will always be an ample supply of what William R. Steinway called "our three-legged brother." They do this late at night and on weekends. Somehow, without MBA degrees or quality control engineers or computer systems or lawyers, they cause old Steinways to rise from the dead. This they do with no more than their minds, hands, and tools, precisely the same stock that Heinrich Englehard Steinweg brought to America in 1850. And once again, in the words of an old Steinway advertisement, "a sense of beauty fills the air—there is a hush of breath while the listener drinks the beauty fills the air—there is a hush of breath while the listener drinks the beauty from each fleeting note . . . Yesterday it might have been Paderewski . . . But whatever the time and whichever the master, the piano remains the same—Steinway, Instrument of the Immortals."

Chapter 34

GOD SPEAKS THROUGH EVERY STEINWAY

Much of recent Steinway history is static on the signal of time. Which master of business administration presides today, or in the future if there is one, is trivial. Which bank gets paid or does not get paid from the proceeds of a legend is ultimately immaterial. The name *Steinway & Sons* will survive, for that is in the nature of the business. Albert Weber has been dead for more than 110 years, and it is a century since his son was led into an insane asylum by his mother. The name Weber can be found today on pianos made in Korea by Samsung. They are cheap and people buy them, perhaps with some vague sense that they are buying a "name brand" or even a German piano. Perhaps there is a paper trail to Albert Weber; perhaps the name is a coincidence, perhaps unrelated, perhaps a legal use of a dormant and unprotected ancient trademark. In the domain of word magic specifics are of no importance.

As long as pianos are made, there is likely to be one, somewhere, labelled *Steinway & Sons*. If the past and present are any indicators, this will continue for centuries. The British journal *Early Music* routinely carries advertisements by the dozen for replicas of clavichords and harpsichords, the keyboard predecessors swept away by pianoforte technology two centuries ago. If this seems, somehow, a small and dark fate, it is not. The Customs Service, whose job today, as in the time of William, is to identify, count, and collect tariffs on all things entering America, tabulated harpsichords entering the United States at rates of four thousand to six thousand per year in the 1980s, easily twice the number of Steinway grand pianos built here. The name, it may be safely forecast, will be known for generations.

The power and the danger of a name is its portability. It may, by some vague consensus and sometimes only fiat, be attached to any object, as the purveyors of radios and refrigerators once wished to do with Steinway. It is not the essence of the thing. A Mrs. Grovene C. Smith of Watertown, New York, wrote to Theodore Edwin Steinway in December 1936. Mrs. Smith had bought a Steinway, and she wrote emotionally of her pleasure in that sound and the joy it brought her. She summed her experience with the words: "God speaks through every Steinway." Mrs. Smith's name joined the list of those who approved: Berlioz, Liszt, Rubinstein, Paderewski, Hofmann, Horowitz, and hundreds of others. Theodore E.'s view was that "the fundamental qualities in a piano which make for superiority are resonance, tone color, sustaining quality, responsiveness of action and durability." It was no accident that three of his five criteria related to sound. The sound of the instrument is the ultimate result.

It might be plausibly argued that there is no "Steinway Sound," that a piano is a piano, and that those who have endorsed the piano over the decades did so for reasons of convenience or gain. Critics who complimented the instrument were paid or suggestible. There is no doubt that in the case of some artists and critics these charges are true. In this view overstrung grands, duplex scales, bent rims, and other aspects of piano technology combine with endorsements in a marketing strategy spanning more than a century, the purpose of which is to create *perceived* value, a socioeconomic excuse for what Thorstein Veblen called "conspicuous consumption." It is also true that thousands of Steinways now sit and have sat unplayed for years in living rooms, their sole function being to send silently the message that in this place resides a person both cultured and wealthy.

The question then becomes, do Steinways sound better? That is unanswerable, for the judgment is ultimately subjective and perceptual, like the preference for one fragrance over another or the color of a tie. The judgments themselves are suspect, for our vocabulary for the description of sound is an impoverished one. Laplanders, old semantics texts report, have twenty different names for types of ice and forty words for classes of snow. If the number of descriptors in a language relates to the importance of the phenomena described, then snow and ice are crucial to Laplanders, and sound is unimportant to English speakers. The sound of a Steinway was described by one critic as "focussed, powerful, clear cutting bass; a middle register that is rich without being oppressive; and a treble that is at once piercing and songful." To this partisan other pianos seemed "fragmented, limited, and idiosyncratic when not palpably peculiar." Conceding that it is difficult to play a fragmented piano, the meaning evaporates from such statements in exponential relation to the time spent examining them. This is the inadequacy of the language and not the fault of the writer of the words.

Professionals who work with sound often resort to analogy in description. A recording with strong high-frequency energy is "bright"; a quiet recording has a "black" background and may have "high contrast." It is no accident that these analogies are often visual; there is a concrete quality to things seen and the names for them that bring a reassuring and unwarranted certitude to the murky and fugitive acoustic milieu.

The vagaries of language are a carapace over the soft tissues of other uncertainties. Medical research has found variability even in apparently simple judgments of sound quality. Consider the following task: a skilled medical practitioner is asked to evaluate the "roughness" of a human voice sounding the letter "A." It might be expected that trained professionals when presented with the same voice at different times would rate it the same. They do not; in the language of science "intra-rater reliability" is low. The evaluator of the voice might rate it at a four for roughness on one occasion and a two on another. If a single trained individual cannot achieve stability of ratings for such signals, it comes as no surprise that even greater variations occur among other persons. In these tests a single voice was often rated across the range from "no roughness" to "very rough" by medical personnel. There was a tangible democracy in this imprecision; the reliability of the ratings of the unskilled were no different in assessing vocal roughness than the ratings of otolaryngologists and speech pathologists. The prognosis for those suffering from vocal abnormalities aside, an apparently simple criterion applied to a mundane sound is sufficient to dash the reliability of judgments on the rocks of uncertainty.

There are other peculiarities no less potent in the domain of the acoustic; not the least among them is that we all hear differently and for each individual hearing changes over time. The effect, called presbycusis, is most pronounced in males, and its essence is a gradual truncation in the range of frequencies heard with age. The nominal range of human hearing is between 20 and 20,000 hertz. One hertz is one vibration per second. The nominal frequency range of the piano, when tuned to A-440, spans from 27.5 hertz at the lowest key A to 4,186 hertz at the highest C. The range encompasses that of an ordinary orchestra, and the oddities begin almost immediately.

The business of partials (called by some harmonics) is central to the sound of the instrument and its perceived quality in the conventional view. If, for example, one presses the A above middle C on an in-tune piano, the fundamental A-440 will sound. So will a series of partials at integer multiples of 440, i.e., 880, 1,320, 1,760, 2,200, 2,640 hertz, et cetera, on up to perhaps the fifteenth or twentieth partial. These vary in both strength and duration, and the tendency over the years has been to "voice" pianos to emit increasing amounts of high-frequency energy so they "project" better and "cut through" the orchestra. Since depressing a single key produces not only a note but a "chord" of partials, the timbre or tone color of the piano is influenced by the relative strength of the partials. The instrument of today would be damned as hideously dissonant by refined auditors of the nineteenth century.

As listeners became accustomed to dissonance (compare the band music of Sousa and Stan Kenton or Schumann and Schoenberg), the sound of the piano changed. The alteration, though slow, was not greeted with universal approval. In 1939 the critic Olin Downes, writing of the last performances of Paderewski, mourned the transformations in piano tone wrought in his lifetime. Mr. Downes was no fan of high partials. Steinway & Sons also resisted the demands of many artists for increasingly bright pianos. Writing in 1935, Theodore E. noted that the "only difference" between a concert hall and living room grand was in the "greater brilliance" of the concert piano. Neither Theo E. nor his Concert and Artists manager liked bright piano sound; their aesthetic was Victorian, not modern, and high partials were to be regulated out of the instrument, not in. Helmholtz had advised the eradication of partials above the seventh, and Berlioz in 1867 praised the Steinways for lessening "to an imperceptible point" the high partials that "render some of the most simple and agreeable chords *cacaphonique*."

The twentieth partial of A-440 is at 8,800 hertz, and measurements show traces of energy there in modern instruments. This is well into the range in which the effects of presbycusis manifest themselves. Though this energy would be easily audible to a child and a twenty-year-old "average" male, an average fifty-year-old male might easily experience diminution in his ability to hear eight kilohertz. At age eighty—more than one piano virtuoso has been active at that age—the ability to hear 8,000 hertz might be reduced by a factor of one thousand compared to a man of twenty. To that virtuoso, the piano does not sound at all as it does to his audience, nor as it did to him in youth.

Yet another vagary intervenes. It is in the nature of the instrument that as it gets louder, the relative proportion of high-frequency energy in a note, the upper partials, increase markedly. In this nonlinear world the timbre of a loud note would be disproportionately altered as compared to a softer one.

While a further level of complexity is scarcely needed, it is nonetheless present. As the player moves up the scale of the piano, the number of partials in a single note reduces. While twenty or more partials are measurable in the midsection and the bass, the high treble has relatively few. By the time the highest G on the keyboard is reached, the typical instrument has but three partials, the highest at 9,408 hertz.

That many in a modern audience will not be able to hear that third partial is likely, and its presence or absence at the ear is mitigated by still another variable: the air through which it travels. On a humid or rainy night the atmosphere itself can absorb much of the energy of the third partial of the highest G, rendering it inaudible to even the youngest in the audience. Distance from the instrument to the auditor is another variable in this circumstance; the piano sound heard in the parquet is not the piano audible in the balcony. The artist, the instrument, the auditor, and the environment are tossed in a salad, the ingredients of which are, ipso facto, never the same. The genius of the Steinways from Heinrich E. through Henry Z. ultimately lay in their ability to persuade millions of persons across decades and continents that in this realm of supreme subjectivity, individual variation, incertitude, and everchanging conditions, there was an absolute best. The assertion, repeated often enough, took on the coloration of fact.

"The universe," admonished the physicist Niels Bohr, "is not only stranger than we imagine, it is stranger than we can imagine." Less cosmologically, but still in the realm of physics, the same view might be applied to pianos. The physical parameters of sound can be measured and have been for centuries. Henry Steinway, dead since 1865, observed vibration with sand and ribbons. C. F. Theodore listened carefully to the results of his creativity with the glass spheroids known as Helmholtz resonators, and since then hundreds of learned monographs have been published on the physics of piano sound.

It is a peculiarity of virtually all these arduously careful studies, covering in their total thousands of pages and spanning more than a century, that the investigators assumed that a Steinway behaved like a Bechstein or a Bosendorfer, and more recently, like a Yamaha. In some ways they do, almost by definition, or they would not be members of the class of objects called Piano. The clear but unspoken message of the scientists is that they believe that the differences claimed by pianomakers make no great difference. Almost anyone who has chanced to hear two pianos side by side or two performers on the same piano knows that this simplifying assumption, while convenient, does not pass the test of experience.

In January 1991 the matter of differences between makes of pianos was investigated. The research question was deceptively simple: are there such differences and, if there are, can they be measured? With the cooperation, alphabetically, of Baldwin, Bosendorfer, Steinway, and Yamaha, four concert grands were brought to Manhattan's American Academy and Institute of Arts and Letters. An auditorium there, built partially underground and therefore providing a silence unusual for Manhattan, is a favorite recording location for classical music. Each instrument was selected by its maker as representative of the type and each was regulated, voiced, and tuned by a concert technician provided by the manufacturer. In the language of pianomen, this was a "concert prep."

To provide the assembled pianomakers a chance to hear their instruments in the same place at the same time from precisely the same stage position, a concert pianist was engaged to play the same Bach, Beethoven, and Chopin works on each piano. The actual performances were by Mordecai Shehori, a virtuoso whose large talents are counterbalanced by an almost equal obscurity. Shehori, who had never so much as seen the instruments before that day, chose to play them in the ascending order of their action weights. Thus the Baldwin came first, followed by the Steinway, the Bosendorfer, and the Yamaha. Two hours later, a perspiring Shehori completed the subjective demonstration of the pianos; each maker was predictably convinced that his instrument performed to excellent advantage. Mr. Shehori had his opinions, as all pianists do. The Baldwin was hard to control and had a "watery, unfocussed sound." The Steinway, due to malfunctioning dampers, inhibited effective use of the pedal. The Bosendorfer could not withstand the power of Shehori's crescendi and its tone became "glassy." For Shehori, the Yamaha was "inspiring"; he was able to extract from it a "finer set of gradations." It felt, thought Shehori, like "a German Steinway." Six months later after a recording session on that Yamaha, Shehori was crushed: "I can't believe it's the same piano. It's destroyed." Thus it has always been for artists in perpetual search for the ultimate instrument. The magical is fugitive.

The man having completed his task, a machine was brought in. Its purpose was to strike each piano key with the same force from exactly the same position. Shehori, hearing this mechanical proxy finger at work, was surprised. "It has good tone." A minute's study of the device revealed the reason: "Just like a good pianist, it keeps its elbow low," diagnosed the virtuoso. The digital recorders rolled as the mechanical finger did its work, and the sounds of the pianos were no longer music but data. Bits became bytes became sectors became files of data at ever higher levels of digital organization.

The composer Rossini's reported description of the Steinway sound as "a nightingale cooing in a thunderstorm" was supplemented by the less evocative but vastly more precise fluorescent hues of computer-generated three-dimensional graphs that plotted the tones, simultaneously showing time, power, and frequency. They are called "waterfall plots," and they transform sound into a cascade of lines something like a contour map that permits the eye to see that which first fell upon the ear. There is a peculiar power in this, for with it the investigator can both look at and listen to sound. Via the computer, sound becomes a malleable thing; it can be sliced, stopped, reversed, inverted, filtered, repeated, disassembled and reassembled, and ultimately compelled to reveal some, but not all, of its secrets.

Things are seen which illuminate the judgment of the artist; the spectrum of the Baldwin is an unusually spikey collection of peaks and valleys with more high frequency energy than any of the other instruments. This is the physical basis of the sound Shehori called "watery, unfocussed." His words connoted a judgment that the graphs do not; the bright, hot sound of the Baldwin is preferred by some, disliked by others. It is simply one coloration on the palette piano.

An observation of the Bosendorfer is also traced on the computer plots. The Bosendorfer will simply not play as loudly as the other instruments. Under powerful hands the spectrum of the Bosendorfer erupts with a series of enharmonic spikes. This is the "banging" for which Paderewski was reviled, but it is easier to bang a Bosendorfer Imperial than the other instruments. The explanation may be found in a bitter conflict between Bosendorfer the man and C. F. Theodore Steinway in the 1870s. Offended by the Steinway claims of technical supremacy, Bosendorfer penned a pamphlet attacking Theodore's duplex scale as a fraud. Theodore was soon circulating his own booklet characterizing Bosendorfer as a fool. One fruit of the personal controversy was a refusal to adopt Steinway construction features in Bosendorfer pianos as did most other Austrian and German manufacturers. The heritage of that battle can still be seen today in the construction of the Bosendorfer's rim, which remains resolutely non-Steinway. It is thin, light, and made of solid wood with a furniture joint in one corner. There are no Steinway-type laminations and no Steinway-like mass.

It can be speculated that the interaction of the light rim with the sound-board might be the source of the Bosendorfer's comparatively lower sonic output, which, for a given key pressure, is about 30 percent to 50 percent below the other three pianos. In terms of its spectrum, it is in the middle, and much like the Steinway. The Yamaha has less high frequency energy and the Baldwin much more. Besides its individual sonics, the Bosendorfer visually reflects a different sensibility. It is spectacularly well finished inside and out. There is not a rough or unfinished edge anywhere; every screw glistens and every metal bit glows. The acreage of its vast top has the flatness and gloss of precision optics. In comparison to this piano, most other objects made by men look like works in process.

Yamaha president Genichi Kawakami's prediction more than twenty years ago that Yamaha would overtake Steinway invests the examination of the Yamaha with an extra interest. In business terms Mr. Kawakami's statement was similar in implication to another renowned forecast: Krushchev's statement to Nixon, "We will bury you." Reports surface occasionally of sightings of precise copies of Steinways bearing the Yamaha name, and other reports confirm Steinway as a target. In a 1981 interview an anonymous Yamaha manager told the *New York Times*, "We are chasing hard, we want to catch up with Steinway." Another commented, "We know we have the best. You see we buy [wood] from a Czech mill that also supplies Steinway, so we know we take the top quality, and that Steinway gets the next best." Steinway, of course, denied that it used any Czechoslovakian suppliers. More recently Yamaha American managers have taken a benign view, disavowing the ambition to exceed Steinway. In eery imitation of the words of Theodore E., a Yamaha concert and artists manager stated, "Yamaha wants to be of service to pianists." Given the Japanese history of success in television, semiconductor memories, machine tools, cameras, automobiles, motorcycles, and many other products, the issue of the sonic characteristics of Steinway and Yamaha pianos has a broader relevance.

Among the oft-repeated Steinway lore is the assertion that the instruments "sing" but other instruments do not. Paderewski's observation that "anyone" could make a Steinway sing but it took a true virtuoso to elicit the effect on an Erard was an extreme manifestation of this view. It is likely that an artist cannot compel or control the effect; it is simply present or absent to some degree. The nature of the singing phenomenon, according to some who hear it, is a subtle variation in the sustained tone of the piano during long notes. The computer reveals that there are, indeed, such effects. The partials making up the note each follow their own course in decay. Generally, the higher partials die more quickly, but for unknown reasons contrary to common sense, partials sometimes strengthen. Some even die out completely, then reappear thousandths of a second later. The result, apparent to the careful listener, is an ever-changing timbre for a note or notes. Though visible on the computer screen and audible to the ear, the effect defies quantification, but inspection reveals that there are more of these variations in the tone of the Steinway concert grand than in the Yamaha. If this is singing, then a Steinway somehow sings more. The utility or importance of the phenomenon is a judgment best left to artists and aesthetes.

Other strange effects manifest themselves in the cool green and blue graphs. On the note E one and one-third octaves above middle C—roughly in the middle of the range for an operatic soprano—the sound of the Steinway drops for about two seconds after being struck, then as if by some magical ingestion of energy, becomes markedly louder for roughly another second before returning to its prior level. The shape of the Yamaha's tonal decay is entirely different. It drops sharply in less than a second, then more slowly for three more seconds. It never exhibits the peculiar, almost animate, rise and fall of the Steinway.

The power of the Steinway bass is another item of persistent comment through the decades, not all of it favorable. Here again the computer confirms the doctrine. Struck with the same sharp force, the note B two octaves and a half step below middle C generates about 35 percent less volume on the Yamaha than the Steinway. There is a further difference. The fundamental at 61.7 hertz—roughly the frequency of the familiar power line hum heard from many electronic devices—is nearly absent in the Yamaha. The Yamaha relies more on the "phantom" bass created by the ear/brain than the Steinway. The Yamaha's fundamental is not only about 60 percent softer than the Steinway's; it exists for a much briefer time.

If power is one distinguishing aspect of the Steinway bass, there is another. Veteran classical recording engineer Marc Aubort speaks of the "growl" of the Steinway's bass as a distinctive characteristic not found in other instruments. The growl can be heard in Steinway grands dating back more than a century to the time of William and Theodore. Not always esteemed, some nineteenth-century critics used words such as "harsh" or "raspy" to describe it.

The computer, acting as a sonic microtome, allows the individual partials to be examined. While the first three partials appear unremarkable to the eye and ear, beginning with the fourth, sawtoothlike serrations grow on the waveform. By some unknown means this "buzz" appears on the higher partials, the combination of which is the growl of the bass. The phenomenon confounds mainstream theories of how pianos work, but it is nonetheless real. Both graphs and the ears confirm that the Yamaha does not growl; the sharp teeth of the Steinway waveforms are rounded on the Yamaha's. It might be said that if Steinway bass growls, Yamaha bass croons.

There are other acoustic fingerprints as well. It is axiomatic among artists that the use of the pedals is critical to performance. Among these the right pedal is the most used. Pressing it raises the dampers that still the strings' vibration after the key is released, and the strings can continue to vibrate freely, creating what can be called a wash of sound. In the conventional explanation of what happens, the strings are said to vibrate sympathetically. In this theory, if middle C is struck, other Cs would begin to vibrate, as would harmonically related Gs, and possibly a miscellaneous note or two, such as the D three octaves above. The computer plots show evidence of this; the lines representing the higher partials rise somewhat, suggesting that unstruck strings are vibrating in sympathy.

This, however, does not explain the complex haze of sound exuded by some pianos when the right pedal is pressed and a note or chord is struck. Striking the E in the octave above middle C with the pedal down on the Steinway causes a blanket of sound to unfold; its source is not the sympathetic vibration of harmonically related strings, but the excitation of an entire chromatic scale (both black and white keys) extending nearly two octaves downward. The means by which the effect is produced are unknown, but a signal processing technique called Variable Frequency Resolution Fast Fourier Transform, which takes longer to say than do, shows a well-defined and in-tune chromatic scale emanating from the Steinway when its dampers are up. The Yamaha produces a much less coherent "scale" with more notes missing and some out of tune. It is more like a noise, and at the ear the Yamaha does not generate a perceptible haze.

There is another effect of using the right pedal, sometimes called the "loud pedal." Striking the same E with equal forces, depressing the *pedale* on the Yamaha causes peak sound level to nearly double. On the Steinway the level increases almost imperceptibly, about 12 percent. In this and other ways, the two instruments have distinctly and measurably different sonic signatures. It is for artists, markets, and history to determine whether or not Yamaha's goal of overtaking Steinway, or for that matter reaching some sort of perceived aesthetic parity, has been achieved. One thing is certain: the phosphors of the cathode-ray tube draw the Steinway and the Yamaha as different instruments.

The computer-augmented analysis that sometimes confirms long-held beliefs is, in one sense, a flashlight with which the caverns of the perceptual and subjective may be explored. All things seen will not be seen at once, all things will not be seen, and things may be seen which are surprising. None could be more curious than the fact that striking a single key on a piano triggers two distinct events that overlap in time, giving the impression of a single note. The partials or "harmonics" that are created by the vibration of the string, itself a colossally complex event involving both longitudinal and transverse vibrations and conditioned by a host of practical departures from the theoretical string of classical mechanics, account for only a portion of the sound which is heard. At musically useful durations it can be a small part. Imagining the partials as rows of corn in a garden as seen from the vantage point of a tall stepladder, the earth between the partials is not black soil, but ground rampant with weeds. The weeds are a form of noise, so to speak, but unlike garden weeds the noise in the piano tone has a crucial function. Without it a piano would not sound like a piano.

A few keystrokes and mouseclicks allow a filter to be built with the computer that removes the partials while allowing the remainder of the piano sound to be heard. With the tonal components removed, the residue sounds as a "bonk." Something like a bongo drum, it is a noise with pitch. Creating an inverse filter and listening to only the partials presents a "zinging" sound. The zing begins slowly and builds to the full form of a sustained piano tone. Its onset is similar to what might be heard if it were possible to run a violin bow across piano strings to excite them. The source of the bonk is likely the hammer striking the string; another computer program demonstrates this by modelling it. When a series of sine waves— representing the partials—is rapidly switched on, they generate a fat spectrum rich in nonharmonic tones bunched at the base of each partial. The spectra of the piano look the same, and this indicates that in the first half-second or so of piano tone the instrument emits not just the note struck and its partials, but literally thousands of other frequencies between the partials. If a half-second seems a short time, it is ample to play two eighth notes at the brisk tempo of 120 beats per minute. In considerable amounts those notes will be made up of what is technically noise.

But this is noise with special characteristics. "Complex systems consist of vast numbers of interactions that engender a degree of uncertainty. This dynamic uncertainty or erratic behavior is classified as noise. Instead of knowing the evolution of a complex process with certainty, we can only predict possible future states of the process," wrote two scientists, West and Schlesinger, in describing "natural phenomena" that contain the same class of noise as the piano tone. The bonk of piano notes follows what is known as the "inverse power law spectrum," the specifics of which are less important to understand than is its ubiquity. The phenomenon is called "one over f" and is written $1/f$. Water flowing over rocks, the length of words written or spoken, the heartbeat of living creatures, the flow of traffic on an expressway, earthquakes, the music of Bach and B. B. King all contain $1/f$ phenomena. The behavior of $1/f$ events defeats causality by definition. This is not the domain of clockwork mechanism; it is both chaotic and common. Some who study these phenomena call them fractals, and it emerges that there is a fractal component in piano sound. The "noise" that begins a piano note follows the $1/f$ distribution. Stranger still, the piano is a device which transforms chaos into order, for from that noise emerges the quasi-coherent sounds of a musical note. These notes are then structured by composer, artist, and instrument into yet another $1/f$ pattern. That $1/f$ events have an aesthetic appeal is acknowledged by many investigators, but the basis of the attraction is a mystery.

A German immigrant and his sons living at 199 Hester Street, city, county, and state of New York, one hundred and forty years ago experienced the fascination of the fractal. This, of itself, was unremarkable; that attraction has been shared by uncountable thousands of pianomen, many no less talented. S. B. Driggs poured a half-million antebellum dollars into his innovative vision of the piano in a frontal assault on convention. The money was gone in a year. Frederick Mathushek sputtered brilliant designs like a pinwheel on Independence Day, then died staring at poverty. Chickering, Weber, and Hale were among the hundreds who also tried and succeeded, to a degree and for at least a while. But the Steinways tattooed both the ghost success and the sound of the piano with *their* name. This demanded the transformation of the subjectively experienced into the objectively believed. In the Victorian milieu of unyielding beliefs in progress, the nature of moral conduct, deterministic science and, above all, an unflinching readiness to judge good and bad, such an accomplishment was possible. There could clearly be a best. Now too many know too much, or perhaps too little, and the absolute is obsolete. Steinway & Sons is an entity that survived beyond its ethos.

Henry Ziegler Steinway is wrapped in the warp and woof of concentration. The 150-year-old bench of Heinrich E. creaks lightly as Henry Z. shifts his weight. Locked in contemplation, he coughs. Through an open window on Fifty-eighth Street at the rear of Steinway Hall the sound of traffic seeps into the room; a distant siren bewails unrecorded tragedy. The likeness of William Mason gazes serenely at the door from a vantage point over the fireplace. A fragmentary thought

emerges from the depths of a half-century's experience. "This tone business . . ."
Contemplative silence returns. Henry Z.'s hand moves to Heinrich's jack plane
that lies on the bench as if left there only yesterday. An enigmatic half-smile
appears. Then Henry Ziegler Steinway speaks. "I give it a few years. By then
the whole piano business may be gone."

NOTES

KEY TO THE NOTES

Three nonstandard abbreviations are used within the notes:

"AA" means "Author's Analysis" and is used to indicate that some mathematical or logical operation was performed on the data cited in the source(s). The nature of such an operation is generally apparent from the context.

"NYT" refers to the *New York Times*, which was known as the *New York Daily Times* for a brief time in the nineteenth century when a weekly edition was published. The *Daily Times* is subsumed under the abbreviation "NYT," and this abbreviation always refers to the daily paper.

"WSD" refers to the William Steinway Diary, a daily journal kept by Mr. Steinway for approximately thirty-five years.

The writer adopted the practice of using the term *op. cit.* only for references originally cited in the same chapter. This arose from the vexing experience of prowling through hundreds of notes seeking a fuller citation. In these notes a full citation will be found within the boundaries of the chapter, except, of course, in cases of error.

1. HIS EXCELLENT CONSTITUTION

3   "Henry E. Steinway was born": Elbert Hubbard, "The Story of the Steinways, Being a Reprint from 'The Fra' Magazine," p. 5. The first four pages, more or less, recount a visit by Luther Burbank during which a girl played Mendelssohn's *Spring Song*. "Luther Burbank didn't care to talk about himself or his work; he wanted me to tell of Steinway . . ." wrote Hubbard. By the happiest of coincidences, Hubbard had visited the Steinway factory just a few days before, where, it may be presumed, he steeped himself in the lore vouchsafed to Burbank and millions yet unborn.

3   "the army of the Corsican": ibid., p. 5.

3   "red tooth and claw": ibid., p. 6.

3   "Up there with the foxglove": ibid., p. 6. Hubbard also informs the future that "several of the motherless children gave up the struggle and cried themselves to sleep, to awake no more."

3   "Father Steinway": ibid., p. 5.

3   "only to find it": ibid., p. 6.

3–4   "Henry Steinway had his": ibid., p. 7.

4   "as often repeated by Mr. Steinway": "Biographical Sketch of Henry Steinway," *Encyclopedia of Contemporary Biography of New York*, vol. 2, pp. 362–68, reprint pagination used here. The biographies of several of the Steinways, of which this is one, were most likely written by William Steinway circa 1882. They were extensively adapted in other biographical accounts of the family as well, and they should be understood to be entirely official but not entirely correct.

4   "they were surprised": ibid., p. 1.

4   "a blinding flash": ibid.

4   "stiff and almost cold": ibid.

4   "forced to earn": ibid.

4   "answered the call to arms": ibid.

4   "The occasion": op. cit., "The Story of the Steinways," p. 13, who also has Heinrich playing a "wondrous jew's harp" after the Battle of Waterloo, p. 12.

4   "A fearful struggle": op. cit., *Encyclopedia of Contemporary Biography of New York*, p. 1.

4   "his excellent constitution": ibid., p. 2.

4   "he enjoyed the reputation": ibid.

4   "greatly admired": ibid.

4   "whole company": ibid.

4   "the liberty-breathing": ibid.

4   "About 1818": ibid. (Hubbard, p. 14, has Heinrich being offered the rank of lieutenant to reenlist.)

4   "There he tried": ibid.

4   "Self-made businessmen": ibid.

5   "his 'masterpiece' ": ibid.

5   "admired and sought to purchase": ibid.

5   "The verifiable": German real estate transaction between Johann Heinrich Roder and Heinrich Steinweg at Seesen, October 7, 1829. From a communication by Dr. W. Noller, Seesen, to Steinway & Sons dated July 20, 1962.

5   "By the time": letter from Nicolas Slonimsky to Theodore E. Steinway,

December 4, 1953. The letter was written to rectify date-of-birth errors for Henry, Jr., and William in Theodore E.'s book *People and Pianos*. For unknown reasons and for much of his adult life, William Steinway claimed he was born in 1836, although he was actually born in 1835. There is no question that William knew the correct year of his birth.

5   "According to the family legend": op. cit., *Encyclopedia of Contemporary Biography of New York*, p. 2.

5   "In Hubbard's redaction": op. cit., "The Story of the Steinways," p. 15.

5   "Musicians came": ibid., p. 17.

5–6   "In another, more": op. cit., *Encyclopedia of Contemporary Biography of New York*, p. 2.

6   "He did value education": Statement of Henry Z. Steinway to the author, July 30, 1990. This is called "The Jacobsohn Institute" in certain accounts.

6   "a four-thousand-square-foot": AA, German real estate sales agreement between Dr. Benjamin Ginsberg and Heinrich Steinweg, January 10, 1850, "*im Herzogl. Contor Seesen.*"

6   "In fact, his birthday": communication of Herbert Noffke, Wolfshagen, Germany, to Steinway & Sons, October 23, 1970.

6   "He was the fourth": ibid.

6   "He was no orphan": ibid.

6   "It was claimed": op. cit., *Encyclopedia of Contemporary Biography of New York*, p. 1.

6   "Connected to aristocracy": op. cit., Noffke, who also determined that Heinrich's father was actually killed by lightning on June 5, 1812, as was one brother.

2. DID A WHITE MAN DO THAT?

7   "We have entered": *New York Herald*, January 4, 1849.

7   "In the twenty-nine": Harry Hansen, ed., *The World Almanac and Book of Facts*, p. 135 ff.

7   "The *Herald* correspondent": *New York Herald*, January 4, 1849.

7–8   "When the Commissioners": Bureau of the Census, *Historical Statistics of the United States*, Part One, p. 105 ff.

8   "The locus": AA, ibid.

8   "At Liverpool": NYT, October 15, 1851.

8   "We came out": ibid.

8   "The tax was not": ibid.

8   "The vessels": NYT, December 15, 1853. This detailed account was written by A. C. Castle, M.D.

8   "Baggage, boxes, and pots": ibid.

9   "Fair weather": ibid.

9   "Bilge water": ibid.

9   "In less than three months": NYT, November 18, 1853.

9   "Though the emigrants": AA, *New York Tribune*, January 27, 1849.

9   "Were travel": AA, ibid., and *Statistical Abstract of the United States, 1989*, p. 615 ff.

9   "Ship *Montezuma*": Commissioners of the Port of New York, *Ship's Manifests and Logs*, April 13, 1849.

9   "Monday, June 11": *New York Herald,* June 11, 1849.

10   "On June 13": Commissioners of the Port of New York, Ship's Manifests and Logs, June 13, 1849.

10   "I, Robert Robinson": ibid.

10   "The tide of immigration": *New York Herald,* June 13, 1849.

10   "There was a strong": Leo Hershkowitz, *Tweed's New York,* p. 9 ff. There was an active and powerful nativist political party among whose members was Samuel F. B. Morse. Only a month before Charles's arrival, the Astor Place Riot occurred. The riot was, at least in part, a demonstration of nativist sentiment against a performance by English actor William McReady. See *New York Herald* and *New York Tribune,* May 9, 1849, *et seq.*

10   "The result was": Richard O'Connor, *The German Americans,* p. 112 ff.

10   "In 1857 a New York": ibid., p. 118.

11   "After Carl Steinweg debarked": Theodore E. Steinway, *People and Pianos,* p. 11.

11   "public records show": AA. Arrest records, charity hospital admissions, almshouse rolls, and asylum reports, City of New York, 1849–1850.

11   "The city's social pathologies": *New York Tribune,* September 9, 1849.

11   "The 1834 epidemic": *New York Herald,* June 13, 1849. The *Herald's* cholera history piece appeared the same day as Charles's arrival.

11   "the most fatal . . . of all diseases": ibid.

11   "By mid-June 1849": *New York Tribune,* September 10, 1849.

11   "Fatalities increased": AA, ibid.

11   "Treatment, such as it was": anon., "Typhus, Typhoid and Relapsing Fevers," *Encyclopedia Britannica,* Ninth Edition, vol. T, p. 676 ff.

11   "Effervescing drinks": ibid.

11   "In the summer of 1849": *New York Tribune,* op. cit.

11   "The bodies of persons": *Encyclopedia Britannica,* op. cit.

11   "Every article": ibid.

11   "Instead, a *chiffonnier*": Citizens Association of New York, *Report upon the Sanitary Condition of the City,* 1867, p. 41.

11   "sent as an *avant courier*": "Biographical Sketch of Henry Steinway," *Encyclopedia of Contemporary Biography of New York,* vol. 2, pp. 362–68 (reprinted).

11   "Given the speed": AA. A typical ocean crossing by steamer took three weeks. Given that Carl (Charles) arrived in June, there was but six months in which he might have "reported" back. A report and response to it therefore took one and one-half months. Carl clearly could not have written more than four letters and received responses to them in the six months before Heinrich sold his home in Seesen—assuming, of course, that the home was sold instantaneously.

12   "On Thursday, January 10": German real estate sales agreement between Dr. Benjamin Ginsberg and Heinrich Steinweg, January 10, 1850, "*im Herzogl. Contor Seesen.*"

12   "approximately $780": *New York Herald,* June 11, 1849. Trade data reported allows the computation of an approximate thaler/dollar exchange ratio.

12   "The amount was": Bureau of the Census, *Historical Statistics of the United States,* Part One, p. 160 ff.

12   "Heinrich Steinweg appeared": *"Herauswanderung,"* photocopied extract of typeset German record, March 20, 1850, no page number.

12   "On Sunday, May 19": Commissioners of the Port of New York, Ship's Manifests and Logs, Log and Manifest of the *Propellor Helena Sloman,* June 29, 1850. Some accounts, most notably *People and Pianos,* p. 15, give the ship's name incorrectly as *Helene Sloman.*

12   *"instrumentenmacher* Heinrich Steinweg": ibid.

12   "The Steinwegs made": ibid.

12   "Ship's records show": ibid.

12   "For purposes of the trip": ibid.

12   "This was the maiden voyage": Charles Hocking, *Dictionary of Shipping Disasters.*

12   "Later that year": *New York Post,* December 5, 1850.

12   "A newspaper report": ibid.

13   "By count": Robert Ernst, *Immigrant Life in New York City, 1825–1863,* p. 200 ff. This valuable work compiles much useful data from the city's corporation manuals and other sources.

13   "Every kind of preparation": *New York Herald,* June 29, 1850.

13   "The evening": *New York Herald,* July 5, 1850.

13   "At the peaks": *New York Herald,* March 19, 1853. The *Herald's* review of past labor actions was inspired by what it perceived as unrest among working men.

13   "That as labor": ibid.

13   "working under wages": ibid.

13   "unhealthy excitement": ibid.

13   "their organizing societies": ibid.

13–14   "The bells": Ronald Filippeli, ed., "New York City Tailors' Strike," *Labor Conflict in the United States.*

14   "owned by John Short": Assessment rolls of the City of New York, 1853. Number 199 Hester is the first known address of the family to appear in city directories. It is possible that they lived elsewhere before moving to Hester Street. Their summer arrival in America may have caused their omission from the 1850 census and, unrelatedly, from city directories published midyear. A Henry Steinveg [*sic*] is listed at 199 Hester Street in the 1851–52 *Doggett & Rode Directory of the City of New York,* p. 507.

14   "Hester Street was and is": photocopy of nineteenth-century map, other identification obliterated, in the New York County Clerk's office showing wards and election districts.

14   "Hester between Orange": The urban geography and structural descriptions in this chapter are based on the *Perris Maps of New York City* for 1853. These very accurate maps show details of buildings, lot lines, types of businesses, locations of city services, and much other information. The maps were often used by insurance companies to evaluate fire and other underwriting risks. The dimensions, such as street lengths, distances, building sizes, etc., were scaled from these elegant maps by the author. The structure at 199 Hester occupied by the Steinways no longer survives.

14   "Number 199": ibid.

14   "Writing a few years later": Citizens Association of New York, *Report upon the Sanitary Condition of the City,* p. 84 ff.

15 "The Steinway family's neighbors": *Doggett's New York City Street Directory for 1851*, Hester Street. This is the first and only known publication of this "reverse" directory.

15 "Across the street": ibid.

15 "At 168 and 169": ibid. *Doggett's* would not print the names of persons residing in what were known as "houses of infamy."

15 "Of the Fourteenth Ward's": AA, *Census of the State of New York for 1855*. At this time New York State had its own decennial census that was taken at a five-year offset to the federal census. Official tabulations do not give proportions. These were computed by the author.

15 "The 'Sons of Erin' ": ibid.

15 "The proportion of": ibid. Manhattan's total population was 607,299 persons, of whom 48.4 percent were native Americans.

15 "If typical": op. cit., *Report upon the Sanitary Condition of the City*.

16 "Whether it was cause": AA, *Annual Report of the Police Commissioner of the City of New York*, 1860.

16 "In 1860": AA, ibid.

16 "The crimes": AA, ibid. Arrest reports for nearby years were also examined; causes of arrest were essentially stable.

16 "Women were arrested": ibid.

16 "At 10 o'clock": NYT, August 12, 1854.

16 "In total": AA, op. cit., *Annual Report of the Police Commissioner of the City of New York*.

17 "Nor did Heinrich": op. cit., *Perris Maps*.

17 "There were ample": ibid.

17 "To reach the *abbattoir*": op. cit., *Report upon the Sanitary Condition of the City*, p. 85 ff.

17 "But fat boiling": *New York Herald*, April 25, 1853.

17 "For decades": ibid. This article reports that the city's 7,000 omnibus horses each worked six hours and covered 168,000 miles daily. This equates to an average of four miles per hour, a rate of travel equal to or faster than the Manhattan bus rider experiences today on midtown Madison Avenue or Sixth Avenue routes.

18 "One month": NYT, August 18, 1853.

18 "While piano*making*": AA, enumeration schedules, New York County, *Census of the State of New York for 1855*.

18 "Lighte, whose name": letter from Henry and Charles Steinway to C. F. Theodore Steinway. Undated, circa 1850. A collection of surviving Steinway family letters is in the possession of Mr. Henry Z. Steinway. Mr. Steinway lent these letters to the Smithsonian Institution for English translation by a group of volunteer scholars interested in the house's history. E. M. Goode of the Smithsonian kindly provided a set of the translations to the author, who wishes to express his gratitude to all involved. In some instances the translations have been modified with the assistance of a native German speaker, Mr. Marc Aubort.

18 "witnessed Carl Steinweg's American citizenship": Court of Common Pleas, New York, June 30, 1854. Carl (Charles) was the first of the Steinways to apply for American citizenship. Ultimately, all male family members

became citizens; the last to be naturalized was Heinrich on January 28, 1863.

18   "Abraham Bassford": op. cit., *Perris Maps of New York City.*

18   "Bassford pianos were": NYT, October 26, 1853, and December 7, 1854.

3. IN THEIR OWN NAME AND STYLE

19   "The pianoforte is": *New York Musical Times,* December 18, 1852.

19   "Not one factory": ibid. The estimate of Chickering's annual output is based on a capacity statement of "twenty-five Pianos per week" appearing in *The Musical World and Times,* May 7, 1853.

20   "A large proportion": Whitworth is quoted at length in Douglass C. North and Robert P. Thomas, eds., *The Growth of the American Economy to 1860,* p. 246 ff.

20   "to this very want": ibid.

20   "Some of these Yankee": op. cit., *New York Musical Times.*

20   "The term 'finishing' ": ibid.

20   "In the action-making": ibid.

20   "a half century later": personal observation by the author of a single-cylinder Cadillac built circa 1903.

20   "Writing to a friend": Christine M. Ayers, *Contributions to the Art of Music in America by the Music Industries of Boston, 1640–1936.* This work begins with the statement, "The writer takes no personal responsibility for the statements in this volume, since they have all been based on the most reputable authorities available to her." p. 2.

20–21   "And most important": ibid.

21   "[W]e looked upon Chickering": op. cit., *New York Musical Times.*

21   "In December 1852": *The Musical World and Times,* December 17, 1853.

21   "upon the interests": ibid.

21   "Bleeding was tried": ibid.

21   "In Manhattan alone": AA, Enumeration schedules, New York County, *Census of the State of New York for 1855.* The official report of the 1855 Census, p. 428, claims thirty-eight pianoforte manufacturing "establishments" in Manhattan and twenty-eight elsewhere in the state, with Erie County (Buffalo and environs) having the next largest concentration of five. Close inspection of the schedules does not confirm the official count of thirty-eight if the criterion of company name is used—ergo, the statement in the text "over thirty." It is possible that the definition used was sites, as contrasted to business entities. Some makers, including Steinway & Sons, manufactured at more than one location in different wards. A further factor complicating the data is that census workers did not enumerate stores, except to count certain types. Small pianomakers operating inside or behind a retail store would likely have been neglected unless there were very obvious signs of manufacturing activity. Data, it seems, are never as they seem.

21   "James Pirsson": *The Message Bird,* June 1, 1850. A "monster piano," approvingly reported the *Bird*

21   "gave up the business": *The Music Trades*, December 2, 1893. These are the recollections, four decades later, of pianomaker R. M. Bent, who worked for Pirsson. In this account Pirsson achieved an $11,000 gain in just one year on property on Leonard Street, circa 1853. The interest on an $11,000 principal constituted a comfortable annual income.

21   "Henry Steinweg, Jr., worked": op. cit., letter from Henry and Charles Steinway to C. F. Theodore Steinway. Undated, circa 1850. The letter mentions autumn, suggesting that it was written about that time of year.

22   "Both Pirsson's home": Vera Brodsky Lawrence, *Strong on Music, Volume I, Resonances*, pp. 608–609. Lawrence, p. 608, states that the Pirsson performances were the "best private chamber music to be heard" in Manhattan circa 1849. The author wishes to express his gratitude to Ms. Lawrence for generously sharing her immense knowledge of Manhattan's musical and social history.

22   "The always-observant Whitworth": op. cit., *The Growth of the American Economy to 1860*.

22   "A fat stack": New York State Supreme Court, judgment index, "*Wake* v._____".

22   "In 1853 one of": Chauncey M. Depew, ed., *One Hundred Years of American Commerce*, vol. 2, p. 513.

If so, it was the early part of the year, as William appears in S&S Production Records as a bellyman for the earliest known Steinway & Sons pianos. The Production Records constitute a unit-by-unit account, and they contain much useful information, including the names of men working on the instruments, type, technical characteristics, construction and sale dates, buyers names, disposition of pianos returned to the factory, and other data. They are often called the "number books."

The actual sale of the assets of Nunns & Company did not take place until late 1854. The *New York Times*, October 2, 1854, contains an advertisement reading: "ASSIGNEE'S SALE OF PIANO-FORTES, TOOLS, PATTERNS & c.—The stock of NUNNS & CO. will be sold at the Warerooms of MCDONALD & BROTHER, No. 292 Bowery, at a great sacrifice for cash. The stock comprises an assortment of grand diagonal and horizontal 6½, 6¾ and 7 octaves, in plain and carved cases. Also several second-hand pianos, from $50 to $125, fully warranted; by order of WM. WAKE, Assignee." Nunns's liquidation was voluntary, as there is no entry in any court record.

22   "One of those scarred": ibid.

22   "William's brother": op. cit., letter from Henry and Charles Steinway to C. F. Theodore Steinway. Undated, circa 1850. The letter indicates an agreement of one year at a rate of three dollars ($3) per week for Charles. This is puzzling, since Charles was at least twenty-one years old, older by half than the typical apprentice, yet the meager wage and specific employment term suggest an apprenticeship. Other questions also arise: If Charles was a cabinetmaker as legend avers, then why did he not work in that better-paid trade? If Charles was learning pianomaking at age twenty-one, then what did he do in Germany between the ages of fourteen (by which, if not before, schooling was ordinarily complete) and age twenty approximately (when he arrived in America)? These questions are respectfully brought to the attention of researchers in Germany.

22   "The despicable 'truck' system": op. cit., *One Hundred Years of American Commerce.*

23   "Largest among them": AA, op. cit., enumeration schedules.

23   "Pennsylvania-born": Nancy J. Groce, *Musical Instrument Making in New York City in the Eighteenth and Nineteenth Centuries*, vol. 2, pp. 354, 390, and 208. Groce's painstaking compilation of the identities, locations and years of operation for hundreds of Gotham instrumentmakers is an indispensable resource. The author is indebted to Ms. Groce for her help in locating obscure but useful material.

23   "Likewise, Lighte's revenues": op. cit., AA, enumeration schedules.

23   "Two to three dollars": AA, Joseph D. Weeks, *Report on the Statistics of Wages in Manufacturing Industries*, p. 289 ff. This would be for a small board with simple ribbing and without bridge fitting or flow-coat.

24   "In one case": *New York Tribune*, March 17, 1854, quoted in *Musical Instrument Making*, op. cit., p. 139. The firm was Bacon & Raven, who noted that their well-paid mechanics were "unmanly and ridiculous" in "parading their wrongs and sufferings before the public, as poor oppressed workmen . . ."

24   "The piano workers": AA, op. cit., *Report on the Statistics of Wages in Manufacturing Industries*. The earnings differential was known among the workmen. See *New York Herald*, March 25, 1853, where a furniture man states: "The varnishers and polishers in the furniture business are not paid nearly as well as those in the piano-forte business . . ."

24   "According to": NYT, November 8, 1853.

24   "The second-largest": AA, op. cit., enumeration schedules.

24   "They formed": op. cit., *Musical Instrument Making*, p. 280.

24   "Apparently hewing": AA, op. cit., enumeration schedules.

24   "At the opposite pole": AA, op. cit., enumeration schedules.

24   "The case work": author's examination of two Nunns & Clark pianofortes of this period.

24   "In the medium-priced": NYT, April 26, 1854, advertisement. The double-number street address told the reader that the firm was of significant size, i.e., that it occupied two consecutive city lots.

24   "Producing five hundred": AA, op. cit., enumeration schedules.

24–25   "George Bacon and": op. cit., *Musical Instrument Making*, pp. 185–86.

25   "Not only": Court of Common Pleas, New York, June 30, 1854.

25   "but a former partner": op. cit., *Musical Instrument Making*, pp. 185–86.

25   "That pioneer": AA, op. cit., enumeration schedules. It should not be inferred that the Steinways were alone among Germans in starting a firm at this time. Albert Weber commenced operations in New York in 1852 and for many years was a formidable competitor. Scheutze & Luedolph, formed circa 1855, won a gold medal for their piano at the American Institute Fair in 1857, and continued to make pianos for roughly two decades. George Steck commenced operations about 1858, and the Decker brothers followed a few years later. Lindeman produced an elegant and extraordinary design called the Cycloid piano. In Baltimore, Knabe began making pianos in the 1830s, perhaps qualifying him as the pioneer German piano manufacturer in America. All these firms survived, at least in name, into the twentieth century, except Scheutze & Luedolph.

25   "A tale oft-repeated": See Theodore E. Steinway, *People and Pianos*, p. 1 ff., for a charming, misty version of what Theodore E. himself called "propaganda."

25   "Legal name changes": Charles and Henry, Jr., both petitioned for legal name changes. These were granted in New York's Court of Common Pleas on June 15, 1864. The dates for their grants of American citizenship were June 30, 1854, and February 18, 1856, respectively. William received his citizenship papers on October 1, 1856, but there is no record extant of his obtaining a legal name change.

25   "Of the legend," New York State Supreme Court, *Steinway* v. *Steinway*, et al., 1876.

25   "As the *Times* explained": NYT, May 3, 1858.

26   "More or less quiescent": *New York Herald*, March 25, 1853, *et seq*. The *Herald* reports on labor actions by the ship joiners, carpenters, and others including furniture and pianomakers.

26   "The pianomakers met": *New York Herald*, April 18, 1853.

26   "James Young": ibid.

26   "Thus the spring": Richard M. Bent in his reminiscences, *The Music Trades*, December 2, 1893, confirms a role for labor unrest, albeit of a different kind: "In the spring of (18)'53 there was a big strike at Raven & Bacon's [*sic*], and the Steinways, who were all very hard workers, got disgusted with the action of the men and went into business for themselves . . ." Bent indicated that some Steinways, most probably Charles and Henry, Sr., were then working at Bacon & Raven. *The American Musician*, March 10, 1888, published an article by Francis Bacon, son of George Bacon of Bacon & Raven, in which he confirmed that two of the Steinways worked for his father; he claimed that "Henry Steinway, Sr." and Charles Steinway "were Bacon & Raven employees."

26   "the Steinways built": enumeration schedules, New York County, Fourteenth Ward, sixth election district, *Census of the State of New York for 1855*.

27   "A city directory": Doggett & Rode, *The New York City Directory for 1851–1852*.

27   "Detailed maps": Perris Maps, 1853, vol. 3, map. no. 23.

27   "The map's legend": ibid.

27   "That the Steinways themselves": S&S Inventory Book, 1856.

27   "There is further evidence": NYT, November 27, 1854, advertisement.

27   "The ultimate evidence": enumeration schedules, New York County, Fourteenth Ward, sixth election district, *Census of the State of New York for 1855*.

27   "There, captured": ibid.

27   "The 'Stimways' ": ibid.

28   "Also at 199": ibid.

28   "The Hester Street": Determined by an examination of several city directories through 1858.

28   "By the time": op. cit., enumeration schedules.

28   "Paid an average": AA, enumeration schedules.

28   "The company legend avers": Theodore E. Steinway, *People and Pianos*, p. 12. Theodore E. was merely reporting that which he had likely been told.

28   "The same still-crisp": Perris Maps, 1853, vol. 3, map no. 37.

28 "Occupied in 1851 to 52": AA, *Doggett's New York City Street Directory for 1851*, Varick Street, and Doggett City Directories, 1850 through 1856.

28 "and in 1856": S&S Inventory Book, 1856.

28 "They, along with": op. cit., *The American Musician*, March 10, 1888.

28 "Krall was later employed": S&S Production Records.

28 "Number 85 Varick": op. cit., Perris Maps, no. 37, and Hagstrom Map Company, *New York City 5 Borough Atlas*, 1987, pp. 10–11.

29 "Reporting on conditions": Citizen's Association of New York, *Report Upon the Sanitary Condition of the City*, p. 33 ff. The surveying physician, one B. M. Keeney, counted 261 dram shops, 101 brothels, and three churches in the southern portion of the Eighth Ward, plus a "large number of policy shops," which were a "great curse to the people, especially the negro population . . ." On Varick Street the "occupants persist in throwing garbage and rubbish into the water closets." As a result the toilets became clogged with faeces, "rendering the neighborhood offensive with insalubrious emanations."

29 "Many families": ibid., p. 37.

29 "The negroes": ibid., p. 40.

29 "There were 'the filthy habits' ": ibid., p. 37.

29 "The moral condition": ibid., p. 38.

29 "The more than forty-five hundred": AA, op. cit., enumeration schedules.

29 "of the 116 firms": AA, H. Wilson, *Trow's New York City Directory for 1854–1855*. The directory also showed that American composer George F. Bristow was selling pianos at 423 Broadway at this time.

29 "just 265 feet": AA, op. cit., Perris map no. 15. In 1993 there was a garage at this location. On the east-facing wall of the adjacent building could be seen the weathered outline of the old Steinway & Sons wareroom.

29 "Second Class Store": ibid.

29 "James Pirsson": AA, op. cit., *Musical Instrument Making*. Though their occupants changed, specific street addresses were often associated for many years with particular trades. Number 88 Walker was a piano retail location for roughly a quarter century, beginning, as far as is known, with Pirsson in 1845 and continuing at least through 1868 when the premises were rented to a vendor named Rudolph Bergin. Number 85 Varick was occupied as late as 1870 by a member of the trade named Jacob Christie. Given the obscurity of their predecessors and successors at these addresses, it may be safely inferred that location was of minimal importance in Steinway & Sons' success.

30 "On the other side": AA, *Doggett's New York City Street Directory for 1851*, Walker Street, and later directories.

30 "In 1854": op. cit. *Trow's New York City Directory for 1854–1855*.

30 "From this location": AA, S&S Production Records, 1855.

30 "According to": ibid.

30 "The total number": AA, op. cit., enumeration schedules. The number was probably not true. An undated letter circa 1850 from Charles and Henry, Jr., to C. F. Theodore indicates that in America ten men could make one piano per week. With fifty-five hands, output should have been about 275 per year—145 percent higher than it actually was. Based on actual output, S&S probably employed about two dozen men.

30   "The balance of 83": AA, S&S Production Records, 1855.

30   "Among the dealers": ibid., and *Musical Instrument Making*, p. 226–27.

30   "In the early Steinway years": NYT, July 1, 1854, advertisement.

30   "less than two hundred paces": op. cit., Perris map no. 15.

30   "In 1855 Chambers took": op. cit., AA, S&S Production Records.

30   "Thomas H. Chambers invites": op. cit., NYT. Chambers was a high-frequency advertiser in the *Times*. See March 22, September 9, October 2, 1854, for other examples of his regularly rotating copy.

30   "Selling nearly as many": S&S Production Records, 1853–58. Hammick sold at least some Steinway-built instruments marked Steinway & Sons. In 1992 the author examined an S&S square that was signed by J. T. Hammick. Unfortunately, the instrument had been abused and was suffering from a cracked plate.

30   "At towns along": AA, ibid.

31   "Hammick also made": AA, ibid.

31   "Also selling for": Enumeration schedules, Columbia County, New York, Eighth Census of the United States.

31   "Blanchard, Chambers, and Hammick": AA, op. cit., S&S Production Records.

31   "A dealer named": ibid. John F. Petri, according to a memorandum by Henry Z. Steinway, dated March 1, 1985, was a piano teacher who began selling pianos for the family in 1855. In 1858 Petri was hired by S&S in New York, and remained an employee until his retirement at age 66 in 1877. J. F. Petri died in 1892. The William Steinway diary (hereafter WSD) indicated a close and trusting relationship between Mr. Petri and the Steinway family.

31   "In Washington": AA, op. cit., S&S Production Records.

31   "The Zogbaums": op. cit., *Musical Instrument Making*, p. 509. Overlapping dates and the unusual surname suggest that members of the same family were simultaneously involved with music retailing in Manhattan and Savannah.

31   "They made": AA, op. cit., S&S Production Records.

31   "and it exists today": Author's inspection of number 483, for which the generosity of Laurence Libin and Stuart Pollens of the Metropolitan is greatly appreciated. The author also wishes to thank Bill Garlick and Roland Loest for their technical assistance and commentary on the instrument during this inspection. As of 1994, 483 had been removed to Steinway Hall in Manhattan. The piano is unplayable and in profound need of stabilization.

31   "Number 483": AA, op. cit., S&S Production Records.

31   "However, according to": ibid.

31   "Surfacing eighty-eight years later": ibid. The destruction of number 484 reflected an attitude common in the piano business: every old piano that survives inhibits the sale of a new one. Not withstanding reverential noises publicly made, the private attitudes of many in the trade are little different today.

31–32   "Speaking publicly": *Leslie's Illustrated Weekly Newspaper*, September 22, 1860.

32   "Its entries begin": AA, op. cit., S&S Production Records. This set is

clearly the original record. Another exists in a collection at La Guardia Community College, Queens, New York. The La Guardia production records are clearly a later emended copy. All references and analysis in this work employ the primary original set. No nefarious intent should be inferred from the existence of two records; the second set was probably produced by a clerk to reduce handling of the original documents.

32 "But the records do show": ibid., 1853–58.

32 "The Steinways themselves": ibid.

32 "Henry was the first": ibid.

32 "A decade later": op. cit., *Musical Instrument Making*, p. 246.

32 "After roughly forty": op. cit., S&S Production Records, 1853–58.

32 "He was replaced": ibid.

32 "the only nonfamily member": WSD, April 30, 1865, reveals that Henry Kroeger was paid $3,000 in cash on that date and a royalty thenceforth of $1 on every square piano and $2 on every grand piano built.

33 "The Steinways' rapid": *New York Musical Times*, December 18, 1852.

33 "Oliver Day": ibid.

33 "buzzing and boring": ibid.

33 "vulgar": ibid.

4. NOT STRICTLY LEGITIMATE, BUT GOOD

34 "Liszt stands there": quoted in Arthur Loesser, *Men, Women and Pianos; A Social History*, p. 369.

34 "He would perform": Dieter Hildebrandt, *Pianoforte, A Social History of the Piano*, p. 107. Hildebrandt also informs us (p. 108) that Liszt did not really play with his gloves on.

34 "The story is told": Harold C. Schonberg, *The Great Pianists*, p. 151.

34 "Two countesses": ibid.

34 "Other devotees": ibid.

34 "His handsome countenance": ibid., account of Henry Reeves, p. 152.

35 "fits of hysterics": ibid.

35 "In one case": op. cit., *Pianoforte*, p. 109. Apparently Liszt's performances sometimes resulted in damage to the piano, with string breakage reported frequently. Given his prodigious skills, it may be inferred that the breakage was intentional and all a part of the show. Lest extraordinary powers be attributed, it should be noted that the instruments of Liszt's time were much less robust mechanically than those built later.

35 "A letter to Liszt": quoted in Allen R. Lott, *The American Concert Tours of Leopold De Meyer, Henri Herz and Sigismond Thalberg*, p. 7.

35 "Max Maretzek": Max Maretzek, *Crotchets and Quavers, or Revelations of an Opera Manager in America*, p. 66. The author is indebted to Vera Brodsky Lawrence for bringing this work to his attention. Among Maretzek's talents was a remarkable command of high Victorian prose; any who seek out *Crochets* will learn, among other things, which opera introduced roller skates and spotlights to American culture.

35 "The other view": ibid.

35 "Justly or unjustly". NYT, November 23, 1852.

35 "when not dismissed": op. cit., *The Great Pianists*, p. 179: "He was a clown

. . ." A minority view on De Meyer is presented by Lawrence, *Strong on Music, Volume I: Resonances*, p. 309, who describes De Meyer as an "Austrian supervirtuoso" and "a formidable master of the flagrantly Barnumesque."

36   "The Lion's first": op. cit., *The American Concert Tours*, pp. 34–35. The debut date was October 20, 1845. According to Lott, De Meyer arrived on October 15, 1845, and departed on June 25, 1847, for a total of 618 days spent in America. His first full concert took place on November 7, 1845.

36   "It is difficult to afford": *New York Herald*, October 21, 1845. Quoted in *The American Concert Tours*, p. 36.

36   "Leopold De Meyer was playing": ibid., p. 50. In the fashion of the time, these were "assisted" concerts with other musicians and were not recitals as we know them today. Also consistent with the practice of the period, De Meyer played only his own compositions and his own opera transcriptions.

36   "During his American sojourn": ibid., p. 112 ff.

36   "Chopin owned": op. cit., *Pianoforte*, p. 139.

36   "Liszt's homes": ibid., p. 142.

36   "A half-century later": Ignace Paderewski and Mary Law, *The Paderewski Memoirs*, p. 219.

36   "Three-quarters": statement of Henry Z. Steinway to the author, July 30, 1990.

37   "De Meyer's performances": op. cit., *The American Concert Tours*, p. 112 ff.

37   "Press opinion on De Meyer": ibid., p. 99 ff. There appears to be a law governing critical opinion: critical ardor falls as a nonlinear and increasing function of the frequency of exposure to an artist. No less than Rubinstein and Paderewski experienced this effect, albeit for reasons both individual and different.

37   "what did damage": ibid., p. 128 ff.

37   "A formidable amalgamation": Vera Brodsky Lawrence, *Strong on Music, Volume I: Resonances*, p. 377 ff.

37   "Before long": ibid.

37   "In response": op. cit., *The American Concert Tours*, p. 128 ff.

37   "We . . . take great pleasure": S&S confidential circular, September 1, 1867.

38   "DE MEYER'S playing": NYT, October 3, 1867.

38   "There were just three": AA, NYT, September 25 through October 30, 1867, advertisements.

38   "On the night": WSD, October 1, 1867. William made the terse entry: "Opening night at our Hall. Leopold DeMeyer's first appearance." William did, however, attend five performances by others within a month.

38   "Beginning his career": NYT, April 8, 1891.

38   "one of the greatest": ibid.

38   "a shrewd stroke": ibid.

39   "of a most interesting": ibid.

39   "With a portfolio": NYT, November 3, 1887.

39   "Legend has that": Theodore E. Steinway, *People and Pianos*, p. 16. Lind's debut at Castle Garden at the southern tip of Manhattan grossed over $17,800 for its 6,000-seat capacity, and many of those tickets were scalped.

Later grosses were almost as high. It is unlikely that immigrant "mechanics" could pay such prices, whatever their devotion to music. To pay, say, three dollars for a ticket required the wages of two or three days' pianomaking.

39   "Leaving Barnum": NYT, November 3, 1887.

39   "The city was": ibid.

39   "It reached a higher": NYT, June 16, 1854.

39   "first musical reunion": NYT, June 15, 1854.

39   "was Louis George Maurice": Stanley Sadie, ed. *New Grove Dictionary of Music and Musicians*, vol. J, Jullien entry.

39   "A survivor": ibid.

39   "While occasional": ibid.

40   "best orchestra ever heard": NYT, March 31, 1860.

40   "So it was": NYT, June 16, 1854.

40   "The price": NYT, June 15, 1854. The inclusion of transportation (horsecar and ferry fares, etc.) in the ticket price was an immensely clever and logistically complex strategy, presumably the work of Barnum. No reports were found of this being done again. An indoor New York audience of 24,000 for a musical event likely stood as a record until the relatively recent advent of stadium rock-and-roll concerts.

40   "The evening's pièce": NYT, June 16, 1854. In what was in large proportion a wooden city lit by open flames, fire held a terror much greater than it does now. Barnum's own museum burned twice, and a few years later the Crystal Palace itself was totally destroyed by fire.

40   "that they should not": ibid.

40   "The fire is reached": ibid.

40   "other devices, not strictly": ibid.

40   "In short": ibid.

40   "The triumph extended": ibid. Municipal inspection of structures and regulation of building public safety was a construct of the undreamt future in 1854. Live load limits, maximum occupancy, the number and placement of exits, ventilation, and other factors bearing upon safety were subject only to the knowledge of builders and the conscience of developers. That the reporter commented on the Palace's stability suggests he may have previously occupied one or another creaking balcony.

40   "In 1860": NYT, March 31, 1860.

40   "Within a few years": S&S catalog, undated, circa 1860.

40   "Carl Bergmann": ibid. Bergmann, a cellist, was later the conductor of the New York Philharmonic. See *Strong on Music, Volume I: Resonances*, p. 546 ff., for an account of the ill-starred Germania Musical Society. The names of Bergmann, Aptommas, and Fry appear in an NYT advertisement from June 15, 1854, and all three also endorsed pianos other than Steinways.

41   "to be clearly understood": NYT, February 18, 1856, quoted in Mark C. McKnight, *Music Criticism in the New York Times and the New York Tribune, 1851–1876*, pp. 178–180.

41   "The evil": ibid.

41   "nothing but a superfluous": NYT, February 16, 1857, quoted, ibid.

41   "In 1855 a tally": AA, Robert Ernst, *Immigrant Life in New York City, 1825 1863*, p. 215.

41   "Between 1855 and 1865": AA, *Census of New York for the Year 1855*, p.

187 ff., and *Census of New York for the Year 1865*, p. 200 ff. Though they could not have known it *a priori*, the Steinways entered a growth industry.

41   "The average American home": *Statistical Abstract of the United States, 1991*, table 930, "Utilization of Selected Media."

41   "television sets": ibid.

42   "But once": *Atlanta Daily Examiner*, February 6, 1858, quoted in op. cit., *The American Concert Tours*, p. 587.

42   "will be cherished": *Mobile Register and Journal*, April 7, 1848, quoted, ibid.

42   "One key": Robert M. Jibou, "Ethnic Hegemony and the Japanese of California," *American Sociological Review*, vol. 53, no. 3, June 1988, p. 353–67.

42   "Roughly half": AA, enumeration schedules, *Census of New York for the Year 1855*. The author sampled national origin for pianomakers and musicians residing in the Eighth, Eleventh, and Fourteenth Wards, not the entire city. These proportions should therefore be considered approximate. By 1875, the *Census of New York* showed a total of 2,540 musicians in the entire state, of which 37.8 percent were German, the largest group. Of the 1,859 pianomakers, 982 or 52.8 percent were of German origin. It is likely that the German concentration in these occupations in Manhattan was higher. For the entire state, the foreign-born comprised 24.4 percent, while in Manhattan that proportion was 42.8 percent. See *Census of New York for the Year 1875*, table 67, "Occupations of the People," and table 2, "Population of New York."

42   "Modern studies": M. D. R. Evans, "Immigrant Entrepreneurship: Effects of Ethnic Market Size and Isolated Labor Pool," *American Sociological Review*, vol. 54, No. 6, December 1989, p. 929–49.

42   "This was true": letter from Henry and Charles Steinway to C. F. Theodore Steinway, undated, circa 1850.

43   "This tradition": statement of Henry Z. Steinway to the author, July 30, 1990.

43   "Not only did Carl": AA, S&S catalogs, circa 1863 through 1883.

43   "When in 1857": AA, S&S production records, 1853–58.

44   "96,000 other German residents": op. cit., *Census of New York for the Year 1855*, p. 110 ff.

5. AN UNFRIENDED PIANO OF THE SQUARE KIND

45   "It is not a long time ago": NYT, May 11, 1864.

45   "The judges were": ibid.

46   "serial number 550": S&S production records. Since 1853 Steinway & Sons has maintained a unit-by-unit running record of instruments built, often with notes as to type and disposition. Inside the firm this was known as the "Number Book."

46   "The jurors were true": ibid.

46   "(Entry) #1541 is the best.": Judges' Reports, American Institute Fair at the Crystal Palace, ms. 1855.

46   "The gold medal": transactions of the American Institute, 1853.

46   "Old gentlemen": NYT, November 15, 1855.

47 "It remained": Production records, S&S.

47 "Steinway & Sons left": S&S catalog, circa 1866.

47 "In 1866 Chickering": NYT, November 23, 1866.

47 "ignorant, arrogant": letter, HS to WS, March 11, 1864.

49 "The Crystal Palace": NYT, July 15, 1853.

49 "When the Crystal Palace": ibid.

49 "The gold medal detonated": AA, S&S production records.

50 "strange polyphonist": NYT, May 11, 1864.

50 "There, in 1825": U.S. Patent Office records, patents dated December 17, 1825, May 24, 1830, December 31, 183X, and October 31, 1839.

50 "Alpheus Babcock": For a general discussion of Babcock, see Loesser, *Men, Women and Pianos*, pp. 462 ff., and for the Steinway perspective see Depew, *One Hundred Years of American Commerce*, pp. 509 ff.

50 "But the iron frame": ibid., p. 510.

54 "All things": author's examination of #483.

54 "Be it known": U.S. Patent Office records, patent No. 8470 issued to Frederick Mathushek.

55 "To his brother": letter from CS to CFTS, December 1, 1864.

55 "Charles did not mention": S&S inventory book, 1857. Known by the family as the "Inventory Book," this continuous financial record contains detailed lists and valuations of partnership assets and obligations. It was used in the computation of net worth, profit, and loss under a single-entry bookkeeping system.

55 "Four decades later": Depew, p. 511.

55 "What William did not write": AA, S&S production records.

56 "The Steinways were democratic": AA, S&S production records.

56 "Common scale": S&S production records.

56 "From New York": Depew, p. 509–511.

57 "Mathushek was a man": NYT, November 11, 1891.

57 "on a single day": NYT, September 20, 1860.

57 "There is no article": *New York Daily Tribune*, March 9, 1865.

6. ANIMATED WITH THE STRANGEST DELIGHTS

58 "From the first day": S&S inventory book, 1856.

58 "At the time the accounts": AA, ibid.

59 "It was a spectacular success": AA, ibid.

59 "Nonetheless, Bergmann": Vera B. Lawrence, *Strong on Music*, vol. 1, pp. 548 and 609.

60 "The Steinway accounts": S&S inventory book, 1857.

60 "Another early endorser": *New York Daily Tribune*, April 16, 1859.

60 "The Reverend Henry Ward Beecher": S&S catalog circa 1866.

60 "Steinway & Sons carried": AA, S&S inventory book.

61 "Of the artists": *New York Daily Tribune*, March 9, 1865.

62 "In later years": newspaper clipping, Henry Z. Steinway collection.

62 "Described by piano parts maker": Dolge, *Pianos and Their Makers*, p. 302.

62 "The nature of": NYT, December 3, 1858.

62 "Their business neighbors": AA, pseud., "The Ladies Man," *The Fast*

Men's Directory and Lover's Guide to the Ladies of Fashion and Houses of Pleasure in New York and Other Large Cities, 1854.

62   "In general, the Germans": NYT, December 1, 1858.

63   "Describing an opera": letter from HS to WS, December 13, 1863.

63   "I really know very little": letter from HS to WS, March 11, 1864.

64   "Our new piano": letter from CS to CFTS, undated, probably 1851.

64   "Father is now working": letter from CS to CFTS, December 1, 1854.

64   "In other letters": letter from HS, CS, and WS to CFTS, March 30, 1861.

64   "The Old Man is done": ibid.

65   "The Prussian Civil Code": Sagarra, *A Social History of Germany 1648–1914*, p. 405, *et seq.*

65   "They begin": U.S. Patent Office records, No. 17,238, issued May 5, 1857.

65   "I have put an action": letter from CFTS to his father, date likely 1857.

65   "I have made a machine": letter from HS to CFTS, September 23, 1859.

66   "Compounding the complexity": Benson, *Audio Engineering Handbook*, p. 1.37.

67   "More remarkable still": quoted in Ehrlich, *The Piano: A History*, p. 57.

67   "The most remarkable player": NYT, March 28, 1859.

67   "Mr. Mills, the pianist": NYT, November 23, 1859.

68   "Ecstatic reports": NYT, February 23, 1860.

69   "We are keen": letter from CS and HS to CFTS, September 23, 1859.

70   "Beginning in late 1856": Lott, *The American Concert Tours of Leopold De Meyer, Henri Herz and Sigismond Thalberg*, vol. 2, p. 489 ff.

71   "Critics slyly noted": NYT, October 2, 1862.

71   "In advertisements": *Musical World*, vol. 20, number 8, August 21, 1858.

72   "Also in Greenwood": Gottschalk entry, Stanley Sadie, ed., *New Grove Dictionary of Music*, vol. G, p. 572. The remains of L. M. G. were apparently deposited there some years after he died.

7. BRINGING TO PERFECTION AN ART INDUSTRY

73   "Yesterday afternoon": *New York Tribune*, August 31, 1860.

73   "Four days later": NYT, September 4, 1860.

73   "Within a week": *Home Journal*, September 10, 1869.

74   "As you can see": letter from CS to CFTS, October 16, 1860.

74   "In 1858": AA, S&S inventory book.

74   "Far uptown": AA, New York State Census of 1855, Federal Census of 1860, and Perris Insurance Maps, ca. 1860.

74   "The ward, reformers": Citizens Association of New York, *Report upon the Sanitary Conditions of the City*, p. 325 ff.

74   "It was in this setting": *Leslie's Illustrated Weekly*, undated clipping.

75   "In roughly three": AA, S&S inventory book.

75   "Continuing, he told the reporters": *Leslie's*, op. cit.

76   "Charles's words": *Leslie's*, ibid.

76   "The report in": NYT, op. cit.

76   "On Fifty-second Street": Undated photographic series.

76   "In the spring of 1859": *New York Daily Tribune*, April 16, 1859.

77   "The Steinways also": NYT, op. cit.

77   "The family had previously": AA, S&S inventory book, 1853 through 1859.

77   "All the heavier": NYT, op. cit.

77   "Print reports of the opening": *Home Journal*, op. cit.

78   "We presume": *New Yorker*, undated clip.

78   "Despite the accomplishment": AA, S&S inventory book, 1859 through 1861.

79   "There are three hundred and fifty": Handbill, "Steinway's New Piano Manufactory," undated.

79   "Steinway & Sons actually": AA, 1855 New York State Census enumeration documents.

79   "Objective evidence": AA, S&S production records, 1855–60.

80   "The production of grands": AA, ibid.

80–81 "Meanwhile, there was": AA, ibid.

81   "The state alike": Steinway in *The Great Industries of the United States*, 1872.

81   "The concept of": *New York Musical World*, January 17, 1857.

81   "Putting his prescriptions": *New York Musical World*, September 12, 1857.

82   "In 1860 the United States": Report of the Eighth Census of the United States.

82   "The compound annual": AA, ibid.

82   "There was only one man": AA, enumeration documents of the Nineteenth Ward, Eighth Census.

83   "In the years": AA, table, "Business Cycle Expansions and Contractions in the United States," *Business Conditions Digest*, January, 1987, p. 104.

83   "Business here is": letter from CS to CFTS, December 1, 1854.

83   "Two weeks later": *New York Daily Tribune*, December 14, 1854.

83   "The Panic of 1854": Hinckernell, *Financial and Business Forecasting*, p. 250 ff.

83   "Two Years later": ibid., p. 252 ff.

84   "A formerly prosperous": *New York Musical World*, November 7, 1857.

84   "Madame Theresa": *New York Evening Post*, appearing in *New York Musical World*, November 21, 1857, p. 724, and NYT, November 11, 1857. Some accounts give Runk, not Rank.

84   "In the 'Faderland' ": letter from CFTS to family, October 12 (?), 1857.

85   "Writing to his": letter from WS to Anna Steinway, October 12, 1857.

8. MEN OF NEW YORK

86   "William is on": letter from CS to CFTS, March 30, 1861.

86   "The wedding took place": WSD, April 23, 1861. William Steinway's diary begins on Saturday, April 20, 1861, with the words, "Daily Diary of Wm. Steinway & wife." Maintained for more than thirty-five years, it contains thousands of handwritten pages and was a key source for this work. The author wishes to express his deep gratitude to Mr. Henry Z. Steinway for making the diary available and permission to quote without restriction.

87   "From headquarters": NYT, April 16, 1861.

87   "The general order": ibid.

87   "In the annual Mayor's Message": NYT, January 8, 1861.

87   "Flags flew": NYT, April 19, 1991.

88   "A special and rare": NYT, extra edition, April 21, 1861.

88   "The Seventh, however": NYT, April 18, 1861.

88   "That day, Friday": NYT, April 20, 1861.

89   "Och! We're the boys": account by J.F.O.B., NYT, May 1861. A light-hearted account of the delights of warfare.

90   "The *Boston*": ibid.

90   "The troops fell in": ibid.

90   "After the ceremony": WSD, April 23, 1861.

90   "Dear Brother Theodore": letter from CS to CFTS, no date. Charles's Fifth Regiment was reported camped on the Battery on April 24, 1861. NYT, April 25, 1861.

91   "The men": ibid.

91   "When the Baltic appeared": NYT, April 29, 1861.

91   "Nearly half were farmers": Catton, *Reflections on the Civil War*, p. 41 ff.

91   "Civilians and": H. V. Boynton in *The Encyclopedia Americana*, 1918 edition, vol. 7, pp. 6–21.

91   "This designation": anon., ibid., p. 666.

92   "William noted": WSD, November 4, 1862.

92   "In one of New York's": Theodore Steinway, *People and Pianos*, p. 25.

92   "Some incident": letter from CS to family, November 29, 1864.

92   "Three weeks earlier": WSD, November 6, 1864.

92   "The attack": op. cit., November 29, 1864.

93   "The election of 1834": NYT, July 29, 1877. An excellent article limning Gothamite propensities for mayhem to the date of publication.

93   "The *New York Times*": ibid.

93   "The police riot": NYT, July 6, 1857. Carries the report of the *Brooklyn Eagle*.

94   "Events began": NYT, July 14, 1863. A detailed and probing account of the riots may be found in Iver Bernstein, *The New York City Draft Riots*.

95   "About five in the evening": WSD, July 13, 1863.

96   "The next day": NYT July 15, 1863.

96   "The most frequent": anon., Report of the Merchant's Committee for the Relief of Colored People Suffering from the Riots in the City of New York, pp. 16 ff.

96   "The Steinways were aware": WSD, July 14, 1863.

96   "Rumors rumbled": NYT, July 15, 1863.

96–97   "On Friday, July 17": WSD, July 17, 1863.

97   "Men of New York": NYT, July 18, 1863.

97   "On Monday": WSD, July 20, 1863.

97   "Two days later": WSD, July 22, 1863.

97   "As a social symbol": Bernstein, *The New York City Draft Riots*, p. 26.

97   "A Colonel": James K. Hosmer, *Outcome of the Civil War*, p. 283.

98   "A barrel of flour": ibid., p. 61.

98   "It was not long": Hickernell, *Financial and Business Forecasting*, p. 270 ff.

98   "On the rising tide": AA, S&S confidential circulars, 1860–65. The majority of these appear to have been written by William, as the prose style is similar to that of the diary and other known writings of William.

99   "Efforts to finance": Hickernell, op. cit., p. 280 ff.

99   "Steinway & Sons, with revenues": AA, table in undated German-language

S&S brochure ca. 1875, no page. Federal income tax records with their financially intimate detail were available for public inspection. Both firms and reporters occasionally took advantage of the open records to assemble data of interest. Nancy Jane Groce in *Musical Instrument Making in New York City During the Nineteenth Century*, p. 70, reports a portion of this data.

9. WITH WOMANLY EYES

101   "The Messrs. STEINWAY": NYT, May 11, 1864.

101   "The monthly rental": AA, S&S inventory book, 1863 and 1864.

101   "Certainly the Steinways": op. cit., May 11, 1864.

102   "Inauguration of our new store": WSD, May 10, 1864.

102   "Adding to his": WSD, ibid. Theodore arrived on the *Hansa* the same day as the store opening.

102   "Theodore Vogel": WSD, May 13, 1864.

102   "Three days after": WSD, May 17, 1864.

103   "In 1854 the Piano-forte": NYT, March 22, 1854.

103   "The aristocracy of New York": October 30, 1857.

103   "In 1859": *New York Daily Tribune*, September 28, 1859. A general overview of S&S employee relations may be found in Aaron Spelling, *Labor-Management Relations at Steinway & Sons, 1853–1896*. This work displays marked sympathy with the labor perspective.

104   "Faced with a united": WSD, October 1, 1863, *et seq.* This strike was brief, ending with a 15 percent increase for the workers only five days later.

104   "Gentlemen bosses": Depew, op. cit., p. 513–14.

105   "But the additional 10 percent": WSD, March 14, 1864, *et. seq.*

105   "Resolve not to allow": WSD, February 25, 1864, *et. seq.*

105   "Henry was pleased": letter from HS to WS, February 16, 1864.

105   "When the piano arrived": HS to CS, March 4, 1864.

106   "William recorded": WSD, March 29, 1864.

106   "That night": ibid.

107   "This is to inform": S&S confidential circular, April 1864, and WSD, April 11, 1864.

107   "All five sons": WSD, May 25, 1864.

107   "It was a peculiar comment": Hermann Steinweg appears on the manifest of the *Helena Sloman* when the family arrived in New York in 1850. He was born December 13, 1836, in Seesen and is mentioned in one letter from CS to CFTS, probably written in 1852, which raises the possibility that he may have returned to Europe at about age fifteen. It is certain that he did not die in New York, and no person with a similar name appears in the Federal Census of 1860. No other information on Hermann Steinweg or his fate is known to exist.

107   "Any joy": WSD, May 28, 1864.

107   "In New York City": AA, New York City mortality data 1855–65. A particularly thorough treatment is found in NYT, February 4, 1859.

108   "Ironically, Charles": letter from CS to CFTS, circa 1852.

108   "We plodded our way": NYT, July 2, 1867.

108   "The statistics": Description derived from an entry in the *Encyclopedia Britannica*, Ninth Edition, vol. 18, p. 855 ff.

108   "Henry very low": WSD, December 25, 1864, *et. seq.*

108   "Nor was he the only": letter from HS to CS, March 4, 1864.

109   "Henry's letters": ibid., and letter from HS to WS, March 11, 1864, and letter from HS to brothers, January 21, 1864.

109   "Henry had advice": ibid.

109   "In some of the same": ibid.

109–10   "The general effects": telephone interview with Dr. Arthur Boothroyd, New York, January 29, 1992. Inferences made from the factual statements of Dr. Boothroyd are the author's.

110   "More can be divined": John R. Pierce, *The Science of Musical Sound*, p. 23 ff.

110   "In addition": Boothroyd, op. cit.

111   "A further factor": WSD, August 6, 1861, *et. seq.* The diary reveals that on February 7, 1862, William and Charles were shooting at a bulletproof vest, apparently to test its properties. A third party present missed the target vest and was required to buy a keg of beer, which was consumed that evening. William does not record that he acquired a bulletproof vest. Charles's handgun was a Colt revolver with a six-inch barrel. William's father and brother-in-law toured the Colt factory on December 11, 1861, suggesting that the Colt was the family's choice in handguns.

111   "Charles and William target-shot": WSD, February 10, 1862.

111   "In the case of Heinrich": Dale C. Wheeler, Alan S. Dewolfe, and Marie A. Rausch: "Audiometric Configuration in Patients Being Treated for Alcoholism" in *Drug and Alcohol Dependence*, vol. 5, p. 63–68.

111   "The first of these": Larry J. Bryant and James L. Fozard: "Age changes in pure-tone hearing thresholds in a longitudinal study of normal human aging" in *Journal of the Acoustical Society of America*, vol. 88, no. 2, pp. 813–20.

112   "Contemporary reports": WSD, December 25, 1862. William, in addition to being a patron of Winkens Brewery, saw Mrs. Winkens socially and may have had a financial interest in the establishment. The diary for May 14, 1870, indicates that he attended an auction of the Winkens properties.

112   "While many in the medical": Susan Squires, Catherine Chichester, Dorothy Cirelli, Laurie Davadio: "Sensory alterations in alcohol abuse" in *Topics in Clinical Nursing*, vol. 6, no. 4, pp. 51–63.

112   "While routine consumption": Rudolph Ehrensing, Peter Stokes, Geraldine Pick, Sandford Goldstone, and William Lhamon: "Effect of Alcohol on Auditory Perception and Visual Time Perception" in *Quarterly Journal of Studies on Alcohol*, vol. 31, pp. 851–60.

112   "Studies have indicated": T. Pihkanen and O. Kauko: "The Effects of Alcohol on the Perception of Musical Stimuli" in *Annales Medicinae Experimentalis et Biologiae Fenniae*, vol. 40, pp. 275–82. The author also wishes to express his gratitude to Dr. Jaclyn Spitzer, New Haven, Connecticut, for her explanations and commentary on the relevant literature.

113   "Alcohol also": Ehrensing, et al., op. cit.

113   "Older and less reliable": Pikahnen, op. cit.

114   "Henry Jr.'s contribution": WSD, March 11, 1865.

114   "They showed": S&S inventory book, 1864.

114   "Find Henry": WSD, March 10 and 11, 1865.

114   "Mr. STEINWAY": NYT, March 15, 1865.

114   "Fair day": WSD, March 13, 1865.

115   "In September": letter from CS to family, September 6, 1864.

115   "In late February". WSD, February 24, 1865.

115   "The family learned": WSD, April 25, 1865.

115   "The president's body": NYT, April 26, 1865. An extensive and occasionally bizarre account of what the *Times* called the "obsequies."

115   "Death sweeps": NYT, April 27, 1865.

116   "This, however, was more hope": WSD, April 28, 1865. William wrote to Theodore "relative to his coming over" on this day and could not have had a response the day before when the announcement of Theodore's participation was announced in the *Times*.

116   "At Barnum's": advertisements, NYT, April 25, 1865.

10. IN MANY RESPECTS ADMIRABLE

117   "I struggle every day": letter from CFTS to WS, undated. Most of Theodore's correspondence is undated. Contextual references place the date of this letter as May, 1865.

117   "His advice to William": ibid.

117   "He had received": letter from CFTS to CS and WS, March 24, XXXX.

118   "Old biographical accounts": anon., "Biographical Sketch of C. F. Theodore Steinway," from *Encyclopedia of Contemporary Biography*, 1883 (reprinted), no page numbers.

118   "By late 1855": the first surviving letter from Wolfenbeuttel is dated December 25, 1855, and describes Theodore's facilities in that place.

118   "But in 1855": letter from CFTS to family.

119   "Wolfenbeuttel, Theodore": ibid.

119   "It is a mystery": CFTS to brothers. No date, but likely between 1856 and 1860.

119   "Time after time": ibid.

119   "With his heightening frustration": letter from CFTS to CS and family, no date, probably 1857–59.

119–20   "If you want to do business": letter from CS to CFTS, September 23, 1859.

120   "Only Germans": letter from CFTS to family, no date.

120   "But the family did find": letter fragment facsimile and translation in Theodore E. Steinway, *People and Pianos*, p. 21.

120   "To this end, the brothers": Lawrence, op. cit., p. 547.

121   "As Charles explained": letter from CS to CFTS, March 30, 1861.

121   "The Steinway effort": letter from CS to CFTS, October 16, 1860.

121   "The next year": letter from HS to CFTS, March 30, 1861.

121   "In 1863 Theodore lured": Scott Goddard, ed., *Letters of Hans von Bülow*, pp. 21–22.

122   "The Bulow debacle": letter from CFTS to CS, April 8, 1864. Bulow's motivations in this extraordinary bit of commercial perfidy are unknown, but he was no admirer of the Steinways, and the reciprocal also seems true. During his 1875 tour of America for Chickering, Bulow told the *New*

York Sun that Rubinstein had advised him that the Steinways were not gentlemen. Bulow claimed that the proof of this was that the Steinways refused to hang a large portrait of him in the window of Steinway Hall when he came to New York.

122   "A socioeconomic world away": letter from HS to CFTS, December 3, 1863.

122   "The partner to whom": Grotrian-Steinweg entry, Stanley Sadie, ed., *New Grove Dictionary of Music*, volume G, p. 78.

122   "The relationship": letter from CFTS to parents, August 21, no year.

122   "In Wolfenbeuttel": anonymous English-language translation of proceedings before the Wolfenbeuttel notary dated April 1, 1858.

122   "Onerous terms": letter from CFTS to family, October 12, 1857. The date of this letter suggests that Theodore and Grotrian may have established their business relationship a few months before formalizing it before the notary.

122–23   "The partnership lasted": *New Grove*, op. cit.

123   "Grotrian's heirs": anonymous English-language translation of proceedings before the Ducal Brunswickian Notary, October 11, 1861.

123   "The strange agreement": ibid.

123   "The Steinways in New York": ibid.

123   "A few instruments": the author encountered one of these instruments at a Manhattan used-piano dealer in 1990.

123   "William offered": S&S inventory book, 1865, *et. seq.*

123   "I am praying": letter from CFTS to WS, undated, probably May 1865. See note for page 117 above.

123   "Christian Friedrich Theodore": WSD, October 26, 1865.

124   "Just a month": anonymous English-language translation of a sales and hire contract before the Ducal Brunswickian Notary, September 1865.

124   "The partners also": ibid. S&S licensed its designs for manufacture by others on at least one other occasion. The Parisian firm of Mangeot Frère had such a license.

124   "Theodore's sister": WSD, op. cit.

124   "In that same month": WSD, October 10, 1865.

124   "Earlier that October": WSD, October 4, 1865.

124   "Albert travelled": WSD, December 31, 1871.

125   "Albert's relationship": WSD, May 2, 1862.

125   "Perhaps significantly,": S&S inventory book, 1861.

11. NO BAD FAITH OR EVIL INTENT

126   "This deponent is informed": New York State Supreme Court, answer of respondent William Steinway in re *Oaks* v. *Steinway*, May 6, 1868. This chapter is largely based on the court's case file, which was discovered by the author in 1992 intact and unopened for more than a century. Hereafter documents from this proceeding are designated as "case file."

126   "a singular case": *New York Herald*, June 24, 1868.

126   "Paris-born": Marriage and birth records, New York County Clerk's office.

126   "They were both": letter from HS to WS, December 3, 1864.

126   "In Havana": ibid.

126   "It brought him": letter from HS to wife, February 5, 1864.

126   "At the funeral": case file, letter from WS to Ernestine, November 28, 1865.

126   "Mrs. Ernestine Steinway": case file from WS to Ernestine, November 24, 1865.

127   "Ernestine Hildegarde": AA, case file.

127   "I was thunderstruck": op. cit., November 28, 1865.

128   "There was, in fact": Last Will and Testament of Henry Steinway, Junior, dated March 4, 1865.

128   "Ernestine Steinway was not": case file.

128   "Theodore moved": *New York Herald*, July 11, 1868.

128   "William's forbidding letter": case file, letter, Ernestine to WS, November 21, 1865.

129   "After five years": ibid.

129   "Another letter": case file, letter, November 28, 1865.

129   "I do not know": ibid.

129   "The marriage was verified": ibid.

130   "The date William wrote": WSD, November 28, 1865.

130   "The man to whom Ernestine": case file.

130   "Powerless and penniless": case file, undated letter, Ernestine to WS.

131   "Ernestine accused": ibid.

131   "On the night of": case file, statement of Dr. Oswald Berkan, June 28, 1868.

131   "Dr. Carl Knocke": ibid., statement of Professor Dr. Carl Knocke, June 28, 1868.

132   "A few days": AA, case file.

132   "I cannot sufficiently": case file, letter from Carl Koch to WS, January 25, 1865.

132   "Each child received": ibid.

133   "I went to Mrs. Oaks": case file, letter from Carl Koch to WS, January 28, 1866.

133   "Ernestine somehow": ibid.

133   "Most honored Sir": ibid.

133   "Mrs. Oaks went to Luneberg": case file, letter from Carl Koch to WS, January 31, 1866. This is the third letter from Koch to WS in only six days.

134   "During the episode": case file, letter from Carl Koch to WS, March 15, 1866.

134   "It is fearful and exasperating": ibid.

134   "Back in New York": case file, letter from WS to Ernestine, February 22, 1866.

134   "Ernestine's response": case file, letter, Ernestine to WS, February 26, 1866.

135   "The Steinways believed": AA, case file.

135   "If anything": case file, letter from Carl Koch to WS, date illegible.

135   "In the spring": case file, letter from Carl Koch to WS, May 1867.

135   "Fifteen years later": WSD, December 2, 1881.

135   "The attempt foiled": WSD, July 17 and 18, 1883.

136   "From America": case file, statement of Carl Koch, June 28, 1868.

136   "Koch wrote William": case file, letter from Carl Koch to WS, December 25, 1867.

136   "The children sang": ibid.

136   "Papers were served": the complaint is dated May 1, 1868, and the case file shows William answered one day before he left for Europe aboard the *Union* with his wife, children, and their nurse on May 7, 1868. Peculiarly, the diary makes no mention of the Oaks complaint or answer.

136   "In July William wrote": WSD, July 12, 1868.

136   "Ernestine claimed": *New York Herald*, June 24, 1868. This is likely a version of the account seen by William in Europe. At this point William would have been unaware of some of the claims of financial fraud, since they were not a part of the original complaint.

136   "She says": ibid.

137   "Rapidity was the essence": *New York Herald*, June 27, 1868.

137   "Van Cott argued": *New York Herald*, June 24, 1868.

137   "Virtually the entire family": *New York Herald*, June 27, 1868.

137   "Attorney Jenks": ibid.

137   "Ernestine's mother": case file, deposition of Marie Miller dated June 11, 1868. Unfortunately, transcriptions of testimony at trial were not archived, so we are deprived of the actual words of family members under cross-examination.

137   "A Mr. Nicholas B. Taylor": case file, deposition of Mr. Taylor, June 10, 1868. He was president of a company with the words "Manhattan" and "Mill" in its name; the full name is occluded by the poor penmanship of a notary.

137   "A Mrs. Robinson": case file, deposition of Mrs. John E. Robinson, June 11, 1868. Mrs. Robinson is identified only as the "wife of John E. Robinson."

137–38   "Judge Van Cott": *New York Herald*, June 27, 1868. These documents were not preserved in the case file.

138   "Ernestine's mother was": case file, statement of Carl Koch, June 30, 1868. Mr. Koch's statement was a somewhat tardy addition to the proceedings.

138   "Attorney Jenks": *New York Herald*, July 11, 1868. The reference to a restraining order is mysterious. Logically (as distinguished from legally) it could only have been sought by William, but when, why, where, or how it was granted is unknown. No trace of the order remains, save the *Herald* mention.

138   "There are some facts": case file, Opinion of Judge Gilbert, August 18, 1868. The judge's full name was Jasper W. Gilbert.

138   "What the judge did not know": Last Will and Testament of Henry Steinway, Junior, dated March 13, 1862. The will filed for probate was dated March 4, 1865.

138   "Judge Gilbert, though": opinion, op. cit.

138   "Judge Gilbert also": ibid.

138–39   "Under the actual circumstances": ibid.

139   "In August of 1868": WSD, August 22, 1868.

139   "Arriving there": WSD, August 31, 1868.

139   "William and Ernestine": WSD, September 3, 1868.

139   "Legal reverberations": WSD, November 28, 1868. In a reply dated June

12, 1868, to William's original answer of May 6, 1868, to her complaint of May 1, 1868, Ernestine expanded her allegations of financial wrongdoing by William. Basically, Ernestine complained that the value of her husband's estate was deflated by the Steinways so as to reduce the wealth transferred to herself and her children. The questions of child custody and estate valuation were handled separately by the court. Close inspection of the surviving financial records of S&S suggests that Ernestine was most likely mistaken. William later sought verification of his handling of the estate in the courts and sued Ernestine Oaks to obtain it. The record is incomplete, but William likely succeeded in obtaining vindication.

139   "The Oakses": Henry Z. Steinway, "Ernestine Hildegarde Muller Steinway Oaks," genealogical note, undated.

139   "There, the two older": WSD, September 19, 1883, and February 15, 1884.

139   "Later Ernestine": WSD, February 29, 1888. Initially they lived in Albany.

139   "she was still receiving": S&S stockholder records, 1955.

12. OF A BURGLARIOUS DISPOSITION

140   "The day was beautiful . . .": J. W. Hoyt, *Report on the Universal Expositions of 1862 and 1867*, p. 92 ff.

140   "Their Imperial and Royal": ibid.

140   "There were, said the minister": ibid., p. 93.

141   "The International": ibid.

141   "Chickering gets": WSD, July 2, 1867.

141   "I get sick": WSD, August 4, 1867.

141   "The award": NYT, June 29, 1867. Among other American gold medals were prizes for locomotives, stationary steam engines, woodworking machinery, cotton, minerals, and artificial teeth. This *Times* dispatch was via the "Ocean Telegraph," which had won a grand prize. William's diary shows that he saw the dispatch, noting that "we head the list." S&S was the first gold medal reported and was followed by Chickering. S. G. White's artificial teeth appear after Chickering, and the roster shows no apparent order.

141   "This was no small": AA, Hoyt, p. 93.

141   "There was no class": United States Commissioners, *General Survey of the Exhibition, Paris Universal Exposition of 1867*, p. 50.

141   "The wildest and strangest": ibid., p. 50 ff.

142   "In total": Paran Stevens, *Report upon Musical Instruments, Paris Universal Exhibition*, p. 5.

142   "Berlioz was enthusiastic": letter, translated by and appearing in the S&S catalog of 1888 and many others. At the time the testimonial was obtained, the music of Berlioz was not universally admired. On January 29, 1866, the *New York Tribune* wrote that the New York Philharmonic wasted time in a "vain endeavor to make Berlioz's fantastic ravings intelligible to a sane audience." The *Symphonie Fantastique* was laden with "mathematic, soulless calculations."

142   "Send our patents": WSD, April 28, 1867.

142   "It was too expensive": letter from CFTS to Petri, apparently 1867. W. F.

Petri was a musician and former S&S agent in Washington, D.C., who joined the firm in New York. Petri socialized with William and was highly trusted. He witnessed the wills of Henry, Jr.

142 "(This was probably": Sadie, op. cit., p. 60.

142 "François Joseph Fetis": Nicolas Slonimsky, *Baker's Biographical Dictionary of Musicians*, 5th ed. See *New Grove* for an extensive entry on Fetis.

142 "There are problems with Escudier": ibid.

142 "Brandus": ibid.

142 "Louis Dachauer": NYT, March 24, 1877.

142 "furnishing the proof": S&S catalog, ca. 1870.

143 " 'Fetis,' observed William": ibid. Stevens, op. cit., p. 10 ff presents an interesting contemporary account containing the opinion that all overstrung pianos have a characteristic that "cannot but be deemed a defect; for the crossing of the bass strings . . . makes the bass too powerful and preponderant."

143 "Though drawn": ibid., *New Grove*.

143 "How this belief was formed": Ehrlich, op. cit., p. 56.

143 "By the time": ibid., p. 59.

143–44 "To the numerous": S&S catalog, ca. 1870.

144 "Fetis did not": op. cit., *New Grove*, p. 511 ff.

144–45 "In 1840": Stevens, op. cit., p. 10.

145 "Today the strings": ibid., p. 11.

145 "The next words": ibid., p. 11.

145 "almost verbatim": ibid., p. 12. Speculatively, it cannot but be wondered if the Steinways did not enjoy an advantage over Chickering as native speakers of German, and their shared cultural background with some of the judges, notably Hanslick and Julius Schiedmeyer.

145 "Fetis followed": ibid., p. 13.

145 "These orchestral pianos": ibid.

146 "We take much pleasure": S&S confidential circular, April 3, 1868.

146 "The pianos of Messrs. Steinway": Stevens, op. cit., p. 14.

146 "Our neighbors do not love us": NYT, July 3, 1867.

146 "The pianist Gottschalk": Louis Moreau Gottschalk, *Notes of a Pianist*. The self-effacing title obscures both the acuity of Gottschalk's social commentary and the charm of his (or his translator's) prose.

146 "AMERICAN PIANOS": NYT, July 4, 1867.

147 "Theodore was late": WSD, July 2, 1867.

147 "Nine days lapsed": WSD, July 11, 1867.

147 "The Paris Exhibition": NYT, July 13, 1867.

147 "Société des Beaux-Arts": ibid.

147 "The advertisement appeared": The concept of display advertising with or without illustrations had yet to appear, and in the *Times* virtually all advertisements ran at the back of the paper. The advertisements were classified by product or service. The classification "Musical" was dominated by the city's pianomakers, many of whom seemed to understand that an unknown piano was an unsold piano.

147 "Along with it": NYT, July 13, 1867.

147 "The Emperor": NYT, July 15, 1867.

148 "Steinway, in its claim": NYT, June 29, 1867.

148   "The official lists": Hoyt, op. cit., pp. 97–98. Hoyt states that he has reproduced the lists. The McCormick reaper was the most decorated American entry at the exposition, accumulating a Cross of the Legion of Honor, a grand prize, and a gold medal. Little note was taken of this in New York.

148   "Honors well merited": NYT, July 13, 1867.

148   "They began": NYT, August 4, 1867.

148   "The *Times* continued": ibid.

148   "In the official": Stevens, op. cit., p. 16.

148–49 "It was later reported": see Loesser, p. 512, and Ehrlich, p. 60. Interestingly, an examination of the surviving S&S accounts reveals no evidence of such massive expenditures.

149   "Between 1866 and": AA, S&S German-language brochure, op. cit.

149   "Just five years": WSD, March 6, 1862.

149   "Ship a fancy Grand": WSD, March 8, 1862.

149   "To my horror": WSD, March 15, 1862.

149   "The International": London International Exhibition, Reports of the Juries, Class XVI. p. 1, ff.

150   "Last among": ibid.

150   "The London *News*": quoted in *Harper's Weekly*, August 23, 1862, p. 541.

150   "So had others": ibid.

150   "Rounding out the trio": ibid.

151   "*London Musical World*": *London Musical World*, August 9, 1862.

151   "The first of these": Hideo Suzuki, "Vibration and Sound Radiation of a Piano Soundboard," *Journal of the Acoustical Society of America*, vol. 80, no. 6, p. 1573–82. There is at least a modest irony in the fact that this work was done on a Steinway during the period when CBS owned the firm, and anxiety in the musical community about the quality of the pianos produced was high.

151   "A piano and violin maker,": AA, U.S. Patent Office records.

152   "E. H. Osborne": WSD, November 25, 1872.

152   "The next day": WSD, November 26, 1872.

152   "Dated December 2, 1872": letter from Chickering to S&S, December 2, 1872.

152   "The Messrs. Chickering": ibid.

153   "Chickering was the first": WSD, December 17, 1872.

153   "A discreet eleven days": WSD, December 28, 1872.

153   "It may have been only": Chickering & Sons, "A Plain Statement of Facts Concerning the American Pianos which were Not to be Exhibited . . .", no date, p. 6. This Chickering pamphlet reveals that the notice appeared in Chicago and Boston papers in December 1873.

153   "Chickering had written": Ibid., p. 7.

154   "As this went on": ibid., p. 8.

154   "You will understand": ibid., p. 9.

154   "The original translation": S&S circular, November 25, 1873.

154   "The only surviving record": op. cit., "A Plain Statement."

154   "The Bohemian": ibid., p. 11.

154   "Archcompetitor Bosendorfer": ibid., p. 12.

154   "Julius Schiedmeyer": ibid., p. 13.

155   "The new Imperial": ibid., p. 15.

155   "The right to give": ibid., p. 16.
155   "When New York's": AA, NYT, 1873–74 advertisements.

13. CONDENSER OF POLYPHONY

156   "About 12 o'clock": NYT, May 22, 1866.
156   "The flames leapt": ibid.
156   "Frenzied efforts": ibid.
156–57 "It appeared to have been": NYT, May 23, 1866. The history of the Academy is bizarre and conflict-laden; it would make an excellent study in the consequences of confounding aesthetic and commercial objectives.
157   "Two weeks after": WSD, May 26, 1866.
157   "early October": WSD, October 2, 1866.
157   "The entire space": AA, undated site plan and WSD, May through October, 1866.
157   "In 1839 the French": Loesser, op. cit., p. 346.
157   "Chickering's hall": Gottschalk, op. cit., p. 76.
157   "An Albany dealer": David Eugene Campbell, *The Purveyor as Patron: The Contribution of American Piano Manufacturers and Merchants to Musical Culture in the United States, 1851–1914*, p. 16 ff.
157   "Albany-based": ibid. Myron Decker subsequently moved to New York City and continued in the trade. There was some confusion between Myron Decker and the Decker brothers, also pianomakers, and the brothers unsuccessfully sued Myron in an attempt to prohibit his use of the Decker name.
158   "Therein lies": AA, S&S inventory books, 1865–71.
158   "One thing which is clear": letter from CFTS to WS, June 16, 1877.
158   "Steinway Hall opened": NYT, October 31, 1866.
158   "Everybody is delighted": WSD, October 31, 1866.
159   "The night before": NYT, October 26, 1866, and WSD.
159   "In 1858 the famed": NYT, December 7, 1876. This account sketches notable conflagrations in public spaces after a theater fire in Brooklyn.
159   "The doors opened outward": op. cit., October 26, 1866.
159   "Steam boiler explosions": ibid.
159   "The premiere concert": NYT, October 31, 1866. The *Times* contains the entire concert program establishing, if nothing else, that the paying audience received their money's worth.
160   "The second concert": NYT, November 2, 1866.
160   "Next into Steinway Hall": WSD, November 17, 1866.
160   "Steinway Hall, as last seen": NYT, October 23, 1868.
161   "Decorations were": ibid.
161   "The normally docile": NYT, January 27, 1865.
161   "Gottschalk was": Gottschalk, op. cit., p. 193. This is the first known case of a demand to play a specific Steinway or nothing at all. S&S is but eleven years old at this time.
162   "Our house is purely": catalog, Chickering & Sons, April 1869, no page.
162   "At the height": NYT, December 13, 1864.
163   "Mason is growing": Goddard, ed., op. cit., p. 13.
163   "That the demand": AA, NYT, January 27, 1869, *et seq.*, and federal census data, New York County, 1870.

163   "One 1858 analysis": NYT, December 9, 1858.

163   "In the ten years": AA, New York State Census of 1875.

164   "It was probably": NYT, February 18, 1864.

164   "Born . . . Theodor . . . 1835": op. cit., *New Grove*, vol. T, p. 781, and also Ezra Schabas, *Theodore Thomas: America's Conductor and Builder of Orchestras.*

164–65   "Thomas was a one-man": AA, advertisements of performances appearing in NYT, 1865–75.

165   "We take great pleasure": S&S confidential circular, October 13, 1870.

165   "Among these were": NYT, December 1, 1873.

165   "William did not attend": WSD, February 28, 1871.

166   "The group William saw": *New York Tribune*, February 24, 1872, and January 15, 1873. The Fisk University ensemble toured for many years.

166   "That William directly": WSD, December 7, 1872. WS earlier met with Mrs. Woodhull herself.

166   "Blind Tom was acceptable": Edward T. James, et al., ed., *Notable American Women, 1607–1950*, vol. 3, p. 652 ff.

166   "Just three months after": NYT, March 6, 1873.

166   "In March": WSD, March 13, 1872.

166   "A child prodigy": op. cit., *New Grove*, Vol. R, p. 743 ff.

166–67   "On March 14": WSD, March 14, 1872.

167   "Then, on June 14": WSD, June 14, 1872.

167   "It contained": WSD, June 25, 1872.

167   "The Graus": WSD, July 12, 1872.

167   "the agreement stipulated": information synthesized from undocumented accounts in Loesser, op. cit., p. 515 ff., and Ehrlich, op. cit, p. 54. Ehrlich, apparently unaware of the tours of Gottschalk, et alia, makes the statement that the Rubinstein tour "inaugurated a uniquely American method of sales promotion."

167   "Thus convinced": WSD, November 9, 1872.

167   "William recorded": WSD, June 21 and June 22, 1873.

167   "Combined with": WSD, May 22, 1873.

168   "Rubinstein and Wieniawski": WSD, September 11, 1872.

168   "To further buttress": NYT, September 20, 1872.

168   "Rubinstein had likely": NYT, September 12, 1973.

168   "Two days after": anonymous, Anton Rubinstein biographical pamphlet, no date.

169   "A letter from": ibid.

169   "Reserved seats": NYT, September 19, 1872.

169   "For Monday": WSD, September 23, 1872.

169   "The *Times* critic": NYT, September 24, 1872. Other accounts, such as those of the *Tribune*, were equally positive.

169   "A portion": ibid.

169–70   "A few jotted words": ibid.

170   "An editorial": NYT, September 27, 1872.

170   "After calling": ibid.

170   "Scathing article": WSD, September 27, 1872.

170   "William's article": NYT, September 28, 1872.

171   "The hall's ventilation": WSD, September 27, 1872.

171   "May Heaven": Harold Schonberg, *The Great Pianists*, p. 261.

171   "The four-hour": Ronald V. Ratliffe, *Steinway*, p. 117. The facsimile reproductions of the Rubinstein concerts number among the few services to truth to be found in this work.

171   "The term": McKnight, op. cit., p. 337 ff.

171   "Two years before that": ibid., McKnight, p. 334 ff.

172   "The May 1873": Ratliffe, op. cit., p. 116–17.

172   "Of the last": NYT, May 20, 1873.

172   "On the last full day": WSD, May 23, 1873.

172   "The next morning": WSD, May 24, 1873.

173   "In 125 words": S&S catalog, 1888.

173   "Liszt wrote": ibid.

173   "By noon": WSD, May 24, 1873.

14. HANS IS EASILY RECOGNIZED

174   "In company": NYT, May 14, 1866.

174   "the famous cheese": Those interested in the history of Liederkranz cheese are referred to John Steele Gordon, "The Liederkranz Lament," *American Heritage*, May–June 1992, pp. 16–17, where it is reported that the cheese is no longer made. The Liederkranz as an organization still exists. Bereft of its famous chorus, political power, and opulent headquarters designed and financed by William, the Liederkranz now dispenses small scholarships, and it exhibits no interest in powers and glories past. Telephoned by the author, an official of the Liederkranz said, "We don't give a damn about the Steinways," and then hung up.

174   "Another well-known": NYT, July 14, 1867.

175   "The German choral": ibid.

175   "At the Philadelphia": NYT, July 19, 1867.

175   "Having formed": NYT, July 14, 1867.

175   "William did not": WSD, July 13, 1867.

175   "Prize concert": WSD July 16, 1867.

175   "The *Times* reported": July 19, 1867.

175–76   "A German undertaker": ibid.

176   "For many years": NYT, February 16, 1866.

176   "A surviving engraving": *Leslie's Illustrated Weekly*, no date on clip.

176   "The New York German": NYT, April 16, 1864.

176   "Even the globe-girdling": Gottschalk, op. cit., p. 117.

177   "One of our reporters": NYT, December 27, 1858.

177   "Discarding all ultra views": ibid.

177   "The crescendo": ibid.

178   "The statewide": AA, New York State Census of 1875.

178   "Covering one": NYT, July 28, 1864.

178   "*New York Musical World*": *New York Musical World*, vol. 18, no. 347, November 21, 1857, p. 424. The editor does provide the source from which this shard of musical news was taken.

179   "There was a Teutonic hegemony": AA, New York State Census of 1875.

179   "Meet Charles Dickens": WSD, December 8, 1867.

179   "Sales of tickets": WSD, November 29, 1867.

179   "William, despite a bad cold": WSD, December 9, 1867.
179   "The hall was filled": NYT, December 10, 1867.
179   "Dickens, claimed the *Times*": ibid.
180   "At the second evening": NYT, December 11, 1867.
180   "William witnessed": WSD, December 10, 1867.
180   "By the second series": NYT, December 16, 1867.
180   "The *Times* described": ibid.
180   "On Christmas Day 1867": December 26, 1867.
180   "dedicated to saving": ibid.
180   "most motherly and excellent": ibid.
181   "John Johnson": ibid.
181   "A few blocks . . . away": WSD, December 24, 1867.
181   "On Christmas Day": WSD, December 25, 1867.
181   "Theodore wrote Von Bulow": letter from CFTS to Von Bulow, April 12, 1875.
181   "Privately to a friend": Goddard, op. cit., p. 13.
181   "William learned": WSD, October 20, 1875.
181   "William was there": WSD, November 15, 1875.
182   "Economic activity": AA, table, "Business Cycle Expansions and Contractions in the United States," *Business Conditions Digest*, January 1987, p. 104.
182   "Pay Hogan $50": WSD, November 13, 1875.
182   "The better the concert": *New York Tribune*, March 25, 1876. The remark was written after an all-Beethoven recital by Von Bulow, one of three he gave as a part of his final New York series.
182   "Many of the pianists": Goddard appeared at Steinway Hall on a bill shared with the soprano Theresa Titjens at the time that Von Bulow was performing at Chickering's. The combination of an internationally renowned *pianiste* and an at least equally famous *prima donna* was most likely an S&S attempt at what would now be called contrapuntal programming.
182   "The tours continued": S&S confidential circular, September 20, 1875. Goddard and Titjens were a part of Max Strakosch's Grand Concert Troupe that season. The Theodore Thomas Grand Orchestra had a similar arrangement for the same musical season.

Supplementing national tours of the eminent sponsored by S&S, a smaller concert room adjacent to the main hall was sometimes the site of serious, if less heralded, musical events. In February 1868, Miss Alida Topp, a student of Von Bulow's, launched a concert series in the smaller hall. The *Times*, on February 10, called the undertaking "hazardous," and the *Tribune* of February 7 called Miss Topp's performance a "dangerous experiment." The *pianiste* had violated custom in two ways: first, she performed "unassisted" in what would now be called a solo recital. Second, she combined the works of Bach, Beethoven, Chopin, Handel, Liszt, and Schumann in a single program called "a historical survey."

Another innovator performing in the smaller hall was Marie Krebs, who in 1871 gave a series of "recitals." These, it seems, were among the earliest usages of the term to describe Manhattan piano performances. Miss Krebs was also fond of forging programmatic alloys, blending Beethoven, Chopin, Liszt, Rubinstein, and Scarlatti with then-radical abandon. Perhaps slightly less adventurous than Mme. Topp, Miss Krebs was occasionally assisted by her singing mother. The programs were considered by the critics to be suitable solely for connoisseurs; these latter were sufficiently numerous to permit Miss Krebs to continue with weekly recitals for three months during the winter of 1871. Also concertizing at the time were Therese Carreño, Annette Essipoff, Arabella Goddard, and Anna Mehlig, all of whom also played Steinways, and whose combined activity made the 1870s something of a golden age for the *pianiste*. Despite obvious musical and sociological significance, this feminine piano peerage seems to have somehow eluded serious study and documentation. For further details see Mark C. McKnight, *Music Criticism in the New York Times and the New York Tribune, 1851–1876*.

183   "The rush to Steinway Hall": NYT, April 3, 1877.

183   "Elisha Gray announced": ibid.

183   "The simple melodies": *New York Daily Graphic*, undated clip ca. April 1877.

183   "*Leslie's Illustrated Newspaper*": undated clip ca. April 1877.

184   "Professor Boscovitz": ibid.

184   "Such was the assessment": NYT, April 3, 1877.

184   "The audience, however": ibid.

184   "solitary muse of the parlor": NYT, September 4, 1887.

184   "Dark, rainy day": WSD, April 2, 1877.

184   "The next morning": WSD, April 3, 1877.

15. THE DESPICABLE DEPRAVED CHARACTER

185   ". . . Tretbar & wife": WSD, December 31, 1875.

186   "Henry Reck": AA, WSD, 1870–75. William saw Reck socially on many occasions.

186   "Dachauer's role": NYT, August 18, 1878 and naturalization records, Manhattan Court of Common Pleas.

186   "Albert was": AA, WSD, 1870–75.

186   "There had been Christmas": WSD, December 24, 1875.

186   "Christmas morning": WSD, December 25, 1875.

187   "On Sunday": WSD, December 26, 1875.

187   "At dinner Monday": WSD, December 27, 1875.

187   "Steigertahl was": New York State Supreme Court, *Albert Steigertahl* v. *Mary Ann Steigertahl*, 1875. The record indicates that the connection was witnessed. William testified that Mrs. Steigertahl feared and hated her husband.

187   "Whether by accident": WSD, December 27, 1875.

187   "The next day": WSD, December 28, 1875.

187   "On Thursday": WSD, December 30, 1875.

187   "On New Year's Eve": WSD, December 31, 1875.

187   "William's brothers": letters from brothers to CFTS, March 30, 1861.

188   "Early in their marriage": AA, WSD, 1861–63.

188   "The number 300": WSD, November 16, 1861.

188   "In the early days": WSD, January 5 and 6, 1862.

188   "At the close of 1866": WSD, December 27, 1866.

188   "William's narrative": WSD, January 22, 1862.

188   "At seven the next morning": WSD, January 23, 1862.

188   "At 1 P.M.": ibid.

189   "The next day William": WSD, January 24, 1862.

189   "Regina's mother": WSD, January 25, 1862.

189   "Stop at Pit": The "Pit" was Pythagorean Hall, where the club rooms of the Liederkranz were located.

189   "Regina's ordeal": WSD, January 28, 1862.

189   "had been raving": ibid.

189   "Two weeks after": WSD, February 5, 1862.

189   "For the year 1865": Bureau of the Census, *Historical Statistics of the United States*, Part One, p. 47 ff.

190   "Dr. Elmer Harris": NYT, December 8, 1867.

190   "Adequate means": ibid.

190   "In April 1863": WSD, April 4 and 5, 1863.

190   "At 7:30 A.M.": WSD, June 4, 1865.

190   "George is so exhausted": WSD, February 6, 1867.

190   ". . . The baby is born": WSD, December 14, 1866.

190–91   "Two years later": WSD, November 11, 1868.

191   "October 11, 1869": WSD, October 11 and 12, 1869.

191   "I telegraph to Theodore": WSD, October 12, 1869.

191   "Georgie and Paula": WSD, October 13, 1869.

191   "In June 1870": WSD, June 4, 1870.

191   "Anna Mehlig": ibid.

191   "There is little": Among the more intriguing but enigmatic diary entries is one dated July 2, 1868: "In afternoon have long conversation with my wife from written memorandum with happiest results. Go to theater in evening with her. Feel very happy."

191   "Analysis of William's diary": AA, WSD, 1867–69.

192   "In his letters": letter from CFTS to family, December 25, 1855, and another, undated.

192   "If so, families": Sagarra, *A Social History of Germany, 1648–1914*.

192   "talked strongly": WSD, May 15, 1875.

192   "He recorded that": WSD, July 5, 1875.

193   "wife tells me she is": WSD, March 1, 1869.

193   "In April": WSD, April 23, 1869.

193   "my wife thinks": WSD, May 16, 1869.

193   "William's diary mentions": AA, WSD, 1875–76.

193   "For the summer": WSD, June 15, 1875.

193   "the building of a bridge": WSD, June 30, 1875, *et. seq.* According to the NYT, January 23, 1876, the overall length including approaches was 1.75 miles. Estimated construction cost was $2 million. In the customary fashion a charter was obtained from the state, and in April 1875 Albert travelled to Albany to expedite political deliberations.

193   "After playing Skat": WSD, September 18, 1875.

193   "Dejected beyond description": WSD, September 19, 1875.

193   "My mental anguish": WSD, September 20, 1875.

193–94   "Have further conversation": WSD, October 3, 1875.

194   "premiere of Arabella Goddard": WSD, October 4, 1875.

194   "I give him minute": WSD, October 6, 1875.
194   "The new extra large": ibid.
194   "For her birthday": WSD, October 11, 1875.
194   "I still have spells": WSD, October 14, 1875.
194   "earnest and long": ibid.
194   "The next day": WSD, October 15, 1875.
194   "At 10:30 A.M.": WSD, October 16, 1875.
194   "The next day, a Sunday": WSD, October 17, 1875.
194   "See Stn playing": ibid.
194   "Yesterday afternoon": WSD, October 20, 1875.
195   "It was not long": WSD, October 21, 1875.
195   "When Regina returned": WSD, October 24, 1875.
195   "In early November": WSD, November 2, 1875.
195   "William bought stilts": WSD, November 3, 1875.
195   "I am still very sad": ibid.
195   "felt a pressure": WSD, November 21, 1875.
195   "Hogan's assistant": WSD, November 26, 1875.
195   "William wrote": WSD, November 28, 1875.
195   "William's depression": WSD, December 4, 1875.
195   "The first snow": WSD, December 8, 1875.
195   "My terrible mental distress": WSD, December 9, 1875.
195   "most exciting conversation": WSD, December 17, 1875.
195   "respecting our future": WSD, December 19, 1875.
195–96 "I continue to feel": WSD, January 13, 1876.
196   "Our sufferings": WSD, January 25, 1876.
196   "In the morning little Alfred": WSD, January 26, 1876.
196   "The next day": WSD, January 27, 1876.
196   "A bizarre telegram": ibid.
196   "It is evident": WSD, February 21, 1876.
196   "We both suffer": ibid.
196   "William told his brother": WSD, February 27, 1876.
196   "After taking supper": WSD, March 4, 1876.
196   "The next day": WSD, March 5, 1876.
196   "The days passed": WSD, March 7, 1876.
196   "In mid-March he forgave": WSD, March 9, 1876.
196–97 "He aided the new college": WSD, March 4, 1876.
197   " 'God,' declared": NYT, May 6, 1871.
197   "Even a female doctor": ibid.
197   "During the night": WSD, March 14, 1876.
197   "The next day": WSD, March 15, 1876.
197   "When William learned": WSD, March 18, 1876.
197   "It was about this time": WSD, March 16, 1876.
197   "William Steinway had": Bureau of the Census, *Marriage and Divorce, 1867–1906*, Part One, p. 165.
197   "only 629 divorces": ibid., p. 38.
197   "Commenting on": NYT, January 5, 1868.
197   "The Chicago situation": ibid.
197   "When Theodore returned": WSD, March 21, 1876.
198   "Bulow was": ibid.

198   "terrible excitement": ibid.

198   "She is dreadfully frightened": ibid.

198   "I read them": WSD, March 22, 1876.

198   "Everybody in high glee": ibid.

198   "It was not long": WSD, March 25, 1876.

198   "I again feel": WSD, March 29, 1876.

198   "I (am) the unhappiest": WSD, April 9, 1876.

198   "I feel very tired": WSD, April 11, 1876.

198   "At the end": WSD, April 12, 1876.

198   "Have conversation with wife": WSD, April 16, 1876.

198   "Soon Cotterill": WSD, April 20, 1876.

199   "After almost a quarter-century": ibid.

199   "Shortly Regina went": WSD, April 22, 1876.

199   "points for my complaint": WSD, April 23, 1876.

199   "watch my wife": WSD, April 29, 1876.

199   "It becomes my settled conviction": WSD, May 3, 1876.

199   "The next day William learned": WSD, May 4, 1876.

199   "I suffer dreadfully": WSD, May 6, 1876.

199   "I introduce my wife": WSD, May 15, 1876.

199   "lovely day": WSD, May 20, 1876.

200   "At 1:40 wife takes leave": ibid.

200   "On the Steamer": ibid.

200   "A week or so later": WSD, May 29, 1876.

200   "I feel a little more quiet": WSD, May 21, 1876.

200   "The jury have found": New York State Supreme Court, Special Proceeding, 1881. New York law requires that commitment proceedings forever remain sealed. The nature of Stern's mental disorder and the circumstances leading to his commitment cannot therefore be learned.

200   "Stern had his sister committed": New York State Supreme Court, Petition on Caroline Hecht, 1877. This was an ancillary matter in which the records are not sealed.

201   "general paralysis": records of the New York County Clerk, December 19, 1881.

201   "When an absolute divorce": Bureau of the Census, op. cit., p. 310 ff.

201   "That R. M. Henry": AA, WSD, May through October 1876.

201   "Charged with fact-finding": New York State Supreme Court, *William Steinway* v. *Regina Steinway*, 1876, hereafter referred to as "case file." New York state law seals divorce proceedings for 100 years. Thereafter they may be examined.

201   "Officially and sufficiently": case file.

201   "True to his word": Complaint in case file.

202   "I feel sick": WSD, July 27, 1876.

202   "disgusted with Pastor Krusi": WSD, May 13, 1876.

202   "On July 28": WSD, July 28, 1876.

202   "I commenced to notice": case file, July 28, 1876.

202   "Louise Krusi swore": ibid.

202   "Mysteriously": WSD, April 20, 1876.

203   "Minna Roesen": case file, July 28, 1876.

203   "William's diary": AA, WSD, year of 1869. The matter of Alfred and his

paternity was not before the court. The complaint finesses Alfred while mentioning George and Paula, who are referred to as "the issue of the said marriage." Nowhere in the diary does William actually state who he thought was the father of Alfred. Contextual inferences indicate that William probably believed Stern the father and definitely believed that he, William, was not.

203	"I have often seen": case file, July 28, 1876.
203	"Pastor Krusi swore": case file, July 28, 1876.
203	"The pastor did not": WSD, May 2, 1876, note in margin and main text.
203	"When she made this confession": case file, July 28, 1876.
203	"Ida, a former cook": WSD, August 3, 1876.
203	"I immediately go up": WSD, August 4, 1876.
203	"A few days later": case file, August 8, 1876.
203	"She saw them both undressed": WSD, August 8, 1876.
203	"The signed English-language": case file, August 8, 1876.
204	"William had left": WSD, June 4, 1869, *et. seq.* At this time Regina was about five months pregnant with Alfred.
204	"Next the referee": case file, August 15, 1876.
204	"the adultery as charged": case file, August 15, 1876.
204	"A day later": WSD, August 16, 1876.
204	"I give him $100 to disburse": WSD, August 17, 1876.
204	"Louise Krusi": case file, August 18, 1876.
204	"very pleasant and cool": WSD, August 22, 1876.
204	"To my unspeakable joy": ibid.
204	"Hardy & Duryea": WSD, August 25, 1876.
204	"The payment": WSD, August 26, 1876.
205	"*Steinway* v. *Steinway*": When the case was officially entered is unknown, but typewritten judgment rolls in the clerk's office now show *Steinway* v. *Steinway*.
205	"The decree": case file, Honorable Charles Donohue, August 24, 1876.
205	"In William's view": WSD, August 30, 1876.
205	"Tretbar has fitted": ibid.
205	"Reck calls": WSD, September 19, 1876.
205	"utterly crushed": WSD, September 20, 1876.
205	"I tell him not to come": WSD, December 17, 1876.
206	"In eveg have interview": WSD, October 14, 1876.
206	"Soon Dachauer": WSD, October 16, 1876.
206	"One day later": WSD, October 17, 1876.
206	"long talk": WSD, October 31, 1876.
206	"R.R fully establishing": WSD, November 1, 1876.
206	"Tell Dachauer": WSD, November 11, 1876.
206	"When Louis Dachauer": WSD, December 30,1876.
206	"Jesuit tricks": CFTS to William, April 17, 1877.
206	"Mrs. Dachauer charges her husband": NYT, March 24, 1877.
207	"to stop all further publications": WSD, March 24, 1877.
207	"all he had": ibid.
207	"A few days later": WSD, March 27, 1877.
207	"house of ill repute": WSD, March 24, 1877.
207	"Marie Dachauer apparently": WSD, April 16, 1877.
207	"Nine days later": WSD, April 23 and 25, 1877.

207   "a party": WSD, June 3, 1877.
207   "The Ocean Telegraph": WSD, June 12, 1877.
207   "Letters from Regina": WSD, August 22, 1877.
207   "In October": WSD, October 16, 1877.
207   "When the tree was lit": WSD, December 24, 1877.
208   "A cable dispatch": NYT, August 18, 1878.
208   "The obituaries": WSD, August 17, 1878.
208   "M.D. NOT DIVORCED": WSD, September 13, 1878.
208   "Judge Lawrence's daily log": New York Supreme Court Log, March 23, 1877, p. 277.

16. BAD BIRDS EVEN THEN

209   "For sometime past": *Music Trade Review*, January 3, 1876.
209   "Aggressively edited": Funding came in the form of extensive advertising. J. C. Freund, the editor, also discussed with William the idea of investing in a print shop. This, however, does not seem to have occurred.
210   "A glance": S&S confidential circular, January 10, 1876.
210   "Against this retail": Bureau of the Census, *Historical Statistics of the United States, Colonial Times to 1970*, p. 284 ff.
210   "Having moved to New York": Nancy J. Groce, *Musical Instrument Making in New York City During the Nineteenth Century*, p. 304.
210   "I do not now remember": *New York Sun*, September 5, 1877.
210   "They were regarded": ibid.
210   "The 'contract' piano": *Doggett's New York City Directory, 1854–1855* lists more than ninety Manhattan piano dealers and makers as well as four action makers, two piano stool manufacturers, two piano hardware suppliers, and a piano leg turner named Charles Charles. Legs and stools were so similar to items produced in the furniture trade that any of the city's dozens of furniture manufactories could also produce them and probably did.
210   "Thomas H. Chambers": Groce, ibid., p. 226 and 227. Chambers prospered sufficiently to acquire a home in Gramercy Park at number 23. Despite the fact that he and William were neighbors and in the same trade, William's diary contains scant mention of Chambers.
210   "and playable Chambers pianos": a Chambers square piano, probably from the 1870s, was examined in the spring of 1992, and thanks are due Mr. Roland Loest for bringing it to the author's attention. That there was no maker's name cast in the plate suggests that the bichord overstrung square was a stencil piano.
211   "It was here": *Music Trade Review*, October 10, 1876, reveals that Hale filed for the new trademark protection on the name "Stanley & Sons," showing that at least one of the alleged similar-sounding names was, in fact, his.
211   "Hale, it was claimed": *Music Trade Review*, November 1875 through March 1876. These stencil names were extracted from multiple issues during the anti-Hale crusade.
211   "Importers of expensive wine": NYT, February 11, 1876.
211   "Many buyers did not": *Music Trade Review*, February 3, 1876.
211   "Counterfeits found their way": ibid.

211 "William claimed": *New York Sun*, September 5, 1877.

211 "J. P. Hale produced": Loesser, op. cit., p. 528. The data cited by Loesser exhibit some internal inconsistencies. Federal income tax data report Hale's revenues in 1869 as $207,355, while Loesser states Hale's manufacturing capacity was twenty to twenty-four pianos per week or 1,000 to 1,200 units per year. Hale pianos were sold at retail for $150, which suggests a dealer price of about $100. Hale's 1869 capacity at these prices must have been in the region of 2,000 pianos per year. In unit terms, Hale's output was therefore likely about the same as S&S in 1869, but Steinway revenues were six times higher. Hale claimed that by 1870 he had a capacity of 3,000 pianos per year.

211 "Much of Hale's output": *New York World*, February 2, 1876.

211 "Out West": *Music Trade Review*, February 3, 1876.

211 "A dealer from Columbus": ibid., November 24, 1875.

212 "In what may be": *Cincinnati Daily Times*, reprinted in NYT, January 23, 1875.

212 "Hale called this": ibid.

212 "Am at store": WSD, March 29, 1877.

213 "By this quaintly precise": AA, S&S inventory book, 1876, and S&S production records, 1876.

213 "America's centennial year": AA, "Business Cycle Expansions and Contractions in the United States," *Business Conditions Digest*, January, 1987, p. 104.

213 "Over nine thousand businesses": Warren F. Hickernell, *Financial and Business Forecasting*, p. 340 ff.

213 "A parlor grand": AA, S&S confidential circulars, 1869–76. The circulars contain wholesale and retail prices for all styles of Steinway pianos.

213 "The Steinway & Sons workmen": AA, Joseph D. Weeks, *Report of the Statistics of Wages in Manufacturing Industries*, p. 289 ff.

213 "In the persistent and strong": AA, Joseph D. Weeks, *Report on the Average Retail Prices of the Necessities of Life*, p. 85 ff.

213 "A proposal": NYT, January 3, 1874.

214 "The falling bricks": *New York Sun*, September 7, 1877. The wall collapsed in December 1870. This was a follow-up story to a great fire at the Hale works that week in which at least nine died. When the blaze leapt to adjoining tenements and destroyed them as well, 120 families were said to be left destitute and homeless. The author learned from inspection of court documents that Hale applied for and received waivers from city ordinances that required fire shutters and doors in his building. Hale seems to have been as persuasive with judges as William.

214 "He was quick": NYT, January 23, 1875.

214 "Equally radical": This description of Hale's distribution system is synthesized from accounts in *Music Trade Review*, November 1875 through March 1876.

214 "While those opposed": *New York Sun*, September 5, 1877.

214–15 "Were it not, men": Alfred Dolge, *Pianos and Their Makers*, p. 339–42. Dolge erroneously gives the year of Hale's arrival in New York as 1870; 1860 or 1861 is more likely.

215   "J. P. Hale's strategy": letter from CFTS to WS, April 17; no year, but probably 1877. In this letter Theodore alludes to Hale's financial interest in Chickering, intelligence he likely obtained from William. No evidence of such an investment can now be found, other than a statement by Weber to that effect in *Music Trade Review*, October 3, 1877.

215   "Theodore was aware". ibid.

215   "He who does not": ibid.

216   "With William's steady hand": WSD, November 14, 1876.

216   "We should be guided": CFTS to WS, op. cit.

216   "Soundboard compression": ibid.

216   "Albert's newly patented": ibid.

216   "I will": ibid.

216   "Theodore advocated": ibid.

216–17   "Controlling about": S&S inventory book, 1876.

217   "Cancellation of promotional": WSD, December 21, 1875.

217   "I make motion": ibid.

217   "William's narrative": WSD, January 31, 1876.

217   "The next day fifteen": WSD, February 1, 1876.

217–18   "In the morning": WSD, February 3, 1876.

218   "But a foot": WSD, February 4, 1876.

218   "I suffer": WSD, February 10, 1876.

218   "In the afternoon with": WSD, February 11, 1876. It is likely that William was in error on the date he visited the *Times*, as the article *appeared* on February 11, 1876. According to the diary, William read proofs the evening of February 11, a clear implausibility.

218   "creating great sensation": WSD, February 12, 1876.

218   "one of the great industries": NYT, February 11, 1876.

218   "CHICKERING, STEINWAY": ibid.

218   "This is that the making": ibid.

218   "William and his allies": NYT, February 12, 1876.

219   "Such names are bought": ibid.

219   "Albert Weber was, more or less": In 1869 Weber had revenues of $221,444, according to the income tax data. Just three years earlier, his revenues were a scant $72,421 and he produced only 266 pianos. Trebling the size of his business in just three years (and it was seventeen years old in 1869) was an impressive feat, and was certainly known to William. By the time of Weber's death in 1879, production was up to 1,700 units.

219   "Banks did not": New York State Supreme Court, *Hale* v. *Phillips*, 1886.

219   "A piano tuner from Poughkeepsie": *Music Trade Review*, January 3, 1876.

219   "In a lawsuit": New York State Supreme Court, *Hale* v. *Phillips*. The *New York Times* ran what was likely a paid piece on December 13, 1877: "So perfectly are Hale's pianos made that other manufacturers buy up large numbers of them, mark their own names thereon, and send them out to their agents and the public to be sold at double the price he charges. . . . Of course he checks this evil whenever he hears of a case, but if a cash order comes to him for 1,000 pianos he cannot always tell who is the real party behind it."

220   "dark ways of the makers": *New York Tribune*, January 13, 1876.

220   "At the same time": New York State Supreme Court, *Weber* v. *Webber*, et al. The case file shows that Webber had the audacity to use cuts from Albert Weber's catalog.

220   "Your uniform love": NYT, February 15, 1876.

220   "I had fought": ibid.

220   "If a little ring": ibid.

221   "Sixty to seventy thousand": NYT, February 17, 1876.

221   "It was American organs": AA, *Annual Statement of the Chief of the Bureau of Statistics on the Commerce and Navigation of the United States*, 1880, p. 83 ff.

221   "The export trade": ibid.

221   "All musical instrument": ibid. Then, as now, America had substantial trade deficits. Deficits were posted in thirty-three years between 1835 and 1885.

221   "In 1885": *Annual Report and Statements of the Chief of the Bureau of Statistics on the Foreign Commerce, Navigation, Immigration and Tonnage of the United States*, p. 91 ff.

221   "The manufacture of piano-fortes": NYT, op. cit.

221   "A new piano war": *New York World*, February 18, 1876.

221   "The *World* dispatched": ibid.

221   "The *World* felt it": ibid.

221   "Pattison lectured": ibid. The reference is to pianist John N. Pattison, who during the 1860s was the recipient of largesse from Steinway & Sons that included a free piano for his home and cash advances. Pattison subsequently defected to Weber and played his instruments at the Philadelphia Centennial Exposition in 1876.

221   "You ought to make it clear": ibid.

222   "Weber's 'insignificant coterie' letter": ibid. This is a reference to NYT, February 15, 1876, in which Weber used the quoted phrase.

222   "When the article appeared": WSD, February 18, 1876.

222   "The *World* reported": *World*, op. cit.

222   "Declared Weber": ibid.

222   "It's all a question": ibid.

222   "Yes, but about the bogus": ibid.

222   "Only the *Music Trade Review*": By Spring 1876 the attention of the trade was shifting to the Centennial Exposition.

17. AGGRESSIVE AND IRREPRESSIBLE MANUFACTURERS

223   "Depart with": WSD, June 7, 1876.

223   "Such was the case": Francis A. Walker, ed., *United States Centennial Commission Reports and Awards, General Report of the Judges of Group XXV*, p. 27 ff.

224   "The Decker Brothers": Nancy J. Groce, *Musical Instrument Making in New York City During the Nineteenth Century*, p. 246. The name Decker, working as a finisher, appears for several years in the production records of S&S in the 1850s.

224   "George Steck": ibid., p. 456.

224   "he had reduced": S&S confidential circular, January 10, 1876. "The retail prices have in all cases been left unchanged, as there is a strong probability that a formidable strike for higher wages will be inaugurated next spring . . ." wrote William to his dealers and agents. The price reduction averaged about 9 percent, a substantial amount.

224   "and in the spring": S&S confidential circular, May 1, 1876. William also streamlined his product line by dropping certain models, but on May 5, 1876, noted that there was "not such a rush for the Style 1 piano in rosewood as I anticipated."

225   "In the first quarter": NYT, April 16, 1876.

225   "We also avail ourselves": circular, op. cit.

225   "We also exhibit": ibid. The term *composite* means "alloy."

225   "A special car": WSD, April 20, 1876.

225   "There the roughly": Francis A. Walker, *The World's Fair at Philadelphia 1876: A Critical Account*, p. 9 ff.

225   "The efficiency": ibid., p. 7.

225   "Crates marked": *Centennial Commission Reports and Awards*, op. cit., p. 32.

225   "Germany was": ibid., AA, p. 32.

225   "upwards of 200": ibid.

225   "Only ninety-eight of the pianos": AA, ibid., p. 34.

225   "At Paris in 1867": AA, J. W. Hoyt, *Report on the Universal Expositions of 1862 and 1867*, p. 93.

225–26   "To begin, the judges": *The World's Fair*, op. cit., p. 33.

226   "The radical defect": ibid., p. 29.

226   " 'The report,' declared Walker": ibid., p. 31.

226   "The report was to be": ibid., p. 32. The judge was "accountable to the Administration and the world." As matters developed in the piano judging, less abstract forces played a significant role.

226   "Judge Henry K. Oliver": *New York Herald*, July 16, 1876. This was the first published report of what was apparently common knowledge in the trade. William monitored the situation closely that spring. On April 15, 1876, he learned that Schiedmeyer was "Juror for the German Empire." On April 21, William received intelligence that "Bristow and Oliver of Boston will probably be taken" as judges. There were many contacts with New York State Centennial commissioner C. P. Kimball, who told William on April 17 of "all the machinations of Chickering through Beckwith," another Centennial official.

      On May 3, 1876 William dispatched Tretbar to visit Bristow, now confirmed as a Centennial juror. Bristow told Tretbar that "he thinks our pianos the best." Events revealed that Mr. Bristow was not a man of fixed opinions on piano excellence. Current musicological opinion confers historical importance on G. F. Bristow's compositions.

226   "Though he was not": The *Herald*, op. cit., reveals that Kupka judged sewing machines at Vienna; the connection, if any, between expertise in pianos and sewing machines remains a mystery.

226   "Great excitement again": WSD, June 8, 1876.

226   "Boscovitz told William": ibid.

226   "I send Blasius". WSD, June 9, 1876.

226   "(He will do all he can": ibid.

227   "who amazes T.": WSD, June 10, 1876.

227   "Unable to find": WSD, June 11, 1876.

227   "Sunday William spent": ibid. This same day William loaned $100 to Pastor Krusi, whose assistance in the divorce was so helpful, and he also encountered Louis Stern. "I am greatly excited," recorded William.

227   "Monday was cold": WSD, June 12, 1876.

227   "The plot thickened": WSD, June 13, 1876.

227   "The week moved on": WSD, June 15, 1876.

227   "great dispute": WSD, June 16, 1876.

227   "Originally the report read": *Music Trade Review*, October 18, 1876, p. 196. The reports at this time were still unpublished and supposedly confidential. What turgid stratagem caused the publication of the early report is opaque, but Chickering himself can be excluded from the list of possible sources.

227   "As ultimately published": *Centennial Commission Reports and Awards*, op. cit., p. 194, report number 382. An S&S confidential circular dated May 24, 1878, states that "we have just been informed of the publication of the Official Reports and Awards . . ." This was nearly two years after the judging.

227   "who spent the entire day": WSD, June 16, 1876.

227   "At 11½ A.M.": ibid.

228   "George Cook": WSD, June 20, 1876. William was also acting as a mediator with the judges: "I beg Schiedmeyer to yield and meet Bristow a little." This failed when juror Oliver objected. It may be presumed that the jurors were pondering report semantics.

228   "Later that Tuesday": ibid.

228   "The reports were shown": WSD, June 23, 1876. George F. Bristow seems to have been a guppy among the piano piranhas.

228   "When William returned": WSD, June 26, 1876.

228   "At the Judge's Hall": ibid.

228   "Schiedmeyer gives me": ibid.

228   "Commissioner C. P. Kimball": WSD, June 27, 1876.

228   "For some reason": WSD, June 28, 1876.

228   "That same day": ibid.

228   "that Matters are not forced": WSD, July 6, 1876.

228   "The *New York Herald*: WSD, July 16, 1876.

228   "WHAT'S THE PRICE": *New York Herald*, July 16, 1876.

228–29   "Although there": ibid.

229   "Three at least": ibid.

229   "A good natured": ibid.

229   "He was a member": ibid.

229   "Julius Schiedmeyer, though partisan": WSD, April 15, 1876. Close research in Europe would yield much of interest on matters Steinway, including Theodore's relationships with Schiedmeyer, Bluthner, Bechstein, Bosendorfer, and other luminaries in the continental piano constellation. This task is recommended to resident investigators.

229   "In a paragraph": *Herald*, op. cit.

229   "The reporter suggested": ibid.

230   "Mr. Gray": If Gray's statement is to be believed, it is more likely that the maker of this offer planned to engage a prostitute.

230   "Gray also claimed": *Herald*, op. cit.

230   "Weber and Bristow": New York State Supreme Court, *Van Dyke* v. *Steinway* case file.

230   "Steinways and Julius Schiedmeyer : e.g., WSD, June 20, June 26, 1876. William entertained Schiedmeyer on the Independence Day holiday, watching fireworks from the roof of Steinway Hall. Seeking respite from the intense heat that smothered the city, they remained on the roof until seven in the morning. See WSD, July 3 and 4, 1876.

230   "Why the paper did not": *Van Dyke* v. *Steinway*, op. cit.

230   "Garbled details": WSD, July 17, 1876.

230   "We read in your issue": *New York Herald*, July 19, 1876.

230   "William personally": WSD, July 18, 1876. William read the letter to a Mr. Connery of the *Herald*, then signed it in his presence. Such formalities were unusual in William's relationships with those he called "pressmen."

230–31 "Though our puff": WSD, July 19, 1876.

231   "George Bristow also": *Herald*, op. cit.

231   "William thought": WSD, July 19, 1876.

231   "At all events": *The World: New York*, July 19, 1876.

231   "The *World* reporter": ibid.

231   "Shortly after": WSD, July 20, 1876.

231   "The next day": WSD, July 21, 1876.

231   "very much excited and disgusted": ibid.

231   "Schiedmeyer would soon": WSD, July 22, 1876.

231   "Pianist Frederick Boscovitz": e.g., WSD, July 26 and 27, 1876.

231   "Tretbar told William": WSD, July 31, 1876.

232   "About eleven hundred persons": NYT, August 20, 1876. The always friendly *Times* reported in detail under the headline "Free Excursion to the Centennial."

232   "Heavy rains": WSD, August 19, 1876.

232   "William remained": WSD, August 20, 1876.

232   "Back in the city": WSD, August 24, 1876. William was at this time opening yet another front in the piano wars. On August 23, 1876, an agent bought a Chickering upright piano, no. 48 611. This William examined and found infringements of Steinway patents. A week later Frank Chickering was served. Averring innocence, Chickering ultimately capitulated.

232   "It was early September": WSD, September 7, 1876.

232   "Detective Hogan": WSD, September 8, 1876.

232   "Kimball wants us": WSD, September 11, 1876.

232   "Gloomy, rainy day": WSD, September 12, 1876.

233   "All day long now": NYT, August 8, 1876.

233   "See Kimball": WSD, September 15, 1876.

233   "William's next step": WSD, September 17, 1876.

233   "William received": WSD, September 28, 1876.

233   "At twenty-eight lines": *Centennial Commission Reports and Awards*, op. cit., p. 146, report number 89, p. 194, report number 382; and p. 146, report number 88, for Steinway, Chickering, and Weber, respectively.

233   "There was a second": ibid., p. 194, report number 380.

234   "The full metal frames": ibid.

234   "Receive our Iron report": WSD, October 12, 1876.

234   "Another factor": NYT, March 20, 1891.

234   "Playing a minor role": WSD, October 7, 1872.

235   "Scarcely one month": WSD, October 27, 1876.

18. THE TRUTH AT LAST

236   "The excitement": NYT, September 30, 1876.

236   "The [award] system": ibid.

236   "In the piano competition": AA, op. cit., *United States Centennial Commission Reports and Awards, General Report of the Judges of Group XXV*, p. 32–35.

236   "Good for what?": op. cit., *The World's Fair at Philadelphia 1876: A Critical Account*, p. 29.

237   "Of the ten million": ibid., p. 26. For those with a penchant for precision, the exact attendance was 9,910,966, of which 8,004,274 or 80.76 percent were paid admissions. The price was fifty cents, with the remarkable proviso that a single piece of money was required. No change was made and two quarters, for example, could not be used. The Treasury printed large numbers of fifty-cent notes for the use of the Centennial Bank, and visitors were sent there to have their bills and coins exchanged for these notes. A major fear of Centennial officials was counterfeit money, and this procedure was thought to reduce the threat. Walker, a man in a position to know, claimed that between 20 and 40 percent of the bills routinely presented to the Treasury for redemption were counterfeit.

237   "The first Steinway": NYT, September 30, 1876.

237   "Immediately below": ibid.

237   "None of these": *Van Dyke* v. *Steinway*, op. cit. Also WSD, October 8, 1876.

237   "The report the jurors": ibid.

238   "At the time": WSD, August 1, 1876. In a meeting with General Oliver, William reported that he "begs me to give him the data for the development of pianoforte building in New York, as the task has been allotted to him to write the introduction to the Jurors reports." Nearly a month later, on August 28, 1876, William sent the general a memorandum. On October 21, 1876, Oliver gave William the key to his hotel room in Philadelphia. William entered and examined the general's piano history, then departed the hotel to meet with Oliver. The extent of William's influence on the report cannot be determined, but it is intriguing that, while generally dismissive of Chickering's claims of iron-frame primacy, Oliver's report also cites a prior claim to overstringing by the genuinely obscure maker Albert W. Ladd in 1853. See *United States Centennial Commission Reports and Awards*, p. 29. Mr. Ladd never obtained a United States patent for his development, which was likely used on square pianos.

238   "Weber's advertisements": NYT, August 16, 1876.

238   "Under the headline": NYT, October 27, 1876.

238   "there were no clues": ibid.

238   "The piece as signed 'SPHINX,' ": NYT, October 27, 1876.

238   "But by the end": ibid.

238   "It was likely no coincidence": WSD, October 28, 1876.

238   "Herbert Van Dyke": *Van Dyke* v. *Steinway*, op. cit.

238   "The 'important news' ": ibid.

239   "While the amounts": ibid.

239   "Over the next month": AA, WSD, October and November 1876.

239   "Van Dyke's own search": *Van Dyke* v. *Steinway*, op. cit.

239   "statements of two prostitutes": ibid.

239   "exceedingly vile conundrum": ibid. In January 1877 William sent employee Nahum Stetson to Philadelphia to obtain that letter and other documents. Stetson reported the "scurrilous letter to Oliver, and letter by Bristow to Cent'l Commission gone, probably destroyed." Stetson did, however, obtain the original judge's reports. WSD, January 20, 1877. Apparently the Commission operated under the modern concept of "sunshine laws."

239   "After eight months of silence": *Van Dyke* v. *Steinway*, op. cit.

239   "At this point": WSD, June 26, 1877.

239   "Hall reported": ibid.

239   "Hall soon delivered": WSD, July 17, 1877. On July 26 Hall received a further $250 for "legal services." In this instance he seems to have delivered the actual scores of the judges for each of the pianos, most likely in the form of Bristow's notes. Whatever his skills at the bar, Hall found courier work between Brooklyn and Fourteenth Street a lucrative supplement, and the obvious conflict of interest does not seem to have inhibited him.

239   "Another front": *Van Dyke* v. *Steinway*, op. cit.

239   "Charles Tretbar": ibid. These letters are among the very few Tretbar documents known to survive.

240   "In an amazing display": *New York Tribune*, January 1, 1878. This interview illuminates the dates of the changes in Weber's awards, at least according to Weber.

240   "Albert Weber's strategic error": NYT, October 27, 1876.

240   "We feel that many": letter from Tretbar to Watson, June 26, 1877.

240   "Tretbar thought the remedy": ibid.

240   "first and highest award": ibid.

240   "When a man's honor": letter from Tretbar to Watson, August 10, 1877.

240   "Tretbar was soon": AA, WSD, August–October, 1877. Tretbar left on August 18 and returned October 28, 1877.

240   "While Tretbar": ibid. for the activities of Phelps, e.g., his attempts to get General Oliver to sign on August 10–14, 1877.

241   "Joseph P. Hale's": NYT, September 4, 1877.

241   "A scene of terror": ibid.

241   "Papers have scathing": WSD, September 4, 1877.

241   "Sun has an acct": WSD, September 5, 1877.

241   "While Charles Tretbar kept": ibid.

241   "When the *Britannic*": WSD, October 28, 1877.

242   "Little time": WSD, November 4, 1877.

242   "THE TRUTH AT LAST": NYT, November 11, 1877. This was designated by the *Times* as a "card," i.e., a paid insertion. At long last readers tracking the piano wars were able to distinguish between news and advertising copy.

242 "THIS IS TO CERTIFY": ibid.

242 "This was a total": *The World's Fair*, op. cit., p. 29 ff, for Walker's discussion of the original rules and procedures.

242 "A week passed": NYT, December 4, 1877. This was also legended as a "card." The new journalistic candor may have resulted from fear of libel actions.

242 "William observed": WSD, December 4, 1877.

242 "Detected and defeated": NYT, December 4, 1877.

242 "Several ocean voyages": ibid.

242 "After again declaring": ibid.

242 "An *honest* man": ibid.

242–43 "As a propagandist": ibid.

243 "Though having much else": ibid. Weber set forth a lengthy excerpt from the Centennial's "Directions for a System of Awards" that, naturally enough, supported his position.

243 "In January 1878": *New York Tribune*, January 17, 1878.

243 "I have just returned": ibid.

243 "Candidly admitting": ibid.

243 "Forgetting, it seems": ibid.

243 "The Steinways have": ibid.

243 "There is no 'war' ": *New York Tribune*, January 21, 1878.

243–44 "But there is a 'war' ": ibid.

244 "Weber, according to William": ibid.

244 "Partially screened": WSD, January 28, 1878.

244 "The next day Mr. Wass": WSD, January 29, 1878.

244 "A day later": January 30, 1878.

244 "SIR: In a recent": *New York Tribune*, February 7, 1878.

244 "Scarcely a week": WSD, February 13, 1878.

245 "Napoleon J. Haines": WSD, February 14, 1878.

245 "Finally, William": ibid.

245 "Freund was freed": February 15, 1878. That there was a Hale-Chickering Weber "combination" was still believed by William. He also thought "that the retail price list of their new pianos will be largely reduced." See WSD, February 24, 1878.

245 "The next day William was charged": WSD, February 28, 1878.

245 "Though the charges": WSD, March 6, 1878.

245 "Freund told William": WSD, March 8, 1878.

245 "In a few weeks": *Music Trade Review* beginning in April 1878.

245 "William did not suffer": WSD, August 23, 1876, *et seq.*

245–46 "These infringements": S&S confidential circular, August 15, 1878. This same issue promotes, for the first time, "ebonized" cases for grands and uprights. This is the familiar black piano finish now considered standard.

246 "the touch would become uneven": ibid.

246 "When an evening meeting": WSD, August 15, 1879.

246 "A credit reporter": WSD, July 25 and 30, 1878.

246 "Assets exceeded liabilities": AA, S&S inventory book, 1873–79, and particularly 1878.

246 "To my great joy": WSD, January 21, 1879.

246 "Albert Weber died": WSD, June 25, 1879.

246   "Obituary notices": WSD, June 26, 1879.

246   "The *New York Times*": NYT, June 26, 1879.

246–47 "After a long paragraph": ibid.

247   "Herbert Van Dyke, the ex-Weber": *Van Dyke* v. *Steinway*, op. cit.

247   "Herbert Van Dyke not only lost": ibid.

247   "John C. Freund": *Music Trade Review*, January–December 1879, and particularly February 18, April 3 and 18, 1879.

247   "John Freund had found": NYT, January 14, 15, and 16, 1880.

247   "At Christmas": WSD, December 25, 1879. As was his habit, William stopped by the store on Christmas Day and found the gifts.

248   "Hale had other": *New York Sun*, October 17, 1883.

248   "DEATH OF JOSEPH": ibid.

248   "The *New York Tribune*": *New York Tribune*, October 17, 1883.

19. FINE LOOKING AND INTELLIGENT MEN

249   "We have met to demonstrate": *New York Sun*, June 22, 1872.

249   "The first to strike": WSD, May 13, 17, and 20, 1872.

249   "The *New York Herald*": *New York Herald*, May 22, 1872.

250   "Precisely that": NYT, January 18, 1870.

250   "The notion of working eight hours": Ronald Filippelli, ed., *Labor Conflict in the United States*, p. 172 ff. This remarkable work is an encyclopedia of the issues, incidents, and leadership of the American labor movement.

250   "In addition to the concept": ibid.

250   "The intellectual wellspring": David McLellan, *Karl Marx: His Life and Thought*, p. 346 ff.

250   "Therefore 'the laborers' ": ibid.

250   "The connection between": ibid., p. 286 ff.

250   "At Steinway & Sons": AA, NYT, June 16, 1872. Other estimates are as low as four hundred; the precise number is much less important than the ratios.

251   "New York pianomaking": NYT, May 24, 1872.

251   "The *New York Times*": NYT, June 15, 1872.

251   "So robust was the piecework tradition": Author's interview with Daniel Koenig, then S&S manufacturing vice president, February 4, 1992. Mr. Koenig stated that about 25 percent of the operations involved in making a piano were still paid as piecework, and that the proportion had been reduced from 50 percent. In Mr. Koenig's view, piecework made it "difficult to instill quality" in "operators," i.e., the employees who actually make pianos.

251   "Workers' earnings": NYT, May 30, 1872.

251   "As compared to": *Historical Statistics of the United States*, Part One, p. 121 ff, and particularly Series D-738.

251   "the laborers, earned": *Report of the Statistics of Wages in Manufacturing Industries*, p. 289 ff.

251   "Very skilled workers": ibid.

251   "Soundboard makers": ibid. The *Report* does not mention Chickering by name, but notes to the wage tables permit unambiguous identification as Chickering.

251	"As it had for many years": ibid.
251	"An average Steinway varnisher": ibid.
251–52	"A Steinway topmaker": ibid.
252	"An 1870 study of pay": NYT, January 18, 1870.
252	"Commenting on the Steinway work force": *New York Herald*, May 24, 1872.
252	"Cuts in the piece prices": AA, WSD, 1865–69. During the 1873 recession the family reduced wages 15 percent. See WSD, November 23, 1873.
253	"Job actions": WSD, May 13, 1872.
253	"To the surprise of the tradesmen": WSD, May 20, 1872.
253	"agitation for the eight hour system": WSD, May 23, 1872.
253	"At that meeting of five hundred": NYT, May 24, 1872.
253	"A committee of 16": WSD, May 23, 1872.
253	"Eight-hour optimism": NYT, May 24, 1872.
253	"Weber's men": WSD, May 25, 1872.
253	"The Steinway men": NYT, June 15, 1872. On May 27, 1872, William wrote: "All the journeymen pianoforte workers strike, except our men, who seem to be unwilling to join in the movement."
253	"inflammatory": WSD, May 28, 1872.
253	"The tactics were": ibid.
253	"Agreeable to": ibid.
253	"The next morning": WSD, May 29, 1872.
253	"What you ask for": *New York Sun*, May 30, 1872.
253	"The demands would": NYT, May 30, 1872.
254	"William then asked": ibid.
254	"This was done by secret ballot": WSD, May 29, 1872.
254	"did not wish to fight": NYT, May 30, 1872.
254	"When the workers reassembled": WSD, May 29, 1872.
254	"An employee": *New York Sun*, May 30, 1872.
254	"Several enthusiastic speeches": *New York Herald*, May 30, 1872.
254	"A committee visited": NYT, May 30, 1872.
254	"If the dealers thought": ibid.
255	"I am much worn out": WSD, May 29, 1872.
255	"That night": S&S confidential circular, May 29, 1872.
255	"True to his word": ibid.
255	"The sixty-dollar amount": AA, S&S prices in effect in 1872.
255	"The dealers": WSD, June 3, 1872.
255	"Over the weekend": WSD, June 1, 1872.
255	"There was the occasional victory": NYT, May 14, 1872.
256	"William received word": WSD, June 2, 1872.
256	"This is reported": WSD, June 4, 1872.
256	"The *New York Sun*": *New York Sun*, June 5, 1872.
256	"William learned": WSD, June 4, 1872.
256	"The next morning": WSD, June 5, 1874.
256	"The *Sun* remarked": *New York Sun*, June 6, 1872.
256	"The next night": *New York Sun*, June 7, 1872.
256	"Other pianomakers": ibid.
256	"That same day": ibid.
256	"Estimates of the total": ibid.

256   "the whole city is in a blaze": WSD, June 7, 1872.

256   "The fact is": NYT, June 8, 1872.

257   "Albert Weber opined": ibid.

257   "while Napoleon J. Haines": ibid. Haines capitulated to the eight-hour demands of his workmen, then aligned himself with the other "bosses."

257   "Propaganda aside": WSD, June 8, 1872. It may be speculated that this decision was a relief to the 150 or so men who continued to work at Steinway's in defiance of the majority of pianomakers. With the factory closed they would not have to endure the disapproval of their peers.

257   "The Eight Hour League": WSD, June 10, 1872. The Eight Hour League was the umbrella organization for the city's various workmen's protective and benevolent associations. On June 19, 1872, the *Times* reported that the League had "taxed" workmen and built a treasury of about $1 million. This was to be used to pay strike benefits according to the account. The amount seems implausibly large for a transient organization, but even if true, the sum was sufficient for only a few weeks' aid to the 40,000 who were expected to march in the demonstration. The million-dollar war chest was likely no more than a bit of propaganda proffered to a gullible reporter, the calculated effect of which was to vex employers and create hope among the workingmen, who were now called "malcontents" by the *Times*.

257   "a grand fizzle": WSD, June 10, 1872.

257   "On Friday evening": WSD, June 14, 1872. The factory had reopened on Thursday, June 13, and about 350 men reported to work. See NYT, June 14, 1872.

257   "Clearing out": NYT, June 16, 1872. The account includes an example of "clearing out" as it was practiced at Phyfe & Company on Forty-second Street.

257   "There being 300–400 policemen": WSD, June 15, 1872. WSD, June 14, 1872, reveals that William met with police Captain Gunner and "we make all necessary preparations to have a large police force on hand." It appears that William did not actually approach the S&S factory. To appear would have been foolhardy. William did see the attack on Phyfe & Company and wrote, "Captain Gunner arrives with 80 Men, charges on the strikers and clubs them over the arm and legs, they running as fast as their legs can carry them."

257   "What he did not know": NYT, June 16, 1872.

258   "Deterred by the large force": ibid.

258   "The strikers": ibid.

258   "They were beaten back": ibid.

258   "Later that day": WSD, June 15, 1872.

258   "The police remained": NYT, June 16, 1872.

258   "departed to their": ibid.

258   "The pianomakers": WSD, June 24, 1872. Many men returned to work by June 17, and by June 24 the pianomakers had all returned to their benches.

258   "William, called by": WSD, June 21, 1872.

258   "Officers' conduct commended": June 24, 1872.

258   "The day before": WSD, June 23, 1872.

259   "It was ninety degrees": WSD, August 12, 1872.

259   "It was to be": Bureau of the Census, *Historical Statistics of the United States*, Part One, p. 121 ff.
259   "Though the depression": WSD, December 4, 7, 9, and 22, 1872.
259   "and national economic activity": AA, table, "Business Cycle Expansions and Contractions in the United States," *Business Conditions Digest*, January, 1987, p. 104.
259   "In his only published": *New York World*, September 30, 1873.
259   "Albert then gave": ibid.
259–60 "Showing a grasp": ibid.
260   "Having explained": ibid.
260   "the trigger for the Panic": Warren F. Hickernell, *Financial and Business Forecasting*, p. 324 ff.
260   "Cooke's firm": ibid.
260–61 "Business failures": ibid.
261   "A meeting": WSD, September 21, 1873.
261   "The German Savings Bank": September 22, 1873.
261   "I was very much excited": WSD, September 23, 1873.
261   "William's small investment": incorporation record, Bank of the Metropolis. William held fifty shares at $100 par. Oswald Ottendorfer was also a minor investor. The bank was a rare case of an Anglo-German joint venture.
261   "that we can have all the greenbacks": WSD, October 4, 1873.
261   "to reduce stock": ibid.
261   "As often happened": WSD, October 4 and 6, 1873.
261   "A lumber shipment": WSD, October 1, 1873.
261   "Business, wrote": WSD, October 6, 1873.
261   "Have good talk": WSD, October 17, 1873.
261   "By November": WSD, November 3, 1873.
261   "Meanwhile, there were": WSD, October 30 and November 17, 1873.
261   "On November 19, 1873": WSD, November 19, 1873.
261   "and the next day": WSD, November 20, 1873. On November 23 William recorded that the "deduction" averaged about 15 percent.
261   "After three months": WSD, November 28, 1873. Equitable Life Insurance was the lender, and the loan apparently solved the S&S liquidity crisis. The next day William acquired his new home in Gramercy Park.
261   "In March 1876": NYT, March 2, 1876. The article revealed that the unions had been decimated by the depression. Membership was down 63.9 percent to about 18,000 men, one-fifth of whom were unemployed. This unsigned piece is an example of impeccable and detailed reporting.
261   "Combining both": ibid. The differential rates of unemployment for union and nonunion workers are mysterious. The unions had no ability to negotiate continuing employment, yet their unemployment rates were lower. This may have been the result of the tendency of some unions to focus on larger and stronger firms (such as S&S) in their organizing activities.
262   "But not all fared poorly": ibid.
262   "The *Times* reporter": ibid.
262   "In January 1876": S&S confidential circular, January 10, 1876.
262   "Business very quiet": WSD, January 15; February 8, 10, 16; March 6, 8, 30, 1876.
262   "On a carriage ride": WSD, March 7, 1876.

262   "On his birthday": WSD, March 5, 1876. William was now forty-one years of age.

262   "The company's debt ballooned": AA, S&S inventory book, 1870–77.

263   "Economist Edward Atkinson": Edward Atkinson, "Low Prices, High Wages, Small Profits: What Makes Them" in *The Century Magazine*, vol. 34, no. 4, August 1887, pp. 368–84.

263   "To do this": ibid.

263   "At Steinway's": author's estimate and NYT, June 16, 1872.

263   "In the winter months": NYT, January 1, 1876.

264   "In January 1877": NYT, January 7, 1877.

264   "The problem began": ibid.

264   "Food was stolen": ibid.

264   "In the winter": ibid.

20. VILE FIENDS, SUCKERS, AND BLOODHOUNDS

265   "A perfect pandemonium": WSD, September 11, 1879.

265   "The comatose union": NYT, September 18, 1879. In its new incarnation, the union—a term now freely used in place of protective and benevolent associations—was called the Order of the United Piano-makers. The term "pianoforte" had also slipped from the lexicon, at least among the workers.

265   "The leaders were men": ibid. The *Times* also noted that the union men were still largely German; since the books were closely guarded by the bosses and warerooms were generally far from the factories, the scope of the union's "mercantile" knowledge was probably overestimated by the reporter. There remains the possibility that there were clerks sympathetic to the cause who supplied commercial intelligence to the union.

265   "Instead, a sophisticated": ibid.

265–66   "At the small sixty-man shop": ibid.

266   "This refined technique": ibid.

266   "After lengthy conversation": WSD, September 11, 1879.

266   "He acknowledged": In 1883 congressional testimony William said, "I myself think labor ought to organize as it has organized. I am not opposed to labor unions, and any labor union that is carried on in a sensible way can do a great deal, not only toward bettering their own condition in the way of wages, but also in equalizing wages in the various cities, and in resisting in times of depression the great deterioration and fall of wages." William did not, however, approve of the "entrance of the socialistic and communistic element in the labor unions" or the exercise of "terror" over workers who did not wish to strike. He believed that strikes were an essential mechanism. They were "a necessity, and should not be legislated against, and cannot be legislated against." He saw strikes as a counterbalance to competitive forces that would otherwise not allow an individual manufacturer to raise his piano prices even if his labor costs increased. Testimony of William Steinway before the United States Senate Committee on Education and Labor, September 27, 1883, p. 1086 ff.

266   "There was only one day's": WSD, February 12, 1880.

266   "On Friday": WSD, February 13, 1880.

267   "This required": WSD, February 13, 1880.

267   "Huge numbers": AA, S&S inventory book, 1879–81.

267   "After the investment in lumber": ibid.

267   "A new response": WSD, February 14, 1880.

267   "On Monday William": WSD, February 16, 1880.

267   "and William seemed surprised": WSD, February 17, 1880. "And even our polishers here do not work," wrote William.

267   "Consulting with": WSD, February 18, 1880.

267   "While William did not have": NYT, February 18, 1880.

267   "The 'Vilest of the Vile' ": NYT, January 7, 1877.

268   "The strikers": NYT, February 18, 1880. Turtle Bay Park was located on Forty-fifth Street. Another meeting site was Wendell's Assembly Rooms on Forty-fourth Street. In the strikes of the 1860s and 1870s, meetings were most often held at the Germania Assembly Rooms far downtown on the Bowery or at Teutonia Hall, also downtown.

268   "The *Times* man": NYT, February 18, 1880. It was also reported that the union was "secret."

268   "precisely centered at": AA, Joseph D. Weeks, *Report of the Statistics of Wages in Manufacturing Industries*, p. 289 ff.

268   "William noted": WSD, February 18, 1880. "Especially the Times," observed William.

268   "The varnishers were demanding": *New York Sun*, February 25, 1880.

268   "Carl Schiff": *New York Sun*, February 23, 1880.

268   "Schiff, reported": ibid.

268   "Six hundred sacrificed": *New York Sun*, March 8, 1880.

268   "At the meetings": *New York Sun*, March 14, 1880.

268   "The *New York Sun*": *New York Sun*, February 29, 1880.

268   "The union set forth": WSD, February 24, 1880.

268–69 "News of the new": WSD, February 26, 1872.

269   "NOVEL AND RADICAL": NYT, February 28, 1880. William recorded the event this way: "At 3 P.M. Boss pianomakers of N.Y. meet and resolve unanimously to make a grand lockout to take place Monday, March 15, if up to March 13th Steinway's men have not returned to work. At same Hotel in eveg, meet Albert Weber, young Haines, Steck, Bacon & F.G. Smith in Committee and draft resolutions, which are given to the press, I take them to the Staatzeitung." WSD, February 27, 1880.

Weber was Albert J. Weber, Jr., then about age twenty-two, who took over the firm after his father's death.

The lockout was not really a new tool; it had been used by the piano manufacturers in February 1864. WSD, February 25, 1864. While the 1864 lockout was directed only against members of the "association," the 1880 action locked out all workmen, irrespective of their sympathies. One result was many new union recruits who received strike benefits if they attended the weekly meetings.

269   "The bosses were": ibid.

269   "The rate of wages": ibid.

269   "A splendid export trade": ibid.

269   "The 'splendid' export business": AA, *Annual Statement of the Chief of the Bureau of Statistics on the Commerce and Navigation of the United States*, 1880,

p. 83 ff. Then, as now, a balance-of-payments argument was popularly persuasive, even if false.

269   "The cost of making pianos": NYT, February 28, 1880.

269   "Last, the society": ibid.

269   "The gauntlet was down": *New York Sun*, February 29, 1880.

269   "The *Sun* reported": ibid.

269   "Instead they talked": *New York Sun*, March 8, 1880.

269   "Taking a page": *New York Sun*, March 18, 1880.

270   "William thought": WSD, March 18, 1880.

270   "There were many expressions": *New York Sun*, March 14, 1880.

270   "William wrote": WSD, March 12, 1880.

270   "J. P. Hale, apparently": *New York Sun*, March 15, 1880.

270   "At their weekly meeting": ibid. NYT, March 25, 1880 confirms that Hale claimed he was closed for repairs.

270   "Haines was accused": *New York Sun*, March 15, 1880.

270   "The workingmen heard": ibid.

270   "The Baltimore pianomakers": NYT, March 20, 1880.

270   "and the Socialist Labor Party": *New York Sun*, March 16, 1880, and NYT, March 23, 1880.

270–71   "We must sweep away": NYT, March 22, 1880.

271   "The bosses ask us": *New York Sun*, March 22, 1880. Similar quotes appeared in the *Times* this date, but it added, "A speaker named Lagrasse . . . denounced the manufacturers as a 'miserable gang of bloodsuckers and curs,' " while an anonymous orator declaimed that "the working men must have war to release the white slaves of the capitalists." The *Times* characterized the event as "the usual mass meeting." In marked contrast, the manufacturers had issued a statement saying, "We shall stand firmly together to prevent piano-fortes, so necessary to educating the young, from being forced beyond the reach of people of moderate means."

271   "A Mr. Frank McCarthy": *New York Sun*, March 22, 1880.

271   "Schiff, one of the": NYT, March 22, 1880.

271   " 'The workingmen,' quoted": ibid.

271   "A cautionary announcement": ibid. It seems that *faux* socialists were also soliciting donations for the strikers and keeping the proceeds.

271   "The union men": NYT, March 17, 1880. The proposal was reported as made to Napoleon Haines. Though he was meeting regularly with Haines and other owners at this time, William's diary makes no mention of Chinese labor.

271   "Mongolians for": ibid.

271   "to the Chinamen": ibid.

271   "The Flowery Kingdom": ibid.

271   "The unnamed capitalists": ibid.

271   "While the skeptical": ibid.

271   "Encountered as a group": *New York Sun*, March 17, 1880.

271   "I don't want": ibid.

271   "We don't want": ibid.

271   "A third declared": ibid.

271   "we shall not be driven": ibid.

271 "William was quoted": NYT, March 17, 1880.

272 "This was no idle threat": WSD, March 17, 1880.

272 "a carload of stuff": ibid.

272 "The first to concede": NYT, March 19, 1880. The meal was claimed to be compensation for the three days of work lost.

272 "Haines, a sophisticated": NYT, March 21, 1880.

272 "The men were to agree": ibid.

272 "to not be controlled": ibid.

272 "do not desire": ibid.

272 "wish to have the same good": ibid.

272 "Haines told": ibid.

272 "Faced with these": ibid.

272 "That night the Socialist": ibid.

272 "We are willing": NYT, March 24, 1880.

273 "The *Times* wrote": NYT, March 25, 1880.

273 "On the *Times* editorial page": NYT, March 25, 1880.

273 "The next day": WSD, March 25, 1880.

273 "The headline": NYT, March 26, 1880.

273 "The Executive Committee": ibid.

273 "William, still rummaging": ibid.

273 "It was in a circular": S&S confidential circular, March 26, 1880.

273 "The piano dealers throughout": ibid.

273 "The great strike of 1880": WSD, March 26, 1880.

274 "I refuse in the case": ibid.

274 "Com. returns": ibid.

274 "A man named Flesse": NYT, March 27, 1880.

274 "William observed privately": WSD, March 26, 1880.

274 "As a final act of celebration": NYT, March 27, 1880.

274 "Though cancelled": WSD, March 29, 1880. This was Easter Monday.

274 "Theodore addressed the men": ibid.

274 "Apparently moved": ibid.

274 "When the Massachusetts": WSD, September 25, 1880.

274 "But the most significant": WSD, March 28, 1880.

274 "In September 1882": NYT, September 19 and 20, 1882. William was in Europe when the strike began and did not return until October 8, 1882.

275 "After nine weeks": WSD, November 22, 1882.

275 "Passage and expenses": WSD, November 11, 1882.

275 "Our victory is complete": WSD, November 23, 1882.

275 "A notice also appeared": NYT, November 11, 1882.

275 "In the opening days of May": *New York Sun*, May 2, 1886.

275 "There were in the city": ibid.

275 "A notable thing": *New York Sun*, May 3, 1886.

275 "As the eight-hour strikes": *New York Sun*, May 4, 1886.

276 "teaching the use and composition": advertisement, *New York Sun*, May 2, 1886.

276 "Most's International": *New York Sun*, May 3, 1886.

276 "The capitalists seem to forget": *New York Tribune*, May 3, 1886. There were many synchronized eight-hour strikes nationwide, and they were by no means constrained to New York pianomaking. Many union men espoused

more moderate sociopolitical views than the pianomakers. The *New York Tribune* reported on April 27, 1886, that the head of the Brotherhood of Locomotive Engineers believed that "there should be no antagonism between Capital and Labor." This was the view of a man who led successful eight-hour strikes against Jay Gould's railroads.

276   "The *Times* observed". NYT, May 3, 1886.

276   "A few days before": WSD, April 26, 1886.

276   "Putting essentially": NYT, May 2 and 4, 1886.

276   "Unlike strikes past": see WSD, April and May 1886. There was no piano manufacturer's group for this strike, and William, after the 1880 and 1882 experiences, made no move to start one. Others, such as the furniture manufacturers, did form associations.

276   "It took the Grand Lodge": NYT, May 10, 1886.

276   "played hide and seek": *New York Sun*, May 10, 1886.

276   "A *Sun* editorial": *New York Sun*, May 11, 1886. The *Sun* may have modulated socially since the 1880 strike. On May 3, 1886, for example, it labelled the Socialist Labor Party "radical." One goal of the party was the passage of legislation mandating an eight-hour day.

277   "Two days later": WSD, May 12, 1886.

277   "Everybody compliments me": WSD, May 11, 1886.

277   "It seems to me": NYT, March 28, 1880.

21. GODFORSAKEN ASTORIA

278   "June 6, 1870": WSD, June 6, 1870.

278   "For reasons unclear": "Business Cycle Expansions and Contractions in the United States," *Business Conditions Digest*, January 1987, p. 104.

278   "At the end of 1869": AA, S&S inventory book, 1869.

278   "and the whole family": AA, S&S inventory book, 1856–69. Rather than pay themselves salaries, the partners took cash from the partnership that appeared in the accounts as a reduction in their equity. If, for example, a partner's share in the firm was $200,000, and he "drew" $25,000, his share in the partnership was then $175,000. Profits in any year were apportioned according to each partner's share at year-end.

278   "advertising in": WSD, April 30, 1870.

278   "The craft they bought": WSD, May 19, 1870. Unfortunately, William's diary reveals neither the price of the yacht nor the cost of the Morgan overhaul.

279   "On this first excursion": WSD, June 6, 1870.

279   "The level of preparation": ibid.

279   "On the return": ibid.

279   "and running aground": ibid.

279   "The voyage": The degree of development may be gauged by the fact that the total population of Queens County in 1870 was 73,803 as compared to 942,292 in New York County (Manhattan), according to Table 1 in *Census of New York for the Year 1875.*

279   "Albert and William": WSD, June 12, 1870.

279   "Albert soon": WSD, June 16, 1870, and July 17, 1870.

279   "At 11 A.M.": WSD, June 22, 1870.

279 "The 'reservations' ": *Long Island City Star and Newtown Advertiser*, July 30, 1869, cited in Aaron Singer, *Labor-Management Relations at Steinway & Sons, 1853–1896*, p. 88. This dissertation exhibits a pronounced prolabor bias, and its writer largely expunges the strong socialist connections and routine threats of violence that were organic to the labor movement of the time.

279 "Communal living": NYT, January 3, 1870. An overview of the more prominent of the manifold variants in American socialist thought and action.

280 "He did not take long": AA, WSD, June–July 1870. Just nineteen days elapsed from the first time William saw the Pike property to the time he purchased it. There is no diary mention of his examining alternative properties.

280 "certain pieces, parcels": undated typeset document, "Abstract of Title," covering William Steinway land purchases, including that of July 11, 1870. This may have been printed up by William to give to potential purchasers of parcels.

280 "On Monday, July 11": WSD, July 11, 1870.

280 "over to view the land": WSD, July 12, 1870.

280 "William had been buying": AA, WSD, 1861–70.

280 "The family even": AA, New York State Supreme Court, *Oaks* v. *Steinway*, case file.

280 "Within a few years": AA, Department of Buildings, City of New York, "Record of Plans and Specifications for New Buildings 1866–1901." These records begin in 1866. It appears that before June of that year, there was no municipal oversight of Manhattan construction. William's Queens land acquisitions took place at a long-term peak in metropolitan construction. In 1871 there were 1,451 building permits granted. This fell to roughly half the 1871 peak by 1876, and permits did not reach 1871 levels until 1883. In 1883, 1,450 permits were granted. In essence, Manhattan real estate entered a twelve-year depression shortly after William bought in Astoria.

280 "One clue": WSD, September 9, 1870.

281 "After William closed": WSD, September 6, 1870. It was decided by this time that all four partners (Heinrich, William, Theodore and Albert) were to hold equal shares in what William called the "country seat."

281 "To my consternation": WSD, December 14, 1870.

281 "The next day": WSD, December 15, 1870.

281 "On December 20": WSD, December 20, 1870.

281 "piercing cold": WSD, December 24, 1870. Another document was quickly prepared when Heinrich became seriously ill. This was a new partnership agreement that was signed the same night by Heinrich, Theodore, William, and Albert. To this time, Heinrich and William owned the factory and Steinway Hall separately, and "rented" them to Steinway & Sons. On December 22, 1870, new deeds were signed conveying equal interest in the factory and hall to Theodore and Albert, i.e., Heinrich, William, Theodore, and Albert now each had a one-quarter interest in the real estate. The new partnership papers were likely drafted because of the property transfers, but full understanding of these transactions requires documents now lost. It appears, however, that Heinrich wanted to ensure that his

sons Theodore and Albert became full partners in Steinway & Sons before he died.

281   "He is very much swollen": WSD, December 31, 1870. There was no celebration this New Year's Eve. "At 11 P.M. we are all in bed, sleeping into the New Year," wrote William.

281   "About 3 P.M.": WSD, January 2, 1871.

281   "The condition": Amelia M. Arria, Ralph E. Tartar, Ph.D., and David Van Thiel, M.D., "Liver-Brain Relations in Alcoholics," *Alcohol Health & Research World*, vol. 14, no. 2, 1990. The author wishes to express his gratitude to Dr. Ralph E. Tartar, who in a telephone interview on August 1, 1991, explained the probable cause and course of Heinrich's condition based on the description contained in William's diary.

281   "lacquer finishes and felts": ibid.

281   "Heinrich, who was": WSD, January 3, 1871. "Father feels very good and is much elated, believing himself to be out of danger," reported William.

281–82   "Father was slumbering": WSD, January 16, 1871.

282   "With what was obviously": S&S inventory book, 1870.

282   ". . . rapidly sinking . . .": WSD, January 18, 1871.

282   "He would insist": WSD, January 20 and 23, 1871.

282   "The senior Steinway": WSD, January 29, 1871.

282   "As a terminal condition": op. cit., Tartar interview.

282   "Heinrich Steinway died": WSD, February 7, 1871.

282   "and were 'splendid' ": WSD, February 8, 1871.

282   "Heinrich's death mask": ibid.

282   "A nineteen-piece band": WSD, February 9, 1871.

282   "with some two thousand persons": ibid. The estimate is William's. Perhaps 500–600 of these were employees; the huge turnout of mourners suggests great stature for Heinrich; unfortunately, no independent record of his life in New York could be found. The "splendid" obituaries, certainly approved by William, reveal nothing about his father, but "puff" the firm. See NYT, February 9, 1871.

282   "During the time": WSD, December 20, 1870.

283   "In 1870": NYT, February 19, 1879.

283   "About ten years ago": ibid.

283   "Cardozo, in less than four years,": NYT, February 25, 29; March 6, 13, 26; April 2, 5, 9, 10, 12, and 20, 1872. Judge Cardozo resigned from the bench but was allowed to continue to practice law, a probable quid pro quo for his silence. In an 1883 suit by a man named Bernzing, who was badly hurt when he fell from a scaffold at the Steinway factory, Judge Van Brunt called on William "relative to a piano" two days after he dismissed the Bernzing action. WSD, January 21 and 23, 1884. If, as Marx believed, religion was the opiate of the masses, pianos may have been the opiate of New York's judiciary.

283   "When William sued": New York State Supreme Court, *Steinway* v. *Oaks.*

283   "I see Jos. Howard": WSD, October 27, 1869.

283   "The price of justice": WSD, June 29, 1870.

284   "Joe Howard also had": When Barnard granted a motion adverse to William's interests, William called on Howard immediately. WSD, December 23, 1869. In 1871 William gave Cardozo two tickets to the Liederkranz

Ball and a $75 box. These the judge returned due to "sickness in his family." WSD, February 13 and 14, 1871.

284   "It was in November": WSD, November 3, 1871.

284   "A few days later": WSD, November 8, 1871.

284   "The difficulty may have": AA, map of Steinway, Long-Island, no date. This detailed map was probably prepared to assist in the sale of property in the development ca. 1880.

284   "When this exercise": ibid.

284   "Roughly thirty acres": ibid.

284   "millions of square feet": S&S catalog, 1884.

285   "There was no detail": e.g., WSD, March 2, 1873, and throughout 1872 and 1873 for examples of micromanagement.

285   "When the foundry": WSD, March 8, 1873.

285   "When pilings": WSD, November 8, 1873.

285   "Myriads of Mosquitoes": WSD, July 7, 1872.

285   "William was also": WSD, July 12, 1872.

285   "Throughout the pioneering": WSD, July 31, 1872, *et seq.* By August 2, 1872, William was unable to leave his bed: "I suffer dreadfully. . . ." By August 7 William was again able to leave his home.

285   "As if this were not": WSD, October 27 and 29, 1872.

285   "a mix of jest and insult": WSD, April 18, 1873.

285   "That Theodore was no admirer": undated document titled "C. F. Theodore Steinway." Apparently compiled as a part of a legal proceeding, this document sets forth the periods of Theodore's visit to America from October 26, 1865, through April 16, 1884, when he departed for Germany, there to remain until his death in 1889. Theodore was granted American citizenship by the Superior Court in Manhattan on May 7, 1872, but he may have knowingly renounced it at a later date by legally declaring himself an "inlander" at Braunschweig.

285   "as did his sister-in-law": WSD, July 22, 1872.

286   "Between 1868": AA, *Complete File (of) Patent Copies, Steinway & Sons.* This bound volume contains all patents in chronological order issued to the house during the years of family ownership. The author is grateful to Mr. Henry Z. Steinway for making it available for study.

286   "Roughly one-fourth": ibid.

286   "The first hairline": ibid. Practice prior to this time required extensive custom-fitting of action parts, one result of which was that repair required the fabrication of more custom parts. The knowledge and skills required were rare, and it is likely that many field repairs were crudely expedient.

286   "obviating": S&S catalog, 1884, p. 8.

286   "Grand Duplex Scale": op. cit., *Complete File (of) Patent Copies*, United States Patent No. 126,848.

286   "The actual live": ibid. The description here applies to the implementation on grand pianos. For squares and verticals, only one end of the string is "duplexed," that end being at the tuning pins. Actual practice varied widely over the years, particularly with respect to the number of treble notes on which the duplex was not muted by felt. Owners of Steinways seeking a brighter and more aggressive treble can experiment with removing some of the felt damping in their instruments without fear of irreversible damage.

On some instruments inspected by the author, the duplex sections have been completely damped by piano technicians and so-called restorers who apparently did not understand the duplex concept.

286   "While other patents": op. cit., *Complete File (of) Patent Copies*, United States Patent No. 204,106.

286   "most important". op. cit., S&S catalog, pp 8 9.

286   "To build rims": op. cit., *Complete File (of) Patent Copies*, United States Patent No. 229,198.

286   "Pianist/teacher/critic": Fanny Morris Smith, *A Noble Art: Three Lectures on the Evolution of the Piano*, p. 119 ff. Ms. Smith also wrote for *Etude* magazine until well after the turn of the century. Now virtually forgotten, her understanding of the interactions of technology and music was profound and singular.

287–88   "As a part": op. cit., *Complete File (of) Patent Copies*, United States Design Patent No. 11,856.

288   "an 1884 brochure": op. cit. S&S catalog, pp. 8–10.

288   "while an 1876": S&S catalog, 1876 p. 1 ff.

288   "Born in Potsdam": *Encyclopedia Americana*, vol. 14, pp. 85–86.

288   "with such a perfect": letter from Helmholtz to S&S, June 9, 1871, as reproduced in S&S catalog, 1888, p. 15.

288   "I have repeatedly": letter from Helmholtz to S&S, August 13, 1873, as reproduced in S&S catalog, 1888, p. 15.

289   "Their instruments": S&S inventory book, 1885.

289   "a fine souvenir": WSD, October 7, 1893. William was suffering severely with rheumatism and was largely confined to his home. He had not appeared at Steinway Hall in more than six months at the time of Helmholtz's visit to New York. It may be that it was not William with whom Helmholtz met, but either Charles or Frederick Steinway.

289   "No evidence": Ellen von Siemens-Helmholtz, *Anna von Helmholtz; Ein Lebensbild in Briefen*, p. 75. The author is indebted to Helmholtz scholar Dr. David Cohen at the University of Nebraska, Lincoln, for this citation and its translation. Dr. Cohen also stated in a telephone interview on October 14, 1991, that his research in Helmholtz's voluminous collected papers revealed no evidence of communication between Helmholtz and any of the Steinways.

289   "Von Helmholtz": letter from Helmholtz to William Steinway, October 6, 1893, as reproduced in undated S&S catalog, ca. 1896, p. 12. This letter was written while Helmholtz was in New York and after his visit to the Steinway factory. There is a semantic ambiguity here, possibly introduced by William's translation: the reference to curvature may have been to bones in the ear, but if so, then the analogy drawn by Helmholtz seems remote. Modern illustrations of the tympanum show a shape that might be loosely interpreted as similar to the curvature of an S&S soundboard. See John R. Pierce, *The Science of Musical Sound*, p. 97. For a glimpse of selected and subtle complexities of the ear, consult A. J. Hudspeth and Vladislav, "The Ear's Gears: Mechanoelectrical Transduction by Hair Cells," *Physics Today*, February 1994, pp. 22–28.

289   "Albert, for one": letter from C. F. T. Steinway to Albert Steinway, no date, ca. 1876.

289–90   "In the case of the calamity": ibid.

290   "newspaper shenanigans": C. F. T. Steinway to William, June 16, 1877.

290   "The damned artists": ibid.

290   "I know very well": ibid.

290   "At the time of his purchase": AA. The precise population of Queens County in 1870 was 73,803, as compared to 942,292 in New York County (Manhattan). *Census of New York for the Year 1875*, Table 1. Growth rate (AAGR) computed by the author using enumerated populations of Queens County for the years 1855 through 1875.

290   "A man named": WSD, October 3, 1889. William Williams was active in Long Island City politics and his brother was a New York City police inspector. In 1894 W. H. Williams appeared, pistol in hand, at a Long Island City hotel, where he expressed a desire to kill former Long Island City mayor Paddy Gleason. According to the *Times* of November 27, 1894, "a lively little scene" followed in which Gleason challenged Williams to shoot him. Apparently drunk, Williams had difficulty in pulling the gun from his pocket. This complication gave two unidentified men the chance to seize Williams and push him into the street. Gleason followed Williams outside and berated him as a coward; Gleason then tried to punch Williams, but the same two men pulled Williams back, and the ex-mayor's blow missed its mark. Williams was then hustled up the street. No charges were filed against Williams, who was formerly Long Island City's police commissioner. Williams's motivation, other than demon rum, was reported to have been remarks made by Gleason during a speech at Steinway village. W. H. Williams was also one of the incorporators of William Steinway's Bowery Bay Improvement Company. Such was one Steinway business associate in Astoria.

291   "There are no records": AA, S&S Inventory Book, 1880.

291   "A decade after": op. cit., *Labor-Management Relations at Steinway & Sons*, p. 103. The statistic of 130 residences is for the year 1881; the population at the same time was stated to be 1,200 persons.

291   "The entire Fifth Ward": NYT, July 4, 1880.

291   "Growth for the last": AA, ibid.

291   "It was not based": Leifur Magnusson, *Housing by Employers in the United States* and Stanley Buder, *Pullman: An Experiment in Industrial Order and Community Planning, 1880–1930*. These are two among many works that document the practices of owners of industrial/residential developments. Magnusson traces their American origins as far back as 1790.

292   "The single-family homes": op. cit., *Labor-Management Relations at Steinway & Sons*, p. 94. Other styles were also built; many were small by contemporary standards, with combined first and second-floor living spaces of roughly 825 square feet; this, however, was opulent compared to many of the city's tenements. Building lots were 25 feet wide by 100 feet deep, roughly the size of a Manhattan lot. William was personally involved in designing and siting the homes. The first group of six were "almost complete" on August 26, 1873, according to his diary.

292   "I consider one of the greatest evils": op. cit., Testimony of William Steinway before the United States Senate Committee on Education and Labor, p. 1087.

292–93   "During a strike meeting": *New York Sun*, March 8, 1880. There is nothing in the diary to support these contentions. Since William was engaged in what was really real estate development, it was not in his own long-term interests to cast out large numbers of Steinway Village residents, no matter what their sociopolitical views.

293   "The reference to coal miners": NYT, August 4, 1877.

293   "Myriads of Mosquitos": WSD, August 19, 1877. The phrase appeared often in William's descriptions of Astoria summers. On this trip to Astoria, William noted that he drove behind two horses "for the first time in my life."

293   "The malaria": NYT, September 26, 1877. William's children were summering at the mansion, and he visited often. The diary makes no mention of the malaria, but William was almost certainly aware of it. The outbreak appears to have been to the west and south of the village by a few miles. Long Island City, though sparsely populated, covered a large area. See also NYT, April 9 and November 12, 1875, and December 14, 1877.

293–94   "Later that same year": NYT, February 18, 1879. This is an indignant review of Long Island City politics to the date of publication.

294   "One growth industry": NYT, October 2, 1881.

294   "When the *Times* visited": ibid. Horse racing results were transmitted to these places by telegraph. In more modern parlance, they were "bookie joints." A few years later an enterprising man with a firm grasp of the potential of high technology and connections, literally, with the telegraph company succeeded in intercepting and delaying the wire reports long enough to place bets on the winners. This worked until his good luck provoked an investigation. Such was life along the Victorian version of the information superhighway.

294   "At the posh establishment": ibid.

294   "Possibly they were there": ibid.

294   "In a strange turn": ibid.

294   "This may well": NYT, June 12, 1880. By 1889, and probably well before, William was eager to show that he had no control whatsoever over the police in the village. See Minutes of the Board of Trustees of Steinway & Sons, May 2, 1889.

295   "Brother Albert": WSD, June 22, 1870. Albert accompanied William on his first visit to Bowery Bay, and was actively involved in planning and management, e.g., WSD, January 27, 1872, where Albert joins a consulting engineer to plan a floodgate on the property, and WSD, November 4, 1873, when Albert terminated the building at Astoria after the panic that fall. Albert was also involved in planning and building the mill, foundry, and keymakers' shop.

295   "Henry William Theodore Steinway": WSD, September 11, 1872. On this date William records that "Henry Steinway commenced to work at our factory yesterday" and also that "Rubinstein is much pleased with our Hall and our grand." Anton Rubinstein had arrived on the *Cuba* that day. Both events proved significant, but in very different ways.

295   "Albert limps badly": WSD, April 21, 1877.

295   "Albert appeared": WSD, April 25, 1877.

295   "Albert said to be sick": May 1, 1877.

295   "See Albert": WSD, May 5, 1877.

295   "malignant bilious": WSD, May 6, 1877.

295   "regular Typhoid fever": ibid.

295   "in 1883 its mortality rate": *Encyclopedia Britannica*, Ninth Edition, vol. XXIII, p. 676 ff.

295   "One possible route": Herbert E. Buffum, M.D., et alia, *The Household Physician: A Twentieth Century Medica*, vol. I, p. 517 ff.

295   "German cure": op. cit., *Encyclopedia Britannica*.

295   "For this two": WSD, May 6, 1877.

295   "Stop at Albert's": WSD, May 11, 1877.

295–96   "We all feel dreadful": WSD, May 13, 1877.

296   "The next morning": WSD, May 14, 1877. At his death, Albert was thirty-six years, eleven months, and twenty days old, according to the death certificate filed with the city by Dr. Schnetter. William was roughly two months past his forty-second birthday.

296   "The notices": WSD, May 15, 1877.

296   "At 6 P.M.": ibid.

296   "Come unto me": The Bible, King James Version, Mt. 11:28–30.

296   "sobbing as though": WSD, May 15, 1877.

296   "uneasy sleep": ibid.

296   "It is raining": WSD, May 16, 1877.

297   "eloquent sermon": ibid. While the funeral of his father attracted two thousand persons, Albert's service was held in the small hall, which seated roughly 350 persons. William, who clearly grieved more intensely for his brother, makes no mention of the aggregation.

297   "William and Henry W. T.": ibid.

297   "short prayer": ibid.

297   "I suffer intensely": ibid.

297   "This was one of most": ibid.

297   "You write that you feel very lonely": letter from C. F. T. Steinway to William, June 16, 1877.

297   "Our old father": ibid.

297   "How come": ibid.

297   "I will now have to finish": ibid.

297   "They were, after all": With the possible exception of the mysterious Hermann, who disappeared from the family record in the mid-1850s as an adolescent.

297   "William now found himself": WSD, June 24, 1877.

297   "received a royalty payment": WSD, April 30, 1865. The royalty was presumably still in effect. William does not record its revocation, although Albert did cut Kroeger's salary to $5,500 during the depression.

297   "By the school term": WSD, December 7, 1870, and January 13, 1871.

298   "During the summer": WSD, July 17, 1872.

298   "Shortly after": WSD, October 12, 1872.

298   "An early clue": WSD, August 22, 1872. This was apparently a group effort in attitude modification involving William, Albert and Reck.

298   "Give H. St.": WSD, December 25, 1879.

298   "William described": WSD, various dates, 1872–91.

298   "I have quite a dispute": WSD, September 23, 1872.

298   "severe reprimand": WSD, August 7, 1872.

298   "being treated": ibid.

299   "that Grandmother is dying": WSD, August 9, 1877.

299   "By eleven": ibid.

299   "The pressing task": ibid.

299   "Later that day": ibid.

299   "Saturday, the day": WSD, August 11, 1877.

299   "family now residing": ibid.

299   "At 1:10 Pastor Krusi": ibid.

299   "About this woman": City of New York, death certificate of Julianne Thiemer Steinway.

299   "By 5:30 P.M.": WSD, August 11, 1877.

299   "The next day": WSD, August 12, 1877. The decision was made while taking a boat ride.

300   "Clear cold day": WSD, December 26, 1879.

300   "Four months": WSD, April 26, 1880.

300   "After revising": WSD, June 26, 1879.

300   "It was a fast vessel": William noted distances made good; unfortunately he did not indicate if he was recording statute or nautical miles. If nautical, the *Main* was steaming at better than 13 knots.

300   "On board": WSD, July 4, 1879.

301   "Great joy": WSD, July 5, 1879.

301   "His first stop": WSD, July 7, 1880.

301   "It was run": Minutes of the Board of Trustees of Steinway & Sons, March 18, 1884, indicate that a "probable separation would take place" since Maxwell "had misapplied funds." William was authorized to settle the matter in a way that "would avoid the necessity of litigation," i.e. without creating a public scandal reflecting on Steinway business acumen. Over the next ten days Maxwell made sundry bizarre demands, such as that he be allowed to retain Steinway Hall, London, and issued threats, not the least of which was that he would sell his stock in the London branch to the British music publisher Chappell. All this came to little, for Maxwell settled for seventy-five pounds sterling. "He then takes leave of me crying," recorded William on March 28, 1884. The next day Maxwell was outbound on the steamer *Oregon*. A few days earlier William had dispatched his nephew Charles H. to tend to the London operation, effectively flanking Mr. Maxwell.

301   "A meeting with": WSD, July 8, 1880.

301   "for the first time": WSD, July 12, 1880.

301   "Tel[egraph] to R.R.": ibid.

301   "his sister Doretta": WSD, July 24, 1880.

301   "Visit the Ranfts": WSD, July 20, 1880.

301   "The next day": WSD, July 21, 1880.

301   "Take dinner": ibid.

301–2   "We drive out": WSD, July 24, 1880.

302   " 'George,' wrote William": WSD, July 25, 1880. George may have been a troubled young man. On September 20, 1879, William told George about the divorce "and what she did," more than three years after the fact. William noted that George had "come to nearly the same conclusion,"

raising the possibility that the son witnessed some aspect of his mother's infidelities.

302   "he saw Ernestine Oaks": ibid. At least one of two meetings may have been accidental.

302   "Julius Schiedmeyer": WSD, July 26, 1880.

302   "He called upon": WSD, July 27, 1880. Dr. Paul was out of town.

302   "*Pianiste* Anna Mehlig": ibid.

302   "answer to a crazy letter": WSD, July 28, 1880.

302   "Checking into his hotel": WSD, August 6, 1880.

302   "After dinner": WSD, August 8, 1880.

302   "After the second": WSD, August 11, 1880.

302   "dispensation": WSD, August 12, 1880. The dispensation was granted on August 13, 1880. It emerges that George lost a marriage-related document from Theodore, and William had to obtain a duplicate. Those with an inclination to the psychoanalytic can speculate as to George's state of mind.

302   "William bought": WSD, August 15, 1880.

302   "The wedding took": WSD, August 16, 1880.

302   "Splendid floral": ibid.

302   "Elizabeth Karoline Ranft": Consular papers of Elizabeth Karoline Ranft Steinway, 1880. These appear to be the functional equivalent of what today would be called a passport, although photographs were not then in use. While in Vienna on his honeymoon, William visited local pianomakers Streicher and Ehrbar on August 20, 1880, but did not call on Theodore's archrival Bosendorfer.

302   "the ladies call": WSD, August 22, 1880.

302–3   "Less than two weeks": WSD, August 31, 1880.

303   "Give her five pounds": ibid.

303   "laid up with Rheumatism": WSD, September 3, 1880.

303   "Ellie and George were seasick": WSD, September 2, 1880. The *Main* was making good up to 360 miles per day, fully 15 knots westbound, and the voyage took about ten days.

303   "When the *Main* reached": WSD, September 10, 1880.

303   "driven to my house": WSD, September 10, 1880.

303   "More than a month": WSD, October 13, 1880.

303   "Nearly six weeks": WSD, October 23, 1880. He also attended a concert at Steinway Hall that evening at which Franz Rummel performed.

303   "One and one-half months": WSD, November 3, 1880.

303   "preside at meeting": WSD, December 7, 1880.

22. WITHOUT COMMENT ON THE ANIMUS

304   "In the busy throbbing": *New York Herald*, December 29, 1892.

304   "leg torn off": ibid.

304   "both eyes destroyed": ibid.

304   "Italian": ibid.

304   "Head nearly amputated": ibid.

304   "a piece of wood": ibid.

305   "When the New York & Long Island": ibid.

305   "and the plan was": "Certificate of the New York and Long Island Railroad

Company," July 29, 1891. The phrase "one account" refers to this document, which may be deemed official, as it was filed with the state. Various newspapers report other proposed routes that conflict, mostly with respect to the eastern and western extremities of the line.

305 "It's murder": *New York World*, December 29, 1892. The *World* at this time was the liveliest of the Manhattan dailies. Innovative page layouts, copious, well-drafted illustrations; and crisp copy featuring murder, mayhem, greed, and corruption, sprinkled with sex whenever feasible, made the *World* the seminal ancestor of today's tabloid television. The *World*, however, was boundlessly more artful and creative, as when it ran an illustrated feature on a do-it-yourself suicide machine that automatically interred its user. The headline for the tunnel explosion read: "DEATH IN DYNAMITE."

305 "For a two-block radius": *New York Daily Tribune*, December 29, 1892.

305 "Horses were knocked": *New York Times*, December 29, 1892.

305 "The scene was": AA, based on examination of illustrations appearing in the *World*, op. cit.

305 "The public are clamoring": *New York Times*, December 30, 1892.

305 "*New York Tribune*": op. cit., *New York Daily Tribune*.

306 "Hearing of the tunnel": WSD, December 28, 1892.

306 "William quickly": WSD, December 29, 1892.

306 "the tunnel company": op. cit., *New York Herald*.

306 "William was not about": WSD, August 13 and 14, 1892. William authorized the payment of one month's expenses of $3,000 at this time in the form of a loan to the New York & Long Island Railroad Company. While his diary indicates that he made attempts to attract capital to the project, none were successful. It is therefore inferred, since there is no evidence of other funding, that at the time of the explosion he was still underwriting construction costs. William first visited the tunnel shaft on October 15, 1892, after returning from Europe, where he spent time at the Wiesbaden baths seeking a cure for his rheumatism. The same day, but after the explosion, a "supplemental" contract was signed with the Inter-Island Construction Company, so it was apparently William's immediate intent to continue tunnel construction. The cause of the tunnel explosion is not entirely clear. It was standard practice to thaw dynamite by covering it with sand and heating it in a steam box to prepare for the day's blasting. Shortly before the dynamite was to be removed from the steam box, it exploded. This explanation was given by Peter McEntee, the foreman in charge of the dynamite, who was blown through a fence by the blast and then charged with manslaughter by Long Island City authorities. (The charges were later dropped.) Had the tunnel been completed during his lifetime, William's extensive Queens real estate holdings would have likely appreciated immensely, a probability he certainly understood.

306 "The dream": WSD, April 17, 1883.

306 "The L.I.C.S.R.R.": Vincent Seyfried, *The New York and Queens County Railway* and the *Steinway Lines*, map, p. 7, photocopy of apparently self-published manuscript.

306 "In public documents": WSD, May 2, 1883.

306 "able to confuse": op. cit., p. 1 ff.

307   "It was Henry Ziegler": WSD, June 6, 1883.

307   "This one was called": WSD, June 16, 1883.

307   "The newly formed": AA, WSD, June 23, 1883.

307   "There was already": map, "Steinway, Long Island," undated, ca. 1883, and Minutes of the Board of Trustees of Steinway & Sons, November 19, 1879.

307   "All inhabitants": op. cit., reverse side, map, "Steinway, Long Island."

307   "The school was very": "Illustrated Pamphlet on the Founding and Development of Steinway, N.Y.," undated, ca. 1896, pp. 19 and 23. This brochure dates the Fifth Ward school as being constructed in 1877 and its capacity as one thousand students. It may be that the capacity was originally five hundred students, as claimed on the reverse side of the map, op. cit.

307   "This was an exercise": AA, Francis A. Walker, *Compendium of the Tenth Census (June 1, 1880)*, Part 1, Table XLII.

307   "In 1880 the entire": ibid., Part 1, Table XIX.

307   "The city provided": WSD, March 5, 1885. On this date William was mediating a crisis between the teachers and Long Island City politicians, who wanted to replace the women with their own needy relatives.

307   "William Steinway was": op. cit., Minutes of the Board, October 26, 1889.

307   "On more than one": e.g., WSD, June 16, 1893.

307   "Later a free": ibid., op. cit., Minutes of the Board, October 26, 1889. This was stocked with donated volumes from the library of C. F. Theodore Steinway.

307   "To all residents": op. cit., map.

307–8   "Neat Two or Three": ibid.

308   "The attention of manufacturers": ibid.

308   "Just four years before": S&S catalog, 1888, p. 16. The cases for all pianos were built at Astoria beginning in 1879, then shipped to the Park Avenue plant. Actions were also made at Astoria, a practice that drove C. F. Theodore to tirades. His concern was the humid sea air and its adverse effect on precision machining and assembly of small wooden parts, of which there were vast numbers in each piano action.

308   "That Steinway & Sons": ibid. An advantage of the Astoria waterfront location was the ability to store huge logs wet. This prevented the cracking of the logs, known by lumber men as "checking." Near the point of harvest, the logs were lashed and nailed together in huge rafts, sails were run up, and the rafts were floated and sailed to Astoria, presumably from northern forests. The crews manning the rafts built shelters on them and sometimes brought their families for voyages that often took weeks. Lumber movement on the St. Lawrence River involved rafts city blocks long, and old engravings of the S&S manufactory show similarly immense rafts immediately offshore.

308   "Although difficult to imagine": AA, *Compendium of the Tenth Census*, Part I, Table XLV.

308   "Of the sixty": ibid.

308   "The status of metropolitan": ibid.

308   "The Manhattan farms": ibid.

308   "The four hundred acres": AA, ibid.

308   "Deducting the cost": AA, ibid., and WSD, September 6, 1870.

309   "William noted with great": WSD, August 5, 1883. On August 12, 1883, again a Sunday, gross proceeds were $142, setting another record and implying 2,840 nickel fares. Since most Sunday fares were likely visitors, it becomes possible to compute that between 1,200 and 1,400 persons were sojourning at Steinway and environs on summer Sundays.

     Fares were set as a condition of the charter, usually granted by the municipality, and could not easily be raised. No mayor or city council would risk the wrath of the electorate by granting increases for the days Monday through Saturday. The occasional horse railroad was able to extract a ten-cent Sunday fare, particularly those that serviced the Long Island grave-yards. It was common practice to combine a cemetery visit with a picnic for the whole family. While the children frolicked among the tombstones and the adult women talked, the men might slip away to one of the dram shops near the graveyard, there to satisfy a thirst or other needs.

309   "Had William": AA, S&S inventory book, 1883.

309   "When Albert Weber": New York Supreme Court, *Weber* v. *Mayer*, et al. This case may represent one of the rarer events in the annals of the court; among the et alia was Albert J. Weber, Jr., and this meant that a mother had sued her son. The failure to distinguish between the Weber firm and the man, Albert J. Weber, Jr., was at the heart of the matter: Albert J. had dispersed substantial sums on the traditional delights of wine, women, and song. Mr. Weber's entertainment expenses (his first wife accused him of spending their wedding night in two whorehouses) exceeded his income. This caused Albert J. to expropriate cash from the firm, essentially draining its liquidity. When creditors foreclosed on Mr. Weber personally, the scan-dal reflected on the firm and closed it temporarily. Shorn of her $100,000 inheritance and the $50,000 due each of her two daughters, Mrs. Weber asked the court to intervene. The Weber firm remained under the jurisdic-tion of the court for many years, but there is no discernible evidence in the voluminous record that Mrs. Weber or her daughters ever received their full inheritance. The lawyers, referees, and receivers received their full pay, and Albert J. Weber was somehow able to continue his dissolute ways.

309   "Another advantage": WSD, August 8, 1883. After reading a report in *Dun's Weekly* that *Music and Drama* was mortgaged to Albert Weber in the amount of $34,210, William dispatched Tretbar to the County Clerk's Office. There another mortgage on Eagle Printing in the amount of $12,740 was recorded, and Tretbar discovered it. The combined mortgages of Freund to Weber were in the amount of $46,950. It is likely that some of the funds diverted from Martha Weber were lent to Freund.

309   "Mr. Weber": ibid.

310   "One of Freund's earliest": *Music & Drama*, January 13, 1883.

310   "As the money": ibid.

310   "Freund claimed": ibid.

310   "the firm is tenaciously": ibid.

310   "Without comment on the *animus*": *Music & Drama*, January 20, 1883.

311   "William's response, sniffed": ibid.

311   "Although neither Freund": AA, S&S inventory book, 1856–65. William

gave very serious consideration to having Freund arrested for libel; see WSD, January 24, 1883. Though the record is far from clear, it may be that William covertly arranged an interruption of the circulation of Freund's paper with the cooperation of the news distributor. Freund was likely spared a libel arrest on the Belmont piece when he took up the Nordheimer-Steinway Hamburg connection. William did not seem eager to have piano buyers understand this arrangement.

311   "blackmail": WSD, March 9 and 13, 1883.
311   "The tale involved": *Music & Drama*, January 20, 1883.
311   "old and battle-scarred": ibid.
312   "As to how far": ibid.
312   "As one of the results": *Music & Drama*, February 3, 1883.
312   "Entirely unknown": op. cit., Minutes of the Board, December 24, 1889. In this meeting William offered to sell the *Pianofabrik* to S&S.
312   "To be perfectly independent": op. cit., *Music & Drama*.
313   "shipping weekly": ibid.
313   "A few of them": ibid.
313   "Readers of *Music & Drama*": *Music & Drama*, February 3 and 10, 1883.
313   "Messrs. Steinway have": *Music & Drama*, February 3, 1883.
313   "More Light": *Music & Drama*, March 10, 1883.
313   "CAUGHT—The Steinways": ibid.
314   "I can state but the truth": ibid.
314   "Freund out": WSD, March 7, 1883. This was written in reference to the *Music & Drama* article dated March 10.
314   "thoughtlessly": WSD, March 9, 1883. The employee, a man identified only as Gruber, was asked to resign. In less than a month Gruber obtained a job as a reporter. WSD, April 8, 1883.
314   "A state of musical terrorism": Emil Liebling was closely allied with the Kimball company in Chicago for many years. William Wallace Kimball, it may be recollected, was a major buyer of pianos built by J. P. Hale, who died in 1883. Where Kimball was obtaining pianos at the time Liebling wrote *Music & Drama* cannot be determined, but Kimball did not begin manufacturing his own pianos until 1888. See Van Allen Bradley, *Music for the Millions*, p. 109, for a truckling account.
314   "J. C. Freund has no blackmail": WSD, March 14, 1883.
314   "BROKEN AT LAST": *Music & Drama*, April 14, 1883.
314   "So there has been": ibid.
314   "beautiful day": e.g., WSD, April 4, 1883.
314   "Having much fun": WSD, April 5, 1883.
314   "Baby Willie": WSD, April 19, 1883.
315   "The policy of the house": *Music & Drama*, July 7, 1883.
315   "Within a few months": WSD, October 23; November 27 and 28, 1883.
315   "William snapped up": WSD, May 17, 1884.
315   "about a week's worth": AA, S&S inventory book, 1883.
315   "William was not long": WSD, July 17, 1884.
315   "The *New York Times*": NYT, May 15, 1884.
315   "Feel perfectly well": WSD, May 15, 1884.
315   "Based on the results": AA, S&S inventory book, 1883.

315   "The national financial carnage": NYT, December 30, 1883, and January 1, 1885.

315–16   "In less than two years": WSD, years 1883–85.

316   "By early 1885": WSD, January 28, 1885. The acquisition and consolidation of the roads was no minor task; it required Long Island City aldermanic approvals, the surrender of a franchise by a reluctant seller, political machinations at Albany, at least one court action, and the persuasion of a number of stock- and bondholders.

316   "immense pit": WSD, April 1, 1885.

316   "On paper": WSD, March 9, 1885.

316   "When the trial": WSD, June 26, 1889. That the gas company was now a valuable asset became clear on March 22, 1889, when the Standard Oil Company offered William $300,000 for it and threatened to open a competitive gasworks. William did not sell to Standard Oil.

316   "Several rabid socialists": WSD, April 1, 1885.

316   "Executives": WSD, April 5, 1885.

316   "Menzl tells me": WSD, April 11, 1885.

316   "pleasure ground": NYT, July 12, 1896. This multipage story, heavily illustrated and incandescent with praise, is William's media masterpiece, the capstone of a life in print.

316   "wooded shores and natural bluffs": ibid.

317   "Bowery Bay Improvement Company": WSD, April 30 and May 1, 1886. The original incorporators were William, George Ehret, the Long Island City politician William H. Williams, Henry A. Cassebeer, William's nephew, and William's son George. The full legal name was the Bowery Bay *Building and* Improvement Company, but William usually used the short form.

317   "*respectable* people": WSD, June 20, 1886 and often thereafter.

317   "heavy riding": WSD, May 30, 1886.

317   "The bathhouse": WSD, June 6, 1886.

317   "Street railway": WSD, June 6, 1886.

317   "At the rate": AA, WSD, June 21, 1886. This was the first weekend that Bowery Bay was officially open to the public.

317   "immense crowds": WSD, June 20, 1886. From contemporary maps it may be learned that the thirsty celebrants of pastoral pleasures had to stagger but several hundred feet to reach the village.

317   "impudent roughs": op. cit., NYT.

317   "I drive them off": WSD, July 5, 1886. William does not divulge whether he merely brandished his weapon or actually discharged it. Since this was the Fourth of July weekend, the sound of gunfire would have been of interest to none but the target. The trespassers on William's beach had come from nearby Rikers Island, not yet a prison.

317   "When the bathing pavilion": WSD, August 23, 1886.

317–18   "Hottest day": WSD, July 17, 1886.

318   "Less than two weeks": WSD, July 18, 1886.

318   "After the pavilion manager": August 12 and 13, 1886. The violent and embezzling managers were replaced with a Steinway family member, Henry Cassebeer.

318   "Later that summer": WSD, August 21, 1886. William had taken a committee of men, apparently the planners of the annual S&S picnic, to Bowery Bay on July 18, 1886.

318   "The picnic of our men": ibid.

318   "all of Long Island City": WSD, August 28, 1886. By this time railway receipts were hovering in the range of $3,000 per week, implying that at least thirty thousand round trips were made each week, with at least half of that traffic on Sundays.

318   "More land": WSD, September 3, 6 and 7, 1886. The Bowery Bay capitalization was increased to $250,000 at this time.

318   "Grand Pier": WSD, May 29, 1887. Cost and dimensions of the pier from NYT, July 12, 1896.

318   "William bought a half-interest": WSD, March 24, 1887. William first became a stockholder in the East River Ferry Company on this date and purchased the New York & College Point Ferry Company in 1890, thereby consolidating Astoria service.

318   "Traffic on the street": AA, WSD entries 1886–91.

318   "Have much trouble": WSD, March 26, 1890.

319   "I have serious apprehensions": WSD, March 18, 1896.

319   "In 1865": Stock certificate in the possession of Henry Z. Steinway.

319   "Under his guidance": WSD, October 17, 1873. William wrote: "Have good talk with Theodore. He fears Albert's machinery improvements more than anything else."

319   "In a report filed": Joseph D. Weeks, *Report of the Statistics of Wages in Manufacturing Industries*, p. 292.

319   "Steinway manufacturing operations": William probably believed that there were efficiencies in automation, notwithstanding that the labor content in the instrument did not obviously decrease. One factor here was the vertical integration at Steinway. Milling lumber beginning with logs and pouring cast iron were not conventionally considered a part of pianomaking. S&S also fabricated most of its own hardware, going so far as to make their own screws. This integration had two benefits: first, there was a greater independence from outside suppliers and the assurance of supply—no small matter during the panics that destroyed thousands of firms every few years. In addition to independence, there was the second benefit—no less important—of being able to maintain absolute quality control. The price paid for assured high-quality supply was probably low efficiency. William wrote in his "Illustrated Pamphlet of the Founding and Development of Steinway, N.Y." (p. 12) that machinery had replaced the "hand labor of at least 900 workmen." This claim seems improbable.

320   "He had likely seen": D. W. Fostle, *Speedboat*, p. 9 ff.

320   "These early engines": ibid.

320   "One was a licensee": ibid.

320   "Gottlieb Daimler": ibid., p. 17 ff.

320   "Daimler and Maybach": ibid.

320   "It was first used": ibid.

320   "But William's diary": WSD, August 17, 1888.

320   "a long talk": WSD, August 22, 1888.

321   "neither version": WSD, February 2, 1889.

321 "It was April 30 1890": WSD, April 30, 1890.

321 "The rent paid": Minutes of the Board of Trustees of Steinway & Sons, November 9, 1889. This was for a building of approximately 2,500 square feet.

321 "We have started": catalog, Daimler Motor Company, 1891. The catalog was clearly written by William.

321 "especially adapted": ibid.

322 "Printing Presses": ibid.

322 "250 feet South": ibid.

322 "at last a demand": WSD, February 22, 1891.

322 "Motor Quadricycle": op. cit., Daimler catalog.

323 "He did so": Leon Mandel, *American Cars*, p. 29 ff.

323 "It would be eight": ibid. Ford built his first quadricycle in 1896, eight years after William acquired American rights to Daimler's inventions. By 1899 Ford's first company failed.

323 "With the slightly": WSD, January 30, 1892.

323 "and by 1893": AA, catalog, Daimler Motor Company, 1893.

323 "The least expensive": ibid.

323 "The most expensive": ibid.

323 "By late 1893": WSD, October 18 and 25, 1893. Gottlieb Daimler himself worked on this vehicle during a visit to America. It was likely built at Daimler's Canstatt works in Germany and shipped to Astoria. Sadly, William does not indicate its fate, for it would have been one of the earliest motor vehicles to operate on American roads.

323 "He must, however": op. cit., *Speedboat*, p. 17 ff. This contains an analysis of the relative merits of competing prime movers, e.g. naphtha, electric, and steam. By any rational measure, the Daimler engine was superior.

323 "A large display": op. cit., "Illustrated Pamphlet of the Founding and Development of Steinway, N.Y.," p. 28, contains William's version of the event. The boat was claimed to make the fantastic speed of 16 mph. There was even a Steinway raceboat, 42 feet long with a 10 horsepower engine. "We are now ready to demonstrate to persons interested in this kind of sport, what we can do in speed, inviting anything of her size afloat to a friendly contest," wrote William in the 1893 Daimler catalog. Under the rules of naval architecture as then known, a vessel's waterline length was a basic determinant of her speed. This was why William conditioned his challenge with the phrase "anything of her size." As a displacement hull, *Our Racer*, as the boat was called, should have made about 10 statute miles per hour.

323 "The summer of 1895": WSD, June 14, 1895.

323 "Daimler Motor Company": WSD, August 2, 1895.

323 "Ever optimistic": For an illustration of the marina, see NYT, July 12, 1896.

323 "Taking a page": WSD, October 3, 1896.

323 "Articles about": e.g., *Horseless Age*, April 1896.

323 "A thick book": *What Owners of Daimler Motors Say*, ca. January 1896.

23. YOU ACT MOST UNWISELY

325   "Harbuckel now accuses": letter from William Steinway to C. F. Theodore Steinway, August 31, 1887.

325   "I must confess": ibid.

326   "In America": Nancy J. Groce, *Instrument Making in New York City During the Eighteenth and Nineteenth Centuries*, p. 392.

326   "Jonas Chickering": Alfred Dolge, *Pianos and Their Makers*, vol. 2, p. 50 ff, politely traces the corporate peregrinations of some lesser-known Chickerings. NYT, February 16, 1893, reports litigation among family members alleging embezzlement of company funds. The *Times* page one headline read "GRAVE CRIMES CHARGED. G. H. Chickering would brand his brother a thief."

326   "Napoleon J. Haines": New York Court of Common Pleas, *Haines* v. *Haines*. This action alleged that a son of N. J. Haines first looted his father's company, then set up a competing Haines piano company. Papers are incomplete, so the outcome cannot be determined.

326   "Maxwell's proposal": WSD, August 29, 1877, and September 8, 1877.

326   "William himself": "American Musical Instruments": in Chauncey Depew, ed., *One Hundred Years of American Commerce*, p. 509.

326   "It is therefore": letter, C. F. Theodore Steinway to William, April 17, 1877. (Year is author's estimate based on content.)

326   "Maxwell, provisioned": AA, S&S inventory book, 1877–78.

327   "William evaluated": WSD, July 7, 1880. "Visit St. Hall am pleased," wrote William.

327   "By the close of 1880": AA, S&S inventory book, 1880.

327   "It was in March": WSD, March 28, 1880. About a year earlier, on March 5, 1879, his birthday, William had written: "Beautiful day, my Rheumatism nearly gone, to store early, letter from Theodore of February 20th, in which to my horror he says that he has offered 45,000 Marks for factory . . ." This raises the material possibility that William was, at best, an unwilling participant in the Hamburg venture. He conceivably feared the defection of Theodore, who may have been quite willing to once again make pianos in Germany independently.

      On June 17, 1877 Theodore wrote William that he wanted to make cheap pianos, and that he could make much money with the name Theodore Steinweg. William's response is lost, as are many intervening letters between the two men, so a definitive answer on the circumstances that resulted in the launch of manufacture at Hamburg will likely never be known.

327   "The lengthy and bitter": WSD, March 1–30, 1880.

327   "Simultaneously": WSD, March 17, 1880.

327   "William later claimed": *Music and Drama*, February 2, 1883.

327   "Often in contention": WSD, March 5, 1879. On his birthday, William had written: "Beautiful day, my Rheumatism nearly gone, to store early, letter from Theodore of February 20th, in which to my horror he says that he has offered 45,000 Marks for factory . . ." This raises the material possibility that William was, at best, an unwilling participant in the Hamburg venture. He conceivably feared the defection of Theodore, who may

have been quite willing to once again make pianos in Germany independently.

In April 1877 Theodore wrote William that he wanted to make cheap pianos, and that he could make money with the name Theodore Steinweg. William's response is lost, as are many intervening letters between the two men, so a definitive answer on the circumstances that resulted in the launch of the Hamburg *fabrik* will likely never be known. Theo lived in Braunschweig, so he was not managing daily operations at the *fabrik*.

328   "Via William unceasing promotion": op. cit. letter from C. F. Theodore Steinway to William Steinway, April 17, 1877. This too was resented by Theodore, who felt that advertising the Steinway system of pianomaking helped their many imitators more than it did Steinway & Sons. Loesser, *Men, Women and Pianos*, pp. 589–90, attributes the success of the German piano industry to imitation of Steinway & Sons, and cites the instruments of Bechstein and Bluthner as cases in point.

328   "Hamburg manufacturing": Henry Z. Steinway, "Arthur von Holwede" (biographical memorandum).

328   "To store at": WSD, March 28, 1880.

328   "After fifteen years": op. cit., "Arthur von Holwede."

328   "William noted": AA, WSD, June 28, 1886, and March 26, 1886.

329   "By 1888": WSD, December 31, 1888.

329   "been in town": Minutes of the Board of Trustees of Steinway & Sons, March 18, 1884. See also a note for page 301.

329   "At the same trustees' ": ibid.

329   "Embezzlers, forgers": WSD, November 30, 1889, tells the tale of Delahanty, a Long Island City alderman, who also ran William's railroads. Mr. Delahanty, William believed, sold seven railway horses and "pocketed the money." On another occasion Delahanty tried to shoot William H. Williams, who himself later tried to shoot Paddy Gleason. Such was Long Island City politics. Somehow dodging the bullets, William had business and political relationships with all three.

A truly bizarre case involved Gustav Milair, aka Miller, the younger brother of Ernestine Miller Steinway Oaks. Milair had tried to cash a forged $5,000 note drawn on S&S. When William confronted Milair, the forger pulled out a gun and threatened to shoot himself. Showing the steely nerve of a character in a dime western but probably acquired in Long Island City, William disarmed Milair. WSD, July 18, 1883.

329   "In another instance": S&S confidential circular, February 12, 1876.

329   "In time William learned": NYT, February 4, 7, and 8, 1889, details the "antics of a bogus count" claiming to be a Steinway relation. The monetary losses were minor, if not trivial.

330   "Henry Steinway a good talking to": WSD, August 22, 1872.

330   "Henry W. T.": e.g., WSD, September 11, 1872, *et. seq.*

330   "Kroeger tells me": WSD, June 24, 1877.

330   "I have quite a dispute": WSD, September 23, 1877.

330   "That same year Kroeger's salary": WSD, January 7, 1877. William's arrangement with Kroeger was secret and brought his total salary to $5,500. This was an immense sum, perhaps twice what William's nephews were later paid. If the royalty negotiated with Kroeger after Charles's death was

still in effect, then Henry Kroeger would have had additional income of at least $2,000 per year. Unfortunately, the very important role of Henry Kroeger at S&S is lost in the fog of time.

330   "At age fifty-four": WSD, October 1, 1879. The business, which initially also rented pianos, was located by 1880 at 24 Union Square, not far from Steinway & Sons. It is unclear when, exactly, Kroeger began making his own pianos.

330   "Pass Kroeger": WSD, September 22, 1887. One reason for the breach in the relationship was that Kroeger or his agents now claimed that Kroeger had been crucial in the design of S&S instruments and had invented many features that the Steinways claimed as their own. William took this seriously enough to write to his dealers on January 1, 1886, and strongly deny a significant role for Kroeger. William also claimed that Kroeger did not resign but was fired, a statement clearly contradicted by William's own diary. On March 13, 1879, Henry Kroeger met with William, and after William refused to restore his salary to $6,000, gave one month's notice. William asked Kroeger to stay until Theodore returned from Europe, and Kroeger remained for about five months.

     William's circular characterized Kroeger's first pianos as "cheap and trashy" stencil instruments, then went on to demean his former employee's current output as an "unseasoned conglomeration from a dozen different owners of cheap workshops." In a discussion by the author with piano technician Bill Garlick, who owned a nineteenth-century Kroeger grand, Mr. Garlick described the piano as "just like a Steinway" and of "excellent construction and workmanship." Mr. Garlick, himself a former Steinway & Sons employee, was unaware that the Kroeger who built his piano was also a Steinway employee for nearly a quarter century. The reader with computer experience will understand that Henry Kroeger built Steinway clones.

331   "Have a scene": WSD, August 26, 1879.

331   "Reprimand both": WSD, December 18, 1880.

331   "Have a fatherly": WSD, February 19, 1885.

331   "H.W.T. Steinway refusing": WSD, May 4, 1885.

331   "insane ideas": WSD, March 29, 1887.

331   "The house was doing": AA, S&S inventory book, 1880–90.

331   "Henry (who never married)": WSD, June 30, 1879, and Minutes of the Board of Trustees of Steinway & Sons, February 12, 1891, when a resolution was passed to charge rent for those occupying company property. Surrounding events make clear that this was directed at Henry W. T. Steinway. The day before, William warned H.W.T. that he risked being fired.

331   "To his credit": AA, Minutes of the Board of Trustees of Steinway & Sons, 1880–90.

331   "Have the most exciting": WSD, March 29, 1887.

331   "The matter of 'valuations' ": AA, S&S inventory book, 1886.

331   "insulting manner": April 17, 1887.

332   "bitterly denouncing": WSD, August 30, 1887.

332   "This Mr. Cassebeer": WSD, September 8 and 19, 1887.

332   "Stand more and more": WSD, October 10, 1887.

332   "Cassebeer has the good sense": WSD, September 24, 1877. That same night William played skat with Cassebeer.

332   "a good talking to": WSD, September 21, 1887. Apparently William hired Delahanty before Cassebeer resigned.

332   "Compel Henry": WSD, October 5, 1887.

332   "For more than a decade": AA, S&S inventory book, 1880–07.

332   "It will be inevitable": letter from William to C. F. Theodore, August 31, 1887. This was written aboard the *Saale*, bound for Europe. The translator is unknown; copy provided by Henry Z. Steinway.

332   "Unfortunately": ibid.

333   "You see": ibid.

333   "Henry Steinway is out": letter from C. F. Theodore to William, September 12, 1887. The translator is unknown; copy provided by Henry Z. Steinway.

333   "I would like": ibid.

333   "In regard to Harbuckel's": letter from C. F. Theodore to William, September 13, 1887. The translator is unknown; copy provided by Henry Z. Steinway.

333   ". . . I only wonder": ibid.

333   "If we paid him out": ibid.

333   "I can only tell you": ibid.

333   "can only have been said": letter from Frederick T. Steinway to C. F. Theodore Steinway, September 16, 1887. The translator is unknown; copy provided by Henry Z. Steinway.

334   "I look at it": ibid.

334   "embitters": WSD, December 2, 1887.

334   "The dark view": S&S inventory book, 1887.

334   "I go for Henry": WSD, April 28, 1888.

334   "Unite upon proposition": WSD, June 24, 1888.

334   "We are unalterably opposed": WSD, July 10, 1888.

334   "Can we use Mexican": WSD, July 31, 1868.

334   "Don't know Mexican": WSD, August 3, 1888.

334   "The year 1888": WSD, December 30, 1888.

335   "Unspeakable mental suffering": ibid.

335   "In the spring": WSD, April 17, 1888.

335   "not handsome": WSD, July 28, 1887.

335   "I conduct Paula": WSD, November 12, 1888.

335   "do not lessen": WSD, December 30, 1888.

335   "the internal dissension": ibid.

335   "one Judge Brady": WSD, January 2, 1889.

335   "While Theodore was": WSD, January 20, 1889.

335   "We agree": WSD, January 21, 1889.

335   "sell at 200": WSD, February 12, 1889.

335   "Theodore's price": AA, S&S inventory book, 1888. Theodore's share of S&S was precisely 26.7 percent. In more modern terms, Theodore was asking about ten times earnings for his equity in a firm that operated with *net* margins on U.S. operations in the range of 25 to 30 percent. His price was about 1.6 times book. Of the book value, the Astoria real estate was now down to 15.8 percent.

335   "Go to store": WSD, March 26, 1889.

335   "William ordered": WSD, March 26, 1889.

336   "My many years anticipation": WSD, March 29, 1889. The same Koch housed Ernestine's children more than twenty years before and was involved on William's behalf in this crisis, apparently serving as his Braunschweig counsel.

336   "See to my horror": WSD, April 12, 1889.

336   "Brunswick authorities": WSD, September 27, 1889.

336   "Theodore had applied": Superior Court, New York County, May 7, 1872.

336   "It has actually come to pass": letter from Werner Reidemeister to Arthur von Holwede, December 11, 1889.

336   "William had arranged": WSD, November 22, 1889. Here William writes letters on the "unfortunate Braunschweig and Hamburg affair."

336   "When the coffins arrived": WSD, January 14, 1890. Among the many elaborate requirements was the need to obtain special zinc coffins, then disguise them so they could not be recognized as such. The bodies were carried in cabins on the steamer, not as freight.

337   "It was Christmas Eve day": Minutes of the Board of Trustees of Steinway & Sons, December 24, 1889.

337   "He proposed to sell": ibid.

337   "He also offered": ibid.

337   "To make matters": ibid.

337   "Cash was not": ibid.

337   "To further sweeten": ibid.

337   "Theodore and William": S&S inventory book, 1888.

337   "In the year 1889": WSD, December 31, 1889.

337   "and returned": AA, WSD, December 25, 1889. Estimated, based on eleven months' earnings. As usual, William was at the hall working on Christmas Day.

337   "In effect, the nephews": AA, ibid. Offsetting this to some extent was the market reality that Hamburg pianos sold for roughly one-third less than New York pianos.

337   "That same year": AA, op. cit., S&S inventory book.

337   "I myself am now": letter from William to C. F. Theodore, August 31, 1887.

338   "lengthy discussion": WSD, December 26, 1889.

338   "fairly well": ibid.

338   "he makes no objection": ibid.

338   "After a hot fight": ibid.

338   "Henry W. T.": WSD, December 31, 1889.

338   "By accepting an appointment": WSD, April 9, 1890. It was apparently not a conflict of interest, by the mores of the time, for William to serve the public as a rapid transit commissioner at the same time that he was an investor in a private company building a tunnel that was a part of the system. Though this offered obvious advantages, the voluminous and fractious public record contains no criticism of William's dual role.

339   "As early as 1870": WSD, May 10, 1870. The same day he declined to run for alderman, William discharged a boy named Adolph Bothner for frequenting gambling saloons.

339   "Ottendorfer": ibid.

339   "William was also": WSD, October 7, 1872. On this date William learned that his resignation from the Committee of Seventy was not accepted. The committee played an important and, of course, controversial role in investigating corruption. The inquiry involved, on both sides, persons who played or would play some role in William's life. One target was the Nineteenth Ward alderman Terence Farley; another was Judge Cardozo, to whom William had personally supplied a piano and ball tickets; a survivor of the epidemic of rectitude, though impeached, was Judge Barnard, who had ruled on certain matters in the Oaks case. Judge Barrett, who set Tweed's bail at an enormous $3 million, would seek William's influence with the German bloc in a future election. John Hoffman, New York's governor and William Havemeyer, soon to be mayor, were or would be members of the Liederkranz. George Jones, editor of the *New York Times*, was energetically anti-Tweed and generous with his coverage of Steinway & Sons. Future governor and presidential candidate Samuel Tilden would soon be William's Gramercy Park neighbor. Why William tried to resign will forever remain an intriguing mystery. Perhaps the most bizarre link to the future involved attorney Wheeler Peckham, an aggressive prosecutor of Boss Tweed. Nearly a quarter century later William Steinway reduced his own examination by Peckham to a series of bon mots as a courtroom full of reporters and even the judge laughed with William and at Counselor Peckham.

      Some sources state that it was Theodore Steinway who sat on the Committee of Seventy. This is incontrovertibly erroneous.

339   "Oswald Ottendorfer": Ottendorfer appears in William's diary as early as 1862. He was nine years older than William.

339   "After a few years": NYT, December 16, 1900.

339   "Ottendorfer was a": ibid.

339   "Ottendorfer established": ibid.

340   "Ottendorfer's $300,000": ibid.

340   "Park Com. McLean": WSD, October 15–20, 1885.

340   "I promise to go": ibid.

340   "he fully approves": ibid.

340   "Apparently a consummate": WSD, July 17, 1865.

340   "Taking a sleeper": op. cit., WSD, October 15–20.

340   "Rushing between": ibid.

340   "When Oswald": ibid.

340   "The next day Maxwell": ibid.

340   "The truce": WSD, November 4, 1885.

340   "Among these were": WSD, April 30, 1885.

340–41   "The day after": WSD, January 23, 1885.

341   "In another case": WSD, November 24 and 26, 1886. The dinner lasted until two in the morning. Loyalty beyond death was another aspect of Van Brunt's character. Nine years after William died, Van Brunt, now a judge with the Appellate Division of the Supreme Court, was a minority of one when he wrote a dissenting opinion favoring the Steinway family in an action against William's estate. It was his last case, as Van Brunt died after writing the opinion. NYT, June 10, 1905.

341   "I have a long": WSD, December 20, 1885. Presumably the post of inspector

general, despite its imposing title, involved nothing beyond the capacity of a young man, nor did the duties impinge greatly on the welfare of the state's citizens.

341   "President Cleveland": WSD, January 8–14, 1886. Ottendorfer received a letter from Cleveland, and communicated the offer to William, "which I of course have to decline."

341   "President Cleveland consulted": WSD, June 13 and 22, 1887.

341   "William also pushed": e.g., WSD, May 8, 1888.

341   "William Steinway did not": The key word here is *direct*. On April 30, 1887, William learned that the Queens County district attorney was "short in his accounts" $20,000 and "would have to run away." William eschewed the chance to save the career of this servant of justice, assistance that would likely have made William a law unto himself in Queens. William did, however, make loans to Long Island City mayor Paddy Gleason totaling $11,800 in 1886 and 1887. The incomprehensibly corrupt Gleason apparently paid William back, freeing him to indirectly accuse William of murder when the tunnel exploded. Gleason's political coat of arms was crossed battle axes, a reference to an incident when he used an ax to destroy a railway station in Long Island City putatively placed by predatory capitalists without proper permission.

341   "The acceptability": WSD, February 20–23, 1888. "Harassed all day by Mayor Grace . . . But in evg. Collector Magone calls with telegram from Pres. and I reluctantly promise to accept temporarily. Sleep but little during the night," wrote William. The immediate issue was the selection of a site for the Democratic National Convention; Grover Cleveland wanted and got St. Louis, but lost the election to Benjamin Harrison. New York was a competing site for the convention, but was this sufficient to cause William to lose sleep?

341   "When the Piano and": NYT, April 25, 1890.

342   "I rise and make": WSD, April 24, 1890.

342   "The claim is made": op. cit., NYT.

342   "Some of our industries": ibid.

342   "I am glad": ibid.

342   "Throughout our land": ibid.

343   "Papers all have": WSD, April 25, 1890.

343   "It was via": WSD, April 9, 1890.

343   "To ensure that": WSD, April 16, 1890. This original commission was short-lived and succumbed to a fatal combination of statutory restriction exacerbated by political machinations. The second commission was formed in December 1890 with many changes in membership, and it was this body that became known as the Steinway Commission. William recorded August Belmont's passing on November 24, 1890. William was appointed to the new commission on December 24, 1890. That same day William learned that the New York City Council passed an ordinance permitting his East River tunnel; Mayor Hugh Grant had discussed the project with William just ten days earlier, suggesting that Grant countenanced both William and his project. Just one day before, William attended a massive dinner of the Reform Club at Madison Square Garden, and was seated with Grover Cleveland at the speaker's table. While not yet at the height of his fame,

William was likely near the apogee of his practical political power at Christmas 1890.

343   "The Manhattan carried": AA, NYT, December 1, 1892.

343   "Collecting over": AA, ibid.

343   "Its officers": NYT, December 24, 1890. This article announced the formation of the second commission, and immediately called it the Steinway Commission. The piece characterized William as "a practical mechanic of wide experience," despite the fact that he had not earned his living using tools for roughly thirty-five years. This description was undoubtedly the inspiration of some person or persons eager to camouflage the group with the colors of populism.

343   "This system consists": ibid.

343   "It is made light": ibid.

343   "Known as the Greathead": NYT, December 26, 1890. The dates of the *Times* pieces suggest what would today be called a "public relations" campaign, artfully managed, was launched by the "underground road" forces. William and his East River tunnel project stood to benefit, but in the bubbling stew of Manhattan politics, management might have come from almost anywhere, save the capitalists controlling elevated roads.

343   "But before Greathead's": NYT, January 6, 1891. Among the more bizarre schemes was a plan for a "viaduct" fifty feet wide running the length of Manhattan, with trains running above the homes, stores, theaters, and hotels that made up its base. A patented plan envisioned a train that never stopped—was "endless" and operated by stationary engines. To get on or off, passengers boarded small trains, then stepped to the main train.

344   "There was such a resurrection": ibid.

344   "There were, without doubt": AA, NYT, December 1, 1892.

344   "Our plans call": NYT, December 15, 1892.

344   "President William Steinway": NYT, December 29, 1892.

344   "little doubt": ibid. This was the public posture; privately on December 6, 1892, William "look[ed] up easterly and westerly elevated lines in case underground Road does not sell." None of this would have been a secret to the elevated interests. Commissioner Spencer was a Morgan partner.

344   "They had already had millions": ibid.

344   "At noon": NYT, December 30, 1892.

345   "The lone bidder": ibid. His name was W. Howland Amory, and he was a former Steinway Commission employee. "If the commissioners had wanted some one to stand between them and an empty form of sale that function would have been assigned to Mr. Amory as willingly, probably, as anyone," commented the *Times*. This skepticism was unwarranted. William's diary indicates that the Amory bid was genuine, if niggardly. On January 3, 1893, Howland Amory appeared at a commission meeting with his attorney to claim the franchise. "Bowers & I make short work with him," wrote William. Whatever Amory's agenda, it was not to provide a fig leaf for William.

345   "Gould, Morgan": Jay Gould himself died about a month before the bidding. His decease would not have altered the strategic position of the elevated road interests.

345   "They were large rocks": AA, NYT, December 1, 1892.

345   "In terms": AA, ibid.

345   "The day after": WSD, December 30, 1892. The immediate request was for an "extension" of the existing routes. This is the only meeting with the men of the financial establishment recorded by William. Their opposition to subways may well have been a factor in William's inability to attract capital to his East River tunnel project, at least before the explosion. Morgan, for example, had the power to influence the course of nations. William may have been naive in believing he could succeed against such forces, and the politicians could only gain by allowing him to champion the ambitious subway plan whether he won or lost.

345   "To my dismay": WSD, January 14, 1893.

346   "Late in 1895": NYT, November 24, 1894.

346   "It is an exceedingly": ibid.

346   "The 'blue laws' ": ibid.

346   "warm Croton water": ibid.

346   "This whole thing": ibid.

346   "No less shocking": NYT, September 8, 1894. The article disingenuously claimed William had never been allied with any political factions.

346   "was to fight it": ibid.

346   "no Democrat": ibid.

347   "silly": ibid.

347   "He should be": ibid.

347   "You, yourself": ibid.

347   "It seems to me": *Musical Courier*, quoted ibid.

347   "the burden": ibid.

347   "In evening at 7 P.M.": WSD, May 16, 1894.

347   "It was there": WSD, June 22, 1892.

348   "Lovely weather": WSD, September 11, 1892.

348   "In addition": ibid.

348   "When the *Herald* correspondent": WSD, September 12, 1892.

348   "Steinway New York": ibid.

348   "A few days later": WSD, September 14, 1892.

348   "He receives me": ibid. At Rubinstein's residence William met Josef Hofmann, "now sixteen years old." A few years before, Hofmann had toured for Weber, igniting a brief but intense national concern with the exploitation of children that cancelled any benefits to Weber from the tour.

348   "not to trouble": ibid. William may actually have been relieved. With the last and only Rubinstein American tour firmly lodged in the pantheon of cultural events, a second tour, no matter how good, would have difficulty meeting public and critical expectations. The mere rumor of a tour would have also started a bidding war for Rubinstein among the musical agents and pianomen, making it a proposition both risky and very expensive.

348   "When William returned": October 9, 1892.

348   "After the international": NYT, October 11, 1892.

348   "Lessen": ibid. Interestingly, the *Times* did not report that William purchased three acres in Seesen for a village park, naturally named in his honor, and which still exists. William's visit to Seesen seems to have generated substantial excitement, including a torchlight parade with the

standard collection of bands and a festival where William addressed a crowd he estimated at 1,000 people with "a fine speech with five dialects that creates the greatest merriment." After dispensing a few "private benefactions," William found himself pestered by "a string of beggars." WSD, September 20–22, 1892.

349   "the facts of this": Minutes of the Board of Trustees of Steinway & Sons, October 11, 1892.

349   "saw Jay Gould": WSD, August 20, 1889.

349   "almost overwhelmed": WSD, April 14, 1890.

349   "the sixtieth mile stone": NYT, March 6, 1896.

349   "All day he was": ibid.

349   "engrossed testimonials": ibid.

350   "Callers, letters": WSD, March 5, 1896.

350   "Steinway, William Steinway": op. cit., NYT.

350   "delightful entertainment": ibid.

350   "a general jollification": ibid.

350   "Having learned": WSD, March 5, 1896.

350   "I am presented": ibid.

350   "I do not wish to spend": William to C. F. Theodore Steinway, August 31, 1887.

24. THE AIRY FABRIC OF A NAME

351   "Ah, yes, if notes": R. W. Gilder, "How Paderewski Plays," *The Century Magazine*, vol. 43, no. 5, March 1892, p. 727.

352   "No pianist has ever": Minutes of the Board of Trustees of Steinway & Sons, April 2, 1892. The words were William's.

352   "When in London": WSD, July 12, 1890.

352   "Thinking the price too high": WSD, September 26, 1890. Rummel, who made little impression on the future, enjoyed a close relationship with William, from whom he borrowed money on more than one occasion. He performed so frequently at Steinway Hall that he was virtually the house pianist. On July 25, 1891, William noted that Rummel "goes to Knabe." By this time the Paderewski contract for the 1891–92 season was signed and Tretbar was making preparations for his American debut. The signing of "Paddy" cannot have pleased Franz Rummel.

352   "Mayer, excellent agent": WSD, October 22, 1890. Tchaikovsky played New York in 1891, opening the New Music Hall on Fifty-seventh Street funded by Carnegie.

352   "Poor little Hegner": WSD, January 4, 1890.

352   "The advent of this gifted": NYT, April 20, 1890. Otto Hegner died in 1907 at age 30.

353   "Without comment": Minutes of the Board of Trustees of Steinway & Sons, January 23, 1891, notes that "153 men were daily employed" at the hall polishing, regulating, and voicing pianos.

     NYT, May 3, 1890 reports that the last event at Steinway Hall was a lecture by the noted critic H. E. Krebiehl, entitled "Precursors of the Pianoforte" with demonstrations on historical instruments. Opined the

Times, ". . . it is doubtful if any other four walls in the country have heard the same amount of good music. To music-loving New Yorkers the news of the close of its career comes like the announcement of the death of an old friend." The night the hall closed for the last time, William wrote: "Work late in my office evg."

353   "Mayer arrived": WSD, March 25, 1891.

353   "sum of $29,280": The contract amount in sterling was converted to dollars using the exchange rate in the S&S inventory book for English assets denominated in sterling at the close of 1891. So far as is known, this is the first publication of the accounting from the records of S&S.

353   "At a hastily": Minutes of the Board of Trustees of Steinway & Sons, March 25, 1891.

353   "It was approved": ibid.

353   "For obscure reasons": ibid.

353   "At the same meeting": ibid. For a total of $3,750 and roughly one-third the per-concert fee for Paderewski.

353   "Chas. H. St. cables": WSD, April 17, 1891.

353   "Meanwhile, Franz Rummel": NYT, April 2, 1891. Rummel did not defect to Knabe until July, so it may be assumed he was still playing a Steinway for these recitals.

353   "it might have been": ibid.

353–54   "That a musical city": NYT, May 3, 1891. The New Music Hall was formally opened May 5, 1891. "Its acoustic properties found to be adequate," headlined the *Times* on May 6, 1891.

354   "Seating three thousand": ibid.

354   "glorious": WSD, May 5, 1891. After the concert, which he attended with his wife, William repaired to the Liederkranz.

354   "dinner with Tretbar": WSD, July 5, 1891.

354   "According to a later": Ignace Paderewski and Mary Law, *The Paderewski Memoirs*, p. 97 ff.

354   "Paderewski also enjoyed": ibid. The warehouse was undoubtedly the converted former auditorium of Steinway Hall.

354   "Paderewski tries our grands": WSD, November 13, 1891. For many years Paderewski played Erards in Europe, also a commercial arrangement. It is conceivable that he had encountered few Steinway instruments before his arrival in America. It was not unusual for artist/pianomaker contracts to absolutely prohibit the playing of a competitor's instrument under any circumstances, including in private homes. Bizarre as this may seem, it was prudent from the pianomaker's standpoint. A few chords casually played and/or an offhand remark were easily inflated into a ringing endorsement.

355   "a most wonderful player": WSD, November 17, 1891.

355   "*Music & Drama*": *Music & Drama*, November 21, 1891. This was a special "supplement," raising the material possibility that it was paid for by Steinway & Sons. The paper at this time appears to have been under the control of Harry Freund, who did not share his brother J. C. Freund's enmity toward William.

355   "He came upon": ibid.

355   "It must be admitted": ibid.

355   "Is he the greatest of all?": *New York Sun*, November 18, 1891.

355	"A slender young man": ibid.
355–56	"He, like the grand old Russian": ibid.
356	"The schedule of 107": op. cit., *The Paderewski Memoirs*, p. 118 ff.
356	"immense receipts": WSD, March 26, 1892.
356	"A perfect pandemonium": WSD, March 28, 1892.
356	"Settlement with": ibid.
356	"The maestro s total": AA, ibid., and Minutes of the Board of Trustees of Steinway & Sons, April 2, 1892.
356	"diamond studs": WSD, December 26, 1892.
356	"Biggest retail trade": WSD, December 23, 1892.
356	"We by far": WSD, December 31, 1892.
356	"Combined with Hamburg": ibid.
357	"and William declared": S&S inventory book, 1891. In addition to the dividend, $5,000 in extra salary was awarded each of the nephews and selected other managers including Tretbar and sales head Nahum Stetson. See Minutes of the Board of Trustees of Steinway & Sons, April 2, 1892.
357	"In late 1890": WSD, November 11, 1890.
357	"The financial situation": WSD, December 1, 1890. William was nonetheless moving ahead with his East River tunnel plan. The accounts that would have shown the borrowings and the repayments are not known to exist and were probably destroyed.
357	"Have a hard tussle": WSD, February 11, 1891.
357	"cost figures": Minutes of the Board of Trustees of Steinway & Sons, January 23, 1891.
357	"In 1887 Henry and Fred": Minutes of the Board of Trustees of Steinway & Sons, December 31, 1887.
357	"Two years later": Minutes of the Board of Trustees of Steinway & Sons, December 29, 1889.
357	"Resolved, that the": op. cit., Minutes of the Board, January 23, 1891.
358	"The pace": Minutes of the Board of Trustees of Steinway & Sons, February 12, 1891.
358	"Two weeks later": Minutes of the Board of Trustees of Steinway & Sons, February 28, 1891.
358	"Mr. Fred T. Steinway": ibid.
358	"Mr. Henry W. T. Steinway": ibid.
358	"In response": ibid.
358	"Resolved that Henry": ibid.
358	"reprimanded for having": ibid.
358	"I give him": WSD, February 28, 1891.
358	"We are again having": WSD, July 11, 1891. WSD, May 19, 1891, states that H. W. T. moved from the S&S apartment.
359	"H. W. T. received": AA, S&S inventory book, 1880–91.
359	"On a Saturday": Minutes of the Board of Trustees of Steinway & Sons, December 19, 1891.
359	"having been cited": ibid.
359	"A thorough investigation": ibid.
359	"it became evident": ibid.
359	"withdraw": ibid.
359	"several": ibid.

359   "were full": ibid.
359   "even C. F. Theodor": ibid.
359   "whether or not": ibid.
359–60   "then stated": ibid.
360   "All the members": ibid.
360   "We are all": WSD, December 19, 1891.
360   "Dear Sir": letter from H. W. T. Steinway to William, December 31, 1891.
360   "We had": WSD, January 31, 1891.
360   "Several months": WSD, April 17, 1892.
360   "Chas. H. St. writes": WSD, July 22, 1892.
360   "the most absurd": WSD, September 14, 1892.
360   "Henry Sues": *New York World*, undated clipping ca. September 1892.
360   "Henry W. T.": ibid.
361   "I am surprised": WSD, October 10, 1894.
361   "squirms and tries": WSD, December 17, 1894.
361   "This action": NYT, February 19, 1895.
361   "In one of these": New York State Supreme Court, *Steinway* v. *Steinway*, May 8, 1893.
362   "I am pained": letter from Sophie Fricke to Addie, February 22, 1899. Fred T. Steinway in America translated this for some unknown purpose.
362   "I would not care": ibid.
362   "In 1900": op. cit., New York State Supreme Court, case file.
362   "Undaunted": New York State Supreme Court, *Steinway* v. *Steinway*, et alia, January 23, 1901. The decision was in favor of the defendants.
363   "and first among": Loans to Gleason were the subject of testimony by William on February 18, 1895. See NYT, February 19, 1895. The surviving record is not clear as to whether these were the same loans that William recorded in his diary; it appears, however, that William may have been personally responsible for them in the event of Gleason's default.
363   "The essence": New York State Supreme Court, *Steinway* v. *Steinway & Sons*, et alia, June 10, 1893, Brief for Plaintiff.
363   *"ultra vires"*: *Black's Law Dictionary*, Fourth Revised Edition, p. 1692.
363   "The remedy asked": op. cit., Brief for Plaintiff.
363   " 'useless wasteland' and 'salt marshes' ": ibid.
363   "squandered": ibid.
363   "practically conducting": ibid.
363   "enormous sum": ibid.
363   "Further claims": ibid.
363   "William, in his testimony": NYT, January 29, 1895.
363   "But no plausible": AA, S&S inventory book 1870–91.
363–64   "Compared to": ibid.
364   "The complaint next": op. cit., case file.
364   "William and nephew Charles": NYT, January 29, 1895.
364   "William's assertion": op. cit., Brief for Defendants.
364   "But the claims of the nephew-errant": op. cit., Brief for Plaintiff.
364   "That a manufacturing": ibid.
365   "They amounted to": AA, contested expenses, ibid.
365   "The alleged frivolities": AA, ibid., and S&S inventory book.

365 "We assert": op. cit., Brief for Plaintiff.
365 "Apparently convinced": ibid.
365 "Computed on": AA, ibid., and S&S inventory book. The number of shares outstanding and the proportion held by various family members varied over time. The 6 percent equity for H. W. T. is an estimate of his average holdings during the period of concern.
365 "The actual items": op. cit., Brief for Plaintiff.
365 "There were donations": ibid.
365 "Argument cannot be needed": ibid.
365 "The court was likewise": ibid.
366 "almost ludicrous": ibid.
366 "show a very serious": ibid.
366 "Addition in the time": AA, ibid., and S&S inventory book.
366 "doubtful claims": op. cit., Brief for Plaintiff.
366 "bad loans": ibid.
366 "Involving famous names": NYT, January 30, 1895.
366 "I find here": NYT, February 20, 1895.
366 "We were very much": ibid.
367 "What does this mean?": ibid.
367 "Papers have absurd": WSD, January 26, 1895.
367 "Harbuckle attacks": WSD, January 29, 1895. "Harbuckle" was the family nickname for H. W. T. Steinway; its originator is unknown, but it is first used in the diary in 1878.
367 "The science": Fanny Morris Smith, *A Noble Art: Three Lectures on the Evolution and Construction of the Piano*, p. 1 ff.
367 "People are not wanting": ibid.
368 "Cigarettes for Paderewski": op. cit., NYT, January 30, 1895.
368 "Judge Beekman": ibid.
368 "William Steinway made": NYT, January 31, 1895.
368 "Mr. Steinway showed": ibid.
368 "Judge and spectators": WSD, January 30, 1895.
368 "Harbuckle helps himself": WSD, January 28, 1895.
368 "This is a most remarkable": NYT, January 31, 1895.
368 "For Cotterill": op. cit., *Steinway* v. *Steinway & Sons*, et alia, June 10, 1893, case file, "Steinway & Sons to George W. Cotterill." This document lists "services" by Cotterill from 1893 through June 28, 1897. No hours are shown, and the sum $25,000 appears on the last page.
368 "Compare these persons": NYT, January 31, 1895.
368 "expended $100,000": ibid.
369 "He had also": ibid.
369 "In the interim": NYT, February 19, 1895. The *fabrik* action was initially tried before Justice Stover.
369 "Glorious news": WSD, March 6, 1896.
369 "bashes him fearfully": WSD, May 7, 1896.
369 "It is proper": *New York Law Journal*, vol. 15, no. 37, May 13, 1896.
369 "conditions and influences": ibid.
369 "in the development": ibid.
369 "a wise one": ibid.
369 "a policy such as this": ibid.

369 "Henry W. T.": ibid.
369 "The plaintiff is not": ibid.
369 "his confidence in the management": ibid.
369 "there is not a single scintilla": ibid.
369–70 "We are entitled": ibid.
370 "If it had not been": ibid.
370 "But by that time": op. cit., "Steinway & Sons to George W. Cotterill," p. 7, shows date of June 1898. William died in November 1896.
370 "His home": NYT, June 28, 1939.
370 "In his eighty-third": *Watertown Daily Times*, June 28, 1939.
370 "In the early 1920s": S&S stock transfer records. These records are not entirely clear, and the author wishes to thank Mr. Henry Z. Steinway for confirming H. W. T.'s stock sale to others in the family.
370 "Young Steinways": statement of Henry Z. Steinway to the author, September 16, 1991.
370 "Henry W. T.": NYT, July 11, 1939.
370 "Of that": ibid.
370 "life interest": ibid.
370 "troubles, vexations": letter from William to C. F. Theodore Steinway, August 31, 1887.

25. THE PECCANT PIANOMAKER OF NEW YORK

371 "It is well-known": NYT, February 15, 1893, editorial. The *Times* of this date carried both a news story and an editorial on the conduct of pianomakers.
371 "William, who was chairman": NYT, February 15, 1893, quote of N. Stetson. It is unclear if the gift to the fair was William's personally or that of S&S; the amount is reported as either $20,000 or $25,000, the larger being more frequent. According to this account, William gave $20,000 and the "Chicago branch of the house" gave $5,000. This would have been Lyon & Potter, a piano dealer in which the family held an interest.
371 "In recognition": WSD, February 2, 1891. The entry contains an unusual item: an undated newspaper clipping reporting the Chicago visit is affixed to the diary page.
372 "Some months": NYT, February 15, 1893.
372 "Joseph P. Hale's": Alfred Dolge, *Pianos and Their Makers*, p. 179 ff.
372 "In Cincinnati": ibid., p. 346 ff.
372 "In 1887": WSD, January 9, 1887. The circumstances surrounding this are unclear, but one result of William's change of Cincinnati retailers in favor of Morris Steinert was the creation of a competitor sufficiently viable to survive to this day. Steinert, who operated what today would be called a retail chain, was buying up to four hundred Steinways per year or about 15 percent of the house's output. During roughly this same period, S&S established captive dealers in Chicago, Philadelphia, and other cities, suggesting a general shift in retailing strategy away from independent dealers.
372 "In Richmond, Indiana": op. cit., *Pianos and Their Makers*, p. 348 ff.
372 "French & Sons": Alfred Dolge, *Men Who Have Made Piano History*, p. 75 ff.

372   "Story & Clark": ibid., p. 376.

372   "The Schiller": ibid., p. 148 ff.

373   "John V. Steger": op. cit., *Pianos and Their Makers*, p. 361 ff.

373   "Kimball, after many": ibid., p. 339 ff. This illuminates the strong business relationship between Kimball and Hale as well.

373   "Kimball had a small hall": Van Allen Bradley, *Music for the Millions*, who also notes that on April 26, 1891, Kimball introduced its first grand piano, a sure sign of artistic aspirations.

373   "All the piano manufacturers": NYT, February 12, 1893.

373   "We are not unpatriotic": ibid. Stetson was speaking for the house because William was at home, almost totally disabled with rheumatism and gout.

373   "Just three days": NYT, February 15, 1893.

373–74   "each firm acted individually": ibid.

374   "The pianos of Peoria": NYT, February 15, 1893, editorial.

374   "Predictably, the traditional": NYT, August 24, 1893.

374   "One was Theodore Thomas": Ezra Schabas, *Theodore Thomas: America's Conductor and Builder of Orchestras*.

374   "national tours underwritten": S&S confidential circulars, October 13, 1870; September 26, 1871; August 31, 1872; and September 20, 1875. The Thomas Orchestra also accompanied Rubinstein at his Steinway Hall debut and made literally hundreds of other appearances there.

374   "and lent the maestro": Loans to Thomas were among the issues at trial in *Steinway* v. *Steinway & Sons*, et alia, June 10, 1893, case file. There were at least two direct loans to Thomas with a total of $8,933.13 that do not appear to have been repaid. William made additional loans to and investments in the American Opera Company and the succeeding National Opera Company, of which Thomas was conductor. The current dollar amount is estimated with a CPI multiplier derived by the author and is only an inexact approximation of the sum.

374   "At Thomas's request": *The Presto*, May 4, 1893. This publication, based in Chicago, was another sign of the westward shift in the economic center of gravity of American pianomaking.

374–75   "A decree issued": Paul and Ruth Hume, "The Great Chicago Piano War," *American Heritage* no. 21, 1970, p. 16 ff. This whimsical piece was also reprinted by Steinway & Sons. There is little here that indicates the stakes in what was deadly commercial combat.

375   "he should have been": *Chicago Herald*, May 11, 1893, quoted op. cit., *Theodore Thomas*, p. 206. Thomas ultimately resigned as musical director of the fair. See NYT, August 11, 1893.

375   "there are some men": *Musical Courier*, quoted op. cit., "The Great Chicago Piano War," reprinted, p. 5.

375   "human chrysanthemum": *New York World*, April 27, 1893. "Nasty article in Herald & World corr. from Chicago," wrote William that day. The next day he made his "first attempt to walk on crutches."

375   "why I should be forced": *New York World*, April 28, 1893.

375   "at liberty": ibid. William clearly played a strategic role, meeting with both nephew Charles and Nahum Stetson at his home, but for the first time in three decades a "piano war" was waged without William Steinway in the front line.

376   "the Council of Administration": NYT, May 2, 1893.

376   "The next day": NYT, May 3, 1893.

376   "Art and Hustlers": NYT, May 13, 1893.

376   "Though undoubtedly a hustler": ibid.

377   "The Boston school": Fanny Morris Smith, *A Noble Art: Three Lectures on the Evolution and Construction of the Piano*, p. 110.

377   *"Every true piano"*: ibid., p. 155.

377   "William Mason": William Mason, "Paderewski: A Critical Study," *The Century Magazine*, vol. 43, no. 5, March 1892, p. 721 ff.

377   "It seems to me": ibid., p. 723.

377   "While fully recognizing": ibid., p. 721.

378   "His piano is": NYT, May 13, 1893.

378   "First it was Charles Tretbar": WSD, March 30, 1893.

378   "On the scene": WSD, May 1, 1893.

378   "This was not": The first indication of William's long illness occurred in January 1893. By February he was virtually immobile.

378   "inflammatory rheumatism": WSD, December 31, 1893.

378   "While gout": Marshall Cavendish, *Marshall Cavendish Encyclopedia of Family Health*, vol. 3, p. 579 ff. As to the medical understanding in 1991: "It is now known that the part played by diet is relatively small . . ."

378   "If inadequate exercise": *Encyclopaedia Britannica*, Ninth edition, Vol. 11, p. 5 ff.

378   "Fellowship, song, and beer": AA, WSD, 1865–80. On November 1, 1885, William recorded: "I drink 10 glasses of imported beer, feel fresh and free of rheumatism," but in general he noted lower consumption when he noted it at all.

378–79   "the depressing consequences": op. cit., *Britannica*.

379   "My hand swells": WSD, January 19, 1893.

379   "I suffer": WSD, January 20, 1893.

379   "By the fourth day": WSD, January 23, 1893.

379   "a fever appeared": WSD, February 2, 1893. By this time William was receiving morphine injections.

379   "Unable to move": WSD, February 9, 1893.

379   "Though Paderewski": WSD, February 3, 1893.

379   "obnoxious award system": February 10, 1893.

379   "shoulders shiny red": symptoms reported in *Marshall Cavendish*, op. cit.

379   "great excitement": WSD, February 27, 1893.

379   "By then": NYT, February 15, 1893, reports sixteen withdrawals.

379   "Sat up in chair": WSD, February 27, 1893.

379   "At 3 A.M.": WSD, March 1, 1893.

379   "almost crazy": WSD, March 2, 1893.

379   "passed a sleepless night": WSD, March 4, 1893.

379   "my Willie": WSD, March 5, 1893.

380   "had Bright's disease": ibid.

380   "This quiets me": ibid.

380   "At 3 P.M.": WSD, March 6, 1893.

380   "suffered dreadfully": ibid.

380   "still quite prostrated": WSD, March 7, 1893.

380	"She, her husband": WSD, March 11, 1893.

380 "She, her husband": WSD, March 11, 1893.
380 "an important resolution": ibid.
380 "A *Times* reporter": NYT, March 12, 1893.
380 "have long articles": WSD, March 12, 1893.
380 "invalid wagon": ibid.
380 "a number of visitors": WSD, March 19, 1893.
380 "It was two more": WSD, April 5, 1893.
381 "Wagon tips over": WSD, April 12, 1893.
381 "A masseur was added": WSD, March 29, 1893.
381 "After a month": WSD, April 28, 1893. Throughout April the annual stockholder meetings of Steinway & Sons, the railway companies, and real estate companies were held. William was represented by proxy. For unknown reasons William did not choose to hold any of these meetings at his home.
381 "Following the typical": NYT, May 5, 1893.
381 "There was other": ibid. There was perhaps another factor at work as well. Chicago papers unsympathetic to Paderewski's choice of pianos had made "uncomplimentary remarks" about both his playing and personal appearance. "He has been unused, even though coming from ignorant sources, to being adversely criticized," noted the *Times*, which also characterized the pianist's personality as "overstrung."
381 "The performer": ibid.
381 "The spiral of fear": WSD, June 28, 1893.
381–82 "The business cycle": AA, table, "Business Cycle Expansions and Contractions in the United States," *Business Conditions Digest*, January 1987, p. 104.
382 "Under the Sherman": Warren F. Hickernell, *Financial and Business Forecasting*, p. 391 ff. The silver act was repealed by Congress in late 1893, but this was insufficient to undo the effects of gold hoarding. Hickernell (p. 398) states: "The cause of the panic of 1893 was the fear that the gold standard would be superseded by the silver standard." One contributing factor to this fear was the suspension of payments in gold by the New York Sub-Treasury. The job of heading the subtreasury was offered by President Cleveland to William on January 8, 1886. As usual, William declined the political appointment.
382 "Mr. Chas. H. Steinway": Minutes of the Board of Trustees of Steinway & Sons, July 28, 1893.
382 "Mortgages were taken": ibid., and Minutes of the Board of Trustees of Steinway & Sons, August 22, 1893. The total of the two mortgages was $275,000. Given that William was reporting short-term rates as high as 75 percent, the interest on the mortgages was a remarkably modest 5 percent.
382 "Nationwide, assets": NYT, July 1, 1893.
382 "and by the end": AA, S&S inventory book, 1893.
382 "President Cleveland's": WSD, August 7, 1893.
382 "Financial situation": WSD, August 12, 1893.
383 "could stand it quite well": ibid.
383 "so nervous and excited": WSD, August 14, 1893.
383 "vividly thinking": WSD, August 16, 1893.

383   "had quite literally": WSD, August 17, 1893.

383   "was received": WSD, August 19, 1893. The picnics were usually held on a Saturday, normally a workday for the men.

383   "I worry very much": WSD, August 28, 1893.

383   "a most terrible one": WSD, December 31, 1893.

383   "far beyond": ibid.

383   "in fact, the only establishment": ibid.

384   "The 'deposits' ": Roughly concurrent with H. W. T.'s legal action, the inventory book ceases to show large liabilities to members of the extended family. William's diary makes no mention of the disposition of these funds, and no detailed records of the transactions survive. The lack of family "deposits" was likely a factor in the cash crunch that forced the mortgaging of the hall and factory. Henry W. T.'s lawsuits might well have toppled the house had willing lenders not been found.

384   "In that worst of years": S&S inventory book, 1893. Of this dividend, William received about $80,000, cash he needed to keep his other ventures operating, since virtually all were losing money.

384   "In the spring": WSD, May 3, 1892. This was a partial sale. Earlier William sold an interest in the gas company to a man named Trask for $165,000. See WSD, April 1, 1890. The record is unclear as to what was equity and what was debt in these transactions, but it seems that William had no interest of any kind in the gas company after the second sale.

384   "a few weeks later sold": WSD, May 25, 1892.

384   "A few months later": WSD, January 5, 1893.

384–85   "The seventeen thousand shares": AA, incorporation documents, Steinway Railway Company. The capital actually paid in is unclear, and it is unlikely that the road(s) earned material profits during the time William owned them. William retained about 31 percent of the stock, assuming that the transaction was in fact completed on these terms.

385   "George A. Steinway": WSD, June 4, 1886.

385   "George started": WSD, September 13, 1883.

385   "At age sixteen": WSD, October 3, 1881.

385   "At seventeen": WSD, October 31, 1882.

385   "sickly child": George was "very weak" at birth, and at the age of one and one-half William feared he would die of some unstated disease. See WSD, June 4, 1865, and February 6, 1867.

385   "The piano company": WSD, June 19, 1869.

385   "to pieces in a few hours": WSD, March 17, 1870.

385   "On another occasion, George": WSD, June 5, 1880. This is the date of the mention; the event happened "many years ago," according to the diary.

385   "Georgie asked": WSD, January 9, 1878.

385   "Am somewhat uneasy": January 12, 1879.

385   "Go home and reveal": September 20, 1879.

386   "no feelings": WSD, July 25, 1880.

386   "the news quite composedly": WSD, January 12, 1882. The diary indicates that Regina's family decided that she was to be interred in France rather than in America, and so it is learned that Regina's banishment was in effect eternal.

386   "Researchers now write": Henri Begleiter, Bernice Porjesz, and Bernard

Bihari, "Auditory Brainstem Potentials in Sons of Alcoholic Fathers," *Alcoholism: Clinical and Experimental Research*, vol. 11, no. 5, September/October 1987, p. 477 ff, states: "Recent findings in population genetics suggest that sons of alcoholic fathers are at a high risk for developing alcoholism." Also Elizabeth Knowles and David Schroeder, "Personality Characteristics of Sons of Alcohol Abusers," *Journal of Studies on Alcohol*, vol. 51, no. 2, 1990, p. 142 ff: "Genetic studies have found that children of alcoholics, especially sons of alcoholic fathers, are at greater risk for the future development of alcoholism than are the children of nonalcoholics." Evidence for biochemical, neurophysiological, cognitive, and behavioral differences is cited.

386   "evoked by *sounds*": op. cit., "Auditory Brainstem Potentials." Also Jaclyn B. Spitzer and Craig W. Newman, "Brainstem Auditory Evoked Potentials in Newly Detoxified Alcoholics," *Journal of Studies on Alcohol*, vol. 48, no. 1, 1987, p. 9 ff, which contains the cautionary statement, "Due to the pervasiveness of alcoholism in our society, studies using larger samples, selected with greater care and definition, are needed to describe fully the impact of alcoholism on neural transmission, as measured using evoked potentials."

386   "Other studies": op. cit., "Personality Characteristics of Sons."

386   "strange malady": WSD, April 3, 1895.

386   "nervous prostration": WSD, March 30, 1894.

386   "With a gift": Minutes of the Board of Trustees of Steinway & Sons, April 6, 1891. George's holdings varied.

386   "For a time George reported": WSD, May 30, 1886.

387   "George's part": WSD, December 27, 1890.

387   "George resigned": WSD, January 8 and January 26, 1891. When William consolidated his street railways, George was once again elected president. See WSD, March 30, 1892. This, however, was likely little more than a corporate convenience, as George had resigned from the S&S Board of Trustees in September 1891.

387   "George was given": Minutes of the Board of Trustees of Steinway & Sons, January 23, 1891.

387   "I worked hard": WSD, January 29, 1891.

387   "ill in bed": WSD, February 12, 1891.

387   "bad news": WSD, March 6, 1891.

387   "deeply grieved": WSD, March 10, 1891.

387   "Before long": WSD, March 27, 1891.

387   "reasons of impaired health": Minutes of the Board of Trustees of Steinway & Sons, September 9, 1891.

387   "George's illness": AA, New York State Supreme Court, Appellate Division, Second Department, *Ottilie Marie Steinway*, et alia, v. *Louis von Bernuth*, et alia, Defendants' Exhibit H. It seems that any family member could tap at will the treasury of Steinway & Sons.

387   "Living rent-free": WSD, September 20, 1891.

387   "had to again make good": WSD, March 28, 1894.

387   "George is in bed": WSD, March 30, 1894.

387   "a long tale of woe": WSD, October 18, 1894.

387   "for help and advice": WSD, October 19, 1894. George's wife Ottilie rarely

saw William socially in the six and one-half years of her marriage to his son. Nonetheless, she appears to have mastered the art of getting along with him.

387–88   "My son George": WSD, October 24, 1894.

388   "About twenty-four percent": Archibald Church, M.D., and Frederick Peterson, M.D., *Nervous and Mental Diseases*, p. 645.

388   "The best-informed": ibid., e.g., ". . . [I]t is in the fragile, nervous constitutions of individuals tainted by heredity that extreme emotions are wont to exert their malign influence."

388   "ALBERT WEBER'S FALL": NYT, October 3, 1896.

388   "luxurious home": ibid.

388   "his revelry": ibid.

388   "white with rage": NYT, September 17, 1896.

388   "You have no right": ibid.

388   "In 1884": New York State Supreme Court, *Weber* v. *Meyer*, et alia.

388   "peculated": ibid.

388–89   "Through all his dissipations": op. cit., NYT, October 3.

389   "At times": ibid.

389   "I'll make three millions": ibid.

389   "Weber has been insane": ibid.

389   "My son George": WSD, November 2, 1894.

389   "The dimmed prospect": WSD, November 4, 1894.

389   "still in bed": WSD, December 23, 1894.

389   "Two months before": WSD, November 29, 1894. William states the family moved "some weeks ago."

389   "William's holiday": WSD, December 24 and 25, 1894.

389   "George's holiday": op. cit., *Nervous and Mental Diseases*, p. 536.

389   "George suffered": ibid., p. 528 ff. William used the phrase "nervous prostration" on October 20, 1894, and subsequently.

389   "Brought to the attention": ibid.

390   "morbid state": ibid.

390   "Neurasthenia": ibid., p. 535.

390   "He removed George": WSD, April 24, 1895.

390   "dress himself": WSD, January 21, 1895.

390   "an unstimulating": op. cit., *Nervous and Mental Diseases*, p. 536.

390   "In the *severer*": ibid.

390   "By May of 1894": WSD, May 12, 1895.

390   "long letter": WSD, April 5, 1895.

390   "I first consulted": New York State Supreme Court, Appellate Division, Second Department, *Ottilie Marie Steinway*, et alia, v. *Louis von Bernuth*, et alia, p. 70 ff.

390   "Both North Dakota": *New York Herald*, July 28, 1895.

390–91   "I told him": op. cit., *Ottilie Marie Steinway*, et alia, v. *Louis von Bernuth*, et alia.

391   "Sales lost": During this time William was often worried about poor sales, e.g., WSD, May 29, 1894.

391   "WHEREAS the said": op cit., *Ottilie Marie Steinway*, et alia, v. *Louis von Bernuth*, et alia, Plaintiff's Exhibit A.

391   "see the said children": ibid.

391 "With a presumably secure": ibid.
391 "If George": WSD, July 9, 1895. George made the trip in a Daimler motor-boat.
392 "On July 13": WSD, July 13, 1895.
392 "relapsed": WSD, December 31, 1895.
392 "To my pleasant surprise": WSD, July 30, 1895.
392 "Before long": WSD, August 28, 1895.
392 "sensible": WSD, August 28, 1894.
392 "habitual intemperance": *Ottilie Marie Steinway, et alia, v. Louis von Bernuth, et alia,* Defendant's Exhibit I.
392 "William paid": WSD, October 10, 1895.
392 "Only one day": WSD, September 28, 1895.
392 "in quite unobjectionable": WSD, September 29, 1895.
392 "A scant thirty-four days": WSD, November 2, 1895.
392 "Via cables": typically, WSD, November 9, 1895, and January 7, 1896.
392 "a great deal": October 21, 1896.

26. FORGIVE ME, I LOVED HIM

393 "He had been ill": NYT, December 1, 1896.
393 "The mayor early": *New York World,* December 1, 1896.
393 "William Steinway died": op. cit., NYT.
393 "A little after": ibid.
394 "As his fortune": ibid.
394 "relentless foes": ibid.
394 "proud of his": ibid.
394 "were earnest": ibid.
394 "he had no taste": ibid.
394 "the history of Steinway Hall": *New York Herald,* December 1, 1896.
394 "endowment": ibid.
394 "His financial standing": op. cit., NYT.
394 "In Long Island City": *New York Evening World,* July 27, 1896.
394 "working with a heavy loss": WSD, March 21, 1896.
394 "William toured": WSD, September 23, 1896.
394 "Paderewski": WSD, April 18, 1896.
394 "old Koven": WSD, June 15, 1896.
394–95 "greatly grieved": WSD, June 16, 1896. Likely among them were nephew Fred, who was fond of fast horses, and nephew Charles, who, by family legend, enjoyed gambling. The track in question seems to have been at Bowery Bay, which had been renamed North Beach in belated recognition of the connotation of "Bowery."
395 "The biggest slate": letter from Fred T. Steinway to William, May 21, 1896.
395 "At the time": WSD, June 12, 1896, and NYT, July 1, 1896, reports the conclusion of William's efforts.
395 "Abbey, Schoeffel & Grau": ibid.
395 "Mr. Steinway's presentation": ibid.
395 "has done more financially": ibid.
396 "a perfect pandemonium": WSD, June 23, 1896.

396   "we are pestered": WSD, June 21, 1896.

396   "Weber failed": NYT, February 4, 1896. William wrote that this was "long-expected."

396   "Gildemeister & Kroeger": WSD, May 29, 1896. Gildemeister was a former Chickering executive who lost his position there when the firm was reorganized. He joined with Henry Kroeger in the making of Steinway clones for a brief time. He then came to S&S and stayed for many years.

396   "Hallet & Davis": WSD, July 21, 1896.

396   "Alfred Dolge": WSD, July 10, 1896. This was indirect; William guaranteed a ninety-day note for $25,000 at the Metropolitan Savings Bank. Dolge failed after asking William for a further $150,000. Yet another money panic was developing, and on November 1, 1896, William noted that short-term interest rates reached 100 percent.

396   "Poor old Max": WSD, July 22, 1896.

396   "Old Mrs. Dachauer": WSD, October 26, 1896.

396   "This is the first time": WSD, November 3, 1896. William had apparently forgotten that he voted for the Republican Ulysses Simpson Grant on November 5, 1872, and against Tweed, a Democrat, in the 1871 city elections.

396   "I still feel quite ill": WSD, November 6, 1896.

396   "remarkably well": WSD, October 31, 1896.

396–97   "I still feel quite ill": WSD, November 7, 1896.

397   "Work til 9 P.M.": WSD, November 8, 1896.

397   "Albert raves": WSD, May 9, 1877.

397   "Typhoid was": AA, *Historical Statistics of the United States, Colonial Times to 1970*, Part 1, p. 63, series 198.

397   "The announcement": NYT, December 2, 1896.

397   "At the Liederkranz": ibid.

397   "From the pianomakers": NYT, December 3, 1896.

397   "The Liederkranz floral": ibid.

397   "A life-size": ibid.

397   "The simple Unitarian": ibid. This choice of faiths was apparently made by a family member; William was not an active member of any religious organization.

397   "After the private": ibid.

397   "When placed": ibid.

397   "A squadron": ibid.

397   "On the left": ibid.

397   "There was an honor guard": ibid.

397   "William had made": WSD, July 16, 1870.

397   "The pallbearers": op. cit., NYT, December 3, 1870.

398   "All twelve": ibid. Only Ottendorfer and Cotterill among the pallbearers played any material role in William's life, and how the others were chosen is unknown.

398   "The members": ibid.

398   "A special section": ibid.

398   "German societies": ibid.

398   "The majestically plaintive": ibid.

398   "He spoke in German": ibid.

398   "nothing could be written": ibid.

398   "Julius Hoffman": ibid.

398   "We thank you": ibid.

398   "Overcome by his feeling": ibid.

398   "All around him": ibid.

398   "gloriously sung": ibid.

398   "Outside on Fifty-eighth Street": ibid.

398   "Behind the hearse": ibid.

399   "The pallbearers": ibid.

399   "As the body": ibid.

27. IMPECUNIOUS PEOPLE

404   *"May 19, 1898.":* *New York Herald*, May 19, 1898.

404   "Charles was also a master": Shortly after Charles took over, S&S financials appeared in the conventional form of balance sheet and income statement; in 1896 Fred caused a ten-year income statement to be cast, the first sign of any formal interest in long-term financial trends. This may have been precipitated by the inquiries of parties interested in purchasing the house, whose questions could have exposed the family to some of the basics of business finance.

William's financial management skill is illuminated by two diary entries only three weeks apart: "I am greatly pleased that St. & S. and I are so well provided with money through my splendid bond sales, that we can stand any amount of panic with comparative non-apprehension," wrote William on December 21, 1895, in the midst of a Wall Street panic. "Our accumulated stock of money melts away like butter under the sun," was the entry on January 11, 1896.

405   "Though William": Daybook of Fred T. Steinway. Unfortunately, the book was sporadic and only covered a few years at the turn of the century. If Fred kept other journals, they may be presumed lost or destroyed. Henry Z. Steinway reports that Fred's wife, Julia, destroyed many of her husband's papers after his death. What little direct evidence exists of Fred's interests and activities comes from the daybook.

406   "in 1896, for example: Minutes of the Board of Trustees of Steinway & Sons, December 23, 1896.

406   "When I saw": op. cit., *New York Herald*.

406   "There is wide": ibid.

406   "On the part": ibid.

406   "That Mr. Steinway": ibid.

406   "Whatever Mr. Steinway": ibid.

406   "a great-hearted generosity": ibid.

406   "The recession": AA, "Business Cycle Expansions and Contractions in the United States," *Business Conditions Digest*, January 1987, p. 104.

406   "The result was": AA, S&S unit production records.

406   "Worse yet,": AA, ibid.

407   "In the record year": AA, S&S inventory book, 1893.

407   "By 1896": AA, ibid., 1896. By the time the dividend was declared, William had died. Undoubtedly, William would have declared a larger dividend, since profits, though diminished, were still substantial. It appears that the

nephews decided to retain the earnings rather than distribute them. Their personal incomes were, of course, proportionately reduced.

407 "At the Bank of the Metropolis": New York County Surrogate Court, "In the matter of the estate of William Steinway, deceased."

407 "Adam Weber": op. cit., *New York Herald.*

407 "A business associate": op. cit., *New York Herald.*

407 "Almost a decade": NYT, January 31, 1904. Somehow the executors were able to forestall public filing and therefore public knowledge of the specific condition of the estate until this time.

407 "but as Tretbar": New York State Supreme Court, Appellate Division, Second Department, *Ottilie Marie Steinway*, et alia, v. *Louis von Bernuth*, et alia.

407 "The result was": op. cit., NYT.

407 "Some of these funds": The loan situation was further complicated by William's endorsement of notes, which were then discounted to the corporation. This practice emerged during the litigation by Henry W. T. Steinway, and was the means by which some of the Gleason loans were handled. See NYT, February 19, 1895. It is possible that still more loans in which William was involved were written off by the house, but surviving records are insufficient to confirm or preclude this. Among the largest items in surviving records was the "Special Expense a/c." Typically much larger than salary, wage, advertising, concert and artist, commission, and interest expense accounts, it was probably here that many financial skeletons were interred. In 1897, for example, "Special Expense" was equal to 35.4 percent of total profits and 6.9 percent of revenues from new pianos sold. Unfortunately, the detail for this account is lost, but fragmentary evidence suggests that some "loans" to artists and others were posted to this account.

408 "Strictly separate": letter from C. F. T. Steinway to William, September 13, 1887.

408 "In the fifteen": AA, S&S inventory book, 1881–95 and Inventory and Appraisement of the Personal Estate of William Steinway, April 5, 1898.

408 "Calls on me": WSD, June 1, 1884.

408 "midway in a recession": AA, "Business Cycle Expansions and Contractions in the United States," op. cit.

408 "Theodor Lemke": WSD, May 22, 1891.

408 "I am pestered": WSD, August 21, 1891.

408–9 "a lattice door": WSD, December 28, 1891.

409 "having dreadful trouble": WSD, January 7, 1892.

409 "almost ground to powder": WSD, January 25, 1892.

409 "the attempts personally": WSD, December 31, 1893.

409 "The *Musical Courier*": WSD, December 19, 1893.

409 "Chiefly from old maids": WSD, December 25, 1893.

409 "pestered all day": WSD, December 28, 1893. It seems that the pleas to William reached a peak each Christmas.

409 "In January 1892": WSD, January 16, 1894.

409 "again plagues me": WSD, January 22, 1894.

409 "they being penniless": WSD, January 10, 1894.

409 "William von Meyerinck": WSD, January 22 and 25, 1894.

409   "but Mrs. von Meyerinck": WSD, July 30, 1894.

409   "a long talk with Rafael": WSD, December 7, 1892.

409   "Joseffy has not": WSD, December 19, 1893.

409   "This day 37 years ago": WSD, December 1, 1895. There was another reminiscence on April 23, 1895: "This day 34 years ago I was married in Buffalo." In general, however, William remained a man more interested in the future than the past.

409–10   "Besides giving money": WSD, April 7, 1894, is a representative entry: "Mrs. Groenevelt and her daughter Celeste call on me, latter plays fairly well, but of course I decline paying for a family of five to go to Vienna for the girl's study."

410   "Not all William's assistance": WSD, October 30, 1894. Thomas H. Chambers died on August 6, 1895, according to the diary.

410   ". . . loaned him $500": WSD, June 7, 1895.

410   "I remain until 9 P.M.": WSD, July 12, 1895.

410   "How much money": Inventory and Appraisement of the Personal Estate of William Steinway, April 5, 1898.

410   "The vastness": AA, NYT, December 2, 1895.

410   "Of the 405 recorded": AA, op. cit., Inventory and Appraisement.

410   "During those final": AA, ibid., and S&S inventory book, 1896.

410   "The *Times*, page one": NYT, August 2, 1897.

410   "Scarcely a year": NYT, July 12, 1896.

410   "was originally intended": op. cit., NYT, August 2.

410   "legitimate means": ibid.

410–11   "where men,": ibid.

411   "where baseballs": ibid. The racial attitudes implied by this activity were not confined to the amusement seekers of North Beach. William recorded that his son-in-law Louis von Bernuth brought home a "large, splendid" black French poodle. The dog was named Nigger, and the children were "literally crazed with Joy over him." The dog ran away, and the maid was dispatched in search. The dog was "caught" at Twenty-eighth Street. See WSD, April 22 and 25, 1895.

411   "that the Klondike": op. cit., NYT, August 2, 1895.

411   "Turkish Sirens": NYT, August 4, 1897. The *Times* of this period vigilantly sought examples of weakness in the city's moral fiber. Upon discovery, these were exposed to public scrutiny so that they might be quickly rectified by constituted authority. Any gains in circulation were likely an incidental but pleasant consequence of this essentially noble purpose.

411   "The 1893 Chicago": Cynthia Taylor Young, "The Way We Weren't," *Northwestern University Dialogue*, Winter 1993, p. 1 ff.

411   "couchee-couchee": op. cit., NYT, August 4.

411   "last and only chance": letter from Charles H. Steinway to "Dear Boys" (presumably including Fred Steinway and Henry Ziegler), July 30, 1897.

411   "the dread calamity": ibid.

411   "To avoid such ignominy": Memorandum of Association of Steinway & Sons, Limited, August 7, 1897.

411   "The rationale": One likely additional factor was that English "capitalists" had approached William in the past about selling Steinway & Sons, in one

instance offering $4.5 million for the house. These offers were refused (e.g., WSD, January 2 and 21, 1889), yet a peculiar item appeared on August 30, 1896, just three months before William died. "Chas. St. writes that Eshelby had brought syndicate matters near realization," wrote William. Eshelby was the manager of S&S, London. The possibility therefore exists that William was exploring the sale of the house through an equity offering before his death. Eshelby's familiarization with "syndication" was probably a factor in Charles's 1897 attempt.

411–12   "We need the United States": *London Statist*, quoted in NYT, June 6, 1898.

412   "why they did not turn south": It is possible that the family felt Wall Street too close to home and the scrutiny of the press, which might have discovered the condition of William's estate and triggered an avalanche of litigation by creditors.

412   "The New York Stock Exchange": AA, NYT, April 25, 1898. From the data in this issue the contemporary market capitalizations of the traded firms can be computed.

412   "Dear Boys . . .": op. cit., letter from Charles H. Steinway.

412   "A telegram": ibid.

412   "The trend": op. cit., Memorandum of Association.

412   "The reduction": ibid.

412   "On the face": ibid. The preferred shares were priced to yield 5 percent and the common 8 percent with the total yield about 6.27 percent. Priced at about 2.35 times book, S&S was not a cheap stock; it was to be listed on the London Stock Exchange.

412   "It was Eshelby": letter from Charles H. Steinway to "Dear Boys," August 5, 1897.

412   "Everything at present": ibid.

413   "The hope was": AA, S&S inventory book, 1896. This is based on the distribution of shares, which were essentially unchanged, but is before syndication fees and other charges, the precise amounts of which are unknown.

413   "Dear Boys": Charles H. Steinway to "Dear Boys," August 13, 1897.

413   "I have no excuses": ibid.

413   "Just at the present time": NYT, August 4, 1897.

413   "It was reported": NYT, August 19, 1897. The English prospectus indicated that the offering was to close on August 12, 1897. The piece contained many errors on the history of the house. A story on how a father prevented his daughter's elopement by pursuing her on a bicycle occupied the next column. The prospective groom planned to puncture the bicycle's tires before trying again.

413   "As announced exclusively": NYT, August 20, 1897.

414   "Secretary of": ibid.

414   "We have not been advised": ibid.

414   "While general": AA, S&S production records 1892–97.

414   "Sales of Hamburg": ibid. and AA, S&S financial reports.

414   "One who was not": daybook of Fred T. Steinway, March–May 1898. At one point, Cotterill also told the nephews that they were personally responsible for William's and Steinway & Sons' debts.

414   "Not long after": op. cit., Inventory and Appraisement of the Personal Estate of William Steinway, April 5, 1898.

414   "in all respects": ibid.

414   "William's $600,000": ibid.

414   "The $214,000": ibid.

414   "The 119,000": ibid.

414–15   "In essence,": AA, ibid.

415   "The New York & College Point": ibid.

415   "William's East River": ibid.

415   "The Ravenswood": ibid.

415   "The shares in": ibid.

415   "In August 1898": Certificate of Incorporation of the Daimler Manufacturing Company, filed and recorded August 3, 1898. The company was authorized for a capitalization of $500,000, and began with fifty shares subscribed at $100 each. Twenty shares were held by Kuebler, with a half-dozen other stockholders owning five shares each.

415   "Though Kuebler": "Annual Report of the Daimler Manufacturing Company," 1901.

415   "American Mercedes": Catalog of the Daimler Manufacturing Company, 1904, p. 1 ff.

415   "but the parent company": D. W. Fostle, *Speedboat*, p. 51 ff. The importers, Smith & Mabley, contracted to import the staggering number of one hundred Mercedes in 1904, and also developed the legendary chain-drive Simplex, a high-performance American luxury automobile quite capable of beating Mercedes in competition. Like William Steinway, Smith & Mabley also built boats. Both understood that the nation's waterways were then better developed than its roads.

416   "In a strange example": ibid.

416   "Brewer George Ehret": NYT, August 2, 1897. Undoubtedly, this was not Ehret's choice. On June 10, 1889, Ehret offered to give William his share in the amusement park if William would "assure everything." William did not assume Ehret's interest, and the diary indicates that Bowery Bay generally continued to lose money. Ehret also had a share in the ferry prior to William's death.

416   "William's Gramercy Park home": NYT, February 2, 1904. The home was later razed, and an apartment building now stands on the approximate site.

416   "Two million dollars": AA, op. cit., Inventory and Appraisement.

416   "The value": ibid. This was about $150 per share, or about 12.5 times 1897 earnings and roughly at book value.

416   "*Town Topics*": *Town Topics*, May 26, 1898, quoted in *Musical Courier*, June 1, 1898,

416   "The *Musical Courier*": ibid.

416   "Events may show": ibid.

417   "On the other hand": ibid.

417   "else his estate": NYT, May 20, 1898. The forcing factor was the story on the estate's difficulties in the *New York Herald* one day before.

417   "there seems now no chance": ibid.

417   "According to William's": Last Will and Testament of William Steinway.

417   "George himself": ibid.

417   "At the rate": AA, S&S inventory book, 1883–92.

417–18   "Many transactions": op. cit., daybook of Fred T. Steinway, March–May 1898.

418   "saved the family's honor": ibid. Precisely what Cotterill did to accomplish the feat was not stated by him. There are many mysteries here; it is unclear, for example, how, and by whom, the banks were persuaded to wait patiently for their funds, particularly those made in the names of others, such as Tretbar and Stetson, both of whom were moderately wealthy as a result of their S&S salaries and bonuses. The case of Daimler is strange also; besides the patent rights, there was a substantial investment in machinery, as photographs of the works clearly show. No trace can be found of a formal sale of the tooling and machinery.

418   "Contingency plans": daybook of Fred T. Steinway, June–September 1899.

418   "Small creditors filed lawsuits,": e.g., New York State Supreme Court, *Rummel* v. *Steinway*. Franz Rummel's wife was the daughter of Samuel F. B. Morse, and she sued for $6,000 loaned William.

418   "but the most significant": New York State Supreme Court, Appellate Division, Second Department, *Ottilie Marie Steinway*, et alia, v. *Louis von Bernuth*, et alia. Ottilie Marie was the minor daughter of George A. Steinway. Related aspects are found in New York Supreme Court, Appellate Division, First Department, *Ottilie C. Recknagel* v. *Charles H. Steinway*, et alia.

418   "The life of George": NYT, September 22, 1898.

418   "the Steinway Hall crowd": op. cit., *Steinway* v. *von Bernuth*, p. 144.

418   "satisfied": ibid., p. 133, testimony of Henry A. Cassebeer.

418   "although my father": ibid.

418   "George lived": ibid.

418   "baker's dozen": AA, *Historical Statistics of the United States, Colonial Times to 1970*, Part 1, p. 165, series 735. In 1896 the average annual earnings of a nonfarm worker was $439. Not until the year 1966 did the average American worker earn (in current dollars) an amount equal to George's stipend from William.

418   "I have just received": op. cit., *Steinway* v. *von Bernuth*, p. 73.

418   "Your children": ibid.

419   "Ottilie's later pleas": ibid., p. 74 ff.

419   "the thing is a matter of business": ibid.

419   "remarked it was entirely": ibid., p. 81.

419   "The income": The amount is conservative. In 1890 S&S paid a dividend of $20 per share, which would have netted George's three daughters $46,000 on the intended 2,300 shares.

419   "the earnings of": AA, op. cit., *Historical Statistics*, Part 1, p. 165, series 735.

419   "STEINWAY SECRETS": NYT, February 18, 1900.

419   "certain weaknesses": ibid.

419   "had no property": ibid.

419   "In reality": WSD, June 13, 1895. William wrote: "I examine all of George A. Steinway's papers, documents and his somewhat foolish will, made April 17, 1894." On June 29, 1895, George signed a new will "written in his

own handwriting" in the presence of William, who obviously approved it, as he provided the witnesses. On July 6, 1895, George signed "all necessary papers." William was clearly in control of the disposition of George's assets.

419   "Louis von Bernuth averred": The diary reveals this as a patent falsehood. On June 17, 1895, William had "a long conference" on the divorce of George with Ottilie's father and von Bernuth. On June 21 von Bernuth was present at a second meeting that included Ottilie, her lawyer, her father, and William that finalized the divorce arrangements.

419   "who told William": WSD, November 2, 1895. The wedding was in the New York papers as well: "Papers state marriage of Carl L. Recknagel and Ottilie C. Steinway," wrote William on December 29, 1895.

419   "knew nothing": op. cit., NYT, February 18, 1900.

419   "This claim": op. cit., *Steinway* v. *von Bernuth*, p. 73 ff.

420   "With the wisdom": op. cit., NYT, February 18, 1900.

420   "collusively": op. cit., *Steinway* v. *von Bernuth*, p. 100 ff.

420   "on grounds": ibid.

420   "fraud upon": ibid.

420   "concealed from William": ibid.

420   "William did": WSD, November 2, December 28 and 29, 1895.

420   "nothing was alleged": NYT, March 10, 1901.

420   "have no possible": ibid.

420   "The family now claimed": New York Supreme Court, Appellate Division, First Department, *Ottilie C. Recknagel* v. *Charles H. Steinway*, et alia.

420   "and it was held": ibid.

420   "at a proper place and time": NYT, June 15, 1899 and March 26, 1901.

420   "Another": ibid.

420   "By the end of 1900": Minutes of the Annual Meeting of Stockholders, April 7, 1901.

420   "What had once been": AA, ibid.

420   "One result": AA, ibid.

421   "Baldwin, whose estate": *Music Trade Review*, March 16, 1901.

421   "appreciation of properties": NYT, February 3, 1904.

421   "William's East River": ibid.

421   "to amount to": ibid.

421   "delphic wisdom": op. cit., *Musical Courier*, June 1, 1898.

421   "cumulative fiction": ibid.

28. MEMBERS OF THE BLOOD

422   "Anyone who has passed": *Music Trade Review*, April 7, 1900.

422   "The proprietors": ibid.

422   "mashers": ibid.

422   "congregate about": ibid.

423   "standing in one place": ibid.

423   "something had to be": ibid. Union Square was a "noted hangout for fairies," according to a reformer in 1914. See Timothy J. Gilfoyle, *City of Eros*, p. 388 and pp. 210–12. Roving phalanxes of prostitutes cruised Fourteenth Street as well, and on Thirteenth there were many bordellos. William

signed a complaint against a Miss Irene McCready that caused the arrest of "10 girls, 13 men" at 74 East Fourteenth Street on October 2, 1865. This was his only recorded strike against the venues of venery that were a part of each Manhattan entertainment district. Steinway Hall, Irving Hall, the Academy of Music, several theaters, and Delmonico's Restaurant were among the establishments nearby, assuring that the area's "fallen women" had an ample and ever-changing clientele drawn from Gotham's more prosperous citizens.

423   "The chair": Minutes of the Annual Meeting of Stockholders, April 6, 1903.

423   "The house": ibid.

423   "not many business houses": ibid.

423   "None could have been": AA, S&S catalogs and price lists, 1897–1904. Missing price lists make it impossible to determine when exactly the house cut prices, but it is clear that they were reduced by the beginning of 1899 and may have been lowered in 1898.

423   "In his thirty-one years": AA, S&S confidential circulars, 1865–96.

424   "The price": AA, S&S catalogs and price lists, 1897–1904.

424   "cheap trade": Daybook of Fred T. Steinway, 1902.

424   "The Steinway buyer": AA, S&S catalog and price list, 1884–85. This pricing structure was maintained throughout the roughly three decades that S&S offered all three types of instruments.

424   "By 1890": Minutes of the Board of Trustees of Steinway & Sons, December 31, 1890. In addition to the last five squares, the house built 758 grands and 1,553 uprights in America. Hamburg built 312 each of grands and uprights, for a total of 2,940 pianos. The squares were not sold out until 1893.

424   "The *Music Trades*": *Music Trades*, May 2, 1908.

425   "A plan was floated": ibid.

425   "commercial uselessness": ibid.

425   "enormous amount": ibid.

425   "Between 1899 and 1904": AA, *Historical Statistics of the United States, Colonial Times to 1970*, Part 1, p. 224, series F-1; Part 2, p. 697, series P-299.

425   "the only Manufacturers": *Music Trade Review*, April 28, 1900. This was a constant claim, and it was made in countless advertisements and articles for more than seventy years after 1870.

426   "In 1891 Steinway": AA, op. cit., *Historical Statistics* and S&S production records.

426   "While industry output": ibid.

426   "By 1900": AA, S&S catalogs and price lists, 1897–1904.

426   "average annual earnings": op. cit., *Historical Statistics*, Part 1, p. 168, series D-780.

426   "The revised strategy": *Music Trades*, May 2, 1908.

426–27   "To this enterprising": *Music Trade Review*, February 9, 1901.

427   "What the twentieth": ibid.

427   "When you buy": *Music Trade Review*, May 19, 1900.

427   "His name was Josef Hofmann": NYT, March 2, 1898.

427   "The 'Child Pianist' ": *New York World*, March 2, 1898. At the turn of the century, the artists associated with Steinway constituted a virtual pantheon of late romantic virtuosi. Alphabetically and incompletely, this included Aus der Ohe, Bloomfield-Zeisler, Busoni, Carreño, d'Albert, Dohnyani, Friedheim, Godowsky, Joseffy (still working off his debts to the company), Paderowski, and Siloti, whose tone production particularly impressed Fred Steinway.

428   "a man of earnest purpose": *New York Sun*, March 2, 1898.

428   "His interpretations": ibid.

428   "No pianist": ibid.

428   "Josef Hofmann recital": daybook of Fred T. Steinway, March 24, 1898. In general, Fred was an anchor to windward when the gales of artistic enthusiasm blew. The "pounding" referred to can be described as the use of excessive force in the depression of the keys. Beyond a certain force, the instrument's output becomes nonlinear with respect to amplitude. Beyond this force, enharmonic partials are produced, and the sound becomes blurred and harsh, but not significantly louder. The peak sound pressure level at which the enharmonicity occurs varies by make of pianos, size of the piano, condition of the hammers and other factors. Generally speaking, concert Steinways of the late nineteenth and early twentieth centuries do not differ in major ways from the instruments of today, and it is difficult to create enharmonic outputs without specific intent, as the instruments have an extremely wide dynamic range. The input/output relationship follows a square law. To double the sound pressure level requires an input force four times greater.

        Based on the large number of reports of "banging" by major artists, it appears that for roughly a decade after the turn of the century, the technique was a stylistic affectation of a number of prominent artists. *Music Trades*, May 20, 1908, shows a panel cartoon of Emil Sauer reducing a concert grand to rubble while playing the *Tanhauser* Overture, then bowing as he is showered with bouquets.

428   "I heard him play!" NYT, April 24, 1898.

429   "The fact that he": September 10, 1899.

429   "there must be": ibid.

429   "Mark [*sic*] came over": daybook of Fred T. Steinway, December 16, 1899.

429   "Mark tries": ibid.

429   "Paddy's secretary": ibid.

429   "Mark wants to create": ibid.

429   "Tretbar dissatisfied": ibid.

429   "Today's Paddy recital": ibid.

429   "as if he had never": NYT, December 13, 1899.

429   "dropped some notes": ibid.

429–30 "the octave repetitions": ibid.

430   "there was always": ibid.

430   "William went so far": WSD, February 3, 1891.

430   "Weber was now": NYT, August 21, 1903.

430   "It is astonishing": *Music Trade Review*, April 14, 1900.

431   "For a long time": *Music Trades*, February 29, 1908. This story reports an

agreement for the installation of the German Welte und Sohne player mechanism in Steinway pianos, an arrangement made principally for the European market. The Welte system was capable of highly musical reproduction.

431 "desired to maintain": ibid.

431 "The significance": *Oregon Daily Journal*, February 25, 1908, reprinted in the *Musical Courier*, March 11, 1908.

431 "There is another phase": *Oakland Enquirer*, March 7, 1908, reprinted ibid.

431 "That is": ibid.

432 "I never heard": *Los Angeles Herald*, March 4, 1908, reprinted, ibid.

432 "about two": *Los Angeles Times*, March 5, 1908, reprinted, ibid.

432 "Let us say nothing": *Oregon Sunday Journal*, March 1, 1908, reprinted, ibid.

432 "elaborate little": ibid.

432 "Locks and Lambasting": *Musical Courier*, March 18, 1908.

432 "The shock-headed": ibid.

432–33 "According to Freund": *Music Trades*, April 18, 1908.

433 "It seems to me": *Music Trades*, March 21, 1908.

433 "It was no accident": AA, *Historical Statistics of the United States, Colonial Times to 1970*, Part 2, p. 697, series 299, and p. 716, series 148 and 152. The Piano Manufacturers Association International reported production of 103,000 in 1992.

433 "Had it been": AA, ibid. and S&S production records.

433 "All stockholders": Minutes of the Annual Meeting of Stockholders, April 3, 1905.

433 "The profits came": AA, S&S financial records.

434 "in line": Minutes of the Annual Meeting of Stockholders, April 6, 1908.

434 "A recession": NYT, October 23 and 24, 1907.

434 "There are sure": NYT, October 27, 1907.

434 "is merely following": *Musical Courier*, May 27, 1908.

434 "For the first time": *Music Trades*, May 4, 1908.

434 "Schwander, who claimed": *Music Trades*, May 11, 1908.

434 "Steinway & Sons are": op. cit., *Musical Courier*, May 27, 1908.

434 "No more": ibid.

435 "Chickering . . .": ibid.

435 "not been on sale": ibid.

435 "a superannuated": ibid.

435 "The Pianola": reprinted in Harvey N. Roehl, *Player Piano Treasury*, p. 7. Originally from *Cosmopolitan Magazine*.

435 "Its production": ibid.

435 "Within the home": ibid.

435 "intends to combine": *Music Trade Review*, April 20, 1901.

436 "both plays and sings": *Music Trades*, August 8, 1908.

436 "This instrument": ibid.

436 "The year 1908": *Music Trades*, August 1, 1908.

436 "Chickering, which": *Music Trade Review*, January 13, 1900, and April 14, 1900. Wanamaker's was then located on Broadway just below Tenth Street.

436   "will be able to market": op. cit., *Music Trades*, August 1.

436   "The care taken": *New York World*, unknown date, reprinted in *Music Trades*, January 18, 1908. The premise for the piece was a search for "a model factory," which, of course, was found in the facilities of S&S.

436   "entire absence of hurry": ibid.

436   "It is not": ibid.

437   "Henry E. Steinway compelled": ibid.

437   "In our establishment": *Systems*, July 1908, reprinted in *Music Trades*, July 25, 1908.

437   "My desk is": ibid.

437   "The heads": ibid.

437   "modern cost-keeping": ibid.

437   "wage-earner": ibid.

437   "If a man is a drone": ibid.

437   "Treat men fairly": ibid.

437   "In a mode": NYT, February 20, 1909.

438   "there was no connection": ibid.

438   "The Aeolian companies": Minutes of the Board of Trustees of Steinway & Sons, March 9, 1909.

438   "The agreement": ibid.

438   "Ultimately, less than": AA, S&S production records, 1909–34.

438   "Enter almost": NYT, January 28, 1912.

438   "these superb": ibid.

438   "Starting at $1,250": ibid. and AA, S&S retail price lists, S&S production records.

439   "In 1910": NYT, June 10, 1909 and Minutes of the Board of Trustees of Steinway & Sons, May 24, 1909. The sale was not officially completed until 1910.

439   "The Harlem railroad": op. cit., NYT, June 10, 1909.

439   "Charles H. Steinway": *New York Sun*, unknown date, reprinted in *Music Trade Review*, January 19, 1901.

439   "It was not until": Minutes of the Board of Trustees of Steinway & Sons, June 5, 1916.

439   "The output": S&S production records, 1896–1913.

439   "But no one": D.W. Fostle, *Speedboat*, p. 111 ff.

439   "and Hamburg production fell": S&S production records, 1914–20.

440   "In February 1917": Minutes of the Board of Trustees of Steinway & Sons, February 6, 1917.

440   "The more than": AA, S&S financial records, 1914–24.

440   "By 1917": NYT, February 7, 1917.

440   "Americanism": NYT, April 4, 1917.

440   "Steinway's treasury": S&S financial records.

440   "Frederick Vietor": *Music Trades*, September 6, 1919.

440   "The German Savings Bank": Permission for Change of Name, Germania Savings Bank, 1917. These documents were filed with the Manhattan County Clerk's office as required by law for the institutions cited.

441   "The answer, among": AA, S&S production records and financial records, 1910–20.

441 "Steinway, the Highest": *Music Trades*, January 25, 1919.

441 "Were we to": ibid.

441 "Business statistics": *Music Trades*, April 12, 1919.

441 "*artisans*": op. cit., August 23, 1919.

441 "A Little Better": ibid.

442 "Gentlemen: In accordance": Minutes of the Board of Trustees of Steinway & Sons, April 21, 1919.

442 "The working class": ibid.

442 "We will absolutely": ibid.

442 "Between 1917 and 1919": AA, *Historical Statistics of the United States*, Part 1, p. 231, series 189, 194, 195, and p. 169, series 813.

442 "The reason": ibid., p. 179, series 977.

442 "At Steinway Hall": Minutes of the Board of Trustees of Steinway & Sons, April 24, 1919.

442 "and some ten thousand": *Music Trades*, September 25, 1919.

442 "The new labor": Minutes of the Board of Trustees of Steinway & Sons, September 30, 1919, reproduces a letter containing these union demands.

443 "The refractory": AA, op. cit., *Historical Statistics of the United States*, p. 169, series 813.

443 "A wage of $42": AA, NYT, November 30, 1919.

443 "closed shop": op. cit., Minutes of the Board, September 30, 1919.

443 "BOLSHEVISM NOT NEW": NYT, December 7, 1919.

443 "The disease": ibid.

443 "We will oppose": *Music Trades*, October 4, 1919.

443 "One month": NYT, October 31, 1919.

29. A DEMOCRATIC AND GENIAL CHARACTER

444 "In the death": *Music Trade Review*, November 1, 1919.

444 "Those who": ibid.

444 "most impressive": *Music Trade Review*, November 8, 1919.

444 "Seldom have": ibid.

445 "The services": ibid.

445 "There was music": ibid.

445 " 'Mr. Steinway' ": ibid.

445 "Substituting": ibid.

445 "A wealth": ibid.

445 "Where William's death": NYT, October 30, 1919.

445 "This, too, was change": *Musical Courier*, May 27, 1908.

445 "Even if all the piano": ibid.

445 "By the time of": *Historical Statistics of the United States, Colonial Times to 1970*, Part 2, p. 700, series P-331.

445 "Of that almost": AA, ibid. and S&S private daybook.

445 "Ten years before": AA, ibid.

445 "In the last year of William's": AA, ibid.

445 "In the last year of Charles's": AA, ibid.

446 "STEINWAY FORTUNE": NYT, November 26, 1919.

446 "Although Charles F. M.": ibid.

446 "Mrs. Marie A. Steinway": ibid.

447 "The will cuts off": ibid.

447 "excepting and excluding": Last Will and Testmaent of Charles H. Steinway, April 23, 1914.

447 "Years later": New York County Surrogate Court records, March 24, 1921, *et. seq.*

447 "It amounted": ibid.

447 "Within a few days". op. cit., *Music Trade Review*, November 8.

447 "In 1904 fully": AA, op. cit., *Historical Statistics of the United States*, Part 2, pp. 697–702, series P-299, P-318 through 374.

447 "Another 6.5 percent": ibid.

447 "One in fifty": ibid.

447 "Twice as many": ibid.

447 "Musicians and": ibid., Part One, p. 143 ff., series D-233–682.

447 "Of these": ibid., p. 716, Series Q-153.

448 "The reason": ibid. Part 1, p. 224 ff., Series F-1–20.

448 "Besides spectating": File, "SAJI," Collection of Henry Z. Steinway.

448 "an extremely valuable": *Music Trade Review*, July 30, 1927.

448 "Focusing on": ibid.

448 "The data for": ibid.

448 "Tabulating": ibid.

448 "Nationally music": ibid.

448 "The recreations": ibid.

448 "Player pianos": AA, United States Department of Commerce data reproduced in Harvey N. Roehl, *Player Piano Treasury*, p. 51.

448–49 "By 1927": ibid.

449 "The date was": Erik Barnouw, *A Tower in Babel*, p. 61 ff.

449 "In the four hours": *Detroit News*, September 1, 1920, quoted ibid.

449 "Publisher William E.": ibid.

449 "Thaddeus Cahill": Greg Armbruster, ed., *The Art of Electronic Music*, pp. 4–11.

449 "aetherially pure": ibid.

449 "After a few years": op. cit., *A Tower in Babel*, p. 72 ff.

449 "Radio Music Boxes": ibid., pp. 78–79.

450 "In 1920": AA, op. cit., *Historical Statistics of the United States*, Part 2, p. 796, series R-93 through 105.

450 "By 1930": ibid.

450 "Unable to compete": AA, op. cit., *Player Piano Treasury*, p. 51.

450 "But at Steinway": AA, S&S production records, 1921–26.

450 "It began": *Advertising Age*, August 25, 1969. The Ayer agency resigned the Steinway account to assume Yamaha.

451 "They began": *Music Trade Review*, April 14, 1900.

451 "One Whole Note": ibid.

451 "The name Steinway": Unfortunately, the author has lost the dates and media for these advertisements. Generally, S&S advertised during this period in *Literary Digest*, *Saturday Evening Post*, *Atlantic*, *Review of Reviews*, *Vanity Fair*, and other magazines. Additionally, the *New York Times* and other papers were used to build Steinway Hall traffic. In some cases, major market dealers, such as Lyon & Healy in Chicago, conducted their own Steinway campaigns in the dailies.

451   "The visual keystone": Much of the art used in Steinway advertisements is still displayed at the hall on Fifty-seventh Street in Manhattan.

452   "His moving fingers": See above note on media. This ad is also reproduced in Ronald V. Ratliffe, *Steinway*, p. 123. This book was produced with the support of the current ownership of Steinway & Sons and is used by them as a sales promotion item.

452   "Under Fred Steinway": AA, S&S private daybook. It is significant that as early as 1875, and perhaps before, promotional expenditures were a "line item" in S&S financial records.

452   " 'Service,' as it was known": Alexander Greiner, "Pianos and Pianists," p. 105 ff. This typewritten manuscript was a gift to Henry Steinway by its author, who was head of the concert and artists department of S&S from 1928 until his death in 1958.

453   "Alexander Greiner": ibid.

453   "The Steinway is": ibid. Brailowsky was a Class D artist. According to Greiner these "included more artists of all kinds than could be listed in the Manhattan Telephone Directory."

453   "about twenty-five dollars per new piano": AA, S&S private daybook, 1920–29. This is the mean expenditure for the period based on C&A operating expenses. It does not include the capital investment in loan pianos, since the data on that constantly rotating stock was unavailable.

453   "i.e., reading glasses": S&S inventory book, 1860. These pianists and a few others such as William Mason also received loan pianos for their homes.

453   "He and his wife": Recollection of Henry Z. Steinway, based on his conversations with Julia Steinway. Mrs. Steinway maintained an active interest in the business for many years after her husband's death.

454   "I think": quoted in Craig H. Roell, *The Piano in America, 1890–1940*, p. 165 ff.

454   "The Baldwin": ibid.

454   "Boy, you ain't": ibid.

454   "There is something": ibid.

454   "Choose": *Music Trades Review*, March 19, 1927. This carries a Baldwin display ad stating that while pianists are "unlike in their racial characteristics," they are "of one mind and opinion—all use Baldwin." The evidence presented was a listing of five artists, all European-trained.

454   "Billy Sunday": op. cit., *The Piano in America*.

454   "an unforgivable orgy": The *Etude*, January 1924, p. 7.

454   "naturally to blame": ibid.

454–55   "Any of you": NYT, October 11, 1924.

455   "We listen to Bach": reprinted in NYT, September 20, 1925.

455   "We are fascinated": ibid.

455   "a new": ibid.

455   "more pianofortes": ibid.

455   "repopularize the": NYT, June 8, 1926.

455   "patron saint": ibid.

455   "This had no": op. cit., *Historical Statistics of the United States*, Part 2, p. 697, series P-299.

455   "In former years": op. cit., NYT, June 8.

455   "The result": AA, S&S private daybook, 1919–25.

456   "It took Charles": AA, ibid., 1902–14.

456   "Per-piano profits": AA, ibid., 1919–27.

456   "Your trustees": Minutes of the Annual Meeting of Steinway & Sons, April 5, 1926.

456   "The year Fred": AA, S&S private daybook, 1926.

456   "By the time": AA, S&S private daybook, 1929.

456   "It was 1928": AA, S&S production records, 1928.

456   "Profits, however": AA, S&S private daybook, 1928.

456   "The London hall": AA, S&S private daybook, 1920–29.

456   "At last demand": op. cit., Minutes, April 5, 1926.

456–57   "but it was not until 1947": ibid., April 6, 1948.

457   "In the spring": ibid., April 4, 1924.

457   "Planned to cost": ibid., April 6, 1925.

457   "A churchlike": In the public areas many of the main architectural elements and furnishings of Steinway Hall still existed in 1993.

457   "based on the drawings": ibid.

457   "THRONG AT OPENING": NYT, October 28, 1925. The first hall opened on October 31, 1866.

457   "More persons": ibid.

458   "What heart too proudly": ibid.

458   "early arrivals": ibid.

458   "had attended": ibid.

458   "In the last paragraph": ibid.

458   "roughly one-fourth the assets": AA, S&S financial records, 1926.

458   "The building": op. cit., Minutes, April 5, 1926.

459   "The medal": NYT, December 23, 1925.

459   "Your trustees": op. cit., Minutes, April 4, 1927.

459   "Since the beginning": ibid.

459   "He was correct": "Business Cycle Expansions and Contractions," *Business Conditions Digest*, vol. 30, no. 1, January 1990, p. 104.

459   "succumbed to a heart": *Music Trade Review*, July 23, 1927.

459   "Mr. Steinway": NYT, July 18, 1927.

459   "the finest radio concerts": ibid.

459   "one of the leading": op. cit., *Music Trade Review*.

30. THE ROAD TO DESTRUCTION

460   "At a meeting": *Music Trade Review*, July 30, 1927.

460   "first cousin": ibid.

460   "For five years": ibid.

460–61   "He even put": ibid.

461   "Though not educated": WSD, April 29, 1895: "My son Theodore is very unruly at school and is frequently punished by having to stay after school." On June 22, after a visit by the headmaster, William donated two $500 prizes to the school but did not specify their purpose.

461   "antiquarian interests": recollection of Henry Z. Steinway.

461   "one of the finest": op. cit., *Music Trade Review*, July 30, 1927.

461   "Yet there was": NYT, October 26, 1952.

461   "To settle": NYT, December 18, 1926.

461   "more like a musician": Telephone interview with Warner S. Shelly, October 1990.

462   "But the life": Interview with confidential informant.

462   "A separation": ibid.

462   "The evidence": AA, S&S private daybook, 1909–39.

462   "During the year": Minutes of the Annual Meeting of Steinway & Sons, April 2, 1928.

462   "The excellence": ibid.

462   "That year": ibid.

462   "This was not": AA, ibid.

462   "Theodore reported": AA, ibid.

462   "Many player": ibid.

462   "This was a reasonable": AA, S&S private daybook, 1920–29. Using the available financial and production data, the author built a computerized historical model of S&S operations that greatly aided in analyses of this type. Ultimately, multiple models were built spanning the years 1885 through 1972.

462   "By 1929": AA, ibid.

463   "Profits slid": ibid.

463   "Used-piano sales": AA, ibid. More precisely, the ratio of used to new piano sales changed, and the proportion of used instruments became a greater fraction of total sales. A similar shift occurred, for example, before the 1907 panic.

463   "absolutely sound": quoted in John K. Galbraith, *The Great Crash of 1929*, p. 31.

463   "the high tide": ibid., p. 20.

463   "Everybody Ought": ibid., p. 57.

463   "the economic condition": ibid., p. 75.

463   "stock prices": ibid.

463   "Economic problems": NYT, July 1, 1930; September 13, 1930; July 28, 1930; August 3, 1930; respectively, for the imputed causative factors.

463   "it will take as long": NYT, May 29, 1930.

463   "Too many people": ibid.

463   "One of the greatest evils": ibid.

463   "The Great Depression": AA, "Business Cycle Expansions and Contractions," *Business Conditions Digest*, vol. 30, no. 1, January 1990, p. 104.

463   "For those employed": AA, *Historical Statistics of the United States, Colonial Times to 1970*, Part 1, p. 164, series D-722 through 724.

463   "Between 1930 and 1933": AA, ibid., Part 2, p. 1038, series X-741 through 755.

463   "Wages would not": AA, ibid., Part 1, p. 164, series D-722 through 724.

463   "Housing prices": AA, ibid., Part 2, p. 640, series N-156 through 167.

463   "automobile sales": AA, ibid., p. 716, series N-148 through 155.

463   "Even radio": AA, ibid., p. 696, series P-288 through 290.

464   "85 percent sales slide": AA, ibid., p. 697, series P-299. The 1920s peak occurred in 1923 with 344,000 pianos sold and reached bottom in 1931 with sales of 51,000, a slide of 85.17 percent. Data were collected every other year, so it is possible that the peak may have been higher and bottom lower by some moderate amount.

464 "Once there had been": AA, United States Department of Commerce data reproduced in Harvey N. Roehl, *Player Piano Treasury*, p. 51.

464 "In 1930": AA, S&S private daybook and S&S production records, 1928–31. This pushed the per-piano advertising cost to an unprecedented $165 per instrument sold.

464 "It is hardly" op. cit. Minutes, April 4, 1934.

464 "We live and die": *New York World*, reprinted in *Music Trade Review*, January 18, 1908.

464 "Only fifty or so": recollection of Henry Z. Steinway, who also remembers that some workers would arrive at the factory driving the taxicabs with which they earned supplementary income.

464 "The remaining": op. cit., Minutes, April 2, 1934. Theodore E. cut his own salary by about 60 percent and paid himself no bonuses.

464 "to a 1901 basis": ibid.

465 "In New York": S&S production records, 1926–33.

465 "For every seven": AA, ibid.

465 "Production in Hamburg": ibid.

465 "Even with the factories": AA, S&S private daybook, 1930–35.

465 "But by 1933": ibid.

465 "Fred came in": note in the collection of Henry Z. Steinway.

465 "Paderewski declines": Minutes of the Board of Trustees of Steinway & Sons, June 10, 1931. These are distinct from the minutes of the annual stockholders' meetings.

465 "The grim responsibility": op. cit., *Pianos and Pianists*, p. 108 ff. Greiner notes that there was not a single artist defection to a competitor. Almost certainly, a contributing factor was that the remaining pianomakers were also occupied with survival issues and were in no position to subsidize artists.

465 "By 1935 concert": AA, S&S private daybook, 1929–35.

465–66 "Waffle irons,": AA, op. cit., *Historical Statistics*, Part 2, p. 694–700, particularly series P-283, 284, 289, 290, 336, 337. The growing availability of refrigerators is particularly interesting. From 5,000 built in 1922, the number climbed to 890,000 in 1929 and continued to grow during the Depression, reaching 2,824,000 in 1936. For the men who made cold a commodity, the Depression was a different experience.

466 "In 1930": AA, ibid., p. 400, series H-873, 874. But by 1932 even this fell by a third; many could no longer afford to escape as often.

466 "Following the World War": Robert R. Updegraff, *The Updegraff Report: a Special Survey*, typewritten manuscript, p. 8 ff. The report is dated 1930.

466 "Radio is the beginning": ibid.

466 "probably the greatest indictment": ibid.

466 "He did what his father": S&S retail price lists, 1929–34.

467 "Here Are the Steinways": "Here Are the Steinways and How They Grew," *Fortune*, December 1934, p. 99 ff.

467 "No mention was made": AA, S&S financial records and production records, 1926–34, S&S inventory book, 1860.

467 "From Heinrich's day": op. cit., *Fortune*, p. 101.

467 "shocked other pianomakers": ibid., p. 103. This canard has been endlessly repeated and elaborated. Actual inspection of a half-century of piano adver-

tising showed that there was nothing unusual about the media, content, or frequency of Steinway advertising as compared to its nineteenth-century competitors, save for a greater emphasis on proprietary technology.

467   "tense and dynamic": ibid., p. 101.

467   "the high, oldtime": ibid., p. 103.

467   "a dark, earthy place": ibid., p. 104.

467   "7,000,000": ibid.

467   "Steinway history": ibid., p. 100.

467   "The Name": ibid., p. 99.

467   "The family turned down": ibid., p. 163.

467   "The sons will learn": ibid.

467   "it was revealed": ibid., p. 153.

467   "Officially": memorandum of Henry Z. Steinway, December 1991. The twenty-month closing is the author's estimate, and it is based on the cited memorandum. *Fortune* claimed twenty-five months, which appears too long. Peculiarly, the Minutes shed little light on the closing and the reopening. They do reveal that only 273 pianos were actually built during 1932, and that the return to work was with seven-hour days in 1933. As of December 31, 1933, 605 men were working at reduced wages and 364 were not, creating an S&S "unemployment rate" of 37.6 percent.

467   "Also claimed": op. cit., *Fortune*, p. 156, and S&S production records. U.S. sales for 1934 were 1,130 units, suggesting that the rehiring of 605 men was very optimistic.

467   "high by nearly half": S&S private daybook, 1934. The actual assets were $9,588,742, of which an astonishing $2,408,981 was inventory.

467   "Safe to say": op. cit., *Fortune*, p. 163.

468   "inventor": ibid., p. 101.

468   "accelerated actions": United States patents, numbers 1,826,848 filed February 18, 1931, and 2,031,748 filed May 18, 1934. These dealt with the method of mounting piano keys and the positioning of lead weights within them for balance; neither represents innovation of the scale wrought by C. F. Theodore or Henry Steinway, Jr.

468   "The first was": op. cit., Minutes of the Board, May 31, 1935.

468   " 'Baby' grands": The origin of this enduring term is obscure, but it appeared in *Music Trades* by March 7, 1908, where Hardman, Peck & Company used it to describe a small grand they offered. Small grands i.e., less than five feet five inches long, of many makers exhibited severe tonal compromises. The Model S Steinway of the 1930s had a very even and well-balanced tone, with power ample for most living rooms. Henry Z. Steinway informed the author that the Model S was the favorite piano of Josef Hofmann.

468   "Perhaps no announcement": *Piano Trade Magazine*, February, 1936, p. 6 ff.

468   "It is our opinion": ibid.

468   "Instead of": ibid.

468   "usual Steinway reticence": ibid. It was also claimed that the basic design was by Henry Ziegler, now deceased; commercial development was the work of Paul Bilhuber, then a member of what was called the "inventions department."

468   "Not merely": op. cit., Minutes of the Board, November 8, 1935.
469   "Dealers could": ibid.
469   "In the first": AA, S&S production records, 1920–39.
469   "had it not been": ibid.
469   "The manufacture of upright": ibid.
469   "By the mid-1930s": ibid.
469   "but one Steinway upright": ibid.
469   "the Haddorff Piano Company": *Piano Trade Magazine*, June 1935.
469   "A number of tricks": ibid. This description is based on photographs of the piano accompanying the article.
470   "Among the more bizarre": ibid., March 1936.
470   "Art Moderne Steinways": ibid., January 1941.
470   "Mini-Piano": ibid., January 1941. This Hardman, Peck instrument was but 36 inches high and 17 inches deep.
470   "Clever folding tops": ibid., August 1935.
470   "Radio manufacturer": ibid., April 1937.
470   "In 1935": ibid., August 1936 and January 1941.
470   "In 1939": ibid., January 1941.
470   "In 1939": AA, ibid., and S&S production records.
470   "The problem": AA, S&S production records.
470   "The first of": AA, S&S production records, catalogs and retail price lists, 1937–40.
470   "Cheap for a Steinway": AA, op. cit., *Piano Trade Magazine*, January 1941. The average 1939 price of a small console piano was $298.44, down 5 percent from 1937. A by-product of the styling frenzy was ferocious price competition and a temporary suspension of H. L. Mencken's rule that "nobody ever went broke underestimating the taste of the American people."
471   "and in 1939": AA, S&S production records, 1937–41.
471   "Eighty years before": Among several such letters is one dated August 21, no year, in which C. F. Theodore opines that his pianinos are ideally suited to New York City because of their small size.
471   "roughly quadrupled": AA, S&S production records, 1935–39 and S&S private daybook.
471   "In 1939 Theodore E.": S&S financial records, 1939.
471   "This did not change": AA, op. cit., production records and daybook, 1929–39.
471   "The new 'economy' models": ibid.
471   "Almost twenty-one dollars": ibid.
472   "I shall never forget": op. cit., *Pianos and Pianists*, p. 221 ff.
472   "Only the black, mute": NYT, March 5, 1939.
472   "tall figure": ibid.
472   "To have seen": op. cit., *Pianos and Pianists*, p. 220. Greiner, it should be noted, was never impressed by Paderewski's talent; his attitude preceded by many years his witness to what can only be called the terminal performances.
472   "Paderewski Collapses": NYT, May 26, 1939.
472   "When it was": ibid.
473   "on a reduced scale": NYT, May 28, 1939.
473   "lordly magnificence": ibid.

473   "I was backstage": op. cit., *Pianos and Pianists*, p. 221.

473   "Ignace Paderewski died": NYT, June 30, 1941.

473   "concerned for both": recollection of Henry Z. Steinway.

473   "temporary": ibid.

473   "American production": AA, S&S production records, 1925–40. The all-time New York sales peak occurred in 1926 with 6,294 units. In Hamburg the peak was in 1928 when 2,602 pianos were sold. Both reached minima in 1932 with 900 and 216 units, respectively.

473   "Continue Hamburg": op. cit., Minutes of the Board, February 28, 1936.

473   "The letter": ibid.

473   "When the Third Reich": recollection of Henry Z. Steinway.

474   "Final result": "Annual Report of Steinway & Sons for the Year Ended December 30, 1939." Why this report is dated December 30 is unknown; the report consists of a profit and loss statement plus a balance sheet that was mailed to shareholders.

474   "Publicly undaunted": *Music Trades*, January 1940.

474   "Mr. Theodore E.": op. cit., Minutes of the Board, October 19, 1939.

474   "By preventing practices": Foster Dulles, *Labor in America*, p. 275.

474   "The result was": AA, op. cit., *Historical Statistics of the United States*, Part 1, p. 177 ff., series D-927 through 951.

474   "Representing the piano": Craig H. Roell, *The Piano in America, 1890–1940*, p. 232 ff. Roell presents a more complete account of this exercise in political fantasy and federal incompetence.

475   "Among the general": ibid.

475   "In a way reminiscent": recollection of Henry Z. Steinway.

475   "not dictated to": As matters turned out, at least one Communist was active in the union leadership. See memorandum, Random Memories About Unionization of Steinway & Sons, by Henry Z. Steinway, February 10, 1988.

475   "Between 1935": AA, op. cit., *Historical Statistics of the United States*, Part 1, p. 177 ff., series D-927 through 951.

31. SLIGHTLY LONGER THAN A BOXCAR

476   "Mr. William R.": letter from Walter Petersen to William R. Steinway, July 3, 1945.

476   "I cannot say": ibid.

476   "Since 1930": AA, S&S financial records, 1930–45.

476   "At the end": ibid. Liquid assets were equal to seven weeks at the 1944 mean burn rate.

476–77   "Steinway sales": *Historical Statistics of the United States*, Part 1, p. 226, series F-31.

477   "Frederick Vietor": *Piano Trade Magazine*, April 1941.

477   "Wages are higher": Robert Heller Associates, *Final Report of April 18, 1941*, p. 2 ff.

477   "operating management": ibid.

477   "violation of sound": ibid.

477   "always represent": ibid.

477   "strong men": ibid.

477   "styling deficiencies": ibid.

477   "loss rate": memorandum of Paul Bilhuber ca. February 21, 1941.

477   "failure to keep up": ibid.

477   "We would counsel": ibid.

478   "Their arrival": recollection of Henry Z. Steinway.

178   "Soon the tradepapers": *Piano Trades Magazine*, May 1941.

478   "To lower the raised": *Piano Trades Magazine*, October 1941.

478   "The message was": Minutes of the Board of Directors of Steinway & Sons, July 16, 1941, reveals that a factory manager named Anderson was hired, and *Piano Trades Magazine*, May 1941, reports the hiring of a controller named Miller, as well as the fact that a member of the Heller consulting firm had joined the S&S board. None of these gentlemen had the long career customarily associated with S&S employment. The trustees officially became directors on June 30, 1941.

478   "On March 12": *Piano Trade Magazine*, April, 1941.

478   "judicious investigation": op. cit., Minutes of the Board of Directors, August 20, 1941.

478   "possibility of": ibid.

478   "best and thoroughly": ibid., December 17, 1941.

479   "Manufacturer of all types": NYT, March 1, 1942.

479   "manufacturers will": NYT, March 4, 1942.

479   "As if to show": op. cit., Minutes of the Board of Directors, September 17, 1941. At this time S&S was also selling radios from the hall.

479   "More than 700": NYT, March 20, 1942.

479   "seek post-war": op. cit., Minutes of the Board of Directors, May 20, 1942.

479   "never about": "Here Are the Steinways and How They Grew," *Fortune*, December 1934, p. 163.

479   "The Name": ibid.

479   "some well-known": op. cit., Minutes of the Board of Directors, July 15, 1942.

479   "no critical materials": NYT, July 2, 1942.

479–80   "The plants, machinery": NYT, June 22, 1942.

480   "By mid-August": op. cit., Minutes of the Board of Directors, August 18, 1942.

480   " 'CG,' in the bubbling": John L. Lowden, *Silent Wings at War*, p. 10. Notably devoid of aggrandizement and written from experience, a full account of American combat glider history in World War II is found here.

480   "Roughly forty-eight feet": ibid., p. 12 ff.

480   "Its envisioned mission": ibid.

480   "Plywood was made": See United States of C. F. Theodore Steinway numbers 204,106, dated May 21, 1878; 229,198, dated June 22, 1880; and 230,354, dated July 20, 1880, for insight into his technology.

480   "By Christmas 1942": op. cit., Minutes of the Board of Directors, December 12, 1942.

480   "Wings for Victory": See "To Holders of Steinway & Sons Stamped 5% Debentures of 1966," March 30, 1943. This advised holders that accrued interest was being invested in "U.S. Government Bonds."

480   "in total": op. cit., *Silent Wings at War*, p. 17.

480   "flak bait": ibid., p. 11.

480   "suicide jockeys": ibid.

480   "When a 137-glider": ibid., p. 48.

481   "wooden aircraft program": NYT, June 14, 1944.

481   "gave themselves unselfishly": ibid.

481   "spearheaded the invasion": ibid.

481   "fabricated by": ibid.

481   "Operadio": op. cit., Minutes of the Board of Directors, May 19, 1943.

481   "A plan to buy": op. cit., Minutes of the Board of Directors, May 17, 1944.

481   "Ultimately more than": Minutes of the Annual Meeting of the Stockholders of Steinway & Sons, April 1, 1946.

481   "As glidermaking": op. cit., Minutes of the Board of Directors, July 21, 1943; August 23, 1944; and September 20, 1944.

481   "Employment slipped": ibid.

481   "In 1944 Steinway": AA, S&S financial records, 1930–45.

481   "the old [Hamburg] factory": op. cit., Minutes of the Annual Meeting, April 1, 1946.

481   "of all the U.S.": ibid.

481   "A dollar of assets": AA, S&S financial records, 1927–46.

482   "postwar production slipped": AA, S&S production records, 1939–48.

482   "As to our Branch House": "Report of the President for the Year 1947," April 5, 1948. Beginning with fiscal 1941, the S&S accounts were audited by Haskins & Sells. Thereafter, the "annual report" took on a more modern, but still terse, form. In this report Theodore formally addressed the stockholders for the first time.

482   "In 1948 Hamburg": op. cit., production records.

482   "It was not": ibid.

482   "Alexander Greiner recollected": Alexander Greiner, *Pianos and Pianists*, pp. 222–26.

482   "to discuss tempos": ibid.

482   "And what kind": ibid.

482   "Philadelphia recital": ibid.

482   "We sold": op. cit., Minutes of the Annual Meeting, April 6, 1948.

483   "He resolutely refused": op. cit., Minutes of the Board of Directors, March 26, 1947.

483   "The suggestion was made": ibid., August 28, 1946.

483   "President Theodore E. Steinway": ibid.

483   "vigorously objected": ibid., September 25, 1946. Other directors were "sympathetic to the suggestion," noted the Minutes.

483   "The Radio Corporation": NYT, March 27, 1947.

483   "No list price": ibid.

483   "for Dumont Laboratories": ibid.

483   "The least expensive": AA, S&S retail price lists, 1946–48.

483   "By October 1947": NYT, October 10, 1947.

483   "It took seventy years": AA, *Historical Statistics of the United States, Colonial Times to 1970*, Part 2, p. 783 ff., series R-2, 105; and Part 1, p. 43, series A-350.

484   "Had those pianos": AA, ibid., series R-103 and S&S production records, 1953. The number of TV sets made in 1953 was 7,216,000. In 1947, 179,000 sets were built.

Notes

484   "in 1938": *Bureau of the Census: Social Indicators III, Selected Data on Social Conditions and Trends in the United States*, 1980, p. 561.

484   "By 1960": ibid.

484   "In 1960 television": ibid.

484   "Despite some probable": AA, Historical time series of industry unit sales were tabulated by Henry Z. Steinway and provided by him. The writer is solely responsible for any observations or inferences made from Mr. Steinway's data.

484   "One of the worst": NYT, July 22, 1949.

484   "few who can walk": ibid.

484   "In the demobilization": op. cit., Historical time series.

484   "By 1950": AA, ibid.

485   "Steinway & Sons": AA, ibid.

485   "There were weekly": recollection of Henry Z. Steinway.

485   "The city of": Theodore E. Steinway, *People and Pianos*, p. 5.

485   "it seemed": op. cit., Minutes of the Annual Meeting, April 5, 1954.

485   "During 1953": ibid.

485   "The Steinway piano": op. cit., quoted in *Pianos and Pianists*, pp. 187–88.

485   "The Steinways have": ibid.

485–86   "That year": op. cit., AA, *Historical Statistics of the United States*, Part 2, p. 716, series Q-148 through 153.

486   "A two-thousand-dollar scholarship": NYT, May 9, 1994.

486   "The proceeds": Minutes of the Annual Meeting, April 5, 1954. The net was $26,875, split equally between the New York Philharmonic and the Musicians Foundation.

486   "The 'Voice' ": Tim Brooks and Earle Marsh, *The Complete Directory to Prime Time Network TV Shows*, p. 799.

486   "With opera": ibid.

486   "Firestone demanded": op. cit., *Pianos and Pianists*, p. 176 ff.

486   "Via some unclear": ibid.

486   "You wouldn't want": NYT, October 20, 1953.

487   "The program began": op. cit., *Pianos and Pianists*, p. 170 ff.

487   "faced his colleagues": op. cit., NYT, October 20.

487   "A tumultuous": ibid.

487   "The guests, reported": op. cit., *Pianos and Pianists*.

487   "In December": Minutes of the Board of Directors, December 31, 1953; and May 19, 1954.

487   "After the expenditure": op. cit., NYT, May 9. Internal records are not entirely clear but suggest that the true amount may have been 5 to 10 percent higher.

487   "Steinway sold": AA, S&S production records.

487   "piano manufacturing": Minutes of the Board of Directors, June 22, 1955.

488   "Steinway & Sons needs": Minutes of the Board of Directors, October 11, 1955.

488   "an office of chairman": ibid.

488   "considerable discussion": ibid.

488   "Kinsmen of Founder": NYT, October 21, 1955.

488   "is a great-grandson": ibid.

488   "Walking through": NYT, October 26, 1952.

488   "Managers were": recollection of Henry Z. Steinway.

488   "steadfast adherence": op. cit., *Pianos and Pianists*, p. 171.

488–89   "furtherance of all": ibid.

489   "child": op. cit., NYT, October 26.

489   "Fools' names": quoted by Henry Z. Steinway, March 26, 1993.

489   "Democratic and": *Music Trade Review*, November 1, 1919.

489   "Industry sales": op. cit., Historical time series.

489   "By 1950": Memorandum of Henry Z. Steinway to the Board of Directors, June 15, 1950.

489   "if Steinway intends in the future": ibid.

489   "if Steinway intends to purchase": ibid.

489   "if Steinway intends to abandon": ibid.

490   "The Steinway building": NYT, April 22, 1958.

490   "Almost exactly": NYT, April 9, 1957.

490   "The three million dollars": "Steinway & Sons Financial Statements and Supplemental Schedules for the Year Ended December 31, 1958," Schedule 3: Property and Equipment Account. These accounts were for management use and were not available to stockholders.

490   "The building cost": There was, however, a gain booked of about $1.5 million, the result of depreciation taken. This funded factory improvements in Astoria, as did the sale of the Ditmars Avenue factory in 1957.

490   "It is my thought": op. cit., Memorandum, June 15, 1950.

490   "The record is silent": AA, S&S financial records, 1948–62. The years of greatest Hammond popularity, based on hall sales volume, were 1953 through 1957.

490   "When policies": AA, ibid. Hammond sales were discontinued by 1963. Hammond had ended its policy of exclusive sales territories, and price competition broke out. Steinway Hall was never a place in which to seek bargains.

490   "sticking to the knitting": quote of Henry Z. Steinway, March 26, 1993.

490   "After bottoming out": op. cit., Historical time series.

491   "compared to 17 million": op. cit., AA, *Historical Statistics of the United States*, Part 2, p. 796, series R-102.

491   "The 1961 dividend": AA, S&S financial and production records, 1954–61.

491   "The sum of these": AA, op. cit., "Steinway & Sons, Financial Statements and Supplemental Schedules for the Year Ended December 31, 1960." A trial on the data for 1966 gave similar results.

491   "Among the strangest": ibid. This was an accrual item.

491   "Under the management": AA, S&S financial and production records, 1954–68. Hamburg production in 1949 was 209 pianos. This climbed to 1,712 by 1959, then remained in the range of 1,700 to 1,800 units per year for the next decade.

491   "The new era": See Harold Schonberg, "More Fizzle Than Explosion," NYT, December 4, 1966, for an acutely perceptive contemporary account of the "Tofflerites."

492   "Total attendance": AA, Bureau of the Census, *Statistical Abstract of the United States*, 1972, p. 209, table no. 333.

492   "It was also tallied": op. cit., NYT, December 4.

492   "Though sales": memorandum, Recapitulation of New York City Area C&A Service, August 23, 1966, and S&S production records, 1956–65.

492   "Each year a few hundred": AA, S&S production records and *Historical Statistics of the United States*, Part 2, p. 796, series R-102. Regression analysis revealed a strong inverse relationship between the change in the number of television households and S&S grand piano shipments using a two-year lag for the years 1950 through 1971. F-ratio = 92.05, probability better than 0.00001, correlation = 0.919, R-squared = 84.41 percent.

492   "The 116-year-old": memorandum of Henry Z. Steinway to The Board of Directors, February 19, 1970.

492   "Even as renowned": op. cit., Minutes of the Board, May 19, 1967.

492   "This did not": ibid.

492   "One of the strangest": NYT, December 7, 1960.

493   "Mr. Gould said": ibid.

493   "protect": ibid.

493   "unduly strong": ibid.

493   "Through a strange": recollection of Henry Z. Steinway and note to the author, date obliterated, ca. April 1993.

493   "There Henry Z.": ibid.

493   "In a 1965": memorandum of Henry Z. Steinway to the Board of Directors, November 18, 1965.

493   "Although he did not": AA, op. cit., historical time series and S&S production records, 1957–66.

493   "Steinway in the late 1960s": AA, "Steinway & Sons Financial Statements and Supplemental Schedules for the Year Ended December 31, 1965 through 1970," Schedules 1 and 2.

493   " 'Road to Glory' ": note by Theodore E. Steinway in the collection of Henry Z. Steinway.

31. SUCH, I AM AFRAID, IS LIFE

494   "The Columbia Broadcasting": NYT, February 10, 1972.

495   "Such an outcome": memorandum of Henry Z. Steinway, "Sale of Steinway & Sons to CBS—A Chronology," January 26, 1986.

495   "Before the appearance": ibid.

495   "The value": ibid.

495   "In the parlance": AA, ibid., and "Steinway & Sons Financial Statements and Supplemental Schedules for the Year Ended December 31, 1971," Exhibit B.

495   "Now we have": letter from Charles H. Steinway to Nahum Stetson, June 27, 1896.

495   "As in the time": ibid., Exhibit A, line item "Good Will."

495   "at the urging": recollection of Henry Z. Steinway, March 26, 1993.

495   "whale oil": At the time, there was no great environmental concern with the use of this substance. The natural lubricant decayed over time, making is desirable to find a stable substitute.

496   "Adjusted by the price": AA, S&S financial records, 1885–1971. By 1891 and possibly before, the warranty period was for five years. See Minutes of the Board of Trustees, September 6, 1891.

496   "the Astoria strike": op. cit., Minutes of the Board of Directors of Steinway & Sons, November 10, 1970.

496   "These leapt": AA, op. cit., Steinway & Sons Financial Statements, Schedule 2, 1966–71.

496   "During this same": Bureau of Labor Statistics, *Employment, Hours, and Earnings, United States, 1909–84*, vol. I, SIC 393: "Musical Instruments, Production Worker Average Hourly Earnings in Dollars," p. 374.

496   "During the first six": op. cit., Minutes of the Board, "Employment Data, 1/1/69–6/30/69."

496   "Attempts were made": ibid.

496   "rework": AA, Steinway & Sons Financial Statements and Supplemental Schedules for the Year Ended December 31, 1966 Through 1971, Schedule 2.

496   "In just five": ibid.

496   "and warranty expenses": ibid. The absolute level was still very low. Production-related warranty expense was only $6.68 per piano, or less than 0.3 percent of 1971 new-piano revenues. Compounding the difficulties was a fixed-cost problem. From a postwar record of 3,729 U.S. pianos built in 1966, 1971 production slipped to a recessionary 3,032—a decline of 18.7 percent.

496   "down where": reprint, *The Music Trades*, May 1972.

497   "In the nineteenth": Committee on Finance, United States Senate, *The Existing Tariff on Imports into the United States, etc., and the Free List*, 1884.

497   "I do not know much": George B. Curtiss, *Industrial Development of Nations*, p. 31.

497   "Yamaha was": *Music Trades*, May 16, 1908. These pianos used American parts for critical assemblies: "Thus it will be seen that in the far-away Flowery Kingdom the superiority of American-made piano actions is recognized," read an advertisement for actionmakers Wessell, Nickel & Gross who themselves once worked for Steinway.

497   " 'Jap piano' ": *Piano Trades Magazine*, April 1937.

497   "The domestic Japanese": AA. Time series of Japanese piano production and exports were tabulated by Henry Z. Steinway and provided by him. The writer is solely responsible for any observations or inferences made involving Mr. Steinway's data.

497   "In 1960": ibid.

497   "By 1967": ibid.

497   "notwithstanding": AA, Bureau of the Census, *Statistical Abstract of the United States*, 1978, p. 708 ff.

498   "dirt cheap, landing": op. cit., Time series of Henry Z. Steinway, "price/unit."

498   "This resulted": memorandum of Henry Z. Steinway, Minutes of the Board, date uncertain, ca. 1967.

498   "overtake Steinway": memorandum from Henry Z. Steinway to Robert G. Campbell, January 19, 1973. This cites a "printed speech" containing these words. NYT, February 22, 1981, indicated that the objective was still in place. "We are chasing hard, we want to catch up with Steinway," said a manager.

498   "For Henry Z.": AA, S&S financial records, 1955–71.

499   "From Hamburg": op. cit., Minutes of the Board, November 4, 1970.

499   "Steinway protests": ibid., November 15, 1971. It is worth noting that the first wave of Japanese pianos landed on the shores of Europe, the result of the distribution system structure there. Unlike dealers in the U.S. who offered only one make at a price point, European dealers often sold several competitive makes. This was similar in concept to a single dealer offering Cadillac, Lincoln, and Chrysler automobiles. Such a structure made it much easier for a "new" maker to place his product on the floor with "established" names, since the European dealer did not risk the loss of his existing brands.

499   "pirated": ibid., May 19, 1967.

499   "to learn the secret": ibid.

499   "that there will be": ibid.

499   "had a shockingly": ibid., March 11, 1971.

499   "claimed credit": ibid.

500   "Sales were infrequent": affidavit of Theodore E. Steinway, May 25, 1956. This contains an extensive record of the trading price and volume of S&S shares.

500   "The bottom": ibid.

500   "In the mid 1950s": AA, ibid.

500   "Rosenwald owned": letter from Henry Z. Steinway to writer, March 26, 1993.

500   "one of the smartest": ibid.

500   "ridiculous": ibid.

500–1 "a sale was the answer": ibid.

501   "eager 'to get' ": ibid.

501   "Dividends": AA, Steinway & Sons Financial Statements and Supplemental Schedules for the Year Ended December 31, 1966 Through 1971, Exhibit B.

501   "Over two dozen": memorandum of Henry Z. Steinway, "Review of Merger & Acquisition Contacts," 1955–68.

501   "The legendary firm": ibid.

501   "In July 1970": recollection of Henry Z. Steinway, March 26, 1993.

501   "anxious . . . leaning . . . make something": op. cit., memorandum, "Sale of Steinway."

501   "CBS had,": op. cit., "Review of Merger."

501   "The next day": op. cit., memorandum, "Sale of Steinway."

501   "In only sixty-two days": AA, ibid. An agreement in principal was reached on February 3, 1972.

501   "CBS would exchange": AA, ibid.

502   "Steinway was actually": AA, on the basis of net margin for the year 1971.

502   "As a practical": AA, NYT, February 10, 1972, which contained CBS financial data and announced S&S acquisition.

502   "Though there is": AA, Steinway & Sons Financial Statements and Supplemental Schedules for the Year Ended December 31, 1955 Through 1971, Exhibit B.

502   "My own feelings": letter from John H. Steinway to "Sam," February 25, 1972.

502   "Up to the moment": recollection of Henry Z. Steinway, March 26, 1993.

502 "Alexander Greiner": op. cit., Alexander Greiner, *Pianos and Pianists*, p. vi.

502 "the heroines": ibid.

502 "Some of us . . .": op. cit., reprint, *Music Trades*, May 1972.

502 "none are getting": ibid.

502 "hostile to manufacturing": ibid.

502 "inner city": ibid.

502 "an opportunity": ibid.

503 "one huge company": ibid.

503 "Last was a": ibid.

503 "We think": ibid.

503 "We are looking": ibid.

503 "It became publicly": *Wall Street Journal*, May 1, 1972. This was the classic "tombstone."

503 "The real powers": recollection of Henry Z. Steinway, March 26, 1993.

503 "Harvey Schein": ibid.

503 "With five levels": organization chart of CBS drawn by Henry Z. Steinway for writer, no date, ca. April 1993.

503 "I continue": memorandum from Henry Z. Steinway to Robert G. Campbell, November 11, 1972. This is a series of more-or-less monthly management reports.

503 "We hoped": ibid.

503 "made clear": ibid., January 19, 1973.

503 "The Japs are here now": ibid., October 19, 1973. S&S had averred buying Everett prior to its acquisition by CBS. See op. cit., Minutes of the Board, November 10, 1970.

504 "for roughly 90 percent": recollection of Henry Z. Steinway, March 26, 1993.

504 "cooperative": ibid.

504 "I find these instructions": op. cit., memorandum from Steinway to Campbell, September 20, 1974.

504 "A bizarre": ibid., October 24, 1975, among other references. December 27, 1976, memorandum states that there are no sales or inventory reports due to "EDP foul-ups."

504 "Maybe I will live": ibid., October 24, 1975.

504 "In this exotic": ibid., October 18, 1974.

504 "people will pay": ibid., October 24, 1975.

505 "As prices": AA, S&S production records, retail price lists, and industry time series of Henry Z. Steinway.

505 "market share atrophied": ibid. In the pre-Japanese era of the early fifties, S&S share ranged between 25 and 30 percent of the tiny grand market that itself averaged about 4,000 units per year. S&S share of the much larger upright market hovered below one percent, certainly within the range of statistical error in the data.

505 "good old pianos": op. cit., memorandum from Steinway to Campbell, November 15, 1974.

505 "the most important": ibid., December 21, 1974.

505 "Let us not forget": ibid., August 22, 1975.

505 "I ask that": ibid., November 23, 1976.

505 "We will rise or fall": ibid., December 27, 1976.

505 "to improve quality": ibid.

505   "That year": ibid., January 21, 1977. Data for the fiscal year 1976.

505   "JOB CHANGES": NYT, June 4, 1977.

505   "unfrocked": recollection of Henry Z. Steinway, March 26, 1993.

506   "the Fender guitar": *Music Trades*, April 1985, states that the firm was founded in 1930 by radio repairman Leo Fender and guitar teacher Clayton Kaufman. The key product was the "Telecaster" solid-bodied electric guitar introduced in 1948. Though initially disparaged as a "toilet seat with strings," the Fender Telecaster became very popular, as did other Fender instruments and amplifiers.

506   "According to insiders": article by Steve Lohr, NYT, August 24, 1980.

506   "Peter Perez was": ibid.

506   "at age 34": ibid.

506   "the practice": ibid.

506   "a delicate balancing": ibid.

506   "1.5 million board feet": ibid.

506   "unhurried pace": ibid.

506   "The virtuosi who": article by Harold Schonberg, NYT, June 22, 1980.

507   "In a convolution": ibid.

507   "This independence": Similar differences were still apparent in the early 1990s, according to piano technician and former Steinway employee Bill Garlick. The writer believes that at present individual variations within type exceed the differences between types when instruments are classified by country of manufacture, and further that critical manufacturing/maintenance operations such as regulation and voicing can swamp subtle mechano-acoustical effects otherwise possibly attributable to country of origin.

507   "We have two factories": op. cit., NYT, June 22.

507   "or use a house instrument": "house piano" is the term used to describe the piano normally found in a particular venue. In some cases, particularly in smaller cities, the house piano is owned by the facility or it may be on long-term loan from a maker or local dealer.

507   "Now the C&A": It is unclear when the practice of renting pianos to artists began at S&S. A memo from David W. Rubin to Henry Z. Steinway dated August 23, 1966, indicated that the practice was in place in New York by the 1956–57 concert season. This was done under the rubric of a cartage charge.

507   "Like all great": NYT, May 18, 1982.

508   "left to direct": N. R. Kleinfeld, NYT, May 26, 1982.

508   "Perez, taking his dismissal": ibid.

508   "devoted much of his time": ibid., May 18, 1982.

508   "a banjo": ibid.

508   "After departing": *Music Trades*, July 1985.

508   "In little more": ibid.

508   "Out of cash": ibid.

508   "Before long, Wurlitzer": ibid., February 1988.

508   "The 1976 postwar": AA, S&S production records, for combined New York and Astoria output. The 1976 combined output exceeded 1966 by only 21 pianos, or 0.39 percent.

509   "In the last years": AA, S&S financial records.

509   "and newspaper inquiries": op. cit., NYT, June 22, 1980.

509 "Between 1971 and": AA, S&S production records, retail price lists, and industry time series of Henry Z. Steinway.

509 "Each one of these": *Music Trades*, September 1985.

33. MY GREAT, GREAT WHATEVER

510 "We're bleeding": New York *Daily News*, August 20, 1985.

510 "It's been a long": ibid.

510 "The company": ibid.

510 "Eight months": *Wall Street Journal*, December 4, 1984. See also NYT, December 4, 1984.

510 "Fender was": NYT, February 2, 1985.

510 "Organ builder": *Music Trades*, April, 1985.

511 "The announcement": Samuel Lipman, "Steinway on the block," *The New Criterion*, January 1985, p. 75 ff.

511 "Handling the sale": ibid.

511 "little more": ibid.

511 "a commercial": ibid.

511 "slogan": ibid.

511 "The profile": ibid.

511 "a star-studded": ibid.

511 "save a national": ibid.

511 "the commitment": ibid.

511 "By one count": statement of John Birmingham to the writer.

511–12 "Senator Jesse Helms": NYT, January 11, 1985.

512 "Known as the 'leveraged' ": John Kitching, "Early Returns on LBOs," *Harvard Business Review*, vol. 67, no. 6, November–December 1989, pp. 74–81.

512 "By 1988": ibid.

512 "For CBS the threat": NYT, February 15; March 1, 2, 6, 8, 14, 16, and 22; April 2, 3, 4, 10, 11, 12, 16, and 22; May 1, 3, 6, and 25; June 8, 19, and 25; July 4, 10, 17, and 30; August 13 and 29; September 4; October 2, 17, 23, and 25; November 2 and 14, 1985.

512 "We are excruciatingly": NYT, April 24, 1985.

513 "We are already": *Music Trades*, March 1985.

513 "And consequently": ibid.

513 "Whatever the situation": confidential source.

513 "My family": NYT, May 31, 1985.

513 "waterfront": ibid.

513 "CBS said": ibid.

513 "offer a good home": ibid.

513 "By August, eight hundred": op. cit., New York *Daily News*, August 20.

513–14 "Artists tell me": ibid.

514 "Price isn't an object": ibid.

514 "Fully aware": ibid. Mr. Meyer officially left S&S on September 12, 1985.

514 "That year": *Music Trades*, May 1986.

514 "This is an exciting": press kit, Steinway Musical Properties, Bruce Stevens speech of Friday, September 13, 1985.

514 "It marks the beginning": ibid.

514 "Let me assure you": ibid.

514   "consultants": recollection of Henry Z. Steinway.

515   "you might find": note from Bruce Stevens to Henry Z. Steinway, September 13, 1985.

515   "talking points": ibid.

515   "my great, great": ibid.

515   "Henry's whatever": ibid.

515   "In these swift-moving": ibid.

515   "the chief executive": op. cit., press kit.

515   "concentrated in": ibid.

515   "James F. Stone": ibid.

515   "Bruce Stevens": ibid.

515   "The company supplies": ibid.

515   "According to": *Wall Street Journal*, March 27, 1991.

515   "This is not": *Music Trades*, September 1985.

515   "acted as a financial": *Wall Street Journal*, December 13, 1985.

515   "Persons close": confidential source.

516   "it is clear": AA, based on CBS offering memorandum, December 1984, and op. cit., *Harvard Business Review*.

516   "Steinway and": ibid., offering memorandum. Five-year mean pretax earnings for the group, including S&S, was $8.9 million per year. With ten-year Treasury bonds in September 1985 yielding 10.5 percent, SMP interest costs were certainly higher. Assuming, for purposes of illustration, a 350 basis point premium to the Treasuries and 10 percent down, annual interest due—with no amortization of principal—would have totalled $6.74 million or 75.7 percent of mean pretax earnings and greater than cash flow in any of the five preceding years. Allowing for amortization over ten years, payments of $9.2 million annually would be required, an amount in excess of mean earnings and 64.3 percent greater than mean cash flow.

516   "I believe that it's good": NYT, September 17, 1985.

516   "In a 1991": interview with the writer.

516   "very rigorous": ibid.

516   "neglecting its dealers": ibid.

516   "no knowledge": ibid.

516   "not very good": ibid.

516   "an infusion of management": ibid.

516   "value-added": ibid.

516   "John McLaren": newsletter, *The McLaren Report*, November 1985.

516   "face a formidable": ibid.

517   "An internal document": AA, "Steinway & Sons 1986 Failure Costs."

517   "This was fifty-seven": AA, ibid. and Steinway & Sons Financial Statements and Supplemental Schedules for the Year Ended December 31, 1966, Schedule 2.

517   "Rework expenses": ibid.

517   "Some of the rise": AA, S&S price lists.

517   "When scrap costs": op. cit., "Failure Costs." There was no breakout for scrap costs in the family management epoch. A comparison on this item is therefore impossible.

517   "He had spent": *Music Trades*, June 1987. By the second quarter of 1994, Mr. Koenig was no longer employed by S&S.

517   "His remarkable": ibid.

517   "documenting and improving": statement of Dennis Bracco, formerly with S&S quality group, to the writer.

517   "A former member": ibid.

517   "According to one": ibid.

517   "operators": ibid. Based on the writer's experience, reference to shop floor personnel as "operators" is also common usage at the executive level.

517   "A May 1988": interoffice memorandum from Dan Koenig to Bruce Stevens, May 25, 1988.

517   "turning point": ibid.

518   "evolved from an organization": ibid.

518   "foggy information": ibid.

518   "we now build": ibid.

518   "gradual rise": ibid.

518   "improve quality": ibid.

518   "guild hall": ibid.

518   "the cultural make up": ibid.

518   "We have": ibid.

518   "evolve into a": ibid.

518   "highest possible quality": ibid.

518   "These declined": AA, S&S memorandums, "Yearly Totals for Rework" and "Yearly Totals for Scrap."

518   "retrograded": op. cit., interoffice memorandum, May 25, 1988.

518   "status quo": ibid.

518   "illogical": ibid.

518   "superior pianos": ibid.

518   "differential": ibid.

518   "probably dumping": *Keyboard*, August 1988.

518   "What they're merchandising": ibid.

518   "The consumer": ibid.

518   "ethics and": ibid.

518–19   "After buying": ibid.

519   "In the time": AA. Peak postwar grand market share was 30.21 percent, achieved by Henry Z. Steinway in 1958. His father averaged 25.7 percent in his last five years heading the house.

519   "I was looking": Edward Rothstein, "To Make a Piano of Note, It Takes More than Tools," *Smithsonian Magazine*, November 1988, p. 143 ff.

519   "The methodology": ibid.

519   "Rothstein later": Edward Rothstein to the writer.

519   "It's really different": Edward Rothstein, "Don't Shoot the Piano," *The New Republic*, May 1, 1989, p. 32 ff.

519   "I get uptight": ibid.

519   "The design": ibid.

519   "In reality": communications of Roy Kehl to the author. Mr. Kehl identified well over two hundred discrete types of Steinway grand designs, and the number of upright and square designs may be nearly as large.

519   "Design changes": The most notable may have been the abandonment of the Teflon action bushing.

519   "For the first": op. cit., *The New Republic.*

519   "injuring the remnants": ibid.

520   "cut corners": ibid.

520   "complaints": ibid.

520   " 'When the market": *Computer World,* March 20, 1989.

520   "add a little": ibid.

520   "ordinary pianos": ibid.

520   "While this was": statement of Bill Strong to the writer.

520   "Sour Notes": *Wall Street Journal,* March 27, 1991.

520   "Sandford G. Woodard": Matthew L. Wald, NYT, March 28, 1991. During 1993 Mr. Woodard left S&S.

520   "The music industry": op. cit., *Wall Street Journal,* March 27.

521   "changes in two of": op. cit., NYT, March 28.

521   "They're living": ibid.

521   "I don't think": ibid.

521   "In early 1989": op. cit., *Wall Street Journal,* March 27.

522   "Garbage": Michael Vitez, *The Philadelphia Inquirer,* May 9, 1991.

522   "Madman": ibid.

522   "vendetta": ibid.

522   "Steinway officials": ibid.

522   "pointing out": ibid.

522   "This particular": ibid.

522   "Notice this piano": ibid.

522   "40 megaton": ibid.

522   "Frank has to be": ibid.

522   "this company is": ibid.

522   "compromised": ibid.

522–23   "fewer than 1 percent": ibid.

523   "another Steinway document": AA, "Steinway Repair—Warranty Units," April 28, 1990.

523   "Soundboard problems": AA, ibid.

523   "In his view": op. cit., *Philadelphia Inquirer,* May 9, 1991.

523   "By 1992": Mr. Yaeger provided a copy of his data set of May 18, 1992, to the writer, who wishes to express his gratitude for same.

523   "But it was not": AA of Yaeger data set.

523   "in fact": ibid.

523   "no meaningful difference": AA, specifically the data failed to meet the significance criterion when subjected to a Chi-square test for proportions.

524   "The forty-eight-inch spruce slice": Forest Products Laboratory, Forest Service, *Wood Handbook: Wood as an Engineering Material,* (Agricultural Handbook No. 72). The dimensional change was computed with the formula and coefficients found in chapters 14-5 through 14-12. Generally, this is a time/temperature/humidity relationship. Chapter 6-8 treats the topic of wood strength and the duration of the load, while Section 3 is a general review of moisture content parameters.

524   "The crack": The wood will be of smaller dimension under lower humidity, in effect contracting and "opening" a crack.

524   "Theoretically": the effect is due to changing acoustic impedances within the string/soundboard/case system. For an accessible general treatment of

acoustic impedance phenomena in pianos, see Anders Askenfelt, ed., *Five Lectures on the Acoustics of the Piano.*

524–25   "Continued dampness": S&S catalog, 1883. These statements were "boilerplate," and appeared in a number of S&S catalogs.

525   "Micheal Yaeger": memorandum of Micheal Yaeger, January 20, 1990. Copy provided to the writer. By 1994 Micheal Yaeger had sold his Connecticut piano store and was reported to be studying law.

525   "I am told": "Here Are the Steinways and How They Grew," *Fortune*, December 1934, p. 160.

525   "The salesman": ibid.

525   "He led her": ibid.

525   "Company records": S&S "number book." The writer is indebted to Roy Kehl for his determination of the number of this singular piano, a Model M, which was likely repaired before its 1942 sale during the wartime piano shortage.

525   "The Steinways have chosen": op. cit., *Fortune.*

525   "the warranty repairs": memorandum from Paul Bilhuber to B. H. Collins, October 27, 1931.

526   "in the greatest number": *Musical Courier*, May 31, 1930.

526   "Rather than fight": recollection of Henry Z. Steinway.

526   "For several years": Boston press kit. According to a company press release in the kit dated January 16, 1992, the Boston was "the result of six years of research and development." This, however, would have required a management decision to build a second line about one month after the Steinway acquisition tombstone appeared in the *Wall Street Journal.*

527   "piano-shaped objects": op. cit., *Keyboard*, August 1988.

527   "When queried": statement of Bruce Stevens to the writer.

527   "This was news": Leslie Helm, *Los Angeles Times*, undated photocopy of clip, but ca. January 1992.

527   "*Designed by Steinway & Sons*": op. cit., Boston press kit.

527   "is manufactured": ibid.

527   "The answer seemed": newsletter, *Museum of the American Piano*, no. 11, January–March, 1991.

527   "A five-feet ten-inch Boston": ibid.

527   "A few blocks": as seen by the writer in February 1992.

527   "The wholesale price": Boston wholesale price list, January 16, 1992. The 83.14 percent markup to "retail" on the Boston was also less than the roughly 100 percent markup on Steinway pianos.

528   "A venerable": Edward Rothstein, "A Conflict of Cultures at Steinway," NYT, November 3, 1991.

528   "The Boston": ibid.

528   "Steinway & Sons is": ibid.

528   "The company": Schuyler G. Chapin, letter to the editor in NYT, December 1, 1991.

528   "modern engineering": ibid.

528   "A century": Fanny Morris Smith, *A Noble Art: Three Lectures on the Evolution and Construction of the Piano*, p. 95 ff. It was exactly a century; this work was published in 1892, and the Boston was officially introduced in 1992.

528   "visually arresting": *Music Trades*, October 1988.

528   "living Steinway artists": ibid.

528   "including Steinway": An S&S "art catalogue" ca. 1900 shows a few custom designs so grotesque that they foreclose the possibility of description. For roughly three decades after the death of William, S&S had an "art department" that designed these custom pianos, of which the two White House instruments—numbers 100,000 and 300,000—are the best-known. Actual casework was often executed by outside cabinetmakers.

528–29 "the longest set": Michael Kimmelman, NYT, June 4, 1988.

529   "The Steinway piano": ibid.

529   "Donations to": leaflet, "The Steinway Foundation"; on back: "Contributions are welcome and may be sent to . . ."

529   "If last night's": Bernard Holland, NYT, June 16, 1992.

529   "inconsistent": ibid.

529   "some wonderful": ibid.

529   "maker of background": ibid.

529   "member of a new": ibid.

529   "A company in need": ibid.

529   "What are you writing?": statement of John Birmingham to the writer.

529   "I'm gonna": ibid.

530   "two other": Annual reports of the Baldwin and Kimball companies, FY 1992.

530   "More difficult": statements of Daniel T. Koenig during the course of a 1992 factory tour given the writer.

530   "Look at that, it's": ibid.

530   "Look at that. They": ibid.

530   "landed quality": ibid.

530   "operators": ibid.

530   "industrial chaos": ibid.

530   "zero quality control": ibid.

530   "archaic": ibid.

530   "Theodore": ibid.

530   "We've done": ibid.

530   "everything about pianos": ibid.

530   "Everybody in the industry": ibid.

530   "In its roller coaster": AA, S&S production records.

531   "befogged": William D. Gramp, *Pricing the Priceless: Art, Artists and Economics*, page 179.

531   "Beginning in late 1991": recollection of S&S union leader Bill Youse.

531   "In 1989": op. cit., *Computer World*, March 20, 1989.

531   "By the fall": Michael T. Kaufman, NYT, November 25, 1992.

531   "The industry": *Music Trades*, April 1993, states that 1989 grand piano shipments were 28,626 and in 1992 were 28,369, a difference of 257 pianos, or 0.9 percent. This is likely within the range of statistical error for the data, as the 1994 report post facto raised 1992 production by 1,000 units.

531   "roughly the same": AA, S&S production records, 1893, 1932, and 1958. The comparison is complicated by the changes in proportion of grands to uprights. S&S currently produces proportionately very few uprights, while in 1893 and 1958 uprights were a substantial factor in total output.

532   "Porsche,": Csaba Csere, "The Problem at Porsche: Price," *Car and Driver*, June 1993, p. 67.

532   "At the time": AA, S&S retail price lists, 1985–93.

532   "In early 1993": ibid.

532   "Under SMP": ibid.

532   "the world s most": S&S advertisement, NYT, January 8, 1993.

532   "have a legendary": ibid.

532   "in a little brochure": S&S booklet, date uncertain, but received from a Steinway salesman in 1992 by the writer.

532   "buyer of a Duesenberg": Anthony Harding, ed., *Classic Cars in Profile*, pp. 61–72.

532   "On that basis": AA, S&S retail price list, 1929. The "New York Retail" for the concert grand Model D was $3,000, in ebony and without a bench. The arithmetic is $100 \times \$3,000 = \$300,000$, the Duesenberg's appreciation factor times the 1929 price of the Model D. To determine the appreciation, the writer scanned offerings of Duesenbergs in *Hemmings Motor News* and auction reports, 1990–92. A like procedure was applied for the Corvette example below.

532   "A new one": S&S retail price list, 1993, and a scan of offering prices for used Model D's in the *New York Times* Sunday classifieds, 1990–92.

532   "same price in 1957": AA, S&S retail price list, 1957 and *Road & Track*, August 1957, p. 22 ff. An ebony 1957 Model L cost $3,690 and the Corvette price, replete with Rochester F.I., 4.11 gears, and Duntov 30-30 cam, was $3,909.52 before the customary haggling. A 5.6 percent discount on the Corvette would have brought the two purchases to price parity.

532   "Other sales techniques": advertisement, NYT, April 9, 1993.

532   "They also offered": These were on sale at the factory to persons taking tours.

532–33   "His moving fingers": Steinway magazine advertisement, reproduced in Ronald V. Ratliffe, *Steinway*, p. 123. Accompanying the copy was an illustration of Josef Hofmann.

533   "anniversary Gift Package": op. cit., NYT, April 9, 1993.

533   "The theory": "The Trend Is Not Their Friend," *Forbes*, September 16, 1991, p. 115 ff.

533   "Buy a piano": One example of this message is found in the advertisement, op. cit., NYT, January 8, 1993. Similar messages have accompanied other S&S price increases.

533   "There is a secular": "What's in a Name? Less and Less: Madison Ave. Worries That Familiar Brands May Be Losing Their Punch," *Business Week*, July 8, 1991, p. 66 ff.

533   "One study": ibid.

533   "*Forbes* reported": op. cit., *Forbes*, September 16, 1991.

534   "built to stand": statement of Henry Z. Steinway to the writer.

534   "In Astoria": AA, S&S production records, 1891–97.

534   "A total rebuild": price quote from A&C Pianocraft, Queens, New York, March 1993. This shop is a pioneer in Steinway rebuilding.

534   "SMP executives": above statements of Daniel T. Koenig.

534   "our three-legged": recollection of Henry Z. Steinway.

534–35   "a sense of beauty": op. cit., advertisement reproduced in *Steinway*, p. 123.

34. GOD SPEAKS THROUGH EVERY STEINWAY

536   "The name Weber": *Music Trades*, May 1989. At this time Samsung, a trading company, claimed $30 billion in annual revenue.

536   "The British journal": *Early Music*, scanned by writer for the years 1990 through 1992.

536   "The Customs Service": *Music Trades*, May 1986. The mean for three years was 4,401 harpsichords and clavichords imported into the United States per year.

537   "God speaks": newsletter, *Steinway News*, no. 22, December 15, 1936. Mrs. Smith's letter was dated December 7, 1936.

537   "the fundamental qualities": ibid., no. 2, October 15, 1935.

537   "Laplanders," Irving J. Lee, *Language Habits in Human Affairs: An Introduction to General Semantics*, p. 92 ff.

537   "focussed, powerful": op. cit., Samuel Lipman, "Steinway on the Block," *The New Criterion*, January 1985, p. 75 ff.

538   "Medical research": Jody Kreiman, Bruce R. Gerratt, Kristin Precoda, Gerald S. Berke, "Individual Differences in Voice Perception Quality," *Journal of Speech and Hearing Research*, vol. 35, June 1992, pp. 512–20. Also Bruce R. Gerratt, Jody Kreiman, Norma Antonanzas-Barroso, Gerald S. Berke, "Comparing Internal and External Standards in Voice Quality Judgments," *Journal of Speech and Hearing Research*, vol. 36, February 1993, pp. 14–20.

538   "The effect": There is a vast literature on presbycusis; for an introduction, see H. F. Schuknecht, "Presbycusis," in *Pathology of the Ear*. Most work focuses on speech recognition, and the author could find no studies specifically relating to presbycusis and music listening.

538   "The business": Hermann L. F. von Helmholtz, *On the Sensations of Tone*, p. 79 ff., and Appendix V, p. 380 ff. Helmholtz would be appalled, perhaps revolted, by the sound of today's instruments.

539   "In 1939": Olin Downes, NYT, May 28, 1939.

539   "only difference": newsletter, *Steinway News*, no. 2, October 15, 1935.

539   "greater brilliance": ibid.

539   "Helmholtz": op. cit., *Sensations of Tone*, p. 70: "Hence I think that I may describe the general characteristic of what is usually called a metallic quality of tone, as the comparatively continuous and uniform maintenance of higher upper partial tones." On p. 76, most tellingly: "On examining a new grand pianoforte by Messrs. Steinway of New York, which was most remarkable for the evenness of tone, I find the damping . . . in the deeper notes on the ninth and tenth partials, whereas in the higher notes, the fourth or fifth partials were scarcely to be got out . . ." This was the result of the fat, fluffy hammers that C. F. Theodore advocated with passion and vehemence. A treble hammer from Vladimir Horowitz's last performance grand examined by the writer was granite-like in its hardness.

539   "to an imperceptible": letter from Hector Berlioz to Messrs. Steinway, September 25, 1867, as reproduced in an 1884 S&S catalog. Berlioz was glad to hear the "minor seventh" harmonic expunged from "the longer strings."

539   "render some": ibid.

539   "It is in the nature": computer-based acoustical analysis for this work, in this case an examination of the spectral energy of individual machine-struck notes at three force levels as displayed by 4096-point Fourier transform, Hanning window with a 50 percent overlap using the Aachen Binaural Analysis System. Signal duration was ten seconds, Note = D4 = 293.66 Hz. fundamental. Piano was a factory-prepared Steinway Model D.

539   "While a further": ibid. Data were taken beginning at A-0 (27.5 Hz.) and ascending in ninths, ending with the highest G at 3136.0 Hz.

540   "Distance from": K. Blair Benson, ed., *Audio Engineering Handbook*, particularly chapter 3, "Architectural Acoustic Principals," for an introduction to a topic of immense complexity.

540   "In January 1991": Though conducted by the writer, who assumes all responsibility for analysis and interpretation, the investigation would not have been possible without those mentioned in the acknowledgments as well as the gracious assistance and support of Virginia Dajani and Ardith Holmgrain at the American Academy. A representative of each maker was present during the actual recordings.

541   "watery, unfocussed": The views on the pianos were communicated by Mr. Shehori to the writer immediately after he had played all four instruments.

541   "I can't believe": statement of Mr. Shehori to the writer.

541   "a nightingale": quoted in Arthur Loesser, *Men, Women and Pianos*, p. 513.

541   "sound becomes": The design of the Aachen Binaural Analysis System is to be commended for the ease with which it makes such analysis and manipulation possible. It is unusually fluent software.

542   "Theodore was soon": pamphlet, *Steinway & Sons in New York—Neue Erfindung der Doppel-Scala und die Unwissenheit des Herrn Bosendorfer in Wien.* Libel law had not yet reached its contemporary state of perfection circa 1875. The writer wishes to thank Mr. Marc Aubort for his informal translation of portions of this document.

542   "is about 30 percent": as measured in dB(A) on Note D-4 with a striking force of eight ounces dropped from a height of six inches with the piano's dampers down. Microphones at a distance of 4.5 feet. The range reflects the variations in the other three instruments. Maximum output for any instrument was 67.0 dB(A) with this protocol while the Bosendorfer output was 59.9 dB(A). Informal tests at other scale points confirm the lower acoustic output of this instrument.

542   "We are chasing hard": NYT, February 22, 1981.

542   "We know we have": ibid.

543   "Yamaha wants": statement of Eric Johnson to the writer.

543   "The computer": The phenomenon can be seen in the waterfall plots of the FFTs.

543   "On the note E": Note E-5, 659.26 Hz. Envelope plot for ten seconds of note, dampers down, after machine strike. This effect is so unexpected that the writer listened to both the main and backup recording systems to determine if the effect was an electronic artifact. These systems were completely redundant and independent; the effect is present in the recordings from both systems, and the possibility of artifact is thereby logically excluded. This amplitude variation may also contribute to the phenomenon called "singing" if same is considered to be a general animation of tone.

543   "the note B": B-1, 61.735 Hz. Characterization based on the examination of 2-D and 3-D FFTs. The Steinway fundamental measured 59 dB; the Yamaha 51 dB for the same force applied to the key. Level was 75.25 dB(A) for the Steinway and 72.1 dB(A) for the Yamaha.

544   "The computer, acting": Fourth-order digital filters were constructed to allow the display and audition of the individual partials. This technique is a modern version of the Helmholtz resonators used by C. F. Theodore to examine partials.

544   "Striking the E": Note E-5, 659.26 Hz. Peak SPL for the Yamaha in dampers-down condition was 91.9 dB; with dampers up, this rose to 96.8 dB. Complex masking effects likely do not allow all the chromatic steps to be heard, but they can be measured, and the result is heard as a "haze," which is perceived sometimes as an additional reverberant quality.

545   "Without it": In terms of electronic synthesis, this is the attack portion of the standard envelope parsing of "attack-decay-sustain-release."

545   "another computer program": The writer modelled the phenomenon in DaDisp, summing the first six partials of note D-4 in proportion to their respective levels in the first 1.5 seconds of a Steinway tone at moderate levels. An FFT with Hanning window was taken, and the characteristic spectrum of a piano was produced with enharmonic "spreading" at the base of each partial. Further operation revealed that this was produced by the "on" transient. The effect is similar to the response of a tuned circuit to an impulse. This phenomenon, like the damper-up "haze," is likely subject to masking effects.

545   "Complex systems": Bruce J. West, Michael Schlesinger, "The Noise in Natural Phenomena," *American Scientist*, vol. 78, January–February 1990, p. 40 ff.

546   "natural phenomena": ibid.

546   "the music of Bach": R. F. Voss and J. Clark, "$1/f$ Noise in Music: Music from $1/f$ Noise," *Journal of the Acoustical Society of America*, vol. 63, 1978, p. 258 ff. The writer wishes to thank Dr. Voss for his examination of the filtered piano tone graphs, his comments, and confirmation of the fractality of the "bonk." Dr. Voss made the significant observation that it is unclear whether the phenomenon is chaotic or random, a topic the writer regrets he could not investigate.

546   "That $1/f$": See Mark A. Schmuckler, David L. Gilden, "Auditory Perception of Fractal Contours," *Journal of Experimental Psychology*, vol. 19, no. 3, 1993, p. 641 ff., for an investigation into the nature of fractal contours that are discriminable.

546   "S. B. Driggs": NYT, May 23, 1859, and New York State Supreme Court, Petition of S. B. Driggs in re Driggs Patent Piano Company for a glimpse of a brilliant and volatile man. At one point Driggs claimed he was the inventor of the overstrung scale made famous by the Steinways.

546   "Frederick Mathushek": NYT, November 11, 1891, and New York County Clerk's Office Bankruptcy Proceedings, Victor Hugo Mathushek.

546   "Henry Ziegler Steinway": his observations to the writer in his office at Steinway Hall.

BIBLIOGRAPHY

WORKS CONSULTED

American Institute. *Minutes of Managers of the American Institute Annual Fairs, 1850–1860.* New York: American Institute, 1860.

Armbruster, Gregory, ed. *The Art of Electronic Music.* New York: Quill, 1984.

Asbury, Herbert. *The Gangs of New York: An Informal History of the Underworld.* New York: Alfred A. Knopf, Inc., 1928.

Association for the Exhibition of the Industry of All Nations. *Official Awards of Juries.* New York: William C. Bryant & Co., 1853.

Ayers, Christine Merrick. *Contributions to the Art of Music in America by the Music Industries of Boston, 1643 to 1936.* New York: H. W. Wilson Company, 1937.

Bagwell, Philip S. and G. E. Mingay. *Britain and America, 1850–1939: A Study of Economic Change.* New York: Praeger Publishers, 1970.

Ballantine, Bill. *The Piano.* New York: Franklin Watts, Inc., 1971.

Barnouw, Erik. *A Tower in Babel.* New York: Oxford University Press, 1966.

Bennett, W. Sterndale, et al. *International Exhibition, 1862: Jurors' Reports, Class XVI.* London: Bell and Daldy, 1862.

Benson, K. Blair, ed. *Audio Engineering Handbook.* New York: McGraw-Hill, Inc., 1988.

Bernstein, Iver. *The New York City Draft Riots.* New York: Oxford University Press, 1990.

Bishop, John L. *A History of American Manufactures from 1608 to 1860.* 3 Volumes. Philadelphia: Edward Young & Company, 1868.

Black, Henry Campbell. *Black's Law Dictionary: Definitions of the Terms and Phrases of American and English Jurisprudence, Ancient and Modern.* Fourth edition. St. Paul, Minnesota: West Publishing Co., 1973.

Bloomfield, Peter. *Fourier Analysis of Time Series: An Introduction.* New York: John Wiley & Sons, 1976.

Board of Commissioners of Public Charities and Corrections, New York City. *Annual Report.* New York: Board of Commissioners, 1870.

Bohme, Helmut. *Social and Economic History of Germany.* New York: St. Martin's Press, 1978.

Boyer, Peter J. *Who Killed CBS?* New York: Random House, 1988.

Bradley, Van Allen. *Music for the Millions: The Kimball Piano and Organ Story.* Chicago: The Henry Regnery Co., 1957.

Brooks, Tim and Earl Marsh. *The Complete Directory to Prime Time Network TV Shows, 1946–Present.* New York: Ballantine Books, 1979.

Bruce, Robert V. *1877: Year of Violence.* Indianapolis: Bobbs-Merrill Company, Inc., 1959.

Buder, Stanley. *Pullman: An Experiment in Industrial Order and Community Planning, 1880–1930.* New York: Oxford University Press, 1967.

Buffum, M.D., Herbert E., et al. *The Household Physician.* 2 Volumes. Buffalo, NY: The Brofly Press, 1931.

Campbell, David Eugene. "The Purveyor as Patron: The Contribution of American Piano Manufacturers and Merchants to the Musical Culture of the United States, 1851–1914." Ph.D. diss., City University of New York, 1984.

Catton, Bruce. *Reflections on the Civil War.* New York: Berkley Books, 1982.

Cavendish, Marshall. *Marshall Cavendish Encyclopedia of Family Health.* London: Marshall Cavendish, Ltd., 1991.

Chickering & Sons. *A Plain Statement of Facts Concerning the American Pianos Which Were NOT To Be Exhibited at the International Exhibition of Vienna, 1873.* Boston: Chickering & Sons, 1874 (?).

Church, M.D., Archibald and Frederick Peterson, M.D. *Nervous and Mental Diseases.* Philadelphia: W. B. Saunders, 1900.

Citizens Association of New York. *Report upon the Sanitary Condition of the City.* New York: D. Appleton & Co, 1865.

Closson, Ernest. *History of the Piano.* New York: St. Martin's Press, 1974.

Colange, L. *Zell's Condensed Encyclopedia: An Abridged Library and Universal Reference Work.* Philadelphia: T. Elwood Zell, 1882.

Commons, John R., et al. *History of Labour in the United States.* 4 Volumes. New York: Macmillan Company, 1918–35.

Bibliography

Curtiss, George B. *Industrial Development of Nations*. Binghamton, New York: G. B. Curtiss, 1912.

Davis, Don. *Acoustical Tests and Measurements*. Indianapolis: Howard W. Sams & Company, Inc., 1965.

Depew, Chauncey M., ed. *One Hundred Years of American Commerce, 1795–1895*. 2 Volumes. New York: D. O. Haynes & Company, 1895.

Directory of the City of New-York for 1852–53. New York: John F. Trow, 1852.

Dixon, Robert L. *The Executive's Accounting Primer*. New York: McGraw-Hill Book Co., 1971.

Doggett's New York City Directory for 1850 and 1851. New York: John Doggett, Jr., 1850.

Doggett's New York City Directory for 1852–53. New York: John Doggett, Jr., 1852.

Doggett's New York City Street Directory for 1851. New York: John Doggett, Jr., 1851.

Dolge, Alfred. *Men Who Have Made Piano History*. Vestal, NY: The Vestal Press, nd.

Dolge, Alfred. *Pianos and Their Makers*. New York: Dover Publications, Inc., 1972.

Dulles, Foster Rhea and Melvyn Dubofsky. *Labor in America: A History*. Arlington Heights, Ill.: Harlan Davidson, 1984.

Ehrlich, Cyril. *The Piano: A History*. London: J. M. Dent & Sons, 1976.

Encyclopedia Americana: A Library of Universal Knowledge. New York: The Encyclopedia Americana Corporation, 1919.

Encyclopedia Britannica. Ninth Edition. New York: Henry G. Allen & Co., 1893.

Encyclopedia of Contemporary Biography. New York: Atlantic Publishing and Engraving Company, 1882.

Ernst, Robert. *Immigrant Life in New York City, 1826–1863*. New York: King's Crown Press, 1949.

Ewen, David. *All the Years of American Popular Music*. Englewood Cliffs, NJ: Prentice-Hall, Inc., 1973.

Filippelli, Ronald L., ed. *Labor Conflict in the United States: An Encyclopedia*. New York: Garland Publishing, 1990.

Fostle, D. W. *Speedboat*. Mystic, Conn.: Mystic Seaport Museum, 1988.

Galbraith, John K. *The Great Crash, 1929*. Boston: Houghton-Mifflin, 1988.

Gilfoyle, Timothy J. *City of Eros: New York City, Prostitution and the Commercialization of Sex, 1790–1920*. New York: W. W. Norton & Company, 1992.

Goddard, Scott, ed. *Letters of Hans von Bulow*. New York: Vienna House, 1972.

Gottschalk, Louis Moreau. *Notes of a Pianist*. Philadelphia: J. B. Lippincott, 1881.

Gramp, William D. *Pricing the Priceless: Art, Artists and Economics*. New York: Basic Books, 1989.

Greeley, Horace, ed. *The Great Industries of the United States, Being an Historical Summary of the Origin, Growth, and Perfection of the Chief Industrial Arts of this Country*. Hartford, Conn.: Burr & Hyde, 1872.

Groce, Nancy Jane. "Musical Instrument Making in New York City During the Eighteenth and Nineteenth Centuries." Ph.D. diss., University of Michigan, 1982.

Hansen, Harry. *The World Almanac and Book of Facts for 1958*. New York: New York World-Telegram and The Sun, 1958.

Harding, Anthony, ed. *Classic Cars in Profile*. New York: Doubleday & Co., 1969.

Harding, Rosamond E. M. *The Piano-Forte: Its History Traced to the Great Exhibition of 1851*. Cambridge, England: Cambridge University Press, 1933.

Hart, Albert Bushnell, ed. *The American Nation: A History*. New York: Harper & Brothers, 1906.

Helmholtz, Hermann L. F. *On the Sensations of Tone*. New York: Dover Publications, Inc., 1954.

Hershkowitz, Leo. *Tweed's New York*. Garden City, NY: Anchor Press/Doubleday, 1977.

Hickernell, Warren F. *Financial and Business Forecasting*. New York: Alexander Hamilton Institute, 1928.

Hildebrandt, Dieter. *Pianoforte—A Social History of the Piano*. New York: George Braziller, Inc., 1988.

Hipkins, A. J. *A Description and History of the Pianoforte*. London: Novello, Ewer & Co., 1876.

Hocking, Charles. *Dictionary of Shipping Disasters*. London: Lloyd's Register of Shipping, 1969.

Holborn, Hajo. *A History of Modern Germany, 1840–1945*. New York: Alfred A. Knopf, 1969.

685

Bibliography

Holmes, Thomas B. *Electronic and Experimental Music*. New York: Charles Scribner's Sons, 1985.

Hosmer, James Kendall. *Outcome of the Civil War, 1863–1865*. New York: Harper & Brothers, 1907.

Hoyt, J. W. *Report on the Universal Expositions of 1862 and 1867*. Madison, WI: Atwood & Rublee, 1869.

Jackson, Jim. *Tuning and Repairing Your Own Piano*. Blue Ridge Summit, PA: Tab Books, Inc., 1984.

James, Edward T. *Notable American Women, 1607–1950: A Biographical Dictionary*. Cambridge, Mass.: Belknap Press of Harvard University Press, 1971.

Kirkland, Edward C. *Industry Comes of Age*. New York: Holt, Rinehart and Winston, 1961.

"Ladies Man." *Fast Men's Directory and Lover's Guide to the Ladies of Fashion and Houses of Pleasure in New York and Other Large Cities*. New York: 1853.

Lanman, Charles. *Biographical Annual of the Civil Government of the United States*. New York: J. M. Morrison, 1887.

Lawrence, Vera Brodsky. *Strong on Music, Resonances*. New York: Oxford University Press, 1988.

Lee, Irving J. *Language Habits in Human Affairs*. New York: Harper & Brothers, 1941.

Loesser, Arthur. *Men, Women and Pianos: A Social History*. New York: Dover Publications, Inc, 1990.

Lott, R. Allen. "The American Concert Tours of Leopold De Meyer, Henri Herz, and Sigismond Thalberg," Ph.D. diss., City University of New York, 1986.

Lowden, John L. *Silent Wings at War: Combat Gliders in World War II*. Washington: Smithsonian Institution Press, 1992.

Magnusson, Leifur. *Housing by Employers in the United States*. Washington: U.S. Government Printing Office, 1920.

Makridakis, Spyros, Steven C. Wheelwright, and Victor E. McGee. *Forecasting: Methods and Applications*. New York: John Wiley & Sons, 1983.

Maretzek, Max. *Revelations of an Opera Manager in Nineteenth Century America. Crochets and Quavers & Sharps and Flats*. New York: Dover Publications, 1968.

Maryland Institute. *The Book of the Exhibition, Tenth Annual Exhibition of the Maryland Institute for the Promotion of the Mechanic Arts*. Baltimore: Samuel Sands Mills, 1857.

McKnight, Mark Curtis. "Music Criticism in the *New York Times* and the *New York Tribune*, 1851–1876." Ph.D. diss., Louisiana State University, 1980.

McLellan, David. *Karl Marx, His Life and Thought*. New York: Harper and Row, Publishers, 1973.

Morris, Richard B., ed. *The Growth of the American Economy to 1860*. Columbia, SC: University of South Carolina Press, 1968.

Newhall, Beaumont. *The History of Photography from 1839 to the Present Day*. New York: The Museum of Modern Art, 1964.

New York City 5 Borough Atlas. Maspeth, New York: Hagstrom Map Company, 1989.

New York City. *Annual Report of the Police Commissioner of the City of New York*. New York: The Corporation, 1860.

New York City Directory for 1851–1852. New York: Doggett & Rode, 1851.

New York City Directory for 1853–54. New York: Charles R. Rode, 1853.

New York State. Secretary of State. *Census of the State of New York for 1855: Prepared from the Original Returns Under the Direction of the Honorable Joel T. Headley, Secretary of State, by Franklin B. Hough*. Albany: Charles Van Benthuysen, 1857.

New York State. Secretary of State. *Census of the State of New York for 1865: Prepared from the Original Returns Under the Direction of the Honorable Joel T. Headley, Secretary of State, by Franklin B. Hough*. Albany: Charles Van Benthuysen & Sons, 1867.

New York State. Secretary of State. *Census of the State of New York for the Year 1875: Prepared from the Original Returns Under the Direction of the Secretary of State by C. W. Seaton*. Albany: Weed, Parsons & Co., 1877.

North, Douglass C. *The Economic Growth of the United States, 1790–1860*. Englewood Cliffs, NJ: Prentice-Hall, Inc., 1961.

Paderewski, Ignace Jan and Mary Law. *The Paderewski Memoirs*. New York: Charles Scribner's Sons, 1938.

Peitgen, Heinz-Otto and Dietmar Saupe, eds. *The Science of Fractal Images*. New York: Springer-Verlag, 1988.

Bibliography

Perris, William. *Maps of the City of New York from Actual Survey*. New York: William Perris, 1853.

Perris, William. *Maps of the City of New York from Actual Survey*. New York: William Perris, 1859 *et. seq.*

Pierce, John R. *The Science of Musical Sound*. New York: Scientific American Books, Inc., 1983.

Ratcliffe, Ronald V. *Steinway*. San Francisco: Chronicle Books, 1989.

Report of the Merchants Committee for the Relief of Colored People Suffering from the Riots in the City of New York, July 1863. New York: George A. Whitehorne, Steam Printer, 1863.

Rodgers, Charles T. *American Superiority at the World's Fair*. Philadelphia: John J. Hawkins, 1852.

Roehl, Harvey N. *Player Piano Treasury*. Vestal, NY: The Vestal Press, 1973.

Roell, Craig H. *The Piano in America: 1890–1940*. Chapel Hill: University of North Carolina Press, 1989.

Sadie, Stanley, ed. *The New Grove Dictionary of Music and Musicians*. London: Macmillan Press Ltd., 1980.

Sagarra, Eda. *A Social History of Germany, 1648–1914*. New York: Holmes & Meier Publishers, 1977.

Schlereth, Thomas J. *Victorian America*. New York: HarperCollins Publishers, 1991.

Schneider, David M. *History of Public Welfare in New York State*. Chicago: University of Chicago Press, 1938.

Schonberg, Harold C. *The Great Pianists*. New York: Simon & Schuster, 1963.

Seyfried, Vincent F. *The New York and Queens County Railway and the Steinway Lines*. New York: Vincent Seyfried, 1950.

Singer, Aaron. "Labor-Management Relations at Steinway & Sons, 1853–1896." Ph.D. diss., Columbia University, 1977.

Slonimsky, Nicholas. *Baker's Biographical Dictionary of Musicians*, fifth edition. New York: G. Schirmer, 1958.

Smith, Fanny Morris. *A Noble Art: Three Lectures on the Evolution and Construction of the Piano*. New York: Charles F. Tretbar, 1892.

Sobel, Robert. *The Money Manias*. New York: Weybright and Talley, 1973.

Spillane, Daniel. *History of the American Pianoforte: Its Technical Development and the Trade*. New York: D. Spillane, 1890.

Steinert, Morris. *Reminiscences of Morris Steinert*. New York: G. P. Putnam's Sons, 1900.

Steinway, Theodore E. *People and Pianos*. New York: Steinway & Sons, 1953.

Stevens, Paran. *Paris Universal Exhibition, 1867: Report upon Musical Instruments*. Washington: Government Printing Office, 1869.

Strachey, John. *The Theory and Practice of Socialism*. New York: Random House, 1936.

Tammany Hall. *A True Statement of the Position of Tammany Hall on the Labor Question*. New York: 1875.

Tremaine, Howard M. *Audio Cyclopedia*. Indianapolis: Howard W. Sams & Co., Inc., 1969.

Trow's New-York City Directory for 1853–54. New York: John F. Trow, 1853.

United States. Bureau of Economic Analysis. *Business Statistics, 1963–1991*. Washington: Government Printing Office.

United States. Bureau of Labor Statistics. *Employment, Hours, and Earnings, 1909–84*. Washington: Government Printing Office, 1985.

United States. Bureau of Statistics. *Annual Report and Statement of the Chief of the Bureau of Statistics on the Foreign Commerce, Navigation, Immigration and Tonnage of the United States*. Washington: Government Printing Office, 1885.

United States. Bureau of Statistics. *Annual Statement of the Chief of the Bureau of Statistics on the Commerce and Navigation of the United States*. Washington: Government Printing Office, 1880.

United States. Bureau of the Census. *Historical Statistics of the United States, Colonial Times to 1970*. Washington: Government Printing Office, 1975.

United States. Bureau of the Census. *Marriage and Divorce, 1867–1906*. Washington: Government Printing Office, 1909.

United States. Bureau of the Census. *Social Indicators III: Selected Data on Social Conditions and Trends in the United States*. Washington: Government Printing Office.

United States. Bureau of the Census. *Statistical Abstract of the United States*. Washington: Government Printing Office, 1977–1990.

Bibliography

United States. Senate Committee on Education & Labor. *Report on Relations between Labor and Capital*. Washington: Government Printing Office, 1885.

United States. Senate Committee on Finance. *Rates of Duty on Imports into the United States*. Washington: Government Printing Office, 1891.

United States. Senate Committee on Finance. *The Existing Tariff on Imports into the United States, Etc., and the Free List*. Washington: Government Printing Office, 1884.

United States. Treasury Department. *Commerce and Navigation Report of the Secretary of the Treasury*. Washington: A.O.P. Nicholson, 1855.

U.S. Forest Products Laboratory. *Wood Handbook: Wood as an Engineering Material*. Agricultural Handbook No. 72, revised August 1974. Washington: U.S. Department of Agriculture.

Wadlin, Horace G. *Strikes and Lockouts, 1881–1886*. Boston: Wright & Potter Printing Co., 1889.

Walker, Francis A. *A Compendium of the Ninth Census of the United States*. Washington: Government Printing Office, 1872.

Walker, Francis A. *Compendium of the Tenth Census of the United States*. Washington: Government Printing Office, 1883.

Walker, Francis A., ed. *Centennial Exhibition, Philadelphia, 1876: Reports and Awards Groups 1–36*. Philadelphia: United States Centennial Commission, 1877–78.

Walker, Francis A., ed. *International Exhibition, 1876, Reports and Awards, Group XXV*. Philadelphia: J. B. Lippincott, 1878.

Weeks, Joseph D. *Report on Strikes and Lockouts Occurring within the United States in the Calendar Year 1880*. Washington: U.S. Government Printing Office, 1886.

Weeks, Joseph D. *Report on the Statistics of Wages in Manufacturing Industries*. Washington: U.S. Government Printing Office, 1886.

White, William B. *Theory and Practice of Piano Construction*. New York: Dover Publications, Inc., 1975.

Winckel, Fritz. *Music, Sound and Sensation*. New York: Dover Publications, Inc., 1967.

Wolman, Benjamin B., ed. *International Encyclopedia of Psychiatry, Psychology, Psychoanalysis and Neurology*. New York: Van Nostrand Rheinhold Co., 1977.

STEINWAY FAMILY AND FIRM DOCUMENTS CONSULTED

Audited, unaudited and interim financial statements, 1885–1972.

Catalogs of Steinway & Sons, circa 1865–1992.

Census schedules, federal, for 1850, 1860, 1870, and state for 1855.

Confidential Dealer Circulars, circa 1861–1896.

Daimler Motor Company catalogs, circa 1890–1896.

Deeds to and title descriptions of Steinway properties in Manhattan and Queens.

Diary of William Steinway, 1861–1896.

Family letters collection.

Federal tax assessments, 1865, 1866.

Frederick T. Steinway daybook, circa 1898–1904.

Historical and biographical memoranda by Henry Z. Steinway.

Inventory Books, 1853–1898.

Last Wills and Testaments of Heinrich Steinway, Henry Steinway, Jr., Charles Steinway, Albert Steinway, C. F. Theodore Steinway, William Steinway, Charles H. Steinway, Frederick T. Steinway, and Henry W. T. Steinway.

Letters Patent, 1857–1980.

Minutes of the Annual Meeting of Stockholders, 1876–1972.

Minutes of the Board of Trustees, later Directors, 1876–1972.

Naturalization papers and consular documents, 1855–1890.

New York City tax assessments, 1850–1860.

Papers in suit, circa 1865–1925.

Partnership agreements, circa 1856–1875.

Private daybooks 1900–1940.

Production records ("number books"), 1853–1980.

Ships' manifests and logs, 1849–1850.

Stock transfer records, 1898–1972.

Bibliography

PERIODICALS CONSULTED

Advertising Age
Alcohol Health & Research World
Alcoholism: Clinical and Experimental
　Research
American Heritage
American Historical Review
American Journal of Economics and Sociology
American Musician
American Scientist
American Sociological Review
Annales Medicinnae Experimentalis Biologiae
　Fenniae
Atlantic
Business Conditions Digest
Business Week
Car and Driver
Century Magazine
Computer World
Drug & Alcohol Dependence
Early Music
Etude
Forbes
Fortune
Fra Magazine
Harvard Business Review
Hemmings Motor News
Home Journal
Horseless Age
Journal of Experimental Psychology
Journal of Speech & Hearing Research
Journal of Studies on Alcohol

Journal of the Acoustical Society of America
Keyboard
Literary Digest
London Statist
McLaren Report
Message Bird
Musical Courier
Musical World
Musical World & Times
Music & Drama
Music Trade Review
Music Trades
New Criterion
New Republic
New Yorker (1869)
New York Musical Times
New York Musical World
Northwestern University Dialogue
Physics Today
Piano Trades Magazine
Presto
Quarterly Journal of Studies on Alcohol
Review of Reviews
Road & Track
Saturday Evening Post
Smithsonian Magazine
Steinway News
Systems
Topics in Clinical Nursing
Town Topics
Vanity Fair

NEWSPAPERS CONSULTED

Chicago Herald
Detroit News
Leslie's Illustrated Weekly Newspaper
Los Angeles Herald
Los Angeles Times
New York Daily Graphic
New York Daily News
New York Daily Times
New York Daily Tribune
New York Evening World
New York Herald
New York Law Journal

New York Post
New York Sun
New York Times
New York Tribune
New York World
Oakland Enquirer
Oregon Daily Journal
Oregon Sunday Journal
Philadelphia Enquirer
Wall Street Journal
Watertown Daily Times
World: New York

INDEX